GW01112080

LEADERS OF THE WORLD

General Editor: ROBERT MAXWELL, M.C.

JÁNOS KÁDÁR

Selected Speeches and Interviews

LEADERS OF THE WORLD

General Editor: ROBERT MAXWELL, M.C.

Other Volumes in the Series

LEONID ILYICH BREZHNEV
President of the Presidium of the Supreme Soviet of the USSR,
General Secretary of the Communist Party of the Soviet Union

NICOLAE CEAUŞESCU
President of Romania and General Secretary of the
Romanian Communist Party

K. V. CHERNENKO
General Secretary of the CPSU and
President of the Presidium of the Supreme Soviet of the USSR

MORARJI DESAI
Prime Minister of India

ERICH HONECKER
Party Leader and Head of State of the German Democratic Republic

TODOR ZHIVKOV
General Secretary of the Central Committee of the
Bulgarian Communist Party and President of the State Council of the
People's Republic of Bulgaria

RONALD REAGAN
President of the United States of America

YURI VLADIMIROVICH ANDROPOV
General Secretary of the CPSU Central Committee and
President of the Presidium of the USSR Supreme Soviet

DENG XIAOPING
Chairman of the Military Commission and of the
Advisory Commission of the Central Committee of the
Communist Party of China

In preparation

FRANÇOIS MITTERAND
President of the French Republic

JÁNOS KÁDÁR

JÁNOS KÁDÁR

First Secretary of the Hungarian Socialist Workers' Party

Selected Speeches and Interviews

WITH AN INTRODUCTORY BIOGRAPHY BY
L. GYURKÓ

PERGAMON PRESS

OXFORD · NEW YORK · TORONTO · SYDNEY · PARIS · FRANKFURT

U.K.	Pergamon Press Ltd., Headington Hill Hall, Oxford OX3 OBW, England
U.S.A.	Pergamon Press Inc., Maxwell House, Fairview Park, Elmsford, New York 10523, U.S.A.
CANADA	Pergamon Press (Canada) Ltd., Suite 104, 150 Consumers Road, Willowdale, Ontario M2J 1P9, Canada
AUSTRALIA	Pergamon Press (Aust.) Pty. Ltd., P.O. Box 544, Potts Point, N.S.W 2011, Australia
FRANCE	Pergamon Press SARL, 24 rue des Ecoles, 75240 Paris, Cedex 05, France
FEDERAL REPUBLIC OF GERMANY	Pergamon Press GmbH, Hammerweg 6, D-6242 Kronberg/Taunus, Federal Republic of Germany

Copyright © 1985 Akadémiai Kiadó, Budapest

All Rights Reserved. No part of this publication may be reproduced, stored in a retrieval system or transmitted in any form or by any means: electronic, electrostatic, magnetic tape, mechanical, photocopying, recording or otherwise, without permission in writing from the copyright holders.

Joint edition with Akadémiai Kiadó, Budapest

First edition 1985

British Library Cataloguing in Publication Data

Kádár, János
    Biography. — (Leaders of the World)
    1. Kádár, János 2. Socialist — Hungary — Biography
    I. Title   II. Series
    335'.0092'4   HX260.5

ISBN 0-08-028178-8 *English Edition*
ISBN 3-921328-01-2 *German Edition*

(Distributed outside Germany under ISBN 0-08-028179-6)

Printed and bound in Hungary

Acknowledgements

The Publishers would like to thank Corvina Press for permission to quote from the undermentioned books:

J. Kádár, *Socialist Construction in Hungary*, Budapest 1962
J. Kádár, *On the Road to Socialism*, Budapest 1965
J. Kádár, *For a Socialist Hungary*, Budapest 1974
The 12th Congress of the Hungarian Socialist Workers' Party, Budapest 1980

and gratefully acknowledge the work of the translators of this volume:

Introductory biography: György Bánlaki and Mária Végh
Speeches and interviews: Sándor Bándy, György Bánlaki, István Butykai, György Fukász, Emil Gárdos, Gyula Gulyás, Judit Házi, Tibor Kertész, András Béla Nagy, Sára Magda, Viktor Polgár, Károly Ravasz, and Mária Végh and of Ursula McLean who revised the translations.

For the pictures, the Publishers would like to thank the MTI (Hungarian News Agency).

Contents

Introduction by Robert Maxwell ix

Introductory Biography
Instead of an Introduction 3
A Working Class Boy in Hungary 9
Above Ground, Underground 24
Light and Darkness 51
Towards the Tragedy 77
Rebirth 100
   With Us or Against Us? 119
Epilogue 149
Notes to Introductory Biography 153

Selected Speeches and Interviews
Address at the 10th Plenary Session of the Central Council of Hungarian Trade Unions, January 26, 1957 169
Address to a Meeting of Csepel Activists of the Hungarian Socialist Workers' Party, January 27, 1957 174
Closing Speech at the May 1957 Session of Parliament, May 11, 1957 177
Reply to the Discussion at the National Conference of the Hungarian Socialist Workers' Party (Abbreviated), June 29, 1957 191
Speech to the National Council of the Patriotic People's Front, June 19, 1959 204
Speech at a Mass Meeting in the Csepel Iron and Metal Works (Excerpts), December 1, 1961 210
Speech at the Budapest Party Conference (Excerpts), October 31, 1962 216

Interview Given to André Wurmser, Correspondent of "L'Humanité", January 6, 1963 — 222

Speech at a Mass Meeting Held on the Occasion of UN Secretary-General U Thant's Visit at Csepel, July 2, 1963 — 234

Interview with AP Correspondent Preston Grover, June 1965 — 238

Conversation with Henry Shapiro, the Moscow-Based Correspondent of UPI, July 2, 1966 — 245

Report by the Central Committee of the HSWP to the 9th Congress of the Party (Excerpts), November 28, 1966 — 260

Conversation with Lajos Mesterházi, Editor in Chief of "Budapest" Magazine, February 1967 — 289

Address to the Session of the Central Committee, November 24, 1967 — 295

A Radio and Television Interview, January 1, 1968 — 303

Speech Made at the Cultural Centre of the IKARUS Body and Vehicle Factory (Budapest), February 1968 — 310

Closing Speech at the 10th Congress of the Hungarian Socialist Workers' Party, November 1970 — 326

Speech at the April 1972 Session of the National Assembly — 335

Closing Remarks at the November 1972 Session of the Central Committee — 348

Quo Vadis, Europa? June 1973 — 357

Address at the November 1974 Session of the Central Committee — 364

Address at the Closing Session of the Conference on Security and Cooperation in Europe, August 1975 — 379

Press Conference in Vienna, December 1976 — 382

Press Conference in Rome, June 1977 — 388

Answers to the Questions of the "Frankfurter Rundschau", July 1977 — 394

Address at the April 1978 Session of the Central Committee — 401

Press Conference at the Crillon Hotel, November 1978 — 425

Report by the Central Committee at the 12th Congress of the HSWP (Excerpts), March 1980 — 430

Closing Address at the 12th Congress of the HSWP, March 1980 — 446

Notes to the Speeches and Interviews — 458

Index — 463

Introduction
By Robert Maxwell
General Editor of the "Leaders of the World" Series

Last year there was a stream of visits between senior Western leaders and Mr János Kádár, First Secretary of the Hungarian Socialist Workers' Party. These were an indication of his stature as an Eastern bloc leader willing to forge closer links with the West, and to adopt the profit motive wherever possible to help make the Marxist Socialist State more efficient and productive.

Sir Geoffrey Howe's first official visit as the British Foreign Secretary was to Hungary, as was Margaret Thatcher's first visit to a Warsaw Pact country. Other Western leaders to travel to Budapest in 1984 have included Chancellor Kohl of the Federal German Republic and Signor Craxi, the Prime Minister of Italy. Mr Kádár's own highly successful visit to France was the first from a top-level Warsaw Pact leader to President Mitterand, and followed a visit to President Giscard d'Estaing in 1978.

Who is the object of all this interest? Born in 1912, János Kádár joined the outlawed Communist Party in 1932. During the war he fought underground, and was captured by the Gestapo, only to escape. Purged in 1951, he suffered severe torture by his country's secret police. Five years later he became head of the Hungarian Socialist Workers' Party and took over as Prime Minister. He asked the Soviet Union to give military assistance in stopping the fighting and bloodshed which had been going on in the capital of the country.

Many thought at the time that he was thrust into office as a direct result of his friendship with Yuri Andropov, but in fact they became firm friends only after Kádár came to power. His leadership, however, was supported from the beginning by the Soviet leadership.

Steeled by a life of tumult, this tall, modest man with simple tastes has introduced changes over the last 20 years which are the marvel of his people and the envy of his neighbours. The New Economic Mechanism has brought about major changes in industry which even allow workers to use State factories out of normal hours to produce goods for their own profit at privately negotiated prices. Factory managers are given greater autonomy, and personal accountability for performance has been increased throughout the economy. This flexibility of approach has brought benefits. Hungary is a member of the IMF and has improved its balance of payments, but her foreign debts are still relatively high. This has meant that the continuous improvement in the standard of living of the Hungarian people has halted over the last couple of years, although a modest resumption of economic growth is expected in 1985.

Kádár's number one priority is the welfare and future of Hungary and her people, to which he has dedicated his whole life. Every problem, every situation, is tackled from the standpoint of Hungary and her place in the world. In this he is a fearless and formidable protagonist. Thanks to his influence within the Warsaw Pact and elsewhere there has been no antagonism between Hungary and the Soviet Union as these policies have been implemented.

Kádár has given Hungary political stability and a high standard of living. Domestic reforms under his rule mean that there are now no political prisoners in Hungary, and internment without trial has been abolished. These advances have persuaded many of the emigrés of 1956 to return home. Kádár's popularity is now at its height, and if a Western-style pluralist poll were to be held in Hungary it would undoubtedly result in his re-election with a massive majority.

This year Hungary will have its first general election with two or more candidates fighting every seat. Kádár takes the view that so long as there is agreement on the peaks of policy — upholding the state and its social system, and supporting its Warsaw Pact alliances — the rest can benefit from a variety of views and ideas about how the economic and cultural life of the nation can develop. He points out that Labour and Conservatives in Britain and Democrats and Republicans in the USA share the same basic principles and views about the organisation of their State and its defence alliances, while the debate between them is restricted to the arrangements for distribution of wealth and power within the State.

Kádár has been criticised for seeking the military intervention of the Soviet Union in 1956, but his philosophy on this is a simple one. Following the Great War, the reactionary forces of 1919 invited the aid of the Western military powers to bring down the Bolshevik revolution of Béla Kun. Similarly, in 1956, Hungary had no alternative but to call for the military help of the Soviet Union to prevent a Civil War.

On the European stage, Kádár is a major player, and enjoys a significance which goes well beyond the geopolitical position of the country he leads. It is an honour to publish his book in our series "Leaders of the World".

Oxford, January 1985

ROBERT MAXWELL
General Editor

Introductory Biography

Instead of an Introduction

I am not unbiased. Nor do I believe that one can think about history impartially – not even about remote centuries, let alone the recent past.

I am not a historian either and am not writing a history-book. What I am trying to do is to sketch the outlines of a man's portrait against the background of his age. I have lived through the thirty-five years during which János Kádár has been one of the leaders of Hungary. I am not trying to be unbiased because, one way or another, I have myself experienced the joys, the mistakes, the achievements and failures of this period. I am not trying to be unbiased as far as Kádár is concerned either. I saw him first at a mass meeting more than thirty years ago. Since then I have met him quite a few times – and not only at conferences, meetings, or in Parliament. I shall not forget his relief when, at the end of many hours of conversation, he leaned back in the rather uncomfortable armchair in his study, lit a cigarette and said with satisfaction: "Well, we've got through that!"

His use of the plural was a mark of courtesy, and it was clear that he was relieved to have fulfilled a task not quite to his liking.

The whole thing started when the owner of Pergamon Press of Oxford, on a visit to Budapest, mentioned to one of the party leaders that he would be pleased to publish János Kádár's autobiography, or a biography of him, in the series they were publishing on significant contemporary statesmen. Kádár refused most definitely. He would not write an autobiography and would not agree that someone else should write his biography. Later I learnt from him that he had also categorically refused to have Hungarian Television do a portrait of him as it had of numerous politicians, scientists and artists of our age. Not even on condition that the film would not be shown, but would be placed in the archives of the television company for posterity.

At this stage I was initiated into the "plot" aimed at making something of the Oxford publisher's plan after all. For while Kádár was adamant that his life was not a public matter, a few of his fellow leaders were just as convinced that it would be to the country's good if the world knew more about this unusual political career.

This is how a compromise was reached – that a selection of János Kádár's articles, speeches and interviews would be published, while I wrote the introduction which would enable even those who had neither lived through the period nor were familiar with it to follow Kádár's career.

It was not easy to get Kádár to agree even to this. Early in our conversations, he told me frankly that he would acquiesce only if he were obliged to do so by the leading body of the party. He only gave way to a resolution from the Party's Political Committee.

This episode is characteristic of Kádár's whole life. "One of the newspapers wrote about me", he said at a press conference in Rome in 1977, "that I am a 'slave to compromise', but I should like to say that I do not consider this expression insulting. I have long been in favour of all compromise which helps the cause I have been working and struggling for".

If we search for János Kádár's secret, we will quite certainly find the motive force of his life to have been his sense of duty. And his sense of reality is basic to not only his makeup but also to his philosophy of life. These two factors have been decisive in determining all his policies.

Frankly, I myself had reservations about undertaking this task. I knew, and feel it is only fair to tell the reader, that this biography couldn't even hope to strive to be comprehensive.

If I had started to work with the thoroughness incumbent upon a historian, it would have taken years to do the necessary research in libraries and archives, to understand how all the pieces fit. I would have had to ask contemporaries who are still alive to check what they remembered against the documents, and to study the history of the entire century more thoroughly. And even after all that, there would still remain details which could not be explored or verified.

I had no alternative but to settle for imperfection. This piece of writing is therefore not a portrait; at most, it is the outline of a portrait. My opinion of the period is, obviously, open to dispute, for in more than one instance it differs from the picture generally accepted. As a citizen, I should be justified in shifting responsibility onto the historians, the ideologists, the economists, and the politicians, by asking why they have not explored the history of this period and of this personality more thoroughly and in greater detail. As the author of this essay, I must answer for my own judgements, for the fact that they are open to dispute and also for the fact that my views may be inadequately founded. Kádár did not read the manuscript, so even to that extent my work has not been checked. I have shown it to a few experts, politicians, and friends whose judgement and competence I trust. There were things they agreed with, and things they disagreed with. When they managed to convince me, I incorporated their views; when they did not, I stuck to my own ideas.

For my own peace of mind, I can only add the following: I think I know the fundamental facts. The exploration of the details is not part of this work. One can outline the essence without clarifying the nuances. For this outline, open to criticism though it is, is nevertheless an attempt to analyze Hungary's recent past and that of the Hungarian socialist movement.

I do not know all the secrets either of János Kádár, or of his time; I cannot, therefore, pretend to completeness, attractive and fitting as that aim would be. What I can do is to write of a man whom I more or less know, and of an age as I have lived through it, either in fact or in my mind. I repeat, I am not a historian, but an observer of history.

I realized in advance that the greatest difficulty would be Kádár himself. Although he undertook to answer my questions out of a sense of duty, and did not even tie these interviews to conditions, I knew that my opportunities were limited.

During the conversations, I did not use a taperecorder and even the notes I only made afterwards. Not that Kádár would have objected. But a few years earlier he told me how much he had been disconcerted when one of his interlocutors had suddenly pulled pencil and paper out of his pocket.

"How can one have a conversation", he complained, "when the other person is taking notes?"

And this from a statesman for whom journalists, press conferences and radio reporters are a part of life. I thought that what I would lose on the swings I could make up on the roundabouts if our conversations were more relaxed and more personal, even if subsequently I had nothing but my memory to rely on.

Kádár is a courteous man. It is part of his makeup, but it is reinforced by his tenet that the higher the post one fills, the more it is one's duty to be patient with others. He set no limits to our conversations; the only thing he insisted on was knowing exactly how much time I needed.

He always receives his visitors with his desk cleared. There are no unresolved files on Kádár's table, no unanswered letters. He is disturbed and irritated by unfinished, unclosed affairs.

"I have no time", he said, "to deal with my past."

I am myself a man of reasonable compromise. I asked for three days. I thought this would be enough to ask him about the most important things and was perhaps not too much to discourage him completely. I think I was not mistaken; he nodded, evidently satisfied. All he asked me was to be sure to stick to our agreement for he allocates his time with great precision.

Of course, I knew that even thirty days would not be enough to clarify all the details. But I also knew that Kádár would be neither able, nor willing to agree to that anyway.

"I am not what I used to be", he said on one occasion. "Nowadays I get tired by the evening."

Kádár was sixty-nine at the time of these conversations; he still works from morning till evening, every weekday, except for one afternoon a week when he watches films. In the mornings he takes his time, potters about comfortably, washes, shaves, smokes a cigarette, gazes out of the window. He lives in a beautiful spot amidst trees and shrubs, in a three-room villa in Buda overlooking the city. There are books and pictures all over the place; in his office, too, thousands of books line the walls. It is the same house as he lived in when he was arrested in 1951. His wife was evicted then, fired from her job, and worked as an unskilled labourer for a long time. Today she is a pensioner; she used to be department head at the Information Office of the Council of Ministers.

For Kádár, the mornings are times of preparation. That is when he thinks through the past day and the one ahead, thinks over his work and his tasks. He concentrates in the way that good sportsmen do before going out on the field. He has often been described as having an instinctive talent. What struck me more was his deliberateness. I have noticed that he speaks to a six-year-old child as he speaks to an adult. When he was a worker, he liked to go into the workshop early to put his bench in order, to prepare and arrange his tools carefully, so that everything would be at hand, and only then did he start to work.

In his office, he first goes through his mail and the most important daily reports. He keeps abreast of the news. And then come the sessions, the talks, and the meetings. In thirty-five years he has never got used to dictating; he writes his letters and speeches himself in pencil. He smokes twenty cigarettes a day, neither more, nor less. He used to be a very heavy smoker.

"The doctors told me", he says, "that I should cut down to ten. I would think it over, I answered. And I was thinking that if I cut down by half now, the next time they would say cut down by half again. So I told them I would stick to twenty."

He works until eight in the evening. His lunch of meat loaf or cold cuts he has in his office. He has his one hot meal in the evening at home. He used to take work home, but not any longer. In recent years, his favourite amusements — an evening at the theatre, hunting, a game of chess, or a football match — have become rare occasions. He has no television set; he begrudges the time he otherwise spends reading.

Legend has it that Kádár is a passionate card player. There are apocryphal stories circulating in the country that important state and personnel matters have been decided during games of *ulti*[1]; I myself know politicians who thought to enhance their careers by perfecting their game. The truth is that Kádár likes to play cards as he likes all games; but cards have never played a significant role in his life. And when he does play cards he concentrates only on the game and on nothing else. The public knows, primarily from Kálmán Mikszáth[2], that political decisions at the end of the last century were often made at the felt-covered card tables. The proletarian game of *ulti* had only to be substituted for the upper class game of tarot and the legend was born.

Today only his greatest passion, reading, continues to be Kádár's daily relaxation. There is no evening when he does not read fiction. He usually has four or five books on hand at a time, reading his favourite ones time and again. First of all come the classical writers, but he is surprisingly well informed on contemporary Hungarian literature as well.

"Nowadays I am not able to follow life as closely as I used to", he says. "But good literature helps." He smiles.

"You writers help one get to know the world. More precisely, you *can*."

Even knowing how terribly busy he is — for what he does each day would be to the credit of a man twenty years his junior — I don't believe that lack of time was the main reason for his reluctance about his biography.

Everything I know about him seems to suggest that János Kádár is a profoundly modest man in the oldest sense of the word. He is a type mostly to be found among wise, old peasants who have lived to see much. These men are ready to speak about the crops, the fields, the affairs of the village and of the world, but they are deeply silent about themselves. Not that they have anything to hide; it is just that their instincts protest against such opening up, and they neither want nor tolerate anyone intruding on their privacy. Modesty of the spirit is an inner imperative as strong as that of the body.

Kádár is certainly this type of person. It is not for me to explain the whys and wherefores; I am simply registering the fact. If he appears in a newsreel, he leaves the room while it is showing. He never listens to himself on the radio nor watches himself on television. He has no official, semi-official, or non-official biography. The terse entries on him in various encyclopedias and handbooks contain some contradictory data; the likely explanation is that he has not read these entries. An English historian has written the only book on him; there, even his birthday is mistakenly given. Few Hungarians could tell you the names of his mother or of his wife. He rarely appears in public, abhors all fuss and ceremony and appears on the television screen and speaks on the radio only when it is absolutely necessary.

The Central Committee gave a lunch in his honour on the occasion of his sixtieth birthday. Fortunately, his toast was published word for word. The unpolished text, the repetitions stemming from the improvisation and the awkwardness of some of the phrases only increase the credibility of what he said:

"Propriety also demands that I should say something, although it is not so simple to speak on such an occasion. I should like to say first that my circumstances were such that in the family where I was brought up it was not customary to celebrate wedding anniversaries, birthdays, or namedays. That was the way I grew up. It is only in the last ten or twenty years that I have met with the custom that it was proper to celebrate such occasions officially and unofficially. I should like to say that it is right that the great events of family life are celebrated. But I have had no part in this. I was not accustomed to it, it is only nowadays that I am getting used to it. I am saying this so that you will understand, comrades, that I feel ill at ease at this anniversary and on such occasions; it disturbs me, I am embarrassed.

"The celebration of birthdays as a family matter is the right thing to do and is also a tradition with our people. I regret that I had no experience of it at the age when one grows up physically and spiritually; I feel this lack, but I can no longer do anything about it.

"It is another thing entirely when such a family occasion as, let us say, a birthday becomes a public and political affair. The way I see it, I understand and consider it right, too, that in certain cases, to the limit which good taste permits, a political and public affair be made out of a purely personal matter, like a birthday. I understand and approve of this on two conditions: that it is within the limits of good taste, and that it is not I who am concerned. Then I approve heartily. But if I am involved, then I confirm what I have already said, that I feel ill at ease, I am embarrassed – I am simply not accustomed to this."

When I was questioning him about his life I always had to keep in mind that he does not like to deal with, or talk about himself. Yet how many details of his life there are which are not documented, about which I could have obtained information only from him. My questions were limited not only by the lack of time, but also by Kádár's character which I had to respect.

Mind you, Kádár is not a loner, not an introvert. He likes company, he likes talking, he likes jokes, he has a good and often a keen sense of humour. He just does not like it when he is in the limelight.

It is no small contradiction that with such a personality he has been a leader from his early youth, and the leader of his country for a quarter of a century. Nothing but his sense of duty can account for this.

As far as I know, he was preparing to go on pension upon reaching retirement age like most workers in the country. But that is not how it was to be. And there is no other reason than that he understood that the country still needed him. For I hardly know a leader less preoccupied with his position than Kádár. For him, the exercise of power is also a daily burden. According to one of his colleagues, there are only two things he is really afraid of: the dentist and power. And power is the more fearful.

For a statesman who has helped guide the fate of a country for so many years, contributing daily to the most important decisions, the whole rhythm of his life determined by this form of activity, it cannot help but be a shock when from one day to another his everyday environment changes, and his whole lifestyle alters as his daily tasks vanish. Nevertheless, I do not believe that Kádár, had he retired, would have become an embittered man, finding neither his place nor a purpose in life, as has happened with several leaders I know who have not been able to cope with this change of lifestyle. When Kádár goes on holiday, he really does get away from it all, from politics, from official and state matters; even the papers he only leafs through. This is also part of his secret: he is an exceptionally well-balanced, disciplined man.

When I say the "secret" of János Kádár, I am not talking about the state secrets which are part and parcel of the life of political leaders in any corner of the world. I am talking about the secrets of the personality, of the individual character, those that are every man's own most intimate. Indeed, this is a personal affair of Kádár's which can be of public interest only to the extent that it helps one to understand his career and his policies.

But Kádár also has another secret, one more important than any other and which really concerns everyone. Those who have lived through the past twenty-five years or so know that in November 1956 the most hated man in the world for several hundred thousand Hungarians was the First Secretary of the Hungarian Socialist Workers' Party, János Kádár. And if we leaf through the leading Western newspapers of the time, we shall find only words like "traitor", "executioner", "Soviet agent", and "tyrant" attached to his name.

Since then, a quarter of a century has passed. János Kádár is still First Secretary of the Hungarian Socialist Workers' Party. And today he is undoubtedly the most esteemed, the most popular man in the country. And anyone who pays attention to the Western press today can see that even the most stubborn enemies of the socialist system write about Kádár's person and policies with respect.

This almost incredible change is János Kádár's real secret, one which is worth unravelling.

A Working Class Boy in Hungary

In 1912, when János Kádár was born, Hungary was a part of the Austro-Hungarian Monarchy. His Imperial Majesty and Royal Highness, Francis Joseph, was sitting on the throne of the empire, with claim not only to an almost endless list of titles and honours, to present-day Austria, Hungary, Czechoslovakia, to parts of Yugoslavia, Romania, the Soviet Union, Poland and Italy, but also to having reigned for an unprecedentedly long time: he was in the 64th year of his 68 year rule from 1848 to 1916.

The tragic fate of his family was as marked as the immeasurable power and longevity of the penultimate Habsburg monarch. His younger brother, Maximilian, Emperor of Mexico, was executed by the victorious freedom fighters of this alien country. His daughter, Sophia, died. His son, Crown Prince Rudolph, committed suicide after shooting his sweetheart. His wife, Elizabeth, was stabbed to death by an Italian anarchist. His nephew, the heir to the imperial throne, Francis Ferdinand, and his wife were killed by a Serbian student, who thus provided a pretext for the outbreak of World War I.

This black chronicle is indicative of more than just the agony of the Habsburg House. Crown Prince Rudolph committed suicide because he could not marry Maria Vetsera: a Habsburg Prince could not marry an ordinary baroness. Francis Ferdinand was more stubborn: he married Countess Sophia Chotek, thereby violating the written and unwritten rules of the 650 year-old dynasty. But he paid a high price for it. Prior to the wedding, he was compelled to admit publicly in front of the Emperor and the Princes that his marriage was a misalliance; this meant that his descendants forfeited all claim to the throne, his wife was entitled to none of the privileges of an Archduchess, and their future children would bear the name of their mother, as if they were illegitimate. This ceremonial admission, which today seems comic but at the time was undoubtedly humiliating, had much graver consequences – the death of the royal couple. For while Francis Ferdinand was entitled to a phalanx of armed soldiers on both sides of the street to secure his personal safety when he visited Sarajevo in 1914, protocol dictated that his wife could not be accorded the same honour. This is how the assailants were able to make two approaches to the Crown Prince's carriage unhindered; after the first, unsuccessful attempt they were able to make a second, successful one.

János Kádár was born in Fiume[3] on May 26, 1912. He was entered in the register as János Csermanek, which was the name of his mother, a young, almost illiterate peasant girl who had travelled several hundred miles from Ógyalla, a village near the Upper Danube, all the way down to the shores of the Adriatic in search of work. Borbála Csermanek was a servant girl in Fiume; at that time, and for many years after, that was almost the only way in which peasant girls who had nothing to exist on in their native village could make a living. On the shores of the Adriatic, Borbála Csermanek fell in love with a young peasant from Transdanubia who was doing military service in Fiume. From then on, their fate was similar to that of the royal couple, though without the pomp and palace, bombs and bullets. The young soldier wanted to marry his love, but his family would not let him. They had a few acres of land; the girl had nothing: she was considered no better than a beggar. As was considered right and proper, the young man was married off to a peasant girl of corresponding "rank", and Borbála Csermanek gave birth to a son out of wedlock. The feudal constraint and custom were just as implacably binding on the poorest peasants as on the royal house.

In those days, it was a great disgrace to be an illegitimate child in Hungary. How János Kádár bore this stigma in his childhood I do not know. One thing is certain: he learned what social prejudice was at an early age.

A girl who had to earn her living as a servant could not afford to have a child. No one would hire a servant girl with a child. Borbála Csermanek had no alternative but to find foster parents for her son if she wanted to get a job. And work she had to, because she had no one to support her. This is how János Kádár came to spend the first years of his life in Kapoly in Somogy County. He has no memories of his birthplace, Fiume, and was already a statesman when he next visited the town. He is not the type to go searching for traces of his past.

Kapoly is, indeed, at the end of nowhere. At the time, there was no railway, or proper road; needless to say, there was no electricity, no plumbing, no sewage, as was the case with most Hungarian villages. During the thirties, I myself spent a part of my childhood in that region, and I remember this beautifully situated, destitute village. There were two winding streets with a little brooklet between them which always dried up in the summer; and at the end of the village there is nothing—the forest begins. Kapoly had about a thousand inhabitants at the time, half of them Catholics, half of them Protestants. Most people were very poor, but both denominations had their own church, as was considered proper at the time. Since most of the land belonged to the Benedictine Abbey in Tihany, the little work there was went mostly to the Catholics. Kádár's foster father was a Protestant. A peasant as poor as Borbála Csermanek, he at least had a roof over his head, could grow a few things in the garden, and could keep animals. His lot, a difficult one at best, was aggravated by his wife's illness; there was no one to do the women's work around the house, and the invalid had to be cared for and attended to.

This is how János Kádár later remembered those years:

"Until the age of six I was reared in Somogy County in a small village where the houses had thatched roofs and were lit by oil lamps. It was a muddy hole, but it was my world; I knew every soul, every tree, bush, hill and stream. For me Somogy and its familiar landscape is virtually my native land; it's there I spent the decisive period when I became conscious of the world, and came to know people and their environment, and my home country. Every region has its own peculiarities: the dialect, the way simple human matters are judged, the customs, the dress, the folk art and many other things which a child born and brought up there absorbs and retains the traces of to the end of his life. Life gave me all this in Somogy, and I cherish it, and not just as a memory, to this very day."

In many respects Kádár's childhood is similar to that of the poet Attila József[4], seven years his senior. But while his childhood memories haunted Attila József to the end of his life, Kádár remembers these years as almost idyllic. This was almost certainly due to his foster parents, particularly his foster father. Except for his wife and his mother,

I have not heard him speak of anyone with such warmth and love as he does of Uncle Sándor. There must have been some profound kindliness in this laconic peasant. From day to day he had to struggle for his daily bread, but the permanent uncertainty of whether he would have work tomorrow must have been even more tormenting. But he never sought oblivion in wine as so many of his fellows did, and never made his family suffer for it: the miserable fate of the poor did not harden his heart. He nursed his wife attentively and grew to love the little boy so much that when his wife died he wanted to marry Borbála Csermanek for the sake of the child.

> "The unfortunate
> who wrote all this,
> immeasurably longs for
> love, so that love
> might keep him from
> committing things
> which he fears to do.
> They beat him for things which
> he would never have done
> had he been loved. He is
> the child they did not love,
> and who they beat also
> because they could not
> bear that they
> do not love him . . . "

This was Attila József's cry of anguish at the end of his life when he was becoming more and more conversant with death. Love could not save him from what he was afraid of. The effect he had on my generation is exemplified by two tragedies. Within a few years of each other, a friend of mine, a noted critic, and an actor, perhaps the most outstanding of his generation, both threw themselves under a train at the selfsame spot as the poet had done, when they could no longer bear to live. Their last act was a symbolic tribute to the idol and mentor of my generation, Attila József.

"I learnt in Kapoly", Kádár says, "that the most difficult fate is bearable if one is loved."

His face is lined, his forehead wrinkled, at times he looks tired. His life can hardly be said to have been an easy one. There is another wise saying of Uncle Sándor's which he has never forgotten:

"Remember, Jani, that a poor man's child always has to work."

"This was the first piece of Marxist education I had", says Kádár. He smiles, but it is clear that he is serious.

Uncle Sándor was merely putting into words what the small child had to learn in life anyway. As soon as he could walk and talk, he had to help with the chores around the house, help care for his foster mother, and help look after the turkeys, the pigs and the sheep.

He recalls a hot summer day when he was around six: it was harvest time, and the whole village was working in the fields. He was playing with three other children of the same age in the barnyard of the only slate-roofed house in the village. A slate roof in those days meant not only wealth but rank, too. The owner of the house was a gentleman, a sort of inspector. One of his sons was a bit "soft in the head", mentally retarded we would say today. Hot as the day was, he insisted that he was cold. He made a fire, and the haystack and the slate-roofed house went up in flames. The church bells were rung to raise the alarm and the harvesters ran back to the village from the fields. The children thought it better to make themselves scarce. But in the evening they had to slink back to the village. The Csermanek child had a clear conscience; it was not he who had set the haystack on fire. But when the inspector saw him, he hit him with his riding whip just the same. The child ran home to Uncle Sándor who listened calmly to all that had happened, and then he said "The only one who may hit you, is the one who gives you bread."

This ancient peasant saying reflects the defiance and pride of the oppressed and the humiliated, and in all probability was very characteristic of Uncle Sándor. But the epilogue of this story is no less characteristic of János Kádár. About fifteen years later he returned to visit the village where he had grown up. By then he had not been to Kapoly for many years. He had come by bicycle from Budapest. Just outside the village, he came across some women. He greeted them and asked if they remembered Jani Csermanek. Of course, came the answer, the boy who set the inspector's house on fire. Kádár was so hurt by being remembered so unjustly that he got on his bicycle and went all the way back to the capital — ninety-five miles away — without going into Kapoly. This soft-spoken, calm, well-balanced man is also dogged and defiant. And he tolerates injustice with great difficulty, although he has had to put up with quite a lot of it during his life.

His contact with Uncle Sándor was not broken even after his mother took him to Budapest when he was six. He always spent the summer holidays in the country, and he helped pay for his school expenses with what he earned in the summer by working in the fields. This was how he was able to finish not only the four compulsory years of elementary schooling, but also the next four years, quite a rarity among the poor. He stopped going to Kapoly only when he became an apprentice, because in those days apprentices got no holidays. Later, when he was already earning, he sent a few *Pengős*[5] to Uncle Sándor, whenever he could. The old man had a house, and the garden produced the necessities, but it was a source of great pride and satisfaction to him to be able to invite his friends for a glass of wine from time to time on these few *Pengős*. I think the self-respect this gave him was as important to Uncle Sándor as the air he breathed. One would like to believe that there are men of his sort still around.

Kádár benefited from his village contacts as a child; he learned to know the rural way of life, so different from life in the city, and learned to love nature so much that he still walks in the forest whenever he can. But living among the peasants for years was good schooling for the future politician as well; he became familiar with their lives, their customs, morals, and philosophy of life from within. In Kádár's youth, Hungary was an agricultural country and remained so for a long time. In the twenties, two-thirds of the population was rural, and half the wage-earners worked in agriculture. A quarter of the arable land in the country belonged to a thousand great landowners, on whose estates 400,000 cotters and day labourers worked – twenty per cent of the population, if we count their families. Eighty-five per cent of the peasant holdings failed to yield their owners enough to subsist on. János Csermanek the child had no idea that his father lived less than six miles from Kapoly, in an even smaller village, Pusztaszemes. Only as an adult did he learn that he had a father and three half brothers. No close relationship ever developed between them.

"Ties of blood are not real bonds", says Kádár. "We lived a lifetime without even knowing of each other's existence. One can neither make up for this, nor remedy it."

His father must have been just as headstrong a man. In his old age he had vasoconstriction, and his leg should have been amputated. He would not allow it. He died rather than live without a leg. Kádár sent a wreath to his funeral. They had met only once in their lives. I think Kádár could never forgive him for having abandoned his mother.

In Budapest, Borbála Csermanek worked as a washerwoman, delivered newspapers, and was assistant caretaker. Those who remember those times know what it was like to be an assistant caretaker. In the social hierarchy, the job was roughly equal in rank to that of a street sweeper. Except that the assistant caretaker was at the mercy not only of the caretaker, but at the beck and call of all the tenants as well. It could not have been easy for a child who probably suffered more from humiliation than from anything else to adjust to this way of life.

It took time for mother and son to make friends. And not only because the child had felt very close to Uncle Sándor and his wife, feeling that they were his real parents, rather than his mother whom he had seen only every now and then. Borbála Csermanek was a difficult woman to live with. She was unstable, quick to lose her temper, and quick to become sentimental. "An ill-starred woman", says Kádár. She was so shortsighted that she finished only two years of elementary schooling, then she left because the letters blurred in front of her eyes. She always saw the world through a haze, was always groping, always had to feel her way among people: all things which hardly made her difficult life easier.

What the child understood least was religion. There is no need to see traces of the ideology of the future Communist leader already existing in the child; there is a much simpler explanation. God did not exist for Uncle Sándor; therefore he did not exist for Jani Csermanek either. But the half Hungarian, half Slovak Borbála Csermanek was a devout Catholic. The child did not understand why his mother sent him off on Christmas Eve to queue for bread when there was still some at home. This was around the end of World War I when the poor started to queue up in front of the bakery in the evening to be sure to get some of the early morning bread. It was very cold and the child was freezing. When he had to pee, he asked a woman to keep his place in the queue and ran home. He peeped through the window and saw his mother decorating the Christmas tree. Then he knew why he had been made to stand in the queue. But he did not quite understand. Before Christmas "at home", in Kapoly, Uncle Sándor would get the small axe, take the child by the hand and they would go out to the woods together to cut a Christmas tree. Jani Csermanek knew that it was not little Jesus who brought the Christmas tree; his mother, however, expected him to believe that it was.

In the evening, the mother prayed. She snapped at her son to pray, too. The child not only did not want to pray, he did not even know how to. Borbála Csermanek put some corn in the corner of the room and made her disobedient son kneel on it. It was a common punishment in those days, one of the mildest ones. "To be put in the corner" was a humiliation: the malefactor became an outcast, he did not deserve to be a part of the world. The corn hurt to kneel on; so the punishment mortified the flesh as well.

When she finished her prayers, Borbála Csermanek went to bed. The child did not move from the corner. Neither of them could sleep. Then the mother begged her stubborn son to come to bed. The offended child would not move. He did so only when his mother tearfully coaxed him.

The childhood of János Kádár and of Attila József differed not only because Kádár was more fortunate in similar circumstances. There was also the difference that he stubbornly resisted when he felt an injustice had been done him, while the much more vulnerable Attila József bottled up wound upon wound inside. Of the two rebels, one became a party worker, the other a poet.

Despite all their initial difficulties, I think that, with the exception of his wife, there is no human being whom Kádár has loved as much as his mother. Until her death, he lived with the *Mutter*, as he refers to his mother. Except, of course, for his years in gaol – there were quite a few of these for Kádár – and the considerable time spent underground. Kádár was already one of the country's leaders when no matter how late he went home he knew he would find his mother awake, waiting up for him in the kitchen, never going to sleep until her son returned. Love and the old peasant sense of duty dictated that she should not go to bed as long as her son was up. And in those days, party leaders seldom got to bed before midnight.

But we are still in 1918, the year when János Csermanek left Kapoly to live in Budapest. By then, not only World War I, but the Austro-Hungarian Monarchy too was nearing the end. In October, the Monarchy made a peace overture to the Entente powers, conceding that the war was lost. The agony of the Habsburg empire lasted only a few weeks longer. The Monarchy fell apart, and in November the new Hungarian government led by Mihály Károlyi[6] decided in favour of secession from Austria.

The symbol of the 1918 revolution was the little Michaelmas daisy (called "autumn rose" in Hungarian) the gentle, modest flower which the soldiers used to replace the Monarchy insignia torn from their hats, and which the civilians put in their buttonholes. The revolution was able to realize only what the country was genuinely unanimous on: peace, independence, and civil liberty. It could not alleviate the economic crisis, and was unable to solve Hungary's greatest problem, the land question. The Catholic Church alone had more than two million acres of land, and there were aristocrats with more than a hundred and fifty thousand acres to their name, while many millions of peasants had not an inch of land. In vain was the law ordaining the distribution of the great landed estates with compensation for the owners enacted; in vain was the example of Mihály Károlyi, by then provisional President of the

Republic, who started to distribute his own lands. By and large, the land reform act remained a dead letter.

In November 1918 the Hungarian Party of Communists was founded by Communist prisoners of war returned from Russia, left-wing Social Democrats, an illegal group called the Revolutionary Socialists, and a few left-wing intellectuals. This party differed from all other political forces in that it did not look on the revolution as completed, but demanded a socialist social order. Although in the beginning there were only a handful of them, Communist influence grew in proportion to the people's discontent. The conflict between the Communists and the government went so far that when in February 1919 the unemployed clashed with the police during a demonstration and several lives were lost in the skirmish, about fifty Communist leaders were arrested.

But this temporary incapacitation of the extreme left could not solve one of the gravest problems of the Károlyi government. Mihály Károlyi and his associates had hoped from the beginning that secession from the House of Habsburg and the proclamation of an independent republic would win the confidence of the Entente, and that the new national boundaries would be drawn in accordance with Wilson's attractive principles of national self-determination. They were disappointed on both counts.

On March 21, 1919 the Social Democratic Party of Hungary and the Hungarian Party of Communists merged and proclaimed the Republic of Councils. The members of the newly appointed government were called people's commissars, and the government the Revolutionary Governing Council, another declaration that the new socialist order differed from the bourgeois system. The Chairman of the Governing Council was Sándor Garbai[7], a Social Democrat; the People's Commissar of Foreign Affairs was Béla Kun[8], a Communist.

These events shook the country, but Kádár has no recollection of them and not just because he was only seven years old at the time. He was totally preoccupied with the fundamental change which had taken place in his life. For he is not the type of person who can adjust to a new environment, to new situations and circumstances from one moment to the next. Many years later this is what he said:

"When I stepped out of the Déli (Southern) Railway Station and caught a glimpse of Budapest, which I later became so familiar with, it had an indescribable effect on me; but this is understandable enough. It was here that I first saw asphalt, hard-surface roads, electric lamps, multi-storied buildings, trams, the underground, motorcars, aeroplanes, cinemas and other formerly unknown wonders. And it was here that I first saw enormous crowds of people who were strangers. All this was at once wonderful, alien and awe-inspiring for me; I confess that Budapest remained alien to me, something I didn't like very much, for quite a number of years."

Kádár has no recollections of the council government either, though it was later to determine his life. What could a seven-year-old child used to the silence of a village in the middle of nowhere notice of the objective changes in the world when from one day to another he found himself in the chaos and traffic of the big city? One had to stand in a queue for bread and potatoes, just as before; there was no more money, there were no clothes, nor toys, nor candy. The Republic of Councils inherited the poverty and misery, and reflectiveness is not typical of small children. Nevertheless, Hungary's society and economy were being fundamentally transformed at a hectic pace. In its first proclamation, the Governing Council pronounced the public ownership of large estates, of factories, banks, and transportation companies. Factories employing more than 20 workers and estates of more than 150 acres were nationalized. The eight-hour working day was introduced, the workers' wages were increased by 20 per cent, medical care became free, sick benefits were introduced, a decree providing for a general pension scheme was worked out, working mothers were guaranteed 12 weeks paid maternity leave, and discrimination against illegitimate children was abolished. In the capital, where about a quarter of a million people lived eight or more to a single room, more than a hundred thousand people were rehoused in the villas and spacious flats of the rich. In Budapest, a workers' university was set up where several thousand manual workers studied management, accounting, and foreign languages in the time they got off work in the afternoons for the purpose. According to the Councils' new franchise law, every man and woman over 18 except for the capitalists and priests had the right to vote and to hold office. The separation of church and state was recognized and all schools and educational institutions were nationalized. A uniform system of primary education was worked out: instead of the former four-grade elementary school, all children were to receive compulsory free education until the age of 14.

It is almost unbelievable what strength and imagination the new system had in those first few weeks and months. The decrees, however, were often passed in haste or were impossible to put into practice: even in the case of those that were not, the implementation seldom went smoothly and was often chaotic. There was no lack of utopianism, either; the leaders of the Republic of Councils lived in the happy belief that socialism would be a brief transition to Communism, which the approaching world revolution would bring about.

This utopianism was responsible for the gravest political mistake of the Hungary of the Councils: the government did not distribute the land among the peasants but created cooperatives on the nationalized estates. Peasants have wanted land from the beginning of time and have supported whoever has given them land: this was one of the secrets of the success of Soviet Russia. The Republic of Councils did not give land to the landless, so the majority of the peasants did not feel the revolution was their own; they did not fight for it as they would have, had they been defending their own land. This fatal mistake had its effects not only during the time of the Republic of Councils, but after its suppression, too, and also after the country's liberation in 1945: one mistaken political decision was enough to influence Hungary's history for half a century. The peasantry did not think of the council government as one which had given them land, and they did not think of the Horthy system as one which had taken their land away.

But the Republic of Councils would have fallen even if its peasant policy had been unexceptionable. The history of the Republic of Councils cannot be understood without remembering that its leaders were convinced that the proletarian revolution would soon triumph in a number of European countries; the Hungary of the Councils would then not be a lonely little island in a hostile sea, but a member of a gigantic and strong union. The Russian Communists shared this hope at that time.

Fundamental to all philosophy of history is the question of whether history is to be judged on the basis of facts only, or on the basis of possibilities as well. History has laws of its own. Neither the great successes nor the great failures are matters of chance, but just how, when and where they come about are not matters of unavoidable necessity. And the more chaotic a period is – and the years following World War I were, indeed, chaotic – the more people's hopes, too, have an air of reality, even if they later seem utopian. This is true not only because the events are almost impossible to comprehend, but primarily because events follow each other in such rapid succession that extremes seem more acceptable than during periods of consolidation.

Now, with sixty years of hindsight, the opinion of a number of highly esteemed historians notwithstanding, I believe that the hopes of a European socialist revolution were not naive messianism but a real possibility. In defeated Germany, there was a revolutionary situation similar to that in Russia and Hungary, and it is more than probable that if the socialist revolution had won in Germany, its flames would have spread at least to Eastern Europe.

The suppression of the German revolution sealed the fate of the other European countries as well. Although fighting and uprisings broke out in Austria, Poland, Czechoslovakia, Yugoslavia, Romania, and Bulgaria, these were isolated incidents. The German failure sealed the fate of the Hungary of the Councils. The Western powers which also tried to suppress the new order in Soviet Russia would not tolerate an alien body in Europe. But whereas the vast Soviet republics were able to resist, Hungary was too small to be able to do so. The Republic of Councils fought, and even had some military victories, but in the end fell to forces which were vastly superior.

On August 1, 1919 it was announced at the session of the Budapest Workers' and Soldiers' Council that the Governing Council was resigning and transferring power to a trade union government. The chairman, the former Social Democrat, Zoltán Rónai[9], did not repudiate the Republic of Councils. He spoke of a compromise which would preserve "the soil of Hungary so that the banner of world revolution might fly high again once the world revolution spreads to other countries".

I do not know whether Rónai himself believed what he said, but I think he probably did. The Hungarian Republic of Councils fell as it had come to life and lived: confident of a utopia. It had lasted 133 days. Twice as long as the Paris Commune.

While the country was roused by revolution and counter-revolution, the Csermanek boy was getting to know the great city, so strange and in many ways so frightening and repulsive. At first, he was considered a country bumpkin; in school when he called a chicken "*pipice*"[10] in good Somogy style, the whole class laughed at him, the teacher included. He had brought a little rooster with him from the village so as not to feel so lonely among the many thousands of strangers. By the way, he still keeps poultry; he sticks to his habits. He sought refuge from the unknown city in nature.

"I lived in the Inner City", he recalled "and then later in the 13th, the 7th, and the 6th districts; gradually, I came to know Budapest quite well. Particularly so, since my mother was an unskilled worker bringing up her two children by herself, and I had to work a lot after school at home and also running errands about the city. But I liked to walk all over the city in my free time, too. In the countryside, I took to the forest, to the fields, and plains, so in Budapest, too, I was always trying to move towards the outskirts where one could breathe more freely and where the horizon was not blocked by a multitude of houses. I discovered the shore of the Danube, the winter docks, Lágymányos, Kelenföld, Gellért Hill, Sas Hill, Városmajor, Szunyog Island, the City Park and the People's Park one after the other, and they all became favourite places."

Anyone who knows Budapest even a little knows that these wanderings entailed many hours on foot. A working class kid had no money to take a tram.

"It was very difficult for me to get used to the city", says Kádár. "Yet today I feel like a true-born native of Budapest. You see? That's what people are like!"

In addition to studying, working and wandering about, there were three passions in the boy's life which must have left him little time for sleep: soccer, reading, and chess. He played football for two years in the junior team of the Sports Club in Hársfa Street. He was proud of the club's yellow and blue striped colours, and put up with his mother's scoldings and slaps for all the shoes he kicked to pieces. He played centre half, and, of course, had dreams of qualifying for the national team. When he became an apprentice he no longer had time to go out to play soccer in the People's Park. He still likes to watch soccer games.

Reading soon became another passion. He devoured all the books he could lay his hands on. Since he mostly had time to read only in the evening, and there was no electricity at home and paraffin cost a lot, he would settle under a street light and read there, often until midnight, although he had to go to work at five in the morning. All his life he has slept little. "I do not really know", he says, "why books fascinated me so much. Perhaps because they opened up new worlds to me. Yet I always put more faith in what I saw than in what I read. But in those days my life was very circumscribed. And then I got so used to reading, that now I would miss it as much as I would miss food."

Chess, too, he played competitively. He joined the Outer-Ferencváros Workers' Chess Club and, needless to say, already saw himself as a prospective international grand master. He did not become one, but even today he follows the events of the chess world, and it is one of his favourite pastimes to sit at home with a book and play through the games of the masters.

Education and sports have always played a significant part in the Hungarian working class movement. Reading and chess circles, gymnastics associations, poetry reading evenings, sports clubs, scientific lectures, and hiking clubs were all as much part of the movement, as talking politics. Whether this was because the working class movement had always been persecuted in Hungary, and so took the form of "neutral" organizations, or because they knew that community life can flourish only in a living community, I do not know, but I think the two things reinforced one another. In any case, a whole team of working class leaders grew up in this environment, and on these traditions.

One experience which probably affected Kádár's whole life had to do with chess. A junior tournament was organized at the Barbers' Trade Union headquarters in Havas Street, with the first prize a book. Sixteen-year old János Csermanek won the tournament and the book. This is how he remembered this episode later:

"When I looked at the book at home, I was amazed. Even the title — *Herr Eugen Dühring's Revolution in Science* (in Hungarian it reads literally: How Herr Eugen

Dühring would transform all the sciences—Translator's note)—was strange to me. I had even more trouble with the content. Till then I had read quite a lot of things from penny dreadfuls like *Mr. Hercules* to Verne and Zola but never a book like this. I was astonished after the first reading. I couldn't get it: it was written in Hungarian, I could read the letters, I understood the words, even certain of the sentences, yet of the whole book I understood nothing. Needless to say, at that time I rated my intellectual capacities very highly. I thought the fault was in the book. I was intrigued by the secret of life. And this book said that life was the 'mode of existence of albuminous bodies'. This irritated me, but it also made me restless and excited my curiosity.

I don't want to make a long story of it. I was captivated by the book. I became more and more immersed in it, I read it for almost eight months, I don't know how many times. My friends pushed me about, they yelled at me, cocked snooks at me, but I persevered. In the end, they tapped their foreheads to show me that in their opinion there was something wrong with me. I cannot say that at that time I fully understood Engels's *Anti-Dühring*, the first Marxist book that I came across, but from then on I thought differently about life than I had done before."

If we look through just the table of contents of *Anti-Dühring* it seems doubtful that the young apprentice with his eight years of schooling could have clearly understood even the words or the concepts used. For we find chapter headings like: "Cosmogony, Physics, Chemistry", "Negation of the Negation", "Simple and Compound Labour", "Capital and Surplus-Value". And paging through the book, sentences like: "With Hegel 'in itself' covers the original identity of the hidden, undeveloped contradictions within a thing, a process or an idea; and 'for itself' contains the distinction and separation of these hidden elements and the starting point of their conflict."

Even a reader with some knowledge of philosophy would be hard put to follow such sentences, and the message of *Anti-Dühring* precisely.

Twenty-five years after Kádár wrote the reminiscences quoted above—that is, fifty-two years after having read the book—I asked him again what role the first Marxist work had played in his life. His answer was very precisely and clearly put, which made me think that he had thought this question through.

"I did not become a Marxist through reading *Anti-Dühring*. In the first place, I had no idea what Marxism was all about. But it is a fact that this book, which I found extremely strange, preoccupied my mind for almost a year. It excited me because I did not understand it. But it was not only the secrets of an unknown world that excited me, but the fact that I sensed in this initially incomprehensible argumentation something of what later became the meaning of my life. I do not believe that after my eight-month struggle with the book I understood Engels's theses precisely. But this book changed the way I thought. It dawned on me that there were immutable laws and connections in the world which, so far, I had not even suspected!"

At that time Kádár knew nothing yet about Marxism, nor did he know that there was such a thing as a working class movement. The laws of the day strictly prohibited any worker under eighteen not only from becoming a member of the Social Democratic Party (the Communist party was banned in Hungary at the time) but even from joining a trade union. Kádár recalls only one organized worker in the workshop where he was an apprentice, and presumes that he never spoke of politics to him precisely because of this ban.

To understand this, we have to turn to history again. The Governing Council had transferred power to a trade union government consisting of right-wing Social Democrats in the naive belief that the latter would be able to save something of working class rule. But the trade union government stayed in power for only five days. On August 4, 1919 the royal Romanian army marched into Budapest, the self-appointed governor, the Habsburg Archduke Joseph, forced the government to resign and appointed an insignificant politician prime minister.

The political capers of the ensuing months could be called a comedy had this period not been a tragedy for the Hungarian Left. According to the data at our disposal, five thousand people were killed, more than seventy thousand were jailed and sent to internment camps, and a hundred thousand emigrated during the first three months following the fall of the Republic of Councils. And probably the data at our disposal are no adequate reflection of reality: for it is not customary to keep records of lynchings.

Governments came and went; at the end of August, Archduke Joseph, the self-made governor, resigned under Entente pressure. The Romanians were taking factories, equipment, food and other goods in great quantities out of the country; they terrorized not only the population of the occupied part of the country, but the government, too: they censored the press, tapped ministers' phones, and even the Prime Minister had to ask the Romanian military command for permission to travel to the provinces. It is no wonder that under such circumstances nobody knew who was really in power.

The victors themselves were at a loss for what to do. They had suppressed a left-wing regime, but they did not know to whom they could transfer power. The states neighbouring on Hungary dreaded all governments which might have striven to revive the monarchy, and therefore distrusted the conservative – and largely aristocratic – politicians right from the start. The Entente would have liked to see the formation of some sort of liberal government in Hungary because they saw this as the best antidote to Habsburg restoration and Communism alike, and therefore turned down the conservative aristocrats who volunteered to form a government.

In the end, and as is usual in such cases, the military took the initiative. On August 9, 1919, the so-called national army consisting of about a thousand men, mostly professional and non-commissioned officers, left camp in French-occupied Szeged for Transdanubia which was not occupied by the Romanians. Blood flowed wherever the detachments went. They hanged, whipped and flogged, branded their captives with red-hot irons, skinned their victims alive and burned prisoners in the engine of their armoured train. There had not been such mindless terror in Hungary since the suppression of the peasant uprising in 1514. The Whites, as the counter-revolutionaries called themselves in contrast to the Reds, surpassed in inhumanity the suppressors of the 1848 War of Independence.

The Austrian imperial general, Haynau[11], had only jailed, hanged or shot the captured freedom fighters, but the methods of the White detachments were as mediaeval as when the peasant king, György Dózsa[12], was burned alive on a redhot iron throne in 1514.

It is a fact that people were executed during the Republic of Councils, too. The state security squads openly and proudly called themselves terrorists in those days. There were about two hundred leather-coated "Lenin boys" as they were known. This detachment, which was later disbanded because of their excesses, summarily executed twelve people throughout the whole duration of their activity. And even if we multiply this number assuming documentation to be inadequate, we get only a fraction of the number of victims which the White terror took. And these terrorists killed, but they did not torture. He who has no ears to sense the difference understands nothing of the 20th century history of Eastern and Central Europe.

The commander in chief of the national army was Miklós Horthy[13], then 51 years old. He came from a family of landed gentry and owned about 1500 acres. A pauper in comparison with the great landlords, and a nobody in the company of aristocrats, he was a haughty lord to all peasants, workers and the middle class. He was a naval officer in the Monarchy, a rear admiral of the fleet, for several years aide-de-camp to Francis Joseph I — a conservative, iron-fisted, not particularly bright officer, who spoke the official language of the Monarchy better than his own mother tongue even when he was national commander in chief. He was not made commander in chief just because he had the highest military rank, but primarily because none of the politicians likely to take part in the pending struggle for power considered him a serious opponent.

In March 1920, Miklós Horthy of Nagybánya was elected Regent of Hungary, and became the *de facto* and to all intents and purposes unrestricted ruler of the country for a quarter of a century.

I have seen this upright, hawk-nosed gentleman in photos and newsreels countless times, and two or three times in person. He usually wore the dress uniform of a naval officer with many medals, and he liked to appear in public on horseback. Hence his nickname: the mounted sailor.

Looking back from the distance of many years, and knowing now the facts of history, the secret archives and Horthy's autobiography, I can only say that he was significant neither as a politician nor as a personality. It is typical, though, that for twenty-four years not a single politician of greater abilities turned against him. All of them recognized his power. He never had a real opponent. The solution of this riddle I leave to historians and philosophers.

Just a few months after his election as Regent, the ultra nationalist Horthy signed the Treaty of Trianon[14] which made three million Hungarians share the fate of other ethnic minorities. Hungary's territory was reduced from 105,000 square miles to 35,000, her population from 18 million to 8 million. Several hundred thousand Hungarians fled to Hungary from beyond the new borders, to live in railway wagons and other makeshift emergency housing for years. The peace terms Horthy accepted were much worse than those both the Károlyi government and the Republic of Councils had refused to accept. Doubtless he had no choice. Or rather, he did have: for someone who came so far into conflict with his own principles ought perhaps to have resigned. But it was typical of Horthy's career that he never resigned, and always claimed that he had no other choice.

The two years following the fall of the Republic of Councils was a period of total chaos. The consolidation of the regime started in 1921 when Horthy appointed Count

István Bethlen[15] Prime Minister. Bethlen, who was the most sophisticated politician of the Horthy era, was the descendant of one of the oldest aristocratic families in the country; among his ancestors we find even rulers of Transylvania. He was a committed conservative. His ten-year term as Prime Minister is rightly regarded as the period of the regime's consolidation. After his resignation, he continued as an *eminence grise*, to influence all significant political decisions in Hungary, and his Anglophile orientation greatly contributed to the pro-German Horthy's slow distancing of himself from Hitler in the course of World War II. He was a short, wiry man with a moustache; though of royal descent, he wore a morning coat in an age when general managers and bankers were resorting to the painfully ridiculous anachronism of parading in the plumed hats, short, braided, fur-lined coats, swords and boots, that were the gala dress of the Hungarian nobility. But even he could not save old Hungary.

The economic consolidation of the country meant that in 1929, the golden age of the Bethlen era, Hungary's output reached roughly the pre-war level. But whereas before the war Hungary's rate of economic growth roughly equalled the European average, after the war the average industrial growth rate in Europe was twice the Hungarian; the country's economic backwardness was growing.

Economically, the Bethlen consolidation meant nothing more than the restoration of the pre-war situation. As for the social sphere, the Bethlen government wanted nothing better than to maintain the pre-war *status quo*. The country was dominated by landlords and magnates who enjoyed the support of the military, the bureaucracy, and the petit bourgeoisie. As in the Monarchy, workers and peasants were not considered equals. That the rich tormented the poor—or, in Marxist terminology, exploited them—was a matter of personal experience to a boy, the son of an assistant caretaker, who had been swineherd, apprentice, and unemployed journeyman[16]. János Kádár was a trained typewriter mechanic, but he did not work in the trade. During his three-year apprenticeship, he did nothing but clean the workshop and fetch and carry for a year and a half, like his fellow apprentices. Then he was taught the trade for half a year, and in the third year, when his employer sent him out to maintain typewriters, he had to say that he was a journeyman. It paid the employers to have the apprentices do the simpler jobs of the journeymen.

That Kádár never worked in the trade was not only because the completion of his apprenticeship coincided with the widespread unemployment of the Depression. He was in his last year when on one occasion he went into the workshop in a torn shirt. His employer was angry; he could not send him out to customers in such a state. He growled at him:

"What are you doing in a torn shirt?"

Need I add that in those days it was natural in Hungary for an employer to use a familiar tone with his apprentice?

"It's the only one I've got."

Kádár didn't say so but I can imagine that by then he was boiling with anger.

"Come and see me on Sunday, I'll give you a shirt."

I know from Kádár that though he was never finicky about food or clothing, even as a child it gave him the shivers to wear someone else's cast-off clothing. This was probably the reason why his reply was so impertinent:

"Why not today?"

His employer just asked him when he was to finish his apprenticeship. Kádár told him.

"Don't even show up the next day. I don't need a man like you."

There were not many people working as typewriter mechanics. Kádár recollects that there may have been around a hundred and fifty in the capital. Of course, everybody knew everything about everyone. This exchange of words contributed to ensuring that Kádár was a typewriter mechanic only on paper.

The boy often discussed their lot with his mother. Borbála Csermanek knew how miserable the life of the poor was, if anybody did. But she would say time and again:

"They are villains, Jani, but you can't do a thing against them. They are stronger than us."

I think these words were spoken by millions of workers and peasants in those days. They knew their poverty and also who was to blame, but they had no hope of changing their lot. The unbridled terror, the disillusionment following the suppression of the revolution not only paralysed the working class movement, it had also broken people's faith.

The change came with the Great Depression of 1929. During the four years of crisis, the output of Hungarian industry fell by 24 per cent, the number of industrial workers by 30 per cent, and there was a threefold increase in the number of the industrial unemployed. Casual work in agriculture fell by 50–60 per cent, and more than half a million of the agrarian proletariat was totally or partially unemployed. A quarter of the capital's population lived on low and irregular benefits, on charity and soup kitchens.

The largest demonstration of workers in the inter-war years took place on September 1, 1930. As early as the summer mass unemployment had made for a heated atmosphere throughout the country. On August 11, the Trade Union Council published an appeal to the workers of Budapest to lay down their tools at 11 o'clock on September 1, to join the unemployed at a mass meeting. The government banned the march. The National Federation of Industrialists decided to keep all factories closed on September 1 to deprive the workers of assembly points. The trade union shop stewards had met and decided to cancel the mass meeting because of the police ban, but called on the workers and the unemployed to express their protest by a "peaceful walk". More than a hundred thousand people came out on the streets, and the peaceful walk soon turned into a bloody clash. During the skirmishes one worker died, seventy demonstrators and a few policemen were seriously injured, and several hundred people were arrested.

This day was also János Kádár's baptism of fire. This is how he remembered it twenty-five years later:

"Since I was unable to find a job in my trade and had to make a living somehow, in the summer of 1930 I was working as a warehouse-hand for a carpet wholesaler in Klauzál Street. I was doing my work one morning quite unaware of the political struggles of the working class, when the warehouse was suddenly closed amidst some excitement, and we were told not to come to work until the next day.

"I looked around and saw that all around the shops and workshops were being closed in great haste. There were few people on the streets. An older worker was passing by the building, shaking his fist, and yelling: 'You just wait, you bourgeois, now we'll get even with you!' He was alone, and had hurt nobody, but I saw that it was he who had frightened the petty bourgeois of Klauzál Street. I heard that the unemployed were demonstrating in Nagymező Street. I rushed there and it was like an abandoned battlefield. The street was empty, and I was walking over the glass fragments of the shattered shop windows. Andrássy Avenue was in a similar state. I set out along the deserted street to go towards the park. There was a police cordon at the Grand Boulevard. I could go no further. It was the same at Király Street. On the corner of Dob Street I met some demonstrating workers on their way back from the City Park. I joined them. They were talking about the clashes in and around the City Park. There was a festive mood, a certain cheerful tension about them, and I was caught up in it, too. A horse-drawn lorry laden with soda water syphons drove out from one of the gates in Dob Street. One of the workers walking beside me yelled at the driver and his mate: 'Why are you working, there is a strike today!' Then the driver struck the worker in the face with his whip. What followed took place within seconds. I did not think, I had come to no decision. To this very day I don't know how it happened but all at once I found myself in the midst of a fistfight between hooligans and demonstrators."

During the fighting Kádár was beaten unconscious. He came to on a bench where he had been taken by his unknown mates. Though he had got involved primarily out of curiosity, his participation in the September 1 demonstration started something in him similar to the process triggered by his reading of *Anti-Dühring*, an experience not entirely digested, and one which he had come by accidentally. These two accidents made for the inevitable: Kádár's life and character were such that he had to encounter the working class movement sooner or later.

Above Ground, Underground

When the Depression was at its worst in August 1931, István Bethlen and his cabinet resigned. In September 1931 János Csermanek became a member of the Hungarian Federation of Young Communist Workers (KIMSZ)[17].

"In the first half of 1931, I spent a lot of time out of work, waiting for a job in the ironworkers' section of the labour exchange in József Street", Kádár recalled in 1956. "People didn't call the state labour exchange the 'spittoon' for nothing. Anyone who had had breakfast, had 20 fillérs in his pocket for a piece of bread and five Levente cigarettes seemed a rich man. As we cursed the industrialists, our stomachs growling, our main occupation was indeed spitting.

"There were also passionate political debates in the 'spittoon'. A few workers influenced by the right-wing Social Democrats kept echoing Peyer's[18] words: 'We must wait patiently, we mustn't make things worse by irresponsible action!' At that time, many unorganized workers, men without class-consciousness, frequented the place. At that time, I was one of them. But the overwhelming majority of these people, including myself, agreed that what the Communist propagandists said was true. We called for struggle and booed at those who bade us be patient. Several times a day we drove out the police who wanted to quieten us down. Earlier I had thought that I was weak and helpless, that I could starve or freeze to death with my whole family without other people as much as noticing. But there I came to understand that there were many, many thousands of us workers, and that we would work and live — if we fought.

"I had broken free of the childish daydreams that had cast a veil over, and had made one forget one's penury; I no longer wanted to be either a football player in the national team, or a chess master; I simply wanted to be an iron worker in employment receiving a decent wage for his work. By then I knew that one must fight for that."

So simple, everyday, and self-evident was the way to a worker's acquiring class-consciousness, the process Marx abstracted into a philosophy of history. It is worthwhile quoting the relevant lines from *The Poverty of Philosophy*: "Economic conditions had first transformed the mass of the people of the country into workers. The combination of capital has created for this mass a common situation, common interests. This mass is thus already a class against capital, but not yet for itself. In the struggles... this mass becomes united, and constitutes itself as a class for itself. The interests it defends become class interests."

Kádár's recollections contain two essential elements, exactly those which Marx designates as basic to acquiring class-consciousness. One was the recognition of the fact that he was not alone. Kádár, who had been an apprentice in a small workshop and had worked for small companies, came to this realization in the labour exchange, where every day he met hundreds of fellow workers who shared his fate. He also recognized that without fighting he would not be able to create the decent life he had always instinctively desired for himself, for his family, and for his fellow men. And this was no less than the recognition of the necessity of the class struggle.

When I asked Kádár why he had become a Communist, he considered his reply for a long time, as he always does when he wants to put something very precisely. This is the essence of what he said:

"It was a matter not of theory, but of interest; at that time I knew nothing about Marxist theory, but I had learned and had come to recognize that I could realize my just interests only by uniting with others. And when I say interests, I am not thinking only of my personal interests. I felt a responsibility for my working friends, and later, however bombastic it might sound, for all my fellow workers. There was also anger in me. We can call it defiance or outrage. It was my conviction — as it is today — that he who works has rights as well. And the more so if he works well. But my experience was that it was in vain that I did my work conscientiously, it was as if I were being given my wages as a favour, and I could never be sure when I would find myself on the dole however well I worked. This offended me, angered me, and hurt my pride. I wanted to live in a world where the worker got what he deserved for his work."

The rest happened like this:

"At the beginning of September 1931 as I was walking in Barcsay Street lost in thought, a familiar voice greeted me. It was János Fenákel, my friend from the HSC football team, whom I had not seen for five years. In the course of our conversation it turned out that the same ideas preoccupied us both, ideas which had very little to do with football. We were both young unemployed workers. I told him what the situation was at home, how I kept looking for a job in vain. I told my friend that I had already taken part in the demonstration of the unemployed and that I knew that we were lost if we did not fight, but added that I had no idea how to go on from there.

"When my friend heard me speak like this, he told me that he was a member of the Hungarian Federation of Young Communist Workers and that I should join, too. It was the first time that I met a man who was a member of an illegal movement, who was a Communist. I was very surprised. I cannot now recall what I imagined Communists looked like at the time, but I was surprised that a young skilled worker, someone just like me, whom I knew well and had played football with as a boy, was a Communist."

His admission into the Hungarian Federation of Young Communist Workers must have left a very deep impression on Kádár, for even after half a century he remembers if not the exact date, the fact that it all happened on a Thursday, around five o'clock in the afternoon, in one of the flats at 22 Paulay Ede Street. It was where the "Sverdlov" cell of the Federation met, a group consisting of three young workers, with a girl as secretary. They told Kádár who Sverdlov was—he had never heard his name before—told him who the Bolsheviks were—he knew precious little about them, too—and what the Soviet Union was: Kádár knew little enough about that as well. They talked about conspiracy, about the movement's illegal and legal work, and Kádár received his first alias, something which was compulsory in the underground. From then on he was called Barna (Brown). Probably because his hair was blond, but Kádár does not remember exactly. What he does remember, however, is that when he was told to be prepared for the permanent threat of arrest from then on, it was not so much the police he was afraid of, as of his *Mutter*'s quarrelling with him if that were to happen.

It did happen, and very soon.

He was arrested for the first time on November 9; he was to spend seven years of his life in jail. At the police station he received the customary sound beating. He was threatened, and promised all sorts of things, but nothing could be got out of him. No charge could be laid, and he was freed three months later. By February 1932 János Barna was already a member of the District Committee, and a few months later he became the secretary of the KIMSZ Central Committee, which meant that he automatically became a member of the Hungarian Communist party.

Today it seems almost unbelievable that a twenty-year-old worker, who hardly knew what Marxism, socialism, the Soviet Union, or the Hungarian and international working class movements were all about, a young man who had no experience of daily politics, could, within half a year of his joining, become the secretary of the illegal Communist party's youth organization.

"I did not really understand", says Kádár "what this post meant. In those days all that mattered was the struggle, that was all that preoccupied me."

What had made such rapid advancement not only possible but necessary was that the growing activity of the working class movement as a result of the economic crisis had made the police step up their campaign against the Communists to an unprecedented degree, with the result that they practically wiped out the entire party leadership. New people were needed in the place of those arrested, irrespective of whether they were experienced or not.

The political police managed to plant a traitor in the leading bodies of the party; he had become a member of the Central Committee and of the secretariat, and had betrayed several of the party's leaders. In 1932, the members of the party's illegal secretariat were arrested and were summarily convicted. The pretext for the proceedings was that Szilveszter Matuska, who was probably working for the police, blew up the railway bridge at Biatorbágy in circumstances which are still not clear to this day. Twenty-one people died in the wreckage of the international express, and many were seriously injured. In vain were the protests of a number of outstanding European politicians and intellectuals – Léon Blum, Thomas Mann, Paul Fauré, Bertolt Brecht, Johannes R. Becher, Ludwig Renn, Anna Seghers, Ernst Toller, Käthe Kollwitz, Karl Kautsky, Henri Barbusse, Romain Rolland, Louis Aragon, and André Gide. Two Communist leaders, Imre Sallai[19] and Sándor Fürst[20], were sentenced to death and executed. As far as it can be determined from the documents at our disposal, 146 people were arrested in 1932 on charges of being Communists, and proceedings were started against another 152. In 1933, more than 300 Communists were imprisoned. This was the time when János Kádár was arrested again. And what he was afraid of came to pass: during visiting hours, his mother took him to task in no uncertain terms for being taken away just when she was making dumplings for the family dinner.

We can only guess at how many members the Communist party had in Hungary in the thirties. Strictly an underground movement, there were, naturally, no records and great care was taken to eliminate all possible traces. Conspiracy does not favour the historians of the future.

On the basis of what can be proved today, there were about 500 members in regular contact with the party leadership. This does not mean that the party had 500 members, much less does it mean that there were so many Communists in Hungary. In an organization based strictly on conspiracy, a contact's arrest, emigration, expulsion, omission or withdrawal meant that dozens lost contact with the party as an organization for a shorter or longer period, or for good. According to conservative estimates, the party had approximately 1000–1500 illegal members active in Hungary in those years, and the number of those who, for one reason or another – for example, because they lived in the provinces – were unable to make contact with the party is estimated to have been about twice or three times this number. The matter of factions is a separate question. There were several groups working in the capital which called themselves Communists, their leaders having quit the party partly for theoretical and political, and partly for personal reasons.

It is not my task here to analyze their extremely complex role, but I think that the majority of their members were convinced socialists who, for reasons of strict conspiracy, sometimes did not even know that they did not belong to the Communist party. At the same time, it is also true that the political police employed the clever tactic of tolerating the activity of these groups from time to time as a means of reducing the membership in the Communist party. There was a great deal of fluctuation in the ring of sympathizers and helpers around the party, and the estimates are so contradictory that I think the numbers cannot be established even today. Inconclusive as these data are, they clearly illustrate that big waves of arrest such as the one in 1932 were enough to wipe out practically the whole party leadership.

It was hardly ideal that a movement exposed to so many dangers should have people with as little experience, practice and knowledge as Kádár for its responsible leaders, and, of course, he was not the only one. But the position of the Communist party and working class movement between the two world wars was anything but ideal.

The Communist movement never recovered from the defeat of the Republic of Councils. Modern history demonstrates, and there are enough examples from the Paris Commune through Spain to Chile, that whenever revolution is defeated by counter-revolution, the revolutionaries are virtually paralyzed for years. This is partly because counter-revolution destroys the revolution's organizations and leaders and without these no movement is combat-ready, and partly because people are paralyzed not only by terror, but also by a sense of defeat.

The most experienced Hungarian Communist leaders emigrated, were imprisoned or executed. The best Social Democratic leaders also had to emigrate, and the leadership of the party went to the right-wing, which considered cooperation with the Communists a tragic mistake.

The movement was just the tip of the iceberg. The iceberg itself, the people, whose freedom, rights, welfare and human dignity the Republic of Councils wished to secure, could, in reality, get precious little from the short-lived and economically drained Council Republic during the months of life and death struggle. The most class-conscious workers who, despite all this, stood by the revolution were killed, tortured, imprisoned or exiled. The masses were exhausted and apathetic; though their backbone was not, their faith was broken. Kádár's mother put their views when she said that the upper class were villains, but there was nothing you could do about them; they were the stronger. In the twenties and the thirties, a worker and a peasant was happy if he and his family did not starve. Whereas in 1921 the trade unions had 150 thousand members, in 1938 there were 110 thousand, and by 1942 only 70 thousand members. In the middle of the thirties, every tenth worker was a trade union member, at the beginning of the forties, every twentieth. During the ten years between 1927 and 1937, an average of one per cent of the workers was on strike annually.

Lenin called left-wing Communism an infantile disorder. Left-wing Communism, the cause of so many errors, mistakes, sins, suffering and horror in the Communist movement, has taken several forms, from the dogmatism which reduced theory to a set of commandments, to Pol Pot's reign of terror in Cambodia. The common root is probably the fanaticism of all revolutionaries, a fanaticism without which no revolution could come about or win. But if blind faith kills reason and the ability to engage in sober analysis, it can lead to the most terrible catastrophe. If leaders see what they would like to see happening and not what actually is happening, one way or another it will inevitably lead to distorted policies. And the more difficult, the more hopeless the situation is, the sooner will people escape into the world of daydreams.

The daydream which held the Hungarian Communist leaders under its spell even after the failure of the Republic of Councils was that the victory of the socialist revolution was possible in Hungary and Europe in the near future. And yet, after the last armed uprising of the German workers, the popular uprising in Bulgaria, and the mass strike in Poland were suppressed in 1923, it became evident that the last post-war revolutionary waves were spent. The Communist International recognized this in theory, but the recognition did not transform practice. The leaders of the Hungarian party, most of whom lived in Vienna or Moscow, totally misread the situation at home and in Europe, and continued to regard the dictatorship of the proletariat as their goal, something that was quite hopeless at the time. It was a harmful policy of messianism; only a revolutionary situation can give rise to a revolution.

The result was the grave error of repudiating alliance with any other leftist forces. In 1925, there was an attempt to seek a way out: Communists and left-wing Social Democrats founded a legal party, the Socialist Workers' Party of Hungary, but it was short-lived. One reason was that its leaders were all arrested and the police managed to frustrate its activity; another was that the Communist leaders in exile were unwilling to give up their dream of the immediate dictatorship of the proletariat.

That they expected a miracle was, in human, psychological terms, understandable. In 1945, when the Red Army liberated Hungary, hundreds of the former supporters of the Republic of Councils could not understand why the dictatorship of the proletariat was not immediately established, and there were several places where local council governments were spontaneously set up, so that the Communist party and the authorities had to intervene.

This, of course, explains but does not excuse the erroneous policies of the Communist leaders during the twenties and thirties. The errors were only aggravated by that inevitable disease of all exiled politicians – factionalism – which afflicted the Hungarian Communists living abroad as well. The moderates grouped around the impressive Jenő Landler[21] were for cooperation with the Social Democrats and the trade unions. The radicals led by Béla Kun, the recognized leader of the Republic of Councils, knew only one goal: the illegal party was to prepare the second dictatorship of the proletariat in Hungary, and was to ally with no one. If we disregard the various deviations and the various degrees of programme modification, we will find that up to the mid-thirties, the policy of the Hungarian Party of Communists was determined by Kun's line.

The strategy was typical not only of the Hungarian party, but of the Communist movement the world over. The Hungarian Party of Communists: this name meant that the party was the Hungarian section of the Communist International. It was the same with the Social Democrats: the Social Democratic Party of Hungary was the Hungarian section of the Socialist International. At that time, as far as organization was concerned, the working class movement still clung to the Marxist principle of one unified party for the workers of the world.

The Communist International broke away from the Socialist International in 1919. For a few years there were attempts to unify the two organizations, but soon it became clear that this was impossible. There were fundamental differences in their aims: the Communists wanted revolution, the Social Democrats wanted to change society through reforms. The tragic fratricidal struggle went to the point where Communists and Social Democrats often hated each other more than the enemy who threatened both. The conflict had the most horrific consequences in Germany, where the antagonism of the two workers' parties contributed to the coming to power of the National Socialists.

Factionalism has inherent laws of its own. For example, truth is often sacrificed to group interest, personal conflict, lack of confidence, and prejudice. Factional conflict was something not only the Communist movement of those days suffered from; its effects were felt in the party decades later, not least importantly in the form of grave human tragedies.

"I knew nothing about these debates in those days" says Kádár. "I was interested only in the struggle, and thought little about theoretical, strategic questions."

Obviously, Kádár wants to avoid giving the impression of being cleverer in retrospect than the party's contemporary leaders, now all dead. But knowing his fundamentally realistic cast of mind, and knowing that he lived among workers and peasants, it is difficult to imagine that he, too, believed in the imminence of the dictatorship of the proletariat. In fact, he has noted a number of times that he had little hope of living to see workers coming to power in Hungary; this, however, did not prevent him from fighting for a cause whose victory he would probably never benefit from.

"There is no need to make myths about the workers", he says. "But we certainly knew the smell of each other's sweat. I had a colleague in the factory, an umbrella-maker. He was a demon for work. He worked at home, too, his whole family helped. But he drank like a fish, and could never earn enough money. Then he joined the Arrow Cross Party[22], and was always shooting his mouth off. When I was already working in the underground, I met him once by chance. He did not go to the police. After 1945, he looked me up at the party headquarters. At the time, I was deputy chief police commissioner. 'What did you do [in the Arrow Cross movement – Ed.] ?' I asked him. 'Nothing', he said. 'When I got drunk I talked a lot. And you know that I often got drunk.' 'Lie low for a few weeks', I told him, 'until things calm down. Then report to the police.' As far as I know, he later became an honest working bloke."

Kádár could not know about the infighting within the party leadership, if for no other reason than because the party worked according to the strictest conspiratorial rules. Each party cell consisted of three or four Communists working, if possible, in the same field. In principle, they knew only each other's code names, but this was often impossible in practice. Only the secretaries of the cells were in contact with one member of the four or five member district committees. There was the same type of conspiratorial contact between the district committees and the Budapest party committee, and the Budapest committee and the secretariat. There was practically no national network. The "Committee Abroad" regularly sent leaders back through clandestine channels to direct the work at home, but they had to be changed frequently to avoid arrest, something they often did not succeed in evading even so.

Working underground, conspiracy and secretiveness were among the strictest rules of the party. At the same time, it is certain that often these rules were not observed, nor could they be. A good example of this was Kádár's recruitment. Let us imagine the situation: a young man accidentally meets another young man whom he has not seen for five years, that is since he was fourteen; after a short conversation, the first informs the second that he is a member of a strictly illegal organization, invites his childhood friend to join, and the other young man accepts at once. This story, whose validity I cannot doubt, particularly since I know several others like it, is not even remotely connected with what is termed conspiracy. Knowing how rigorously Kádár insisted on the rules of the underground later, I consider this case typical: probably many of those who got into the movement in their youth did so through similar coincidences. I would even hazard the guess that without this accidental recruitment, the party would probably not have survived. Suitability often had to be proved not before, but after admission.

It is a fact, however, that the violation of the rules of the underground and of conspiracy, or just the remotest suspicion of it, was often enough to get someone dropped from the movement. They were not expelled from the party, unlike those who broke under police torture and talked; nor was their party membership suspended, as with those who opposed the party leadership on some political question; it was simply that contact with them was broken. Incidentally, in those days it was not so simple to expel or suspend someone. Not only because, naturally, no records were kept and nobody had a membership card; a few people at most knew of each Communist's party membership. Letting the party membership know that someone had been expelled was quite a headache. The real names of those expelled and the code names of those suspended were printed in publications issued abroad and smuggled into the country, and those produced at home, but these publications did not reach every party member. This is how people who proved to have been police agents and were publicly exposed could continue to work in the movement for quite a long time after.

The opposite also happened, and probably more often. All conspiratorial, strictly illegal organizations of this sort, organizations permanently under police surveillance and in constant danger from planted informers are inevitably hotbeds of distrust and suspicion.

An ambiguous sentence, a wrong emphasis, an inaccuracy, a mistaken combination of various facts were enough to give rise to suspicion. And it was a merciless rule of the underground that contact had to be severed immediately with anyone regarding whom there was the slightest shadow of a doubt, for he was then a danger to dozens of people. Ruthless as it may seem, in the underground there is no room for charges, for evidence, or testimony or defense, nor can there be: the very suspicion is tantamount to a sentence. How many Communists were dropped from the party through sheer suspicion no one will ever know. But we do know of a whole series of terrible tragedies when unjust suspicion crippled the lives of honest and loyal people for years, decades, and sometimes for all their lives. In many cases, the wounds inflicted and suffered during the cruel years in the underground have yet to heal even half a century later.

And it was not only political suspicion that could lead to ostracism. It was enough if one did not have the proper circle of friends and acquaintances, if one attracted too much attention, became too widely known, did not adhere to the "obligatory" moral norms, or was deemed potentially dangerous to the party in any other respect. The tragic expulsion of Attila József, for example, had ideological, artistic, and human reasons. There can be no doubt that the poet deviated from party ideology in a number of questions; for example, he professed the synthesis of Marxism and Freudism. It is also a fact that none of his contemporaries or comrades recognized his poetic genius during his lifetime. Cruel as it might seem, however, a gravely neurotic man undergoing psychoanalysis, who was trying to let his doctors in on his innermost secrets, could not be a member of an illegal organization.

Under the circumstances, vigilance was, of course, a primary requirement in the movement. But an excessively suspicious, captious or just ill-natured man could not only embitter many lives, but could also do a lot of harm to the movement. I heard from Kádár that during World War II, when he was already a member of the secretariat, he got a message from another secretary of the Central Committee who was under arrest. It came through a bribed prison warden, and was to the effect that one of their comrades, a well-known Communist highly-placed even today, was a traitor. Kádár asked through the bribed guard why he thought so. The reply: the man said he would do anything for his sweetheart. And anyone who would do anything for a woman would be capable of betraying the party.

Today, in the quiet of peace time, one can smile at this story, or groan in despair. But at that time, in the shadow of the prison and the gallows, it was bitter reality.

The same member of the Central Committee charged a third member of the secretariat, too, with being a traitor. His grounds: 400 *Pengős* were missing from the party funds which he handled. At that time, this was a clerk's monthly pay. And there were hardly any proper accounts kept of the party's money with vouchers and receipts. As always, Kádár listened to common sense: he could not imagine that someone would embezzle 400 *Pengős* when he was handling several tens of thousands, particularly when the political police would have been willing at any time to reward him for treason with enormous sums of money. But the charge remained, and the third member of the secretariat was dropped from the party with the understanding that he could clear himself after the Liberation. That is what they told him, and he agreed with the decision. In a similar situation he would have done the same, he said. In fact, he did manage to clear himself after the Liberation.

Should we condemn the secretary of the Central Committee for these allegations? We can, and in a certain sense, we must. Particularly because he played a less than noble role after 1949. But we also have to bear in mind that he returned to Hungary from the Soviet Union at the risk of his life, and spent almost ten years in jail where not even his name could be beaten out of him. There are people who are heroic in some situations, and very fallible, even criminal in others.

Should we pass sentence on Kádár for expelling, against his own conviction, a leader of the party whom he knew and respected? We can, and we must, and he himself is not proud of this act. But let us recall for a moment that under permanent threat as the underground was, personal conviction and the sense that one was a good judge of character were not strong enough arguments against suspicion. Who would have dared put the lives of dozens of people, perhaps the whole movement, just because he thought he might be right?

Kádár smiles when he tells these stories. But the smile does not hide the lines on his face.

I know another story. Kádár did not like one of the leaders of the party, and considered his activity harmful. But after 1956, when he was attacked, he came to his defense: he reminded his listeners that when this man was being taken by detectives to a secret meeting before the Liberation he threw himself under a tram rather than expose a comrade.

One can understand this movement only if one is familiar with its woof and warp alike.

I have run ahead in time, but let me dwell upon the inter-war years a little longer. I do not believe that a period, a system, or an organization can be understood without knowing its workaday, everyday life. Anyone who today reads that a leader of an illegal party exchanged information on the most closely kept secrets of the organization through a prison guard might presume either that the Communists had an enormous, well-organized machinery or that they were mad.

The reality was more simple. During the Horthy regime, the prison guards were not particularly well paid; they were usually peasant boys who stayed on as soldiers, and then turned prison guards. Even so there were many applicants, because a small but steady salary, a pension, and the free uniform were better than permanent uncertainty, or working in the fields from dawn to dusk. But a badly paid servant is corruptible not only because he needs the money, but also because he feels no loyalty to his master.

The Communists had no large, well-organized underground apparatus. But they had a few well-operating illegal channels which they had built up with great care. One of the most important of these was the means of remaining in contact with the jailed leaders, for sooner or later almost all their leaders were jailed. They subjected this contact to careful testing; from the meaningless, misleading messages they sent in and out of prison it would immediately have become evident if they had been reported to the police. The real messages were sent only after several test runs.

But the danger of betrayal was still there. There is no illegal work without risks.

But let us get back to the thirties. When Kádár got into contact with the movement, the Communists insisted on the necessity of strict asceticism — another "infantile disorder": he who serves the world revolution neither could nor should have a private life. Kádár knew the working class very well, and knew that workers take to asceticism like cats take to water. Fate had burdened them with enough misery and need for sacrifice; why should they voluntarily deny themselves the few good things they might enjoy?

No matter how compelling Kádár felt party discipline to be, he was unable to ignore his common sense.

"I was arguing and struggling with myself", he says, "but in vain. I was unable to subordinate reality to any kind of theory."

He was not thinking of himself. But he thought that if the party were to try to win over the workers only after they had stopped drinking, smoking, playing cards, and cursing, then the party had had it, and so had the working class. And he hadn't become a Communist for that.

"In the spring of 1932", he recalled, "as a member of the northern territorial committee of KIMSZ, I had a conversation with a young Communist, a working girl, the secretary of the illegal cell at the Silk Works. The cell there had 4 members, and they had not recruited a new member for months. I asked her why. The comrade said that they had not admitted new members because all the girls working there had no interest in serious things like their economic position or politics. They were interested only in the cinema, in lipstick, in beautiful clothes, and boys, the comrade said. And something to the effect — in a tone of despair — that their morals were not irreproachable (though she used a much stronger expression).

"At first I did not know how to answer her; I just sat silently, and pondered. The secretary of the KIMSZ cell at the Silk Works had been the member of the illegal Communist movement for 6 months at the time of that conversation. Six months earlier she herself had been exactly as she now — looking down at them from the superior heights of a six-month-long illegal past — contemptuously described her fellow working girls to be. She, too, had been interested in the cinema, in beautiful clothes and boys. But not *only* in the cinema, in beautiful clothes and boys. If she had been, it would hardly have been possible to make a Communist out of her. And what a sin it would have been against the movement if the KIMSZ member who had started to talk with her eight months earlier had judged by appearances, and had said with a wave of the hand that it was not worth dealing with her because she was interested only in the cinema, in beautiful clothes, and boys."

The essence of Kádár's later policy is already detectable here. As Brecht pointed out, the people cannot be dismissed: one must live, work, and manage with the people one has in a given country. But such a time was still far into the future; many trials and detours were ahead of Kádár and the Communist movement before this principle could be realized.

Primary among these trials were the pitfalls of the Hungarian political scene of the thirties and forties. This was determined by two factors, whatever government ruled the country. The first was hostility not only to Communism and Social Democracy, but also to all progressive left-wing aspirations and thoughts. The second was the demand for territorial revision. Anyone who did not espouse these two basic principles had no chance of playing a role in Hungarian politics.

Horthy's Hungary was a rather strange type of state. Though in fact everything depended on the personal decision of the Regent, the verbal clashes that took place in Parliament were sometimes as stormy as those in the most developed bourgeois democracies. There was a multi-party system, but nobody threatened the absolute power of the government party, which changed names several times. That no one did was small wonder in an electoral system in which the secret ballot was introduced only in 1938; until then, 199 out of the 245 Members of Parliament were openly elected on the pretext that secretiveness did not befit the Hungarian national character. The franchise was restricted to citizens over 30 years of age with six years residence in a given electoral district, and with six years of elementary schooling. Aristocrats with family-trees going back several hundred years, Jewish bankers, army officers, priests, diplomats were all to be found in the succession of governments, and initially, one or two "token peasants" as well, but they were soon left out. The press was relatively free but the substantive political and social questions were often decided in various secret, semi-secret, and legal organizations like the Etelközi Szövetség[23] (Etelköz Federation), the Magyar Országos Véderő Egylet[24] (Hungarian National Defense Society), Revíziós Liga[25] (The League for the Revision of the Trianon Peace Treaty), the Ébredő Magyarok Egyesülete[26] (Society of Awakening Hungarians), the Kettős Kereszt Vérszövetség[27] (Dual Cross Blood Federation), and the Turul Szövetség[28] (Turul Federation). Their names say a lot about the age and its spirit. Hungary must have been the first country in the world where a large amount of foreign currency was forged "for patriotic purposes" in an official institution, the army's Cartographic Institute, if not with the government's knowledge, at least that of the Prime Minister. The chief of police was one of the main defendants in the trial finally held under foreign pressure. The government was not even shaken by this international scandal, while the opposition MP, who had declared in Parliament that a government which allowed such things to happen could not remain in office, was beaten up in broad daylight by former members of Horthy's officer corps.

The German National Socialists' rise to power had a decisive effect on Hungarian politics. Not only Horthy, but the Anglophile István Bethlen knew that they could realize their plans for territorial revision only with German assistance. And Germany left no doubt as to what she had in mind. "Anyone who wants to sit at the table has at least to help in the cooking", Hitler told the Hungarian Prime Minister when the latter paid a courtesy call. Hungary became a prisoner to her own policy. The government put all its eggs in one basket: the revision of the truly unjust Treaty of Trianon; it thus not only plunged the country into catastrophe, but made a settlement of the border question impossible in the long term as well. It is an illuminating, though for us tragic, example of the dialectics of history. Germany first annexed Austria, then partitioned, and the next year occupied Czechoslovakia. Hungary also got her share of the prey. The first Vienna Award of the Axis powers returned about 4,600 square miles to the mother country together with a million people, most of them Magyars. The second Vienna Award in 1940 returned about 16,500 square miles of Transylvanian territory to Hungary along with two and a half million people, of whom one million were Romanians.

Up to that point, the assistance Hitler required was only economic and political. But in 1939, Germany attacked Poland and World War II broke out.

The Prime Minister of the Hungarian government at the time was Count Pál Teleki[29]. It is worth dwelling upon his personality, because he was a characteristic figure of his time. He was a descendant of one of the most ancient aristocratic families in the country, an outstanding geography scholar, and a follower of István Bethlen. He was one of the men behind the moves to overthrow the Republic of Councils. As Foreign Minister, he was a member of the delegation which signed the Treaty of Trianon which he himself roundly condemned. He was Prime Minister from 1920, the year flogging was re-introduced in Hungary. He had to resign as Prime Minister because he supported the return of King Charles IV. He participated in the Franc forgery project, was a supporter of research in the social sciences, and was the country's chief Boy Scout. As Prime Minister, he saw that the Second Anti-Jewish Law[30] was passed, and withdrew from the League of Nations. After the outbreak of World War II, he tried to convince Great Britain that he was cooperating with Hitler under duress. After the partition of Poland, he provided humane refuge to more than 100,000 Poles. At the same time, he joined the German–Italian–Japanese tripartite treaty. He signed a perpetual non-aggression treaty with Yugoslavia. When Hitler attacked Hungary's southern neighbour, and Horthy and the cabinet decided on Hungary's participation in the military action, the deeply religious Pál Teleki committed the deed for which his religion gives no forgiveness: he committed suicide. His farewell letter to the Regent is one of the tragic documents of Hungarian history:

"Your Excellency,

We have become faithless – out of cowardice – to the Pact of Everlasting Friendship based on the Address of Mohács. The nation is feeling it, and we have thrown away the nation's honour.

We have taken our stand by the side of blackguards, for not a word of the trumped-up atrocities is true. Neither against Hungarians, nor against Germans! We shall become grave robbers! The basest of nations. I have not restrained you, I am guilty. Pál Teleki."

Hungary's reasons for entering World War II were primarily domestic. The interests, the ideology, the lifestyle of the ruling circles in the social system which came into being after the defeat of the Republic of Councils all impelled the country in that direction. For twenty years, they had been impressing on the nation that territorial revision, which would solve everything, was the country's fundamental goal; and later, that every inch of land regained was to the credit of the Germans; and they proudly professed that they had been anti-Communist before Hitler ever was. All this could hardly have resulted in anything other than Hungary's entry into the war when Germany attacked the Soviet Union.

What would have happened if she had not? It is possible that the pro-German faction would have ensured Horthy's overthrow, although in the light of the contemporary balance of power, the probability seems small. It seems much more probable that the Germans would have occupied the country sooner rather than later. Had this happened, many things would have turned out differently for Hungarian history, and not only at the peace conferences. In 1945, the nation would have started a new period from a different position, with a different kind of self-respect. Hungary's leaders of the day forfeited this opportunity.

The National Socialists' rise to power had a profound effect on the world Communist movement too. The terrible shock when the strongest Communist and Social Democratic parties of Western Europe, the German, were liquidated, their members executed, beaten to death, jailed or shut up in concentration camps put an end to the deplorable fratricidal struggle between them. In 1935, the Seventh Congress of the Comintern declared the struggle against Fascism to be its supreme goal, and called on Communists to join forces with Social Democrats, trade unionists and all democratic forces. The Executive Committee of the Socialist International lifted its ban on forming a united front as early as the end of 1934.

It was not easy to put a popular front policy into practice. People who had been calling each other class traitors one day were hardly able to digest that they were brother workers the next. Undoubted differences remained between the policies, strategies, tactics, organizational structures and principles of the Communists and the Social Democrats. In Hungary, it made a considerable difference that the Social

Democratic Party and the trade unions were legal, and strove to avoid being banned at any price, while the Communists were still only able to work underground. Cooperation with the democratic forces was made almost impossible by the fact that at this time the bourgeois politicians in opposition were still unwilling to have anything to do with the Communists.

The situation was not made any easier when the Comintern dissolved the Central Committee of the Hungarian Party of Communists in 1936. The Comintern was right in claiming that though the leadership had, in principle, accepted the necessity for a popular front policy, it had hardly changed earlier practices. Béla Kun was unlawfully arrested; he died in prison, and was rehabilitated only in 1956.

After the Central Committee was dissolved, the party leaders in Hungary, acting on the basis of false, mistaken or misinterpreted information from Vienna, dissolved the party organizations in the country; the result was total chaos. The temporary leader designated by the Comintern started to reorganize the Communist party from Prague. The basic idea was for Communists to infiltrate the legal organizations of the Social Democratic Party and the trade unions.

This is how János Kádár, just released from jail, came to join the 6th District organization of the Hungarian Social Democratic Party. There he was the steward of a group of ten, liaison man for a youth group, district secretary, and member of the district Executive Committee. In the summer of 1941, he became the head of the Budapest territorial committee of the Hungarian Party of Communists.

"Cooperation with the Social Democrats was no problem for me", Kádár recalls. "Most of them were the same kind of working class persons as me. Even if we did not think alike, our lives were alike, so we understood each other."

During the five years he spent in the Social Democratic Party, he not only learned legal party and trade union work, but he also came into close contact with a stratum which he hardly knew before. The Social Democratic Party's group of doctors and artists belonged to the 6th District and for a while Kádár acted as liaison with them. János Kádár, who was brought up in the countryside, and grew up among workers and the petty bourgeoisie, was able to say from then on that he knew the life of all working strata from the inside – something which, of course, it never crossed his mind to put in so many words.

Kádár worked in all sorts of places, wherever he could get work, at a carpet wholesaler's and at a medicinal herb factory, among others.

"I never thought", he says "that the camomile which filled the fields in my childhood was a commodity, and a valuable one at that."

He smiles.

"What kind of work did I do? Today, the refined term is a 'material handler'; in plain language, I was drudging."

I do not think that this work hurt Kádár's self-esteem. To begin with, in those days he was already preoccupied first and foremost with the working class movement; but he also likes to work at any sort of job. He is the type who is incapable of doing a bad job.

"I have always worked properly wherever I was", he says.

Péter Veres[31] writes of the seasonal workers and the navvies working on the railway that they worked well out of sheer pride; it would have been a shame to do otherwise. This is how Kádár remembers it:

"I was working as a journeyman at a small firm where we knew what orders had been placed. We learned that there were orders for only two months, and once these were completed we would be fired. We decided to "pace" two months' work to last four. And that is what we did. I must say that I had worked before and afterwards, but never suffered so much. I half worked, half didn't. We struggled and suffered. It is bad for a man not to do real work."

He also knew that he could be relatively independent in any place if he worked well. And this was very important to him.

"When I was taken on, I always asked the boss to tell me what my job was, and leave the rest to me, and he would be satisfied with my work."

He found being bossed about very hard to take. It was much worse than the hardest work.

Wherever he worked, he observed and learned. He watched how the work was organized, how the marketing was done, how and why people were hired and fired, how production went and by what methods they tried to increase it.

"Perhaps I was lucky", he says "to have worked at so many places. This way I learned more."

He observed people in particular. His curiosity about people is insatiable even today.

"Once a comrade asked me to let him go with me to a factory. This was sometime in the sixties. He told me that he wanted to meet some interesting people. I was amazed. I had never met a person who was of no interest. Every human being is interesting."

This is an honest statement, although it may seem naive. I have observed several times how passionately interested he is in people. When I talked to him privately for the first time in my life, he spent an hour asking me where I had come from, who my parents and family were, how I grew up, how I worked, how my days went, what my hobbies and aspirations were. I think it is people that interest him the most of all.

He worked longest in an umbrella factory employing a hundred people. When he was let out of jail, one of his friends recommended him to the owner. In those days, prisoners had their heads shaved, so he could not deny where he had come from. He told the boss why he had been in jail. He got the job nevertheless.

"From this point on, I was a 'legalized Communist' in the factory. This was very good, I did not have to pretend and lie all the time."

He recalls and praises this factory to this day. The boss bought the silk and the steel himself, and exported the finished umbrellas himself, or sold them to wholesalers on the home market.

It is worth pondering on people's lives, for they tell us a lot about history. The boss, who was of Jewish origin, perished in a concentration camp. His wife, who had studied economics in the United States and had introduced the Bedeaux-system in their factory, settled in England after 1945. Kádár, the material handler, the delivery man, the general factotum and errand-boy became what he is today.

The boss was fair to him not only when he took him on. One day Kádár got a summons from the police headquarters to appear the next day. The summons gave no indication why. He did not know whether they just wanted to question him on some matter, or whether he had to serve the five months of his temporarily suspended sentence. In any case, he left a letter behind with one of his acquaintances asking the boss to give his working-papers and pay to his mother if he were jailed. The boss not only did that, but when Kádár was let out half a year later — he had to serve the suspended sentence after all — sent a message to him that he would take him back at the factory if he promised that he would not carry on Communist activities there.

"I promised", says Kádár. "What else could I do?"

He smiled.

"But I didn't promise I would not engage in trade-union activity. We fought for and won a two weeks' paid holiday, a very great achievement at the time."

He served his sentence in Szeged, in the infamous Csillag prison. He was taken there by train handcuffed to another prisoner in a normal third-class carriage. The two guards sat facing them. There, too, he observed the people. Those who entered the compartment could not immediately see that they were prisoners. Then they noticed the handcuffs.

"There were some who turned back at once. Others tried to pretend that they noticed nothing. But there were some who offered us cigarettes. Although they had no way of knowing what we were guilty of."

In Szeged, they were led through the city handcuffed. It was Candlemas day, bright and sunny, the streets swarming with people.

"And I was terribly angry that these people were just smiling and talking while we were suffering for them, too."

Today he smiles at his former fury.

"By the same token, I should have been angry with the whole country. Well, it's hard to be objective."

At the Csillag prison they knew how to handle prisoners. The new arrivals were stripped naked between two sets of bars and all their belongings were taken away. Then the barred doors were opened and between the next two sets they got their prison uniforms, mess-tins, and blankets. The political prisoners could move around freely during the day behind the innermost set of bars. They were taken for a walk at noon, when the other prisoners were locked in their cells.

Kádár looked forward to meeting his fellow prisoners, particularly because he knew that Mátyás Rákosi[32] was also a prisoner at the Csillag. Rákosi, one-time people's commissar in the Republic of Councils, was an internationally recognized leader of the Hungarian Communist movement. He had returned to Hungary from the Soviet Union on instructions from the party. He was arrested in 1925 and sentenced for life. After spending sixteen years in jail, he was deported to the Soviet Union where he became the leader of the Hungarian Communists in exile.

The first meeting between Rákosi and Kádár almost miscarried. When Kádár went up to the Communist prisoners, there was a robust man standing in the middle of the group.

"I thought he was Rákosi and I was just about to greet him. Then a short, putty-faced man came up to me and introduced himself as Mátyás Rákosi."

Kádár recounted that Rákosi was the leader of the Communists in prison, too, and gained a number of concessions for the political prisoners from the governors. He held an interesting seminar on the Republic of Councils which was of special interest to Kádár because he hardly knew anything about that period. Only works vilifying Communism were published in Hungary on the dictatorship of the proletariat, and it was the first time that he met a man who had personally taken part in the Council government.

It was in the umbrella factory that Kádár met Judit Szántó, Attila József's common-law wife, and then, through her, the poet, too. Kádár's memory is phenomenal: to this day he recalls that he heard Attila József for the first time at the end of September 1931 in the Kazinczy Street headquarters of the Precious Metal Workers' Trade Union, where the poet was lecturing a working class audience on "Proletarian culture". The poet was 26 at the time, Kádár 19. Later he heard his poems in reading clubs on a number of occasions, and he liked them a great deal. Even today he considers Attila József's poetry an important element in his life.

"He was interested in all the significant questions of the class-struggle", Kádár wrote in 1971, "and was particularly preoccupied with the cultural affairs of the working class. Basically he was quite right, though sometimes impatient in his struggle to end the sectarian isolation of the working class movement. This led to arguments. He was very sensitive to the widespread lack of understanding even on the part of people he would have expected support from. He was defending not something he thought, but something he knew to be true."

Judit Szántó was an umbrella maker, recited poetry and was a Communist. There was nothing very surprising in this: there were many people in the working class movement whom today we would consider a little odd. Her husband had emigrated, he lived in Moscow with their daughter. Later he married Béla Kun's daughter.

"Judit was a skillful propagandist", says Kádár. "She did nothing but read her daughter's letters to her fellow-workers in the lunch break. The little girl wrote that she was learning to play the piano, and that they were planning to spend their summer holidays in the Crimea."

No explanation was necessary. The umbrella makers knew that the man Judit Szántó was living with was a writer, as was her husband who lived in the Soviet Union, that he made practically no money so that she supported him, and her pay was barely enough to keep the wolf from the door. Sometimes they could afford to pay rent and buy fuel, sometimes they could not.

When Kádár met Judit Szántó, Attila József was becoming more and more neurotic, and she lived in permanent fear that he would commit suicide. One day she was so worried that she asked Kádár to go to their flat to see how Attila József was; she was not able to leave the factory, but Kádár, who was a messenger, could.

The women working in the factory often asked Kádár to see to this or that of their chores, and whenever he could he tried to satisfy the requests. I am all the more inclined to believe this as I have had opportunity to observe his thoughtfulness; it is one of his basic characteristics.

Yet Judit Szántó's request was unusual. Kádár rang the bell in vain, and then entered the flat with the key she had given him. Attila József was lying in bed — at noon, something almost unheard of for Kádár — and was sound asleep, or at least seemed to be. Kádár was frightened, and started to shake Attila József.

"He was a thin man of slight build", says Kádár. "As I was shaking him, I was afraid he would break in my hands."

Finally the poet woke up from his dazed sleep, and then it was his turn to be frightened: how had this stranger got to his bedside, and why was he shaking him? Kádár finally managed to explain the unusual situation, and then they started to talk. He told Attila József that he had heard his lecture, and liked his poems, and the poet slowly calmed down.

What the greatest poet of the age wanted most was to be loved. To be loved for himself and for his poetry. Had he got that, perhaps he would not have ended under a freight train.

Kádár met Attila József once again at the request of Judit Szántó, although by that time Attila József was no longer living with her. The poet was living at his sister's boarding-house, editing an ephemeral periodical — as Kádár recollects, just a few issues were published — in which Kádár found the theoretical articles obscure.

"We argued", says Kádár. "Well, to the extent it was possible to argue with him. He was so convinced he was right that he tolerated no contradiction. That was the first time I heard the phrase 'national Communism'. I did not understand it. For me Communism was internationalism. Now I understand what Attila József meant. Something not very different from what Lenin had in mind when he emphasized the significance of the national features in socialism. At most, it was a case of mistaken emphasis; but after all, he was a poet and not a politician."

"She was a tough woman", he says of Judit Szántó. "She suffered in silence, but was like an exclamation mark. It was impossible not to notice, particularly for a man as sensitive as Attila József. She was the same in the movement, too: strict, uncompromising, puritanical. I knew more than one like her among the Communists at the time.

"The derangement of Attila József's personality was aggravated not only by his inability to support himself, but by the thought that Judit Szántó sustained him by hard work, self-discipline, and sacrifice. Who can bear it when another person sacrifices him or herself for him?"

I am not trying to solve the secret of Attila József's tragedy; I am writing about János Kádár. But the way one relates to a genius is very revealing.

The 7th Congress of the Comintern gave a great boost to the Hungarian working class movement. There were more strikes from 1936 on, trade union membership grew at a rate not seen since the Great Depression, and many Social Democratic Party branches doubled their membership. More than a thousand Hungarian volunteers fought on the Republican side in the Spanish Civil War, and many hundreds fell. The Communist party carefully organized the illegal route to Madrid through Prague.

Although Kádár was a convinced internationalist, he felt he had to fight at home.

Hungary's entry into the war strengthened not only the Right, but also the Left. A growing number of groups sought an opportunity to cooperate in the fight against Fascism. In the autumn of 1941, there were two significant demonstrations: one at the memorial torch to the Prime Minister of the first independent Hungarian government, who was executed in 1849, the other at the grave of the leader of the 1848 War of Independence. In the famous Christmas issue of the daily *Népszava*[33] (People's Voice), the most significant opposition personalities took a stand against Fascism, the war and German influence. In addition to Social Democrats and Communists, there were articles by populist writers representing the peasantry, by Endre Bajcsy-Zsilinszky[34], the former leader of the "racial purists" and Horthy's friend, who was later a key figure in the resistance movement, as well as by Gyula Szekfü[35], the most significant conservative historian and ideologist of the age, a close associate of István Bethlen's, who became Hungary's first ambassador to Moscow after 1945.

The first legal body uniting the anti-Fascist forces, the Hungarian Historical Commemorative Committee, was formed in February 1942, on Communist initiative. On March 15, the anniversary of the 1848 War of Independence, a demonstration was organized at the statue of Sándor Petőfi[36]. The progressive forces sought to find a common platform in Hungarian history, in 1848 and Petőfi, something everyone considered his own. At earlier demonstrations, there had been a few hundred people, sustained by the faith of tens of thousands and the hopes of hundreds of thousands more. Even this had been no small number in a country at war, when one of the major goals of these demonstrations was to end the war. But the number was hardly enough to influence the policy of a government with such a smoothly-running repressive machinery. Tens of thousands were expected at the March 15 demonstration. But a resolute warning from the Ministry of Home Affairs persuaded the leadership of the Social Democratic Party to forbid their party members to take part at the eleventh hour. The Social Democrat leaders thought that the survival of the party was at stake, and perhaps they were right on that point. What they failed to see was that the survival of the Hungarian nation was at stake, and not just that of Hungarian social democracy.

In the end, several thousand people took part in the demonstration at the Petőfi statue: Communists, Social Democrats who defied the ban, people from the National Peasant Party[37], the anti-German bourgeoisie, progressive intellectuals and left-wing youth. What was planned to be a silent demonstration soon resounded with chants calling for a separate peace, for worker–peasant alliance, and for an independent, free, and democratic Hungary. Finally the crowd was dispersed by the police.

The government hit back hard. Árpád Szakasits[38], the Secretary-General of the Social Democratic Party, was arrested, and more than 400 left-wing Social Democratic Party officials were sent to do forced labour at the front, sent to what was practically certain death. In April 1942 all branches of the security forces, the political police, the gendarmerie, and the military's counterintelligence service set out to liquidate the Communist party. Three of the six members of the Central Committee were arrested; two of them died under torture, the third was executed. More than 200 Communists were sentenced to jail, others were interned, or sent to do forced labour; very few returned.

In May 1942, Kádár got instructions to go underground. Until then, he had been the member of an underground movement working under conditions of legality. Except for his illegal work, his life had not differed much from other people's: he had a registered flat, a job and family. But from then on, he was a member of an underground movement living in illegality; a month later he became a member, then the secretary of the Central Committee. János Kádár took the place of Ottó Korvin[39], who had been sentenced to death; of Sándor Lőwy[40], killed by forced-feeding; of Imre Sallai and Sándor Fürst, who had been executed; of Ferenc Rózsa[41] and Károly Rezi[42], who had been tortured to death; and of Zoltán Schönherz[43], who had been hanged.

After the tough crackdown on the left, Horthy dismissed his pro-German Prime Minister, and appointed Miklós Kállay[44], one of Count István Bethlen's associates, in his place. The period of "playing both sides of the political fence" had started in Hungary.

Many consider Kállay to have been an outstanding tactician, a man able to lead the ever more aggressive German empire by the nose for two years. I see his role differently. Undoubtedly he recognized that Hungary should try to get out of the German alliance, but the most he could achieve was to play for time.

Horthy's and Kállay's responsibility is only augmented by the fact that they saw what was coming. In a lecture to the generals in the autumn of 1942 the chief of staff of the Hungarian army was already questioning the Germans' ability to win the war. In January 1943 the Soviet troops routed the poorly-armed, and poorly supplied and equipped Second Hungarian Army at the Don. In February the Sixth German Army was annihilated at Stalingrad. In May the German and Italian troops surrendered in Africa. In July the Allies landed in Sicily, and Mussolini's dictatorship fell. In October the Italians declared war on Germany.

Meanwhile, Kállay kept sounding the Allies about the possibility of withdrawing from the war. But he made conditions as if Hungary had won the war. The Allies replied that Hungary should negotiate a ceasefire with the state with which it was actually at war, the Soviet Union. This was something Horthy and his associates were not prepared to do.

In the end, Hitler got fed up with the insubordination of his ally. In March 1944 he summoned Horthy and informed him that German troops would occupy Hungary. It is not the task of this book to clarify what happened at that meeting; typically, different accounts have been given by all the participants. It is a fact, however, that Horthy did not resign and did not call on the country and the army to resist.

The Germans entered Hungary with eight to nine divisions, and with carefully prepared lists of names. In a few days, the Gestapo arrested more than 3,000 people with the help of the Hungarian political police. They arrested all the leaders who were unreliable from the German point of view: Social Democrats, Smallholders[45], bourgeois liberals, royalists, and Jewish capitalists. Horthy's former Minister of Home Affairs and confidant was jailed. István Bethlen went underground. Prime Minister Kállay sought political asylum at the Turkish Embassy for a while, and was later arrested. The Communists were not arrested because by then all the leaders of the party were underground.

The Regent appointed an insignificant pro-German diplomat general as Prime Minister in Kállay's place. And he issued a statement according to which the German troops had marched into Hungary on the basis of a preliminary agreement.

After the German occupation the opposition parties and trade unions were banned, and the shipments of Hungarian agricultural and industrial goods to Germany were stepped up. The First Hungarian Army was sent to the front again, 100,000 Hungarian citizens of German origin were drafted into the SS, and the deportation of the Jews started. There were about 800,000 people in Hungary who counted as Jews on the basis of the anti-Jewish laws. Half of them were killed, mostly in concentration camps.

As a result of the occupation, the Allies started the regular bombing of Hungary. In June 1944 the Allies landed in France; in July German officers and politicians attempted to assassinate Hitler. In August after the Red Army broke through the German–Romanian front, Romania asked for an armistice, and then declared war on Germany. Two weeks later Bulgaria also withdrew from the war.

Horthy decided to act – in true Horthy style. Replacing the insignificant pro-German colonel-general, he appointed a pro-Regent colonel-general as Prime Minister. After much hesitation, he brought himself to send a secret armistice delegation to the Soviet Union – without informing either the government, or his own Prime Minister.

The long hesitation gave the Germans time to prepare for the overthrow of the government. Ferenc Szálasi[46], the Arrow Cross leader, was already at the German Embassy. In September Skorzeny, the man who had freed Mussolini, arrived in Budapest charged with the task of occupying the Castle Hill area and arresting Horthy. At the beginning of October, SS General Zelewsky, the man who suppressed the uprising in the Warsaw ghetto, was sent to Hungary. First the Germans arrested the commander of the Budapest army corps, which was of key importance, and then kidnapped the Regent's son.

That day, on October 15, 1944, Admiral Miklós Horthy of Nagybánya, Regent of Hungary, informed the country over the radio that he had concluded an armistice. The Germans frustrated this astonishingly amateurish breakaway attempt in a few hours. Horthy's proclamation was broadcast on the radio at noon; by evening, Ferenc Szálasi's takeover proclamation was being read on the air.

There are various versions of the details of this tragic day. But no explanation can change the facts. Few people have left the historical scene so dishonourably after a quarter of a century of rule as Miklós Horthy. He was unable to save either his country or his regime; nor could he rescue his best friends and the people most faithful to him.

Hungary's new ruler, Ferenc Szálasi, the head of the Arrow Cross Party, was a man of even lesser capabilities than Horthy. He was National Leader with the Regent's authority, Prime Minister and Supreme Warlord, that is, Commander in Chief of the armed forces. He selected his cabinet from the leaders of ultra right-wing parties and groups.

The Arrow Cross Party had time enough only for devastation and murder. A sort of intoxicated, irresponsible mindlessness prevailed in Hungary during those months; as the contemporary song said: "The world is but a day." The Arrow Cross rabble (it is difficult to call this mob anything else) carried off, tortured and executed people. They armed children and sent them against the Soviet tanks with rifles in their hands. Fifty thousand of the 150,000 Jews living in Budapest were dispatched to Germany on foot; many of them, mostly women and children perished on the way. Seventy thousand of the capital's Jews were fenced off in a ghetto in an area where until then 7,000 people had lived. One hundred thousand soldiers and about half a million civilians were taken to Germany. True, some of them left voluntarily. There were some who rightfully thought that they would be taken to task in the months to come. But most of them simply believed what the propaganda machinery had been hammering into their heads for years, that the Russians would cut a foetus out of its mother's womb. According to the records of the Arrow Cross ministries, of doubtful accuracy at best, 55,000 wagons of goods were taken to Germany from Hungary.

On April 4, 1945 the Nazi troops were driven out of the last Hungarian village. Hungary was liberated.

But to get back to Kádár: in 1942, György Goldman, the outstanding sculptor, had looked him up in the umbrella factory and told him to go underground immediately; the wave of arrests was such that not a single known Communist was safe.

However, it was not that simple. Since Kádár could not now go home, he had neither money, nor clothes, nor a place to stay. He went to the factory office and asked the accountant to give him his wages and two weeks' holiday pay. The woman asked no questions, but gave him the money, although she could hardly have had any doubts as to why Kádár had to disappear so suddenly.

The greatest problem was where to stay. In those days, the Communist party was not yet equipped to provide illegal flats for members in trouble. By March 1944, the time of the German occupation, the Communists had managed to build up their illegal network to such an extent that in a number of cases it was they who provided the Social Democratic leaders in hiding with flats, money and forged documents. For example Kádár, who had a flair for drawing, was a specialist in official stamps. He learnt how to do it from Endre Ságvári[47]; the stamp was a round wooden plate; the letters were painted on with a hairline brush. Initially he made passes and documents for himself; later, for others, too. But it took a long time for this network to become established.

There was a ring around the party of former members who did not rejoin after they had once been arrested. They could be asked for money, but not for a place to stay; they were afraid of the risk involved. But there was another ring, too: left-wing intellectuals, working class sympathizers, toughs known from prison, and mostly Jewish merchants who, partly out of conviction, partly by way of providing for the future, helped the Communists.

Kádár flitted from flat to flat, helped sometimes by luck, sometimes by chance. Once in the street he met a worker he had been on good terms with at the umbrella factory. Naturally, the man knew that Kádár was a Communist and that he was hiding.

"Do you need money?" he asked.

Kádár did not need money; but he did need a place to stay. His acquaintance had an idea: his brother's lodger had been drafted into the army not long ago.

"But if I get caught, your brother will get it in the neck, too", Kádár warned him.

"Suits me fine", said the friend, his eyes twinkling, which leads one to believe that the relationship between the brothers was not all that good.

In the evening they went off to the sprawling tenement house in Ferencváros where the brother of Kádár's acquaintance lived.

"By that time, I had got accustomed to looking around thoroughly before entering a place", says Kádár. He saw that in the inner courtyard, on the ground-floor two men were going from flat to flat. That they were detectives was written all over them.

"I thought I was on the spot, all right; I hadn't even moved in, and they were already looking for me."

It turned out that the detectives were looking for a robber. But this lodging did not prove to be a lasting one either. The brother-in-law of the acquaintance's brother was in the gendarmerie, not in itself a problem, because Kádár had excellent forged papers; but this particular gendarme had the habit when he arrived in Budapest at night of kicking the door and yelling: "Open up! Police!" It is understandable that Kádár moved on.

Kádár was concerned about his mother, too. Since he could not go home, he waited for her at the printers' where she got the newspapers she sold.

"I am going away, *Mutter*."

"Where?"

"Just away."

His mother knew then what it was all about.

"And what will happen to us?"

"You wouldn't be better off if I were arrested."

He saw his mother once more before the country was liberated. He caught a glimpse of her in the street, by chance. She was stumbling, short-sighted, carrying a large pack of newspapers. Kádár did not approach her. He had instructions to avoid all who knew him. The underground requires even harsher discipline than the army.

"She seemed even smaller than she was", says Kádár.

Soon it turned out that he was able to provide for his mother financially. Better than when he was working.

"I have never had so much money as in the underground. I did not even spend all I got."

The party had money aplenty. "Moscow gold!" But it came not from Moscow, as the propagandists claimed: it hardly could have done so for all contact with the Comintern and the Committee Abroad had been broken since the outbreak of the war; the money came from well-to-do middle class people, intellectuals and artists. Some sympathized with the movement; some with one or another of its members; there were some who frankly said that they expected service in return when the Communists got into power. In those days, many people already felt that great changes were in the offing in Hungary, and people are not stingy in such times, particularly people with full purses.

The worst thing about being underground, recalls Kádár, was that he had to go "to work" during the day so that his landlord would not sense something "fishy" about him. He had to wander about, to walk the streets for ten hours a day, ride on the trams, or go and sit in a cinema or a pub, carefully avoiding all the places where there might be police raids, and always watching whether or not he was being followed. A proper disguise was a part of the conspiracy. Since Kádár usually wore knickerbockers and a peaked cap, in the underground he wore a suit and tie, and carried a briefcase and an umbrella. He grew a moustache, too; his wife recalls a very ugly copper coloured brush.

In 1942, the police did in fact manage to liquidate the Communist party organization. As Kádár recollects, of the 400 to 450 party members they had regular contact with, only about a dozen or so remained in contact with the illegal leadership. The three-man secretariat immediately started searching for the Communists who had escaped, to clarify the reasons for the arrests, and to try to rescue those arrested. By January 1943, they had already contacted as many as 70 to 80 party members, and had gained a lot of experience in illegal work. Small as the number was, it shows that whenever the police decimated the party, it was always able to reorganize itself.

Analyzing the reasons for the arrests, they concluded that the party was unable to withstand a cleaning-up operation of the scale following on the March 15 demonstration. This time there had been no police spy, informer or traitor among them. They came to the conclusion that only by going completely underground would it be possible to avoid arrests in the future. This also meant, however, that relations with other left-wing forces were practically terminated, and Communist propaganda activity was also significantly cut.

Despite all this, the political police started another large-scale operation against the party at the beginning of 1943. In May 1943, Kádár met Árpád Szakasits who advised the Communists to abandon all underground activity and to fight against Fascism only by legal means. This was in the heyday of the Kállay period, when the Social Democrats hoped that the government would withdraw from the war. Incidentally, Horthy's soundings on the possibility of an armistice were always, typically, accompanied by an anti-Communist campaign. Even at that stage, the Regent imagined that the Communists would have no role in Hungary's future.

Kádár did not heed Szakasits's suggestion, and tried to persuade the general secretary of the Social Democrats to join the underground struggle. Szakasits, however, refused to hear of it, afraid that the party and the trade unions would be banned. After that, contact between the two parties was broken off for almost a year, until the German occupation, when the Social Democrats, by then also underground, accepted the Communists' standpoint.

"Whoever wants only to survive and nothing more, will perish", said Kádár, with two years' experience of the underground behind him to Szakasits, in hiding for only a few days.

But let us return to 1943. In order to facilitate cooperation between Communist parties and other anti-Fascist forces in the various countries, the Executive Committee of the Communist International dissolved the Comintern. Around that time, the position of the Hungarian party was as catastrophic as it had been a year earlier. Kádár, who at that time was leading the party, recalls that they had permanent contact with only eight Communists. They therefore decided to disband the Hungarian Party of Communists. The formal aspect of this decision was that the Communist party in Hungary was the Hungarian section of the Comintern, and the Comintern had dissolved itself. But the real point was to minimize to some extent the police persecution which was totally paralyzing the party's work.

"We who adopted the resolution to disband the Hungarian Party of Communists in 1943", Kádár wrote in 1956, "regarded the Peace Party[48] as a Communist party working under a different name, and that's how I still see it today."

The name Peace Party did not originate with Kádár. He suggested Worker-Peasant Party but his fellow leaders voted against this.

There has been much argument as to whether this change of name was well advised. Radio Kossuth, the broadcasting station of the exiles in Moscow, continued to speak only of the Communist party. The Communists at home believed that this was due to lack of information. It was only after the Liberation that they found that this was the way the Committee Abroad or the Moscow Committee led by Mátyás Rákosi — it had neither an official name, nor a specific function — wanted to let them know that they condemned the change of name.

I think the move had only limited significance. Although they did not manage to mislead the police, the appeal of the Peace Party resulted in the formation of peace committees, particularly in the countryside where the Communists had had no influence before. And although the change of name caused some confusion among party members, the party did succeed in establishing contact with other anti-Fascist parties and individuals, though the German occupation had a great deal to do with this. In the autumn of 1944, the party's name was changed to the Hungarian Communist Party.

In April 1944 the Red Army was approaching Hungary. The Communist leaders felt the time had come to establish contact with the Communists in exile, and to coordinate their plans. Originally they wanted to send Endre Ságvári across the front, but finally it was Kádár who went.

"I was worried that Ságvári would come to harm", says Kádár. "And you see what came of it. That's how much good intentions are worth."

His eyes are very bitter. And how many such wounds he bears!

Endre Ságvári lost his life at the end of July 1944 in an exchange of fire with detectives.

Kádár left for Yugoslavia to reach the Soviet troops with the help of Tito's partisans. He was caught at the border. Fortunately he had good papers; all the time he insisted that his name was János Lupták; he was a deserter, and had had enough of the war. He says that at the trial he clicked his heels so smartly that the military judge was quite moved by what a strapping soldier he was.

Kádár feared not only the death sentence, but also acquittal; in the latter case, he would be taken before his release to the detention centre, where he was sure to be recognized; he had spent more than enough time there for that to happen. In the end, he was sentenced to two years and was taken to the army jail in Conti Street. He cogitated about how to let the party know what had happened to him for a long time. Then he wrote a letter to an acquaintance who he knew would recognize his handwriting; since he would not understand why the signature was

"Lupták", he would be sure to show it to his sister, who was in contact with the party leadership.

The ruse worked. The party leadership immediately hired a lawyer, and promised him 2,000 *Pengős* if he got "Lupták" out of prison. The money was handed over to the lawyer in a gateway by the woman who today is Kádár's wife. She had to pretend that she had scraped the money together with great difficulty.

Kádár describes the lawyer as a "wily old fox"; Kádár could relax, he kept repeating; he would take care of everything.

"The more he told me to relax, the more worried I became", Kádár says.

He knew that he could be exposed at any time and for a Communist party secretary that would probably have meant death.

Only later did he learn that he escaped exposure by a hairsbreadth. When Horthy wanted to talk to the opposition leaders before the withdrawal, they looked for János Csermanek, too, because they knew he was the leader of the Communist party. There was only one man even among the Communist leaders who knew that Csermanek was Kádár—his illegal name by that time—and that Kádár was the Lupták serving his sentence in an army prison. And he decided not to reveal Lupták's identity. Fortunately, for the Arrow Cross soon came to power.

Lupták therefore remained Lupták and the lawyer did indeed do his utmost to have him set free, but meanwhile the Arrow Cross takeover intervened. The prisoners in Conti Street were taken over to the jail on Margit Boulevard.

"When we were lined up", Kádár says, "I saw a few familiar women comrades among the prisoners. I gestured to them not to recognize me. I was lucky."

The prisoners set out for Komárom in November 1944 on foot; they were to be put into wagons there and taken to Germany. The party leadership assigned several details to free Lupták on the way. One group followed the prisoners on bicycles, armed with pistols and hand-grenades; another followed in a car in officers' uniform. They found the batch of prisoners, but not Lupták. Kádár had escaped at Nyergesújfalu with a few Yugoslav partisans, and walked back to Budapest. This was not easy, as the roads were full of checkpoints. Kádár put a plank on his shoulder, and at every check-point said that he was taking it to the next village. Again he was lucky and got home.

In May 1944, while János Kádár was in jail under the name of Lupták, the Hungarian Front was formed with the Peace Party, the Social Democratic Party, the Smallholders' Party, the royalist Dual Cross Blood Federation and the Peasant Party taking part. Typically, the leaders held their meetings in the house where the Minister of Home Affairs lived. By that time, all the opposition parties were calling for a freedom fight against the occupying Germans. The Hungarian Front wrote a memorandum to Horthy in September 1944, calling on him to withdraw from the war, to declare war on Germany, and to form a new government with Hungarian Front and army participation. The Regent received the leaders of the Social Democrats and of the Smallholders a few days before his abortive attempt to withdraw, but the discussions did not go beyond meaningless generalities. The head of the military counterintelligence negotiated with the Communists. László Rajk[49], who was secretary of the party and just out of prison, asked the army for weapons with which to arm the workers in case of a withdrawal. The general, however, wanted a list of the workers the Communists considered trustworthy. They parted company with little confidence in each other.

The leaders of the Hungarian Front were aware that Horthy was planning to withdraw, but did not know when. It turned out that no one else knew either. The Front organized a general strike for October 17, and was taken by surprise by the Regent's proclamation of October 15, and its total failure.

Perhaps the only good thing about October 15 was that after Horthy's proclamation, a few imprisoned opposition politicians were freed, Endre Bajcsy-Zsilinszky among them. It was under his leadership that the Hungarian Front was transformed into the Liberation Committee of the Hungarian National Uprising. They entrusted Lieutenant-General János Kiss[50] with organizing the military resistance, but the Arrow Cross "Censure Board" – this was the new name given to the political police – planted an informer into the network; the military leaders were arrested, and János Kiss and two of his associates were executed. Endre Bajcsy-Zsilinszky, deprived of his parliamentary mandate, was also executed. As an organization, the Liberation Committee fell apart.

Though it was of small military significance, there was, nevertheless, some armed struggle against the Arrow Cross and the Germans in Hungary, first of all in Budapest. Communists, young Social Democratic workers, deserters, and left-wing youth blew up German cars and ammunition, freed prisoners, and attacked Arrow Cross headquarters. There were several armed groups fighting outside the capital as well; partisans, exiled Communists, and captured soldiers were parachuted from aeroplanes dispatched from the Soviet Union. Roughly 2,000 to 2,500 people took part in the armed struggle against the Germans and the Arrow Cross.

One of those fighting was Jenő Csermanek, János Kádár's younger brother. Kádár has always been proud that it was not he who recruited his brother into the Communist party. He was not even aware of his membership. The boy came to join the movement and later the armed struggle of his own accord. Of course, he did not know that his brother was the highest contact-man in the Communists' Military Committee. Jenő Csermanek died in 1948; he was hoisting the red flag on the balcony of their flat on May 1, when the balcony of the war-damaged building collapsed.

Having returned to Budapest, Kádár had again to look for a place to stay. By then, it was easier than in the initial underground period. A well-known actor with good contacts with the upper middle class helped him out. One of his friends, a Baroness, was looking for a caretaker for her villa in Pest. The Baroness was staying at her country estate; by then, air attacks on the capital were an everyday occurrence. Besides the "caretaker", only an old French lady companion, a maid, and the housekeeper lived in the villa. It was an ideal hiding place.

"Never in my life did I have it so good", says Kádár. "The maid brought me breakfast in bed every morning."

The problem came when the Baroness returned one evening unexpectedly. Kádár politely introduced himself as the new caretaker; the Baroness told him that she had come home because she had heard that the maid had been stealing the linen.

Kádár was surprised: "Are a few sheets worth risking getting bombed for?"

"What is mine is mine", said the Baroness.

The next morning when the maid brought in his breakfast she informed him that the Baroness had been arrested on charges of hiding Jews. The detectives were waiting for the caretaker in the housekeeper's flat.

"They told me to wake you up, Sir, but I said I couldn't because you would be very angry."

"Later", says Kádár, "I reasoned it out that the maid had probably reported the Baroness to the police so as not to get into trouble for stealing."

It is characteristic of the times that such an immensely rich and well-known person could be arrested on the basis of a denunciation like that.

Kádár was trapped; in the end, he slipped out of the villa, calmly walked by the housekeeper's flat, heard the detectives calling to him, but did not stop. He quickly stepped outside the gate, locked it from without, and ran. He was exceptionally lucky to have encountered such clumsy detectives.

It is characteristic of Kádár that he felt it his duty to get her keys to the divorced husband of the Baroness. He went to his office but did not find him there. He put the keys into an envelope and left.

The siege of Budapest followed, and then there really was nothing to do but try to survive. Kádár was hiding with two other party leaders. By then they did not adhere to the rules of conspiracy. Caught together, or one by one, it made no difference: they would be executed anyway.

It is part of Hungary's bitter history that after 1945, one of the men he was hiding with became Head of the State Security Authority (ÁVH)[51], the body which arrested Kádár in 1951. The other was one of the defendants in the Imre Nagy[52] trial in 1958.

Kádár and his comrades tried to get across the front. They were hiding in Zugló, on Hungária Boulevard, in a damaged house; the Soviets were only a few blocks away. But then, for some reason, on that particular spot the front ground to a halt. Two hard, nerve-wracking weeks followed until the last German and Arrow Cross detachments left. But the Soviets did not come. The first Soviet soldier appeared only half a day later. What Kádár had hardly dared believe had come to pass: he was liberated.

Light and Darkness

An eyewitness once remarked that he who has not seen the Ides of March of 1848 has seen nothing. I could say the same thing about 1945.

However, the comparison is not precise. In 1848, the nation rose to fight for its freedom. In 1945, Hungary had lost the war, the capital and part of the country was in ruins, the people were hungry and cold, and freedom was won not through an uprising but by the Red Army.

Nevertheless, 1945 and 1848 had something in common. The whole nation sensed the fundamental change; words, emotions, and debates were heated and oratory filled the air.

"I was 33 years old at the time of the Liberation", János Kádár recalled 20 years later. "I didn't think I would live to see the day, but I thought that afterwards everything would be simple and easy. But nothing was simple."

Even the first encounter with a Soviet patrol which Kádár and his comrades met was not free from difficulty, as they did not know the password which Communist leaders had been given. At the very least, the soldiers must have wondered at the three wildly gesticulating men trying to prove in broken Russian that they were the leaders of the Hungarian Communist party. Of course, they had no way of proving it. Luckily, the soldiers dismissed them with a shrug; in a war, such things may have a lot worse consequences.

The next day, Kádár and his comrades fortunately ran into Zoltán Vas[53]. Vas had spent sixteen years in prison with Mátyás Rákosi and went to the Soviet Union with him. He was sent to Budapest with the combat troops to find the Communist leaders in hiding and to organize the public administration of the city. Vas executed his mission with characteristic flair. For example, says Kádár, he appointed a tram conductor as police chief in Kőbánya, because the man wore a uniform. He immediately got hold for Kádár and his comrades of a horse and cart which was driven by a young Soviet soldier. Vas explained to him that he was personally responsible for the lives of the Hungarian Communist leaders and sent them back to Hungária Boulevard, adding that he himself would join them soon. They did not see him for a whole day.

Things certainly were strange in the Hungary of those days. On November 7, 1944, the Communist leaders who returned from the Soviet Union formed the legal Central Leadership of the Party in Szeged, the first liberated Hungarian city. On November 28, László Rajk, the secretary of the illegal Central Committee of the party, was arrested in Budapest. The democratic parties formed the Hungarian National Independence Front in Szeged on December 1. The military leaders of the Liberating Committee of the Hungarian National Uprising were executed by the Arrow Cross men on December 8. The Provisional National Assembly met in Debrecen on December 21 and elected the Provisional National Government. Endre Bajcsy-Zsilinszky was executed on December 24. The provisional government approved the decree on land reform on March 17, but the city of Esztergom, thirty miles north of the capital, was still in the hands of the Germans.

The provisional government was a national unity government, embracing all anti-German forces, including Horthy's men. Indeed, they had the largest number of cabinet posts. Colonel-General Béla Dálnoki Miklós[54] became the Prime Minister. He was the commander of the former First Hungarian Army who went over to the Red Army after Horthy's proclamation. Unfortunately, he was accompanied only by a few of his officers, as he did not take his troops with him. Horthy's chief of staff, who had also gone over to the Soviets, became Minister of Defense, although he played a still unclarified role in the failure to issue any orders to the Hungarian army following the Regent's proclamation. The commander in chief of the gendarmerie, whom Horthy sent to Moscow to conclude the armistice agreement, also became a minister, as well as the son of the suicide Count Pál Teleki, who had also been a member of the armistice delegation. The Communists had three ministerial portfolios, the Social Democrats and the Smallholders two each, and the Peasant Party one.

This ratio did not correspond to the real power situation in any way. The political forces which constituted the base of the Horthy regime for a quarter of a century were practically wiped out by 1945. Some switched allegiance to the Arrow Cross, or at least tacitly recognized their power and thereby compromised themselves completely; others got to Germany as prisoners of the Nazis and did not return after they were liberated, while others left the country voluntarily or retired from politics. The purpose of including Horthyist politicians in the provisional government was probably to disorientate the Hungarian troops still fighting on the German side and the administration in the unliberated part of the country. I do not think it met with all that much success, because Western Hungary was largely unaware of the existence of the provisional government.

The first elections to the National Assembly held in November 1945 gave a more accurate picture of the political situation in the country. No Horthyist party ran in the elections. The Smallholders' Party won an absolute majority with 57 per cent of the vote. The Communists and the Social Democrats got 17 per cent each and the Peasant Party 7 per cent.

The past of the Smallholders' Party was as contradictory as its present and future. It is difficult to establish when it was formed, as it had so many predecessors, under many names and with many political programmes. Sometimes it would unite with the right wing against Bethlen, and at other times with Bethlen against the Social Democrats. From the beginning of the forties, under the influence of Bajcsy-Zsilinszky, it pursued an unambiguously anti-German policy. The most successful year for the party was 1935 when it got ten per cent of the vote. The party was banned after the German occupation.

Before the Liberation, the name of the party was Independent Smallholder Agricultural Workers' and Citizens' Agrarian Party.

Simply put, it meant a peasant party, but they did not want to use this name because the word "peasant" itself was also used as an insult at the time. After 1945, they dropped the word "agrarian" from their name to indicate that the party represented the entire population of the country, with the exception of the workers.

The Smallholders' Party was indeed the rallying point for everyone with doubts about socialism and the working class movement. I knew quite a few of its leaders and members at the time, and still keep in touch with some to this day. Among them were peasant politicians, bankers, left-wing intellectuals, confirmed anti-Communists, conservative right-wingers, liberal democrats, anti-Semites, Jewish capitalists, members of the petty bourgeoisie, one-time members of the bourgeoisie who had joined the resistance, military officers, nationalists, well-meaning teachers, deeply religious people, atheists. It is no wonder that in 1945 this heterogeneous party represented the majority of the country. In the summer of 1945 the Smallholders' Party had almost one million members.

The Communist Party's 17 per cent share of the vote in the 1945 elections was an almost incredible achievement. Eight hundred thousand people voted for the Communists in the first free elections in a country where for a quarter of a century one could only hear or read that they were ungodly villains, traitors, murderers; it was a party which had been forced underground and decimated time and time again, with a few thousand members at most. In February 1945, the party had 30,000 members, in May 150,000, in October 500,000, mostly in Budapest and a few large industrial centres. It seems to me that the Communist party was able to survive the period when the number of active members shrank to a dozen because hundreds of thousands of people were behind it even if precious little trace of it was evident at the time.

We have another election result from 1945. The first municipal elections were held in Budapest in October. The Smallholders won with 290,000 votes, but they barely beat the Social Democrats' and the Communists' joint ticket which got 250,000 votes. The political situation in Budapest was different from that in the country at large and the fate of the country was primarily determined by the capital.

The majority of the Communist Party's leaders of the time judged the election results differently. They still had not shed the illusions nurtured since 1919 and thought that the majority of the people wanted workers' power. They hardly knew anything of, or were unwilling to take note of what had happened in Hungary since the suppression of the Republic of Councils, how public opinion had developed, what effect religion and a quarter of a century of counter-revolutionary propaganda had on the minds of the masses. They expected the certain victory of the two workers' parties in the elections. One of the tragic repercussions of this disillusionment was that a few years later they thought that they had to govern a Fascist people, and that this fact justified repressive measures.

Although not formally, in practice six people constituted the leadership of the Hungarian Communist Party. We have already mentioned Rákosi, who was elected Secretary-General of the party in February 1945. Ernő Gerő[55] had participated in the Communist movement since the Republic of Councils; nowadays many believe that he was an expert in economic affairs. "Long live Gerő, the bridge builder!" was one of the slogans in those days, because he was in charge of the reconstruction of the country. Although this is true, I see the role of this politician, cold, lacking in emotion, incapable of maintaining human relationships, quite differently. Together with Rákosi, he was probably the most responsible for what happened later.

József Révai[56] was the favourite of the intellectuals and of some of the younger members. Unlike Rákosi and Gerő he was an excellent speaker. Starting as a poet and an anarchist, he had also been active in the Republic of Councils. He was a good political writer, a rigid ideologist, a rude, tyrannical man.

Mihály Farkas[57] was born in Upper Northern Hungary and from there went to the Soviet Union. His intelligence was average and, as it later transpired, his feel for politics was about the same. History allotted him the worst role—he became the "hangman".

In addition to the Moscow émigrés, there were two men in the highest echelon of leadership who had not been in exile. One was László Rajk, who was born in 1909.

He was a student of the liberal arts in Hungary's most famous elite school, the Eötvös College[58]. He was first arrested at the age of 23 for Communist organization. After his release, he became a construction worker and in 1935 he was one of the leaders of the construction industry strike. He fought in the Spanish Civil War where he was the political commissar of one of the international brigades. He was injured at the front and the French interned him. After the Nazi occupation of France, he was taken to Germany and put in a concentration camp, from which he escaped, to be arrested in Hungary, then later released, and arrested again; he only avoided execution because the leaders of the Communist party offered to do a deal with his brother, who was an Arrow Cross state secretary in the collapsing regime: if he would save his younger brother, he also would be saved in his turn.

Consequently, Rajk was not sentenced to death, but sent to a concentration camp; from there he returned to Hungary by barge on the Danube. This strong-built, broad faced, fiery-eyed man had many admirers after 1945, particularly among the youth and the intellectuals. He knew them and spoke their language.

The other leader was János Kádár. From the forties on, the two of them had alternated in leading the party. They hardly met; when Rajk was under arrest, Kádár led the party, when Kádár was in jail, Rajk was in charge.

I did not know László Rajk personally. I only saw and heard him several times at meetings, demonstrations, and debates. He was different from Kádár and had a sparkling, extroverted personality. During this period I also saw and heard Kádár a few times. He was quiet, thoughtful, calm, restrained. To stereotype is to oversimplify, but I think it is true: Rajk was every inch an intellectual, Kádár a worker. I did not know then that Kádár was esteemed primarily by the former illegal Communists, many of whom were in important posts in those days. They had shared practically every day of the underground period. Rajk spent a long time in Spain, France, Germany, and consequently the older party members knew him less. He got to play a really significant role only in the post-war years. That led to his tragedy, too.

For some reason Rákosi returned from the Soviet Union a few months after his fellow-leaders. Kádár says that he personally was looking forward to Rákosi's return. Until then the Communist Party was led by Gerő. Kádár's career in the new Central Leadership started with Gerő announcing at one of the first meetings that Kádár was to be severely reprimanded for the dissolution of the Hungarian Party of Communists. Kádár swallowed hard. First of all, he did not understand who had made that decision when they were the leaders of the party.

"Can I say something?" he asked.

"Are you still trying to defend what you did?" snapped Gerő.

This is a small matter, but very revealing: the exiles were generally formal in addressing one another, while the Communists who had remained in the country were on familiar terms with each other. Formal language is typical of a hierarchical order, while the familiar tone is that of a community.

"The devil defends it", shrugged Kádár.

I think it is one of his fundamental characteristics that if he runs up against a wall, he stops but without abandoning his convictions.

"What I did not at all understand", he says "is how it was possible to punish someone without giving him the chance to defend himself. We were no longer in the underground movement."

Shortly after he received his next severe reprimand, when the Ministry of Home Affairs had no money to pay a salary to the policemen of Budapest. At that time Kádár was the deputy police chief of Budapest.

"I reported it to the minister", said Kádár.

"Do not report to the minister, but to the Central Leadership", retorted Gerő.

Kádár remained silent. He does not like to defend himself.

This was another reason why Kádár looked forward to Rákosi's return. He thought that the style of leadership would then change. He did not yet know that Rákosi had told his comrades in Moscow that once home they would have to do everything themselves because the party leaders in Hungary were useless.

Those who knew Rákosi better say that he always prepared carefully for every conversation and negotiation. He always surprised his partners by being very well informed. Those who met him at that time remember him as a clever, witty conversationalist, who was pleasant and attentive when he wanted to be. In any case, he behaved differently from the icy Gerő, the offensively sarcastic Révai, and the gruff Farkas.

In those days Kádár, like so many others, was swamped with work. He was the deputy chief of police, then the head of the personnel department of the party, a secretary of the Budapest party committee, a member of the Political Committee, the secretary and later deputy secretary of the Central Leadership, and a Member of Parliament. By that time, Kádár was his official name, too; he had become so used to it underground that he changed his name with the permission of the Minister of Home Affairs.

He didn't find time to move his mother to Budapest — she had spent the end of the war in Kapoly — until May 1945. By that time he had a flat, the first flat of his own. His mother grumbled and bickered with her son for having neglected her for so long.

"Why did you become a policeman?" she complained. "It will get you into trouble, you'll see."

"Once I went to hold a meeting at the MÁVAG enterprise", says Kádár. "*Mutter* was sitting in the hall, she had gone to visit the parents of one of my acquaintances; we had been in jail together and they had all come to visit us together."

It was the first time that his mother had heard him speak in public.

"By that time she had glasses, and could read. She was trying to understand the pamphlets. She wanted to understand my world."

After the Liberation, slogans played a significant role in the life of the country. A concise, to-the-point slogan meant more than a substantive study.

The first slogan of the Hungarian Communist Party issued in Szeged in November 1944 was: "There will be a Hungarian rebirth!"

Not many shared that belief. A well-known Hungarian writer wrote in his diary that a hundred years would pass before the country recovered from this catastrophe.

This pessimism was not unfounded. Not only the bridges of the Danube and the Tisza, but also a great many of the smaller road bridges had been blown up. Forty per cent of the railway tracks were destroyed. Of the 70,000 railway wagons, 50,000 had been taken to Germany and half of those left in the country were damaged. Only six ships remained out of a total of 300. Ninety per cent of the factories and enterprises had suffered some degree of damage. Seventy per cent of the country's livestock had been taken to the West or slaughtered. Forty per cent of Hungary's national wealth was destroyed. The extent of the damages exceeded the 1938 national income five times. More than half a million Hungarians had been killed during the war.

The capital suffered the most. Budapest was literally in ruins, without electricity, water, gas, transport, postal or telephone services. The newspapers were filled with personal appeals from families seeking missing members; some had been deported, some taken away by the army or the Levente[59] organization, some had become prisoners of war, or disappeared on the front, some had just fled the country, often not knowing why. As soon as the first trains started — but on foot and bicycle too — tens of thousands fanned out to the villages, taking their remaining clothes, shoes, linen, tools, nails, and whatever else they could find to barter for food. The currency depreciated rapidly. The one-million strong capital was starving. Undoubtedly, the most important task was the reconstruction of the country.

The Provisional National Government did not repeat the mistake of the Republic of Councils: it rapidly introduced a radical land reform. Fighting was still going on in Hungary when the government decree on the "Elimination of the System of Large Estates and on the Provision of Land for the Tillers" was published. On average, 650,000 farm hands, agricultural labourers and holders of dwarf plots were given 7 acres of land each. The land distribution affected more than two million people, one quarter of the country's population. The Hungarian peasantry experienced much suffering and hardship in the years to follow, but life was never again the same as before 1945.

Understandably, the distribution of land turned a significant social and political force, the Catholic Church, even more against the new order. The Church was the largest landholder in the country, owning about one and a quarter million acres.

Owing to its historically negative role and its enormous wealth, the Catholic Church has never been the "national church" in Hungary, as for example, it is in Poland. In Hungary's case, the Protestant churches could better identify with the nation because they had lived through persecution and oppression just like the exploited people and the nation itself with its curtailed independence. The Catholic Church's centuries of political backwardness probably weighed just as much in turning it against the new order after 1945, as its loss of wealth and power.

The head and Primate of the Church was Cardinal József Mindszenty, Archbishop of Esztergom[60]. Mindszenty is now dead. Knowing his life and memoirs as I do, I am positive that he was narrow-minded and backward as a person and as a Church leader, not only in the political, but also in the philosophical sense. He did immeasurable harm not only to the country, but especially to Hungarian Catholics. After the Liberation, when he demanded a say in Hungary's fate not only in his capacity as head of the Catholic Church, but also as the "first baron of the realm", he discredited not only himself, but also his religion and Church by this anachronistic feudal idea.

But, unfortunately, anachronism has deep roots in Hungary. If in the thirties big merchants and bankers could parade in plumed hats and short coats trimmed with fox fur, with swords at their sides, claiming to be descendants of ancient Hungarians, there is no reason why a lean high priest of petty bourgeois origin could not call himself the first baron of the realm in the forties. Public political ridicule could not prevent many hundreds of thousands of politically inexperienced people, religious and devoted to the Church, from heeding the Primate's words. Thousands of destitute peasants did not want or did not dare to occupy the land allotted to them, fearing not only God's punishment but even more the rumours that the landlords would return and then God help those who had dared to plough their lands. The Hungarian peasant carried in his genes not only György Dózsa's revolt but also the horrible fate that befell him. And they remembered well what followed the overthrow of the Republic of Councils: the corpses of their fathers and brothers hanging in the main square of the villages.

However, this is not the whole truth. The predominant majority of the peasantry welcomed their plot of land, the fulfilment of a century-old dream. I knew priests who had dedicated their whole lives to teaching, who, as teachers, were second to few in the country; priests who were not only shepherds to their flocks, but also taught poor people beekeeping, fruit planting and market gardening; nuns who cared for the sick with more devotion than their closest relatives. In my view, it is against these that the head of the Catholic Church sinned the most. He deprived them of their vocation. They wanted to serve the people, but owed obedience to the Church.

I do not know what considerations led Mindszenty to decide that there was no need for a Christian political party in Hungary. There could have been either a Christian democratic or Christian socialist party, most probably with no small influence. It is not a sufficient explanation that the Primate did not think much of either democracy or socialism, not even in their Christian versions.

Mindszenty ignored the fact that the people he had sent into the political arena while he remained head of the Church and a baron had to work under different conditions. When the Parliament declared Hungary a republic in February 1946, only one MP voted against it, although the Primate had opposed the liquidation of the monarchy and he had a number of supporters in the House. However, no one who wanted a career as a politician in Hungary in those days could publicly vote for continuing the Hungarian Monarchy. This would have been anachronistic beyond measure.

The Communists and the Social Democrats would have liked to have seen Mihály Károlyi become the President of the Hungarian Republic; he had returned after almost thirty years in exile. The Smallholders' Party would not hear of it – partly for political, partly for personal reasons. The first President of the new Hungarian Republic was the leader of the Smallholders' Party, Zoltán Tildy[61]. He was a Protestant minister, a well-intentioned, diplomatic man, though not particularly strong-willed, who had led the party together with Endre Bajcsy-Zsilinszky during the war. Ferenc Nagy[62], another leader of the Smallholders' Party, of peasant origin, was appointed Prime Minister. He was tougher, more decisive and more right-wing than the President. Another member of the Smallholders', Béla Varga[63], was elected Speaker of Parliament. There is nothing more to be said about him apart from the fact that he was a Catholic priest. Béla Kovács[64], also of a peasant background, became Secretary-General of the Smallholders' Party. He was a man of great vision and the party's most distinctive politician.

Let us go forward a few years. President Tildy was put under house arrest a few years later after his son-in-law was executed for spying. In 1956, he was a member of Imre Nagy's inner cabinet; he was sentenced at the same time as Nagy and he died not long after his release from prison. Prime Minister Ferenc Nagy did not return from his visit to Switzerland in 1947. Later, he became a farmer in the United States and one of the leaders of the Hungarian émigrés. He tried to return in 1956, but Austria expelled him. At the end of the seventies he wanted to visit Hungary, but he had a fatal heart attack before the trip. Again there is nothing more to say of Béla Varga other than that he was a leader of the Hungarian émigrés and was always financed by the Americans. Béla Kovács was arrested in 1947 by the Soviet authorities. In prison he learnt Russian, read Marx and Lenin, and after his release he became the director of a state farm. In 1956, although seriously ill, he was a member of Imre Nagy's inner cabinet. He was not among those prosecuted and was elected an MP in 1958, shortly after which he died of a heart attack.

Perhaps these few portrait sketches serve to show how heterogeneous the Smallholders' Party was. Furthermore, the leaders mentioned belonged to the centre. The right wing of the party, representing a significant force, demanded the amendment of the land reform, an offensive against the left-wing parties, and the prevention of nationalization. They failed to get the upper hand, but not for lack of trying.

The Left's response was the creation of a Left-Wing Block with the participation of the Communists, the Social Democrats, the National Peasant Party and the Trade Union Council. It was around that time that the slogan "We won't give back the land!" was born, and then at the Left-Wing Block's rally, attended by more than 300,000 people in Budapest in March 1946, there was a second major slogan: "Expel the people's enemies from the coalition!" At that time, the government consisted of nine members of the Smallholders' Party, four Communists, four Social Democrats and one Peasant Party representative.

For many years Árpád Szakasits had been Secretary-General of the Social Democratic Party. He was a former construction worker, who later became a journalist and a published poet. Kádár characterizes him as a man who had his heart in the right place. I think this description is accurate; I knew him quite well. He was honest, and not exactly decisive. His party was anything but united. In those days, the Social Democrats' right wing was no longer represented by Károly Peyer, the former leader of the party, who had been a supporter of compromise with the government ever since the suppression of the Republic of Councils. Even his imprisonment by the Germans failed to enhance his stature. The fiery-eyed and fiery-tempered Anna Kéthly[65] was originally the spokesperson of the Centre, but later she moved increasingly to the Right. I often heard her speak; she was an outstanding speaker, a romantic person. The left wing was led by György Marosán[66], the former baker and trade union leader, who by that time was urging a merger with the Communists.

Again, let us look ahead at events. After Tildy's removal, Szakasits became the President of the Hungarian Republic. In 1950 he was arrested. Released in 1956, he died as a member of the Presidential Council of the Hungarian People's Republic in 1965. Kéthly was also arrested in 1949. In 1956, she was a member of Imre Nagy's inner cabinet. She left the country and died in exile. Marosán was also imprisoned and released only in 1956. In July of that year he became a member of the Political Committee, and after November 4 was appointed Minister of State in the cabinet. In 1962, he resigned from the Political Committee. He is a grey-haired, perennially youthful old man, a pensioner who swims regularly even today and belongs to a workers' choir.

The National Peasant Party did not represent a politically significant force, but added a bit of colour to Hungarian political life. It was made up of radical writers and destitute peasants. Its leader was Péter Veres, a former agricultural labourer, seasoned by prison, who became a sober-minded and wise writer. He wore peasant boots and an open-neck white shirt even when he was the Minister of Defense and was called Uncle Péter by the whole country. I liked him tremendously, perhaps best of all his contemporaries, although I differed from him on almost every issue. His party lacked unity just as much as the others. Ferenc Erdei[67], one of the most significant sociologists in the country, led the left wing. The right-wing leader was Imre Kovács[68], the outstanding publicist.

These people's subsequent careers went as follows: until 1956, Péter Veres was the president of the Hungarian Writers' Union. On October 23, he addressed the demonstrators at the statue of General József Bem[69]. After 1956, he was an MP. Kádár, who respected him, wrote of him after his death: "Over the years there were serious differences and clashes of views on three important issues between Péter Veres and the Communist party; he was wrong on two, but right on one."

After the Liberation, Ferenc Erdei headed various ministries. On October 23, 1956, he attempted to speak to the hundred-thousand-strong crowd from a balcony of the Parliament building, but was booed. He was a member of the committee which conducted negotiations with the commanders of the Red Army in Hungary on November 3. He was arrested but later released. He then said he would never get involved in politics again. Quite frankly, I did not believe him. He became the head of the Patriotic People's Front, and later of the Hungarian Academy of Sciences. The upgrading of the agricultural sector is also to his credit.

Imre Kovács, who once wrote a moving book on the misery of Hungarian peasant, left the Peasant Party in 1947 and became the leader of one of the right-wing parties. Then he left the country and was one of the leaders of Hungary's political emigrés until his death. He either could not or would not recognize what had happened meanwhile to the Hungarian peasantry, whose advocate he had once been.

To illustrate the atmosphere and tone of the political debates, I quote from the official record of the Parliamentary proceedings on February 8, 1946:

"János Kádár (CP): Distinguished House! I consider the speech of the previous speaker, my fellow MP, Dezső Sulyok[70], which is also the speech of a spokesman for the majority party, extremely harmful and negative for our country. [Noise and protest in the Smallholders' Party. Shouts of "Because he is a Hungarian! Because he sides with his country! In the end he will be beaten up for it!" Pandemonium.] Glad as we were yesterday to welcome the Prime Minister's statement that he condemns and opposes national chauvinism which can only bring the nation to ruin [Cries from the Smallholders' Party: We do too!" Ignác Sári (SHP) "This isn't it! This is not chauvinism!" Mihály Farkas (CP): "The worst kind of chauvinism!"], today it is with equal regret that I have to state that this all too necessary stand and this all too necessary condemnation are not fully shared even within his own party. [Noise and interruptions in the Smallholders' Party ranks: "Yes, they are!"] To assist and to adopt the reasoning of that chauvinism, which has ruined and impoverished our country in the last quarter of a century and still not to be satisfied with the extent of its devastation [A voice in the Smallholders' Party: "Don't you speak of chauvinism!" Interruptions from the Smallholders' Party bench: "He does not understand the meaning of the term!" Noise], to assist chauvinism and to give voice to it in Parliament, I consider extremely harmful to the country's interest. [Mátyás Rákosi, Minister of State: "That's right!" László Orbán (CP): "Read Tito's speech." Noise. Jenő Némethy (SHP): "Tito does not direct the fate of the world!" Continuous noise.]"

In contrast with the other, politically most heterogeneous parties, the leadership of the Hungarian Communist Party was united. It had no Right, Left or Centre factions and it was not only the fact that Hungary belonged to the Soviet sphere of influence on the basis of the agreement among the allied powers, but also this unity that contributed to the Communists' having an influence in the country considerably greater than that reflected in the election results.

Under left-wing pressure, the National Presidium of the Smallholders' Party announced in March 1946 that the leader of the right wing, Dezső Sulyok, and nineteen of his fellow MPs were expelled from the party. The liquidation of the Smallholders' Party had begun.

Undoubtedly, the constant pressure by the Left, and particularly by the Communists, was a contributing factor. But there is also no doubt that this extremely heterogeneous party, uniting voters and leaders of the most diverse views, essentially carried within it the seeds of its own dissolution.

The turning point in the breakup of the Smallholders' Party and in the shift in Hungarian politics and power relationships came when a group called the Hungarian Fraternal Community or Hungarian Community was eliminated. Several factors were involved in this extremely complex case, the details of which are yet to be fully clarified. This secret society was created before the war, like so many similar organizations. As far as I know, it did not engage in any meaningful activity. In 1947, however, an anti-republic plot was discovered. Among its leaders was one of Horthy's colonel-generals, whom the Regent had designated Prime Minister before the Arrow Cross coup, high ranking military officers, a former minister and several MPs of the Smallholder's Party who were influential in Parliament. The Committee of Seven directing the plot was making preparations for a coup to restore the monarchy and it wanted to use the members of the Hungarian Community, several of whom belonged to the Smallholders' Party, towards this end.

The state security bodies acted in haste, perhaps politically motivated. They arrested the leaders of the organization when they only had proof of an isolated plot, but no proof of to what extent and who among the members of the Hungarian Community had been drawn into the conspiracy, that is, who among the leaders of the Smallholders.

At first all four parties of the government coalition — the Smallholders included — sharply condemned the plot, but the Communists and the Left continued their pressure, making the situation more acute, and this led to the break-up of the Smallholders' Party. Béla Kovács, Secretary-General of the Party, was arrested, Ferenc Nagy, who was in Switzerland at the time, did not return, Béla Varga, the Speaker of Parliament, left the country. The Smallholders' Party expelled many of its MPs, several were arrested, while others withdrew to found new parties.

The 1947 election reflected reality better than that of 1945 in that it was not a heterogeneous Smallholders' Party which opposed the Left, but the Democratic People's Party professing Christian ideals, the Hungarian Independence Party, which used the former slogan of the Smallholders' "God, Country, Private property", and the Independent Hungarian Democratic Party — I do not know whether the last named had any programme other than getting their leaders elected. The three opposition parties were organized by former Smallholder leaders. These parties, together with a few opposition groups, obtained 40 per cent of the vote in 1947. The Smallholders' Party, which before that had an absolute majority, lost 2 million votes, 1.8 million of which went to the breakaway parties. The Communists became the country's strongest party with 1.1 million votes, or 22 per cent of the vote.

During these years Kádár was engaged primarily in organizing the party. Party membership grew at incredible speed. By September 1946, at the time of the Third Congress of the Hungarian Communist Party, there were 650,000 registered party members, 150,000 of them in Budapest. Incidentally, three reports were given at the congress. Mátyás Rákosi reported on the domestic and foreign political situation of the country and the tasks facing the party, Imre Nagy spoke on agrarian policy and János Kádár on organizational questions.

The membership of 650,000 was hardly realistic. However well and efficiently the Communist Party worked after the Liberation, it is unthinkable that over half a million people in Hungary had become convinced Communists in a year and a half.

It is a historical fact that many became party members out of self-interest and careerism. This applies not only to the Communist Party. In the years of the coalition, the parties delegated their own people to all government posts; whoever wanted to fill a post had to belong to one of the parties. Even cinema licences were distributed on a coalition basis. There were some who wanted to conceal their past with a party membership card and could count on the protection of their parties during screening.

The parties were hunting for new members and voters to increase their electoral base, and they were not too particular about their applicants' motives. Consequently, the sad situation arose whereby long-standing Communists, who had been unable to withstand the tortures of Horthy's police and had confessed, and so implicated others, were expelled by the dozen, while tens of thousands were admitted whom nobody knew anything about.

There was also a distorted, false ideology. One of the party leaders later admitted that their view was that only those who entered the party after the Liberation were absolutely trustworthy.

This was because the old party members could have been police informers if they had lived in Hungary, Trotskyists if they had lived in the Soviet Union, and imperialist agents if they had lived in the West. This paranoia manifested itself in the terrible show trials.

Kádár saw it differently. This is how he put it in his report to the congress in 1946: "Together with careerists and other elements who do not belong among us, people infected by the corrupting influence of Fascism who have not yet been completely cured have also got into our party."

Kádár's opinion, as can be seen in the contemporary press and documents, in essence coincides with his policy after 1956. However, I do not mean to imply that his views have not changed at all and he saw everything the same way that he does today.

"The mistakes committed by the party during those years are my mistakes, too."

This must be true as far as daily politics are concerned, but some of his basic principles formulated then have not changed to this day; the phraseology is almost the same, which implies that the elements of his world outlook crystallized thirty years ago. Particularly when we know that he does not read his earlier speeches and writings.

"The path of development is sound when the masses of people become convinced through their own experiences that the party exists for them.

"Those who do not want to accept the fact that they exist for the people and not the people for them often do more harm to the party than our enemies.

"We are convinced that the enemies of the Hungarian people underestimate the political maturity of our people. During the recent difficult years, the Hungarian people have learned much, they are becoming more and more mature politically, their understanding improves from day to day, and they have come to recognize their enemies and their friends. For this very reason the party which will have done the most for the Hungarian people will become the strongest party in Hungary.

"In protecting peace, all honest people of whatever party affiliation or non-affiliaton are our allies.

"The leaders of certain organizations of our party, and their number is not small, have yet to recognize the real significance of the relationship between the party and the masses. Comrade Rákosi pointed out at the Central Leadership meeting on February 10 that the consolidation of the power of the working class had led to the harmful practice on the part of the leaders of certain party organizations whereby they started to abandon the method of convincing people through education and turned to the use of administrative means and bureaucratic methods. These functionaries have been causing and cause immeasurable harm to the relationship between the party and the masses."

Quoting Mátyás Rákosi was not just a polite gesture. The same principles were present in other Rákosi speeches in those years. I do not know whether this was honest or done out of tactical considerations. The sharp change took place later.

However, it is worth noting a seemingly insignificant but, in my opinion, important factor, the difference between Rákosi's and Kádár's personalities. The 1946 Christmas issue of *Szabad Nép*[71] (Free People) published interviews with Rákosi, Kádár and Mihály Farkas. It is a rare document because Communist leaders seldom make public statements on subjects other than politics. Here are Rákosi's and Kádár's answers to *Szabad Nép*'s questions:

"For me", said Rákosi, "one of the great experiences of 1946 was the Communist tour of the villages when the working people of the countryside and of the towns met each other. Many of our comrades think that such small tasks are dreary, yet without them we cannot convince people who have only heard the Communists slandered for 25 years that our principles are right. I have always listened with the greatest interest to the little incidents which emerge in the course of the tours of the countryside and which show what a tremendous experience it is for working people of the towns and the countryside to meet each other. I was particularly touched by one of these stories. The workers touring in one of the villages near the Danube took away with them an elderly widow's old window-frames saying that they would bring them back next Sunday repaired. The next day the backward, misled and reactionary elements of the village started to ridicule the old woman, saying, 'You will never see your window-frames again because it has never happened yet that the Communists bring back something once they have laid their hands on it.' And, indeed, our comrades did not show up on that following Sunday. The anti-Communist villagers reacted with malicious glee. But the old woman was all the more pleased when the comrades concerned reappeared in her village two weeks later and put up the now repaired, nicely painted, and newly glazed window-frames, excusing themselves for the delay, which was because their lorry had broken down the previous Sunday. The widow happily told the visitors that for the past two weeks the village had spoken of nothing but her 'stolen' window-frames. 'They were wasting their time', said the widow. 'I knew the Communists keep their promises. And I was right.'"

Kádár told the reporter the following anecdote:

"I am an old sportsman. As a young ironworker during the twenties I kicked around the ball with the Hársfa Street boys as a member of the Vasas Juniors in the ankle-deep sand of People's Park. We used to play a good three hours, and the score was usually 15 : 11. Later, I became a fan, and, as befits a self-respecting ironworker, a Vasas fan at that. Now, thanks to the honour entrusted in me by their club members, I am the chairman of the Vasas club and proud of my team, the best Hungarian workers' sports club. So I am an expert on football *ex officio*. But even more as a fan. I do not want to describe the psychology of the fan but I must tell you that the fan certainly knows how to select the team better than the coach, and knows how to play better than the players, not to mention the fact that he knows a hundred times more about running a game than the referee. The well-known and learned comments from the stands prove this: 'I would have put Szilágyi as center!' 'The ref is nuts!' 'You jackass! That wasn't offside!' And that is the way I was myself for 16 years and, although I wasn't necessarily yelling during the games, I was one of those who knew everything better.

But I had a small accident this summer. Somebody came up with the idea of organizing an HCP-Peasant Party soccer game. The great match took place at the Üllői Street stadium. I too put on a Tee shirt and shorts. Our entry, as we ran out onto the field all in a line, was terrific. Nobody tripped. Then came the surprises. The first, deepest impression was voiced by either Comrade Köböl[72] or Comrade Apró[73], who said: 'Say, this field looks a lot longer from down here. How are we going to keep running backwards and forwards?' I don't want to make this story long because then I could say that the Peasant Party tricked us, for, with the slogan that they are a young party, they had nine college kids in their team. By contrast, the knees of our veterans creaked like a rusty key in a lock. I don't want to go into the details, but they beat us three nothing. (I ask the comrades typesetting this to set the previous sentence in small letters, perhaps it will escape Comrade Rákosi's attention.) Anyway it was at this game that the cocksureness of being a fan changed, because we saw how difficult it was to play soccer and how easy to yell and criticise from the sheltered stands. We couldn't even walk straight for a few days after the game. I just had enough strength to get off the high horse I had been sitting on as a fan for 16 years. I started seeing the game differently, but it is also a part of the fan's psychology that he is not consistent. At the recent *Vasas–Fradi* match, I was at it again. 'It would have made all the difference if Szilágyi had played centre forward during the first half.' I am once again the old, all-knowing spectator. I know everything better than the coach, the players and the referees. I am incorrigible. I am a fan."

Rákosi had either made up or believed that childish story. Such old ladies exist only in fairy-tales and not in the Hungary of 1946. It is highly unlikely that any old peasant woman would have left her house without windows – What if it should rain? – and surely none would have said things like "the Communists keep their promises". Rákosi thought that with stories like that one could win the support of the people. He did not know that people only laughed at such things. And when harder times came they no longer laughed. Kádár was just telling a story. What he said had no educational purpose: he did not want to make propaganda. Yet there is a philosophic core to his story. To my mind, his career proves that experience and a grasp of reality becomes wisdom at a certain stage.

Two significant domestic events preceded the 1947 election. Those who thought that Hungary would not recover from the devastation of the war for decades were mistaken. Yet in the beginning many things seemed to support that notion. Hungary set a world record in inflation. Whereas in December 1945 there were 765 billion *Pengős* in circulation, by July 1946 there were 47,349,492,000 billion. I do not know what this sum means but I do know that the workers took their pay home in a bag and by the next day it had practically no value at all. The state succeeded in creating a new and stable currency in an almost unbelievably short time, by August 1, 1946. One new *Forint* was worth 400,000 quadrillion *Pengős*. I do not know the value of this either, but I do know that nobody exchanged the money and the discarded banknotes printed on inferior paper were lying in piles on the streets. The young Hungarian state made politics out of this too: it called the new money the *Forint*, in contrast with the *Pengős* introduced by the Horthy regime. And the money, to the surprise of many, proved stable. Bit by bit, food, and rather poor quality clothing and shoes were available even if in limited quantities. The three-year national economic plan adopted in 1947 aimed at reaching the level of the last pre-war year in three years in respect to both production and the standard of living.

Meanwhile, the peace treaty between the victorious and the defeated states was concluded in the autumn of 1946. Hungary was allotted the fate which Horthy and Szálasi and their like deserved. The ally of Hitler's Germany again found herself with the borders dictated at Trianon after World War I whereas it was the leadership of the country, and not the Hungarians themselves who were responsible for their participation in the war on Hitler's side. But those who direct world affairs think in terms of states and not in terms of peoples and nations. Czechoslovakia had been dismembered by the Germans. Yugoslavia had fought against the *Third Reich* throughout the war. Romania had quit the Axis alliance and turned against Germany before Hungary did. The victorious Allies could hardly be expected to sanction the border readjustments executed with Hitler's blessings.

The country and its leaders were resigned to the peace treaty because they knew they could not expect anything else. The politicians and public opinion were primarily preoccupied not with the peace treaty, but with the domestic political struggles.

In connection with the 1947 elections, it is said even today that fraud was committed and the Communists became the strongest party only through cheating. The first part of the sentence is true, the second is false. The notorious "blue cards" were used in the elections without the knowledge and approval of the CP leadership. Those who were away from their normal residence (riding) could vote several times by using these cards. According to calculations which seem authentic, the Communists obtained no more than two mandates this way. In a 411-seat Parliament it made no difference. Undoubtedly, this unwise and counterproductive move caused grave moral harm; it was a prelude to a sad period when some Communist leaders thought that any means could be used to further the interests of working class power. As the old proverb says, even the road to hell is paved with good intentions.

After the 1947 elections, the opposition made one more desperate attempt to gain power. The leaders of the parties who had seceded from the Smallholders' Party tried to convince their former party to quit the coalition and to form a government with them. This came to naught just as the attempt of right-wing Social Democrats to form a coalition government with the exclusion of the Communists failed. In the end, the new government was formed with the Smallholder Lajos Dinnyés[74] as Prime Minister and the ministries divided among five Communists, four Smallholders, four Social Democrats and two Peasant Party members.

Following the 1947 election victory, the Communists achieved another significant result in 1948. The right-wing and centrist leaders of the Social Democratic Party had either resigned or been expelled and several of them had left the country and the two working class parties merged in June 1948, and adopted the name Hungarian Working People's Party. Szakasits was named President of the Party and Rákosi became its Secretary-General, with Mihály Farkas, János Kádár and György Marosán as his deputies.

The country's domestic political situation seemed to have stabilized. The left-wing government coalition led by the Hungarian Working People's Party had a comfortable majority, its power was threatened neither by the opposition nor by any social stratum. The banks were nationalized in 1947, factories employing more than 100 workers were taken over in the beginning of 1948 and the denominational schools were abolished in the summer of 1948. There was much to indicate that a stable and quiet period would follow in Hungary. This was reflected by Kádár's March 1948 speech in Parliament:

"From the very first day the basic principle of our policy has been the cooperation of all democratic forces in the interest of undisturbed and more rapid development. Our attitude did not change even when the Hungarian Communist Party became the country's strongest party numerically as well. On the contrary, everybody can feel that the coalition has become more stable, since the fortnightly crises of the previous period are things of the past, and we hope that the future will be even freer of shocks and crises. We wish to establish an ever firmer alliance of all the democratic forces of the Hungarian people. It is the wish of the entire Hungarian people and also in the interest of the country to have the constant party polemics replaced more and more by joint creative democratic work. An opposition which genuinely accepts democracy and exercises constructive criticism is compatible with our system of democracy and can render a genuinely useful service to the country."

This view concerning the multi-party system was not just Kádár's own opinion, but the official stand of the Communist party. This is what József Révai, the party's leading ideologist, wrote in the September 26, 1948 issue of *Szabad Nép*: "In Hungary, there is a people's democracy, a coalition; there are classes, and the differences between the working class and the peasantry have not disappeared; in such circumstances we would not take a single step towards the elimination of classes by the formal abolition of parties."

This was also János Kádár's opinion, and not only then; even today he thinks it would have been correct to retain the multi-party system. That is not how it turned out. Rákosi emphasized the importance of liquidating the "old forms and institutions" at the November 1948 meeting of the Central Leadership and at its March 1949 session he unambiguously stated in his Secretary-General's report that the mere existence of the other parties constituted a "reserve-force" for the class enemy. The parties threw in the towel or were shut down one after another; Hungary has had a one-party system since 1949.

What caused this fundamental political change which, of course, manifested itself not only in the liquidation of the multi-party system?

Kádár said in one of his speeches: "I became a member of the then illegal Hungarian Young Communist League in September 1931. At one of the cell-meetings at which five of us were present, our secretary gave a brief report on the international situation. Since that was my first such meeting, I paid very close attention and I will never forget it as long as I live. The secretary of the cell used the expression that the international situation was complicated. That was more than 45 years ago, a long time, and since then I have heard many reports on the international situation and almost all of them started the same way."

Alas, however characteristic this story is of our age, it is a fact that the international situation in 1948 was even more complex than usual. The times were gone when the Red Army and the troops of the Western powers fought as allies against Fascism, the common enemy, and the king of England sent a ceremonial sword to the victors of Stalingrad. Churchill, who was the Soviet Union's ally in World War II, openly reverted to his former self and proclaimed afresh the struggle against Communism in his Fulton speech. Because of her industrial and military strength, and not least her atomic bomb, the United States became the world's leading power. After Roosevelt's death, the ultra-conservative Truman became President. He considered the Soviet Union the number one enemy of America and the Western World. What Hitler had counted on in the last days of his life and what at the time was unimaginable, came to pass: the Western Allies and the Soviet Union were regarding each other as enemies. The beautiful, but brief dream that the immeasurable sufferings of the world war would be followed by a period of calm came to an end.

The three Western great powers created the Federal Republic of Germany in 1949, implying that they considered the Soviet Union and not Germany as their main enemy. In 1948, the Western European Union was established, which in 1949 became the military organization called the North Atlantic Treaty Organization, NATO.

In 1949, the Communists won the Chinese civil war. In 1950, when the United States intervened militarily in the war between socialist North Korea and South Korea led by the dictator Li Sin Man, the Northerners stopped the American advance with the assistance of the People's Republic of China. It was probably an even sorer point with the American leaders that the Soviet Union produced her first atomic bomb in 1949, an event which had been forecast by American experts for 1954, or for 1952 at the worst. Thus the permanent danger that the United States could at any time launch a nuclear attack on the Soviet Union without the latter being able to respond was removed, but the nuclear arms race which is still crippling the world today was on.

In this tense international situation the Soviet Union was still in the same situation it had practically always been in ever since its formation: its survival was in peril. There had been civil war, interventions, blockades, military attacks. Nobody will ever be able to say how many Soviet citizens suffered a violent death at the hands of various enemies during the thirty years of Soviet power, but their number can be estimated as at least thirty million. There has hardly been another country or social system in world history which has sacrificed so much blood to survive.

The Cold War, which could have turned into a shooting war at any time, froze not only inter-state and world economic relations, but also the domestic politics of the Soviet Union and the people's democracies. They thought that ensuring democracy and individual liberty in a time of siege was not the most important task of the state.

However, such a view was not inevitable. The Soviet Union lived through the most dangerous period of her history during Lenin's life, and Lenin did not believe that domestic repression was the most effective means of defense against the outside threat. But after Lenin's death Stalin became the leader of the Soviet Union and political methods changed.

Communist leaders in exile, who had lived in the Soviet Union during the thirties and forties, had a rough idea of how Stalinist policy would react to the Cold War threat. The Communists who had not been in the Soviet Union had no conception of this.

"I have thought this over repeatedly", says Kádár, "and had someone told me in 1948 what would happen in the following years, I would not have believed a word of it. It was so unimaginable that I would have thought it a feverish nightmare."

I do not believe that the multi-party system is the basis of democracy, but its elimination by force undoubtedly indicated something. The Marxist classics never claimed the one-party system to be the institutional political system of socialism; in the Soviet Union after 1917 the other parties destroyed themselves by taking the side of the Whites in the civil war. In Hungary, where the coalition parties accepted the socialist state system, the elimination of the multi-party system was not a historical necessity, but the manifestation of the concept that not only opposing views, but even minority views, were not to be tolerated.

Although it was not expressed in so many words, uniformity and agreement with everything became the main requirements in almost all spheres of life. Parallel with that, a misconception started to emerge that there was some sort of a perfect central Brain which decides everything, and the enterprises, plants, offices, citizens, and villages had no other task than the ever more perfect implementation of these decisions.

Other nations had the same experience. Poland was the enemy of Nazi Germany during the war, and members of the bourgeoisie, nationalists, Communists and anti-Communists by the hundreds of thousands fought against the occupiers. In Czechoslovakia, a developed industrial state, there had been a liberal bourgeois democracy when she was dismembered and annexed by Germany. In Bulgaria the Czar, in Romania the King, had ruled, sometimes with Fascist leaders. Both states were backward agrarian countries, but both turned against Germany in the end. In Hungary, there had been a semi-Fascist, semi-feudal, but in certain respects liberal regime which ended in a Fascist dictatorship. How was it possible to shape the domestic policy, the economy, the social structure and political institutional system of such different countries according to a single model?

Yugoslavia was the only socialist country unwilling to accept the requirements of uniformity. This was not in respect of the one-party system, which again shows that this was not the crucial question. Contrary to other Eastern European countries, in Yugoslavia there was only one party after the 1945 victory. But the League of Yugoslav Communists thought that an international organization – the Information Bureau of Communist and Workers' Parties, which was founded in 1947 as the successor of the Comintern – could not determine the policies of the various socialist countries in all their detail.

In June 1948, the Information Bureau condemned the League of Yugoslav Communists and branded its leaders as nationalists and anti-Soviet. The 1949 resolution called the Yugoslav leaders traitors and imperialist agents striving for the restoration of capitalism and plotting against the other socialist countries.

The Yugoslav crisis must have been the final reason for the radical change in Hungarian domestic politics, for the creation of a political atmosphere which theretofore had been not only unknown but also unimaginable in Hungary. In June 1949, the population of the country was shocked to learn from the newspapers that László Rajk, Foreign Minister of the Hungarian People's Republic, and member of the Political Committee of the Hungarian Working People's Party, had been arrested and charged with being a party to an anti-state conspiracy.

We have come to the most tragic chapter of the Hungarian working class movement. Communists were jailed, forced to make false confessions, tortured and executed by Communists.

It is not the task of this book to clarify the reasons, the mechanism and the exact history of the show trials. I know dozens of people, one or two are friends, who fell victim to these terrible trials. I have read a number of memoirs about these times and I know a few people who were the executors. One of the mysteries of the show trials is that both the hangmen and the victims are enigmas themselves.

No one can know the whole truth about the trials. I think that even if the most secret files of the most secret archives were opened — although I doubt that any such exist — the exact truth would still remain undiscovered.

I do not know the reasons behind the trials. But it is not sufficient explanation to say that in an increasingly tense situation, under the threat of what seemed like imminent war, Rákosi and Co. believed that there was a need for an iron-fisted dictatorship in Hungary and therefore it was necessary to eliminate from political life — sometimes from among the living — those people whom they suspected of possibly turning against them at some future date. It is not sufficient to say that they wanted to demonstrate the imperialist danger and the validity of the decision against the Yugoslavs through the trials. The international aspects cannot provide an exact explanation either, because in some socialist countries not a single politician was executed — and this only aggravated Rákosi's crime. The least credible explanation is that they wanted to eliminate the opposition within the party. All these reasons are true, but they are in no way the whole truth, not even in combination.

In Hungary, there was no opposition force in 1949 which could have overthrown the regime or could even threaten it seriously. The only thing that Rákosi and Co. feared was that a part of the party leadership might turn against them. It was a manifestation of the terrible distortion of power that they were convinced that their personal power was indispensable to the security of the social system.

Their fear was nonsense because in 1949 neither László Rajk, nor any other Communist leader represented a basically different political line; they respected Rákosi and recognized him as the leader of the party. Nonetheless, this distorted logic was at work, at the root of the trials. The arrested bourgeois politicians got relatively light sentences, the former Social Democrats on the whole received heavy ones, but only Communists were executed. Among the latter, the proportion of top level military and police officers was especially high. These were people who, in fact, had armed force at their disposal but it did not even enter their minds to turn it against either socialism or Rákosi and Co. The predominant majority of the victims were Communists who had lived in Hungary or in a Western country before the

Liberation, and therefore were alien and unreliable as far as Rákosi and his associates were concerned.

Undoubtedly, knowing their character, past, careers and ideas, the majority of those executed would probably not have endorsed Rákosi's policies and methods in the long run. Therefore, Rákosi's instincts were right in that respect. This is true even if there were exceptions both among those victimized and those who were not.

I once knew an outstanding Communist leader who all his life was unable to understand why he had remained free when his whole life, his role in the underground movement, his circle of friends and personality predestined him to be one of the victims. I have known two brothers, both of whom were state secretaries; the more capable suffered no harm, the other spent several years in prison.

It is not my task to pass judgement; I do not even know the precise details. I wish to illustrate the mechanism of the structure by saying that only the three or four highest ranking political leaders and perhaps the chief of the State Security Authority were privy to the essentials, the ramifications and the political meaning of the show trials. However unimaginable it may seem today, not only were the rest of the Political Committee uninitiated, but also those who prepared and conducted the trials. This, of course, does not acquit either the guilty or those who were politically responsible.

"In retrospect, many small things jelled in my mind", says Kádár. "Just before the Liberation, Gábor Péter[75] once told me that he would like to be in charge of the political police. I could not understand it. If the party delegates me to be a policeman, I'll do it, as in fact I did. But why would anyone aspire to be a policeman? Then, a few years after the Liberation, Gábor Péter started complaining that Rajk did not allow the State Security Authority to work independently, that he poked his nose into everything. Later he said of Pálffy[76] and Sólyom[77] that the Horthyist military officers still showed in them. I told him to go to hell with such idiocy, but I did not attribute any particular significance to his remarks. Not even later, when Mihály Farkas repeated the same charges against all three almost word for word."

At that time Rajk was Minister of Home Affairs, György Pálffy head of military counterintelligence, László Sólyom the police chief of Budapest, Gábor Péter head of the State Security Authority, and Mihály Farkas the secretary of the Central Leadership responsible for the armed forces. These charges only lent colour to the subsequent much more terrible and false ones.

One Sunday, Rákosi invited Kádár to his home. Gerő, Farkas, and Révai were already there. Kádár noticed immediately that Rajk was not present although even officially he belonged to the highest level of the party leadership.

"I came to realize only later", says Kádár, "that these four men regularly discussed all important issues before their submission to the Political Committee."

It soon became clear why Rajk was not present. Mihály Farkas informed us that according to the reports of the State Security Authority László Rajk was suspected of being an agent of the American intelligence service.

"I could not speak, I was so astonished", says Kádár. "Then all I could say was that it was impossible."

Farkas argued that they had got the reports from reliable agents working in Switzerland. Kádár protested. Gerő and Révai remained silent. The relatively brief debate was closed by Rákosi saying that even if it could not be proved, if Rajk was suspect, he should not remain Minister of Home Affairs, but should take over the foreign affairs portfolio and Kádár should become Minister of Home Affairs.

"I immediately understood", says Kádár, "that Rákosi had already decided on this question without me. I also understood why Rákosi had invited me to arrive later than the others. Révai was very pale, and so was I, I think."

In September 1948, László Rajk was appointed Foreign Minister, and János Kádár Minister of Home Affairs. According to a contemporary press report Kádár said upon assuming office: "It is an honour and a great task for me to continue and advance László Rajk's creative work successfully." To which Rajk replied: "I don't think this is good-bye."

There is no way of knowing what Rajk really felt. Was he offended or suspicious? There is no witness or proof, but I don't think he was. Not only because he remained a member of the Political Committee, the highest ruling body of the Party, but because in those days it was natural for Party leaders to be entrusted with different posts. By way of illustration, let me mention three Communist leaders figuring frequently on government lists. Imre Nagy was Minister of Agriculture between 1944–45, Minister of Home Affairs 1945–46, Minister of Food 1950–52, Minister of Requisitions 1952, Deputy Prime Minister 1952–53, and Prime Minister 1953–55 and in 1956. Ernő Gerő was Minister of Commerce and Transport in 1945, Minister of Transport 1945–49, Minister of Finance 1948–49, Minister of State 1949–52, Minister of Home Affairs 1953–54, and First Deputy Prime Minister 1952–56. Erik Molnár[78] was Minister of Public Welfare between 1944–47, Foreign Minister in 1947 and 1952–53, Minister of Justice from 1950 to 1952, and again in 1954–56.

The change of portfolios itself would not have made Rajk suspicious. There is no way of knowing whether he felt any distrust directed at himself. But it is certain that he had no idea of the horrors awaiting him. He could not have imagined that anything like that could happen in the movement for which he had struggled all his life, in which he believed and of which he was proud. This was also pertinent to the age.

László Rajk's arrest by the State Security Authority on May 30, 1949 was a major turning point.

The Rajk trial was intended for the public, and attention was paid to appearances. Tibor Szőnyi[79] and András Szalai[80] were the first to be arrested. Szőnyi lived in Switzerland during World War II and after the war he established contact with the United States intelligence service upon the instruction of the Communist Party to enable Hungarian Communists living in exile in Western Europe to return to Hungary with its assistance. Szalai was a member of the illegal Hungarian Communist party; he was so brutally tortured by Horthy's police that he almost died. His wife fought with the Yugoslav partisans.

The three main points of the charges were based on the biography of the principal defendants, but on utterly false data: Rajk and his accomplices were agents of the American intelligence service, Yugoslav spies, and informers of Horthy's police.

The army general and the police colonel figuring in the trial were intended to prove the fourth main charge: armed conspiracy. To lend it all more colour, a Yugoslav diplomat, one of the leaders of the Serbo-Croatian minority in Hungary, and a former left-wing Social Democrat politician were also among the defendants.

I am certain that we will never learn what exactly happened between László Rajk's arrest and execution, and not only because the main witness, Rajk, is dead as are, as far as I know, all of his co-defendants. I think Rajk himself, even if he were alive, could not say what exactly took place in his mind. Perhaps only a Shakespeare or a Dostoyevsky could tell us. Was he tortured? Probably. But Rajk had been in police interrogation rooms quite a few times and they could never break him. Did they keep him awake for days or weeks to break his will? Did they subject his nervous system to constant 180-degree turns: surrounding him with total silence, then with terrible noise, sometimes with blinding light, sometimes with total darkness, by torturing him, then talking to him as a comrade? Did they threaten him with the extermination of his family or did they feed him hopes that they would let him live? They did all these things to quite a few prisoners. Did they give him narcotics as Mindszenty said they did when he wrote about his own case in his memoirs? But there is no narcotic which can make someone confess in public day after day to deeds which he did not commit. His prosecutors were so sure of themselves that the trial was broadcast live on the radio.

Rajk, deathly pale, stood in front of the microphones reciting his phony confession in a colourless tone, but fluently: he was an American agent, a police informer, an accomplice of the Yugoslav Fascists, preparing a coup-d'état, and he wanted to have the Communist party leaders assassinated.

Those who know this confession, but never have restless nights, are not real Communists.

We do know how others behaved in similar circumstances. For example, there was the former hussar officer, one of the military leaders of the resistance movement, a staff officer of the democratic army after the Liberation, who, upon instructions, commanded the execution in 1949 of Major General György Pálffy, his friend, comrade and superior. When he, too, was arrested, he asked for a glass of brandy and the confession they wanted him to sign. He had no illusions. But let no one call him a cynic. He fought for a cause at the risk of his life and went to the gallows without disowning that cause.

The most general and palpable explanation is that Rajk was persuaded that his confession served the interests of his party and of the international working class movement; he was led to believe the bizarre notion that a trial like this and these confessions would disturb the public, and fortify their resistance against the enemy.

I do not believe that it was as simple as that, although there is some truth in it: more so than in other explanations. But I should like to make two additional comments. The main defendant of one of the show trials said in his final statement that perhaps he could have saved his life, but what meaning would his life have, if he could no longer be a Communist. Kádár takes a similar view of Rajk's tragedy. In his opinion, a completely broken man stood in the courtroom, a man who was deprived of his honour, beliefs, purpose and meaning in life, disowned by his party, people, comrades and friends, a man for whom everything he knew about the world and believed in was completely confused and who had only one desire, death, because he was unable to continue living like that. Kádár's opinion is important because he had to live through the same thing himself not much later.

I cannot solve the mystery, nor is it my task to do so. I can only say that the country should bow to the memory of László Rajk, 40, former would-be teacher, political commissar of the international brigades in Spain, Secretary of the Hungarian Party of Communists, Minister of the Hungarian Republic, member of the Political Committee of the Hungarian Working People's Party; to György Pálffy, 40, former captain of the Hungarian Royal General Staff, head of the military committee of the underground Communist party, chief inspector of the armed forces of the Hungarian Republic, major general, Deputy Minister of Defense; to Dr. Tibor Szőnyi, 46 year-old doctor, member of the Central Leadership and the Organizing Committee of the Hungarian Working People's Party, head of the cadre department of the party; to András Szalai, 32 year-old engineer, deputy head of the cadre department of the Hungarian Working People's Party; and to their companions. Their fate should never be forgotten. More unbiased Hungarian citizens of more peaceful ages and calmer times, those who did not know the victims or those who sacrificed them, will perhaps think differently. I am their contemporary; I neither want to nor am I able to forget.

A still open question is why hundreds of thousands of people believed these terrible and impossible charges, which contradicted all logic and human experience. It is not a sufficient explanation that the victims confessed, speaking against themselves. Not only because according to the fundamental rules of law a confession without supporting evidence — and there was none — is worth nothing. The country learnt of Rajk's arrest and the charges against him in June, and could only hear and read Rajk's confession in September. I think there were few Communists who did not believe the charges before the confessions were heard, although quite a few knew Rajk and his arrested companions personally. Party discipline paralyzed not only the victims' minds, but the minds of party members' too.

And at that time discipline was not the result of orders, or fear, but of conviction, belief, dedication to a cause. They could imagine that Rajk was somehow a traitor, but not that the leaders of their party might be capable of fabricating such a thing. And indeed the latter was the more unbelievable. The reality of these terrible trials was beyond all human imagination and knowledge. This explains why the people who did not believe the charges against Rajk were those who suspected the Communists of every evil under the sun anyway.

"I had to wait another two years for my turn", says Kádár.

After a while it became obvious that his turn would also come. Let us not believe the story made up after 1956, and which was sometimes reported as fact, that he had persuaded Rajk to confess. Nor should we accept the story that as Minister of Home Affairs he had knowledge of the preparations for the trial. By that time the State Security Authority did not come under the Ministry of Home Affairs, but had become an independent body subordinated directly to Mihály Farkas. He told Rákosi and Co. that he did not believe that Rajk was guilty and he protested against his arrest. I have already mentioned that Kádár and Rajk had hardly met during their years in the underground and their subsequent relationship was no closer, so he was unable to contradict either the charges or Rajk's confession on the basis of personal impressions.

"Nevertheless, I believed that my insight into a person's nature could not be mistaken to such an extent", he says.

Firstly, one small detail caught his attention in the confession. Rajk said that he had secretly met the Yugoslav Home Affairs Minister Rankovich in a hunting lodge in Hungary.

"Rajk was a clever man", says Kádár. "He had learnt not to take unnecessary risks. Why did they not meet in Yugoslavia, in complete safety?"

He asked Rákosi the same question. This cannot be true, he said. And if this is not true, can we be certain that the rest is?

This mode of thought is typical of Kádár. If he does not feel that some seemingly insignificant detail is true, then he is unable to accept the whole.

Rákosi stopped him by saying something about the unimportance of details. Only the main thing mattered and that was that Rajk was guilty.

It is small wonder that the air, already rather chilly in Hungary at that time, froze around Kádár. He repeatedly asked to be relieved of his ministerial duties because he was unable to work in such an atmosphere.

"Rákosi did not understand that", he says. "One of our comrades who was in a high position once went to see him. He asked Rákosi to be allowed to work as a doctor again, because he did not feel up to his position. Rákosi did not understand him either. He told him that it was impossible: nobody who has once tasted power can give it up."

In June 1950, János Kádár was relieved of his post as Minister of Home Affairs and became a department head at party headquarters. At the same time, he remained a member of the Political Committee and of the Secretariat.

"At that time, Rákosi was not only hinting that I was not innocent either", says Kádár, "but for months he had been urging me to confess my guilt."

One of his colleagues who often met him at that time says he could see nothing to indicate his inner tension. Apparently he lived and worked just as before. Binding party discipline, which, I think, by that time was a means of defense, too, determined his life to such an extent that he did not even speak to his wife about the impossible situation in which the Secretary-General of the Party suspected one of his deputies of treason.

He was arrested in May 1951.

"Believe me, I felt relieved. I thought that nothing could be worse than permanent uncertainty."

There is also a story, which many have published as fact, that Kádár was exceptionally brutally tortured in prison. This is not true, but the mental torment was even more agonizing. While the interrogation was in progress, he was not left alone for a single second; there were two interrogators with him in the cell day and night. Kádár in his stubbornness insisted on one condition to the last: he was unwilling to implicate anyone else in his confession. The charge did not differ much from the one against Rajk. He was sentenced to life imprisonment. By that time, who knows why, arrested leaders were no longer executed. There were no other public trials apart from the Rajk trial, and I do not know the reason for that either.

"The sentence was a terrible disappointment", says Kádár. "I almost had a breakdown."

He had had enough of everything, the sordid lies, the sullying of his ideals, his principles being trampled underfoot. He had hoped to be sentenced to death and executed.

This is seemingly contradicted by one of his speeches in 1958. Then he said: "There have been two occasions in my life when it seemed I'd have to die. The first was in 1944, the other later. A lot of things have been said of me—particularly in 1956; people said things like 'Kádár is hysterical, he's had a nervous breakdown', although it is one of my characteristics that I am calm by nature, and can take a lot of mental strain. When it seemed the time had come to die, I was pretty calm when I thought over where I had been, and what I had done in my life; in 1944, I felt that there really was nothing wrong. If that's how things were, I'd just have to die. The people would live, the Soviet troops would arrive, and socialism would triumph. The second time, I was in trouble. Then it seemed as if I'd have to die under circumstances when all my comrades, all my brothers, all whose opinion I esteemed, all who I had worked with as a young man would think that I had betrayed the Communist cause. And this, believe me, is a terrible thing. At that time, I was not fighting for my life. What I did want very much was to live to see the day when people would know that I was not a traitor to the Communist flag."

In my view, the contradiction is only apparent. I can imagine that someone can have enough of life and, at the same time, still want to see his honour cleared. In any case, let us be cautious in passing judgement about situations which an average person cannot even imagine.

Kádár spent three and a half years in the Conti Street prison, where he had already been an inmate as János Lupták, the deserter. The highest ranking leaders were kept in this prison at that time and were totally sequestered not only from the outside world and from one another, but even from the guards. Kádár did not hear a word, nor was he allowed to meet or talk to anyone for three years.

"It was not the first three years which were the most difficult, but the last six months", he says.

Not the years when he thought that never in his life would he see anything other than the whitewashed walls of the cell and the iron door, but the six months when the rehabilitation procedure was already under way, when the interrogators and guards were calling him "comrade": these were the hardest to bear. When he knew that he would probably be freed and he would get back not only his freedom, but his honour, too.

"As long as they treated me as a spy, a criminal, an enemy agent", says Kádár, "I had patience. But when they called me 'comrade', it was difficult for me to bear it any longer. How long would they keep me in prison if they knew me to be innocent?"

The interrogating officer who headed the rehabilitation procedure (incidentally, he had headed Kádár's interrogations, too, but then the tone had been somewhat different) repeated time and again that the comrades—that is, the leaders of the party—were very busy and he could make no decisions without them. Kádár, completely isolated from the outside world, had no way of knowing of the power struggle among the leaders of the Hungarian party on which the rehabilitation of those innocently arrested depended. He did not know that the head of the State Security Authority had been arrested in 1953. And not for his breaches of the law.

There was a tragicomic episode during the rehabilitation of János Kádár and his companions. One of his fellow-defendants stubbornly refused to revoke his false confession against himself on the basis of which he had been illegally sentenced. He said that whenever he had revoked a confession his fate had taken a turn for the worse.

The desperate state security officer, impeded in his work, begged János Kádár for help in persuading the stubborn co-defendant to confess that he was not guilty.

"Damned if I was going to help the police", says Kádár.

Kádár was released in the autumn of 1954. He was 42: in his prime, as they say. His hair had thinned, his complexion had become yellowish, his eyelids twitched, his hands trembled. Those who do not know Hungarian history might have thought there was no corner of hell which he had not seen. But there was. And we will meet him there, too.

Towards the Tragedy

The illegal trials were only a part of the process as a result of which the country became increasingly gripped by fear. Many people were interned without being formally sentenced: the leading officials of the Horthy era, higher ranking military, police and gendarmerie officers, better-off citizens and their families were deported from the capital and their homes and possessions confiscated. In the countryside lists of *kulaks*[81] were drawn up and inclusion was often decided not by the person's actual financial situation, but by intrigues, personal enmity or by chance. "Vigilance" became the foremost political requirement and wherever there were any shortcomings the "hand of the enemy" was detected, instead of a search being made for the real cause of the problem. The clerk or the foreman who forgot to lock his desk drawer or left a file out was in trouble. He was lucky if he got off with just having his name put on a black-list. Falsehood saturated the whole country; shock-workers were designated for propaganda purposes and, by various tricks, their norms were overfulfilled a thousand per cent, and they tried to get the rest of the workers to believe that it was only up to them to follow suit.

All this was based on the twisted ideology that the class struggle was necessarily becoming more and more acute. After the outbreak of the Korean War the country lived in a state of tension. Rákosi and his associates exaggerated the real danger immeasurably and this determined their policy, their social and economic decisions.

The Committee of National Defense was created in November 1950 composed of Rákosi, Gerő and Mihály Farkas.

In the following years, this committee of three, the existence of which was unknown to the Cabinet and to the Central Leadership of the Party, decided on every important and many insignificant issues facing the country. The following slogan applied to the whole country: "Let us follow as one the wise leader of our people, Mátyás Rákosi!"

The period of "splendid winds"[82] following the Liberation was over and not only in political life. The volume of industrial production in 1949 exceeded that of the last pre-war peace year by 28 per cent, but from then on serious difficulties were revealed. The leadership set the totally unrealistic aim of transforming Hungary's agrarian-industrial structure into an industrial-agrarian one in five years. The investment estimates of the Five Year Plan were set at 28 billion *Forints* in 1948. This sum was raised to 35 billion in the spring of 1949, to 51 billion at the end of the year, to 60 billion in 1950, and to 85 billion in 1951. Ninety per cent of all investments were allocated to the development of heavy industry and two thirds of all industrial investments went to mining and metallurgy. The slogan was that "Hungary should become the country of iron and steel!" This one-sided and forced plan, which was impossible to fulfil anyway, was inevitably at the expense of light industry, the service sector and agriculture, i.e. everything that served the consumer.

Agricultural production in 1948 amounted to only 80 per cent of the pre-war level. In order to solve the problem, collectivization was to be pushed at a forced pace. This is how Rákosi put it: "Within 3 to 4 years we have to evolve this question to the point at which 90 per cent of the peasantry will cultivate its land under socialist common cooperative cultivation."

Apart from the terrible syntax of the sentence (the spread of jargon through poorly written pamphlets was also characteristic of the period), this goal was wishful thinking, just like the forced pace of industrialization. In 1953, 38 per cent of the country's arable land and 32 per cent of the agricultural workers belonged to state farms or cooperatives. In many places the cooperatives were organized under duress, which caused not only human tragedies, but discredited both joint farming in particular and the socialist system in general.

The growth in the number of cooperatives did not lead to an increase in agricultural output. The cooperatives gathered in the poorest or landless peasants, who had the least farming experience. There was a shortage of animals and machinery; as much as 70 per cent of the harvesting was done by hand. The cooperative leaders were picked not on the basis of expertise but political reliability, or more exactly, of who was presumed reliable. The various central bodies decided what and how much a cooperative had to produce on the basis of various considerations, among which one certainly did not figure: what the cooperative was suitable for. The peasants came to know mainly the disadvantages, and hardly any of the advantages, of collective farming. In the beginning of the fifties, the income of the peasants in the cooperatives fell by two thirds, almost as much as that of the individually farming peasants. This explains why it was impossible to get the majority of the peasantry to join the cooperatives even by force.

Yet everything was done to make their life more difficult. The system of compulsory deliveries was introduced and the delivery quotas were constantly being raised while the purchase price kept dropping. Up to three years imprisonment could be imposed on anyone who "sabotaged" the compulsory deliveries. The fact that yields may be better one year and worse the next was completely disregarded. In 1952, for example, the weather was so bad that in many places the yield did not even cover the needs of a family, but the compulsory delivery was raised regardless. These were the years when peasants bought flour, poultry and eggs in the urban centres if they could, in order to be able to fulfil their compulsory delivery quotas.

A scapegoat had to be found for the fiasco and the scapegoat in this case was the rich peasantry. Seventy thousand families were put on the kulak-lists; increased tax and delivery obligations were imposed on them, in many places their machines, farm buildings and even their houses were confiscated. These measures led to decreased production and often achieved exactly the opposite of their desired political aim. Even the majority of the former cotters, the destitute day-labourers, who really did not care for the bullying rich peasants, were indignant at this unjust and inhuman persecution, and particularly so when often diligent, honest middle-peasants were put on the kulak-lists.

It is no wonder that people fled the villages and the various measures prohibiting this were in vain. If for no other reason, they were impossible to enforce because the rapidly developing industry demanded labour. By 1953, 100,000 peasants went to work in industry from the cooperatives alone. And what was quite unprecedented was that the peasantry often left the land for which they had been struggling for centuries. There were more than 4.2 million acres of land unclaimed, and there was no one to cultivate it.

Naturally, the catastrophic agricultural situation also affected the urban population. In 1951, rationing was introduced for a number of basic foodstuffs and industrial products, and queueing started again outside the shops. I was a soldier at the time and I took bread home from the barracks for my family. The constant raising of norms basically meant a decrease in salaries, and the annual Peace-Loans constituted a form of taxation. In 1952, the real wages of workers and employees were 20 per cent lower than in 1949.

That the mood of the country was not as bad as the economic and political situation — and perhaps it is not the passage of time and the romanticism of my youth that make me say it — can be attributed to a strange national schizophrenia. The Communists whose relatives and friends were arrested knew at the same time that Hungary had started on the road towards socialism after all. Kádár says that once he had the following thought in prison: I am a prisoner and may well die a prisoner, but there is popular rule in Hungary and that is more important than my fate. Although the peasant hardly had his daily share of bread, his son went to secondary school and university, something which previously would have been almost unimaginable. The wage of the worker decreased, but his brother was a factory director or military officer. In 1951, more than half of the roughly 25,000 leading state officials had been workers or peasants before the Liberation.

Three years later, the Central Statistical Office studied the social origin of the leading personnel of eighteen industrial enterprises, three counties, and eight ministries. In the 18 large enterprises, one thousand of the 1,500 people in managerial posts were of worker or peasant origin. Out of the 280 council leaders in the three counties 200 had earlier been workers or peasants. Forty per cent of the leading officials of the eight ministries were workers. This unbelievable degree of social restratification concealed many of the catastrophic blunders and mistakes of the new order.

A compulsory eight-grade primary school system was introduced. In 1953, two and a half times as many youngsters went to secondary school as in 1937 and sixty-five per cent of the children's parents were workers and peasants. The number of university and college students grew three and a half times and fifty-five per cent of them were children of workers and peasants. All this happened in a country where a few years earlier it was hardly possible for a child of a manual labourer to go to secondary school or to university. Forty-three thousand adults studied what was taught in the higher grades of primary school to make up for what they had had no opportunity to learn as children: 24,000 workers attended secondary school, 9,000 went to university, and 30,000 unskilled labourers were being trained to become skilled workers.

Book publishing increased threefold compared to 1938 and books, which were extremely expensive before the Liberation, were sold very cheaply. In 1953, there were 10,000 public libraries in the country with more than one million registered readers; practically every village and factory had its own library. Between 1949 and 1953, the number of cinemas grew three-fold, primarily because electricity was brought even to villages in the middle of nowhere. Young and old sang, danced and acted in 18,000 art groups.

I know very well that it was not to the advantage of everyone, not even to that of the country, that diplomas and leading positions were distributed on the basis of class origin. Later it also led to human tragedies. I also know that the worker and the peasant who went home from the library, the cinema, the cultural group, cursed roundly because there was no bread, no meat, no milk, no shoes; because the norm had been raised again, the compulsory delivery quota increased again, and arrogant and heartless officials trifled with them, the "working people", while they read of their own glorification in the newspapers every day. But they would borrow another book, go to the cinema, dance and sing all the same, and they knew that they could never have lived like this under the old system, not even if there were some who had been making more money then.

The greatest motivating force was one's child. "We will not eat the hen today which will lay the golden egg tomorrow" proclaimed Mátyás Rákosi. That is to say that today we must tighten our belts in order to lay the foundation of the future. Marx called this original capital accumulation, which is scientifically true, but Rákosi's slogan was mere pragmatism, the ideological rationalization of the given state of politics and the national economy. But millions of people did not read Marx and did not think like Rákosi. For them, the future meant their child, for whom they were willing to make any sacrifice, to work and sweat, to face poverty, deprivation, and even injustice. A few years before, the life goal of the majority of workers and peasants was to have their children work for the post office or the railway company. And then came a system in which, with all its mistakes, their children could become engineers, doctors, accountants, ministers, or professors.

In a certain sense Stalin was indeed the leader of his people; he knew that a people was willing to suffer for its future. But Rákosi was searching only for good sounding reasons and slogans to conceal reality.

Every new social order is born amidst immeasurable suffering. Historical experience has shown this to be as inevitable as labour pains.

To recognize and to feel the suffering is not only a moral but primarily a political prerequisite for the leaders of a country. This was one of the secrets of Lenin's greatness. I am not greatly interested in whether a politician weeps at home for his people. The important thing is whether or not an awareness of the suffering of his country and his class is reflected in his policies. I condemn Rákosi and the others not because they lived in villas surrounded by ancient parks, while the people lived in subdivided flats, because they had food in abundance while ordinary citizens could hardly buy lard, and generations grew up without having seen chocolates or lemons. I do not believe that during World War II Churchill ate the same food as the deprived British people, that he hid from the bombs in primitive shelters and bought rationed clothes like his compatriots. But he represented the interests of Great Britain and led his country magnificently during the World War, in England's most catastrophic period.

True, we would expect a different approach to life from a socialist leader who professes the principle of the people's power. But the cardinal crime of Rákosi and Co. was not that they did not identify themselves with the people in their way of life, but that they did not even take note of the suffering, the anguish, of the country; and, what is more, even expected people to pretend that everything was in the best possible order. This gave rise to a day-to-day tissue of lies that it is difficult for people to bear in any social system. And this is even more the case under socialism, which professes social justice.

It was Rákosi's special and personal crime that he who had spent sixteen years in prison and was saved from the gallows only by the world-wide solidarity of his comrades, sent innocent people to prison and to the gallows without batting an eyelid. Could he have acted otherwise? Despite all contrary opinions, I think he could. I do not believe that events pose no alternatives for leaders and that there is no room for manoeuvre. I do not share the vulgar-Marxist thesis that the individual has essentially no role at all in history. The period of the so-called personality cult is the best counter-example here when, day in and day out, this theory was being voiced while at the same time enormous power was concentrated in the hands of individuals. I think that Stalin's personality influenced the history of the Soviet Union and the Communist movement of the whole world to a significant degree, although, of course, it would be a grave mistake to attribute all its errors and achievements to him, and not to search for their economic, social, political and historical reasons.

Joseph Vissarionovich Stalin, the General Secretary of the Communist Party of the Soviet Union, one of the most puzzling, and to this day insufficiently analyzed, leaders of the 20th century, died at the age of 74 in March 1953. His death shook the world Communist movement like an earthquake. The Soviet Party changed Stalin's political course almost immediately and this change considerably influenced Hungarian politics, too. The June 1953 Resolution of the Central Leadership of the Hungarian Working People's Party condemned the cult of the personality, the lack of collective leadership, the weakening of the worker–peasant alliance and the mistakes in economic policy. The resolution declared that the rate of industrialization must be radically reduced, and the ratio between heavy and light industry changed dramatically. The peasantry was to be given significant assistance and relief, and the standard of living of the population was to be fundamentally increased.

It was an epoch-making resolution. Had it been implemented, Hungary would surely have avoided the tragedy of 1956.

The June party resolution put a new leader in the focus of the country's attention. Replacing Mátyás Rákosi, who remained the First Secretary of the Party, Imre Nagy, then 57, became Hungary's Prime Minister.

The short, stubby, bespectacled Imre Nagy was known as a professorial figure although he came from a peasant family. He was a worker; in World War I he was a prisoner of war, and became a Bolshevik; he took part in the battles of the Republic of Councils, was arrested, and emigrated to the Soviet Union in 1928, where he was one of the managers of Radio Kossuth during World War II. Together with Gerő, Farkas and Révai, he belonged to the four-member leadership which returned to Szeged from Moscow during the war to establish the legal Communist Party. In the committee, Imre Nagy was Gerő's deputy, that is, one of the most significant leaders among the exiles. He was a member of the Political Committee of the party from 1945 but was dismissed in 1949 for not approving forced collectivization. At the next party congress he was again elected to the Political Committee, and from 1950 he was Minister of Food, then Minister of Requisitions, that is, the supreme executive of a policy with which he had disagreed only the previous year. I do not know if Imre Nagy had changed his opinion, nor do I know why he got back on the Political Committee.

Although he had played a leading role since 1945 and from 1952 was a Deputy Prime Minister, the country really came to recognize his name in 1953. The general public immediately saw Imre Nagy as a peasant politician and as a politician of national stature. Not only because he was presumed to have different ideas about the peasant policy and to attribute greater significance to national characteristics, but also because millions of Hungarians had found those features lacking in Rákosi's policies, and therefore assumed that Rákosi's successor as Prime Minister would support such principles. We hope the historians will clarify what really happened in the Hungarian political leadership in 1953, to what extent the change can be attributed to world political, personal and principled reasons, and to what extent Imre Nagy's views, the changed party policy and the pressure of public opinion played a role in the changes. At present I can only say that the three-year rivalry between Rákosi and Nagy, and the tragic factional infighting, plunged the country into catastrophe.

In the beginning it was not mentioned publicly that there was a difference of views between the two politicians. Perhaps I am not mistaken in saying that the stubborn insistence on the myth of party unity, which existed less and less, became a decisive obstacle in the way of the renewal of the Communist party. The two speakers at the Communist activists' meeting in Budapest in July 1953 were Mátyás Rákosi and Imre Nagy. I remember well that the whole country sat by the radio, listening as Rákosi, speaking about the June party resolution, continued to emphasize increasing industrial production, while Nagy underlined the need to increase agricultural production and individual consumption. Undoubtedly the latter policy held greater appeal for the country. Everyone sensed the difference between them, but both of them behaved as if they were saying the same thing.

They protected the semblance of unity even more at the 1954 congress of the Hungarian Working People's Party which, also in the name of unity, was opened by Imre Nagy and closed by Mátyás Rákosi. Here is what Nagy said: "The theoretical-political unity of our party is the granite foundation on which the happy socialist future of our working people, and of our beautiful homeland is being constructed." And Rákosi: "Our party's main strength... lies in... unity. We must therefore guard the unity of our party like the apple of our eye, like our dearest treasure."

I do not doubt either Rákosi's or Nagy's faithfulness to their principles or that they believed not only in their concepts, but also in their historical roles. Rákosi probably thought that he provided continuity in the Communist movement in Hungary going back to the Republic of Councils. Perhaps the Communists made mistakes at times, but this movement represented the vital interests of the Hungarian people. I did not know him personally, I only saw and heard him, like every Hungarian citizen, at mass meetings and countless times in newsreels. He was not an attractive man, but he was a clever and cunning politician. In the mud-wrestling of daily politics he was probably far superior to Imre Nagy. And he must have been helped by his past, which accorded him a special authority.

I did meet Imre Nagy a few times. I knew him as a scrupulous and reserved man, a politician thinking through his principles. Reading and re-reading his writings from the spring and summer of 1956 his later role is almost unbelievable today. His language and style hardly differed from that of Rákosi; he was thinking in the same terms. In 1953, he probably perceived his role as being to prove that the policy hallmarked by Rákosi's name was capable of renewal.

The biggest problem — and I say this from a distance of almost 30 years — was that neither Rákosi, nor Imre Nagy realized that only those who had their roots in Hungarian reality could bring about the continuity and renewal of Hungarian radicalism, of the Hungarian Left, and the Hungarian Communist movement. Both of them had been in prison and in exile too long really to know Hungary. Neither their partnership, nor their historical role was fortunate. For both of them politics meant committee infighting rather than state leadership.

Yet their good programme brought welcome achievements in the beginning. New vineyards, and new orchards were planted here and there. And he who plants a fruit-tree or a grape vine has confidence in the future, because the first harvest is years away.

The food situation was better in the autumn of 1953 than at any time since 1949. The real income of workers and employees grew by 20 per cent and that of the peasantry by 10 per cent. The internment camps were closed, the evictions were invalidated, the summary trials ended. The country gave a sigh of relief. Not only did fear lose its grip on people, but again there was an inclination to work because people saw not only the purpose but also the future security of their work. Ilya Ehrenburg called this process the thaw in his world-famous novel.

One question was fatally, if understandably, ignored. In 1953, not one word was mentioned in public about the injustices committed against the Communists and other left-wing leaders unlawfully sentenced. Rákosi knew well that his mistakes and sins could be forgiven, but if it became known that innocent people had been forced to make false confessions, imprisoned and executed on his instructions and with his knowledge, he could not remain in his post.

The victims of the tragic trials have Rákosi's downfall as compensation for their lives and their immeasurable sufferings. Rákosi and Co. fell above all because it was impossible to ignore the victims' corpses, their memory, the horrific injustices. But the country also paid a heavy price.

According to an often told story, upon listening to the report of a Communist leader just freed from jail Rákosi asked him:

"Why did you not inform me that you had problems of this kind?"

The story is probably exaggerated, but it is true in essence. Rákosi and Co. pretended that they knew nothing of the falsehood of the trials, as if only Gábor Péter, who tricked them, too, had been responsible.

Rákosi summoned Kádár not long after his release.

"He received me by saying", Kádár says, "that he was glad to see me. What could have I said? I was not glad to see him, but I was glad to be alive and out of prison. I did not know much about the political situation. I had certain impulses, which I never liked to give way to. I did not know how the country or the people lived, I did not know what was happening in the world."

In the total isolation of prison, Kádár had only learnt of Stalin's death after a considerable delay, from a novel by a Hungarian writer.

Rákosi asked Kádár what he wanted to do — as if that depended on Kádár.

"I told him that so far I had earned my living in three different ways. I used to work in the Ministry of Home Affairs, but I didn't think I felt like working there again."

"That isn't in the cards", interjected Rákosi.

"I used to be a worker and I think I could still do a useful day's work."

"That is out of the question", said Rákosi.

"Of course I knew that", says Kádár. "He did not summon me to put me in a factory as an iron worker. And then, I said, I had been a party worker, too."

"That would be the suitable thing", said Rákosi. "The post of secretary is vacant in two districts"; he asked Kádár which one he would choose, the 8th or the 13th district.

"Angyalföld, the 13th district", I told him. "I only learnt later that the secretary's post was not vacant in either district", says Kádár. "They created a vacancy for me."

He did his work in the mornings. In the afternoons, visitors, who were dissatisfied with the leadership, became more and more numerous: Communists, former Social Democrats, left-wing bourgeois politicians. Some had been in prison, some had been ministers in the past years. Rajk was dead, Mihály Farkas had disappeared from the scene in disgrace, Révai was seriously ill, Gerő, as usual, was shrouded in silence. Kádár's political role strengthened continuously.

Rákosi was not so stupid as to be unaware of this. He kicked Kádár upstairs: he was nominated to become the First Secretary of the Pest County Party Committee. Kádár protested, asking to be left in the 13th district, where he grew up, where he had thousands of acquaintances. Rákosi would not budge and Kádár had to go.

This was in 1955, when it was already evident that after the sound programme of 1953 and the promising upswing, the policy went bankrupt again. The economic situation deteriorated, primarily due to the ill-devised industrial policy and no less to the inconsistent and contradictory implementation of decisions. The biggest problem, however, was the split within the party leadership and the state of uncertainty among the 850,000-strong party membership. By 1954, the personal struggle between Rákosi and Imre Nagy was obvious, even to the uninitiated. A section of the party membership still trusted Rákosi, not knowing his role in the illegal trials, and many of them were responsible for local violations of the law or at least for the unthinking implementation of erroneous policies. Other Communists attributed all positive changes to Imre Nagy. This mass of almost one million people, just like the majority of the population, did not know what to think because there was one set of guidelines one day and different ones the next. As newer and newer statements were made, the guidelines remained only empty words, which further harmed the credibility of words. The power struggle between the two leaders and their factions contributed greatly to the tragedy of the country.

Probably the greatest difficulty was that a large part of the population no longer had confidence in the party leadership and saw no party programme which might have restored the confidence that had been undermined for years. And it is very difficult to lead a country without confidence and credibility; in certain situations, it is impossible. Rákosi had lied too often and had done too much harm to be trusted. Imre Nagy tried to please all sides, which was enough only to win over a minority. Kádár was not in a position, and was not well enough known, to have a say in policy decisions.

In the meanwhile, the matter of the still unclarified trials came more and more into the focus of public opinion; there was still no public mention of them, although the country became ever more preoccupied with the question as more and more innocently imprisoned people were released.

Finally it was history that put Rákosi in a position in which he no longer could remain silent. In May 1955, a delegation headed by Khrushchev, First Secretary of the Soviet Communist Party, visited Yugoslavia to settle relations between the two states and the two parties. Subsequently, the parties taking part in the work of the Communist and Workers' Parties Information Bureau agreed to invalidate the Bureau's strong condemnation of Yugoslavia of 1949.

Now Hungary also had to settle relations with her southern neighbour. And that could hardly be done without clarifying the matter of the Rajk trial, where a great many of the charges had involved Yugoslavia and the Yugoslav leaders. So in the summer of 1955 – two years after the party's 1953 resolution! – Rákosi was obliged to mention the trial at a sitting of the Central Leadership. He wanted to defend his own position and the part he had played, and he lied: far from an explicit declaration of Rajk's innocence, he insisted that Rajk had concealed many things from the party. At the November session of the Central Leadership he repeated this slander and stated that Gábor Péter and his associates had wanted to discredit the Yugoslavs through the Rajk trial. These half-truths, Rákosi's blatant defense of his own role and the shirking of his responsibility satisfied no one, and dissatisfaction with him grew.

By then, the Rákosi group was again all-powerful in the leadership. In April 1955, the Central Leadership expelled Imre Nagy from that body and from the Political Committee, and he was dismissed from the post of Prime Minister as well. The new Prime Minister was the 33-year-old András Hegedüs[83]. Rákosi's strategy during those years was to put relatively young, unknown and inexperienced people who posed no threat to him in the top leadership positions. Mihály Farkas was also dismissed from the Political Committee; in 1953, for some unknown reason, he had become a faithful adherent of Imre Nagy. True, only for a year, when he again switched to Rákosi, but by then it was too late. Imre Nagy was expelled from the party itself in December.

The 20th Congress of the Communist Party of the Soviet Union convened in February 1956, finally presented the solution the Hungarian party had been unable to come up with. The resolution passed declared that world war was not inevitable; it took a stand for peaceful coexistence between different social systems, and emphasized the importance of national characteristics and specific historical conditions in socialist construction. In his famous speech, Khrushchev dealt for the first time with the grave violations of the law committed in the Stalinist period, with the personality cult, and with the offences against democracy and collective leadership which had occurred.

This was the second chance Hungary's politicians had after 1953 to set their house in order. Kádár maintains even today that the catastrophe of 1956 could have been avoided if the Hungarian party had learned the lessons of the 20th Congress in time.

But even then Rákosi did not give up; his fatal crime was that he put his personal power before the interests of the country and the party. At the sitting of the Central Leadership where he reported on the Soviet party congress, he claimed that the 20th Congress justified Hungarian policy. Speaking about the mistakes revealed at the congress, he said that these had already been remedied by the Hungarian party. Although several members of the Central Leadership criticized him for all this – something that earlier had been unheard of – Rákosi still had enough power to have his way. Summing up, he declared: "In my opinion, the authority of the party is growing."

A policy based on such lies and self-deception could only lead to catastrophe. Five difficult months after the 20th Congress the Hungarian leadership had still made no decision on any fundamental issue. The political atmosphere within the country was by then explosive. A great many people, particularly young people and intellectuals, were openly protesting. There were party meetings which lasted three days because of the number of speakers. By then, several primary organizations were demanding that Rákosi be dismissed. In June 1956, there was a bloody clash between dissatisfied workers and the armed forces in Poznan, Poland. This was the final warning for the Hungarian party. What should have happened long ago, finally came to pass in July. The Central Leadership relieved Mátyás Rákosi of his posts as first secretary and a member of the Political Committee; János Kádár and György Marosán were elected to the Political Committee. Kádár became secretary to the Central Leadership.

The newly elected members were invited into the assembly hall where the Central Leadership met. Kádár was seated with the presidium. Mihály Farkas was sitting down in the hall. There was a draft resolution to expel him from the Central Leadership and from the party. Farkas spoke in defense of himself, and tried to shift all responsibility for his mistakes onto others; finally he broke down in tears. The Central Leadership expelled him from the party.

"I watched him leave the room head bowed", says Kádár. "I could not feel sorry for him."

The resolution had three serious shortcomings, three reasons why it could not change the fate of the country. The first was that it came too late. The second was that although Rákosi was dismissed, it was for "reasons of health", and not explicitly for his serious mistakes and crimes. The third fatal mistake was that the man chosen as first secretary of the party was Ernő Gerő, Rákosi's closest associate. No radical departure from the former mistaken policy could be expected of Gerő; besides, a large section of the population rightly felt that essentially the leadership remained in the hands of the Rákosi group which by then lacked all credibility.

There are some who believe that if Kádár, and not Gerő had been elected leader of the party in July, the October tragedy could have been avoided. Kádár is of a different opinion.

"Analyzing the events in retrospect", he says, "I don't believe that such a purely personal change could have prevented the catastrophe at that stage."

The tension was too great by then, and the time too short. It does not seem likely that Kádár could have saved the situation in July, although probably many things would have happened differently if he had led the party and not Gerő. On the other hand, he would have had to appear on the scene much more burdened by the past when the time came.

Gerő's leadership meant hardly any change from former methods. It is characteristic of the situation that Kádár had to protest to the Political Committee that his telephone was being tapped and his mail opened. In the meantime, tension was growing within the country. But that was not Gerő's primary concern; he was busy trying to convince the leaders of Hungary's allies of the new leadership's good intentions. One party delegation after the other went to China, to the Soviet Union and to Yugoslavia.

Following a resolution by the Central Leadership, the remains of László Rajk and his fellow-martyrs were given a solemn reburial on October 6. As György Marosán recalls, when Kádár called for the ceremonial funeral at the sitting of the Political Committee, Gerő whispered nervously with the Prime Minister and the Minister of Home Affairs, and then announced that they did not know where the bodies had been interred.

At the funeral, hundreds of thousands paid their last respects at the bier of those who had literally given everything in the service of a distorted people's power: not only their lives, but their honour, their integrity, and their principles. Those who attended the funeral, saw the crowds, and did not realize that this tragic ceremony was the prologue to Hungary's tragedy were quite lacking in political acumen. I must confess that there were many of us like that. The feverish country did not realize that she stood on the brink of the grave. This tragic funeral was such a shock that the members of the Political Committee met that very evening and decided to propose the arrest of Mihály Farkas. A few days later, Imre Nagy was re-admitted to the party upon no small popular pressure. But all that could not forestall what was to come.

The Hungarian tragedy of 1956 is tragic among other reasons because so many unrelated, totally contradictory elements were involved in it that in many people's minds the various truths cast doubt on each other or cancel each other out, even today.

On his 60th birthday, Kádár described the matter very precisely: "In 1956, a grave and critical situation arose, the scientific name for which is counter-revolution. We are aware that this is the scientific definition of what occurred in 1956. But there is also another term which we may all accept: it was a national tragedy. It was a tragedy for the party, for the working class, for the people, and for many individuals. The way had been lost, and that led to tragedy." That a Communist leader has called a counter-revolution a national tragedy well illustrates what a complex process we are talking about.

The atmosphere in the country was just as complex. How many kinds of Communists there were! Convinced dogmatists, who throughout it all remained certain that they had done everything in the best possible way. Convinced dogmatists who tried to counterbalance what they had done, to save face in their own and the country's eyes, by becoming the spokesmen of extremist elements, often turning anti-Communist in the extreme. Honest people, for whom every word of every party resolution had been gospel truth. Careerists who were interested only in their own prosperity. Members of the old illegal party who had come to know Rákosi's prisons just as well as they knew Horthy's, and who were seething with hatred. Old "illegals" who likewise had been in all the prisons, but when it came to the defense of the socialist social order, took up arms even if it meant fighting side by side with their former jailers. State Security officers who had tortured Communists without hesitation when this was demanded of them, and when they realized what they had done, shot themselves. State Security investigators who had found pleasure in torturing people, and fled the country at the first opportunity. Workers who had become good managers; and workers who had been poor managers. Workers who had remained workers, and had retained their socialist conviction even on years of bread and dripping and beans. Workers who had grown lethargic, and those who had had enough. Destitute peasants brought up on onions, bread and beatings from the gendarmerie; socialism had given them nothing, but had made doctors, engineers and teachers of their children. Peasants brought up on beatings from the gendarmerie, who had learned to beat their fellows. Intellectuals who were Communists and remained so. Intellectuals whose conscience could not bear their sense of being accomplices in what had passed. Intellectuals who had espoused socialism from one day to the other with the same extravagant enthusiasm with which they later became its enemy. Those who had seen the Liberation as adolescents and were fired by the enthusiasm of those first years, and those who had shared in only the most difficult years; those who had found that a man's origin was more important than the person, and words more important than deeds. There is no need to go on.

There were people of middle-class origin whose factory, shop or basement workshop had been taken away. There were members of the genteel middle class who in the old system had kowtowed to their bosses in white shirt and tie, and kowtowed in the new system without a tie because then that was the fashion. Of the bourgeoisie who were politicians or were active in politics, there were some whom Rákosi had imprisoned, and some who were made ministers. We cannot be sure that the former were the worse politicians or the less decent men. We cannot be sure of the opposite either. There were teachers who heartlessly taught young people catchphrases one is ashamed even to pronounce, and there were those who even in those years loved Vörösmarty[84], Ady[85], Kossuth[86], Rákóczi[87], mathematics, and biology, and taught others to love them as well. There is no need to continue this list either.

There were those who used and some who abused the opportunities offered, and there were some who were deprived of opportunities. There were those whose hearts bound them to their families and their social class, while their minds bound them to the social system they lived in. There were others for whom it was the other way around. No one can accuse them of having been naive, of having been quick to believe and easily disillusioned. They were taught that what had been established was perfection itself; who will blame them for having felt confused, or for rebelling when experience proved it all to be otherwise.

Even the enemy was of all kinds. There were those who had hated the new system from the beginning. There were those who hated it from 1947, 1948, or 1949, as their experiences warranted. And those who hated it from 1955, or 1956. There were those preparing to take revenge for the past ten years, and those who had become reconciled to defeat. There were those who did not turn against the ideals of socialism, and yet took up arms against it.

On October 17 the party committee within the Hungarian Writers' Union requested the convening of a special party congress. On October 22, the undergraduates of the largest universities in the country decided to re-establish the Union of Hungarian University and College Students. The leaders of the Petőfi Circle[88] proposed that Imre Nagy and his associates should be included in the party leadership. The Budapest Technical University passed a decision to organize a mass demonstration the following day to express solidarity with the Polish Communists. On the previous day, the Central Committee of the United Polish Workers' Party elected Gomulka, illegally arrested in 1949, as the party's first secretary. The other universities in Budapest joined in the call for the demonstration.

At that time, Hungary's highest state and party leaders were out of the country for a week. They were having talks in Yugoslavia. This was a catastrophic decision on Gerő's part. Important as it was to normalize relations with Hungary's southern neighbours, the country should not have been left without leadership in such a situation. Gerő returned on the morning of October 23; he was met at the railway station by the leaders who had stayed at home, who asked him to convene the Political Committee immediately. Gerő was surprised; he knew hardly anything of what had been going on. From the railway station they immediately went to the party headquarters. Gerő, Kádár, Révai and Hegedüs were seated at the head of the table; the rest of the members of the Political Committee were along the two sides. First Gerő gave a rather lengthy account of his talks in Yugoslavia. He still did not comprehend that the country was on the verge of an explosion. During the sitting, people who were not members of the Political Committee kept coming into the room. This was to be characteristic of the following two weeks: spheres of authority and function ceased to operate, and decisions were increasingly made by those who happened to be present. In connection with the planned march, the Political Committee decided not to permit the demonstration, but the armed forces were not authorized to open fire. Several members of the Political Committee were charged with explaining to various organizations and institutions why the decision was the right one. Kádár was to go to the Radio and the Trade Union Council. After he and a few others left the party headquarters, the Minister of Home Affairs announced that he could not undertake to prevent the demonstration without authorization to fire. Those present finally decided to permit the demonstration after all. This was also characteristic of the coming period: decisions were reversed within hours. By that time, Kádár had managed to convince some leading people at the Radio that it would not be right to permit the demonstration. Then he went over to the Trade Union Council. Except for saying that the party relied on the workers he had not much to say to the trade union leaders. They had not much to say to him either. He was recalled to party headquarters from the Trade Union Council by telephone. He arrived around seven o'clock in the evening. Meanwhile, the Political Committee had decided that Gerő should speak on the radio at eight in the evening.

"As for what was happening in the city", says Kádár, "I didn't really know".

The demonstration started with a few thousand students, but the crowd soon swelled to a hundred thousand, and marched through the city overjoyed, singing, yelling and waving flags. I still recall some of the slogans: "Workers and students are of one mind; let every Hungarian join us!"; "We'll no longer stand all the fraud; open trial in the Farkas case!"; "We're fed up with all the mistakes; let's have a new economic policy!"; "Soviet–Hungarian friendship, equality, freedom!" They marched to the statue of József Bem, where the president of the Writers' Union delivered a short speech which no one could hear; then they marched to Parliament, filling the gigantic square, and demanding that Imre Nagy speak to them.

Imre Nagy did not come, and the crowd became more and more restless. One of the well-known leaders of the former Peasant Party went out on the balcony, but he was booed so vehemently that he did not even try to speak. The crowd called for Imre Nagy.

Allegedly, Imre Nagy made the hundred-thousand-strong crowd wait for hours because he would not speak to them until requested to do so by the party leadership. I do not know whether or not this was true, but it sounds plausible.

One delegation after another went to get him, and Imre Nagy finally came to the Parliament building. By then, the square had been equipped with loudspeakers. When he appeared on the balcony, a hundred thousand people fell silent. He passed by me, and I saw that he was nervous.

"Comrades!", Imre Nagy began, but the salutation was drowned in boos. "We are not comrades!" came the chorus from several directions.

What Imre Nagy said then is not significant. He left the balcony, biting his moustache, surrounded by his supporters. I do not know what he — who for forty years had always called everyone comrade — felt at that moment. How simple it would be to say on the basis of the above that by October 23, 1956, the Hungarian people had had enough of socialism. But that is not how it was. I stood in the square myself, marched with the crowds, personally knew hundreds of marchers who were convinced Communists, and saw thousands of people truly, enthusiastically believing that it was the dawn of a new and better socialist era. True, here and there there were already national flags from which the crest of the people's republic had been cut out; and at times there were cries of "Russkies go home!" but such slogans were at that time soon shouted down.

The question of who fired the first shot at the Radio, where the armed conflict broke out, has been long and often debated. Now, twenty-five years later, this debate is almost incomprehensible. Why should it be considered a crime for the state to try to put up an armed defense of its Radio building when it is attacked? No government in the world would act otherwise. But in Hungary it was long claimed in their defense that those guarding the radio only returned fire. As if this were a merit, and its opposite a crime.

This attitude was a significant factor in the tragedy of October. In 1956, all sincere Communists in Hungary, all decent leaders had a bad conscience on account of the sins of the Rákosi era even if they had had no part in it, or had, in fact, been one of the victims. There was no escaping the sense of collective responsibility. And by then everybody knew or felt that these crimes had contributed to the insurrection. How many other things had also contributed became clear only later. In my view, this sense of collective guilt and an abhorrence of violence had much to do with the leadership's attempt from the very first moment to contain the uprising without bloodshed. The intention is understandable, but the result proves that it was not to the purpose: it led to much bloodshed.

By the way, it was the attackers who fired the first shots at the Radio building. The documents and reminiscences all indicate this, but I was there myself. In the evening, a few people clutching spent cartridges in their hands appeared in the Parliament building and yelled that the State Security soldiers were murdering people at the Radio. A committee was sent to check on what was going on. Who decided to send us, and how I got into this committee I don't know to this day. I mention this just to illustrate the atmosphere of those hours.

We went down to the square, and stopped a truck with a gigantic red, white and green flag on it. How it got there, and why it took instructions from the makeshift committee, are some of the other things I don't know. Anyway, it took us to the Radio. Near the Radio, that is, because the street leading to the Radio building was blocked by overturned and burning cars.

"Watch out, they're shooting!", yelled a friend of mine whom I had met accidentally in the crowd, while we were trying to get through to the Radio building, yelling that we were coming from Parliament. I had served in the army, and knew the whistle of bullets. A State Security detail was standing beside the Radio building with bayonets fixed. How I got to the front of the crowd pressing towards them I don't know. We screamed at each other, to link arms, so that the crowd wouldn't push us against the bayonets. We screamed at the young officer in command of the detail to order his men farther back, or they would run us through with their bayonets. Standing in front of the detail with a pistol in his hand, he screamed back that we'd better calm the crowd, because shots had been fired and stones thrown at his men. We were all screaming; we had to, to be heard above the din. Meanwhile, bullets were whistling by; it was not the State Security men who were shooting; they were standing motionless. I was only a few yards away from them, and saw that many of them were trembling, who knows whether from nervousness or fear. Then a command came from the building; the detail backed away, bayonets still fixed and the door slammed shut behind them. The crowd flooded the street in a matter of seconds.

There were several thousand people milling around the Radio building at the time. Their recollections of what happened will probably differ. But everyone who was there is bound to remember that a mechanized military unit backed up by tanks arrived at the Radio building. The leader of our delegation, a well-known poet and a high-ranking military officer who taught literature at the military academy, tried to find the commander of the detail. He couldn't; nobody knew where he was. The documents and the recollections are contradictory, but one thing is certain: the detail had no ammunition. Neither for the tanks, nor for the hand weapons. They had received the command to push back the crowd besieging the Radio building without using arms.

It was at that point that we went back to Parliament. Our "delegation" had dwindled to half; the others had drifted away in the crowd. I have no idea who the others were. By the time we got back, the square in front of Parliament was empty, the building was dark. The guards did not let us in. There was no longer anyone there, they said. We wanted to go over to the party headquarters building nearby, but we were stopped by armed civilians. Polite but nervous, they told us to go away; we had no business there.

The Central Leadership and the Cabinet were in session at the party headquarters; this, of course, we did not know at the time. The Political Committee was transformed; Imre Nagy, among others, became a member, and he was appointed Prime

Minister during the night. Early in the morning, Imre Nagy spoke to the nation on the radio: he called what had happened a counter-revolution, declared martial law, and announced that the government had asked the Soviet troops stationed in Hungary to help quell the uprising.

For on October 23, 1956, besides the hundred thousand people who marched in the streets hoping and calling for the renewal of the system, there had been armed individuals who occupied the Radio building, the international telephone exchange, the editorial offices and printing shop of the party's central newspaper, some arms depots, and some police stations.

I went back to the Radio on the morning of the 24th. During the night, the rebels had occupied the Radio building; the broadcast came from a porter's lodge through a line switched to the Parliament building with the help of a microphone and a record player affixed to an old radio. Whoever wanted to could enter the building. I saw the corpses lying in the courtyard. Almost all of them were State Security soldiers even younger than me. The stiff corpses were laid one on top of the other, like wood for a funeral pyre.

A great many Hungarian historians consider the armed attacks of October 23 to have been precisely planned and executed actions. I can't quite accept this version myself. The explosion was too sudden to have been prepared so precisely. Certainly there were well-trained, well-instructed foreign secret agents in Hungary. And certainly there were illegal organizations in Hungary with plans for an armed coup d'état; but they could never have pulled it off without the mass demonstration. I do not believe that all this was the execution of an overall, precise, preconceived plan directed from above. There is no intelligence service or illegal organization perfect enough to have worked out and executed a thing of this sort.

I differ from a number of Hungarian and foreign commentators in my evaluation of the request for Soviet support as well. In my view, the Hungarian leadership were not mistaken in requesting military assistance from the Soviet Union on November 4. By then they had no other choice if they wanted to save the socialist social order. On the night of October 23, however, it was a mistake to request Soviet intervention. At that time the Hungarian armed forces might still have gained control of the situation had they been given unambiguous orders. The self-confidence of what was, at any rate, a divided leadership had been undermined by the grave mistakes of the past years and this lack of self-confidence and unity also contributed to the catastrophe: it made it easy to believe that the Hungarian Communists and the armed forces were impotent, and that was not true on October 23rd and 24th.

When I asked Kádár about these days, his reply was slow and considered; it is difficult to find words for something that was so difficult even to comprehend.

"The situation which emerged was something that not only I, but nobody anywhere in the world had ever gone through. There was no theory, no recipe, no experience to help. We needed time to rally, to recover our strength."

In the speech delivered in Parliament in May 1957, he had the political and moral courage to put it this way:

"This is how we arrived at a situation which was the disgrace of the leadership and not the disgrace of the people: to the thousands upon thousands of people in all parts of the country who waited for instructions, guidance and direction from the centre, who demanded weapons and who saw what should be done better than we who were in the leadership, to them we could not honestly give the guidance which a leadership in that kind of situation should."

Although in the first days the country was still directed by the party leadership, one individual came more and more to dominate. There can be no doubt that the key person of October 1956 was Imre Nagy. There came about the tragic situation in which a Communist Prime Minister helped counter-revolution to develop.

It only added to the chaos that for ten days the leaders practically did not leave the Parliament building. They got to know of what was going on in the city and in the country only indirectly, through various intermediaries, and such information was not objective, nor could it be.

On October 24, the government ordered a ban on public meetings, imposed a curfew, and called on the rebels to lay down their arms. The orders were never enforced; the curfew was suspended time and time again, and the deadline for the surrender of arms was put off repeatedly.

On October 25, the Central Leadership relieved Gerő of his post and chose Kádár to be the party's first secretary. Kádár spoke on the radio: "The demonstration of a section of the youth, which started peacefully in accordance with the aims of the overwhelming majority of the participants, degenerated after a few hours, in line with the intentions of anti-democratic and counter-revolutionary elements who had joined it, into an armed attack against the state power of our people's democracy. The attack must be beaten back. The main thing is to re-establish order, and the conditions for peaceful, constructive work. The problems must be solved without delay." In his radio speech of the same day, Imre Nagy, too, called what had happened counter-revolution.

On October 28, a six-man presidium took over the party's direction; the chairman was Kádár. After a two-day debate, on October 31, the leadership announced the dissolution of the Hungarian Working People's Party, and reorganized it under the name Hungarian Socialist Workers' Party. Kádár's opponents have often reminded him that he dissolved the Hungarian Communists' party on two occasions.

"Nothing else could be done", Kádár says. "The party had fallen apart, had lost its credibility, it had to be reorganized. I am not trying to make excuses: when we started to debate the matter, there were six of us in the room, the leadership. When the resolution was passed, there was a crowd of more than thirty people. In those days, almost all decisions had to be made like that."

That a party of 850 thousand disintegrated so quickly was not primarily due to the fact that the rebels occupied one party headquarter after another, and had started persecuting Communists. Several leaders went underground in the first days of November, took their family to safety, or escaped abroad. More important was the fact that the party's members were paralyzed in part by the agonizing sense of responsibility already referred to, in part by the lack of leadership, and in part by the fact that Imre Nagy and those around him changed their views very rapidly, and by then, power was, for all practical purposes, in their hands. In his radio speech of October 28, the Prime Minister termed what earlier he, too, had called counter-revolution a revolution; he announced that the Soviet troops would leave Budapest, that the State Security Authority would be disbanded, that the rebels would be coopted into the armed services, that low wages and pensions would be raised and wages in general reviewed, and that a new cabinet would be formed. His purpose in taking such a stand was probably to calm the country and the capital. But by that time, events had already gone too far. The rebels did not keep the terms of the cease-fire; after the Soviet troops left the capital, and the internal security organization, the only government force that was in any way combat-ready had been disbanded, the state no longer had an armed force at its disposal. There should be no mistake: it was not only the investigative body of the State Security Authority, which had been guilty of violations of the law, which was disbanded — the majority of the officers concerned had been dismissed or arrested by October 23 — but also the State Security Authority's armed units, in which young conscripts served under young and likewise decent officers. It was these men who had defended the Radio and the government buildings, and they were the ones killed at the siege of the Budapest party committee headquarters. The composition of the various armed groups was extremely diverse, and changed as events developed. In Budapest, there must have been a few thousand people involved, the predominant majority young men, with quite a few criminals, restless lumpen elements, and teenagers eager for adventure. There were Horthyist army and gendarmerie officers and Arrow Cross men among them, but there were also high school and university students, workers, apprentices, and even Communists. As matters got out of hand, the criminals and the right-wing mob came to form the majority.

Unfortunately, there were counter-examples: for instance that 32-year-old worker, a member of the Hungarian Working People's Party, whose mother, brothers and sisters had died in concentration camps, and who headed one of the most bloodthirsty of the armed groups in October, and even after November 4. Who can account for such things?

But there were other types among the rebels as well. There was, for example, József Dudás[89], the leader of the armed group which occupied the press and editorial offices of the *Szabad Nép*, a group which called itself the "Committee of the Hungarian National Revolution".

There is contradictory information as to who exactly Dudás was, but it is certain that he had already been active in politics before the Liberation. He was, allegedly, a Communist party member; according to others, he was a police agent, a member of the delegation Horthy sent to hold talks in Moscow; after the Liberation, he ran for Parliament as a candidate of the Smallholders' Party and he was arrested for membership in the Hungarian Community. In contrast to most armed groups, Dudás and his supporters had definite political goals. They published a newspaper, issued appeals and leaflets, did not recognize the Imre Nagy government, then held talks with the Prime Minister, addressed a letter to the UN, and occupied the Foreign Ministry. In addition, they set up a political investigation group, and arrested, sentenced to death, and executed people. As far as can be established, the proportion of older men of ultra right-wing political background was higher in this group than in the other armed details.

In October 1956 the prisons were opened up and all the prisoners released: thieves, former Fascist henchmen, SS men, robbers, war criminals, burglars, Arrow Cross men; altogether nine thousand common criminals and almost four thousand political prisoners were freed. Some of them felt that they had not much to look forward to, and left the country immediately. Others lay low; but many of them joined in the fighting. In every case that is not one of class revolution – and many things can be said of 1956, but not that it was a workers' or peasants' revolt – the underworld plays a great part in the ensuing chaos. That is how it was in October, even if many of the hardened criminals really did, for a while, feel that they were the champions of freedom and revolution. Not a piece of bread or a pair of shoes disappeared from the broken shopwindows. These were the days when people tended to see everyone released from prison as one of Rákosi's victims – a strange example of mass hysteria and false consciousness.

Equally indicative of the differences among the fighters were the three leaders of the counter-revolutionary armed forces. I knew Pál Maléter[90], who became Minister of Defense on November 3, personally. A distinguished-looking professional soldier, he had been captured by the Soviet forces during the war. He volunteered to undergo anti-Fascist training, became a Communist, and returned to Hungary in command of a parachute detachment of partisans. A senior officer of the Hungarian armed forces after the Liberation, in 1956 he was the heavy-handed colonel in command of the forced labour units where young men considered politically unreliable because of their origin, and so not to be trusted with guns, were drafted. On October 25, he was commanded to go with tanks against the main rebel centre, the 19th century barracks once named after the Empress Maria Theresa, and after the Liberation after György Kilián[91] who died a hero's death as a partisan. Maléter first started a shoot-out with the rebels, and then switched sides; for the man in the street, he was the best-known figure of October besides Imre Nagy. He was executed.

Colonel Sándor Kopácsy[92] was the police chief of Budapest in 1956. At one time I respected this Communist worker who became a police officer, and then a commander. He served in leading positions throughout the Rákosi era; in October 1956, he was a member of the seven-man executive committee of the Communist party. It was he who gave orders to the police not to shoot at the rebels, and then provided them with large quantities of weapons. He was sentenced to life imprisonment, and was released a few years later under an amnesty; he left the country with a passport from the Hungarian People's Republic. Since then he has been living in the West; he wrote his memoirs which, to put it mildly, are not exactly factual.

Major-General Béla Király[93] became the commander of the national guard, the armed units organized on the basis of an agreement between the Imre Nagy government and the rebels. During the war, he had been an officer of the general staff; after the Liberation, a field-officer of the Hungarian armed forces. He was arrested in 1951 on charges of espionage, and was released in 1956. After November 4 he tried to continue the armed struggle, but left the country in a few days. He became one of the leaders of the right-wing Hungarian émigrés.

The armed counter-revolution culminated in the siege and occupation of the Budapest Party Committee headquarters. In contrast to the chaos at the party headquarters and in Parliament, there was relative calm at the offices of the Budapest Party Committee, probably due in great part to Imre Mező[94]. Mező was no ordinary man. He came from a peasant family of ten children so poor that he learned to read and write only as an adult. Finding no work in Hungary, he emigrated to Belgium; it was there that he became a Communist. An officer in the Spanish Civil War, he later joined the French Foreign Legion recruited against the Germans, and helped prepare the Paris uprising. After the Liberation, he was secretary of the Budapest Party Committee, but was pushed into the background, to be reinstated again as secretary of the party committee in 1954. He and Kádár thought very highly of each other; Kádár visited him on October 29 at the party headquarters in Köztársaság Square, where he, too, had worked.

"I had no other advice to give him", says Kádár, "than to pay no heed to who was first secretary in name, and to take over the leadership of the party committee."

His face is very bitter; he was fond of Mező.

Next day, the various armed groups launched a coordinated attack on the party committee headquarters which was defended by 50 security guards most of them armed only with rifles. The defenders asked the Ministry of Defense, the Ministry of Home Affairs and Imre Nagy himself for help, but in vain; no help came. By the afternoon, the party committee headquarters fell. Imre Mező, who stepped out of the door with a white flag in his hand with two other men was mown down by a round of machine-gun fire. Then came the atrocities: the film accounts and the photos have travelled the world over. There was a captured defender whose heart was cut out, another was hanged by his feet, another was pulled through the square tied to a truck; some were beaten to death, and some jumped from the third floor window to escape torture.

The rebels claimed to have attacked the party headquarters because there was an underground prison under it, where hundreds of innocent people were being kept. They were digging up the ground with heavy bulldozers for days, searching with dozens of detectors, the newspapers and the radio reporting day by day on the cries for help heard coming from the victims of the underground cells. The correspondent of *Magyar Nemzet*[95], the newspaper of the Patriotic People's Front—and hardly a sensationalist paper—wrote this: "Thursday, the men working at one of the shafts finally heard some voices speaking low. The request for help came from very, very far off. 'Free us! We are prisoners! We want to live!', came the hollow voice from below. 'How many of you are there?', they asked. 'One hundred and forty-seven' came the answer."

There was no prison under the party building, but the mass hysteria was not to be contained. Which says a great deal, and not only about those who incited it. It also shows that a great many people thought the worst not only of Rákosi and his associates and the state security men, but of the Communists as a whole.

Another fundamental contradiction of 1956 was that Hungary had a Communist Prime Minister—and a Communist government—at a time when the anti-Communist hysteria was at its worst. But not for long. On October 30, Imre Nagy announced the end of the one-party system, and three days later—in the meanwhile, Hungary had had practically no government—formed a coalition government of Communists,

Smallholders, Social Democrats and Peasant Party representatives. New parties mushroomed, more than fifty, according to some estimates.

It was typical of the government coalition of 1956 that, with one or two exceptions, all the parties were represented by right-wingers. In the Social Democratic Party, for example, Árpád Szakasits who had been general secretary of the party for years, and György Marosán, his deputy, got no say, although they had both been in Rákosi's prisons; they were considered too left-wing. One can imagine what views those to the right of the Social Democrats had, not only on the Communists, but on socialism in general.

Events accelerated unbelievably on the international political stage as well. Taking advantage of the chaos in Hungary, Israel, Britain and France attacked Egypt which had nationalized the Suez Canal a few months earlier. The Soviet leaders visited all the socialist countries to discuss the crisis in Hungary and Egypt. Ferenc Nagy, the former Prime Minister, returned from America to Vienna. Miklós Horthy called on the United Nations to intervene in Hungary "in defense of human rights". At home, Imre Nagy announced Hungary's withdrawal from the Warsaw Treaty and declared the country's neutrality. József Mindszenty spoke on Budapest radio and called the government the heir of the fallen regime.

A typical episode: a mass meeting of former political prisoners was announced for November 1 in one of the largest Budapest cinemas. The idea was for war criminals, Communists, Arrow Cross men, right- and left-wing Social Democrats, Horthy's police toughs, ultra right-wing and moderate bourgeois politicians to discuss matters together.

Kádár, who was also invited, did not attend the meeting. That was the day he announced on the radio the formation of the Hungarian Socialist Workers' Party. The following parts of his address are worth considering for the light they shed not only on the situation of that moment, but also on his later policy:

"In this fateful hour we appeal to those who were led to the party which degenerated into an instrument of tyranny through the blind and criminal policy of Rákosi and his clique by loyalty to people and country, and by the desire to serve the pure ideals of socialism. This irresponsible policy has unscrupulously frittered away the moral and ideological heritage which you acquired through honest struggle and the sacrifice of blood in the old days, fighting for our national independence and democratic development.

"We are talking to you frankly. The uprising has come to a crossroads. Either the Hungarian democratic parties will have enough strength to stabilize our achievements or we must face an open counter-revolution. The blood of Hungarian youth, soldiers, workers and peasants was not shed to replace the Rákosi-type despotism with the reign of counter-revolution. We did not fight in order that the mines and factories should be snatched from the hands of the working class, and the land be taken from the hands of the peasantry. The uprising either secures for our people the basic achievements of democracy – the right of assembly and organization, personal freedom and safety, and human dignity – or we sink back into the slavery of the old feudal world and with this into foreign servitude.

"The new party breaks with the crimes of the past once and for all!

"It defends and will defend the honour and independence of our country in the face of all attacks. On this basis, the basis of national independence, it will build fraternal relations with every progressive socialist movement and party in the world. On this basis, the basis of national independence, it wants friendly relations with all countries, far and near, and first and foremost with the neighbouring socialist countries.

"It defends and will defend the achievements of the Hungarian Republic, the land reform, the nationalization of the factories, banks and mines, and the indisputable social and cultural achievements of our people.

"It defends and will defend democracy and the cause of socialism, not by the servile imitation of foreign examples, but in a manner and way in keeping with the economic and historical characteristics of our country, relying on Marxism–Leninism freed from all dogmatism, on the teachings of scientific socialism, and on the revolutionary and progressive traditions of Hungarian history and culture."

A great many people in Hungary did not notice, did not sense, that someone had unfurled a banner, had announced a programme. In chaotic times of frenzied emotions, it is fine catchwords and seductive illusions that spark enthusiasm and not a calm, sober, and realistic evaluation of the alternatives. The turbulent country paid no heed to this self-possessed and determined voice.

Perhaps I am not mistaken in thinking that the speech reflected Kádár's views of the day before, when he still had hopes that the counter-revolution could be averted by reorganizing the party. That's how long a single day can be in times of tumult.

The "either-ors" he presented were already a foregone conclusion by the time he had finished his speech. The terrible deaths of Imre Mező and his comrades had such an impact on the history of 1956 and of Hungary, that it brought Kádár's own decision to a head.

"It was terribly difficult to come to a decision", he says. "We were living not a day, but an hour at a time, dead tired, dispirited, and without precise information. All we really had to rely on was instinct and experience, rather than facts which we did not have, or had not enough of. And one is unwilling to give up hope, particularly when the fate of a country is at stake. But then the moment came when I could no longer hope that the events would not lead to counter-revolution. And however difficult the decision and what followed was, still it was easier than it had been when I was not yet able to decide and did not yet see the solution."

On the evening of November 1, 1956 János Kádár left the Parliament building together with Ferenc Münnich[96]; the next day, half a dozen other leaders followed. It is typical of the conditions of the time that although a Minister of State was sought for a while, soon everyone resigned himself to the fact that he had disappeared.

Rebirth

At dawn on November 4, 1956 Radio Szolnok announced that an eight-man Hungarian Revolutionary Workers' and Peasants' Government had been formed under János Kádár's leadership. The government's concise programme was also broadcast: national independence, the defense of the socialist system, the re-establishment of the legal order, and friendly relations with all socialist states. The government announced that it had asked the Soviet Union to send Red Army units to help re-establish order in the country.

A small cabinet, and a laconic government statement.

"It wasn't all that simple", says Kádár. "There were people included in the cabinet who did not even know about it. Even people whose whereabouts we weren't sure of. All we knew for certain was that they agreed with us. And there was definitely no time to work out a detailed programme. We could not wait, we had to act."

This is his account as given at the national party conference in June 1957:

"On the 1st of November, although on the 2nd or the 3rd they still included my name in a list of cabinet members, I broke all contact with the Imre Nagy group. The others, Comrade Münnich and the rest, had all done the same. On November 2nd we began partly indirect and partly direct talks with the Soviet comrades, with the leaders of the People's Democracies, and with other leaders of the international working class movement about the need to take up the struggle against the counter-revolution, and about the kind of support they could extend to the Hungarian People's Republic. These talks began on November 2nd, on the 3rd the decision was taken, and, so as to lose no time, the attack began on November 4th, because every day was costing the lives of hundreds of brave Communists and loyal Hungarian patriots."

According to the credible recollections of a high-ranking Yugoslav diplomat, Khrushchev and Tito met in Brioni on November 2. Khrushchev reported to the Yugoslav head of state that after consultation with the Polish, Romanian, Czechoslovak, Bulgarian and Chinese leaders the common view had emerged that if they did not intervene in Hungary there would be a civil war. If UN troops were to go into Hungary as they had into Korea a few years earlier, it would mean the threat of world war. Tito agreed, and emphasized that the counter-revolution had to be defeated not only by force of arms, but also politically. Khrushchev informed him that Kádár and Münnich had left Budapest.

János Kádár gave this account to Parliament in 1958 when he asked to be relieved of his post as Prime Minister and recommended Ferenc Münnich for the office:

"When, on November 1 and 2, 1956, we saw the need for a new government, saw the need to break with the traitors, Comrade Münnich was certainly one of the first to take the initiative – if we must and can speak of such matters – and almost became the Prime Minister. I am now letting you in on a "trade secret". It was Comrade Münnich who recommended that I take charge of things as Prime Minister, since he had spent a lot of time out of the country, and people knew less of his ideas and what he'd done."

When Radio Szolnok announced the formation of the new government, Imre Nagy was in Parliament. He informed the country and the world in a brief radio statement transmitted in four languages that the government was in its place and its troops were fighting. After that he immediately left the Parliament building and went to the Yugoslav Embassy where he and about two dozen of his associates were given diplomatic asylum.

The same day at dawn, the Soviet troops entered Budapest again. There was fighting for 4 or 5 days, mostly in the capital. The Soviets used neither the air force nor the artillery, only armoured units. The tanks attacked the insurgent centres without infantry cover, and when they had destroyed them – and unfortunately, they were mostly blocks of flats – they went on, so that the insurgents could regroup. The insurgents threw Molotov cocktails onto the tanks; charred, shrunken corpses could be seen lying on the streets, a ghastly sight.

"I took part at a meeting in the Putilov factory in Leningrad in 1957", says Kádár. "A woman was introduced to me whose husband had died in Budapest in 1944, and her son in 1956. It was hard to look her in the face."

The fighting ended in a few days and not only because the army did not clash with the Soviets. The fact was that few people saw any sense in fighting after November 4, although it was rumoured that they had to hold out for only a few days longer, the UN troops were coming. By then, a section of those armed were looting shops and robbing department stores. Others stopped fighting after a day or two and went home to their families or left the country. Unfortunately almost 200 thousand people left Hungary with them, mostly young people, and for the most diverse reasons.

There were some who, rightly or wrongly, were afraid of reprisal; others feared that a Rákosi-style tyranny would return again; and others had always been enemies of socialism. But there were also Jews frightened by the anti-Semitism that had flared up here and there during the counter-revolution; young men hungry for adventure, those who believed that life was much more beautiful in the West, and others who saw it as a way of solving their family problems. Most of them probably did not exactly know why they went; they just went with the others, driven by the terrible uncertainty, by hopelessness and fear. "As for the people who in their confusion fled from here at the end of 1956", Kádár noted in Parliament in 1958, "I must tell you frankly that we feel very sorry for them."

When the weapons finally fell silent in mid-November, several main streets of the capital again looked like battlefields; the streets were in ruins, the windows broken, the walls full of shell holes, the shop windows smashed, the electric cables torn out. People queued for bread, milk and potatoes for hours. There was no public transport; a curfew was in effect at night, and armed patrols made their rounds of the streets. There were people who once again felt that life would not be normal in the country for years.

And in the public squares there were the small mounds, the graves of those who fell in the fighting. In many cases, they didn't even know who lay there. Time and again trembling people would lean over the makeshift crosses to decipher whatever fading inscription there was, searching for lost children, brothers, and husbands.

"I am very sorry", said Kádár in May 1957, "for those who died on the other side of the front, because they'd been deceived."

For the time being, there was no question of political, social and economic stability. The strikes continued; the population, primarily the Budapest population, had not worked since October 23. The curfew was lifted only in April 1957. In many places, the workers' councils, revolutionary and national committees founded during and after the counter-revolution had taken over not only the direction of the factories and offices, but also the state administration. Foreign pressure was very strong, and not only through propaganda. Time and again, the United Nations tried to intervene in the events in Hungary. There were illegal groups working within the country; various Western intelligence services were sending agents, money and weapons to Hungary. They had as their slogan: "In March we start again!" The government could probably have brought the situation under control sooner if it had employed force. By then it would have been able to; well-armed, reliable security units were being formed one after another, and the police force was reorganized. For the time being, however, they conducted talks. The new leaders had to work out and coordinate their political ideas. There was no detailed programme, no strategy worked out, and the situation changed from day to day. Often they had to improvise and work things out as they went along. On several issues, they were uncertain; they did not know what to do, which direction to try for a way out of the chaos. It was proposed that they negotiate with Imre Nagy who was at the Yugoslav Embassy (incidentally, Imre Nagy was unwilling to take part in such talks); and there was also the idea that Imre Nagy should establish an independent peasant party.

The leaders gathered at Szolnok left for Budapest in armoured cars during the night of November 6; the 23-member Provisional Central Committee of the Hungarian Socialist Workers' Party met for the first time on December 2. Who had elected this body? Obviously, it was self-appointed. In that situation, no other solution was possible.

"We sat for three days", says Kádár. "Everybody spoke, several times. The hall vibrated with tension. Because at the time the 23 of us were unanimous on only one question: socialism had to be saved. But as to how, there were almost as many ideas as there were people.

"And our ideas took shape right there, in the course of the debate."

Kádár attributed such great significance to that sitting that he returned to it a quarter of a century later at one of the sessions of the Central Committee:

"To this day, it's worth considering the lessons to be drawn from that session: different views clashed, and we kept arguing until we came to a consensus. In the end, we all agreed on the major, on the most important questions. Real and lasting unity can only come about in this way, through lively, open, principled discussion. The rest followed naturally. After we closed the discussion and arrived at a consensus, for a long, long time we were able to defend consistently and to a man the stand we had jointly taken. There's something of permanent value here for today, and for the future."

The basic principle was that people were to be won over by argument if possible, and not by force. To that end, they held one talk after another with the most diverse people, groups and organizations. They tried to incorporate into the leadership whoever they could; not only Communists, but also former Social Democrats, Smallholders, and Peasant Party members, initially, with little success. Distrust and uncertainty were so deeply rooted even in old, experienced politicians and leaders that they could not be dispelled in a matter of days or weeks. There were some who said that they did not agree with the new leadership, others who wished to stay out of politics in the future, others who said that they would not dirty their hands again, and still others who were playing for time. Later, quite a few of them changed their minds.

By then the economic position of the country was catastrophic, although relief supplies were continuously arriving from the other socialist countries. The devastation of the fighting had caused 3 billion *Forints*' worth of damage; production losses amounted to 20 billion *Forints*. Food was in short supply, as was fuel and clothing. If production did not start, the Hungarian economy would collapse; the Central Workers' Council called for a general strike on December 11.

"Still, nobody can say that we were not utterly patient", noted Kádár in his report to Parliament on the government's previous six months of activity in May 1957. "After the cabinet was formed, we repeatedly called on the fighters to stop the hopeless struggle and lay down their arms. Not all heeded our words; these we were forced to crush by force of arms. Realizing that armed resistance was doomed, the counter-revolution turned to political weapons. The aim was still to overthrow the Government. For that purpose, they formed various 'revolutionary committees' and a so-called Central Workers' Council, and sent them to join in the fray. We wanted to give time for those perhaps well-intentioned men involved in these bodies to return to the right path. With this in mind, the government passed a resolution on November 12 that the 'revolutionary committees' and other similarly named new-fangled social bodies were to operate as forums of political discussion, were to help in the work to be done, but were not to try to take over leadership from those in charge. For example, they had no right either to hire or fire workers. These committees, however, failed to comply with the government order; what is more, they formed a 'central executive board of revolutionary committees' – a new counter-revolutionary centre. Thus we had no choice but to issue a decree on December 8 banning all 'revolutionary committees' and other bodies whose activities were counter-revolutionary.

"In the same manner, a long political war had to be fought against the Central Workers' Council and the territorial workers' councils, too. There were decent, honest men in the workers' councils, too, but essentially these councils were being used by the counter-revolution for its own ends. The government was patient with them, as well. We repeatedly talked to the members of the Central Workers' Council, trying to explain to them that they were on the wrong course, pointing out to them who it was that they were actually aiding and serving. These talks, however, were to no avail. Again through no fault of ours, the situation became so acute that it was clear that the Central Workers' Council was acting on instructions from Western radio stations, from Radio Free Europe. We were forced to disband the Central Workers' Council and the territorial workers' councils."

This overheated, extremely tense atmosphere – when people harboured grievances and suffered from a guilty conscience, when despair and suspicion, uncertainty and doubt were in the air – was not suitable for the creation of a decentralized power structure, or for the institutionalization of the citizens' right to have their say. And while the national committees and the workers' councils contained people who desired the renewal of socialist Hungary, there were also people in them whose sole purpose was to overthrow the socialist system.

In the middle of December, demonstrators clashed with the security forces in a provincial town; there were several casualties and a hundred wounded. Two days later, a regional party secretary was murdered.

After that, the government resorted to force. The leaders of the Central Workers' Council were arrested, as were the most vocal opposition intellectuals, unknown and well-known people alike. Imre Nagy and his associates were taken to Romania. Summary courts were introduced. Difficult times followed.

Feelings ran so high that people lost their ability to discriminate: all those arrested were considered to have been either unjustly victimized or to be malicious criminals. I myself was imprisoned at that time and know who my prison-mates were. A seventeen year old apprentice who was captured with a rifle in his hand and sentenced to fifteen years in prison. The guard consoled him after the trial; if he worked well in prison, his sentence would be commuted. The chairman of the National Committee in a provincial town, a high-ranking civil servant in the Horthy regime, sentenced to death, who repeated time and time again that had he known that the Imre Nagy government had not been sworn in by the Presidential Council he would never have accepted a position in a regime which had not been legally sanctioned. A double murderer who had served six prison sentences, a man whom his cell-mates feared so much that they committed the gravest sin possible in prison against him: they reported to the guards that he had a knife. For a time, there were just the two of us together in the cell, and he spoke of the revolution as the greatest experience of his life, something that had purified him of all his sins. A general, formerly an officer in Horthy's army who had attended a military academy in the Soviet Union after the Liberation; he had given weapons to the rebels upon instructions from his superiors. The young headmaster of a secondary school who had recited *"Talpra magyar"* ...[97] on the crowded main square of his native town on October 23; he was reported by his deputy, an unfrocked priest. A well-built, handsome young man, who told me his story in a whisper one night so the others wouldn't hear: when he fled the country in 1950, he had stabbed a border-guard with a knife he had hidden up his sleeve. He joined the Foreign Legion, and fought in Africa and Vietnam. He crossed the Hungarian border on November 1 with a short-barrelled submachine gun, six rounds of ammunition, and four hand grenades. A university student who had stood sentry at the front door of one of the National Committees, and had saved dozens of state security men by taking them prisoner, and finding civilian clothes for them to wear instead of their brand-new police uniforms. There was a priest who said his prayers most of the day; it was he who said to a former Smallholders' Party MP: "Sir, one can tell the Smallholders by the fact that they never put their necks in the noose for their principles." I have no idea why he was arrested. There was a chauffeur who claimed to have saved four of the victims at the siege of the Budapest Party Committee headquarters; he took them to hospital. He could not prove this, but many testified that he had been in Köztársaság Square. A lathe operator, who had knocked the red star off the top of his factory. Many people were charged with this same act; in prison they were called "*csillagszórók*" (literally, star-casters). A university lecturer who called on his students to fight for freedom and democracy. A pickpocket who exercised his fingers for four hours a day so as not to get out of practice. He would have to make a living by it, he said, for he had no other skills; he was sentenced to death and executed for murder.

Historically speaking, the most tragic fate was that of Imre Nagy, who was sentenced to death and executed along with three of his supporters; the other defendants at the trial were sentenced to prison terms. In any political trial, the issue of whether the sentence is a just one is open to dispute. What is certain is that this court procedure was not a show trial as Rajk's had been. What was the road traversed by Imre Nagy, a Communist for forty years who had spent a third of his life in the Soviet Union, who had himself initially called what happened a counter-revolution, that led to November 4 and the gallows is yet to be clarified. His tragedy is unquestionable, as is the country's tragedy which he helped cause.

However painful it is to say so, the political trials were a necessity; circumstances being what they were, life could be normalized only by taking a hard line. Within a few years, however, all political prisoners, even those serving a life sentence, were let out. But the rigour was necessary also for another reason: if the party leadership wanted to eliminate the dogmatic opposition, it had to settle accounts with the right wing.

On November 4, many of those who joined the leadership had committed the grave errors of the previous years. The party had 38 thousand members on December 1; it could hardly be choosy about its cadres, but had to work with whoever was willing. This served to reinforce the fear many people had that a new Rákosi era would follow in Hungary though Rákosi himself was gone.

That was not what Kádár wanted. Though he saw October as a counter-revolution he also saw it as a national tragedy; for this reason, 1956 could come to mean not only bankruptcy in the history of Hungarian socialism, but also the start of its rebirth. "The government is determined not only to safeguard the achievements of the past 12 years with all its might, but also to make a clean break with all the mistakes which had impeded socialist construction in Hungary in past years" — was the way it was put in the first declaration of the Revolutionary Workers' and Peasants' Government.

In December 1956, the party's Provisional Central Committee declared that the counter-revolution had had four fundamental causes: Rákosi and his clique had monopolized the leadership of party and state from the end of 1948 on, and had committed grave mistakes and crimes; the party opposition around Imre Nagy had failed to safeguard people's power; there were significant counter-revolutionary forces in Hungary; and that the imperialists had participated in the Hungarian events, their final aim being the overthrow of the whole socialist community.

At the time, this resolution was a political decision that determined the party's policy. Now, more than a quarter of a century later, we can safely say that it is accurate also as historical analysis. It is a rare case of political analysis made in a chaotic situation that stands the test of time. It is certain that there were many things that the leadership of those days did not see well or clearly, but the basic principles were well-founded, and so it was possible for matters to unfold. Kádár stressed emphatically time and again that it had taken the four causes together to lead to counter-revolution. Others thought differently. In the summer of 1957, I was called to appear as witness at a trial where the judge declared, hammering the table, that now he saw how justified the political trials of the late forties and early fifties had been, and what a mistake it had been to release those convicted, for it was they who had prepared the counter-revolution.

The open debate broke out at the national party conference in June 1957. More than 60 per cent of the 348 delegates were under forty; 80 per cent of them had originally been workers.

The first cut and thrust came when József Révai interrupted one of the speakers. Kádár, quite out of character, brought his fist down on the table:

"In our party, Comrade Révai, it is not the custom to interrupt the speakers, nor will it be!"

Révai and a few other leaders who had had significant roles in the Rákosi era had been included in the Provisional Central Committee at Kádár's specific request.

"I thought", says Kádár, "that if there were differences of opinion within the party they should be reflected in the leadership, too."

By then Révai, the leading ideologist of the Rákosi era, was seriously ill; he had suffered a stroke. One of his hands was paralyzed; he limped up the rostrum with a cane and had difficulty in speaking. The line he took was all the harder. He declared that criticism of the mistakes of the past weakened the fight against the counter-revolution. He complained that the older, reliable party members were being pushed into the background.

His speech triggered such a storm of protest that nobody supported him, although Kádár today estimates that about a third of the participants agreed with Révai.

"Why are you shouting, if you're in the right?", Kádár asked one of his associates after the latter had spoken.

His own opposition to Révai was very calmly and soberly put, but was most determined:

"There is another flag alongside the party's flag: the flag of the fallen leadership. But this flag lies on the ground torn, and I am convinced that it will never fly again. The fallen leadership — and it is no accident that I use this expression, in political life such things are not unusual — fell under such circumstances and in such a way that it can never again return to lead the party."

What gave special weight to the debate was that the Communist Party of the Soviet Union replaced Stalin's closest associates in the presidium during those very days; the restoration of the Rákosi era in Hungary with or without Rákosi was, at that time, still a real danger.

The policy of the HSWP met with unexpectedly rapid success. By the end of December the party already had 100,000 members; in April 1957, there were 227,000, by June, 345,000 members. I do not say that there were no careerists and opportunists among them, people looking out only for their own welfare, but certainly the majority were not of that kind. What is more, I know someone who told me explicitly in the summer of 1957 that he had joined the party in order to get ahead in his profession more quickly; I know him to this day: the intervening years have made a convinced Communist and a decent man of him. The party was reborn as fast as it had fallen apart in October 1956, which shows that it was the leadership that had become bankrupt, not the party itself.

The unsettled, sceptical country calmed down. Industrial production in 1957 exceeded the 1955 level; real wages increased by 14 per cent. Almost half a million people gathered on Heroes' Square on May 1, 1957 to listen to János Kádár, the man they had been striking and protesting against half a year earlier. There was no organized procession, only those went who wanted to.

"I think", said Kádár ten years later, "that those half a million people, citizens of Budapest, who met there again, were those who had decided early in 1945 to rebuild Budapest and to rebuild it for the working people, those who in the tragic autumn of 1956 decided that they would not allow the destruction of all that the working people had created with their own blood, sweat and toil here on the two banks of the Danube so that the future might be a socialist and a beautiful one."

The photo of that mass meeting is still there in Kádár's study.

"That was the first time I felt that we had got over the worst of it", he says. "Frankly, I had thought it would take a lot longer."

When Khrushchev visited Dunaújváros with Kádár in 1958 and they were greeted by thunderous applause, Khrushchev remarked how glad he was, because he had feared that the weapons of the Soviet soldiers had made deeper wounds in the Hungarian people.

"I replied", says Kádár, "that I was glad, too; a year and a half earlier half of those people would have been shouting 'Russkies go home'."

The consolidation of power was completed in January 1958, 14 months after the establishment of the Workers' and Peasants' Government. Then Kádár asked Parliament to relieve him of his post as Prime Minister so that he could dedicate all his time and energy to leading the party.

János Kádár, who does not like to appear in public, never delivered so many speeches nor made as many public appearances as during that period. He felt, rightly, that his personal presence was indispensable, and he made himself do it.

Rereading his speeches, writings, and statements of those days one is surprised to find that many basic elements of his future policy were already expounded in them. I am not saying that in 1957 he saw and judged everything as he was to do in ten or twenty years' time; a lot of things which today constitute his policy are present then only as personal impressions or fragmented ideas. But I should like it to be seen that Kádár's world view and system of thought were well-formed 25 years ago, and have undergone no essential change since. It is indicative not only of him, but of Hungary's history as well, that some of his ideas could only be realized many years later, and that some have not been realized even to this day. Politics is a complex, interdependent system of recognition, formulation and realization; its two poles are truth and possibility.

It is almost symbolic that the speech he delivered to the country on the radio on November 4, 1956 was published in the newspaper under the following headline:

We are in this responsible position in such difficult times not to say fine things, but to speak the truth and to act in the people's interest.

Speaking of the mistakes of the past, he wrote:

"If we don't want to commit a grave crime against the interests of the party and the people, we must not forget the mistakes of the past. For our part, we will not forget them. We know that the mistakes of the former leaders lost the party and the nation a great deal of respect; our task is to use every possible means to prevent these mistakes from occurring again. We are well aware that these mistakes had an adverse effect on development: they undermined the dictatorship of the proletariat in Hungary, led to justified bitterness among the masses, and thus contributed to the fact that the counter-revolution was able to drive a wedge between certain groups of workers and the party. The counter-revolution could thus provide favourable conditions for an all-out attack on our people's republic."

On power:

"We have found that power is not only a great force for good, but also entails a great many dangers for both the party and for the individual Communist. Self-satisfaction and over-confidence can be a very grave danger for the party after it has come to power. I think it is no exaggeration to say that this is the greatest lesson we have had to learn, especially in the course of the October events. For after we came into power, some of the comrades in leading positions – and even comrades in lower posts – were under the illusion that every instrument of power – the police, the public prosecutors, the judiciary, the army, and so on – was in their hands, so that they were in the position to 'settle accounts' with their enemies; it was less important to win the day-to-day support of the masses. I think that this, primarily, was at the root of the mistakes committed. Had this attitude not come to dominate practically all spheres of the party's activity, had we continued to pay constant and close attention to what the working people, especially the working class thought and said about the job the party was doing – as indeed we did between 1945 and 1948, when we had to give answers to every question the people put to us – then our coming into power would not have coincided with a period of grave mistakes."

" 'If you want to know what someone's like, put him in a position of power', an old proverb says. There can be no doubt that power is, indeed, a great test of character. I think, however, that a Communist always has two great tests to pass. The first great test is when the Communist stands alone in the face of the enemy. This is a difficult test, for his life is at stake. Think, for instance, of the comrades arrested by the Horthy-regime! A great many of them lost their lives. Many of them stood this test wonderfully. Rákosi was one of those who did. In 1947, there came the new test: we came into power. And some of those who had withstood the first test in an exemplary fashion failed this second one. They began to think that they knew everything, they began to isolate themselves from the masses for whom they had so long fought. That is how it came about that the only people who were left around those in power were those who praised them. If day after day one reads in the papers and in books only that one is brilliant and infallible, one comes to believe it oneself."

On the party:

"There were times when the bane of the party's life was that we conducted ourselves at the party meetings as if we were attending a bad Catholic church service. We managed to assemble somehow, and a high priest sort of person stood up, and said what he was supposed to say; the rest listened to him with devout attention, and then went home. In these "sermons", to stay with the metaphor, there were things like don't steal, don't be a scoundrel, don't be a careerist; instead, work decently, respect the people, respect your parents, and so on. To this, everyone said Amen. And then, when they dispersed, a significant number of the participants set about doing all kinds of nasty and wicked things, quite the opposite of what had just been talked about. But then, to get rid even of our pangs of conscience, we Communists, too, had our own confession: it was called self-criticism. There were people who called themselves Communists and thought they could carry on like a bad Catholic who behaves like a scoundrel all year long and then goes off to church at Easter tide, confesses his sins, and then, reborn and reassured, goes out in the street; and on the Tuesday after Easter, starts the whole thing all over again.

"Now that the party's prestige is growing, we must be careful to avoid sectarian isolationism, and must make sure that every decent unselfish working person willing to fight, work and make sacrifices for the cause of socialist revolution will find his way into the party, especially the workers. But let these be the only ones to come. Let no one be a party member because it's the thing to do, or for personal reasons. It is better for the party, for the working class, for the whole nation if the party is surrounded by a great host of well-intentioned sympathizers and friends than to have the mass of those who waver in times of trouble within the party itself. This is one of the lessons that October has taught us.

"If it is hammered into people's heads that all good things are thanks to the party, then they will hold the party responsible for all bad things, too, which the party had nothing to do with. From 1949 on, we kept saying that all things are thanks to us. We wanted praise for every little thing. The masses had got used to thinking that the party is responsible for everything. They thus came to hold the party responsible even for shortcomings that were the sins of centuries. The party should be more modest, and then it will have much greater influence on the masses.

"The Communist who acts as if he ruled the people, or as if he stood above them, is not a good Communist. The good Communist is someone who stands at the head of the people when it comes to work, to fighting, in times of trouble; he stays with the people through thick and through thin, and leads them. What is needed the most is for party members to respect and esteem those workers who are not in the party, to see in them citizens who have equal rights in every way; their behaviour should be a clear expression of the fact that Communists have no more civic rights by virtue of their party membership than any other person."

On leadership and the people:

"If I may now be permitted to say something good about the government and the present leaders of the party, I should like to point out that these men are quite conscious of the fact that they are not perfect, and for that very reason want to adhere very strictly to the principle which requires that the masses be able to understand the leadership and the leadership the masses; this is needed if they are to make progress. There can be no doubt that the present leadership is not seen by the masses as standing on the kind of pedestal that the previous leadership was seen as standing on for a long while, surrounded by haloes of every kind, and quite convinced that they were infallible. We might and indeed must say that great crowds followed this leadership with their eyes shut. We today must pay the price for this.

"In people's consciousness, the old is always there to burden the new, the past the present. We need only take a backward glance at history to see this. For instance, there was a time when the people thought it just for a woman to be burned at the stake if it was said of her that she was allied with the devil. What is someone who wants to help the people make progress to do in such a situation? Is he to support the burning of witches just because it's a matter of custom and heritage, and because the masses concur with this practice? I myself think that whoever wants to act with full consciousness of his responsibility must first of all be very clear on what it is that serves the interest of the people and of progress; then he must act on it. He must be just as clear on another basic fact: whether the people understand him or not, he must have the personal courage to stand up before a crowd and tell them that what they want to see done on this or that issue is not just and not possible.

"Theory is for the sake of practice; it has no other sense or function. We learn not for the sake of learning, but so as to be able to work better. But this is not true the other way around, and this is a very important difference. Practice is not for the sake of theory. Practice is life itself. Why do I emphasize this? Because there exists such an anti-Marxist mode of thinking in the sciences. There were instances of this in the movement as well; there were those who felt that the masses existed so that they might test their theories on them. But the masses do not exist so that people might test more or less well-constructed, abstract theories and theses on them. It might happen in the case of such experimentation that the given theory can withstand the test, but this is rare; for the most part, the patients being experimented on die of the experiment, and in the end, the masses knock out the brains of those who'd thought the thesis up."

On the peasantry:

"I think that the worker–peasant alliance grew stronger between 1945 and 1949 in the fight for the land reform and when socialist industry was being built up; and it grew strong when what had been achieved had to be safeguarded, for instance in 1946 when the land that had been distributed had to be defended; and it kept growing right until the Communists came into power. Subsequently, this alliance, too, became a looser one, and for two reasons. The first was that mistaken methods were used in the socialist transformation of the countryside (what I'm thinking of here is the use of force, of pressure, and similar means); the second reason was the faults in the system of compulsory deliveries. Not because a system of compulsory deliveries was introduced as such, but because of the faults in the system in operation. For the prices paid for the produce and the means used to secure these compulsory deliveries were such that in the end they became untenable; and this led to a serious weakening of the worker–peasant alliance. The violations of legality, the mistakes committed in this field, also played a part.

"The main problem with our rural consumers' cooperatives was that they did not function as cooperatives in the true sense of the term. These cooperatives could better be called secondary government stores, for the spirit of the cooperative movement was not to be found in them ... When the rural consumers' cooperatives become capable of fulfilling their real, vital function of helping the peasantry solve its marketing problems and helping to supply the peasantry, then they will be genuine cooperatives, will fulfil their specific function, and will even promote the socialist transformation of the villages. What sort of cooperative is it, what kind of cooperative movement can we talk about when it makes absolutely no difference to the village population whether they have a government store or a cooperative, so thoroughly identical are the functions they fulfil! A cooperative of that sort is no true cooperative.

"Whenever I see a private farmer who clings with his last breath to his own little farm it never occurs to me to say he's a scoundrel or a public enemy. For he doesn't cling to his farm because he's an enemy of the cooperative, but because from his childhood he can remember the awful circumstances he grew up in, and the insecurity that was the bane of the poor. The lesson he drew from it all is that as long as he clings to his little farm he will be able to keep his head above water; once he lets go of that, he will drown. That's the reason why a number of small-scale farmers find it very difficult to join the cooperatives. We must understand this, and not talk to them like enemies, and even less so since the time will come when they will be members, too. Force must not be used. What's important is to enlighten them. People don't like to be pushed around."

On foreign policy:

"We are dedicated to peaceful coexistence. As far as we're concerned, this is no empty phrase. It is in our interest to establish and maintain normal inter-state relations with all countries, whatever social system they have."

On the churches:

"We are of the opinion that the wise ecclesiastical dignitaries are those who free the priest and his flock alike from their conflicts of conscience. And free them they can. All that is needed is for them to adhere to the tenets of their faith – for a priest and a flock without faith is no priest and no flock – and as well as this, to accept people's democracy, and adopt the construction of a socialist society as their social programme. In such a case, there can be no conflict of conscience: a man need not then consider whether in obeying the Pope he is being disloyal as a citizen, or whether in being a loyal citizen, he is neglecting his religious duties to the Pope."

On the economy:

"Every worker must know, and work with this in mind, that living standards are related to production; one has more to distribute, can get and consume more only when and where there is increased production to show for work.

"How to direct the economy is a question that is yet to be settled in the party and among the country's leaders alike. The old practice of paralyzing all local initiative and of centralizing everything is known well enough. We cannot yet say that everything is in order, either in people's minds, or in practice. For instance, the higher organizations have not yet surrendered to the lower those jurisdictions without which we cannot expect independent local action for the benefit of the national economy; on the other hand, they tolerate a kind of anarchy, the undermining of central economic direction in a way that jeopardizes Hungary's socialist construction as a whole. This, too, is the type of problem that we need to find theoretical answers to. Certain theses are already given, and are clear: for instance, Lenin's thesis that in the dictatorship of the proletariat, democratic centralism is also the appropriate method of economic control. To adapt this to Hungary's circumstances, and to teach people how things should be done, this, too, is a task that the party must undertake in the future.

"Every decent person knows that more money for lower achievement is abnormal, and can lead to no good if it becomes permanent practice; in the same way, everyone knows that it is unjust to maintain a wage system in which the diligent and the negligent, those who do a good job and those who do a bad one, all get equal pay."

On youth:

"What took place among Hungarian young people in the course of the October events is a lesson to the young people themselves, but is an even greater lesson to the adults, a much, much greater lesson. What is it that the adults ought to have learned? The following: young people are always inclined to idealize; they seek ideals, at times individuals whom they can look up to as paragons. This is a natural law that we cannot change. But to prevent anyone's taking advantage of it, it is very important that nobody should be made an idol in the eyes of our young people, and that no idealistic picture of the realities of life should be drawn. For let's not forget: those young people who were supporters of people's democracy and the idea of socialism more on emotional than on rational grounds found that there was a contradiction. Socialism, as it is usually described, is a very fine thing; but we have never let it be known that we do not yet have a society of this type; it is only now being born, amidst torments, struggles, problems and difficulties in the same way that any other new world is born. If we told our young people that we already had socialism, we did not tell them the truth. And when we speak about given individuals, we have to be equally careful, because it is a terrible blow to young people when they find themselves disillusioned and indeed they did find themselves in such a situation. They suffered such disillusionment because they based their beliefs not so much on rational, as on emotional, grounds. For this reason, they were greatly shaken. This is a lesson for the future. We should always be sparing of grand words and superlatives. I think we should be very frugal in our use of them. Let's take a very good look before we say that something or someone is 'the most'; for we shall be called to account if it turns out that even the positive or comparative form of that adjective is inappropriate."

On the struggle on two fronts:

"In my view, nationalism and bourgeois pseudo-democracy are hostile ideologies that have burst upon us from the outside and have made their way into our ranks; dogmatism and sectarianism in politics, on the other hand, are our own products. These developed within the working class and the party, and are not 'alien' views if we consider their theoretical nature; but they are harmful views. The former are hostile views, the products of the class enemy; the latter came into being within the working class. It is this that we must keep in mind in our fight against them. Within the party, we must fight first of all against dogmatism and sectarianism, for these are the immediate impediments to our ability to fight effectively against the views and policies of the class enemy."

On the people's front:

"We Communists do not wish to bear the responsibility of leading the nation alone. The past years have taught us that it is a mistake to exclude non-Communists from the sphere of politics. We want to draw people of the most diverse convictions into the conduct of our affairs, on the one condition that they are supporters of socialism."

On national unity:

"I'll tell you honestly, we had to take strong measures to break up the 'national unity' that came into being in October. Why did we have to break up this 'national unity'? Because it was reactionary in its aims. Its leaders were anti-socialist elements. Now we are in the discussion phase; we define our position so that the front may be clearly drawn, so that it may become evident who is on one side, who on the other. The debate must be carried on by ideological and political means. The goal is to create a new national unity on a socialist basis. This, however, will take years."

On democracy:

"The party can and does have an influence on the army, on the police, and other administrative bodies, but this is not the same as having won over the majority of the working class, the peasantry and most of the population to our ideals and policies, not the same as having solved the task of leadership. For if we want to replace ideological influence and political persuasion with the use of force, our real ideological and political influence will, in fact, grow smaller even if there is no ostensible resistance.

"Everyone who knows anything about life knows that there are questions on which differences of opinion exist. Communists can disagree with non-Communists, and with Communists as well. Whenever people think, there will be shades of opinion in their thinking, differences great and small. Nor is this to be deplored. What is deplorable is if we do not speak of these differences."

And finally, some ideas that are close to being a philosophy:

"I have not forgotten the statement some writers made about ten months ago, when they lamented the fact that words have lost their meaning. I am of the opinion that the writers, even those whom we rightly rebuke or reprimand, were correct in some matters; and if we think back over the past years, we must admit that a lot of words have lost their meaning through having become dissociated from the content and essence of what they refer to. But if there's anything that can be said to characterize the Hungary of today then it is that words have regained their meaning."

Many years ago I wrote a book on Lenin; in the course of it, I had to make notes on some 50 volumes of his life's work. I know very well what a variety of Lenin portraits can be drawn on the basis of selective quotations, sentences, and analyses taken out of historical context. I hope that I myself have not drawn a distorted picture with the collection of quotations above. Twenty-five years or so of political practice, I feel, authorize this selection of sentences spoken as many years ago.

Hungary's life after the consolidation of power was determined by two basic factors: the socialist transformation of the countryside, and one sentence of János Kádár's.

We have already spoken of how the Hungarian peasant came to own land after 1945. By 1955, however, there was the grave contradiction that while industrial production was three times what it had been in 1938, agricultural production had not really grown at all. That this was so had nothing to do with the peasants, but with the mistaken agricultural policy.

The basis of the Rákosi era agricultural policy was that the peasant must be beset by compulsory deliveries, taxes and discriminatory prices until he grew weary of it all, and joined the cooperative. Typically, a separate Ministry of Requisitions was created to oversee the compulsory deliveries in 1952. The idea proved to be a bad one; nor did it lead to the results desired. Thirty per cent of the arable land in the country was in the form of cooperative farms in 1953; their yield was only two-thirds of what was produced on private farms. As pressure eased the badly-managed cooperatives, many of which had come into being under duress and had also suffered from state policies, broke up one after another. In the spring of 1957, only ten per cent of the arable land was being farmed cooperatively.

One of the first measures the government took after November 4, 1956 was to scrap compulsory deliveries. The leadership did not think the time right for the creation of new cooperatives. Although the peasants had been surprisingly calm during the October events, their ancient distrust of "townspeople" which the Rákosi era had confirmed made it imperative for the new leadership to try to win their confidence.

The party leadership was sharply divided on the matter of agricultural policy. Some maintained that the peasants must be forced into the cooperatives by economic pressure.

"This sectarian policy", Kádár recalled in 1962, "appeared in the December 1958 sitting of the Central Committee in the form of the proposal that taxes on the peasantry be raised by 700 million forints the following year. Dögei[98] explicitly said that those prosperous peasants should be fleeced. It's dreadful even to think what would have happened had we accepted this proposal: at one fell swoop we would have lost everything which the party's policy had gained in the previous year and a half. For we must not forget that in the minds of millions of people (the masses of workers and peasants, as well as the intellectuals) the bitter lessons of the past years were still vivid, and they could not help but still wonder whether all that really was a thing of the past."

The Imre Dögei mentioned by Kádár had been a landless agricultural labourer; he was a fanatical Communist, one of the first to join Kádár in November 1956; he was Minister of Agriculture until 1960.

Another view was that collectivization ought to be carried out only at the rate that the state could make perfect preliminary material and economic provisions for. Kádár had this to say on the subject later: "One can hardly imagine a cooperative being set up by first building cattle barns, pig pens and granaries in the middle of a village where all the land is privately tilled and only then inviting the peasants to join."

Finally it was agreed that the political preconditions were more important than the economic. Once public opinion in the country indicated that the people had confidence in the leadership, collectivization could take place, and indeed, needed to be carried out. Kádár, who most resolutely opposed the use of force, warned that a voluntary act was not the same as a spontaneous act. The matter could not wait until the peasants joined the cooperatives on their own initiative. He knew peasants well.

"I don't want to start quoting the classics", he once said, "but you all know that very fine thought of Lenin's that the peasant is at heart both worker and capitalist. When he's working, he works like a worker; but as soon as he becomes the owner of his produce, as soon as he takes it to market, at that self-same moment he starts thinking like a capitalist. This peasant works amid great hardships all year, blaspheming and cursing the state and the tax office, time and again he decides to leave it all, for he feels that he is living like an animal. But as soon as his produce is safe in the loft, he becomes a capitalist. If, let's say, the propagandists worked splendidly (they don't yet work so well) and succeeded in winning the peasant over to the idea of socialism, even then it would certainly be the case that for eleven months of every year the peasant would make up his mind to join the cooperative; but in the twelfth month, when his produce is in his hands and is his to sell, he would say that he'll just wait another year."

Organizing the cooperatives was a difficult task because a great many peasants felt that something was being taken away from them which was their own. And this was understandable.

"The peasant", says Kádár, "had struggled all his life to get a hold of at least a small piece of land. Everything he had ever seen and experienced told him that land was the only security, that land was life. Is it surprising that he clung to it?"

As I remembered it, collectivization took place within a few months. I was there, and witnessed terrible tragedies, even bloodshed. I saw a son who disowned his father for joining the cooperative, and a father who disinherited his son for joining. Unfortunately, I saw force as well, not the kind that uses a whip, but psychological duress. I saw propagandists who dealt with peasants as heartlessly as if they were not human beings, and propagandists who grieved with the farmers. A woman who left her husband, and a man who left his wife. I saw a peasant who signed the paper that he'd join, and then hanged himself. The country was in turmoil.

Examining the documents, I came to realize how my memory had deceived me. Three hundred and forty-three thousand peasants joined the cooperatives in the winter of 1958–59; 34 per cent of the arable land came under cooperative ownership. A further 380,000 joined in the winter of 1959–60, so that 56 per cent of the arable land was then cooperative. When 340,000 peasants more joined in the winter of 1960–61, the socialization of Hungary's countryside was complete; 93 per cent of the country's cultivated land was in cooperative or state hands. "This", wrote Kádár in 1961, "together with the consolidation of the workers' government, is unquestionably the greatest social development in Hungary since the defeat of the counter-revolution in 1956."

Why were these three years blurred into one in my mind? Probably because I lived among peasants and saw the change in only one of these years: heard their cursing, their doubts, their protestations. Let no one have illusions: all fundamental change like this which affects the lives of millions is unbelievably difficult. Not only because it is always hard to change one's way of life, one's lifestyle. Things were hard because common stables and storage buildings were indeed needed, and in most places they simply were not to be had. The livestock perished, the grain was lost, and if a peasant weeps for anything this is what he weeps for, perhaps even more than for himself. People had no experience in collective farming, they were not really keen on it, and they lacked competent leaders.

This period of Hungary's history will one day be written in detail. All the suffering, and what it gave birth to. For my part, I am writing about János Kádár; right in the middle of collectivization, at the party congress of 1959, he said:

"I promised myself not to disclose the numerical results achieved county by county, because if any kind of mistaken rivalry were to begin in this sphere, it could completely ruin the possibilities open to us. With the intelligent use of our present resources, however, in the coming months we can take a step forward that will enable the cooperative sector to achieve a decisive superiority in our agriculture. We have recommended and recommend again that our comrades should consider the possibilities and think in the manner of Communist revolutionaries. We recommend the responsible men of the counties to stop a bit after completing a certain task, and examine where they stand in the realization of what they had set out to do, talk over their experiences, and then continue their work having taken all this into consideration."

Kádár had good reason to give such a warning. It was the first time since 1956 that the local authorities failed to carry out a decision of the party leadership on a massive scale. In March 1959, the Central Committee passed a resolution to suspend the organization of cooperatives; nothing was more important than for the peasants to be able to work undisturbed during the spring and summer.

"I repeated at least a dozen times", says Kádár, "that collectivization was not an end in itself. The aim was not to have ever more cooperatives, but to have the countryside produce more and of better quality. I talked in vain."

Despite the prohibitions and warnings, the local authorities set up new cooperatives by the hundreds, thus considerably hindering production, and making quite a few mistakes in their great haste. The cart had started rolling downhill, and could not be stopped; it could hardly be slowed down. The spokes broke and the harness snapped in the rush.

Today, twenty years later, when both production results and the mood of the countryside serve as unambiguous justifications of collectivization, it is easy to say that the decision was the correct one to take at the time. But what if the results and the public mood were not what they are today? Then this would indicate the decision to have been an incorrect one; but worse than that, the decision would probably have ruined the country's whole economy, not to mention the lives of hundreds of thousands of people.

Today it is an ever more hotly debated issue the world over as to what extent the state has the right to interfere in the spontaneous socio-economic processes, and to what extent such intervention makes sense. Socialism is probably the most radical example of state intervention, save for the totalitarian, and usually extreme right-wing dictatorships. Marxist ideology posits a goal-oriented society; at the present level of development and probably for a long time to come, this implies the necessity for the state to try and guide society towards the common goals. Such centralized management can make for distortions; there are, unfortunately, enough examples of this in the history of the socialist social order. Yet I believe that it is not only the principle that is justified; the practice, too, is necessary. As far as I know, history shows that not a single new social order was born in a decentralized framework. The most that can be done is for state management to intervene in the socio-economic processes not arbitrarily, in exclusive pursuit of power and ideological goals, but so as to ensure the closest possible harmony between ideals and reality, goals and possibilities.

The turning point we've been discussing in the history of the Hungarian countryside — and Hungarian socialism — was a matter of more than the correct decision brought at the right time, although this latter time factor was very significant. Had collectivization been started as early as 1957, when power was not yet consolidated, when the new leadership had not had the opportunity to gain the people's confidence, the peasantry would probably have resisted as desperately as before 1956. Had the transformation been postponed to a later date, it would have caused serious social, economic and political problems. The rightness of a decision is always linked to the aptness of its timing. But the right decision in 1959 would have been in vain had it not been followed by an appropriate and relatively consistent peasant policy. If present-day reality unambiguously shows the decision taken more than twenty years ago to have been the right one, it has a great deal to do with the correctness of the policy pursued throughout the intervening years. Even right decisions can be made ineffectual by mistaken policies.

In 1945, the Hungarian Left, primarily the Communists, started life anew in the messianic spirit so well put by the anthem of the period: "By tomorrow we'll have stirred the whole world". The first years seemed to confirm this faith: the country's recovery from the devastation of the war was almost unimaginably rapid. The period following 1949 which made an ideology of this faith destroyed its substance in reality.

Nobody had such naive faith in 1957; everybody thought that the way out of the catastrophe would be much longer and more painful. Kádár, for his part, frankly admits as much. The consolidation of power by the spring of 1957 and economic recovery by the end of 1957 were unbelievably quick results which nobody had expected. It remains for historians to analyze the exact reasons; I only register the fact.

The fundamental transformation of the countryside took place at a similarly unexpected pace. Hungary's agriculture was stable and had started to develop dynamically ten years after the enormous shock of collectivization: in 1970, production exceeded the 1960 level by 30 per cent, in 1980, by 70 per cent. Collective farming had proved beyond a doubt to be better than private farming in Hungary.

All this could never have come about had the peasantry, unsettled and wavering at the start, not found their place relatively quickly in the new socio-economic order. It was not easy. Hundreds of thousands felt that they had been deprived of the meaning of their lives, of their only treasure, their land. I will not easily forget the peasants with their vacant stares, the weeping women, nor the desperate hope voiced over and over again: "They will return it some day, won't they?" And my just as desperate protestations that no, the land would not be returned; they should try to become reconciled to that, and resign themselves to working on collective land, collectively from now on.

The peasantry had suffered a terrible shock; they had lost their land, and moreover, their whole life had changed. Men who had budgeted their days and hours themselves, who had felt that they were their own masters even if they had to work from dawn till dusk had to get used to taking orders. It was very difficult. But in the course of ten years — and that is not a hopelessly long stretch even in one man's short lifetime — Hungary's peasants have grown accustomed to collective farming, and have come to accept it; I think very few of them would want their old land back today. To my mind, this proves that the peasant policy was right as much as the production results.

It would not have happened this way without the political principle which Kádár formulated as follows:

"No new social system, no new world can be born without pain and agony. That is why our party considers it a duty to fight for the new, to realize this new world with minimizing problems as far as possible for society and each individual alike; such problems do not benefit society in any way, do not accelerate or aid the birth of the new order, and so should be avoided, if possible."

Naturally, these problems could not always and everywhere be avoided. But in essence, perhaps they were.

There was a certain sentence of which, to paraphrase John Reed's famous book, I could say: it shook Hungary. The sentence was spoken by Kádár in December 1961: "He who is not against us is with us!"

The sentence is not one original to Kádár. Both Stalin and Rákosi had often used its opposite: "He who is not with us is against us." Lenin had used both, on more than one occasion. Probably none of them knew that the sentence itself, and the idea, is several thousand years old. "He who is not against us is with us", and also its opposite, "He who is not with me is against me", were words reported as coming from the mouth of Jesus by three of the Evangelists, Matthew, Mark and Luke.

In the New Testament, John told Jesus that there was a man who had exorcised a devil in His name: but, because he was not willing to join the disciples, they had forbidden him to do so again. Jesus told them not to interfere with him, for he who was not against them was with them. But when people doubted Him, and said that His power came not from God but from Satan, Jesus demanded absolute faith, and declared that he who was not with Him was against Him.

These two conflicting ideas constitute one of the basic schemes of human thought. They apply to the relationships of man to man, as much as to relationships between groups, classes, and countries. Lenin, rightly, made use of both. When Soviet power was engaged in a life-and-death struggle, everyone who did not support them in that struggle was an enemy. But when the danger was no longer acute, everyone who did not attack the social order was considered an ally. Rákosi's slogan was false and politically harmful because he used it when there was no real threat; he thus alienated hundreds of thousands who could have been won over with patient understanding.

To illustrate the storm that was unleashed by this sentence of Kádár's, let me here quote an article of mine which appeared in a Budapest weekly a few weeks after Kádár's speech.

With Us or Against Us?

MARGINAL NOTES ON A SPEECH

At one time a conductor, who would have preferred to weed the strawberry seedlings in his garden, was expected to raise high the red banner although he carried only the flag and not the symbol. At one time the accountant, who would have liked to take his three children to the cinema, was expected to read *Capital* although he did not understand it and was only intimidated by the difficult text. At one time the house-painter, whom his friend asked to paint his flat on Sunday, was expected to paint slogans on the factory wall although he wrote only the words (but not his faith) on the grey building. The following tenet was hammered home constantly: he who is not with us is against us. He who does not say yes, says no. And since man is fallible, many, who did not agree with what was said, said Yes in unison anyway. But a faith that is faked takes a heavy toll and the extorted enthusiasm discredited even truth until even the voice of the numerous true believers seemed false within the masses of people constrained to agree. The backbone of people given to brooding, doubting, fretting and reluctance bent.

What they say today is that eight hours of work a day is one's duty as a citizen. Design machines, build bridges, drive the tram, heal the sick, plough the land, work more and work better for yourself and the community so that everyone can have a better life, and then weed your strawberry seedlings, go to the cinema, paint your friend's flat if that's what you want to do. Don't claim a faith if you haven't got it; if you are middle class don't profess to be the proponent of the *Manifesto*, no harm can come to anyone if they don't.

What has happened? Are petit bourgeois, strawberry-seedling-weeders, cinema-goers, refrigerator-buyers, cottage-builders being reproduced in this country? Are people taught rock-and-roll instead of revolutionary songs? Are they being allowed to languish and be indolent, instead of being fired with enthusiasm?

What I think has happened is simply that at last the country is led by individuals who have received a mandate from the people and who, in turn, believe in the people. For there is nothing sadder and more humiliating than a mature people being treated like children in short pants. But those who believe in Man know that the number of restrictions must be reduced to a minimum; the freedom which gives birth to order should be restricted only by those prohibitions which are indispensable for social coexistence. Those who believe in Man know that at the most pyramids, but not the future, can be built by servants with bent backs. Those who believe in Man have the patience to wait until everyone finds the correct path by his own efforts, relying on his own experiences, by his own free will, compelled only by facts. And those who believe in Man also believe that he will have the necessary acumen and strength.

Of course, to acquire this patience those who lead the country by the authority of the people had to feel that the social system entrusted to them is strong. And most of all they know that the leaders and the led agree by and large on the goal and the means, because the goal is just and the means are true.

I think this is how it must have happened. Somehow like this the time of wisdom has come after so many trials and so many difficult battles, when the senseless and harmful law could be changed and it could be said and we could hear that he who is not against us is with us. The time has come when faked approval is a greater sin than remaining silent; when hypocritical consent is the fault, not arguing; when Man's most sacred duty and right is not just nodding in agreement, but what elevated him from among the animals, creative thinking, with which he can make his lengthening but still all too short life more and more meaningful.

And this is only the first step. It can be only the first step that nobody is forced to wave the flag if they don't agree with what it symbolizes. That no one is obliged to say yes to something if he is not convinced of its truth. If the conformist yes-men and good-for-nothing leave the ranks of those who approve only out of conviction, the latter will only be the stronger for it. Because there are and there will be people who can proclaim with repute that what happens in this country happens by our will. And the new law guarantees that their army will grow. Strength and truth by themselves act as magnets. The faith of those who know and profess that it is a service and a duty, not a merit, to be a socialist in this country today, will make its mark on those who are brooding, sceptical, fretting and reluctant; on all those who are not against us, and who are, therefore, with us.

The above was an article I wrote many years ago. As can be seen, it made no mention of whose and what speech was being discussed. There was no need; the whole country was talking about that sentence. We get a better idea of the times if I add that a large part of the Hungarian press protested against this article. It was one of the mildest manifestations when one of my critics gave as the title to his piece: "One Who Went Too Far". I got my share of criticism at the Writers' Union conference, too, where, among others, one of the leaders of the party proved on the basis of this little piece, as on an anatomical chart, how many diseases contaminate Hungarian intellectual life: anarchy, right-wing deviation, the negation of the class struggle, revisionism, the underestimation of the role of ideology, petty bourgeois tendencies, and I do not recall the rest.

This article and the attendant storm is interesting because it illustrates the extent to which this one sentence of Kádár's had stirred public opinion and political life. I do not want to defend the shortcomings of that article, but today, from a distance of almost twenty years, comparing it with Kádár's ideas and policies then and since, I still believe that it did not misrepresent the essence of Kádár's train of thought. In other words, those who did not agree with that article did not agree with Kádár himself, or did not understand his policy. There were not a few of these.

This is also indicated by the fact that Kádár felt it necessary to return to this sentence at the 8th Party Congress a year after it had been said.

"I should like to say a few words about a slogan which has caused a considerable stir. I am referring to the phrase, 'He who is not against us is with us'. The first and most important thing which must be put on record here at the Congress, too, is that this statement is, of course, not a scientific thesis but simply a political statement which refers to the relationships between people."

Kádár's precise choice of words explains why so many failed to understand them initially. It was not that they did not agree with his policy — of course there were people like that, too — but they were looking for a historical-philosophical meaning in the slogan rather than the reflection of reality in politics.

Kádár continued with irrefutable logic. Of course, I am saying this in retrospect, because at that time it was not that simple at all. When we are thinking in historical terms, particularly about periods of extremely rapid change, we are often amazed when we view ourselves as we were twenty-thirty years ago. It is surprising how fast we forget. Those who did not live during that time cannot understand what happened, if they are not familiar with the political frame of mind of the country, the class, the leading strata which are just as decisive factors in a given historical moment as the economic or social situation.

This is how Kádár reasoned at the party congress:

"Let us take the simplest example. In the Hungarian People's Republic all people who earn their living by work — and do not spend their days and nights plotting and making bombs — go to their jobs in the morning and work; they are actually with us even if perhaps this is not a conscious attitude on their part. If in the country the general policy is sound, then socialist society is being built in industry, in agriculture, in intellectual life; everyone who works is building a socialist society."

This was the objective, irrefutable reality which Kádár recognized, and this recognition has since determined the fate of the country in many respects. The cause behind the lack of comprehension and the attendant perplexity might well have been the fact that in previous years too much emphasis was put on what people thought and said, and less on what they did. In the Rákosi period policy was only called Marxist but it often deviated from the most fundamental principles of Marxism.

Kádár continued speaking in a subjective vein since different policies can originate from the same facts.

"Broad-mindedness in this case is good and useful because Communists — and, as a matter of fact, all more or less normal political trends — should not strive to add to the number of their enemies, or to push those people into the enemy camp who, on the strength of their positions or views, could be brought into our own camp."

This is already the basic principle of Kádárian politics. He could have drawn a different conclusion from the recognition that whether people in the depth of their souls agree with the prevailing social order or not, whether they are the proponents of or indifferent to some ideology, they are nevertheless building socialism by their work. He could have concluded that public opinion can be disregarded. Unfortunately, we have seen socialist systems senselessly turned into one-man dictatorships.

But here we have to stop for a moment. There has hardly been a political category more often misunderstood or misrepresented than the dictatorship of the proletariat. Particularly since the middle of the 20th century, when the word "dictatorship" entered everyday language as a synonym for Fascism and we have come to equate dictatorship with authoritarianism, with tyranny. And undoubtedly in certain periods the history of the socialist countries had tyrannical features.

But according to Marx's definition the dictatorship of the proletariat is not a system of power, but a social category. Marx calls all class societies dictatorships and all states repressive powers because he considers the withering away of classes and of the state the precondition of freedom. In other words, the dictatorship of the proletariat is none other than a social order in which power is in the hands of the working class just as the dictatorship of the bourgeoisie in Marxist terminology means bourgeois society. Let us add that according to Marxist theory, by eliminating exploitation the proletariat creates the possibility of eliminating its own class rule in favour of the creation of a classless society and the liquidation of the state as the ruling class' organ of repression.

With this sketchy presentation I should like to draw attention to the fact that the categories of Marxist philosophy of history and the terminology used by Marxists in this respect often do not coincide with the everyday meaning of these words and not only in respect of the dictatorship of the proletariat. The state, for example, has not only repressive functions in the stricter sense of the word within the social order but it also has administrative, legislative and other functions, although these serve the interests of the ruling class, too. That is why Marx calls these collectively repression, which does not mean violence in every case, again in the everyday and not the abstract sense of the word.

As long as there are class societies, in every state the ruling class enjoys advantages by which it ensures its rule. In feudalism, they were primarily prerogatives, in bourgeois society they are material advantages. In socialism, even in its present, not yet crystallized form, it is more complicated, which has caused considerable difficulties and still does so today. Even in its most distorted form, because of its very nature, the gap between the richest and the poorest in socialist states is nowhere near as great as it unavoidably is even in the most developed bourgeois societies by their very nature. The ruling class does not have the financial power in the personal sense to retain and consolidate its rule. I suppose that this so far unexplored contradiction is partly responsible for violence, repression and tyranny having played, and being able to play, a role in a young and still weak socialist system.

The direct advantage of the ruling class in Hungary in the forties and the fifties was, first of all, that many workers and poor peasants became leaders in the political, state administration and economic spheres, and, being in positions of power, they ensured the rule of their class personally, too. Similarly, being of working class or peasant origin meant an advantage in secondary school and university admissions, in promotions, appointments and wages. Consequently, the rest of the population suffered a disadvantage because of their class position.

This state of affairs was changed by the Kádárian slogan. Kádár recognized that the best interest of the working class, of the rule of the proletariat, is not the maintenance but the elimination of its own class privileges. This is how he put it: "It's only the entire people who can put this policy into practice; it's only the whole people who can build socialism."

A change took place in the interpretation of class relations in the organization of cooperatives. Time and again the Leninist theory was raised in connection with the peasantry, according to which the workers' rule should rely on the poor peasantry, make an alliance with the middle peasants and fight against the rich peasants. The way Kádár justified the historical rephrasing of this principle is typical of his realism and dialectical world outlook:

"Nowhere did Lenin say that we must rely on the *former* poor peasantry, ally ourselves with the *former* middle peasants and fight against the *former* kulaks."

After the formation of the cooperatives, the contradictions between the various peasant strata flared up again and again for a few years; it could not have been otherwise since they showed even in their approach to life and character but the disadvantageous position of the rich peasants and the privileged position — often only in theory — of the poor peasants had in effect ceased to exist.

Then followed the elimination of all discrimination on the basis of social origin, particularly in the case of children and young people. "It would be unjust", said Kádár, "to restrict these young people's opportunities for education because of the class position of their parents before their birth." Class background ceased to be a factor in university admissions and job promotions, although this did not happen from one day to the next and its cessation quite often met strong opposition.

"It had also occurred to me", says Kádár "that the majority of former capitalists, landowners and bourgeoisie became reconciled to the loss of their factory, their land and their businesses. But what they cannot become reconciled to is their children's career opportunities being curtailed and I understand that. Is it good for the worker, I asked myself, if we artificially create such tensions, and is it good if talented young people cannot apply their talents for the good of the country only because their fathers were exploiters at one time?"

After the "year of the change" — as the political jargon called 1947–48 — which brought a decisive change in Hungarian history even if many things took a turn for the worse afterwards, religious people also felt themselves at a disadvantage, regardless of whether they were born counts or welders. There were both ideological and political reasons for this. According to the classic Marxist dictum, religion is the opium of the people, and it was thought that people can be and must be forced to break free of this addiction. It is also a fact that the majority of the Church leaders did not accept the new social order and that part of the clergy attacked the system, overtly and covertly. Although churches were not closed, and nor were they turned into party headquarters, which is what some people had been threatening to do, and church attendance was not forbidden, the regime responded by excluding people professing their religiousness from advancement. This has also changed. "While we are different in some ways, we are the same in others", said Kádár. "The difference between us is that one of us writes the name of God with a small 'g', the other with a capital, but both of us write Man with a capital." He had also put this fine principle in a more practical way: "We believe that socialism is not built first for the materialists, and then later for believers; it is the society of all working men, and is being built for all. If, however, that's how it is, then everyone should take part in its building. What we have to agree on first of all with believers is on building socialism. For everyone knows that, for example, a two-room centrally heated flat with a kitchen and bathroom is bigger than a one-room flat, whether a believer lives in it or an atheist, and that it's better to live in the two-room flat than in a one-room cold water flat. This is clear enough. If, however, we tried to reach a consensus with believers on the issue of whether there's a God or not this would take a very long debate indeed, and it would be a very grave mistake if in the meantime the building of socialism was suspended."

Parliament's election of a Catholic priest as Deputy Speaker in 1961 symbolized the easing of tension between Communists and believers. The final and comprehensive settlement of the relationship between the state and the Catholic Church, was hindered by József Mindszenty's refusal—even to the extent of defying the Pope—to give up his position as head of the Church. When he left the American Embassy and Hungary in 1971, the relationship between State and Church was settled.

Political prisoners were released mostly due to an amnesty. Ninety-five per cent of the people convicted for counter-revolutionary activities were already free by 1962. At the time of the visit to Hungary of the Secretary-General of the United Nations in 1963 Kádár had the following to say on this question: "We were tough when it was necessary, but we reached a point when an amnesty could be granted. The amnesty indicates the very strength of our regime. No one is imprisoned in Hungary today because of political offences. When meting out punishment we were also guided by humanitarian considerations. When we were compelled to take drastic measures we felt that it was much better to keep a tight rein on a few individuals than to have many ordinary people misled—either by their own stupidity or by deception to fall victim to something which they themselves did not start."

It seems impossible, even hypocritical, to speak of humanism in connection with punishment. But it is a fact that the government released every political prisoner as soon as order was consolidated to the extent that those freed could not have posed a political threat even if they turned against the system again—something which, with one or two exceptions, did not happen. Kádár did not make Rákosi's mistake; he did not forget how bitter is the bread of prison.

Those who left Hungary after October 1956 also received an amnesty. "We welcome the return of every decent person who wants to live and work in Hungary", Kádár said. "To those Hungarians who have gone abroad and have taken root there, we say: remain good friends to your old homeland, and bring honour to its name." I think there are only a few people who have not returned for a visit since then; many of them spend their holidays in Hungary year after year and the number of those who return when they reach pension age or whose last wish is to be buried in Hungary is on the increase.

Today, when every year millions visit Hungary from the West and millions of Hungarian citizens travel abroad, one may recall with a smile that Kádár listed increased tourism as an achievement at the 8th Party Congress. In 1958, 26,000 Hungarian citizens travelled to the West, in 1961, 43,000. If we consider that between

1949 and 1957 practically no tourist crossed Hungary's Western border from either direction, then these numbers are not to be scoffed at.

The change in interpreting the tasks of the party and party members also played a role in putting this key concept into practice. The party was the leading force of the country both before and after 1956. According to the Leninist definition, the Communist party is the voluntary association of people who are aware of the role and goals of the working class, and who represent its interests and power. This function of the party was immeasurably distorted after 1949. This was partly because a few people had absolute control over the party, and bad example is infectious particularly when it is systematic: petty tyrants operated in every area of the country and in every sphere of life, and ordering people about was their prevalent method. This was partly also because the party had one million members but this did not mean that there were one million Communists. Many joined the party out of either justifiable or unfounded fear and this involved not only those who were concerned for their jobs. My mother, a nursery school teacher, was a party member until 1956; although she came from the poorest of working class families, she would have been called a conservative petty bourgeois according to the phraseology of the day. My brother, a clerk, was not interested in politics although he was a party member. And they and their like were not the worst. The worst were the careerists, the tyrants, the overzealous, the denunciators, the self-seekers, the flunkies. A party diluted in this way could have no real self-respect, nor could it command respect. At the same time, it was proclaimed that the party members were considered special, superior to others. This was the crux of the problem of the Hungarian Working People's Party — it believed it ought to rule over the country.

The Hungarian Socialist Workers' Party had 100,000 members at the end of 1956, and 500,000 in 1962. I do not claim that there were no unprincipled careerists, or opportunists among them. But I think that the majority of the party members were Communists and most of them were aware that they were not infallible, superior beings.

"I have always professed", says Kádár "that things are going well when we have many non-party members who we would like to see join the party and very few party members who we would like to see outside of the party."

So that people should not regard membership of the party as a stepping stone in their careers it was necessary to make advancement possible for non-party members, too.

"It was not easy to have this accepted by many people, good and honest Communists among them", says Kádár. "They did not understand how we can profess the leading role of the party, but have non-party members directing party members and filling important leading positions in the government and the economy."

In addition to the old habits and personal interests, poorly understood ideology also has a significant role not only in the minds of the people, but in political life, too. Particularly if a state openly professes and accepts the significance of ideology.

The party organizations had been forbidden to issue instructions to the state and social organizations even earlier. But even more important was the party's emphatic declaration that its task is not to rule but to serve the people. This could be called a sophism since the party remained in charge. Nevertheless, I would not call it a sophism, since I know both the previous and the present practice. The frame of mind in which those in power exercise power is not indifferent.

Of course, the decisive factor is how the mechanism of leadership is institutionalized. There were changes in that respect, too. The party was no longer directed by the arbitrary will of three or four people. Kádár has been a first among equals among his fellow-leaders right from the beginning; but it is also a fact that the leading bodies, the Political Committee and the Central Committee, have become real bodies of leadership again and the scope of authority of local party organizations has also grown.

The party was burdened by another grave legacy. It had to prevent — and convince the country that it was capable of doing so — a recurrence of the grave mistakes and crimes culminating in the show trials of the period preceeding 1956. Several people who played a major role in those events, among them Mihály Farkas and Gábor Péter, were put on trial and convicted. All were freed in 1962 under the amnesty. Rákosi, Gerő and twenty odd associates, who were primarily responsible for what had happened, were expelled from the party. All those who had had any connection with the illegal proceedings were removed from the Ministry of Home Affairs, the prosecutor's office, the courts and the party's disciplinary organs. At the same time, proper respect was accorded to the victims; their families were provided for and rehabilitation came not only to those who had been in prison, but also to those unjustly brushed aside, among them veterans of the Republic of Councils and the Spanish Civil War.

The question may arise — as it did at the time — whether Mátyás Rákosi, the one primarily responsible for these crimes — should have been put on trial? I think not, although it would have been legally justified. It was in the vital interest of the country and of the Communist movement to end the terrible practice whereby fallen politicians were imprisoned almost automatically. It had to be stopped even at the cost of leaving guilty people legally unpunished. Rákosi was never again allowed to return to Hungary. He died in 1971.

What is the guarantee that the crimes of the past cannot be repeated? My answer is that there is no absolute guarantee. There is no constitution, legal system, social and political structure which could totally exclude the possibility of tyranny raising its head in any country, and not just in Hungary. Naturally, the more elaborate and more democratic the machinery of power is, the better it can thwart tyranny. But a similarly important guarantee is to transform the country's system of political norms, so that people will instinctively refuse to tolerate tyranny. And to condition the politicians, too, not to desire and aspire to tyranny and not to consider it as a panacea. I do not claim to know how long this process might take in the life of a country. But Hungary has taken no small steps in the past twenty years to impart these defensive reflexes to her citizens.

Kádár had to fight a tough battle before it was accepted that a policy based on his dictum was not some sort of liberalization, a tactical step, a necessary transition, a compromise, but an organic part of socialist development. Again let us not make the mistake of thinking that what we consider natural today likewise seemed natural twenty years ago. It was not natural for many people, because they had learned things differently and were accustomed to different things. Whoever thinks that in Hungary everything is decided by a central will, that there are no political struggles and differences of views, is fundamentally mistaken. There was a lot of giving and taking of blows until the Kádárian policy became consolidated.

The essence of the policy "He who is not against us is with us" is trust. After the initial enthusiasm, as Rákosi and his associates encountered ever new difficulties they thought that if the country did not share their wishes, or not in the same way, then the people were either hostile or stupid. This was the twisted concept on which they based their policies; according to the infamous expression they had to build socialism with nine million Fascists. Their activities and methods were determined by this concept. It was Rákosi's favourite saying that you cannot make a silk purse out of a sow's ear. He did not believe that people change or can be changed.

"Suspicion was at the root of all the evil", says Kádár. "Yet an entire people cannot be suspect. This people is our people and we Communists are for the people. Whoever was appointed to a post of responsibility was there to serve the good of the people. And you cannot work for the good of the people despite the people."

Twenty years had gone by since Hungary's Liberation; they were stormy years which sorely tested the nation. Even for an individual it is hard to cope with fundamental changes every three or four years and much more so for an entire country. But Kádár could rightly say in 1964: "The dreams of the past are today's reality. We have the basis for the national unity."

The usual sober Kádárian approach. He did not speak of having already achieved national unity, but only that the basis was already there. Even that was an enormous achievement eight years after 1956, and three years after the transformation of the countryside. As a result of the Kádárian dictum, the predominant majority of the country was indeed united on the fundamental issues. We were justified in hoping at the time that after so many trials, a calm, relaxed period would follow. I am not ashamed to say that we were somewhat optimistic.

"If we go back to the morning of November 4, 1956, then I can state that we are happy with what we have achieved through hard struggle. But if we start out from what we want to achieve in industry, agriculture, public education, culture and living standards, then we must be very dissatisfied."

Indeed, a new and serious problem, the necessity to transform the nation's economic life, was already hammering at the door by the mid-sixties.

There is a widespread view that the reason for all the troubles, errors, hardships of the socialist countries is that socialism was established not in the economically and socially developed countries, as Marx had imagined, but in the underdeveloped ones. From the end of the forties, Hungary lived in the atmosphere of the Cold War, with a siege mentality. This also explains why she aimed to be "a country of iron and steel". It was not an easy task for a primarily agricultural country poor in natural resources. Hungary was the bread basket of the Monarchy while industry developed mostly in Austria and Czechoslovakia. The roles were the same in the German–Italian–Hungarian alliance during the thirties.

Yet Hungary became an industrial-agricultural country within fifteen years. But at what a price! The great projects, first of all in heavy industry, were completed at a forced pace beginning at the end of the forties. The result was that industrial production grew by 50 per cent between 1950 and 1952 and the standard of living decreased by 20 per cent.

The totally centralized management of the economy was not a fortunate matter either. All production quotas were set centrally; they thought it was possible to determine at a desk in the capital what and how much every production unit of the country had to produce. This structure was organically linked to the power structure in which all significant decisions were centralized in the hands of a few people.

It did not turn out to be all that expedient that, contrary to the original ideas, practically all the production units of the country were nationalized; not only the factories, and the plants, the banks, but the coffee shops, restaurants, shoe repairers, locksmiths, barbers and grocery shops, too. With slight exaggeration, I could say that the ideal picture the leaders of the time had in mind was of a single foundry, a single bakery, a single food trading company, a single cooperative in the whole country which then could be managed centrally at the press of a button.

It was another peculiarity of the period that quantity was the sole consideration in production. There was a realistic basis to this as it was impossible to mine as much coal, to produce as much steel, to make as many clothes and bake as much bread as was needed to satisfy the suddenly increased demands. Quality was not a consideration even in the case of export products because the other socialist countries had the same shortage problems and there was a buyer for everything in every quantity, irrespective of quality. Yet Hungary, ideology notwithstanding, tried in vain to become self-sufficient as she had to import the indispensable raw materials and pay for them with products.

Although this centrally managed gigantic machinery did work, it was creaking all the way; not only were the cog-wheels breaking and people falling in between the wheels, but the whole structure was threatened with collapse. Incentives were essentially eliminated from economic life, which did not exactly boost people's enthusiasm for work. On the one hand, fantastic one thousand per cent overfulfilment of norms was achieved—those who worked in the trade knew best that it was a lie—and, on the other hand, as soon as performance increased the norm was raised, too, and overfulfilment became compulsory. This led to a situation whereby the factories, production units, brigades, and workers aimed at a 103 per cent fulfilment which was enough to gain praise for overfulfilment, but not enough to lead to the revision of the plans and norms. The slogan of the day said that "Work is a matter of honour and glory" which eliminated the very fundamental Marxist category, interest, from economic life.

These changes were accompanied by an unbelievable increase in red tape. Not that this was a new development in Hungary; in the inter-war period the most insignificant clerk occupied a considerably higher rung in the social hierarchy than the best trained skilled worker. One was a gentleman, the other working class. Why should not tens of thousands of workers and peasants seek "gentleman" status for themselves and their children? Many were delegated by the party to desk jobs although they would have preferred to stay at the work bench or in the fields. I have known many like that; their lives often ended in tragedy.

There was no mercy: centralized management demanded millions of statements, reports, and statistics and somebody had to prepare, process, file and store them. I myself prepared, supervised and passed on such statements; I know that the Hungarian economy was managed on the basis of figures culled from mountains of paper which hardly reflected reality. The distorted form in which interest was allowed to manifest itself in economic life was that everybody touched up his report according to his own interests. Even if there had been an infallible Central Brain which could have decided everything, it would have made the wrong decisions because it received false figures. Although the most striking faults of economic life diminished somewhat during the sixties, the structure remained essentially unchanged and new problems appeared. First of all, there was a shortage of manpower. The rapidly developing industry had two great reserve pools of labour, rural Hungary and women. The number of people employed in industry doubled between 1950 and 1965, while the number of agricultural workers fell by half. During these fifteen years, the number of working women increased by a million and many of them were in industry. By the mid-sixties, however, these reserves were exhausted and industrial expansion could no longer be attained by quantitative factors.

It was also a considerable problem that by then the population's basic needs had been met and people were unwilling to buy just any sort of product. The enterprises were also unwilling to buy shoddy goods, and the foreign markets even less willing to accept them. Nevertheless, the factories were churning out products because they had a vested interest primarily in quantitative production and it did not matter to them whether or not the products could be sold. The warehouses were packed to the roof as more and more unmarketable goods accumulated.

When a man eats his fill every day, and has clothes and shoes – let us not forget that this was not the case for at least the quarter of the country's population before 1945 – he begins buying things like a refrigerator, washing-machine, television, and a car. And although the artificially created lack of equilibrium between the heavy and light industries was restored from the mid-fifties on and supplies to the population improved continuously, another problem appeared, the lack of services. People want the bathtub tap repaired if it is dripping, their cars regularly serviced, and the washing-machine, television set and radio repaired. The large and medium-sized enterprises focusing on quantitative production were unsuitable for meeting this task. The lack of the previously closed locksmith, plumber, carpenter and other workshops could really be felt only now.

This shortage gave rise to the so-called second, or "black" economy whereby the mechanic, the carpenter, the painter undertook jobs in other places either after regular working hours or often during working hours. They often charged very high prices, but the customers were at their mercy because they could not wait until the state enterprises and cooperatives could get around to doing the job. This also meant that the government lost a considerable amount in taxes.

It was no less a problem that the centrally set prices did not correspond either to actual costs or to world market prices. Most products were subsidized by the state for the most diverse reasons, so that it was impossible to determine not only which product was economical to produce but also whether a company was in the black or in the red.

The history of the revision of the economic mechanism tells us a lot about Hungary's political, intellectual and scientific life. The necessity for reform was seen as early as 1957, but at the time it was discarded after fierce debate. It came up again at the beginning of the sixties, and it was stressed at the Central Committee session in December 1964. At the beginning of 1965, Kádár announced in Parliament that in a year's time the fundamental reform of the economic management would be put on the agenda. Hundreds of economists, politicians, and experts took part in the debates, the planning and the preparation, and Kádár announced at the 1966 Party Congress that the new economic mechanism would be introduced on January 1, 1968. At the 1970 Party Congress he reported that the reform had been launched and was functioning well. In the beginning of the seventies the reform process was halted, but in a few years it continued with increased efficiency and impetus.

This is how Kádár put the essence of the reform in his 1965 speech to Parliament: "Except for the agglomeration of industrial plants, we've made no radical change in economic organization, or in economic management in the past few years, in part because we quite rightly wanted to achieve stability. Now, however, there are more and more indications that we must thoroughly re-examine our system of economic management, and work out the means of its rational development. A strongly centralized economy is slow and cumbersome. It is partly on this account that a portion of the goods produced with considerable labour using costly raw materials has failed to meet the demands of the market, domestic and international, and has remained on stock. It is particularly important to produce goods that are up-to-date now that, under the circumstances of peaceful coexistence, competition between the two social systems is growing, economic competition included. We have to present goods that are modern and competitive in price and quality alike on the international markets if we are not to lose out. On the Western markets, that is. But I must add that the times are over when the socialist world accepted poor-quality, useless goods from us, just as the days are over when we accept such goods from anyone. Unfortunately, the economic incentives we have at the moment are more likely to promote the quantitative overfulfilment of the plans, rather than economical production and improved quality. The fact is that the system of incentives and bonuses often works counter to considerations of quality."

A number of other basic questions of the reform were also defined in his speeches and writings. It is only on the rarest of occasions that Kádár uses technical terms, even the simplest ones. And this is not just a question of disposition.

"The task of politics", he says "is to think with the mind of the average man. And people do not experience economic and philosophical categories, but real situations and conditions."

In one of his speeches he quoted a Hungarian living in Canada who said that he would like to work in Hungary and get his wages in Canada. Since material incentives were very little used, people did not overwork themselves in their jobs. This then showed up in the national income and in the wages that could be paid. On another occasion, Kádár said that if a peasant gets 16 Forints for a unit of work, that is how he will valuate socialism. If he gets 42 Forints, then he'll valuate it accordingly. Once Kádár observed: "In the old days, among the horses hitched to a coach was a trace horse, which had to do no more than to look good, because the other four pulled the coach. A country, a people, cannot live in such a manner that four pull, and one just handsomely waves its mane...."

Of subsidies, he had this to say: "Six years ago if a man went into the tavern and asked for two decilitres of wine he received a state bonus of 80 fillérs for consuming it. For the wine-drinker paid less for the wine than what it cost the state."

The service industry did not escape his scrutiny either: "Permit me to quote to you a letter written by a woman who lived in the capital to her husband who was away working in the provinces: 'The hole in the wall of your room is still there. The workmen were supposed to come on Monday. But they didn't, because they were at a wedding. Tuesday was a holiday; Wednesday they came, but it was raining, and they said they couldn't work in the rain; they'd have to wait until it stopped. Now, they're waiting for it to stop raining. But I'm hopeful that by the time you come home, the hole will have disappeared.' I read this letter in a book about the 1880s; its writer lived in Paris, and was the wife of the great impressionist painter, Renoir. But it's the kind of letter that a lot of people could have written who're living in Budapest today."

I remember well how impatiently part of the population awaited the introduction of reform in the mid-sixties. And how worried the other half was.

"The reason why we had to work on the concept of the reform for three years", says Kádár, "was not because the economists had no ideas. There were economic plans, but in judging the reform one had to take into account the social and political effects. Initially, the Central Committee was not unified, and neither was the country itself. The maintenance of stability was more important than anything else at the time; the shock of 1956 was still too near. So we went on debating as long as we could to achieve unity."

The above is characteristic of Kádár's behaviour and way of thinking. As he once said: "I'm the kind of warrior who always likes to know how many people will follow me when I shout 'Charge!' Otherwise one can't fight. If I've five men behind me, I make for a rampart that I can take with just five men; if I've 150, then I can take on a more difficult task."

This is how he argued in 1956 when he also negotiated constantly, although I think, he knew from the beginning that he would not convince all of his partners. It was the same with the transformation of the countryside, and at the time of the call for national unity. Let us not think that every new proposal and thought originates from Kádár. He himself also learnt, and not a little, from reality and from others. And when he had worked out an idea he knew that being right is not enough if significant sections of the population do not accept it. Therefore, he tried to convince those holding differing views, without abandoning what he himself wanted.

It is typical that, as early as 1962, Kádár had formulated one of the fundamental requirements of the new economic mechanism, one which he has not managed to get fully accepted by public opinion even now, in the second flowering of the reform: "The manufacture of uneconomical, obsolete products must stop, and the productive capacity thus saved be put to sensible use. This will also require a certain planned regrouping of the work force."

Seventeen years after these words were heard at the 8th Party Congress, one of the largest factories in the country laid off three hundred people for whom it could not provide work. There was nation-wide indignation and the press and television discussed the case for weeks – three hundred people out on the streets! Of course, nobody was thrown out into the street, but those people had to change jobs. Nothing like it had happened in the country for twenty years.

Many things have gone wrong in Hungary during the past thirty years. But one thing is certain: from the sixties onwards the population grew accustomed to not being threatened by even the shadow of insecurity. A person had to steal before he was fired from his job. Regardless of his job performance, and whether or not his work was needed, his job was secure. He was protected by the law, by the shortage of manpower, by bad regulations and by a misinterpreted humanism. As far as employer and employee were concerned, undoubtedly the latter was at an advantage; he could change jobs at any time if he had an argument with his bosses, if he did not like his environment, or if he was offered more elsewhere. This applied to the majority of workers, skilled and unskilled alike. They could always find new jobs.

It is understandable that in a country where unemployment affected and threatened hundreds of thousands of people, it was an enormous achievement to have total job security. And it is understandable that the country clung, and still clings today, to this achievement: it does not see or does not want to see the disadvantages which stem from it. It is one of the explanations why reform was so difficult to introduce, why it stumbled and halted and why it is still struggling with difficulties today.

"I have said many times", says Kádár, "something that there should be no need to say at all, since everybody knows it: it is not true that there is a shortage of manpower in Hungary. The truth is that manpower is not where it is most needed. Of course, everybody always agrees with me and then they go home and wait for others to put their house in order."

We have often witnessed the interesting situation whereby thinking people become enraged when they see work slow down at one place because there are not enough people, while at another the workers are kicking their heels because there is not enough work; in one factory production shows a deficit, in the other expensive machinery stands idle. And these very same people indignantly protest, citing the violation of the principles of socialism and humanism, when attempts are made to change the situation in a way which would affect them.

The fault is, of course, primarily not in people, but in the structure. The greatest difficulty in the initial period of the reform was probably that nobody knew exactly at what rate and to what extent the economic system can and must be transformed without endangering the economic and social equilibrium. There were some who hurried the process and some who slowed it down. In any case, the economic reform was started in 1968. The following train of thought well illustrates the great significance Kádár attributed to this matter:

"I believe that the task of reforming our economic management is of significance comparable to what we did in 1956 to safeguard working class power, and in early 1960 to reorganize agriculture. Why? Because if we think in the spirit of Leninism, and live and work as Communists, we must always put the question that is essential for a revolutionary: which is the link in the chain that is of the utmost importance from the point of view of our socialist revolution? I'm not saying—and I hope I'm not being misunderstood—that the reorganization of power or of agriculture is not important, only economic reform. What I want to emphasize is that today, and in the next few years, as far as the country's internal development is concerned, reform is the link in the chain on which the appropriate progress toward socialist revolution and the further growth of working class power depend. I ask you to consider the matter in this light, and to deal with it accordingly. It needs no further explanation. People have accepted and have acquiesced in the fact that the people's democracy is viable; the socialist reorganization of agriculture has taken place in circumstances and in the manner appropriate to it. And now the question is being put: where do we go from here? The way forward for us is the reform of economic management. To all appearances, this is an economic question which, however, has repercussions for the stability of our power and our system, for the political mood of our working class: has repercussions for the kind of confidence it places in the party, and for the way it will follow the party and the Communists. That's how weighty a question this is."

Nevertheless, the implementation of the economic reform was halted in the beginning of the seventies. Several leaders who were known to be proponents of the reform were dismissed from their positions in 1974. There were disquieting rumours throughout the country about the return of a hard line policy, about the failure of the reform; indeed there was even talk of Kádár being pushed into the background. I met Kádár briefly at a reception in the Parliament building a few days after the Central Committee session. He was tired and worried.

"How are things?" he asked. "Is there a panic?" "There is no panic", I said, "but there is a great deal of uncertainty. Many people are afraid that the clock will be turned back."

As with most people, it is also noticeable with Kádár when he is very decisive, which he was at the time.

"We have to be careful of many things", he said. "But there is no turning back. You can tell that to anybody you meet."

It is a fact that at that time there was tension between the workers and the peasants. Since the middle of the sixties the standard of living of the peasantry had been increasing at a very rapid rate, and this was not the case in the towns. In the villages new family houses with all modern conveniences mushroomed in the place of the old mud huts. During the seventies I myself have been to several homes where, in addition to various agricultural machinery, the family had two Western-made cars. In Hungary this is rare, even among intellectuals with the highest incomes.

Those who thought that the economic reform gave more to the peasant than to the industrial worker forgot that, economically, the peasant started from a much lower level. And the extra incomes produced in the household plots were obtained not in an eight-hour working day. The number of so-called mixed families, which had both worker and peasant members, was on the increase, so basically the interest of the two classes could not be totally separated. In addition to the sense of security, the will of the peasant to produce could be stimulated only by material incentives, while continuously improving food supplies for the workers and the urban population, the equilibrium of the national economy and the public mood of the whole country depended on this. It was great mistake to think that real tensions could be solved by restricting the more realistic financial motivation of the peasantry instead of working out a more realistic motivation for the workers. Those who wanted to raise the standard of living of the workers by curtailing the incomes of the peasants would have achieved the opposite, and there were several things indicating this at the time of the halt to the reform. When the peasant feels that surplus labour to turn out surplus produce is not economical for him, he stops doing it.

It was also an undoubted fact that the income of the majority of private craftsmen and tradesmen, whose numbers increased after the introduction of the new economic mechanism, far exceeded the income of the workers. But equally this problem could not be solved by once again restricting the private sector, and claiming that the high incomes irritated other workers. It had already become clear that the slow state enterprises were unable to solve the question of services, and the lack of a solution to that problem irritated the population at least as much. The unsettled state of this question was plainly signalled by the spread of the "second economy" which had ever increasing consequences not only economically but socially and morally, too.

I cannot unequivocally condemn the fact that in Hungary, barely thirty years after she had emerged from the semi-feudal socio-economic system in which various prerogatives played a decisive role, the spirit of egalitarianism prevailed and many considered it a mockery of socialism if some could afford a luxurious villa, a week-end cottage, a car and overseas travel while others had everyday financial worries. But egalitarianism should not lead us to forget that the outstandingly high incomes were, with few exceptions, due to outstanding talent or surplus labour, or they came from sectors where the state had not managed to solve the problems of an appropriate production and distribution mechanism. In most cases the spread of unjustified and immoral supplementary incomes, tips and petty bribes can be attributed to similar causes and not because the new economic mechanism had released the genie of petty bourgeois mentality from the bottle, as was believed and avowed by many.

The so-called "refrigerator socialism" debate broke out well before the introduction of the new economic mechanism, stirring public opinion. Many believed that abundance was dangerous and if a consumer mentality overtook Hungary, if people strove to have cars, refrigerators, week-end cottages, if owning private property was on the increase, the petty bourgeoisie would be socially reproduced. There is some truth in this, and the recent period proves it; but I cannot imagine a socialist society which is not striving to improve people's welfare. It is possible to urge people to accept asceticism; in acute situations it is even necessary. But in the longer run it is unimaginable. Socialism must find means other than restricting incomes to motivate people to pursue other things besides wealth as their goal in life. To work this out, and to implement it is one of the most important tasks of this social system.

According to Marxist theory, in a socialist society everybody receives his share from the national income according to his work, and under communism, according to his needs. We have been professing this principle for decades and for decades we have not been adhering to it. We encounter egalitarianism here, too; in a certain sense rightly so. There are some whose work is a hundred times more valuable to the country than that of the average person; yet I do not believe that it would be right to reward him a hundredfold, if for no other reason than that, in our social system, he simply would not know what to do with such a sum. At the same time, it is wrong not to differentiate between people working well and badly, honestly and unconscientiously, with talent or without. Engels's formula that in socialism general fairness and justice cannot come about is a bitter law, but it is a law nevertheless. One man is born strong and talented, the other weak and untalented, and society is unable to equalize these aptitudes.

In general, everybody agrees with the principle that wages should be determined according to the work performed, but it is not so simple to implement this principle. The reason for this is not only the strong and in many respects understandable egalitarian spirit, but also partly poverty, and partly the faulty economic structure. Here is the drawback to the fact that socialism has come about in economically underdeveloped countries; social justice demands that every worker receive a certain wage. This also means that nobody can receive wages above a certain level. Hungary has managed to avoid an economic crisis so far because she has adhered to the basic principle that one cannot distribute more among the population than is produced by society.

There were general political, ideological, conceptual and economic reasons for the debates surrounding the economic mechanism, for the slowing down and uncertainty of the reform. With slight oversimplification I could say that there was a struggle between egalitarianism and incentives, central management and independence, abstract public interest and specific individual and group interests, quantity and quality, price subsidies and world market prices, and doing things the old way and taking risks.

The difficulties do not mean that the Hungarian economy is bankrupt. On the contrary, growth has been permanent in practically all spheres of life, so much so that the population grew accustomed to it. Nowadays it is quite a problem to inform the public in a way which will ensure that they see things realistically.

Compared to 1950 figures, in 1980 the national income grew fivefold, gross industrial production more than eightfold, construction activity six- and a halffold, agricultural production two- and a halffold, both exports and imports more than twentyfold, real income more than threefold, the construction of flats two- and a halffold, nursery capacity more than tenfold, kindergarten capacity fourfold, the number of students studying in secondary schools and institutes of higher learning threefold. While 37,000 foreigners came to Hungary in 1950, in 1980 there were more than 14 million, more than the population of the country. The number of Hungarians travelling abroad in 1950 was 19,000, in 1980 more than five million. In 1950, 47 per cent of the population received free medical care, and in 1980 all Hungarian citizens. There were 600,000 radio and 16,000 television sets in the country in 1960, in 1980, there were two and a half million of each.

I can still recall my childhood when neighbouring families gathered in front of a crackling radio set to listen to the Budapest station because that was the only one the set could pick up, and I recall the time as an adult when tenants of a whole apartment house squatted in front of a television set. The highest ranking persons I knew before the Liberation was a colonel and one of the directors of Hungarian Radio, and neither had a car. In 1980, Hungary's population owned one million cars.

The world-wide price explosion which took place in the middle of the seventies put Hungary in a very disadvantageous position. Today she has to export 20 per cent more than five years ago for the same quantity of import products, 35 per cent more than she had to export in 1950, and 60 per cent more than before World War II. Nineteen-eighty was the first time since 1957 that the national income, gross industrial production, imports and exports, as well as the real income of the population, decreased in comparison with the previous year.

Though a little belatedly, the world economic crisis decided the fate of the Hungarian economic reform. There was no turning back. This is how Kádár put it in 1976: "Instead of lamenting and philosophizing over the changes in world market prices, we should see what we can do here at home to balance the country's payments. I might add that we have in fact had to examine a whole series of things under pressure of the circumstances; but to tell the truth, had these circumstances not come about, even so, sooner or later, we would have had to re-examine these same issues in the course of our building of socialism here at home."

Four years later, at the party congress, he summed up his views as follows: "The adverse changes in external economic conditions have shown up the weak spots in our economy and the shortcomings in our work more clearly. Although we realized that the adverse changes in the market had to be combated by a change in the product structure and selective industrial development, economic management in practice was unable to adjust well enough, fast enough and flexibly enough to the changed conditions. The switch-over to intensive methods of economic management, the improvement in the efficiency of production and the streamlining of production and the product structure lag behind the rate required by the circumstances, and the rate made possible by the present-day technical and technological level of the national economy."

If today, under considerably worse world economic conditions, we can be more optimistic than in the mid-seventies it is primarily because both the country and the leadership recognized that the significant transformation of the economic structure and mechanism is an unavoidable necessity even if it leads to new social tensions. We still do not know how to do many things; there is too much wrangling, time and again we come up against backwardness, conservatism, comfort-seeking, the narrow interests of people, groups and social strata. The world political situation is not favourable either, but the recognition and admission of the necessity of change is there. This is why there is hope that Hungary will be able not only to restore her economic equilibrium, but also to work out an economic structure which is suitable for the creation of a developed socialist society.

It is widely known of Kádár that he is not very fond of travelling: he has said this many times publicly. As far as I know, he was in the West for the first time when he was 48 and, even then not on his own initiative. It was Khrushchev's stubborn conviction that personal meetings between the leaders of the various countries could enhance peaceful coexistence, and that personal acquaintance, even if there was no agreement, was more useful than faceless impersonal confrontation. The first and so far only occasion when the United Nations delegations of the socialist states were headed by the heads of government was the General Assembly session in October 1960. János Kádár arrived in the Unites States on the ocean-liner Baltika. "We are convinced that the day will come when relations between the United States and the Hungarian Peoples' Republic will be good", Kádár had said in October 1958. "Only one factor is required for this: that those who are at the helm in the United States should accept and recognize that there live in the region of the Danube and Tisza rivers a people who are adherents of a socialist society, who are building such a society, and who will never be swayed from it."

At the time that Kádár spoke these words relationships between the United States and Hungary were tense. József Mindszenty had been granted asylum at the American Embassy in Budapest. The Hungarian government had declared the American ambassador a *persona non grata* and in a diplomatic note had demanded a reduction in embassy personnel. It was obvious that the leaders of the United States had no wish to become reconciled to the fact that Hungary was a socialist state. Time and time again they put the so-called "Hungarian question" on the agenda in the United Nations; they gave significant material and moral support to the Hungarian emigré leaders who declared the Kádár government illegal; they dispatched spies and agents to Hungary to organize further uprisings, or at least disturbances. The Hungarian authorities were not idle either; 15 years later they made it public that the new supreme body of the Hungarian emigrants, the Revolutionary Council formed in Strasbourg, was organized by a member of the Hungarian intelligence service.

Relations between the two states were no better in 1960. It was only in 1962 that the United Nations passed a resolution dropping the "Hungarian question" and treating Hungary like any other member state.

The reception in New York reflected these tensions. The American authorities did not at first want to allow the Baltika to dock at one of the official piers and the huge ship had to wait before receiving permission to dock. Groups of demonstrators, partly Hungarian emigrants and partly, according to Cyrus Eaton, people hired and trained by the American intelligence services, followed Kádár everywhere in New York. That their placards and slogans yelled in unison were not flattering is self-explanatory. Not that their organization was perfect. For example, the group demonstrating in front of Kádár's hotel shouted "Tito go home!" On top of all this, the American authorities restricted Kádár's freedom of movement.

This is the report Kádár gave Parliament upon his return: "The restrictions put on our freedom of movement in New York were unworthy, unjust and insulting. But I had another feeling, too, one that I expressed to a reporter of *The New York Times*. 'Look', I said to him, 'this restriction on my freedom of movement was insulting, but not unpleasant. For one thing, I was in pretty good company. As you know, four people have been accorded this 'honour': Comrade Khrushchev, Comrade Mehmet Sehu, Fidel Castro and I. The company, therefore, was not bad. I couldn't help recalling February of 1932 when, on my way out from prison, I was accosted by a head official of Horthy's Ministry of Home Affairs who informed me that I, being a Communist, was not to leave Budapest. I said to the New York reporter: 'It's not the first occasion that I've been told not to leave a certain area. The first time it was one of Horthy's Fascist police. That injunction,' I said to the reporter, 'is no longer in effect; that official, along with the entire system he served, is a thing of the past; as for me, the young Hungarian worker of yore, I'm still here, in fact I'm in New York! I cannot think that such latter-day restrictions on movement will be much longer-lived than the one placed on me long ago by Horthy's head official'."

Kádár delivered a speech at the UN General Assembly session. Near the end of his speech he changed from his businesslike address to a personal tone.

"Our delegation has come here to attend the United Nations General Assembly session. The United States and the Hungarian People's Republic maintain diplomatic relations. The United States authorities, therefore, have a double reason for guaranteeing us, here in New York, the rights and circumstances that international practice requires. Despite this, the United States authorities have informed me of a measure restricting my movements, a measure that offends my people and my Government. Although this treatment reflects adversely not on us and on those of our colleagues who've been treated similarly—nor on our peoples—but only on those who have devised it, I protest against it on principle. I personally have often been the target of attacks in this hall. Allow me, therefore, to make a personal remark. I am a Hungarian worker. For my ideological convictions, I have had to suffer a great deal of persecution from Horthy's Fascist system, and from the German Fascists who occupied my country at the time. But I have always acted in accordance with my convictions and conscience. A man can make mistakes and be in error, but I feel I am serving a just cause, and I am proud that at a grave moment in history, I took a stand for my working class and my Hungarian people who have suffered so much, and that I, together with my faithful colleagues, was where I had to be, and did what I had to do."

At this point, applause broke out in the General Assembly hall of the United Nations' Organization—it was the first time since October 1956 that this had happened when somebody championed the social order in Hungary.

Twenty years have gone by since his "introduction" to New York, and Kádár, who does not like to travel, has been travelling quite a lot, particularly in the mid-seventies. He led the Hungarian delegation to the Helsinki Conference on Security and Cooperation in Europe in August 1975. He visited Poland and Cuba in December. He went to the Soviet Union in February 1976, to Bulgaria and Czechoslovakia in April, to the German Democratic Republic in May, again to Berlin to the Conference of European Communist and Workers' Parties in June and to Austria in December. For years hardly a week has gone by without Kádár receiving a foreign statesman, politician or party leader. Perhaps it is not national chauvinism to say that Hungary, ten-million strong, has become a factor in world politics.

The basis for this is the decade-long policy which Kádár defined as follows: "We'd like people both near and far to know and understand that if the Hungarians say 'yes', they mean 'yes'! And when they say 'no' they mean 'no'! When we take something on, we stand by it with honour; and if we can't support something, we don't hesitate to say so. Responsible political leaders are always hoping for a predictable partner. We are decidedly committed to being predictable. We want to be faithful allies to our allies, and are just that. And when it comes to dealing with the other side, when we discuss something and agree on something, we are fair and honourable partners who keep our word, and are determined to be such in the future."

It was not easy for Kádár to assimilate the twin notions of patriotism and internationalism, or that of peaceful coexistence. His youth, his upbringing, his personal experiences were not such as to lead him in that direction.

"I grew up in an age", he says "when the national flag was the symbol of the Horthy era, the concept of the motherland meant the existing social system. I hated that regime and held its symbols and system of ideas in contempt. It took time until I learnt that the red-white-and-green is the symbol of the nation, and not of Horthy and his associates, and that the motherland is the land of the Hungarian people, and not that of the Horthy regime."

Patriotism is primarily an emotion, while internationalism is the product of the mind. Kádár's emotions made him an internationalist; he is a proletarian of the kind Marx talked of.

It was a part of his youth to hate all systems of exploitation. He became a real statesman when he learnt that peaceful coexistence with the capitalist states is in the basic interests of his class and nation and of the international working class movement. This could not have been easy, particularly after the spokesmen of these countries had reviled and slandered him for years.

What had never posed a problem for him is his relationship with the Soviet Union. He lived to see the distortions of the personality cult, himself paying a terrible price for them; but none of this could alter his conviction that the socialist order was unimaginable without the Soviet Union.

"It's been written so often that I am a Soviet hireling", he says. "They can write what they like. For me it's as simple as two and two: if I did not live in Hungary, but in Australia, my opinion would still be that the Soviet Union is the greatest strength of socialism."

He smiles.

"And they don't understand when I say that if it's raining in Moscow it's not necessary to open our umbrellas in Hungary. Because they don't understand the essence of internationalism. We should not copy each other, that is to no one's advantage; what we should do is appreciate what the other does well, and learn from what hasn't worked somewhere else. We have never been ashamed to say that we have a lot to learn, and we're glad that we have someone to learn from."

It is well known that he liked Khrushchev; their relationship was built on the common struggle. I remember well what a shock it was to many Hungarians when Khrushchev was dismissed. The Stalinist period was still too close and the fear was very real that the change could mean a return to the old policy, to the old methods.

Kádár was in Poland that day. When he got back, the whole country waited to hear what he would say. I was there when he got off the special train at the railway station. He did not wait until he got to his office, did not wait to consult and to be informed. He spoke to the country as soon as he got back. Calmly and frankly.

"A great variety of events have occurred in the past week. There was some news that we were very happy to hear, and some that was a source of surprise. I want to tell you this frankly and honestly. As you know, there have been personal changes in the top leadership of the Soviet Union. Comrade Khrushchev, who asked to be relieved of his post on grounds of his age and poor health, has been relieved of his post, and Comrades Brezhnev and Kosygin have been elected to take his place. In every country and in every party a matter of this nature is up to the party and the country to decide on. For my own part, I think that Comrade Khrushchev deserves a great deal of credit for his fight against the Stalinist personality cult, and for the fact that there is still peace. He worked for peace. I think that those hundreds of thousands of Hungarians who greeted Comrade Khrushchev in the past, and this year, too, when he visited Hungary, and greeted him cordially as the representative of his country and his people, and as the indefatigable champion of liberty did well to greet him, and need have no second thoughts about it. As far as we're concerned, what is essential and decisive is that the policy of the Hungarian Socialist Workers' Party and the Hungarian People's Republic on the issues of peace, of peaceful coexistence, on the socialist countries' commitment to unity, and on the international working class movement has changed not one whit, nor will it change in the future."

A storm of applause shook the railway station. Kádár cleared his throat, and continued:

"In matters of human relations, relationships can vary greatly from person to person, for everybody is different. But I should like to emphasize that the Hungarian Communists, and every Hungarian who has the cause of socialism at heart—and they are the majority—will always respect the representatives of the great Soviet Communist Party, the great Soviet state, the great Soviet people, and will always be willing to meet and cooperate with them as good comrades. They are the most faithful allies of our people, their strongest support on the international scene. The comrades who have now replaced Comrade Khrushchev in positions of leadership, Comrade Brezhnev and Comrade Kosygin are well known to us, are our friends; they are known to represent the political line—have been its advocates in the past—that the Communist Party of the Soviet Union has again taken a stand for, declaring that they are following the 20th, 21st, and 22nd Congresses, and are dedicated to the preservation of peace and to the unity of all progressive forces on the international scene. That's how it is; there has been no change. And there will be no change as far as Hungarian–Soviet relations are concerned either."

Rákosi, too, had been forever lauding the great Soviet Union, the great Soviet party, the great Soviet people, always putting the emphasis on the word "great". His policies, however, hardly encouraged people to give credence to that adjective. Whereas the truth is that the Soviet Union, the Communist Party of the Soviet Union, and the Soviet people are indeed great. And not only in the quantitative sense of the word. Kádár was able to make the country understand this, because for him, great and small do not mean dependence, a relationship of subordination, but a fact. His policy restored the nation's lost and violated self-respect. The words truly had regained their real meaning, because for Kádár, cooperation with the Soviet Union and the other socialist countries means respect for other peoples, a deeply felt internationalism, and the true representation of national interests.

Peaceful coexistence is in no way just rhetoric for Kádár. Nothing proved it better than his insistence on it even during the years when the majority of the Western states did not exactly strive for such a relationship with Hungary. The vile attacks, insults, and allegations against him did nothing to change this; he always subordinates his own person to his principles. He put what he had in mind very precisely: "We mean by peaceful coexistence not merely the absence of war, but a comprehensive mode of existence of countries of differing social systems, one which presupposes normal political relations, economic and cultural cooperation on the widest possible scale, individual contacts, and mutually advantageous agreements."

Time proved him right even if today the atmosphere of world politics is somewhat cooler again. The Hungarian People's Republic has diplomatic relations with 126 countries, with practically all the states of the world. Exports to and imports from non-socialist countries are thirteen times what they were in 1957.

"I don't believe", says Kádár, "that the world's fate depends on Hungary. We are a small state, one of the smallest on this continent. Nevertheless, I think that we, too, have a task and a responsibility in shaping the world."

Paradoxically, the formation of the two big world systems did not diminish, but increased the importance of the small countries. And not only in the sense that a small state's erroneous policy can force its allies into situations they do not desire.

In a world which has become extremely diverse, countless different interests, intentions and approaches must be reflected within the alliance systems, too, by way of a reminder to all states to be patient, flexible and understanding, lest the world come to its extremity. To do so is the task of the small nations, an opportunity they have never before had. It is not only the fate of their own peoples that they can improve on or endanger by wise or unwise policies, but they also exercise influence on alliance systems affecting several hundreds of millions. Accordingly, their role in world politics is much greater than what their population, strategic or economic strength in themselves would enable them to play.

Kádár considers it his right and his duty to think not only in terms of his own country, but in terms of the fate of the world. "The age we're living in", he said in one of his interviews, "is a decisive age. It can prove to be a blessing to man, and it can prove to be a curse. It can turn out to be an age when peoples prosper, an age of harmonious cooperation between nations, but it can likewise turn out to be the age of the final destruction of man. It's the fate of mankind that's being decided now. Our generation has the task of securing mankind's future. We have, in essence, come to the crossroads: the encouraging prospect of the harmonious coexistence of nations, of a growing number of fruitful bilateral and multilateral contacts between them is one alternative; the danger of a thermonuclear holocaust that will destroy all of human civilization is the other. Clearly, everything must be done to prevent the outbreak of another world war. I sincerely hope that our age will go down in world history as the age which founded mankind's peaceful future, which cleared the way for the full realization of the ideals of democracy and humanism, for the national development and social progress of all peoples, for their joint solution of the world's problems, and for the free development of the personality of each and every individual."

This statement was made in the course of an interview with *The New York Times*, one of the most prestigious of the American – and the Western – dailies eighteen years after János Kádár had been humiliated, booed and catcalled in New York.

Nowadays, I often hear Western politicians, journalists and tourists on a visit to Hungary sing praises which I consider exaggerated: to the outsider, reality often seems more beautiful and simpler than it is to those who live in it day by day, who know the problems and the headaches from the inside. To tell the truth, I must add that I like it just as little when foreign visitors look at everything here through dark glasses; it is not only their knowledge of the country which leaves a lot to be desired. As in the case of a report which appeared in one of the authoritative Western papers not too long ago, declaring that there was no bread, and no sugar in Hungary, that fuel was available only on the black market, and that there were no bookshops.

There is bread in Hungary and there is sugar. There is fuel and there are bookshops, too. But these are no great reasons for satisfaction.

At the beginning of the seventies, there was a lively debate concerning the country's name: there were some who proposed that it be changed to Hungarian Socialist Republic.

Kádár took a stand against the change both at the Party Congress and in Parliament.

"The official name of the country", he says "should reflect not its goals, but the real state of affairs." And Hungary's name is the Hungarian People's Republic to this day.

"We are fond of the expression 'socialist'", said Kádár. "We are people of socialist conviction; we speak of socialist industry, socialist agriculture, socialist commerce. In the primary sense of the term, this is all true: in Hungary, industry, commerce and agriculture are, by the very nature of things, socialist. If, however, I consider the details, the possible and the actual shortcomings, at the moment I would prefer to say 'industry', 'agriculture', and 'commerce', and keep saying it until millions of people start saying 'this is indeed socialist industry, socialist agriculture, and socialist commerce'."

There were four decisive stages in Hungary's development into a socialist society: the nationalization of the means of production, the consolidation of power, the collectivization in the countryside, and the introduction of the new economic mechanism. Thirty years were needed for all this. When the economy will be developed enough to be called socialist, nobody knows for certain. For my part, I don't think that there is an imaginary finishing line, and that beyond that we can call ourselves a socialist society. Certainly, we can hardly speak of the full realization of socialism until social relations, and the value system and thinking of the predominant majority of the population become socialist.

This is how Kádár put this:

"For us to complete the construction of a socialist society we need considerably more developed means of production, higher standards of scholarly work, of education and of culture, and a higher standard of living as well. We are very well aware that socialism means not only a larger slice of bread, a home of one's own, a refrigerator and perhaps a car, but that first and foremost it means new social relations and new human relations. Socialist construction is not only an economic task; it must provide for the evolution of a life worthy of a complete human being in the true sense of the word, must provide for harmonious contacts between the individual and society, and for their development."

Social and economic change has, of course, significantly transformed human relations as well. People change once there is no exploitation, if they are guaranteed a job, clothing and their daily bread, if their material needs are at least moderately well met, if the basic conflict between city and village is resolved, once a stable legal system is established, once men and women have equal civic status, and once everybody receives at least eight years of general education. Nevertheless, I believe that the development of a socialist type of public life is as important as a socialist economy.

Democracy in the literal, widest sense of the word means the people's power. In this sense, there is democracy in Hungary.

The other sense of "democracy" is a form of state organization; this is the everyday sense of the term. Though the word and the idea are of Greek origin, the meaning evolved in bourgeois society where equality before the law, constitutional government, universal suffrage, parliament, and the system of political parties came to replace feudal absolutism, and the closed caste system of aristocracy. This was the period when the word democracy, as a form of organization, went over into everyday usage, and became virtually a synonym for parliamentarism built on a multi-party system. In this century, it came to represent the opposite pole to Fascist dictatorship, and, to many minds, the embodiment of freedom.

Far be it from me to take anything away from the significance of this political system for the achievement of civil liberties; socialist democracy, however, has a different meaning both as a concept and in practice. This is why it is a mistake to compare the two; it is not only the proponents of the bourgeois social system who are mistaken in calling socialism to account for its lack of this structure; the Communists are just as mistaken to denounce bourgeois democracy because it does not square with their system of values. The virtues, faults, mistakes, development and short-comings of a social system must be assessed in terms of its own system of norms, and not in comparison with a differently structured state system.

According to Lenin, the essence of socialist democracy is not that people elect others from time to time to exercise power on their behalf, but that the people themselves participate in the exercise of power.

There can be no doubt that working out the structure of direct popular representation and allowing for this mechanism to take root will be a much more complicated and much longer process than the development of parliamentarism. A multi-party system is not absolutely necessary for it, nor is it excluded; the political spectrum is much wider than what party struggles can reflect of the differences of interest and of opinion within a society. The classical forms of people's representation were the Paris Commune and the Soviets in Russia.

Hungary developed a state structure of her own: a system of locally elected councils; a parliament whose members continued to be chosen at general elections, but not according to the rules of a multi-party system; at the same time, the constitution of the Hungarian People's Republic specifies the Marxist–Leninist working class party as the leading social force. If we consider, in addition, the various social forums with national jurisdiction such as the trade unions and the Patriotic People's Front, we can see that Hungary has attempted to shape the state structure of people's power through various types of institutional systems.

"Democracy", said Kádár, "cannot be 'introduced' merely through legislation. The 'introduction' of the parliamentary system is easier, because for the majority of people all the public life this involves is that every so many years they vote for some party or other. Universal – if not day-to-day – participation in public affairs is a much more complicated matter. The first thing that is needed is the right to it. Then the opportunity to participate is needed, in order that the right to it be more than just dead letter. What is necessary beyond that is that people should feel the need to participate, that they should avail themselves of their rights and their opportunities."

In Hungary, these rights are given, as are the opportunities; and, as far as I know the country, the people do feel the need to have a say in public affairs. I think that the major shortcoming is that our system of political institutions has not been sufficiently thought through in all the details.

According to Marx's definition "being radical means to go to the root. The root of man is man himself." Socialist society is not the goal, but the necessary precondition of the emergence of socialist man. And recent decades have taught us that the transformation of man is a most slow and difficult process, particularly when we are talking not about individuals, but a people.

There was a time when it all seemed so simple: we thought that a socialist was someone who placed the public interests ahead of his own. Such self-denial, however, while imaginable for a time, certainly cannot serve as a basic principle. The heroic age is over; a consolidated socialist society looks back with respect at the heroes who sacrificed their lives for the cause, at the shabbily dressed pioneers working from dawn to dusk on empty stomachs, but cannot regard them as examples to be followed. Rather the example is looked for in those who are able to coordinate public interests with their own, those who strive to harmonize their individual goals with those of society. Socialist man is communal man. The elaboration and realization of socialist democracy is of key importance because socialist man is unimaginable without some form of participation in public life.

This is how Kádár writes about this in memory of Péter Veres:

"He felt everything belonged in his sphere of competence, this ceaselessly thinking, restless man. He felt everything that happened around him was his business. He could never look disinterestedly or indifferently at anything, great or small. He was of the opinion that however difficult or even insoluble a problem seemed, one couldn't just shrug one's shoulders. There were those who said: 'Uncle Peter thinks he knows everything; he has an opinion on everything.' But this commenting on everything was due not to some self-important need to be in the limelight, to some itch to show off; it was, rather, due to his passionate interest in public affairs. He never forgot that history and society were created and shaped by the working people; it was the people's duty and right to know something about life, morality, politics, and the economy, to talk about such things, to speak up on matters of public interest."

The demand and the need for such participation is formulated in the country every day; ideas, desires and theories are being voiced, but they have, as yet, to be realized.

When one writes about a contemporary, one must interrupt the story more or less arbitrarily at some point. For this story, there is a fairly obvious point at which to do so. János Kádár, in addition to being a member of Parliament and the Presidential

Council of the Hungarian People's Republic, as well as of the National Committee of the Patriotic People's Front, is the First Secretary of the Central Committee of the Hungarian Socialist Workers' Party. The supreme body of the Hungarian Socialist Workers' Party, the Party Congress, last met in 1980. This is the point in time to which I have traced the outlines of Kádár's life against the background of Hungarian history. In Hungary, the party's social and political role is different from that played by the parties in bourgeois democracies. The Hungarian Socialist Workers' Party is at once a mass party, and the leader of society, as the Constitution specifies. The analogy frequently drawn that the Political Committee corresponds essentially to the governments of the bourgeois states, and the Central Committee to their parliaments is not to the point. The executive bodies of the state in Hungary are the ministries and the councils; the Political Committee has no executive functions, and the Central Committee has no legislative rights; and the analogy fails to take into account the highest party forum, the Party Congress.

The Hungarian Socialist Workers' Party gives political leadership partly through its central bodies, partly through its local organizations and partly through the party members taking part in the country's political, social and economic life. All fundamental national issues are decided by the Central Committee on the basis of the Political Committee's recommendations.

This is not to say that the present structure is ideal, that the mechanism of the party's operation or the division of labour between party and state is perfect. What has been said in connection with the democratization of state political life essentially holds good for democratization of the party level as well.

A few figures might be of interest. The Hungarian Socialist Workers' Party has 800,000 members in 24,000 primary organizations. One per cent of the members had joined the party before the Liberation, 16 per cent between 1944 and 1948, 9 per cent between 1949 and 1956, and 74 per cent after 1957.

Twenty-nine per cent of the party's members are industrial workers, 6 per cent are in agriculture, 41 per cent are intellectuals and white-collar workers, 16 per cent are pensioners, and 8 per cent work in other jobs. On the basis of their original profession, 63 per cent of the party members are workers, 12 per cent are peasants and 25 per cent are intellectuals and white-collar workers; 6 per cent of the membership is under the age of 30, 26 per cent is between 30 and 39, 27 per cent is between 40 and 49, 24 per cent is between 50 and 59, and 15 per cent is over 60 years of age.

Twelve per cent of the party members have not finished eight years of general school; 25 per cent have finished general school, 46 per cent secondary school, and 17 per cent have attended university or college.

Seventy-two per cent of the party's members are men, 28 per cent are women. The numbers show that the pre-Liberation party membership is slowly dying out. It is no mistake to put their numbers at eight thousand, although earlier on I had estimated that there had been only a few thousand illegal Communists. The eight thousand alive today include former Social Democrats and the Communists who had spent the inter-war years in exile. The other data are clear reflections of actual social changes: relatively large numbers joined before 1948 when the movement was on the upswing: the number of those who joined between 1949 and 1956 is surprisingly small, considering that party membership was the largest in those years: only 70,000 people joined the party during this period. Three-quarters of the party members, the predominant majority, joined after 1956. It is particularly noteworthy that the Hungarian Socialist Workers' Party has almost 300,000 members old enough to have been members of the Hungarian Working People's Party, too, but who did not join the party then.

The significant difference between the current and the original occupations of the party members shows considerable social mobility. Three-quarters of the party members were originally industrial and agricultural workers; now, only one-third of them are. Even not counting those who have in the meanwhile, retired, there are 300,000 former workers and peasants now in intellectual occupations.

From the figures for schooling, we see that the proportion of those who have not finished general school is much higher among party members than for the population as a whole; so is the proportion of those with university degrees. The former are workers and peasants who had no opportunity to learn in the old regime. The latter figure shows that the proportion of party members is highest among the country's most highly trained citizens.

The ratio of men to women in the party likewise fails to reflect the population figures, where the ratio is roughly 50–50. But unfortunately, it does reflect the actual situation. The discrepancy is due not only to the fact that Hungary's women acquired equal civil rights barely half a century ago. It also shows the socially, economically and psychologically determined differences in the roles men and women play in public life at present, the differences in the interest they take in it. Nine per cent of the party membership and 17 per cent of the country's population is between the ages of 18 and 29. As far as I can see, this indicates that the party is out of harmony with the way young people think, not so much in its policies, but its structure and everyday practice. It is some help that 60 per cent of the members received into the party in the past five years were not yet 30 years of age.

It is interesting to take a look at the composition of the Political Committee, the party's executive body, all the way back to the Liberation. All the more so since so far there has been no mention of Kádár's associates and colleagues after 1956; I felt that the assessment of their role is beyond the scope of this work. Yet Kádár himself has often emphasized their importance: "I cannot differentiate between my own personal work and the work of others" he said on his 60th birthday.

The average age of the Political Committee elected in 1945 was 41: the youngest member was 32, the oldest 53. Six of them were workers, five were intellectuals. Six came from the Hungarian illegal movement, five from exile in Moscow. All of them had been to prison for their political activities. The majority of those who had been in exile were around 50, those from the illegal movement were under 40. More of the first group were intellectuals, more of the latter workers.

The average age of the Political Committee elected in 1948 after merger with the Social Democratic Party was 47 years; the youngest was 35, the oldest 60. Nine of them had been Communists before the amalgamation, five of them Social Democrats. Twelve knew the prisons of the Horthy regime from the inside. Nine of them were workers, five intellectuals. The former Communist émigrés and the Social Democrats represented the 50 year-old generation, the illegal Communists were under 40. There were more workers among the "illegals" and the Social Democrats, and more intellectuals among those who had returned from exile.

The average age of the Political Committee chosen in 1957 was 50: the youngest member was 36, the oldest 71. All of them had joined the party before the Liberation. Nine were Communists, one of them an émigré, two had been Social Democrats. Originally, eight of them had been workers, three intellectuals. Eight of them had been imprisoned before the Liberation, three during the Rákosi era.

Today, 23 years later, three members of the 1957 Political Committee have passed away. One is still a member of the Political Committee; with one exception, the rest are all members of the Central Committee.

Seven of them have retired, but continue to fill important posts; Speaker of Parliament, Chairman of the Patriotic People's Front, Vice-Chairman of the National Trade Union Congress, and President of the Hungarian Partisan Association.

The average age of the Political Committee elected in 1980 was 56. The youngest member was 38, the oldest 68. Six members were originally workers, two peasants, and five intellectuals. Five of them had joined the party before 1945, seven between 1944 and 1948, one after 1956. Eight of them had always been Communist party members, two had been Social Democrats, and two joined the party after the merger. There is one woman on the Political Committee.

These changes in the composition of the Political Committee well reflect the changes in the Hungarian Communist movement over the past 35 years. After the Liberation, young men who had been underground – mostly workers – and older, experienced emigrants – mostly intellectuals – were elected into the leading body of the party; after the merger of the two workers' parties, it was again mostly older Social Democrats of working class origin who were elected, men who had, however, been working as independent party functionaries for some time. It is characteristic of that body that practically all of its members had been in prison under the Horthy regime. The predominant majority of the members of the 1957 Political Committee were illegal Communists who had been workers for most of their lives, and had served prison terms for their beliefs. The composition of the 1980 Committee was different: the majority of the members had joined the party after the Liberation.

The continuity is provided by the person of János Kádár. He was the oldest member at 68; he had been a member of the illegal and later of the legal Communist party, and a member of the Social Democratic Party; he was a worker, but a leader of the party for the past forty years; he had been imprisoned before the Liberation and in the Rákosi era; except for five years of forced intermission, he has been a member of the Political Committee since 1945.

There is continuity not only in his life, but also in the philosophy of life which determines his policies. "You get to know an idea", he says, "you accept it, and want to see it realized. Then theory clashes with reality; nothing turns out the way you imagined it initially. Only common sense helps, a sense of reality, a feel for what elements of the ideal can be realized given the actual possibilities. Without this, theory becomes dogma, and does not help but hinders the ideal. Dialectics cannot conflict with logic, because what is not logical is not dialectical either."

I don't know when he coined this philosophy of life in so many words, but this approach finds expression in his entire political career as far back as one can trace it.

In the eyes of most people, Kádár's greatest virtue is that he put the country back on its feet after the bankruptcy of 1956. People do not forget that ten years after the total chaos they were already living in relative peace and prosperity.

"For a country which has suffered as much as ours", says Kádár, "the most important thing was finally to have a little peace and security, a time when it could rest, recuperate, and gather strength and self-confidence."

Hungary has indeed been exposed to enormous shocks during this century: World War I, the fall of the Monarchy, the Republic of Councils, the White Terror, Trianon, World War II, Arrow-Cross rule, the Liberation, the year of the change, the Rákosi era, 1953, 1956; it is too much even to think through, let alone to live through and process with one's mind and instincts.

There was a period when many people grumbled about the stubbornness of Kádár's policy, its unshakeable insistence on balance and security. I myself have resented the sluggishness, the laziness and indolence born of calm. Human life is very short; we consider every day, month and year that passes by a tragedy. The time units of history are different: decades slip through its fingers as minutes do through ours, and a century, an unattainable span of time for most men, is but a moment in history.

Yet how many things happened during these years, too. Nineteen fifty-seven: the consolidation of power; 1960: the countryside was transformed, the lives of millions disturbed; 1961: a consistent policy of alliances unfolded, again changing the lives of hundreds of thousands; 1968: economic reform, the country stirred; the beginning of the seventies: a halt, a period of hesitation; the end of the seventies: things started moving again.

Those who see only the consolidation, the equilibrium, have not really understood Kádár's role. His policy was radical in 1956 on the peasant question, on the creation of national unity, and on the transformation of the economic structure. It was an economic policy that proved capable of correcting its own mistakes at the second attempt, what is more, the goals that this economic reform set became a national programme that transformed the entire social structure. It was during these years that, just because of her domestic development, Hungary became a factor in world politics.

"Sometime after the Liberation", Kádár says, "a comrade, a woman, complained to me that she was ashamed that her father had been a capitalist. She was a very decent, brave woman, we had fought in the underground. 'Why are you complaining?' I asked her. 'You've come a longer way; you've abandoned prosperity for the movement. It was all much simpler for me; I became a Communist because every day I saw how they were fleecing me.'"

It's up to the reader to decide whether János Kádár's career had really been that simple.

Epilogue

A warm day in early summer. The cars stop before we reach the limits of the county where we're heading. A cooling bag is taken from the boot; we drink a glass of beer. It feels good in the great heat.

Kádár arrives everywhere on the dot. Whenever he received me, his door opened right on the minute. We had stopped so as to arrive right on time at the first town where the county leaders were waiting for us. The traffic had not been stopped for us along the way.

We toured the county for three days, and stuck to the schedule set to the minute. Except on one occasion; but more about that later. On the way home, we stopped again on the outskirts of Budapest. Kádár took out his watch.

"I told my wife I'd be home around six."

It was half past five.

We had arrived at the county seat, at the guest house of the municipal council in the evening. At dinner, Kádár took the spoon from the waiter's hand.

"I'd rather help myself."

He is a light eater, and does not like his plate full. He belongs to the generation which learned that it is a sin to leave food on your plate.

Late in the evening we walked through the deserted park to the baths nearby. Kádár is a steady, relaxed swimmer; you can see that he did not learn it from a professional swimming instructor. He lets the lukewarm spring water splash over him for a long time. His body is well-proportioned; he is in fine form—one would not think that soon he'll be seventy. I have seen him a lot more tired, a lot more tormented in the past.

The next morning we get up at seven. Breakfast at eight, followed by the report of the county leaders at the headquarters of the local party committee. Kádár's reply is brief: he has nothing special to say; recently he has spoken in public several times, and could hardly say anything new. It is primarily the local functionaries' task to solve the county's problems. He came much more just to look around, to make acquaintances, to visit; he had not been to this county for quite a while.

The cars leave for one of the country's largest metallurgical works. First the managers of the company give an account of their work, then we tour the village-sized plant by bus. We stop several times to get off; Kádár chats with the people.

At one o'clock, lunch in the factory. Kádár retires for half an hour, and concentrates on his afternoon speech. There'll be a mass meeting in the Cultural Center in the afternoon. The hall is packed; it's very hot. Kádár speaks off the cuff, only now and then glancing at his notes. After the meeting, a cold drink. Kádár takes off his coat and tie. Ten minutes rest.

We set off for the town on foot. Kádár puts on his jacket, ponders a little, sighs, then knots his tie.

"It would be better without a tie. But I don't want people to think me lacking in respect for them."

We are going through the new parts of town: we visit a food store, and a pensioners' local party organization. Kádár pays a short visit to the home of the First Secretary of the county party committee. The guest pays his respects to his host. In the evening, there's dinner at the hotel with the leaders of the County Patriotic People's Front. There's a priest, a party worker, an actor, a worker, a university professor, a policeman, and a managing director among them. Kádár speaks briefly. We get home after midnight, and talk for another hour in the lobby of the guest house. The next morning at seven it starts all over again.

The only time when we were unable to keep to the schedule was on our tour of the town. I do not know how many people thronged the streets in that city of two hundred thousand; sometimes it was so crowded that it was hardly possible to find a way through; there must have been at least fifty thousand people. Kádár walks calmly in the crowd, sometimes smiling, raising his hand to greet someone. The people around him applaud, and smile; many of them have a few flowers in their hand, and wave with them. Kádár stops now and again to greet someone, to exchange a few sentences with him.

It may seem a trifling matter, but I noted it. I was present in the Cupola Hall of the Parliament building when the Secretary of State of the United States of America, after more than 30 years, returned St. Stephen's Crown, which had been taken to the West by the Hungarian Nazis and had been safeguarded in the US ever since. I saw the American Secret Service men: their face muscles tense, their eyes roving about all the time, their arms bent to enable them to draw their weapons immediately. It was not difficult to recognize them: there was a little button in one of their ears, and some sort of instrument on their wrist into which they spoke now and again. The guards in civilian clothes escorting Kádár were as relaxed as he was. They stepped closer only when they had to make way through the crowd.

I know what mass hysteria is like. I also know how it can be artificially incited, how it can be staged. I have seen countless films and newsreels of madly celebrating crowds. I have heard the rhythmical, ceaseless clapping as Rákosi was applauded. But I have never seen anything like what there was during those days. This was not a triumphal procession, it was not mass hysteria: there was no delirious cheering, no rhythmic applause, no hurrahs. People surged all over the streets in the sweltering early summer heat wearing just swimming suits or shorts, or stripped to the waist. Wherever we went, they crowded the balconies, filled the windows. Women in aprons, wooden spoons still in their hands, waved in the doorways where they had run down from the kitchen. Older men lifted their hats.

People do not adulate Kádár, do not idolize him, do not celebrate him. They love him. With an intimate, joyful respect. I fancy I know all the country's problems, troubles and difficulties; like most thinking people, I, too, am occasionally overwhelmed by despair seeing the almost insoluble problems in the world and in the country. Not infrequently I feel that in the last twenty-five years we have moved no more than a few grains of sand if we measure our achievements by our aspirations. But I have never been more certain than on that day that János Kádár *is* Hungary.

Kádár is not a man easily moved. Life has made him of hard metal. But that evening he was unable to conceal that he was touched by all this affection. He would not be human if he had not been moved. In difficult times, in the spring of 1957, he said in Parliament:

"Confidence, Comrades, is so great a thing that it scares you occasionally. So is affection, at least to men of conscience. For affection and — I dare say — also gratitude and confidence, if taken seriously, impose so great a responsibility upon a man that it is not so easy to be equal to it."

"The seed has borne fruit", I said to him, probably with pathos; I myself was moved by the experiences of the day.

He drank a sip from his glass; he drinks slowly, with moderation.

"It's not me that all this is addressed to. It's our policy."

"You have been the leader of the Hungarian party for fourteen years now. What do you see as your greatest accomplishments? What are your greatest disappointments? And what are your personal plans for the future?", he was asked in 1971 by a UPI correspondent.

"Everyone who recalls conditions fourteen years ago and takes a look at the Hungarian People's Republic of today knows that a radical change has taken place due to the unity, struggle and work of tens and hundreds of thousands, of millions of people; they have been years of great achievements. Most important to me is that I have had a share in this process, the knowledge that my personal efforts were not in vain, and that I have contributed somewhat to the results accomplished.

"Of course, anyone can suffer disappointments. As for me, I have never been spoiled by life; it has always compelled me to think realistically, and so I have been able to endure the inevitable disappointments fairly well. I have never had any special plans for myself and don't have any now. Long, long ago I became wedded to an ideal and, by and large, have done all that service to this ideal calls for or permits me to do.

"Finally, I should like to add a point to what I have said. The personalities involved always play some role in the events. But as far as the political line of the Hungarian Socialist Workers' Party is concerned, it must not be assessed as the policy of one single person or of, say, five or fifteen people, but as one which is deeply rooted among the masses of our country, and established on firm and lasting foundations."

My youth, my young manhood had been overshadowed, darkened by the personality cult and everything that went with it. I hated it. It chokes me, it depresses me to this day. Yet I have lived through the last quarter of a century, and I have also read Marx:

"It would, of course, be very comfortable to make world history if we were to start the struggle only on condition that our chances were guaranteed to be optimal. On the other hand, it would be a very mystical thing if 'accidents' had no part to play in it. These accidents, naturally, themselves are part of the general course of development, and are compensated for by other chance events. But how fast or slow events move very much depends on such 'accidents', among them the character of the men who head the movement."

To no insignificant degree, the past quarter century of Hungary's history can be attributed to such an "accident". Perhaps from a distance of centuries, posterity will pay attention more to the "general course of development", and will hold that the fate of the country would have evolved much the same way even if someone other than

Kádár had become the leader of the party in 1956. As a contemporary, I can only say that the fate, the everyday lives of hundreds of thousands, of millions would probably have been very different, and I cannot study history in such abstract, unbiased terms as to forget the people who live history. Not only has Kádár identified with the country, the country has also identified with him. This is why I dare to write the bombastic sentence: János Kádár is Hungary.

Kádár seldom speaks about himself, especially in public. In October 1958, not an easy time for the country, when he spoke in Angyalföld at the meeting where he was nominated for parliament, he felt it necessary to say the following:

"Every life is different: some are like this, some like that. For my part, I became a Communist at 19. I cannot claim to have made no mistakes. I've made my share of mistakes, some of them big enough for three. I've also done good. What I can say for sure, and this is something that not even my enemies will dispute, is that I'm a Communist. The rank of Prime Minister—that's a very different thing. The rank of First Secretary of the party—that's a very different thing, too. But there's a rank that's above all else, and that is that a man can call himself a Communist and a man. Whoever can call himself a Communist and a man has the highest rank. Anyone can hold a post of any kind. I've seen prime ministers who later weren't prime ministers. I've seen first secretaries—later they weren't first secretaries. But whoever is a Communist and a man will always stay a Communist and a man, he'll always keep the highest rank. I can only say: my intentions, my thoughts, my feelings have always been those of a Communist ever since I became a Communist. And I'll do my best to remain one as long as I live."

It was this speech which he concluded with the heartrending confession I have already quoted: "When it seemed that the time had come to die, I was pretty calm when I thought over where I'd been, and what I'd done in my life; in 1944, I felt that there really was nothing wrong. If that's how things were, I'd just have to die. The people would live, the Soviet troops would get here, and socialism would triumph. The second time, I was in trouble. Then it seemed as if I'd have to die under circumstances when all my comrades, all my brothers, all whose opinion I esteemed, all who I'd worked with as a young man would think that I'd betrayed the Communist cause. And this, believe me, is a terrible thing. At that time, I was not fighting for my life. What I did want very much was to live to see the day when people would know that I was not a traitor to the Communist flag. This day means that you here know. And that's enough for me."

Notes to Introductory Biography

[1] A popular card-game played with Helvetian cards (sometimes referred to as Magyar cards) by three or four players.

[2] Mikszáth, Kálmán 1847—1910
Great Hungarian writer. In his novels he frequently depicted the corrupt political practices of his age. Among these were the famous tarot parties of Kálmán Tisza, Hungarian Prime Minister (1875—1890), where important political issues were decided around the card table.

[3] Fiume
The Italian and Hungarian name for Rijeka, at present the second largest city of Croatia, Yugoslavia. In 1779 the city and its environs became an autonomous corpus of the Hungarian crown; after World War I, in 1920, it was declared a free city. It was annexed by Italy in 1924, becoming part of Yugoslavia after World War II, in 1947.

[4] József, Attila 1905—1937
One of the greatest Hungarian poets of the 20th century. Attracted by Marxist ideology, he was a member of the illegal Communist party. In 1932 he launched a short-lived literary periodical (*Valóság*), and in 1936 he became one of the co-founders of the review *Szép Szó*. In the early thirties the Communist party broke contact with him partly for ideological reasons and partly because his psychoanalytical treatment was considered a security risk. He committed suicide.

[5] Hungarian currency between 1927 and 1946 introduced following the great wave of post-war inflation. One *Pengő* was exchanged for 12,500 paper-crowns, the previous currency. Eventually the *Pengő* itself fell victim to an unprecedented inflation following World War II, and was succeeded by the *Forint*, the present Hungarian currency.

[6] Károlyi, Mihály, Count 1875—1955
Born of a high aristocratic family, he became the leader of pacifist politicians during the years of World War I. Towards the end of the war, he emerged as an influential figure and formed the Hungarian National Council composed of his followers, Bourgeois Radicals and Social Democrats in October 1918. He was Prime Minister and Minister of Foreign Affairs November 1918— January 1919. After Hungary was proclaimed a republic, he was elected the first President (January—March 1919). As President, he passively supported the Communist takeover in March, but he left Hungary in July 1919 before the defeat of the Council Republic, and lived in emigration until 1946. In 1947 he became Hungarian Ambassador to Paris, but in June 1949 he resigned in protest against the show trial of László Rajk. He lived in exile in France until his death. His ashes were returned to Hungary in 1962, and reburied in a mausoleum.

[7] Garbai, Sándor 1879—1947
Social Democrat politician, construction worker. Chairman of the National Trade Union of Construction Workers (1903—1919). Chairman of the Governing Council in 1919, Minister of Public Education in the Peidl government. He went into exile and became a leading figure of the centrist Hungarian Social Democrat émigrés in Europe.

[8] Kun, Béla 1886—1939
Journalist, Social Democrat, founder of the Hungarian Communist party. Leader of the Republic of Councils in 1919, a prominent member of the Third International. As a young Social Democrat, he was mobilized in the Austro-Hungarian Army at the outbreak of World War I, became a POW in 1916 and joined the Bolsheviks. He received training in Russia and returned to Hungary after the collapse of the Central powers in 1918. He founded the Hungarian Communist party

on Nov. 24, 1918. Imprisoned by the government of Mihály Károlyi, Kun was released on March 21, 1919, and, on the same day, was appointed People's Commissar of Foreign Affairs, a dominant position in the Communist–Social Democratic coalition which came about with the fusion of the two parties. In April 1919 he became People's Commissar of National Defense as well. After the collapse of the Republic, he fled to Vienna. He remained an influential figure in the émigré Hungarian Communist movement as well. He settled in the USSR and was later accused of Trotskyism. He was arrested in 1937 and died in prison.

[9] Rónai, Zoltán 1880–1940
Lawyer, Social Democrat, politician. He was Undersecretary in the Berinkey government, and People's Commissar of Justice in the Republic of Councils. In 1919 he emigrated to Vienna and was active among the émigré Social Democrats. Later he moved to Belgium, where, at the time of the German invasion, he committed suicide.

[10] Diminutive word for chicken, used by peasants while feeding them.

[11] Haynau, Julius Jakob, Baron 1786–1853
Austrian general whose military career was overshadowed by his notorious brutality. During the revolutions of 1848/49 he campaigned in Italy, repressing a rising in Brescia. Moving to Hungary in command of an army corps in 1849, he was appointed the Chief Commander of the Austrian forces in Hungary. After the defeat of the War of Independence, he was entrusted with full powers, and instituted a reign of terror until 1850.

[12] Dózsa, György c. 1470–1514
Szekler soldier who won a reputation in the anti-Turkish struggles at the beginning of the sixteenth century. He organized a crusade against the Turks, but the movement changed into a war against landlords in 1514. His peasant army was eventually defeated, and Dózsa was executed with unspeakable barbarity.

[13] Horthy, Miklós 1868–1957
Regent of Hungary (1920–1944). He was War Minister in the counter-revolutionary Szeged government in 1919 opposing Béla Kun's Communist government; he took over power after foreign intervention led to the defeat of the Republic of Councils. As regent he ruled virtually as a dictator, but allowed parliamentary forms to function. He supported the Axis powers in World War II until, yielding to German pressure, he ceded power to the extreme-rightist Arrow Cross Party in October 1944. He was interned in the castle of Wilheim, Bavaria, where he fell into American hands in 1945; he was set free in 1946. He died at Estoril, Portugal where he lived after 1949.

[14] Part of the system of peace treaties worked out in Paris in 1919 and 1920. It is called the Trianon Peace Treaty because the section dealing with Hungary was signed at the Trianon Palace in Versailles on June 4, 1920.

[15] Bethlen, István, Count 1874–1946
Hungarian statesman, Prime Minister from 1921 to 1931. A skillful conservative politician, he greatly promoted Hungary's economic reconstruction. In 1935 he left the ruling party he himself had founded and went into political opposition. In 1943–44 he was the principal figure among conservative forces seeking rapprochement with the Allies. He died as a POW in the Soviet Union.

[16] Skilled worker who works for a master craftsman or tradesman.

[17] Hungarian Federation of Young Communist Workers, founded in December 1918, active during the years of the Horthy regime, and especially from 1925 until 1936; after that young Communists, among them Kádár, cooperated in the Youth Committee (OIB) of the Social Democratic Party. On October 28, 1944, it was reorganized as the Young Communist League (KISZ).

[18] Peyer, Károly 1881—1956
Fitter by trade, right-wing Social Democrat. Secretary of the National Federation of Hungarian Miners and Founders (from 1918). He was Minister of the Interior in the Peidl government (Aug. 1, 1919— Aug. 6, 1919) and Minister of Labour and Public Welfare (November 1919— January 1920), Member of Parliament (1922—44). Following the German occupation of Hungary, he was taken into concentration camp. After his return, he became increasingly isolated within the Social Democratic Party because of his anti-Communist views. He was expelled from the party in 1947 and joined the bourgeois radical movement. He left Hungary not much later and settled in the United States.

[19] Sallai, Imre 1897—1932
Clerk, Communist leader. He helped to organize the Hungarian Communist party. During the Republic of Councils he was deputy director of the political department of the People's Commissariat of the Interior. Afterwards he was exiled to Vienna, then worked as a scientific researcher for the Marx–Engels–Lenin Institute in Moscow. He returned home in 1931. He was arrested, sentenced by the summary court and executed together with Sándor Fürst.

[20] Fürst, Sándor 1897—1932
Clerk, Communist leader. Between 1929 and 1931 he was in prison. He was released on parole and became a member of the party Secretariat. In 1932 he was arrested again together with his fellow members, and in the course of two weeks he was sentenced by the summary court and executed together with Imre Sallai.

[21] Landler, Jenő 1875—1928
Lawyer, Social Democratic and Communist politician. A leading figure in the pacifist movement during World War I, he managed the Executive Bureau of the Hungarian National Council in 1918. As a left-wing Social Democrat, he urged the fusion of his party with the Communists in 1919. After the Communist takeover he became People's Commissar of the Interior. Later on he was put in charge of railways and navigation, and was commander of the Third Army Corps. After the resignation of the Kun government, he went into exile and became active in reorganizing the Hungarian Communist movement. He died in France.

[22] Extreme-right Hungarian party, borrowing much of its ideology and methods from the German Nazis. Formed in 1936, it united several national-socialist factions under the leadership of Ferenc Szálasi. The party gained 16.2 per cent in the elections of 1939, and by the early forties its membership rose to 300,000. On October 15, 1944, following Horthy's unsuccessful attempt to break away from the Germans, Hitler placed Szálasi into power, who then willingly cooperated with them in continuing the war, and in the deportation and extermination of the Hungarian Jewry.

[23] The most important among the various secret associations in the Horthy era. Formed in 1919, its leader was ostensibly Baron Berthold Feilitzsch, but its actual head was Horthy himself. Its membership consisted of extreme-rightist military officers, aristocrats and senior civil servants. At the time of its formation, the association aimed at the introduction of a military dictatorship. Later, when Prime Minister Bethlen himself became a member, the association accepted Bethlen's more moderate policies.

[24] An organization of military officers of all ranks formed in 1918. During the Horthy era it became a mass organization of reserve officers and non-commissioned officers, the rich peasantry and the petty-bourgeoisie.

[25] The name speaks for itself. To achieve their goal the members conducted energetic propaganda campaigns in Hungary and abroad; in England they enjoyed Lord Rothermere's support.

[26] Counter-revolutionary organization formed in early 1919 for rallying the extreme-rightist, anti-Semitic groups of the intelligentsia and lower middle-classes. Its strength and significance gradually diminished during the consolidation period in the twenties.

[27] Secret association formed in 1919 by Horthy's officers in the town of Szeged. Its purpose was to prepare for a military action to regain Hungarian territories lost in World War I. The association kept in close contact with similar military organizations in Germany.

[28] The strongest youth organization during the Horthy era. In contrast with other religious conservative youth organizations, the Turul advocated a racist ideology (Turul is the name of the sacred bird of the ancient Magyars). During World War II, part of its membership turned against the Germans.

[29] Teleki, Pál, Count 1879—1941
Professor of Geography at the University of Budapest from 1919. Combining politics with an academic career, he became Minister of Foreign Affairs in April 1920, serving as Prime Minister from July 1920, until his resignation following Charles Habsburg's first restoration attempt. Founder of the Christian National League and chief of the Hungarian Boy Scouts, he became Minister of Religious Affairs and Public Education in 1938, and again Prime Minister from 1939 till 1941. When the Germans marched against Yugoslavia through Hungarian territory, he committed suicide.

[30] The law on "the restriction of Jewish expansion in public life and in the economy" was passed on May 5, 1939. It extended anti-Jewish measures among others to those who themselves were not Jewish by faith, but had one Jewish parent or two Jewish grandparents. As a result of this law 60,000 Jews lost their jobs.

[31] Veres, Péter 1897—1970
Peasant writer and politician belonging to the circle of the so-called "populist" intelligentsia. He wrote extensively on the conditions of the Hungarian poor peasantry. At the end of 1944 he became the head of the National Peasant Party; he served as Member of Parliament from 1945 to 1970. In 1947—48 he was Minister of Defense; later, from 1954 to 1956 President of the Writers' Union. He became a member of the Presidium of the Patriotic People's Front in 1968, and continued writing until his death.

[32] Rákosi, Mátyás 1892—1971
Hungarian Communist, leader of the Communist party from 1941 to 1956. An adherent of Social Democracy from his youth, Rákosi returned to Hungary a Communist in 1918 after a period as POW in Soviet Russia. He served as Deputy People's Commissar of Commerce, and later People's Commissar for Social Production in the Republic of Councils, but with the triumph of the counter-revolution in Hungary, he was forced to flee to Moscow. In 1924 he returned to Hungary to reorganize the Hungarian Communist party, but was arrested in 1925 and was sentenced to eight and a half years. Still in prison in 1935, he was put on trial again and was sentenced to life imprisonment. In 1940 he was extradited to Moscow, the recognized leader of the Communist party. Returning to Hungary in 1945, he became the Secretary-General of the Hungarian Communist Party. He was State Minister (1945—49), Deputy Prime Minister (1945—52) and Prime Minister (1952—53). In 1953 he ceded the premiership to Imre Nagy, but remained the First Secretary of the party until July 1956 when he emigrated to the USSR; he lived there until his death. In 1962 he was expelled from the Hungarian Communist party for his grave political crimes.

[33] Political journal founded in 1877. From 1880 to 1948 the journal was the main organ of the Hungarian Social Democratic Party. With the fusion of the SDP and the Communist Party in 1948, the journal was taken over by the National Trade Union Council.

³⁴ Bajcsy-Zsilinszky, Endre 1886—1944
Hungarian politician and journalist, leading figure in the Hungarian independence movement. As a politician he started out as a right-wing opponent of Bethlen's during the twenties. In the early thirties he gradually distanced himself from pro-German rightist forces and became an active organizer of anti-German forces. On March 19, 1944 the Gestapo arrested him following a fierce gun-fight. He was released thanks to the Lakatos government's efforts, but was shortly discovered by Arrow Cross terrorists. He was executed on Christmas Day, 1944.

³⁵ Szekfű, Gyula 1883—1955
Conservative historian, professor of history at the University of Budapest from 1924, and increasingly anti-German as the war wore on; the first ambassador of the new Hungary to Moscow (1946—1948); Member of Parliament from 1953; member of the Presidential Council from 1954.

³⁶ Petőfi, Sándor 1823—1849
One of the greatest of Hungarian poets, active in the 1848 revolution among the radical youth. On the eve of the revolution he wrote the poem *Nemzeti Dal* (National Song) which became the Marseillaise of the Revolution. On March 14, 1848 with his friends he wrote up the requests of the Hungarian nation in the famous Twelve Points. Later on, he took an active part in the Transylvanian campaigns and rose to the rank of major. He disappeared at the battle of Segesvár.

³⁷ Political party founded in 1939 by populist intellectuals. After 1945 the NPP closely cooperated with the Communist Party and was included in the coalition of governing parties. It was dissolved in 1949.

³⁸ Szakasits, Árpád 1888—1965
Stone cutter, Social Democrat and Communist politician. Head of the Department of Public Administration of the Commissariat for Internal Affairs in the Republic of Councils (1919); after three years in prison, Secretary-General of the Social Democratic Party (1938—42; 1945—48); State Minister and Deputy Prime Minister (1945—48); Minister of Industry (1948); President of the Republic (1948—50). Following the fusion of the Social Democratic and Communist parties in 1948, he became the Chairman of the united party. He was arrested on false charges in 1950 and was released in March 1956. In 1958 he became the Chairman of the Journalists' Union and an MP. In 1958 he became member of the Presidential Council, and in 1959 member of the Central Committee of the HSWP.

³⁹ Korvin, Ottó 1894—1919
Bank teller, Communist leader; one of the organizers of the Hungarian Party of Communists (KMP) in 1918, member of the first Central Committee. During the Republic of Councils, he headed the political department of the People's Commissariat of the Interior in charge of eliminating counter-revolutionary organizations. After the fall of the Republic of Councils, he was arrested, sentenced, and executed.

⁴⁰ Lőwy, Sándor 1906—1929
Baker. Secretary of the underground KIMSZ and member of the party's Central Commitee. He was arrested and sentenced in 1927. He joined the hunger strike of Communist prisoners in Vác Prison and died in consequence of forced feeding.

⁴¹ Rózsa, Ferenc 1906—1942
Architect. He joined the working class movement in Germany. He returned home in 1931. From 1932 he worked for the party; in 1941 he became a member of the reorganized Central Committee, then of the Secretariat as well. In 1942 he edited the underground *Szabad Nép* (Free People). He was captured and in a matter of a few days was tortured to death.

⁴² Rezi, Károly 1909—1942
Textile worker. He joined the Communist party in 1933, and was the leader of the Újpest workers

and organized the unemployed. During World War II he took part in the anti-Fascist national liberation movement. He was arrested and tortured to death in three weeks while being interrogated.

[43] Schönherz, Zoltán 1905—1942
Electric engineer. He was secretary of the Hungarian branch of the Slovak Young Workers Association. From 1936 to 1938 he was responsible for organizing the anti-Fascist league of Slovak and Hungarian youth organizations. He organized the Communist movement in his home town of Kassa after its reannexation to Hungary. During 1939—40 he stayed in the Soviet Union, then returned home and became a member of the freshly organized party Secretariat, and of its Central Committee as well. He was arrested, sentenced to death by court martial on charges of treason, and executed.

[44] Kállay, Miklós 1887—1967
Lord lieutenant, Undersecretary for Commerce (1929—31); Minister of Agriculture (1932—35); Prime Minister of Hungary from March 1942 to March 1944; Minister of Foreign Affairs (1942—1943). After the German occupation of Hungary, he was captured and put in a concentration camp by the Germans. In 1945 he moved to Italy and in 1951 settled in the USA.

[45] Party of the landed peasantry founded by István Szabó (of Nagyatád). In 1922 it merged with Bethlen's party to form the United Party (Egységes Párt). During the economic crisis the Smallholders' Party was formed again in 1930 by Zoltán Tildy, Tibor Eckhardt and others. In the thirties the party increasingly shifted into opposition and rejected the German orientation of the Hungarian government. Under the German occupation of Hungary, many of the party's leaders were arrested and the party itself was banned. In December, 1944 the party's representatives played an active role in the provisional government. In the elections of 1945 the party gained 57 per cent of the votes and played an important role in the political life of the country until 1948—49.

[46] Szálasi, Ferenc 1897—1946
Army officer, Fascist leader. In 1930 appointed Major in the Staff Service. He elaborated his own political programme which was an eclectic mixture of anti-Semitism, Fascism and nationalism. In 1935 he retired and formed a National Socialist organization, called Party of National Will. In 1936 he formed the Arrow Cross Party and won a number of seats in Parliament. He was imprisoned in 1937 (till 1938). On October 15, 1944 Hitler placed him in power and he became the "nation's leader". His regime was responsible for the deportation and annihilation of hundreds of thousands of Jews and for an unprecedented wave of terror within the country. In early 1945 he escaped to Germany where he was later captured by American troops. He was sentenced to death by a Hungarian court and was executed in 1946.

[47] Ságvári, Endre 1913—1944
Jurist, leading figure and martyr of the anti-Fascist working class resistance movement. He joined the Social Democratic Party in 1936, and, after 1940, led its National Youth Committee. Following his arrest for anti-Fascist activities, he joined the illegal Communist party and played a major role in the Popular Front movement. He was a regular contributor to the *Népszava* in the early forties. In July 1944 he was killed in a fierce gunfight with detectives sent to arrest him.

[48] Cover organization for the Hungarian Communists after the disbanding of the Communist party from June 1943 to September 1944.

[49] Rajk, László 1909—1949
Communist politician, member of the illegal Communist party from 1931. He fought in the Spanish Civil War and was later interned in France from where he was taken to a concentration camp in Germany in 1941. He escaped and returned to Hungary where, in September 1944, he became the Secretary of the illegal Communist party, but in December of that year he was arrested

and taken back to Germany. He returned to Hungary in May 1945. His positions from then on: Member of the Central Committee and of the Political Committee of the Communist party (1945—1949); Party Secretary of Budapest (1945); Deputy Secretary-General of the Communist Party (1945—1946); Minister of Home Affairs (1946—1948); Minister of Foreign Affairs (1948—May 1949). He was arrested on false charges in May 30, 1949 and was executed in October of the same year. He was rehabilitated in 1955.

[50] Kiss, János 1885—1944
Lieutenant general; retired in 1939 in protest against the German orientation of the Hungarian military leadership. In November 1944 he became the organizer of the military branch of the Hungarian resistance movement. He was captured by Arrow Cross detectives and executed in December 1944.

[51] It was first the state security department of the police (ÁVO); after 1948, it functioned as an independent body. In 1953, it was again placed under the supervision of the Ministry of Home Affairs, and disbanded in 1956. Its detective agencies were guilty of violations of the law.

[52] Nagy, Imre 1896—1958
Hungarian Communist leader. Taken POW by the Russians in World War I, he joined the Bolsheviks and worked in the Soviet Union. In 1921 he was sent back to Hungary; until 1927, he organized the Communist peasants of Somogy County. He was jailed; after his release he worked in the Comintern. He returned to Hungary at the end of 1944 and became a member of the Central Committee and the Political Committee in 1945. He was Minister of Agriculture (1944—45) and Minister of Home Affairs (1945—46). In 1949 he was expelled from the Political Committee, but was then again co-opted. He was Minister of Food (1950—52), and Minister of Requisitions (1952); Deputy Prime Minister (1952—53) and Prime Minister (1953—55). In April 1955, he was condemned as a right deviationist and had to give up all his state functions. In December of the same year he was expelled from the Communist party, to which he was again co-opted on Oct. 13, 1956. From Oct. 24 to Nov. 4 he was again Prime Minister. On November 4, after the Soviet troops returned to Budapest, he fled to the Yugoslav Embassy. He refused to cooperate with the Kádár government, and in consequence was interned in Romania. In the spring of 1958, he was condemned to death on charges of counter-revolutionary activity and executed.

[53] Vas, Zoltán 1903—1983
Communist journalist and politician, member of the illegal Communist party from 1919. He was arrested in 1921 and was sent to the Soviet Union in an exchange of prisoners. In 1924 he returned to Hungary and was again active in the illegal Communist movement. In 1925 he was imprisoned and was rescued by the Soviets 15 years later, in 1940, in an exchange of prisoners. He returned to Hungary after the war and became Government Commissioner for Public Supplies in Budapest (1945), and then, in the same year, the Mayor of Budapest (1945). He was Secretary of the Supreme Economic Council (1946—49); President of the National Planning Office (1949—53); member of the Central Committee of the Communist party (1945—56); member of the Political Committee (1948—53). In October 1956 he took part in the Imre Nagy government, and was later interned in Romania from where he returned in 1959. He devoted the rest of his life to literary activities.

[54] Miklós, Béla, Dálnoki 1890—1948
Staff officer and general, he was the Chief of Regent Horthy's military bureau, and general adjutant; he later became the Commander of the First Hungarian Army. In October 1944, he went over to the Soviet side with one of his troops. He was Prime Minister of the provisional Hungarian government from December 1944 till November 1945, and member of the Supreme National Council from January to November 1945.

[55] Gerő, Ernő 1898—1980
Member of the Hungarian Communist party from 1918, he emigrated to Germany in 1919, after the fall of the Republic of Councils. He returned to Hungary in 1922 and was arrested and sentenced to 15 years' imprisonment. He was extradited to the Soviet Union in 1924 and settled there. He took part in the Spanish Civil War and returned to Hungary in 1944. His positions afterwards: Minister of Commerce and Transport (1945); Minister of Transport (1945—49); Minister of Finance (1948—49); Minister of State (1949—52); First Deputy Prime Minister (1952—56); Minister of Home Affairs (1953—54); member of the Central Leadership and of the Political Committee from 1945; First Secretary of the Central Committee of the Hungarian Communist party from July 21 to Oct. 25, 1956. On Oct. 28, 1956 he went to the USSR, and returned to Hungary in 1960. He was expelled from the party in 1962 for grave political crimes.

[56] Révai, József 1898—1959
Communist leader, journalist, founding member of the Hungarian Communist party in 1918. After the collapse of the Republic of Councils he emigrated to Vienna, but came back to Hungary several times, illegally. In 1930 he was arrested and imprisoned till 1934 when he moved to Czechoslovakia and later to the USSR. He returned to Hungary at the end of 1944 and became a member of the Supreme National Council in 1945. He was member of the Central Leadership and of the Political Committee from 1945. His membership in the latter ceased temporarily in 1953, but he was again co-opted in July 1956. He was Minister of Public Education (1949—1953) and Deputy President of the Presidential Council (1953—1958). After 1956, he was a member of the Central Committee.

[57] Farkas, Mihály 1904—1965
Member of the Czechoslovakian Communist party from 1921, he was imprisoned in 1925. He played an important role in the Communist Youth International (1929—37). During World War II, he lived in the USSR, and worked for the Hungarian broadcast of Radio Moscow. He returned to Hungary in 1944 and became Member of Parliament and member of the Central Committee of the Communist Party. He was Undersecretary of Home Affairs (1945). From 1945 he was also member of the Political Committee, and Deputy Secretary-General of the party. He was Minister of Defense (1948—53). In 1955 he was expelled from the Central Committee because of his role in the show trials. In the summer of 1956 he was expelled from the party, lost his stripes and was put on trial. He was imprisoned until 1961. After his release he worked as an editor in a publishing house.

[58] Founded in 1895 on the pattern of the Ecole Normale Superieure, the College served the education of university students. It was dissolved in 1950.

[59] Para-military organization for boys between the age of 13 and 21. Formed in 1921, it served to compensate for the abolition of general conscription by the Trianon Peace Treaty. In 1944 the Arrow Cross government conscripted the proper age groups to fight on the Austrian and German fronts.

[60] Mindszenty, József 1892—1975
Roman Catholic Primate of Hungary (1945—73), who took an extreme-rightist stand after the Liberation. He was sentenced to life imprisonment in 1949. In 1956 he sought refuge in the American Embassy of Budapest where he spent 15 years. He left Hungary in 1971 and settled in Vienna.

[61] Tildy, Zoltán 1889—1961
Reformed Minister, one of the founders of the Smallholders' Party, Member of Parliament from 1936. After World War II, he became President of his party (1945—46) and from 1946 till 1948 he was President of the Hungarian Republic. He resigned in 1948 and for several years he was under house arrest, but he was rehabilitated in August 1956. From October 25, 1956 he joined the Imre Nagy government as State Minister (until Nov. 4, 1956). He was sentenced to six years' imprisonment, but was released three years later.

⁶² Nagy, Ferenc 1903—1979
Smallholder, politician, member of the Smallholders' Party from 1927, member of Parliament from 1939. He was arrested by the Gestapo in 1944. He became Minister of Reconstruction (1945) and Speaker of Parliament in 1945—46; he was Prime Minister from 1946 till 1947 when he travelled to Switzerland; he resigned his post from there. He later settled in the USA.

⁶³ Varga, Béla 1903—
Hungarian politician, Catholic prelate. In 1937 he became Vice-President of the Smallholders' Party, and was a Member of Parliament from 1939. He took part in the underground anti-Nazi movement. In 1946—47 he was Speaker of Parliament. In 1947 he left Hungary and settled in the USA.

⁶⁴ Kovács, Béla 1908—1959
Hungarian politician, member of the Smallholders' Party. Undersecretary of Home Affairs in the Provisional government in 1944; Minister of Agriculture (1945—46); Secretary-General of the Smallholders' Party (1946—47). In 1947 he was arrested and imprisoned until April 1956. On October 25, 1956 he became Minister of Agriculture in the government of Imre Nagy and held his post until October 31 of the same year; he was State Minister Nov. 2—Nov. 4, 1956. In 1958 he was elected to Parliament.

⁶⁵ Kéthly, Anna 1889—1976
Social Democratic politician, member of the SDP's leadership from 1928 till 1948. Deputy Speaker of Parliament (1945—1948). In March 1948 she was expelled from the party because she opposed the fusion of the Social Democrats with the Communists. She was arrested and sentenced on false charges in 1949. She was released in 1954 with amnesty. In November 1956 she became State Minister in the Imre Nagy government and was active in reorganizing the SDP. On November 3, 1956 she went to Vienna and later settled in Belgium.

⁶⁶ Marosán, György 1908—
Former baker, member of the Social Democratic Party from 1928. In 1939 he became Secretary-General of the National Union of Food Workers. He was imprisoned for one year in 1942. In 1943 he became Secretary of the SDP, and held his post until 1947 when he became Deputy Secretary-General of the SDP. After the fusion of his party with the Communists, he was Deputy Secretary-General of the Communist party and member of the Central Committee and the Politbureau (1948—50). He was also Party Secretary for Budapest. He was Minister of Light Industry in 1949—50. In 1950 he was arrested on false charges and was rehabilitated in 1956. He again became member of the Central Committee and of the Political Committee in July 1956, and became Deputy Prime Minister (July 30, 1956—October 24, 1956). He was State Minister (1957—60), Secretary of the Central Committee (1958—62), and member of the Presidential Council (1960—62). In 1962 he resigned all his posts and retired. He was expelled from the Central Committee in 1962. He left the party in 1965, but re-entered it in 1972.

⁶⁷ Erdei, Ferenc 1910—1971
Economist, politician, a founder of the National Peasant Party in 1939, Secretary-General of the party (1945—1949). He belonged to the left wing of the populist movement and wrote extensively on the living conditions of the Hungarian peasantry. In 1944 he became the Minister of Home Affairs in the provisional government until November 1945. His positions: State Minister (1948—49); Minister of Agriculture (1949—53); Minister of Justice (1953—54); Minister of Agriculture (1954—55); Deputy Prime Minister (1955—Oct. 31, 1956); Secretary-General of the Hungarian Academy of Sciences (1957—64 and 1970—71); Secretary-General of the Patriotic People's Front (1964—70); Member of the Presidential Council (1965—71).

⁶⁸ Kovács, Imre 1913—1980
Writer, leading figure of the Hungarian populist movement, a founding member of the National Peasant Party. In the coalition period he was active in the NPP, but he became increasingly

isolated because he opposed the party's cooperation with the Communists. He left the NPP and joined the Independent Democratic Party. He emigrated in 1948 and settled in the USA.

[69] **Bem, Jozef 1794—1850**
Polish officer active in the 1830 Polish uprising. Following its defeat, Bem emigrated and became the victorious hero of the 1848—49 Hungarian Revolution. He was made commander of the Transylvanian Hungarian troops in November 1848 and succeeded in clearing Transylvania of all hostile armies. However, in 1849 he suffered defeat at the decisive battle of Segesvár. Bem became the common symbol of both Polish and Hungarian independence struggles; this is why his statue was chosen for the demonstration on October 23, 1956.

[70] **Sulyok, Dezső 1897—1965**
Lawyer and politician, Member of Parliament from 1935 to 1939 and from 1945 to 1947. He played a dominant role in the Smallholders' Party but was expelled with his followers in 1946 and formed the short-lived Freedom Party. He left the country in 1947 and later settled in the USA.

[71] Journal of the Communist party from 1942 to November 1956.

[72] **Köböl, József 1909—**
Joiner, party functionary, Communist since 1926. He studied in Moscow during 1934—36, and participated in the work of the Hungarian Communist party from 1939. He was sentenced to eight years' imprisonment in 1942 but escaped. After 1945 he worked with János Kádár at the Budapest Party Committee. In 1949—1950 he was deputy mayor of Budapest. During 1950—55 he was secretary of the builders' union, from 1954 member of the secretariat of the Central Leadership, later member of the Central Committee as well. Between 1957 and 1961 he was Deputy Minister of Building and Urban Development; MP from 1946 to 1958; in 1956 Secretary of the Budapest Party Committee; since 1961 he has been department head in the Central Planning Office.

[73] **Apró, Antal 1913—**
House painter, a member of the Communist party since 1931. Department head of the Central Committee (1945—48), Secretary-General of the National Council of Trade Unions (1948—51); member of the Political Committee (1956—80); Member of the Presidential Council (1948—51), a member of government at the head of different ministries, and as deputy chairman of the Council of Ministers (1952—71); Speaker of Parliament since 1971.

[74] **Dinnyés, Lajos 1901—1961**
Politician, belonging to the left wing of the Smallholders' Party, Member of Parliament; Minister of Defense (1947); Prime Minister (1947—48); Deputy Speaker of Parliament (1958—61). From 1951 to the end of his life he was director of the National Library of Agriculture.

[75] **Péter, Gábor 1906—**
Former tailor, member of the secretariat of the illegal Hungarian Communist party from 1943. In 1945 he became Commander of the Political Department of the State Police in Budapest, and later became the commander of the State Security Authority (ÁVH). He was removed from his post and arrested in 1953 and was sentenced to life imprisonment in 1954. He was released in 1959 and worked as a librarian.

[76] **Pálffy, György 1909—1949**
Staff officer in the Hungarian Army. In 1939 he left the army in protest against its German orientation. In 1942 he joined the illegal Communist party and worked simultaneously in the Smallholders' Party as well. In the autumn of 1944, he became the head of the military section of the Hungarian Communist Party. In 1945 he became head of the Political Department of the Ministry of Defense, and in 1948, he became Deputy Minister of Defense. In the same year he became

member of the Central Leadership of the Communist party. In May 1949 he was arrested on false charges and was executed. He was rehabilitated in 1955.

[77] Sólyom, László 1908—1950
Army officer, member of the illegal Communist party from 1942. As a staff captain he was pensioned off in 1941, following Hitler's declaration of war against the USSR. During the German occupation of Hungary, he was active in the illegal resistance movement, and was arrested in November 1944. In 1945 he was appointed Chief of the Budapest Police and in 1947, the Chief of Staff. In May 1950 he was arrested on false charges and was executed. He was rehabilitated in 1956.

[78] Molnár, Erik 1894—1966
Historian, Communist politician, member of the illegal Communist party from 1928. He became Minister of Public Welfare (1944—47); Minister of Foreign Affairs (1947—48); Ambassador to Moscow and Helsinki (1948—49); Minister of Justice (1950—52); Minister of Foreign Affairs (1952—53); President of the Supreme Court (1953—54); Minister of Justice (1954—Oct. 31, 1956). He was member of the Central Leadership of the party from 1948 to 1956. After 1956 he worked as a university professor and Director of the Institute for Historical Research of the Hungarian Academy of Sciences.

[79] Szőnyi, Tibor 1903—1949
Doctor of medicine, member of the illegal Communist party from 1930. In the thirties he lived in Vienna, and was a leading figure in the party's illegal apparatus. He returned in 1945. He became a member of the party's Central Leadership, and head of the Cadre Department in 1947. He was arrested on false charges in 1949 and was executed. He was rehabilitated in 1955.

[80] Szalai, András 1917—1949
Lathe operator, Communist politician. He was arrested as a Communist in 1933 and again in 1942. After 1945 he became the Deputy Head of the Cadre Department of the Central Leadership of the Communist Party. He was arrested on false charges in 1949, and was executed. He was rehabilitated in 1955.

[81] Russian word for rich peasant.

[82] "Splendid winds" *(fényes szelek)* was the song of the Popular Colleges movement (1945—49). The colleges served the education of poor and disadvantaged students at all levels of education. The movement was dissolved in 1949.

[83] Hegedüs, András 1922—
Communist politician, member of the illegal Communist party from 1942. Active in the Communist youth movement from 1941 to 1948; member of the Central Committee and the Political Committee from 1949. Minister of State Farms and Forestry (1952—53); Deputy Prime Minister (1953—55); Minister of Agriculture (1953—55); Prime Minister (1955—Oct. 24, 1956). In October 1956, he went to the Soviet Union and returned in 1960. He became Deputy President of the Central Statistical Office (1962—63); Director of the Sociological Research Group of the Hungarian Academy of Sciences (1963—68). In 1973 he was expelled from the Communist party.

[84] Vörösmarty, Mihály 1800—1855
Hungarian poet, one of the greatest figures of Hungarian romanticism. He participated actively in the political and cultural struggles of the Hungarian Reform Age. He became Member of Parliament in 1849 and, following the dethronement of the Habsburgs, he became judge of the Court of Appeal. After the defeat of the Revolution, he lived in hiding for two years, but returned to his family in 1850. Although he was never sentenced, he never returned to public life.

85 Ady, Endre 1877—1919
One of the greatest lyrical poets of Hungary. He was leader of the much-debated modern school of poetry. A radical sympathizer, he contributed to several radical newspapers; his articles rank among the best in twentieth century journalism. In World War I, he adopted a pacifist attitude and prophesied the Károlyi Revolution of 1918.

86 Kossuth, Lajos 1802—1894
Hungarian statesman, leader of the 1848 Revolution and War of Independence. In his youth he had been active in the reform movement, and was imprisoned for his writings (1837—40). After his release he became editor of the *Pesti Hírlap* (Pest Journal) and the leader of the Hungarian opposition (1847—48). In the government of the victorious March Revolution of 1848, he first held the post of the Minister of Finance. Later on, he became the leader of the fight to protect the endangered Revolution. After the dethronement of the Habsburgs, he became Governor of Hungary in April 1849. Following the defeat of the War of Independence, he fled to Turkey, and lived in exile, mostly in Italy, where he died.

87 Francis II, Rákóczi 1676—1735
Prince of Transylvania, son of the elected prince Francis I Rákóczi and Ilona Zrínyi, the brave defender of Munkács Castle. He started his freedom fight against the oppression of the Viennese court in 1703. In 1704 he was elected Prince of Transylvania; in 1705 Ruling Prince of Hungary. After a series of military victories the tide turned against him, and in 1711 he left Hungary for Poland, later England and France. After 1717 he lived in Turkey. His ashes were returned to Hungary in 1906 and reburied in state at Kassa.

88
Discussion group organized by the Young Workers' Organization (DISZ) in late 1955. It played a great role in propagating the views of revisionist Communists around Imre Nagy. The circle dissolved in November 1956.

89 Dudás, József ?—1957
Hungarian politician active in the pre-war illegal Communist movement in Transylvania, he was a member of the delegation sent by Horthy to Moscow to negotiate a cease-fire with the Allies. In the summer of 1945 he joined the Smallholders' Party. Arrested in 1946, Dudás spent eight years in prison. On Oct. 28, 1956 he and his armed group occupied the offices of the *Szabad Nép*, the Communist party newspaper, and announced the formation of the Committee of the Hungarian National Revolution. In his newspaper entitled *Magyar Függetlenség* (Hungarian Independence) he put forward his own political aims and denied the legitimacy of the Imre Nagy government. On Nov. 2 he occupied the Foreign Ministry building. He was condemned to death and executed in January 1957.

90 Maléter, Pál 1917—1958
Army officer. He fell prisoner to the Red Army in 1944. He attended Partisan School in the USSR; after his return to Hungary, he was made staff officer in 1952. In October 1956 he was entrusted with recapturing the Kilián garrison in Budapest, but he went over to the rebels and became Deputy Minister of Defense in the Imre Nagy government (Nov. 1—Nov. 2, 1956). From Nov. 3 to Nov. 5, 1956 he was Minister of Defense. He was sentenced to death and executed in 1958.

91 Kilián (Killián), György 1907—1943
Locksmith. He joined KIMSZ and the Hungarian Communist party in 1929. He studied in the Soviet Union in 1930—31. Returning home, he took over the leadership of the KIMSZ Secretariat. He was imprisoned in 1932, emigrated to the Soviet Union in 1939, and fought in World War II after 1941. On his way home, he parachuted into Poland from a military plane and disappeared.

[92] Kopácsy, Sándor 1920—
A police training officer from 1945 to 1953, he became Chief of the Budapest Police in 1953. He held his post until October 1956 when he became Commander of the Revolutionary National Guard. He was sentenced to life imprisonment in 1958. In 1963 he was released with amnesty. In 1975 he settled in Toronto, Canada.

[93] Király, Béla 1912—
A Staff officer in the Hungarian Army, he defected to the Russian side with his troops and became a POW in 1944. After his return to Hungary in 1945, he joined the Communist Party and became Commander of the Military Academy (1947—51), and as major general, Inspector of Infantry (1948—50). In 1951 he was arrested and sentenced to death, but his sentence was commuted to life imprisonment. He was released in 1956 and became Commander of the National Guard at the end of October. In November he escaped to Austria. He settled in the USA and became professor of history at Brooklyn College of the City University of New York.

[94] Mező, Imre 1905—1956
Former worker, Communist politician. In his youth he lived in Belgium where he joined the Communist party in 1929. He fought in the Spanish Civil War and was later active in the French resistance. He returned to Hungary in 1945 and worked within the party and trade union apparatus. In 1954 he became the Secretary of the Budapest Party Committee, and in July 1956, he became member of the Central Committee. When fighting broke out in October 1956, he led the defense of the Budapest Party Headquarters; he was shot by the insurgents on November 1, 1956.

[95] Political daily printed in Budapest. Founded in 1938, it was the organ of the intelligentsia opposed to German influence; it took an anti-Fascist stand during World War II. It was banned after the German occupation of Hungary. It began to appear again in 1945; since 1954 it has been the newspaper of the Patriotic People's Front.

[96] Münnich, Ferenc 1886—1967
Communist lawyer, Commander in the Red Army, Commander of the 11th Brigade in the Spanish Civil War, editor of the Hungarian broadcast of Radio Moscow during World War II. After 1945, he was General and Chief of the Budapest Police (1945—49); he was dismissed after the Rajk trial, and appointed Envoy to Helsinki (1949—50). Envoy, later Ambassador to Sofia (1950—54); Ambassador to Moscow and Ulanbator (1954—56); Envoy to Belgrade (Aug. 7, 1956 — Oct. 25, 1956); Minister of Home Affairs (Oct. 25, 1956 — Oct. 31, 1956); Minister of Home Affairs and Deputy Prime Minister (Nov. 4, 1956—1958); Prime Minister (1958—61); Member of the Central Committee and of the Political Committee from 1956.

[97] The beginning words of the poem *Nemzeti Dal* (National Song) written by Sándor Petőfi on the eve of the March Revolution of 1848. The poem calls on the Hungarian nation to rise and free itself from foreign domination.

[98] Dögei, Imre 1912—1964
Factory worker, politician, member of the illegal Communist Party from 1944. He became member of the Central Committee of the party in 1946. In 1951—52 he was Speaker of Parliament. He was Minister of Agriculture from 1957 to 1960. In 1960 he was Ambassador to Peking and Hanoi. In May 1960 he was expelled from the Central Committee because of his leftist views and anti-party activities; in 1962 he was expelled from the party as well.

At a meeting in Budapest, 1945
At the 3rd Congress of the Hungarian Communist Party, 1946
Accepting the office of the Minister of the Interior, 1948, with László Rajk on his right

4

5 6

4. *At the May 1957 session of Parliament*
5. *Visit to the countryside, 1956*
6. *With his wife in Győr, 1959*
7. *Speech to the UN General Assembly, 1960*
8. *Mass rally in Debrecen, 1961*

9

10

9. *With the writer Péter Veres at a national conference of the Patriotic People's Front, 1961*
10. *At harvest time on a cooperative farm, 1961*
11. *At the October 1961 session of Parliament*
12. *At the first national conference of socialist brigade leaders, 1962*

13. Speech in the Kremlin Congressional Palace at the 1963 Soviet–Hungarian friendship meeting
14. Hunting with President Tito, 1963
15. At the wall of the Kremlin, where the urns of the outstanding personalities of the working class movement are placed, 1963
16. With Leonid Brezhnev in Moscow, 1963

15

16

17

18

17. In his study with the writer
    Mikhail Sholokhov, 1965
18. In Mongolia, at a luncheon given
    in honour of the Hungarian Party
    and Government Delegation, 1965
19. In the horticultural section of a
    cooperative farm, 1965
20. Visit to the countryside, 1965
21. In the Ganz-Mávag Factory in
    Budapest, 1967

22

23

22. With Olympic pentathlon champion András Balczó, 1968
23. In a textile factory, 1968
24. Visit to the 13th district of Budapest, 1969

25

26

25. With Leonid Brezhnev at the 10th Congress of the Hungarian Socialist Workers' Party, 1970
26. At an intermission of the 10th Congress, 1970
27. At the Hungarian Lawn Tennis Championship, 1971
28. In a district of Budapest, 1971

29

30

29. Greeting Fidel Castro at Ferihegy Airport, 1972
30. With Olympic boxing champion László Papp, 1972
31. In Budapest, 1973
32. At the 1973 May Day Parade

33. Visiting a Helsinki market with President Kekkonen, 1973

Selected Speeches
and Interviews

Address at the 10th Plenary Session of the Central Council of Hungarian Trade Unions

JANUARY 26, 1957

Dear Comrades,

When we began the fight to overcome the counter-revolution, we had an increasing number of conflicts in the closing stages of the armed struggle with organizations and groups which in name were workers' institutions, but in their endeavours and objectives undoubtedly served the counter-revolution. Such a description also applies to what was known as the Budapest Central Workers' Council. I cannot state that all the members of this workers' council were traitors to the working class. But you know as well as I do that the way the organization operated as a body, and the actions taken by it, were designed to serve the objectives of the counter-revolution.

In the early days the counter-revolution demanded that there should be neither party nor trade union organizations in the factories.

The counter-revolution wanted to smash the party and trade union organizations, quite apart from its desire to overthrow the Revolutionary Workers' and Peasants' Government.

In the debates at that time I made this clear: as long as there is a working class, they will also have their own party; that was the case during the Horthy regime, and after the Liberation of Hungary from Fascist rule in 1945; and it will continue to be the case until a socialist society is completely established. And my opinion about the trade unions is the same.

There was also a lot of dispute concerning the railways. In my view the people who put forward the idea of setting up a workers' council at the headquarters of the Hungarian State Railways were guided by military considerations, and not by considerations representing the workers' interests. A workers' council at the headquarters of the Hungarian State Railways would have been a military institution; and as such it would have served the counter-revolution instead of the revolution. Everybody knows that. The comrades on the railways were in need of a good union. What they had in mind was a trade union organization which was knowledgeable about the railwaymen's life, which did not turn a deaf ear to their grievances, and which could represent their interests.

We had differences of opinion with the Yugoslav comrades on the subject of the workers' councils. Comrade Kardelj[1] said that in his opinion it would have been a correct step on our part to hand over power to the central workers' councils. During my debate with Comrade Kardelj I told him that they did not know the central workers' councils so well in Belgrade as we knew them here in Budapest. Certain workers' councils neither represented nor served the workers' interests.

I should also like to say a few words about relations between the party and the trade unions. This is associated with a particular slogan: "Independent trade unions".

In the course of my discussions I often had the opportunity to say that personally I completely accepted the formulation adopted by Lenin regarding relations between the party and the unions. If there is anyone who can phrase it better, well, we will consider it.

According to the Leninist position, independence is a political concept and in this sense the unions cannot be independent either of the revolutionary party of the working class or of their different militant organizations.

However, there is another very important concept. It is self-reliance, something that I can recommend for my part. It is intelligible and clear to everyone: the unions must be the self-reliant organizations of the working class.

In this connection the question arises: why, under our conditions are the party and the unions not independent of one another? Because both of them have a common basis of ideology and principle. In his report to the session Comrade Gáspár[2] stated that the unions are based on Marxism–Leninism. I think it would be unreasonable to challenge this point at a meeting of the leading body of the Hungarian trade unions. The unions are based upon socialist foundations and are on the side of the workers' power. These are the common points of principle and objectives which bear evidence to the fact that the party and the unions are not politically independent of one another.

So far as self-reliance is concerned, a harmful practice evolved in the past with regard to relations between the party and the unions. It was harmful from the point of view of the party, and also from the point of view of the unions; therefore, it was harmful from the point of view of the whole working class. The correct practice is that the party should be the leading force of the working class in terms of ideology, ideas and policies; and in this capacity should exert an influence on the unions. But it is quite evident that the unions should lead their own lives on the basis of those common ideas. If this fails to be the case, it will be harmful to the party as well, because it will not enhance the party's authority to interfere with the everyday life and problems of the unions by giving them orders.

What I also mean by self-reliance is this: it is not expedient for the different party organizations to take decisions binding on the trade union organizations in analogous spheres of authority. The party may, and in some cases must, take decisions on issues which are being considered by the unions as well, and it must make its position clear.

However, this position is binding only for party members. When party members come out in support of this position in a trade union body, the weapon they adopt must be one of conviction and principle. They must prove that their position is the correct one. It is not permissible to say, instead of putting forward arguments: do this or do that, because this is in line with the decision taken by one or another of the party organizations.

There is an additional point concerning self-reliance: in our view, a union leadership can command authority only when it has the confidence of the working people. If, for instance, a leadership whose composition has been meticulously calculated in advance is imposed on the membership in an office, there will be no confidence in that leadership, and, for that matter, the members will refuse to follow that union. This is our opinion. Historical experience has taught us not to commit the same mistake twice.

It has been a fundamental error in recent years that in some of the union organizations an attempt has been made to ensure party leadership merely by a numerical majority of party members. This is a path which cannot possibly be followed. It is possible that in a union body or organization, there are only three party members out of ten people but they must be able to lead that body not because they are in the majority, but by the authority they command, by the thoroughness of their Marxist knowledge, and by the force of their conviction.

It goes without saying that the proportions vary from organization to organization. It may well be the case that in the lowest level union organizations the ratio of non-party people is higher; on the medium level, their proportion is not so high and on the highest level it is lower still. This is not attributable to statistical norms but to the fact that the leaders, the people that the masses will have confidence in, are necessarily those who have had more experience in political matters, in theoretical questions and in union activities.

That is why we are not afraid of the masses electing their union leaders.

The unions must be built in this sound manner so that the members become convinced from everyday practice of the self-reliance of the unions. It is a Leninist principle that the union movement is the revolutionary school for the working masses, and for this reason great care must be taken of their self-reliance. The union will never be a school if someone can only be a union member after recognizing all the tenets of Marxism–Leninism, and every detail of all the resolutions of the party as being binding. I hope that the healthy proportion in keeping with Leninist principles will be restored, and that the ratio of party members to other working people will be substantially lower in the unions.

This is one of the reasons why it is important for the unions to act as a vast school for the working class.

I must also comment on the right way to serve the workers' interests, and the interests of the working people. This is the trade union's primary duty. The unions must safeguard the day-to-day interests of the working class, as well as their fundamental and general interests. It is in the fundamental interest of the working class that the building of a socialist society be carried on at an adequate pace; that the completion of this should be accomplished in Hungary; that Hungary should become a socialist country free from any sort of capitalist exploitation. It is the duty and interest of the trade unions to serve this fundamental objective. The other duty is to serve the day-to-day interests of the workers.

I should like you to recall the winter of 1945–46 and the spring of 1946. At that time the working class was in an extremely difficult situation materially. There were trade union activists who went to factories to check the wildcat strikes, and who emphasized very rightly the need for the workers to hold their own, and continue to work, as otherwise it would be impossible to stabilize the country's economic situation. Other activists, however, acted the other way: they also went to the factories but what they told the workers was that it was impossible to work on empty stomachs so they had to be given adequate pay before they would work. That was a sort of "division of labour" which, in my view, failed to promote the aims of the working class, nor was it a credit to the trade union movement. It must be noted, however, that it is possible to gain temporary popularity in this sort of way. But experience has also shown that only those who tell the truth can acquire real respect from the masses. It is wrong to underrate the masses; they are not stupid; they have historical experience to draw on and they are capable of making a distinction between a really good leader and one merely playing on mass emotions.

When on November 3, 1956 we were thinking of forming the present government, believe me, I knew only too well that we were not going to be welcomed with bouquets of flowers. I was well aware what we would have to face but I was convinced that truth was on our side and that the people would understand our action, would approve and appreciate that we were coming out in opposition to the counter-revolutionary flood, and that we were saving the Hungarian dictatorship of the proletariat.

It is the simplest thing in the world to draw up a list of demands. You need to have only a very little union experience to be able to draw up a very long list of demands. Satisfying these demands, and by this I mean translating them into practice, is a little more difficult.

Let us take the strike issue, for example. Well, we already have the demands, or as Comrade Gáspár put it here in more correct terms: the list of justified claims.

Now the question is this: how can they be met? Let us go on strike! It is possible to stage a strike ... We have already had a strike which was the first of its kind in the world: it was a strike complete with all comforts, including the door-to-door delivery of food supplies.

Comrades, there are partial strikes—struggles in support of day-to-day needs. Here, too, it matters who the struggle is being waged against. For instance, if I am employed in a factory and the owner is a capitalist, the point at issue is this: how much of the profit should be his and how much should be taken away for wages for the working class. This is a simple, clear and intelligible problem. But you always have to know to whom or to what you put your demand and who or what is the owner of the factory. If the factory belongs to the working class, to workers' power, the situation is quite different because income is virtually transferred from one pocket to the other.

There is also the general strike. If it is staged in a capitalist country, it is termed a political strike, a struggle for power. If it happens to be staged under the dictatorship of the proletariat, its political content is much the same, for it is also a political struggle, a struggle for power, but it is waged against the power of the working class. That is why I say that to declare the right to strike is not useful.

Of course we can argue generally about whether the declaration of the right to strike is useful in a state engaged in socialist construction. But here and now approval of a strike initiated and provoked by counter-revolution and staged by misled workers can in no way be correct policy. For it is quite obvious that, irrespective of what those taking part wanted, this strike was the rearguard action of the counter-revolutionary attack launched against the Hungarian People's Republic.

In material terms this strike has not been to the benefit of the working people. What was involved was a sum of 9.5 to 10 billion forints paid without any work being done for it. At present we are very much in need of money to increase the salaries of, for example, technical and intellectual workers and teachers, and the wages of workers and other categories of the working people. Only the counter-revolution profited from this policy; in economic terms, the strike meant an additional deficit for the working class. A declaration of principle to be made now would willy-nilly be approval of a strike which caused harm and ran counter to the workers' interests. This is the truth about the right to strike.

There is another issue: production is the basis of life. The present state of affairs is that wages today are higher then they were on October 23, 1956, while the value of what is produced is lower. This is not the case everywhere, but in quite a few places. The miners have done a splendid job in defending their honour. I can tell you, comrades, that what is being performed at the moment by the miners is to the credit of not only the miners themselves but to the working class as a whole. For example, the miners of Nógrád County are at present producing 82 per cent of their previous output under much worse conditions. At the same time I know of a factory in which there is no change in the total number employed, but wages are 20 to 25 per cent higher than they were, while the value of the output is as low as 34 per cent of the former production.

Under such conditions it is impossible to increase the living standard of the working class. And at this point I must tell you very openly and frankly that great attention must be paid by the unions to the issue of production, because this is the fundamental means of raising the workers' material standards.

In conclusion I want to ask my audience to represent the interests of the working class in the most effective manner possible under our present conditions. I appeal to you to lend a helping hand in strengthening workers' power, in the political struggle. This is not a party question; it is an issue associated with the regime. If you detect any counter-revolutionary villainy, do not hesitate to take action against it.

Offer help in safeguarding our material interests. Contribute to increasing the value of production so that we can have something to distribute. Everyone must do a good job in his or her own field so that we can make more rapid progress.

Address to a Meeting of Csepel Activists of the Hungarian Socialist Workers' Party

JANUARY 27, 1957

Dear Comrades,

The struggle over the past few months has in essence been waged for power. The defeated bourgeoisie fought to regain power. Essentially the struggle was about who should own the factories and the land. The bourgeoisie now rack their brains for how to damage the workers' power. Whatever form such harmful attempts assume, we must take action against them. An important precondition of this is that the workers should see things clearly and wage a united struggle to strengthen further workers' power. If every worker was thinking about how to help this country in the best way possible, if some people had not forgotten what it was like when power was in the hands of the bourgeoisie, we would be much further forward today. In fact the development and consolidation of revolutionary workers' unity is one of the most important objectives which Communists must struggle to achieve, shoulder to shoulder with former Social Democrats and all honest working people.

Grave mistakes have been committed over the past years; on many occasions the principles of socialism have been seriously violated. Even today errors occur, but they can and must be eliminated. It cannot be allowed that the workers should be taken in by the manipulations of counter-revolution; it cannot be tolerated that the enemy should exploit some of our errors and shortcomings to launch a concealed or open attack on workers' power; it is not permissible for any honest worker to turn against workers' power. On the contrary: the workers must do everything in their power to defend the achievements of workers' power.

Turning to the efforts designed to create an anti-Communist atmosphere I can state that the charges that the Communists are "Stalinists" or "Rákosiists" are today very much outworn. That is why the counter-revolution, the reactionaries, try to achieve their objectives by adopting different methods; they devise various lies and false charges in an effort to remove Communists from their positions. Naturally, armed force cannot offer any defense against methods of this kind. It is, therefore, necessary for Communists to come out firmly in opposition to all kind of lies and intrigues and to give the working people complete information.

So far as the question of religious instruction is concerned, the major capitalist countries successfully adopted optional religious instruction as early as the 18th and 19th centuries, during the bourgeois revolutions. This correct principle, however, is today translated into practice very strangely in a number of places in this country. Without asking their parents, children are compelled to opt for religious instruction by a form of spiritual terrorism. One-time monks and discredited instructors have shown up in quite a few places; and there are places too where those failing to opt for religious instruction at school are virtually persecuted. For its part the government issues and enforces the necessary decrees in order to put an end to this spiritual terrorism. However, the party organization must also help in putting things right in this field; they must take up the cudgels against the violation of the liberty of conscience. First the counter-revolution mobilized the men to fight, then it wanted to win the support of the women; today it tries to take advantage of the children, as the next best thing; we can see that some instructors in religion, including quite a few brand new ones, carry on incredibly shameful and shameless attempts to poison the souls of the children.

As regards the issue of the workers' councils: the activities of the Central Workers' Council of Csepel, which has now resigned, served the objectives of the counter-revolution and implemented the "advice" offered by Radio Free Europe, instead of serving the interests of workers' power. That is why it declared its own dissolution. Shortly before it was dissolved Elek Nagy himself, the leader of the Council, admitted during his discussions with the government that an action like its dissolution would be worse than a direct provocation. However, not long after the discussions the dissolution of the Council was declared, a move that met the demands suggested by the enemy.

The workers' councils were established during the confusion of the counter-revolution, and thus several inappropriate elements managed to work their way into them. However, the presence of such elements does not necessarily mean that the whole workers' council must be discarded. The objective is that the workers' councils should be managed for the benefit of the workers, and the benefit of the whole people, and be converted to the right way of doing this, if necessary at the expense of recalling some of their members or expelling those not fit for the job.

It goes without saying that the mere existence of the workers' councils is not a magic device which can settle all problems at one stroke; but after a proper reshaping of the councils an attempt must be made to see that they serve the interests of workers' power everywhere, and play an important role in the further development of constructive work in the right direction, in the struggle to raise living standards and to strengthen our people's democratic order. It is one of the important tasks of Communists to promote the above objectives. The workers' councils can only perform really useful and successful work if they are led by the Communists, the party of the working class. This objective, however, cannot be achieved by giving orders. Instead, the party membership must carry out devoted work to achieve this goal.

The strength of the party must be restored as soon as possible. The enemy fears the strength of the party, and the idea of this strength being restored completely in the shortest possible time. Every worker, every workers' council member who wants to work and is working for the cause of the working class must be made aware of the fact that the party's strength is a decisive factor in consolidating workers' power and national prosperity. Ideological struggle is also necessary if the whole working class is to understand this issue. The battle of ideas must also be fought out because it is now coming very much into the forefront in the wake of the armed struggle.

The working class and their allies, the working peasantry, constitute the principal base on which the party and government rely.

The party is the leading force, the general staff in the struggle for power. Without the party, the working class cannot come to power nor can they retain it. Evidence of this is the series of events that took place on October 23. What lies behind these events is that there was treachery inside the party, so the party did not have the strength to intervene in the drift of events; this made it possible for a series of counter-revolutionary actions to take place which constituted a deadly threat to people's democracy.

Regarding some of the problems related to the party, several people have complained that the party's programme and rules have not yet been drawn up. In fact to prepare them is an urgent task. But even at this stage two points, two fundamental issues of our programme, are quite clear: one is the complete building of a socialist society and the other is crushing the counter-revolution while strengthening our power. Everyone can see these objectives quite clearly before the programme is worked out in detail.

The question may well arise whether or not the HSWP will be a mass party. The reply to this question will be given by the iron laws governing life; but even if the HSWP is not going to be such a mass party as the HWPP was, it is certain that it will be a strong, unified party defending the people's interests.

The party must take care that the purity of Marxist–Leninist ideas are maintained. In the ideological confusion brought about by the recent events, it was often emphasized that the leading force of the nation must be the intellectuals or the youth, and not the working class. Views of this kind must be discarded. The working class is the leading force which exercises power in close alliance with the working peasantry. As for progressive intellectuals, they support the working class and the workers' and peasants' alliance.

Let me comment on the issue of the party's political line.

We must firmly dissociate ourselves from the Rákosi-type sectarian policies, and no less from the policies of the group led by Imre Nagy and Losonczy[3] which betray the working class.

Care must be taken that a uniform line predominate in the ranks of our party: there should never be a double line disrupting our ranks. We must constitute a unified force in the struggle being waged against counter-revolution. By taking advantage of the justified dissatisfaction of the masses, the counter-revolution went into action with the aim of overthrowing people's democracy. This struggle which is being waged even at the present moment was launched by counter-revolution and so it must be opposed by the firm weapon of revolution without which socialist consolidation is out of the question.

The people who have been misled will be given adequate information to open their eyes, but those who resort to weapons against people's power will find that the arms will be struck from their hands, and those who hatch plots against our state will find themselves up against the weapon of the dictatorship of the proletariat.

Speaking about the prospects, it must be said that many people tend to be pessimistic today because unemployment has appeared and because we grapple with economic difficulties. This pessimism, however, is not justified. But it is up to us to eliminate the difficulties and bring our problems under control within the shortest possible time. To this end unity in decision and the united strength of the Communists are necessary. Our party's developing strength – the membership stands at 150,000 today—constitutes a major force, a mass force. Conscious of their conviction, Communists must carry on with their struggle without fear. The wrongs must be put right and this needs the joining of forces. If every working person is determined to defend workers' power at his own post, the day of final and complete victory will come earlier.

Closing Speech at the May 1957 Session of Parliament

MAY 11, 1957

Honoured Parliament, Comrades,

I think that everybody who has followed the debate in Parliament with attention will agree with me that the current session of Parliament bears the marks of some new, healthy features in our public life. This debate, the discussion and the contributions made to the report, or following the report, were not formalities; the speakers spoke about essentials. Words have regained their meaning.

I have not forgotten the statement some writers made about ten months ago, when they lamented the fact that words have lost their meaning. I am of the opinion that the writers, even those whom we rightly rebuke or reprimand, were right in some matters; and if we think back over the past years, we must admit that a lot of words have lost their meaning through having become dissociated from the content and essence of what they refer to.

But if there is anything that can be said to characterize the Hungary of today then it is that words have regained their meaning.

Very many of us have been actively taking part in social life for many years. Often it happened that at gatherings, meetings, or some form of study, we talked about the dictatorship of the proletariat, and talked about the fierce hatred felt by the bourgeoisie because they had lost power. However, during those years, those words were separated from their content, they were separated from their essence. We often talked about the dictatorship of the proletariat, but we did not think of what it meant.

In the stormy, bloody days of October, however, the whole nation learned what people's power was, and we also learned what the revenge of the former exploiting classes thirsting for vengeance meant. And the same applies to other words as well.

The discussion here is also characterized by human closeness. I believe that here in Parliament there is nobody who can, for some momentous reason, think more of himself than of the others. There is nobody among us whom we can look at with wonder.

Maybe this is a problem, but I think it is also useful, because we have reached a close human relationship; we realize what the other is right about, we also notice his faults, and I think that, luckily for our system, we also dare to tell him of them. And only in this way can collective wisdom assert itself, and to some extent already does assert itself; it is the kind of thing that we Communists interpret in our party as hundreds of thousands of party members together constituting the wisdom of the working class. This is how that popular wisdom asserts itself, which — I repeat — is rightly represented by this Parliament, if we have the courage to hear the voice of the people, take that voice into consideration, and express it in words!

During this discussion, very many intelligent, practical remarks have been made — even if not in the form of sharp words — almost as criticism. When the miner who is Member of Parliament for Veszprém County said, for example that it is wrong that a very considerable part of the eight working hours gets lost as far as the national economy is concerned, this can be taken as criticism, because the managers could also have noticed this already since, as the speaker said, they were expected to take measures to remedy it. A comment of this type was also made when our friend Z. Nagy[4] noted that relatively little had been said in the report about agriculture. Our Minister of Finance did not discuss agriculture in more detail either, and the new Minister of Finance can take this as the first criticism of him as well, and what is more, as a justified criticism.

Another question also raised by our friend Z. Nagy was that it would be good if the agricultural cooperative movement and the rural consumers' cooperative movement did not represent completely different lines and did not develop completely separately, independent of each other. This was not the first time this observation has been made, and the time will come when we shall have to devote a lot of attention to it.

The main problem with our rural consumers' cooperatives was that they did not function as cooperatives in the true sense of the word. These cooperatives could better be called secondary government stores, for the spirit of the cooperative movement was not to be found in them. Let us not dwell any longer on whose fault this was, but change is needed, that is certain.

To the great satisfaction of us all, the system of compulsory deliveries has been abolished, and we will not restore it. Naturally, this presents a new problem. I remember a peasant worker, I cannot recall where, who went to a district council in Transdanubia and asked whether compulsory deliveries really had been abolished, and it took half an hour to explain to him that they had indeed been abolished. He then said: "Well, isn't there some document you can show me?" The man had the official document on hand and showed it to him. The peasant was satisfied, and moved towards the door, but then he came back and said: "Well, this is all right, now I understand that compulsory deliveries have been abolished, and I am satisfied. But would you tell me now how the townspeople will get their bread?"

And there is a series of similar questions. When the rural consumers' cooperatives become capable of fulfilling their real, vital function of helping the peasantry solve its marketing problems and helping to supply the peasantry, then will they be genuine cooperatives, will fulfill their specific function, and will even promote the socialist transformation of the village. What sort of cooperative is it, what kind of cooperative movement can we talk about if it makes absolutely no difference to the village population whether they have a government store or a cooperative, so thoroughly identical are the functions they fulfill! A cooperative of that sort is no true cooperative, and our friend Z. Nagy is quite right when he brings it up.

Sensible comments have been made on many other, similar specific questions, and the task is for the respective competent ministers to note them well and deal with them.

Nevertheless, the most important thing about the debate is that there is an agreement on the main questions.

Parliament — unequivocally, with an absolute majority — sharply condemns the counter-revolutionary uprising in October as an attempt to restore the regime of capitalists and landed estates and the Fascist state. This has become absolutely clear from the contributions, and from the responses to the contributions. It has also become clear that the overwhelming majority of the Members of Parliament are supporters of people's democratic power and of the people's democratic state, and I mean this in the sense of the inner content of these terms — that this state must ensure the building of a socialist society, and in the last analysis, the complete building of socialism.

There is also agreement concerning our foreign policy. Our foreign policy, rightly, is anti-imperialist, it relies on the international forces of socialism and peace. It is aimed at strengthening the unity of the countries of the socialist community, and within this, Soviet–Hungarian friendship which is of special importance from the point of view of our nation and country. The majority in Parliament — as can be seen — also agrees with this.

Respecting this there is also agreement that, although we are not supporters of the policy of military blocs, we regard the Warsaw Treaty as a justified organization of self-defense for the forces of socialism and peace. We are supporters of the Warsaw Treaty Organization, therefore we are also supporters of the stationing of Soviet troops in Hungary as long as we are confronted by aggressive imperialist endeavours, by the aspirations of the forces of imperialism.

There is also agreement on another aspect of foreign policy: we are dedicated to peaceful coexistence. As far as we are concerned, this is no empty phrase. It is in our interest to establish and maintain normal inter-state relations with all countries whatever social system they have.

Take the United States. The United States, which really is a world power and has great strength, can dispose of Hungary with a wave of hand, because — think the leaders of the United States — what is Hungary, what does she signify in the world? They are profoundly wrong, because she does signify. Through money, machinations and putsches — which they are stirring up and trying to impose in Jordan now, and which they also tried to do in Hungary — imperialism can achieve temporary successes. However, with all this they are only preparing for their own complete defeat on a world scale, because nowadays not only the so-called Communist states are opposed to these imperialistic endeavours, but so are all those states and nations who wish to live in freedom and independence. There is no need to substantiate in detail that government circles in the Hungarian People's Republic are not engaged in upsetting, let us say, for example, the social system in Austria. I do not think that it is even necessary to raise this question. However, upsetting the internal social system of the Hungarian People' Republic is included among the objectives of government circles in certain countries, for example the United States; this is equally clear to everybody. Therefore, when we say that we are supporters of peaceful coexistence, then in our case words and deeds correspond to each other. The American imperialists, and even more so their publicists, also speak of peaceful coexistence and present themselves as supporters of peace. However, in their case words and deeds are diametrically opposed on this question.

From the point of view of peace and quiet and the life of our people, from the point of view of our development, it is a very important and good thing that there is complete unity in the country's principal legislative body on these main basic questions. I am also convinced that this complete unity is an expression of the views, intentions and wishes of not only the 298 MPs present here, but also of the vast majority of the Hungarian people who agree on these basic questions as well.

The agreement which has been evident over these main questions logically and naturally leads to the conclusion that the absolute majority of Parliament sharply condemns the policy of the Imre Nagy government which in all these questions, in the final analysis, betrayed the power of the working class and socialism, betrayed the nation and the cause of national independence.

We have heard very many sharp, critical statements in the debate about the policy of the Imre Nagy government, and I tell you honestly that the criticism and opinions voiced here are only variants, somewhat refined by the parliamentary atmosphere, of the sharp and harsh judgement which we meet with when the working people gather together in their masses! And they are quite right.

Agreement on the main questions logically leads to the approving realization that – and the MPs have expressed this in their contributions – in the given situation at the time, it was inevitable and legitimate to create a new leading body which advocates the cause of the people and safeguards the basic interests of the people.

Therefore, if I have understood the debate correctly, and it is difficult to misunderstand it, Parliament endorses the establishment of the Revolutionary Workers' and Peasants' Government and the main line it has been following so far. And I tell you at once that Parliament has given the government the moral and political support which is absolutely necessary if it is to continue the work successfully. And I thank this Honoured Parliament for this.

The debate has reflected agreement on the main questions, but it has also revealed differences of views on certain issues. In my opinion, it is useful and good that this has been revealed by the debate. I tell you honestly that if such a feature is already a healthy concomitant of our current domestic political development, then this will increasingly be the case later. There is something festive in our present gathering, and this is good, because Parliament has just drawn up the balance of a historic turning point. However, existing differences of views on certain particular questions must also increasingly come out in the course of everyday work. Why do I say this?

I welcome the manner in which our fellow MP Beresztóczy[5] started his contribution, his emphasizing the points on which there is no agreement. Why is this good? Because undoubtedly, there are differences in our views.

The overwhelming majority of the MPs are not separated by different ideological views of the type our fellow MP Beresztóczy—in my view, correctly—emphasized for his own part. However, everybody who knows anything about life is aware that different views on certain questions do exist. There are differences of view between Communists and non-Communists, and there can also be differences between Communists. Between thinking people, there are slight, smaller or bigger differences of views. And there is nothing wrong about this. It is only wrong if we are silent about them. I think that what, let us say, we Communists understand on the Central Committee of our party, or for that matter, what is understood at a meeting of the leadership of the Patriotic People's Front, or any other body fulfilling some sort of social function, also applies to Parliament in a certain sense.

With this, I do not want to offer Parliament the Leninist principle of democratic centralism, but that really is the way things are. What is the correct way to proceed? If life puts a question on the agenda, let us discuss it and then decide on it. However, if we reach a decision, then we should implement that decision and defend it together, honestly. I do not think that this means the introduction of some sort of a Communist reign of terror; on the contrary: we would like it if we debated a question in due time, decided on it in due time and started in due time to implement the decision with joint forces.

Or let us put it another way. Parliament is meeting in the limelight of the utmost publicity; through the radio and press the public knows of our discussions, nevertheless the question does arise which is better: if here we debate a little on certain issues on which there is no agreement, or where we have not established a stand on them, but outside Parliament we jointly support the resolution adopted; or that while we sit here everybody seems to agree on everything but as soon as we leave Parliament everybody begins to explain things differently and represent a different stand?

I think it promotes the cause of the people if, when we work out a decision here, we express our opinion, but when a decision is made, each MP regards it as his moral obligation to represent it honestly in life, in his everyday work, in the area of his own profession.

As our fellow MP Beresztóczy has raised the issue, he should not take it amiss if I draw a parallel. I was Secretary of the Communist Party in the 13th district not long ago and we talked about the experiences of the past years. I told him that there were times when the bane of the party's life was that we conducted ourselves at the party meetings as if we were attending a bad Catholic church service. We managed to assemble somehow, and a high priest sort of person stood up, and said what he was supposed to say; the rest listened to him with devout attention, and then went home. In these 'sermons', to stay with the metaphor, there were things like don't steal, don't be a scoundrel, don't be a careerist; instead, work decently, respect the people, respect your parents, and so on. To this, everyone said Amen. And then, when they dispersed, a significant number of the participants set about doing all kinds of nasty and wicked things, quite the opposite of what had just been talked about. But then, to get rid even of our pangs of conscience, we Communists, too, had our own confession: it was called self-criticism. There were people who called themselves Communists and thought they could carry on like a bad Catholic who behaves like a scoundrel all year long and then goes off to church at Easter tide, confesses his sins, and then, reborn and reassured, goes out in the street; and on the Tuesday after Easter, starts the whole thing all over again.

There are people who sit among the Communists, call themselves Communists, and think that behaviour of this kind is conceivable and can be reconciled with a genuine Communist attitude. People of this type listen to the correct instructions and say that it is all right, but afterwards they work by easy stages and incorrectly for one or two years, and when the responsible leaders bring them to task, they exercise self-criticism nicely, become transfigured, and two days later, they continue with their mistakes where they left off. This cannot be so. This cannot be so, and it has to be changed.

Our fellow MP Beresztóczy started out by emphasizing where he disagreed with us. This outspokenness can be applauded, because in this way it is at least clear, for example, on what questions and to what extent Parliament can rely on our fellow MP Beresztóczy. Now, for example, I as a party official, for I am that also as a result of my plurality of offices, know that I cannot rely on my fellow MP Beresztóczy to convert devout Catholics to convinced Communists.

Our fellow MP János Péter[6] said that they had been there in the countryside during the difficult days and had waited for word about what to do, and the word had not come. A similar question was raised by Comrade Ilku[7], Comrade Csikesz[8] and others as well. What is the essence of the matter in this case? I think we owe it to the Hungarian working class, to the Hungarian working people, and to the honour of the Hungarian Communists, soldiers and policemen to say: the reasons behind the uncertainty and inability evident during the events of October on the part of the masses and certain bodies of the army, on the part of the Communists and the police should not be sought in the masses. That much we owe to the honour of our own people, because when we say that the Hungarian people defended the cause of socialism, it is gospel truth, Comrades. Because every sort of historical merit has been mentioned here, it has to be said that the historical merit belongs to the Hungarian working class—and perhaps not even our working peasant-brothers will get angry with us over this—who since the autumn of 1918 have been fighting for people's power, have shed much blood in the struggle, but have never relinquished their goal. And it was not by chance or accident that the Hungarian people, tormented by an especially villainous form of capitalism and exceptionally strong remnants of feudalism, was the first in the world, after the peoples of Russia who suffered under similar oppression, to win the power for the working people. In my opinion, this is one of the most important historical facts which the Hungarian nation can be truly proud of!

Unfortunately, I cannot discuss in detail the personal experiences of the days of October, but I should like to say something about this as well. If I view the leadership —and here I have to take the party and the country leadership as one— then I have to tell you the following. The leadership of the time can basically be divided into two groups. One was the group that in July resolved that we would correct the mistake, and I am convinced that had we been able to pursue the July line, even if not without internal debates, differences of views, difficulties and dissension, then within a year, and without great harm and sacrifices, we could have eliminated the mistakes. This is an important question. One half of the leadership was led by this endeavour and determination.

In all honesty I have to tell you that this part of the leadership was in a state of serious confusion during those grave days. Speaking on my own behalf, I can tell you that it was not easy to understand what was happening in the drift of the events. And it was even more difficult to foresee the next step, what should be done. So it was difficult to realize what was happening and it was difficult to see what to do. Therefore, there was uncertainty on the part of the better and honest part of the leadership.

At the same time, the leadership included another part, and here I have to speak of the Imre Nagy group, which we did not fully know about at the time. This also has to be said, because I cannot deny that I voted for Imre Nagy to become the Prime Minister. And I shall never deny it, because I did it in the conviction and belief that despite all his faults Imre Nagy was still an honest man, that he still stood on the side of the working class. Later it turned out that this was not true!

What was the case with this leadership? This part of the leadership was not in the same situation as the other part, which did not know exactly what was happening. Imre Nagy and his supporters did know, because in part they themselves were behind it. Therefore, they had no difficulty in knowing what was going on. Consequently, they also knew what they wanted, and they were able to compel, through every sort of pressure, the other part of the leadership to go along with them for a while in that uncertain situation.

This is how we arrived at a situation, which was the disgrace of the leadership and not the disgrace of the people: to the thousands upon thousands of people in all parts of the country who waited for instruction, guidance and direction from the centre, who demanded weapons and who saw what should be done better than we who were in the leadership, to them we could not honestly give the guidance which a leadership in that kind of situation should.

This is how we came to see the drift of events when we realized that it was no longer possible to go further along the way we were going. And I was also certain, although the situation looked different at the time, that the vast masses of the Hungarian people would understand that we had to make a break and we had to take the road of open struggle. I believe that the prestige of the leadership consists not in concealing all this, but in honestly talking about it.

I could not deal in detail in my report with that aspect of the October events which threatened peace, the peace of mankind. Several of the speakers referred to this. That danger was enormous, and there were even two variants of that danger. One variant was the following. The counter-revolution, the face of which has become adequately evident during this debate as well, was an imperialist and chauvinist counter-revolution imbued with a desire for revenge — as everybody knows. Everybody knows Hungary's historical situation too. Hungary has five neighbouring states.

There is not one among the five which does not possess territory which once in the course of history, for shorter or longer periods, very long or not so long ago, belonged to Hungary. This is a historical fact. We follow the right path when we reject nationalistic revanchist ideas; and on this question we return to the ideas of Kossuth, as all our endeavours, in the spirit of socialist thinking, are aimed at implementing the principle of peaceful, fraternal coexistence and of joint struggle along with the peoples of the Danube Basin. And we are right in doing so, because this is in the interest of the Hungarian people. However, those gentlemen cared little about the interests of the Hungarian people, and I declare that had they once got power in their hands — one does not have to say much, possibly just if they had had the possibility to strengthen the elements of their power, let us say for two or three weeks — Europe would have been in flames along three borders of the country. This is obvious even to the blind and to fools.

There is another variant as well. There are comrades of mine — I know their views — for whom evaluation of the person of Attila Szigeti[9] represents a very serious problem of conscience. They knew him — I do not know since when — at a time when he worked in a positive way. Well, even if Attila Szigeti did not personally give the order for those 34 democrats to be shot dead on the Main Square of Győr, or for them to be burnt, there was a very serious affair involving the rival government in Transdanubia. It was meant to be not an episode in some puppet-show, but a bloody historical reality. The basic idea behind the counter-government in Transdanubia was to turn Hungary into a second Korea. Not in the form of a North and South Hungary, but in the form of a West and East Hungary, and imperialism sought to create a new seat of war here in the heart of Europe. In the course of history, nobody has been able to start a local war in the heart of Europe: it always turned to a world war; therefore our fellow MP János Péter is fully justified in warning that this aspect of the events must also be emphasized.

The question of the Patriotic People's Front has been raised. I cannot give a programme, or define the organizational form for the Patriotic People's Front here and now. However, I can refer to historical antecedents. The germ of the Patriotic People's Front was born sometime during the Second World War in the form of the Hungarian Historical Commemorative Committee, the Hungarian Front and other organizations of similar designation. It later became the Hungarian National Independence Front, and the Patriotic People's Front is its direct continuation historically. At the time it was born, it had a living content; there was no need to seek for such a content, because it was born in the spirit of national unity, and at that time too, at the initiative of the Communists. I say this not out of party pride, but for the sake of historical truth. There are many — Darvas[10] and others — who took part in it.

I think that while we are sighing here that the masses are waiting for the Patriotic People's Front to become a reality, the masses are already somewhat ahead of us. Because in reality, what has taken place before our very eyes since November 4, the increasing activity in public and political life, in fact already means that the masses are ahead of us, and that the outlines, the germ of the Patriotic People's Front, whose content in my view is life itself, have already come into being over the past six months.

Look, there was May Day; or there were the four rallies organized under the aegis of the Communist party and the Revolutionary Workers' and Peasants' Government! It is well known that there are still sharp polemics among our people. Let us not deceive ourselves! If there are seven million adults in Hungary, seven million of them do not say "Long live the Hungarian Socialist Workers' Party and long live the Revolutionary Workers' and Peasants' Government!" There is also opposition to this Government in the country. We should not deceive ourselves! About eighty, one hundred, one hundred and forty thousand people gathered at the invitation of the Party and the Revolutionary Workers' and Peasants' Government at the four rallies in Budapest. Nobody counted how many people were out at the Budapest rally on May Day, but I think we do not say too much if we reckon that there were certainly two hundred thousand. It is beyond doubt that throughout the whole of the country, six to eight hundred thousand people gathered. You should compare the figures! The Hungarian Socialist Workers' Party, let us say, has three hundred thousand members in the country, and correspondingly less in Budapest. At the rallies called by the Party, three, four, five times as many people as the number of party members appeared. What sort of people are they? They are non-Communist, honest workers, peasants and intellectuals who agree on the main questions – and in my view, this is the content of the Patriotic People's Front today – agree in condemning of the counter-revolution, the defense of the People's Republic, and the building of socialism.

Our task, and maybe a special task of Comrade Apró, because at this time he is the passive President of the Patriotic People's Front, is to channel this healthy stream, which in my opinion has already found its source in the people, into a suitable and sensible form in the interest of the Patriotic People's Front, and in this way to increase its strength as well. This is our task.

Here I wish to mention that Z. Nagy is indeed right when he says that the building of socialism is not a party question, it is not only a question for the Communists. This stands to reason. I do not intend to get involved in party questions too much, but I should like to say this much: let there be no mistake about it: we Communists have always known that the party is not an end in itself.

The party does not exist for its own sake, the function of the party is to fight – with the guidance of the scientific world outlook of the working class – for the interests of the working masses, to lead, unite and organize the popular forces. This is the reason for the existence of the party. We do not agree that the party is destined to serve its own ends.

Other questions have also been raised. Comrade Gáspár discussed the reasons behind a certain discontent felt by the workers. For example, they could not have a say in factory affairs in a way that would also have benefited the cause. There was dissatisfaction concerning other questions, living standards and similar issues.

I should like to deal here with another issue: the relationship between the leaders and the masses. I believe that the leadership can perform their duty only if they never disregard the thinking and will of the masses.

What is needed for this? First, they must be there among the masses, to ask the people what they are concerned about, and to answer their questions. Otherwise, we do not even know what the masses want.

One cannot hide from the questions of the masses. There are always questions which occupy the masses, which they expect to be answered, and they have to get an answer from somebody. If we do not answer, the enemy does and in line with their own interests. Therefore, the leadership must be there among the masses. One should not be afraid of them, or of their questions! If our standpoint is correct, we can always safely tell it to the masses.

I would also add, that in my opinion, the task of the leadership is not to realize the desire and will of the masses. I say this, however strange it may sound. In my opinion, the task of the leadership is to realize the interests of the masses. Why do I make this distinction? In the recent past, we witnessed the phenomenon that certain categories of workers acted against their own interests on quite important questions. What is the task of the leadership in this case? Should they mechanically implement ideas which are not correct? This is not the task of the leadership. The task of the leadership is to represent the interests of the masses.

The opinion and desire of the masses should always be known and taken into consideration. These usually coincide with progress, but if they do not, then the masses have to be educated in this direction. This is also a task of leadership. It involves among other things that anyone who asserts the right to be esteemed as a leader – and there is no qualitative difference between a village and a national leader, because it is an honour and dignity to be a leader in a village as well – must also always have the courage to say what is in the interest of the masses. This applies whether it is met with applause, or whether at first it is received with disapproval! In my opinion, the masses will give ten times more esteem to a leader, and a leadership in general, which also has the courage to say if the masses are not right on some question, than to one which wants to gain esteem by courting the masses and through demagogy. Because, they will later understand that the standpoint of the courageous leader was correct, and will therefore esteem him, whereas later people will not regard the demagogic leader as a leader. It is possible to achieve momentary success. However a leadership will only have prestige if they always answer the questions of the masses, and always in accordance with their interests and not from some momentary mood. This leadership will be the best, because they become inseparable from the masses.

On the question of youth: what took place among the Hungarian young people in the course of the October events is a lesson to the young people themselves, but it was an even greater lesson to the adults, a much, much greater lesson. What is it that the adults ought to have learned? The following: young people are always inclined to idealize, they seek ideals, at times individuals whom they can look up to as paragons. This is a natural law which we cannot change. But to prevent anyone's taking advantage of it, it is very important that nobody should be made an idol in the eyes of young people, and that no idealistic picture of the realities of life should be drawn. For let's not forget: those young people who were supporters of people's democracy and the idea of socialism more on emotional than on rational grounds found that there was a contradiction. Socialism, as it is usually described, is a very fine thing; but we have never let it be known that we do not yet have a society of this type; it is only now being born amidst torments, struggles, problems and difficulties, in the same way that any other new world is born. If we told our young people that we already had socialism, then we did not tell the truth. And when we speak about given individuals, we have to be equally careful, because it is a terrible blow to young people when they find themselves disillusioned like that, and indeed they did find themselves in such a situation. They suffered such disillusionment because they based their beliefs not so much on rational as on emotional grounds. For this reason, they were greatly shaken. This is a lesson for the future. We should always be sparing of grand words and superlatives. I think we should be very frugal in our use of them. Let's take a very good look before we say that something or someone is 'the most', for we shall be called to account if it turns out that even the positive or comparative form of that adjective is inappropriate. This is a very important lesson.

However, in my view, there is no reason for despair. Because, I remember that during the world of Horthy — and you should forgive me for this thought, but I regard it as important — I was already a young Communist worker in 1932 when there was a certain trial of Communists at the Eötvös College. The press of the time gave broad coverage to it, and — again I do not mean it as an allusion to the Catholic Church, — but *Nemzeti Újság*[11] and *Új Nemzedék*[12] carried editorials of the kind that could almost bring one to tears. They wrote that the Eötvös College trial was a proof that the youth of the ruling class had gone over to the working class. What was the point of interest in the trial? A Communist youth organization was unveiled, with some forty-odd people involved, and those arrested included two or three of the children of the wealthiest landlords in the country, the children of industrialists, the child of the deputy head of the Budapest city police, as well as the child of his "vitéz" (title awarded to servicemen during the Horthy regime — The Editor) cousin, and *Új Nemzedék* and *Nemzeti Újság* were justified in writing in a tone of despair that "the Communists have captured our own youth".

I believe that what happened in 1932 was logical. It is the path of human progress that the rising working classes win over those children of the ruling class who tend towards the good. This is normal. The abnormal is what we witnessed recently — that counter-revolution and Fascism could win over the most vacillating of the children of the workers.

By what sort of ideas? There are people sitting here who know those ideas. Can it be tolerated or allowed that ideas of homicide, exploitation and the plunder of national independence should rally under their banner even five Hungarian children of worker or peasant origin? This is not normal. We have to draw the necessary lesson so that this will never happen again. Only then will we have a right to tell young people that they also have to draw a lesson for themselves.

There is another question here, ideological in character, which we also have to deal with. Our fellow MP Parragi[13] made the following demand: the government should display tolerance and humanity, and we should show that the barriers are not closed either within the country or at the border for those who wish to return. In my view, this is a correct demand, a right demand, but it needs a certain amount of amplification. In my opinion, all this is also required in dealing with those who are guilty. And we have gone a long way in this respect.

Special mention should be made of this when we fight against mistakes; we should really fight against mistakes and not against people. Why is this important? We want people advocating mistaken views to relinquish their mistakes, but if we link them for ever with their mistakes and hit them continuously, non-stop, and label them as wrong-thinking people so that the label sticks to them till their death – this does not ensure a healthy solution of the problem.

Let us fight against mistakes without any apology. We hit the mistake very hard, and with the mistake we also hit the man who makes it, but if he relinquishes his mistake, then he can find the right path himself. Tolerance and humanity, unfortunately, have to be complemented with severity towards criminals. And I tell you honestly that if we think about it, it is not true that those one hundred and seventy thousand or however many people who left the country in their first madness are enemies of the Hungarian people. It is not true, and quite a few of them have already returned. That it means a sacrifice on the part of the nation, that is absolutely true, however.

The same applies to the dead. I am very sorry for those who died on the other side of the front, because they'd been deceived. Therefore, we have to be severe with the criminals, because nothing is more precious for us than the life of the people. There is concern over this, too. There are also comrades sitting here with whom I have recently had talks, who are worried about what will happen to legality. Since we are always advocating "the dictatorship of the proletariat" and speaking about "punishment" and so on, will not the question of legality again be a problem?

I do not think that it will. Why not? For the following reason: because if it happened in the past – and unfortunately, it did happen – that somebody was pointed at as guilty, then the task was to prove that he was a guilty man. This was a bad point of departure, and it also meant that some crime was invented which the person involved had never committed. What is the situation now? Is there need to do any such thing? Do we have to look around and say "I have not seen an enemy around here for three weeks now!" In this respect, we are not so badly off! There are enough real criminal acts against the people which undoubtedly have to be examined and certainly punished in the most severe manner.

To avoid making mistakes, two things are required. First, we should take up and examine the facts, and then we find the man who is responsible. Second, I say that the crime has to be punished, and not the man. The two often go together, but it also has to be said that if somebody did not commit a capital crime, he will have to find his way back to life sometime. Crime has to be severely punished, and if somebody commits a capital crime then he has to receive a punishment which goes with capital crime. Why should crime be prosecuted? In order to deter others who have not yet committed crimes against the people. And in this way I believe tolerance and humanity can also be observed, alongside the obligatory defense of the life of the people, because that cannot be given up. Because if the instigator is not arrested and punished, then that is a crime against the thirty young people whom he will tomorrow and next week incite against their own interests and their own people.

On economic questions: we cannot go into the details. There is already the need to work, and Parliament will then have to debate the annual plan, because this will also serve as a guideline for later work. It is correct that in addition to industry, we also deal with agriculture and other questions. However, here I would like to mention the following:

We have been compelled to take measures which are not pleasant: the authorities have had to increase the price of certain goods. Now things are as follows: we have got into a certain situation. However, we also have to say how we got into it. Some of the measures involved legalize the living standards achieved, and some mean that we have decided on a certain standard of living. There were workers' commissions and I do not know what other sort of organizations at the time when there was no central control. They took a cheque, went to the National Bank, encashed it and paid for whatever occurred to them. Well, part of this had to be legalized; we had no other alternative, and possibly it would not have been correct to do otherwise. The government also decided on wage increases and the abolition of compulsory deliveries, and this accounted for a certain increase of the living standards. Now, price increases are naturally bitter medicine, and certainly it also sours the wine if the price of it goes up. At the time when people came to us with various wage demands, we argued with them. And I tell you that there were also people in the trade unions, the first to recover strength, who proposed wage increases — which were already publicised in the papers before we even sat down to talk — which made the hair of anybody who had any understanding of finance stand on end. Everybody wanted to be a good boy. I argued with the Comrades and told them that this was not a good division of labour. I talked to trade union leaders, who came with proposals for wage increases. They were the good people and we, the government, were the bad people who said no to their proposals. I talked to journalists. They argued that we should guarantee more freedom and allow criticism. I told them: this was not a good division of labour. What sort of situation is it when the only task of the government is to make mistakes, and the task of the journalists is to write about them? I do not wish to settle for this for life. It has to be assumed that the government can sometimes do something good, and the journalists can sometimes make mistakes — so that we should work with an equal division of labour, because otherwise I would immediately switch and go over to the trade unions. I also can make demands that no Prime Minister would say well and good to. Or, if I were a journalist, I, too, could single out mistakes which would be difficult to explain. So that this is not a division of labour.

Well, what is all this about? We told people: listen, this strike complete with all comforts, is a carnival which will have to be paid for. They came to us and said "We will not work" — not representatives of genuine workers, but those who were in a position to take a stand of this kind; "We will not work until this is fulfilled, until that is fulfilled." We told them: people, we are not shareholders in a mining company, or industrialists. If you speak on behalf of honest workers, then it concerns your own affairs. You take revenge not on us, but on yourselves if you do not work for two or three weeks. It was a difficult period, and now it has its consequences.

Now, we have had to draw up a balance. And the result was that we had to make a choice. Should we take back the wages? It is not correct to reduce the living standards of people living on wages. Something has to be done. Is it our duty to establish a balance between the wages, the incomes and the stocks of commodities?

Certainly, it is our duty! However, are we obliged to sell our industrial goods, and sometimes the wine, at the expense of the public, at a price which means that with every litre of wine we also give five Forints as a present from the nation to the person who drinks it? Or is it permissible that in the case of some goods, the buyer puts his money down on the table, but the effect is the same as if he was given an additional 180 Forints at the cash desk, because he was kind enough to buy them? This cannot be so!

It also has to be said that increasing prices is not a trend in our economic policy, but now we have to restore order, and this involves the same sort of measures in economic life as we were compelled to introduce in political life. And economic life will also return to normal! The question has to be looked at in this way. I know that there would be louder cheering if I said "We shall increase wages by another 10 per cent here or there", or if we reduced the price of some goods by 30 per cent. However, our duty is to ensure the stability and balance of the national economy, and in this way to safeguard living standards. This is why we had to take measures of this kind.

In conclusion: as I see it, there is confidence in the goverment, and I tell you honestly that it is very good to see this confidence, and it is needed. I should also like to tell you how we feel about our own assignment, at least I would like to tell you about it on my own behalf. I believe that the others also feel the same about it.

We, Comrades, before becoming members of the Government, also lived and — at least, I so believe — all my colleagues feel the same way about it: our personal demand from life is to live in the manner of an honest Communist and an honest person.

We do not have any other special ambitions, at least as far as I am concerned. There were years when I had had enough of glory as well, and at the time I resigned from posts which were by no means low because I became convinced that I did not need them. However, now we feel that duty has placed us here. I tell you, although it is perhaps not good to joke about a serious matter of this kind, but I imagine it somehow, that around November 1 six million Hungarian adults could have been legitimate claimants for the post of Prime Minister. Because the task in question was to take a stand, and take things in hand, and I tell you honestly — I don't think anybody questions it — that the situation in which a government had to be formed, and work had to be started, was anything but enviable. And I tell you that at the time I could not see keen competition for ministerial posts either.

Still, we have honest, well-intentioned friends and supporters who stand a little to one side as far as we are concerned. They approve of what we are doing, but they will wait a little longer, until we wash the linen even cleaner, and they will appear on the scene of the battle when the day of eternal peace arrives.

There are people of this kind. We are not angry with them. We are convinced that they will help, if they still have a conscience and loyalty to the people. We do not urge them on, because we are glad to see that, since the government came into existence, and has been fighting and working, every day more and more people have come to support it. For us, there is no greater reward for work, and we would like to meet this confidence with honour. Because confidence, Comrades, is so great a thing that it scares you occasionally. So is affection, at least to men of conscience. For affection and — I dare say — also gratitude and confidence if taken seriously, impose so great a responsibility upon a man that it is not so easy to be equal to it, especially under the difficult circumstances in which we are working.

Therefore, I thank you for the confidence you have expressed. I ask you to accept my report and support our government in the struggle and work which has to be done.

Reply to the Discussion at the National Conference of the Hungarian Socialist Workers' Party (Abbreviated)

JUNE 29, 1957

Delegates to the Party Conference, Comrades,

The Executive Committee and the Central Committee decided, when organizing this Conference, that the radio should not broadcast what was said here, and that the full proceedings should not be published by the press, so that we might discuss the party's present most important problems in a completely informal manner. We wanted the Conference to be really a working conference and devoid of all formality, and therefore we did not even invite delegates from fraternal parties. We wanted to finalize a whole series of controversial issues in order to establish a clear situation in the party, so that afterwards we could engage in the work of construction with assurance. In my opinion the debates which have taken place at the Conference confirm the correctness of our decision, because we have indeed spoken openly and frankly about the various problems.

Our Conference has received numerous greetings, and I propose that the Party Conference should publish its gratitude for these warm greetings in the press.

We have, however, also received some criticism, and many people thought it wrong that so very little about the Conference appeared in the press. These comrades are right, and we must be sure that we place the material of the Conference at the disposal of the party membership in some suitable form, possibly in a pamphlet. We have been talking about a good many questions which it will be worthwhile to discuss in the future; in fact it is possible that one or two topics will be included in the autumn educational material as well.

In addition to this, it is also necessary that a series of meetings of activists should follow the Conference, at which the delegates will outline the more important questions debated. At the activists' meetings they should strive to reflect the atmosphere of the Party Conference and also the impressions they got here. Following this, they should discuss the material of the Conference at party membership meetings.

I believe we may conclude without exaggeration that the atmosphere of the Party Conference has been good, that there was an open discussion on principles, and that the delegates were active. Among the results of the Conference we may list that it was completely united on the necessity for further struggle against the counter-revolution. And this is of decisive importance from the point of view of the party.

We cannot, however, remain silent about the fact that there is a difference of opinion in our party over the evaluation of the past. Comrade Révai's standpoint diverged slightly, but on essential matters, from that of other speakers and contributors. Although here at the Conference only Comrade Révai had a divergent opinion on this question, it was not by accident that I said that there is a difference of opinion in the party over the evaluation of the past. We had already heard some of these views — although not so precisely expressed — before the Party Conference.

The mistakes of the past will sooner or later come off the agenda, but Communists must never forget the experience gained from evaluating the work of the former party leadership, otherwise great danger will threaten the future work of the party. In appraising it, a strict adherence to principles must prevail.

Comrade Révai warned us against any misunderstanding in connection with his remarks, because they were in no way intended to be the unfurling of the flag of "Stalinism" or "Rákosiism." We who stand on the basis of Marxism–Leninism, do not recognize these expressions, although it is a fact that such expressions exist. They were invented by the enemies of Communism, the traitors to the party took them over and so did those who were confused by revisionist views. After losing the armed struggle, the enemy attempted on the pretext of persecuting "Stalinists" and "Rákosiists" to force Communists out of their positions. These catchwords, therefore, represented in essence yet another attack by the enemy. Our party — and naturally the Central Committee too — immediately took up the struggle against this kind of differentiation between party members.

Our standpoint on this question is unmistakable. In our opinion there are neither "Stalinists" nor "Rákosiists," and so we cannot speak of their flag. Nevertheless, there does exist another flag alongside the party's and that is the flag of the fallen leadership. But this flag lies broken on the ground, and I am convinced that it will never be raised again. The fallen leadership — and it is no accident that I use this expression, in political life this is not unusual — fell in such a manner and in such circumstances that they can never again return to the leadership of the party.

In the spring of last year, Communists, embittered by the party's difficult position, were angry at Comrade Rákosi. I too was angry, yet until the last minute I maintained — as also did others — that the struggle must be conducted against the mistakes and not against the person of Mátyás Rákosi. Together we wanted to find a way out, a way to develop, because we were afraid that otherwise the party would undergo a great upheaval. We did not cling to Mátyás Rákosi's person because we had liked him. Earlier on we did indeed like him, but by the spring of 1956 this was no longer possible. Nevertheless, this was our standpoint because we loved the party and the working class. It was not our fault, or the fault of the party membership, but Mátyás Rákosi's, that we did not succeed in putting our concept over. And however great the historical merits which Rákosi may have, we cannot forgive him this serious error.

It is a great pity that such an outstanding leader of the Hungarian working class movement cannot be included in the textbook of the party school as a model to young Communists. But he has only himself to blame for this; nobody can play with the fate of the party, not even Mátyás Rákosi.

When Comrade Révai stepped up to the rostrum, he held the flag of the party in his hand—figuratively speaking—and said that he was speaking under that flag. Later, however, he waved the broken flag of the fallen leadership in the hall. Comrade Révai declared that he was in agreement with the political line of the Central Committee, in agreement with the report, with the draft resolution, and the draft party rules. For us this is very important, for Comrade Révai is not just anyone in the Hungarian working class movement. He is a venerable, sincere Communist, to whose name a portion of the party's history is attached. Comrade Révai can, if he wishes, help a great deal in the party's struggle, but precisely because he does not fill just any kind of role in the party, he can also cause a great deal of harm. We ask Comrade Révai to help us in our struggle, and not to cause harm.

Comrade Révai raised questions—and this was why I said he waved the flag of the fallen leadership—which we have already heard from the members of the former leadership. He talked of a black list, of internal exile, and spoke about many hundreds of suffering comrades, the undeserved treatment of the State Security Authority (ÁVH), and so on. I have no reason and no right to assume that Comrade Révai deliberately supported the former leadership by his remarks. I believe and hope that that was not the case, yet by repeating these slanders he unwittingly voiced the slogans of the fallen leadership. It is with such slogans that the members of the former leadership attack the party, while they are fighting for their personal interests.

Comrade Révai agrees that in reorganizing the leadership we did not include those former leaders who would have hindered our work. This was tactically correct, said Comrade Révai. We are pleased that Comrade Révai agrees with us on this question, but I must say that it was not a matter of tactics on our part, but a stand over a matter of principle, and a politically necessary step.

As far as the black list he mentioned is concerned, it never really existed. But we undoubtedly did have to examine person by person who should hold posts in the party in the future, and who should not. We were led by considerations of principle and policy in our judgement. Naturally we recorded our decision on paper too. When the Executive Committee first called a meeting of activists, we discussed with the 280 odd comrades who were present the fact that we must look around to see on whom we could count in our work, who were to work in the party apparatus, and who were not. I listed the names of about 18 comrades who should not for various reasons work on the staff of the party's headquarters. I must stress that there were various reasons; I did indeed mention the names of comrades whom we could not consider simply for reasons of health. It was this list that certain people later unjustly called a black list.

We can at the most speak about internal exile in our country in the sense that former members of the Arrow Cross Party, and some writers too, consider our system irksome and oppressive because there is no legal opportunity for them to carry on activities against it. In the case of Communists, however, in my opinion we can in no way speak of internal exile. Yet, as I hear, allegedly hundreds and hundreds of comrades live in internal exile; that is, there is no chance for them to help make amends for the common mistakes which were committed with the party. We have for various reasons been unable to place some comrades into posts. In the overwhelming majority of cases they are decent, honest comrades, and the party must fight to place them in state, economic or party posts in keeping with their abilities as soon as possible.

How were these comrades removed from their posts? In most instances the counter-revolution drove them out. It will be recalled that while we here in Budapest were working on strengthening central power, at the grass roots the counter-revolution was still raging at full force. For weeks, although we were the masters of the situation at the centre, in the factories the workers' councils ruled. Under the leadership of the hostile elements hidden in the workers' councils, the fight against us was carried on with full force. Hundreds and hundreds of people were sacked from ministries and trusts. Since then we have restored these comrades, with very few exceptions, to their positions.

The situation of those, however, who left the party apparatus, is a different question. On November 4 we considerably reduced the party apparatus, because we did not consider it sound that it should be oversized. We do not underestimate the importance of the party apparatus. There will undoubtedly be need for a certain number of full-time party-workers – in certain places we have recently even increased their number – but we are very careful not to swell the apparatus unjustifiably. Party bureaucracy is even more dangerous than that of state, not only for the party's activity, but also for the people. As a result of the reductions in staff, many comrades have been left without employment who, even if they have made mistakes, are decent, honest Communists. We will do everything to find them jobs as soon as possible. But we protest against anyone forging a weapon against the party out of this. It is not the crime of the party, and the Central Committee that such a situation has come about. At the time we said to these comrades: there is a fight on, we are unable to concern ourselves with appointments, you too must seize arms and join the emergency security forces. If working class power triumphs, if things get back to normal, your position, too, will be settled. If working class power falls, then not only your life, but the life of the whole people will be in danger.

The enemy naturally noticed at once that a great number of comrades had joined the emergency security forces. At least six provincial Fascist delegations called on me (among them those from Borsod, from Tata, and from Nógrád County), and as many from Budapest, and took me to task, wanting to know what the "Rákosiists" and the "Stalinists" were doing in the emergency security forces. Well, I gave them a proper reply, so that the whole pilgrimage of delegations ceased.

Let me stress again, however painful it is, that there are still a few hundred comrades without jobs at present – not only those of whom Comrade Révai was thinking, but unknown people in the countryside, who were ousted from machine stations and co-operative farms, who were possibly just helpers at the district party committees, riding their bicycles to and from work – and perhaps the position of these affects us more painfully. Still, we cannot allow the party to be attacked because of this.

The enemy are seeking a banner, they would like to find a legal forum of some kind, and would be delighted to have it within the party, because they could begin the old song-and-dance all over again. If the party tolerated the unfurling of the former leadership's flag, a new factional struggle would ensue within the party. Various disaffected people would gather around this flag. There are plenty of people with grievances in Hungary, among them those who fought against the party, and now that we have struck back, they have taken offence.

Perhaps the supposition that the right and the left wing could meet under one banner is surprising, but the idea is not mine. Sometime in August last year, when Mátyás Rákosi's removal was still very recent, and we had not yet solved the Imre Nagy problem, Comrade Révai remarked: the party must be careful or we may live to see the two of them in one faction fighting against the Central Committee. I am convinced that if they had the opportunity today they would indeed be fighting in one faction against the Central Committee. I am basing my supposition on the fact that I know the present political standpoint of both of them.

Although we are "guilty" in the eyes of Rákosi and Imre Nagy, our conscience is clear. Naturally we are not infallible, undoubtedly we have all made mistakes; perhaps at critical times we were uncertain, we have taken wrong steps, but we do not regard ourselves guilty, not even in the October events, because we have always endeavoured to act correctly, in the interests of the party and the people.

Comrade Mesterházi[14] raised the point that something ought to be done to make the leadership more popular. I believe that this is not necessary. If the leadership works well, it will become popular with the masses, it will win their confidence and respect. Naturally, it is not by any means the same to the party whether the leaders have prestige or not, because this is connected with the party's prestige. The party's struggle is more effective if the leaders are respected, which does not mean that they cannot be criticized. We accept justified criticism if it is made at the proper place and in the proper manner, but we shall not allow the leaders to be discredited.

The enemy, who now have no open political platform, are seeking hard for points to attack. They are returning to their old, tried and tested methods and are endeavouring to foment factional strife. They brand one comrade as being left-wing, another as right-wing, and strive in every way to bring about dissension. For example, when Comrade Révai came home, the very next day three American journalists came bursting in on me and excitedly asked whether Comrade Révai would be included in the government. I said that unfortunately Comrade Révai was ill, so that for the time being this was out of the question – after which they departed in disappointment. The enemy are endeavouring to foment dissension in every way wherever they can. I recall, for example, when László Rajk came home in July 1945, he had not even set foot in the party headquarters when the enemy struck up the chorus that there were two factions in the party and that there was a life-and-death struggle between them. They alleged that Rákosi was the leader of the "Muscovites," and that the Hungarians acknowledged Rajk as their leader. At that time we all laughed at this, for there was no sign whatever of any factional strife. We were actually working in fraternal understanding, and within the party there was the greatest unity imaginable. But the enemy kept up their tune persistently, and I am convinced that finally Comrade Rákosi too succumbed to the enemy's psychological influence. The enemy strove to sow dissension within the party then, and are striving to do so now too. In our Central Committee, even if there are differences in views and great debates, there is unity on the main issues, and we will not in the future either allow the members of the party leadership to be grouped according to various shades of opinion.

In connection with Comrade Révai's remarks, I should like to touch upon another complex of questions, and that is the December Resolution. Comrade Bakó put things very well in my opinion, when she said that the December Resolution must not be trifled with.

Even if there are faults in the December Resolution, in its main points the Central Committee's evaluation has proved correct, and today nobody can work usefully for the party who does not fully identify himself with the essentials of this resolution. The four factors enumerated in the resolution are closely linked with each other, and if any one of them had been missing, there could not have been a counter-revolutionary uprising. For this very reason — namely that all four factors are important and mutually influenced each other — it is inadmissible for comrades to pick and choose among them at pleasure or according to their own earlier work, deciding which they will accept. I do not claim that the resolution is a political masterpiece, but I repeat that its essential points are valid, and we need not withdraw it.

Let us examine this question more closely. Would not the imperialists have willingly attacked us earlier, say in 1951, if there had been an opportunity for them to do so? Or would not the Horthy Fascists have willingly seized arms against us years ago? And would not the Imre Nagy type of traitors have acted even earlier if the party had been weak? When the party leadership was still united and was welded with the membership, and the party was welded with the people, then there was no possibility of a counter-revolution. This is the historic merit of the Central Committee led by Mátyás Rákosi. But the fact that in 1956 the leadership was no longer united, and a rift appeared between the membership and the leadership as well as the party and the people, is the historic crime of the same leadership. No one can ever whitewash them. Had the unity of the party and with it the party's striking power not weakened, then Imre Nagy would have schemed in vain, the Horthy Fascists and imperialists would have attacked in vain; they would have had nothing to gain in Hungary. And on the basis of these experiences we declare that in the interests of the party and the dictatorship of the proletariat we do not compromise regarding the party's unity.

This question is very important. Although Rákosi and Imre Nagy are not in the country at present, they still have followers in our party. These two kinds of malcontent groups can organize into one faction splendidly — or at least act together — because they are both opposed to the present party leadership, and to the political line which this party leadership represents. This is why we must safeguard the party's unity with fire and sword, and on the basis of the December Resolution at that, because in this we have fully set out the main questions of our party's policy.

It is one of Comrade Révai's old habits that he likes to carry his thoughts to the point of absurdity. Now, exceptionally, I too shall do this. Let us suppose that several centres of leadership were to come into existence outside the Central Committee. For example, the Táncsics Circle would become one such auxiliary centre and Comrade Révai would become another. The reason I mention these examples is because the comrades working in the Táncsics Circle[15] and Comrade Révai himself are all irreproachable Communists, whose respectability and readiness to help cannot be doubted. How would this supposition look in practice? If somebody were not satisfied with the views of the department for agitation and propaganda, he would simply stroll over to the literary department of the Táncsics Circle, and it is quite certain that there they would express an opinion on this same matter that was a shade different. And the person concerned would accept the one which was most to his taste. Or let us assume that over some question or other Comrade Révai's opinion were to be asked, possibly by someone who is dissatisfied with certain measures of the party and the government. This could happen to someone who is also a very decent and respectable Communist. Would it be proper if, in opposition to the Central Committee, he turned to Comrade Révai as a forum? Such a danger exists, and we ask Comrade Révai to reckon with it. Just because we consider Comrade Révai to be an honest comrade of irreproachable morals, one who enjoys great prestige, and has historic merits, this danger exists. It is no secret, comrades, that our Central Committee has debated a very great deal during the past seven months over Comrade Révai's person. And I have always stood for the view—and not because I want to apologize to Comrade Révai, or anyone else—that the party needs Comrade Révai. I am, of course, not alone in thinking this. We esteem Comrade Révai as an open, straightforward man. However, there are still problems in our cooperation, and Comrade Révai should understand this. I am thinking, for example, about his first article which *Népszabadság*[16] published. We argued a great deal at the time about whether we should allow the article to be published. Not a single person in the Executive Committee agreed with every one of the assertions made in the article. Nevertheless we published it, because we thought that the article contained many valuable conclusions. And indeed, it was proper to publish it, for it gave strength to the struggle against the counterrevolution. In my opinion Comrade Révai's contribution here was also useful. Mainly because it evoked a healthy reaction from the participants at the Party Conference with its apologies for dogmatism, sectarianism and the mistakes of the former leadership.

As far as the merits are concerned, as I already stressed in the report, it is still early to be sharing in the glory. In any case, the glory is due first of all to the working people of the Soviet Union and the fraternal countries. If there is anyone in Hungary who has honours in defending working class power, then it is the Hungarian working class, which has for decades fought unceasingly for the socialist revolution. It is one of our greatest matters for national pride that, after the Soviet Union, the Hungarian proletariat and the Hungarian people were the first to achieve working class power. This working class fought for 25 years against Horthy Fascism. And this working class fought after the Liberation too. And if the leaders of today did not exist, a dictatorship of the Hungarian proletariat would still exist, because the Hungarian working class would have found their own people. The government could not have achieved results if the idea of the socialist revolution had not lived in the masses.

Now I shall turn to the questions of the fight against revisionism. In this connection Comrade Révai said we must fight against the conciliatory spirit with regard to revisionism. I fully agree with this.

The other side of the struggle against the enemy is that the traitors must be brought to justice. We consider it our task and duty to throw light on all aspects of the October counter-revolution and whoever is guilty, whoever is a traitor, must be punished. This is now under way.

To be able to fight effectively against the enemy, the party must act unitedly. In this connection we must clearly see the old mistakes and must not repeat them. The strengthening of state power and our struggle against the enemy, as well as the tasks of economic and cultural construction, must be solved in combination with the constant enlightenment of the people, and in accordance with our own specific conditions. The necessary measures of reprisal must, therefore, be linked with explanatory work, in order that the people may see that these reprisals are being taken in the people's interest, and not because of some kind of Communist or individual vengeance.

The unity of the party and the armed forces is necessary for the fight against the enemy. When we began this fight, we thought that we should first strengthen the party among the working class and in the armed forces. If the party is strong in these two spheres, we need not fear for the people's power.

We must cherish, respect and help the army, the police, the Workers' Militia, in a word, our armed forces, and we must instil public opinion as a whole with this spirit. Love of the party also includes criticism. If, therefore, we see mistakes in the armed forces — as anywhere else — we must criticize them severely, but this should take place on a basis of love and should serve the good of the armed forces.

The Workers' Militia which was established recently is one of the greatest achievements of the party and the Hungarian dictatorship of the proletariat, for it is the armed proletariat. But the view that only the Workers' Militia is our armed force, is wrong. This is an insulting and unjust conclusion in relation to our soldiers. Our armed forces are first of all the army and the police, and then the Workers' Militia. From the point of view of power, it is most important that we strengthen, foster and help the spirit of comradeship and unity among the various sections of the armed forces. Let us not permit anyone to sow dissension amongst them.

Speaking of the armed forces, I should like to clarify a few matters in connection with the State Security Authority. Never have any of us made any distinction between our martyrs, whether the persons concerned were enlisted men of the State Security Authority, or not. Such a distinction would indeed be disgraceful. We honour equally the memory of the martyrs who fell defending working class power, whether they were Soviet or Hungarian soldiers, or civilians. But we must not only revere the memory of those who fell, but must also honour those among the living who were disabled or wounded in defense of our working class power — or simply took part in the fighting, and later in the armed restoration of law and order. All other things being equal, we must ensure preferential rights to them, or their children, in admittances to the universities, in filling appointments, and so on.

In connection with the defense of the state, I must also speak about something else. In our country the situation now is that there is no State Security Authority. In abolishing the independent state security body we were motivated partly by political and partly by financial considerations. But the Ministry of Home Affairs and the police have a political department. We believe that these bodies must be the strong arm of the dictatorship of the proletariat. And the bodies concerned with state security must be supported by both the party and the people. Their work in the interest of the people is made easier if they feel the people's love and support, and if we praise and defend them. We must be careful, however, that the spirit of avant-gardism should not be revived in the circles of our state security bodies – the spirit which believes that every other sphere is unreliable, and only the State Security Authority is reliable. If we allow this view to come to life again, we will dig the grave of the dictatorship of the proletariat with it, comrades! Our esteem for the members of the State Security Authority, our reverence for their dead, and the interests of the defense of people's power command us to pay attention to these matters.

Comrades, I should like to deal with a question of principle. Several people have raised the question of what kind of principle the party's unity is founded upon, the unity of will, and so on. I should also like to point out another source of danger to this unity. In the summer of last year a few of Comrade Lenin's hitherto unpublished letters were made public. In one of them Comrade Lenin wrote, not word for word, but in essence, that the bare fact that the Bolshevik party in its struggle relies on two classes, the working class and the peasantry – and this fact is also reflected within the Central Committee – always carries within it the danger of a split in the party. It is worthwhile thinking about this. I do not claim that Imre Nagy had been a stool pigeon or a spy from his early youth on. It is not good to think of people in this way. I believe, however, that to the Hungarian people it is fully clear that in October he betrayed the party and the people. But if Imre Nagy ever was a Communist, and if his political line diverged so far that it culminated in betrayal, then it happened because of the fact mentioned by Lenin. The most important aspect of our party's unity is that, within the alliance of the workers and peasants, we must never forget the leading role of the working class, and the fact that although the party relies in its struggle on two labouring classes, the working class and the peasantry, the party is nevertheless the revolutionary party of the working class. The party can only fight and work effectively for the peasantry, too, if we do not forget this. Is there a danger that we will? Indeed there is! And in the government and the party leadership I have more than once met decent, honest Communists who drew a line of demarcation between themselves and Imre Nagy, but still did not notice this danger.

For example, the Ministry of Agriculture submitted a proposal to the Council of Ministers that we should give back 280,000 holds of forest land to the peasantry. I asked why we should do this? The reply was: the peasants would welcome it wholeheartedly. I said that this was not a principled reason! We need not fear that in our country agriculture will be pushed into the background. We have active fighters for agriculture in our party headquarters who would provide the peasants with all the earthly goods in the world, from investments and machines to old-age pensions. It is good and necessary, too, that someone should fight so well to carry out the tasks entrusted to him. But the Central Committee must not forget that the party is the party of the proletariat, which leads the workers' and peasants' alliance, and that we are fighting for socialism. We are convinced that it is only on this road that we can honestly serve the interests of the peasantry, too, and that the peasants also will be truly happy and without care only in a socialist society.

Two other questions were raised here to which I should like to reply. The question of youth and the Young Communist League (KISZ). At the time the Young Communist League was formed, the requirement that we should rally only the most class-conscious young people and those who were most loyal to the cause of socialism in the Young Communist League was a correct one. Today, in the period of consolidation, we may dispense with the "mosts" — class-consciousness and loyalty to socialism are sufficient. I believe in the present situation that this is a sufficiently high requirement.

I have one more remark to make in connection with the naming of the Young Communist League. One or other of our young functionaries was concerned that the name of Young Communist League would not be a good one and the university students might even beat up some of the first people to join, because of it. I replied that that would not be such a great misfortune either — they beat us up too, when we were members of the young Communists' organization — let them also fight, and take a courageous stand. If need be, the grown-ups will help them. Now it transpires that the situation is not so perilous after all. The enemy has been shattered, and confused young people are beginning to come to their senses and to talk in a normal way about the Communist youth. If there is any party member who is ashamed that he is a Communist, he must be asked to hand back his membership card, and we must take note that we cannot count on him. But if he professes to be a Communist, then he should always and everywhere feel it his duty to fight against mistaken and hostile views, to fight for the objectives of the party and proclaim the truth of the party. Communist courage is needed, comrades, because even the enemy respects those who fight for their convictions.

I also wish to deal with our relations with the non-party masses. In the organization of the party it was — I think, correctly — our basic principle that the number of our party members should be smaller than the party membership of the HWPP. We feel that the numerical proportion of the party in comparison with the class is on the whole sound. It follows from this that we do not even want to enrol every former member of the HWPP into the party. But if this is our aim, then we cannot be angry with those former HWPP members who do not want to join the HSWP. They must on no account be placed at a disadvantage because of this decision. Among the non-party people, it is generally the former HWPP members who stand closest to us; it is particularly with them that we must establish contact, and thus also broaden our basis among the non-party masses.

Everyone agrees that nobody should join the party for carreerist reasons. Nevertheless, proposals have been voiced here that if a former party member in a leading post does not wish to join, then he must immediately be removed from his post. In several instances this has happened. This is not correct, comrades. The laws of our People's Republic ensure that, with the exception of party posts, any other public office may be filled by non-party people. This principle must also be put into practice. This does not mean that tomorrow we should draw up a list in which we demand a non-party prime minister, and similar appointments, but that this principle — and this is the essence of the matter — should be realized in practice. Why? If we remove a factory manager who is otherwise good at his post because he has not joined the party, we will give such an impetus to organizing the party that we shall be unable to stop it. Because if one manager sees what has happened to the other he will think, "Hum! Kovács has been removed because he did not join the party. Well, we'll see about that." He will rush at once to the party secretary and say to him: "Look here, old man, my mother-in-law has been ill up to now," – or he will put forward another pretext – "but now I want to join the party." If they remove one today, tomorrow twenty will join. Are these people enemies? One must assume that they are not. Of course, there may be some among them who are. But a man who likes his work and wishes to support his family, and therefore clings to his position, is no enemy. However, if somebody joins the party only to ensure his position, he does not strengthen the party, but weakens it. For this reason let us be consistent. It is not right to say it is good that the party membership is not nine hundred thousand – and at the same time to be angry with every former party member who did not join in November. We cannot say that non-party people can hold office, and then remove every functionary of any rank who does not join the party. If we do this, then neither the party membership nor the people will understand just what we want! What must we take into consideration in filling appointments? No person can hold a state, economic or other appointment who is not loyal to the Hungarian People's Republic, not loyal to the dictatorship of the proletariat. And I assert that if we apply this one requirement, then we can drive every enemy of the people's power out of responsible office, without forcing people into the party who would not strengthen the party but weaken it.

If we take a look at the composition of this Conference, we must conclude that the proportion of women among the delegates is low, only just over six per cent. This is not a good sign. The counter-revolutionary period, by its very nature, did not favour the social activity of women, and to some extent this is an extenuating circumstance. But we must not be reconciled to this situation, therefore we must quickly make up the deficiency in this area. I propose that we apply the principle that when there is a possibility of placing a man or a woman into an appointment, all conditions being equal, then – at least until the unfavourable imbalance changes – the decision should be in favour of the woman.

I shall now turn to the question of national unity which has been debated so much in the youth movement and in the sphere of literature. I shall be very brief! We can identify ourselves with the standpoint of the Chinese Communist Party which says: "Unity – debate – unity on a new basis."

I must say frankly that we made considerable efforts to shatter the "national unity" that existed in October. Why did this "national unity" have to be destroyed? Because it was rooted in reactionary soil. Its leaders were anti-socialist elements. We do not want unity of that kind. We are now at the stage of the debate when we define what we stand for so that the battle lines should become clear and it becomes evident who is on one side and who is on the other. The debate must be carried on with the weapons of theory, principle and politics. The aim is to bring about a new national unity on a socialist basis. This, however, is still the task of years. Of course, we shall have to get down to it tomorrow, and we can already achieve some results this year. But in order to bring about a national joining of forces resting on a socialist basis which embraces the absolute majority of the people – and the overwhelming majority of the writers — we must continue to work persistently and seriously for a long time to come. We must apply wise methods and wise tactics, which means at present that the guilty must be punished, the misguided helped, those diverging to the left or to the right convinced by arguments, while those standing firmly beside us must be strengthened.

Comrades, as regards economic questions I am now unfortunately not able to go into details. I agree with those criticisms which state that, in comparison with our other tasks, we have lagged very much behind in the sphere of economic and cultural work. There is, of course, a historical reason for this. In our present situation the most important thing was the strengthening of the party and state power. We must begin to solve the economic questions with the realization of the one-year plan, and for this we must mobilize the forces of all of society. We must make it the personal concern of every worker to protect social property, to be thrifty, and take part in socialist labour emulation.

There is a tremendous amount of initiative in this sphere, which the journalists and radio workers are popularizing. But it would be good if we got out of the habit of thinking in terms of extremes, and learned to write and speak with a restraint which suits the actual situation.

There was mention that in addition to the one-year and three-year plans we would need a long-range plan for certain tasks. For example, we should prepare a ten-to-fifteen-year long-range plan for the development of Budapest, the better exploitation of sandy areas, the improvement of alkaline regions, and the solution of our energy problems. When they are prepared, these plans must be submitted for extensive discussion.

Little has been said at the Conference about a certain strengthening of private capital. The party supports the activities of small-scale industry which satisfy the demands of the population. We also respect the useful activity of private retail trade. But inasmuch as some types of trading activity cause harm and increase speculation, action must be taken against them. We should not at once take administrative action, we must strive to convince the people concerned with wise words and make them see reason. But if speculation continues to grow rampant and cause harm to the working people, it may be necessary to take stern measures. There is no doubt that, as in the political struggle, in economic matters too, we must defend proletarian power. Of course, the most effective way to struggle against speculation is to have an adequate quantity of the necessary goods available.

Over the question of the workers' councils I agree with Comrade Révai. We cannot approve the trends which aim at abolishing them by administrative measures. We must strive to see that the workers' councils carry on their activities in the interests of socialist construction.

Let me call your attention to the fact that in the course of the struggle against nationalism, the particular Hungarian conditions must also be taken into consideration. It is true that for centuries the nation was oppressed, and our glorious national uprisings played a progressive role in the history of our country and of mankind. But we have often stressed this circumstance far too one-sidedly, and did not point out that at the same time the Hungarian ruling classes — in the name of the whole nation, quoting them as their authority — oppressed other peoples. The old ruling classes instilled into the Hungarian people, together with the demand for national independence, a national arrogance, and the false, nationalist consciousness of superiority over the fraternal peoples who live side by side with us. We condemn this; this is not our progressive heritage.

As in every other sphere, so on the national question, too, theoretically correct and precise definitions are very important. Without these we cannot call ourselves Marxists. Such a correct definition is, for example, that true patriotism fuses with proletarian internationalism. But, comrades, we must formulate this so that it can be understood by the entire people, because the idea of the unity of patriotism and proletarian internationalism is difficult for ordinary people to understand. It is understandable to them, however, if we say we are Hungarians, we are patriots, but the Hungarian Fascists are mortal enemies to us and our people, in the same way as the Fascists and imperialists of any nation. At the same time, however, the working people of any country who are fighting for international proletarian solidarity, are our brothers.

Finally I wish to speak about the tasks of the party, about party work. How do we stand in this sphere, comrades?

Even when we recognize our great results we must not forget the fact that there is no single area of state and economic, cultural and party work where we have achieved the old standard.

We can easily establish what per cent we have achieved in one or another field of production, but we are unable to show what per cent we have attained in party work! Unfortunately, today we cannot say that things are in perfect order about any area of party work. Now it is particularly in the economic and cultural spheres that party work must be intensified, because in the areas of power, political work, and party building, we are somewhat ahead. Among various strata of the party membership, and particularly among the intellectuals, there is still uncertainty. The enemy has infiltrated into certain areas among the office and administrative workers, and perhaps the peasant organizations too. In state affairs and in economic work there is a great deal of laxness, a lack of discipline. There are still many confused views; in fact, there are even hostile elements in the ministries and elsewhere, too. What is to be done, therefore? What is the way out of these troubles? In such a situation it is even more important that the party's affairs be in order. Only the party can help, with its work of organizing, mobilizing, stimulating and criticizing. For this reason, too, we must guard the unity of the party like our most precious possession, and develop the party in a healthy manner.

About the draft resolution: let me inform you, comrades, that the Drafting Committee has already incorporated into the final draft resolution about 60 per cent of the proposals received partly in spoken, and partly in written form. I shall enumerate them only by topics: we have incorporated in the text proposals about the patriotic and internationalist education of the youth, about the role of the trade unions and the state bodies in connection with labour emulation, about Hungarian–Soviet friendship, about the duties of individual Communists with regard to the everyday troubles and cares of the working people, and other subjects. The Drafting Committee did not take into consideration a whole series of proposals because they were already in the original text in a different form. I ask, comrades, that you adopt the amended draft resolution. I also ask the Party Conference to approve the party rules.

In conclusion, comrades, I should like to stress that the heated debate was extremely useful, because it clarified problems, and on this basis the whole party can act unitedly. In fact we can count with assurance not only on the action of the party members, but also on the masses of the people, because we place in the forefront of our struggle those demands of public interest with which every honest working man can unhesitatingly identify himself, and with the solution of which we can strengthen our whole people's power. As far as our internal affairs are concerned, I propose that, on the basis of the experiences of this Conference, we should turn over a new leaf within the party. Let us close the past, and turn our eyes to the future. The important thing now is, by exploiting the favourable circumstances, to activate party members, and the whole working people, to advance, to force back the enemy more and more, and to have courage to proclaim our views and truths everywhere.

And in the party organizations let us debate our affairs wisely, calmly and patiently, then adopt good resolutions and require that they be strictly observed. Whoever infringes the implementation of the party's resolutions, and the party discipline which requires it, must be severely dealt with. The task, therefore, is, comrades, to strengthen the party's unity, to fight for the people's fundamental interests — and the party will thereby be strengthened, in the same way that this Party Conference is also strengthening our party.

Speech to the National Council of the Patriotic People's Front

JUNE 19, 1959

We summarized and published our principal task for this year in the Central Committee resolution adopted last March. We decided that we would recommend to the working people that in a number of main fields we reach the targets set for the end of the Three Year Plan this year. Of course this does not mean that the Three Year Plan will be completed in two years in all respects, but refers only to a few of the most vital fields. This is one of our central tasks. The other is to consolidate the cooperative farms, and the achievements reached last spring. All this also involves the further strengthening of the foundations of socialism, of our system, and our state; but it also means that we can improve the standard of living of the working people this year. More precisely: on the one hand, we are raising the standard of living, and on the other, are creating the conditions for a somewhat more substantial advance in living standards, after the successful closing of this fiscal year.

The words "we recommend" were not included in the text by accident. They, too, were intended to convey that it is not up to the Central Committee only, nor even to the party alone, to achieve these aims. It is up to the masses of the working people! If they accept our recommendation – and the signs are that they will – and honour their obligations, then we will achieve our aim.

I am convinced that every thinking man and woman is aware that the contents of the Central Committee resolution of last March are not designed to serve any narrow party interests, but the interests, in the full sense of the word, of our entire people, the national aims of our people. And they will serve them well. That is why we have recommended them to our people. The Central Committee is confident that, if we join forces, our plans will be realized. We should not forget, however, that our recommendation was made in the last month of the first quarter of this year. The first quarter, however, ended very quickly, so in actual fact, we will have to achieve all that we have braced ourselves to do in three quarters of a year. Not that this is impossible, but it will require an effort. It is particularly good to remember this now, when we are entering a time of year – July and the first half of August – when, because of holidays, output is usually not as high as in other months of the year. Nevertheless, we are sure that we will manage. One of the main bases for our confidence is that the working people have already pledged themselves to do a major part of the necessary work; and the actual results so far show that they will be as good as – or even better than – their word. But it will be necessary to work to achieve all this.

The Patriotic People's Front is the kind of movement which must reckon with the peasant way of thinking as an important factor. For this reason we ask them to remember that since the Liberation the industrial workers have borne the brunt of the public burdens of our state.

We mean no offence, but we must remind the peasants of 1945 – 46, a time when the industrial workers, starving and working almost for nothing, put the nation's life back to normal, repaired transport and communications and rebuilt the factories while at the same time – and this was the wish of the working class, so it is not meant as a reproach – large numbers of peasants improved their financial position. The very inflation which undoubtedly caused much hunger to the workers, was favourable for the peasantry. Old mortgage debts and new loans dissolved into thin air almost in a matter of days – the peasantry were freed from their debts. And now look at our March resolution. We suggest that the industrial workers overfulfil their plans, turn out more manufactured goods, and, where necessary, reduce costs and improve productivity. These objectives are becoming more and more difficult to achieve every year, for when slackness is rampant and productivity low, it is easier to improve productivity or overfulfill the plan. This year these tasks are more difficult.

By contrast, all we expect of agriculture is that the plan is fulfilled. That is a tremendous difference. Even this year the working class is shouldering a great burden – that is why we are asking the masses of the peasantry and the intellectuals to show appreciation of the workers. Our working class is making efforts to solve tasks which are calculated to benefit the entire people, the entire nation. This is what gives us Communists the moral ground for urging the entire people – non-party people as well—to do their utmost so that our great objectives may be achieved. Not one part of the fruits of their labour will be distributed so that only the Communists, party members or members of the KISZ will share in them; everyone will get their share—the peasants and the intellectuals, too. This is natural and correct.

We Communists—true to our party's traditions—are preparing again for our Congress by wanting to do something for the public good.

This is our tradition. This is the way we like to celebrate.

Of course, other matters will also be discussed at the Congress which concern not only Communists. One of them will be the political line of the party. Those members of the Central Committee who are present here have no right to speak on behalf of the Congress. But we may speak about the ideas which engage our attention. We believe that the Congress will endorse the line which the Central Committee has been pursuing since November 1956.

In essence the main line of our policy is to continue to build a socialist society, to complete that building, and subsequently to establish a Communist, classless society.

That is the essence of our policy, and this does not change—this main line will presumably be endorsed by the Congress. I would like to go into this matter in a little more detail, for, while our political line is known, its interpretation and application in given instances and in given situations is an ever new task.

Take the cooperative farm movement for example, which concerns not only the peasantry—it is a vital question for the working class and the intelligentsia, and also for the entire people. We are handling it with the responsibility due to one of the most crucial issues of our national life; indeed it has a bearing upon social development and the future of the nation. It was with full responsibility that on two occasions our Central Committee discussed the development of agriculture. We decided what was to be done, and we have carried it out. As for the results, we may say that they have surpassed expectations. We actually consider the development of the cooperative farm movement necessary for two reasons. One is that we are convinced that this is the way in which the peasantry can advance. The task is, therefore, to carry through the socialist reorganization of agriculture in line with the political conditions, if possible without loss of time or momentum. There is another reason too: it is in the interest of our national economy as a whole. In the age of advanced farming methods, the age of machines, only large-scale farming can secure better harvests.

How should we go on from here then? Should we re-establish the large estates, call back the counts and the landowners? It is my feeling that even some of the kulaks are saying: We don't need that! Leave the working peasants alone! So we must take the other road. That road on which the peasant is not a beggar in the world when large-scale agriculture comes into being, but is master of his life and his land. We are taking this road, just like the other socialist countries. We must not allow any misunderstanding on this score. But it must also be said that from time to time we will decide, with due care and consideration, how we should continue to progress and what must be done.

The decisive factor is, of course, the political preconditions of progress. These were given last December—as the results show.

And what about the economic conditions? Some people held the view that we should create the economic conditions for the cooperative farms first and that only then should the cooperatives be formed. That sounds reasonable, but it is not how it was in reality, in the cooperative farm movement. How can you go to one section of the population and ask them: give us a few thousands of millions so that we can create some sort of base for the agricultural cooperatives, because we hope that if that's done, then our peasant brothers will join the cooperatives. In reality nothing happens like that, that's not sound thinking. What was the peasant's dream in times gone by? The peasant would like to have lived on his own little estate: one dreamed of six *holds*, another of eight; of how there would be two horses, or oxen, cows; of fattening a pair of pigs, and so on. Did any of this come true? Some of it, yes; indeed alongside the big estates and the millions of poor peasants who had nothing, there were a few thousand peasants who realized their dreams. First he went to his relatives for a loan, to the bank for credit at a usurous rate of interest; he began to work by taking half the crop himself, half going to someone else; he rented something too, and then finally there were his few wretched *holds:* his whole lifetime's work and indeed sometimes his son's whole lifetime's work too, had gone in the realization of this small peasant's dream. And if there was one bad season, if there was some natural disaster or a crash in agriculture or on the market, then one bad year would carry off the "dream" which had perhaps taken father and son 70 years of blood and sweat to put together.

So we have to make a start. If we had first invested in everything which we had dreamed about, and only then started to behave as though everything was held in common, then we would have been like a peasant with nothing but a pair of trousers. We must create a socialist framework, because the peasants already know that if the state gives them no more than a twisted sickle, even then their strength is increased 50 to 100 per cent through the strength of the collective. The clear-headed joint decision, the common will, the collective endeavour, multiplies strength. This is the road of life. The state will also help you; but you must also help yourselves.

By all this I do not mean to suggest that the economic conditions can be neglected. They are, of course, important, but they must not be the conditions determining the development of the cooperative farm movement. We cannot accede to the position of taking a step forward only when all the economic preconditions are to hand. But once we have taken a step forward, immediately the obligation arises to consolidate and strengthen our gains economically, as fast as we can! Economic conditions, therefore, must not be placed in the way of the development of the movement, but it would also be a sin to forget about them. Let us send machines, let us provide all the support to promote the consolidation and strengthening of the cooperative farms. That is the course we are following. This is a manifestation of our Central Committee's policy and how this policy is implemented.

Contrary to hostile slanders, the development of the cooperative farms does not entail a fall in the standard of living. The sum devoted to strengthening the cooperative farms, far from lowering living standards, will raise them year by year. The millions of Forints expended on consolidating the young cooperatives reveal the healthy features of our economy, at the same time strengthening them. The economy which got over the shock caused by the counter-revolution in a very short time, and which today can boast of some fine achievements, is able to devote substantial sums to strengthening agriculture, without jeopardizing living standards. Our policy is straightforward and clear. It serves to develop agriculture, and to further the interests of the entire people.

We are developing our existing cooperative farms – that is progress too, as it contributes towards the consolidation of the cooperative farm movement. That is our task at present. After that, we will investigate the political and economic conditions for further progress. We are not oracles, we are Communists, and the basis of our decisions and our correct policy is a careful analysis of the given situation. To one Western inquirer I said: "We're not going to do you the favour of spoiling the relations between the party and the broad masses of the working people by advancing faster than is made possible by the actual situation. But neither will we do you the favour of marking time when we are capable of advancing." We are now looking at the facts as they are. At one time, we suffered from the sickness of not seeing things as they were in reality, but as we would have liked them to be. We have recovered from this. It would be best if nobody had suffered from this sickness, but if somebody must suffer from it, then it is better that the sufferer should be some American publicist rather than us Communists. "Now *you* are not capable of seeing the realities", I told the visitor, "or if you do, then you try to see them as you want to. This can be seen from your criticisms and invective. There is nothing in them to influence the Hungarian people. Earlier, unfortunately, a part of them were influenced, but only when there really were troubles to be stirred up and we were silent about them. Now we are not silent about our own mistakes, while you write and talk such nonsense that you have completely lost your credibility. If you don't want to throw your money away completely, then tell your 'distinguished' colleagues that they should lie more cleverly." As for the heart of the matter, we are investigating questions related to the further development of the cooperative farm movement with a full awareness of our responsibilities, with resoluteness on matters of principle, and with the circumspection of a party called upon to lead a country.

We will also continue to strengthen and deepen the healthy features of our public life. We would like to see useful, substantial and fruitful discussion whenever people come together to discuss important public affairs – for instance, at conferences of the Patriotic People's Front. Let those taking part exchange views, let them argue and talk, let them expound their views, and once they reached an agreement that will benefit the community, let them work in unity. In general, we intend to continue to deepen the democracy of our system. This also involves raising the standards of parliamentary life. The democracy of our system today is of a much higher order than that of any capitalist country. And we certainly will continue to improve it. But if this should make anyone wonder if next year or the year after the enemies of our system will enjoy greater freedom, I can assure them that they will not. For just as it is our duty constantly to strengthen the democracy of our system for the benefit of the people, so we are aware of our responsibility to the people and the future of the country and of our obligations with regard to the enemies of the system. There are a few other aspects of our policy, which I only mention in order to confirm your belief that they will continue; indeed, some of them we will try to strengthen. For example, you know about our penal policies. People who crossed the limits of forbearance were imprisoned, while those who committed crimes against the people which could not be overlooked—historical crimes—incurred the severest of penalties. To those who, in common parlance, were muddled, we said: "Be sensible, and work!". This was correct policy, as evidenced by the results, for there was quite a lot of muddled thinking; but, I assure you, eighty per cent of those who were mixed up have by now come to their senses and have in the past two years worked honestly and decently.

Then there was the amnesty. We have gone on record—officially and unofficially—a number of times to say that not a single person will be pardoned in this country so long as there are attempts abroad or on the part of hostile circles to coerce us into this. And if they want no amnesty in Hungary, then they're welcome to try to bring pressure to bear on us. Only when this has ceased, and we consider the time has come, will a further amnesty be granted. There was one this year, and it was by no means inconsiderable, as a very substantial proportion of convicted persons were released from prison.

The Patriotic People's Front has scored a victory and the Hungarian people have passed the test with honours at the election. This was something that both permits and justifies leniency towards erring sons of the people. That is the reason for the amnesty last spring.

We take the work of the Patriotic People's Front very seriously, we count upon it and back it. The political alliance of Communists and non-party people is doing useful service to the cause of socialism and is speeding up our progress. Cooperation between Communists and non-party people, work in the People's Front and the policy of a People's Front have resulted in substantial successes. We will continue to pursue this policy.

We Communists have also devoted much attention to the problem of the cult of personality. We are aware not only of what happened, but also of what may still occur. In a difficult situation, people with good intentions begin to work; by and by they do some things well, successes are scored, achievements made; the masses begin to talk about this and appreciate them because of their good work. Gradually, some of the leaders who are working successfully begin to believe that they know everything, that they are infallible, and they pay no heed to what people say. In connection with this, during the period of preparation for the Congress, we ask our own people once again to examine their methods of work, their relations with other people, to deepen their relations with the masses still more lest the old errors return.

The appeal of socialism must be made stronger and socialist enthusiasm stirred up more effectively—that is an important matter, and it will be done successfully! Day after day, our political leaders and economic executives see the enthusiasm with which ordinary people are working at the workbench, and in the villages, on the cooperative farms! It is our duty to be worthy of—not superior to, only worthy of—our people, of the fight the masses of the Hungarian working people have fought these last forty years. If we—whether of the party or of the Patriotic People's Front—are worthy of the people, we will surely be working well for the cause of progress.

Speech at a Mass Meeting in the Csepel Iron and Metal Works
(Excerpts)

DECEMBER 1, 1961

Dear Comrades,

I heartily greet the working people of Csepel on behalf of the Central Committee of the Hungarian Socialist Workers' Party and the government of the Hungarian People's Republic.

Comrades! Nearly five hundred kilometres from Moscow and almost two and a half thousand kilometres east of here, there lies a large Soviet industrial town with one million inhabitants, bearing the name of the great proletarian writer Gorky. No doubt many of you have read Gorky's novel *Mother*, and I recommend that those who have not, should do so, because this book is an epic of the life and struggle of a revolutionary worker. In this book Gorky wrote about living people and events that actually took place. Its heroes are the workers of the Sormovo Factory. The factory has revolutionary traditions. In the revolution of 1905 the workers of the factory were among the first to rise against Tsarist tyranny; later they fought for the victory of the Great October Socialist Revolution, and today too, they are in the forefront in developing the Soviet Union's industrial production. It was this town and this factory—which today bears the name of Red Sormovo—which I visited, as a representative of Hungarian Communists, and the Hungarian working people, at the time of the Twenty-Second Congress of the Communist Party of the Soviet Union. I took part in a factory meeting similar to the one being held here today. We talked about our common problems, and at the end of the meeting one of the workers of the Red Sormovo Factory said that on behalf of the factory's workers he wished to give me a red flag and a model of a ship built in their factory. He asked me to present them to the working people of Csepel who live far away, yet are so close.

I thought it would be fitting and proper if I also conveyed in person this heartfelt, fraternal greeting to the working people of Csepel which the workers of Red Sormovo extended to me.

In recent years I had two particularly memorable meetings with the working people of Csepel. The first was a meeting of Communist party workers in January 1957. The second was a friendly get-together in the spring of 1958, when I came out to Csepel with Comrade Khrushchev. Local party and economic executives frequently urge government leaders to visit them, stating that this helps them in their work. I believe there is some truth in this! But when we attend such meetings, our purpose is not only to help the comrades working here, but also to gain fresh strength for our own work. For we, members of the party's Central Committee and the government, gain strength and confidence when we feel that our cause is just and has the approval and support of the Hungarian working people.

The most significant international event in the recent past was the Twenty-Second Congress of the Communist Party of the Soviet Union.

The Central Committee of the Hungarian Socialist Workers' Party, our entire party, fully and without reservation agrees with the line of the Twenty-Second Congress, and with the new party programme adopted at the Congress. We are firmly convinced that our party and our government are working in the spirit of Marxism–Leninism, and that their activities have been imbued for over five years with the revolutionary principles laid down by the Twentieth CPSU Congress which have further developed Marxism–Leninism.

The Twenty-Second Congress of the Communist Party of the Soviet Union is following and further developing the line of the Twentieth Congress. Consequently, we are convinced that the essential policies of the Hungarian Socialist Workers' Party have also been strengthened by this Congress.

The Twenty-Second Congress of the Communist Party of the Soviet Union repeatedly and firmly condemned the personality cult. If the Communist Party of the Soviet Union had not overcome the personality cult in good time, then the Twenty-Second Congress could not have decided to build a Communist society within 20 years, and it could not have taken such a firm stand in support of the policy of peaceful coexistence. The personality cult, and everything stemming from it – dogmatic distortion of theory, sectarian views, arbitrariness in the party and in state life, the violation of socialist legality – has retarded and obstructed socialist, Communist progress, disrupted the party and caused damage to the contacts between the party and the masses.

We can hardly appreciate to the full the great achievements registered by the Central Committee, headed by Comrade Khrushchev, which has been fighting since 1953 to eradicate the personality cult. Not everyone agrees with this, however. You know that the Albanian leaders, Enver Hoxha and Mehmet Shehu, do not agree with the condemnation of the cult of Stalin's person, and the personality cult in general. They do not agree with it first of all because the personality cult, and everything that goes with it, is thriving in their country at present. I need not describe to you what the personality cult means in the life of a party and a people, for you were able to see and judge it for yourselves in the early 1950s. The Albanian leaders are not pleased with the condemnation of the personality cult, but the international Communist and working class movement agreed with the Soviet Union and the Central Committee of the CPSU when they publicly criticized and condemned the Albanian leaders for being unable to rid themselves of the personality cult. It should also be noted that among the 80 delegations attending the Congress there was one, the delegation of the fraternal Chinese party, which did not find it proper to criticize the Albanian leaders publicly.

The Hungarian Communists, the overwhelming majority of the international Communist movement and almost every one of the fraternal parties, supported the stand that public criticism was indeed necessary. In the case of a mistaken attitude, patience and internal discussion are possible – perhaps even necessary – for a time in order to let people in the wrong come to their senses. But if there is no sign of a change of attitude, then an open stand and public criticism are undoubtedly in place. The CPSU has taken an open stand before the whole world against the faults of the Albanian leaders stemming from the personality cult. This was moral courage, which shows that we are right, and the masses, the peoples, support us.

I can assure you, on behalf of our party's Central Committee, that our party membership, Hungarian Communists, like the entire Hungarian people, are familiar with the personality cult and want no more of it! People have had too much of arbitrariness within the party and of the practice of failing to observe the law which had begun to thrive in our state life. We have done away with the personality cult. Work is proceeding normally both in party and in state life. I believe all of you feel and know this. Whoever takes part in party work or public affairs knows from experience that the kind of situation which should prevail in a socialist state has developed in our country, both in the revolutionary party of the working class and in public affairs. The rule of law is a matter of major importance for the people. By this we mean, of course, not only that no one will be jailed for something he did not do, but also that the spy should continue to tremble and thieves should continue to go in fear, because part of the socialist rule of law is that the guilty should fear the power of the law. We have done away with the personality cult and we shall prevent its return!

What problems do we have in connection with the personality cult, once we have done away with it? It has been a decision in our country that neither streets nor factories can be named after living persons. We adopted this decision five years ago, and we have observed it since. But such names have remained from earlier times; after a while we shall change them. It is, however, not the name that is decisive, but the spirit that prevails in the factory or on the cooperative farm. Even more attention must be paid to overcoming the erroneous views persisting in people's minds. Although the personality cult no longer exists, there are still people who think in a dogmatic, sectarian manner. We are fighting against these views, because they can cause very great harm.

Seven or eight years ago many people in our country believed that everyone alive was suspect. Do you still remember that? Some people would have liked best to organize a party of ten members in our country, because at the end perhaps they no longer trusted even themselves. What went on at that time? Take a man and begin to tell him: you arouse suspicion, you are flirting with the imperialists. At first he becomes frightened, then he trembles. With these methods they kept hustling people over to the enemy side until finally a few of them really were pushed over to them.

We have overcome this harmful attitude. Now it is not the Central Committee which needs to interfere when, for instance, in one of the branches of the Metal Works somebody longs to play the big boss, the dictator. For there are Communists in the Metal Works who put such persons in their place. And that is how it should be.

This is a good opportunity to keep an eye on how people are acting in public affairs, how they are administering public funds. Generally, officials are performing their job in a normal way. But there is still a tendency towards selfishness, towards extortion, that is, to grabbing everything which can be acquired for nothing. When such an inclination is combined with a leading position, it becomes a public menace. We must see to it that nobody misuses his position. We have certain service enterprises, like pipe-fitters, plumbers, electricians. Nowadays — and this must be said frankly — the plumber still goes out more quickly when the ceiling of an enterprise manager's flat begins to leak than if something goes wrong in the flat of an unskilled worker. Everybody knows this to be true.

Therefore we demand that people in leading posts who exercise authority should sooner forego the rights they are entitled to than misuse their authority and those opportunities inherent in their position.

How do we picture the struggle against the old views? We should not call a man to account for the sectarian views he held eight years ago. We have already overlooked that. He should be carpeted though if he continues to profess his sectarian views today. If five years ago we told people who committed leftist or rightist mistakes: look, you made mistakes, but we do not consider you enemies, come back to the right path, work, and we shall forget what happened, then we cannot take them to task now after five years for the old mistakes, because this would not be fair and honest. Everybody knows who committed mistakes, what kind these were and how he went about correcting them. He who has corrected his errors should be left in peace; while those who have not corrected their mistakes should be taken to task in the light of the lessons of the Twenty-Second Congress and warned to correct these wrong views and practices, otherwise they are bound to face unpleasant consequences. We shall not tolerate anyone in the party who does not regard all activities of the party as being based on confidence in the masses. We can only advance together with the masses. It is most important that relations between the party and the people should be strengthened constantly and continuously.

The Communist Party of the Soviet Union has once again given great help to all the Communist and workers' parties by its firm stand against the remnants of the personality cult at the Twenty-Second Congress. In this connection various questions arise. We hold the view that the CPSU is a party which has accumulated tremendous experience because of its historical past; therefore it is a party from which every Communist and workers' party can learn.

So the question arises: is there a leading party in the international Communist movement; are there possibly more leading parties? The parties throughout the world in the international Communist movement are now acting with full independence and equal rights. So there are no superior or subordinated parties in the international Communist movement, and there is no need for a special leading party — either for one, or for more. What is needed then? From time to time the Communist and workers' parties of the world should convene, discuss common experiences, draft a common line and a common resolution, and each should consider these obligatory — just as at present the Moscow Statement of 1960 is considered binding by the Communist and workers' parties in their activities. In our opinion the responsibility of each Communist party is equal: each Communist party is responsible to its own people and to the international working class movement.

Another question raised was whether the resolutions of one party's congress are binding upon another party; are the resolutions of, say, the Twentieth or the Twenty-

Second Congress binding on other parties? The truth of the matter is that not a single party has ever put forward such a demand. It is self-evident that the resolutions adopted by the congress of a party are binding only on its own members. They are binding on the Communist Party of the Soviet Union and its members; they are not binding on us. But in our opinion, we Hungarian Communists are obliged to study and apply in practice all the revolutionary experiences which can be utilized. If the Twentieth or the Twenty-Second Congress of the CPSU gave us an ideological weapon which can help us in our struggle, it is our duty to study and apply this to conditions in our country. This is how we look upon this Congress. We are convinced that the Twenty-Second Congress of the Communist Party of the Soviet Union gave a powerful ideological weapon to all the Communist and workers' parties in the world and thus to the Hungarian Socialist Workers' Party as well. This Congress gives tremendous new strength and impetus to the struggle of our party also.

Of course, some people do speculate. Their line of reasoning is as follows: see, they have removed Stalin's coffin from the Mausoleum, so a new season is opening for the rightist. I have even heard the opinion expressed that we ought to rehabilitate the persons who demolished Stalin's statue here. Please do not mind my speaking about this now, but it is a very important matter. I say that if that statue were still standing, then we should now adopt a decision to have it removed in January or February. But those who demolished Stalin's statue here did not do it because Stalin had faults, but because they hated Communism. We shall, therefore, never rehabilitate them.

One can hear nowadays that perhaps the revisionists were not sinners after all, for they too were castigating the personality cult. There are quite a lot of people who did not join the party after 1956 and are now thinking that there will be some sort of liberal trend in the Communist partics including our own. This, of course, is an error. The principles on which we build our party are still the same after the Twenty-Second Congress as they have been during the last five years. You know who can be a member of our party. I do not wish to dwell on this in detail, but I could put it quite simply. I suggest that we observe the following: we must aim to have as many non-party people as possible whom we should be pleased to see in our party. This is one of our aims. The other is that there should be as few party members as possible whom we should be pleased to have outside the party. On this basis we get our bearings properly. Let us judge people on the basis of our policy and always consider whether the party will become stronger if one person or other becomes a party member, or whether the party would be stronger if we expelled others. This is the foremost requirement in building the party.

I would like to end by recalling the past struggles and the glorious revolutionary traditions of Csepel and the Csepel works.

At one time we used the term: Red Csepel. Of course, one can always tack the adjective "Red" on to the name if one wants to, but this is not absolutely necessary. It is much more important that it really should be "Red" Csepel in work, steadfastness, culture and socialist firmness. On the basis of Csepel's revolutionary past and its achievements in socialist construction I can say: the workers of Sormovo sent this flag to a good place, and I resolved to take it and hand it over to Csepel, because Csepel deserves it for its historic past, and present achievements.

Csepel's work has also left its imprint on this year's results. It is a great thing that you have increased production by 11 per cent instead of the planned 8 per cent in comparison to last year. Just before the meeting we toured the Metal Works. This factory has grown so vast that one day is hardly enough to walk through it. This factory is, both in a figurative and in an actual sense, a battleground for the new, for the new Hungarian industry.

What did I like in this factory? First of all, the noticeable flow of socialist creative work. You are full of plans which help the development of socialist industry. There are many young executives in the factory. Of course, youthfulness is a relative concept. I do not know whether your idea of a young person is the same as mine. To me, people around 40 years of age — who are executives of big departments and shops — are still young. Here, they say "He is young, but he knows his job." Yes, he is driven by socialist, Communist enthusiasm. He has the training, and he knows how to handle people!

Comrades, cherish and cultivate this spirit in this factory, as we must cherish and cultivate it throughout the country. Then progress will be faster.

I would like to ask you now to accept officially from me this red flag which the best Soviet working men and women in the city of Gorky have sent to you with genuine fraternal love, as a symbol of fraternal Hungarian–Soviet friendship. I ask you to be loyal to this friendship, to be loyal to the socialist ideals of our people in your work, in your conduct and in your culture.

There is still great pleasure to come from those results which we have so far achieved, and which we will achieve in the future.

I wholeheartedly wish every worker in the factory good health and the best of success. I ask you to bear in mind constantly that the Central Committee and the government are unshakeable in upholding the cause of Communism. The foundation of our struggle is the confidence which you and the whole Hungarian people will give us in the future as you have in the past five years.

Speech at the Budapest Party Conference
(Excerpts)

OCTOBER 31, 1962

Dear Comrades,

In this period of preparation for our Congress it is important to get a proper picture of the unity of our party, and of the political situation within it. Our party's ideological unity is firm, so it is also firm politically and organizationally. This unity also expresses the great power of our party's main political line, the fact that it is based on the unshakeable foundations of Marxism–Leninism and enjoys the fullest and maximum support of the masses.

During the last twenty years our country has gone through numerous historical changes of a positive and negative character, through many important events which severely tested socialist thinking, the Communist movement and the international revolutionary movement.

These changes of fortune steeled and consolidated the ranks of the Hungarian Communists and taught them to shy away from revisionism which leads to class betrayal, and also from the dogmatic, sectarian tendencies which are so destructive to Communism. The struggles of the six years since the counter-revolution have proved that Hungarian Communists are adherents of pure and inviolable Marxism–Leninism, of cohesion with the people, of a genuine, true and undistorted Communist policy.

Are there any debates in our party, among us Communists? Yes, there are. During the past six years the Central Committee stimulated, encouraged and prompted the entire party membership, when any problem of the revolutionary movement was raised in any party organization, to make a comprehensive examination of each and every question; to give free expression to all opinions in connection with all problems, and to decide the standpoint of the party and party organizations on the basis of a thoroughgoing discussion on all aspects of the question. We are convinced that this — i.e. creative discussion — is not a formal matter, but the indispensable condition for party unity based on ideological and principled foundations. This is real strength, because people who can freely express their opinion, approval or doubts, and who listen to convincing counter-arguments during a discussion, will leave a meeting knowing that it is their own decisions that they are setting out to implement. This gives our party great and multiple strength.

The Central Committee of the party is now following a method which is well known both to you and to the public throughout the country. When the party takes a stand on matters affecting millions — and the Central Committee's resolutions are as a rule of such a character — we are not satisfied with a thorough and searching examination and discussion of the tasks by Communists only. We involve the broadest circles of non-party workers concerned in the implementation of the resolution, on all possible occasions.

In what does the strength of this method lie? It does away with the need for discussion afterwards. It is equally true under capitalist dictatorship and the revolutionary dictatorship of the proletariat that when the party goes into battle, it can rely only on as many people and as much strength in each issue as it succeeds in convincing of the justness and correctness of the cause or of its stand. We should never mislead either ourselves or the party on this score. Explaining, answering questions, and persuading those who are unsure is indispensable!

The general unity of our party depends primarily on the extent to which the Central Committee is firm and cohesive. Things often occur which our half-a-million members know nothing about, because it is physically impossible, by the nature of things, for them to know about everything. In such a situation the Central Committee takes a stand. The Congress is given the task of evaluating the work of the Central Committee and, if necessary, criticizing it.

The useful and creative pre-Congress discussions raised a number of questions. On some issues, and they came to the forefront, the great majority of the party membership understands and approves of the position of the Central Committee, while a minority does not understand or understands it poorly, or understands it properly but does not agree.

I am not going to take these one by one, but I would like to dwell, with your permission, on three debated questions.

The first is the abolition of the categories classifying student youth according to social origin.

Although officially this refers to students, in essence, in actual fact and in its direct repercussions, it affects admission to the universities. Does the directive state who should be admitted to the universities and colleges? Not at all; but it makes clear that there must not be one single category of Hungarian youth which is excluded, from the outset, from the possibility of admission. I believe that if we get to the kernel of the matter, then this is its concrete and direct practical bearing.

Looking at it from the perspective of the weighty problems of the class struggle — by limiting the problem to its essentials, i.e. that a not very large stratum of Hungarian youth should not be deprived of the chance to enter university or college — I do not think that this is a big problem. At least not as weighty as many well-intentioned polemicists consider it to be. Some people even go so far as to sound the alarm, saying that our proletarian homeland is in danger. If the Congress approves the proposal to abolish categories based on social origin, this principle may be applied by September next year. Let us presume that a number of such young men are admitted. Taking September 1 next year as the starting point, it would take ten years for these people to be in a position to perhaps endanger the safety of our proletarian homeland — if they wanted to, and if conditions made it possible; this ten-year period is based on the growing length of studies and the years of practice following it. By that time social development will have advanced so much that not a single person will even remember these problems. The topics of our discussion in September and October 1962, will by then be forgotten by everybody. The distinctions among student youth on the basis of social origin were correct and just at a certain period of our historic development. We had some historical catching up to do: we had to ensure the admission to the universities and colleges of the sons and daughters of the working class and peasantry who for generations had been denied opportunities for education. This was a Communist stand; it was beneficial and helped the cause of the party.

But Comrade Lenin warned us that every slogan is bound to become outdated because of changing circumstances and relations, and if we stubbornly cling to a slogan, it becomes a dogma, which is no longer a help but becomes detrimental to our cause. As far as this problem is concerned, we must realize that continued restrictions would become harmful to the cause of socialist construction, instead of helping it.

The question arises: how can we ensure the admission of working class and peasant youth to the universities and colleges from now on? This question is justified.

It is my personal conviction that our society must extend assistance and support to those working-class and peasant youngsters who start with a definite personal handicap, so to speak, because of the lower cultural standards of their parents; they cannot get the same help in their studies at home as is given to the children of parents with higher education. I am convinced that if we tackle this problem correctly and turn our society's attention to this task, then the help will be forthcoming. Instead of fewer working-class and peasant youths, more will enter the universities and colleges than at present.

I would like to ask those who are concerned with this problem not to maintain these categories in their minds mechanically, and not to judge on the basis of whether the parents were workers or peasants before 1938, not to take only this into consideration. Instead they should pay greater attention to youths who are qualified to enter and are, in fact, enrolled at universities, and whose parents are working in the foundries, digging coal in the mines or tilling the soil for our people even today, and should extend greater assistance to them. In this great discussion we are apt to forget a very essential internal factor of this matter, namely that as a matter of course we should help those parents who are working in the factories, mines, fields or other spheres of productive labour. They must be given greater social assistance and help in doing away with whatever handicaps their children may face, so that their children may study at the colleges and universities under pretty much the same conditions as others.

Why do the directives state that we should end categorizing student youth according to their social origin? Because although this always referred in principle to universities and colleges, there was a period when party work and work in general was unfortunately quite bureaucratic, and subjected the entire student youth to scrutiny, registering them on the basis of their parents' occupation in 1938, something which was never necessary. They stated that if we must know at university admission level what the student's parents did in 1938 – whether they were workers, peasants or something else – then we should know it in case of secondary-school students as well. And they went ahead and registered secondary-school students. This reasoning led to the following: if we must know what the parents of the secondary-school student did in 1938, then we must start registering this information in the sixth grade of the general schools at least. And that is what they did. Now let us take a young man who will be 18 next September. According to present statistical data his average life expectancy is at least another fifty years. And he will develop into somebody. Who he will be depends to a great extent on us and our society. And we do not want to raise the children of the former exploiting class to become disillusioned hooligans with a shattered life, but to be honest, decent, staunch and fully-fledged builders of socialism. This is a Communist standpoint, and also stems from the interests of our socialist cause. It would be unjust to place a child born after the Liberation into a position which is to his legal detriment in any respect because of something which existed in another world, another society, six to eight years before he was even born. Let me add something else: I believe that we should also consider that there are many former capitalists who have become resigned to the fact that their lives as capitalists are finished, and who acknowledge this, but cannot accept that the roads of life are barred to their children.

The second debated question is the policy of alliance. The party's policy of alliance is one of class alliance. The question of class alliance is often confused with relations to people, although this is an entirely different problem. Class alliance is based on cooperation, under the leadership of the working class, between the working class, the peasantry and the intelligentsia, and the stratum – and an important one at that – of the urban petty bourgeoisie. The decisive factor in this class alliance is the nature of its basic principles and the reason for its establishment, together with its objective. The underlying principle of our alliance is our ideology; its objective is the building of a socialist society. This policy of alliance is therefore correct and gives strength to our cause.

The next problem is unity, alliance – and again I am using this term although this is not a class alliance – and collaboration with non-party people. I use this term because I recently read the statement in an article by Lenin that Communists must establish everywhere, in all spheres of work, an alliance with non-party people. This actually means cooperation, working together, or – as we used a different term in connection with another problem – the principled demand that non-party people should also be appointed to leading positions. The gist of the matter is that this cooperation is established on the basis of socialist principles and in the interests of building a socialist society. And this is decisive.

What are our demands in the case of non-party people? That they should be faithful to the cause of socialism, should be loyal citizens of our People's Republic, should want to work for the building of socialism – this is our first demand. The second is that they should be well-trained specialists. These are our two demands. We are not, therefore, faced with the alternatives of placing in some position either a reliable working-class revolutionary who is not good in that particular line, or a non-party expert who is good professionally but can be suspected of a reactionary, counter-revolutionary attitude.

The preparations for the Congress are also linked with the selection of cadres. Many discussions have taken place on the strengthening of local party committees. At times it happened that a man who was described as a fine man, a master of his trade, a decent man who knew how to work for socialism was under consideration. To play safe, we checked up on his party membership, on whether he joined two or twenty years ago. It turned out more than once that he was not even a party member. The wonderful thing in this is that we have been working with people for years; we actually hear them speak up for, and see them take a firm stand on, the building of socialism; we label them good comrades and then it turns out that they are not even party members. This is fine. Our fond desire is becoming a reality, namely to have very few people in the party whom we would prefer to be outside the party's ranks, and to have very many people outside the party whom we would gladly accept as comrades, as party members. This is something to be pleased about, it is a fine thing and we should strive to have many more such cases. It is on this basis and under such circumstances that the demand is raised to have non-party people in leading posts.

Objections have been raised by comrades on several occasions that very little has been said lately about appreciating Communists, while we keep on talking about appreciating non-party people. Is this so? We have to admit self-critically that it is. The party and functionaries speaking on behalf of the party, in various places and over several years, have hardly dwelt on the appreciation of Communists, while they have continuously advocated that non-party people should be honoured. The question might be raised whether this is right or wrong. Is it a Communist standpoint or isn't it? Well, it would not be difficult at all for the Communist party to keep on endlessly praising Communists. What would this lead to? It would be quite dangerous, like the famous phrase of Stalin that the Communists are people of a special mould. Would it be in line with our world outlook to divide mankind into two categories, supermen and second-rate people? This would not be right, it would not be a Communist, a Marxist–Leninist position. Let us just keep on praising non-party people, and wait until non-party people start praising Communists. This is much better than the other way around, with Communists applauding Communists and non-party people applauding those who are outside the party's ranks. It is far better if Communists have words of praise for non-party people, while the non-party people have good words, which spring from conviction, to say about Communists. It is not actually correct for me to say that we will wait for that time – because that time has already come. We have reached a point in our country when non-party people speak with a great deal of appreciation about Communists – and this is a healthy state of affairs, it is good. This is what we should tell those comrades who ask in good faith why the party has for several years been saying so little about the recognition and appreciation of Communists, while talking all the time about non-party people. You can see for yourselves that this has led to the appreciation of Communists. Generally speaking, this whole political line can only be evaluated in its overall effect and its entirety, in a Marxist–Leninist manner. One cannot separate and isolate the problems, the policy of alliance, the placement of non-party people in leading posts, and the ending of categories according to social origin; they should be taken in their entirety, together and in their total effect.

What was the result of the policy consistently followed during these six years? It can be summarized as follows:

The leading role of the working class in our society's life is firm and cannot seriously be contested by anybody. It is incontestable, not because this is prohibited by law, but because the working class, the leading class of society, have achieved undivided recognition by the other classes and strata of society owing to their consistency and – this is the proper term to use – heroism, to their efforts and struggles, thus proving that they are indeed the force destined to lead society.

As we are discussing the consistent policy of six years, let us compare the leading role of the party with the situation six years ago. It is an incontestable and generally recognized fact that Communists enjoy a greater, more sincere and more profound esteem than before. Considering the essential problems of the struggle, we can state that during the last six years capitalist, private ownership of the means of production did not grow stronger, but it was socialist ownership, the common ownership, which gathered strength; this took place to such an extent and under such conditions that we can point to a tremendous change, because we have laid the foundations of a socialist society. To this one should add the unrestrained, creative atmosphere prevailing in our country, which cannot be questioned by anyone. This is the most surprising fact to a visitor from the West, no matter who he may be. Let me add to this the establishment of a continuously strengthening, broadening and consolidating popular-national unity, based on a platform of socialist construction and the safeguarding of peace. All this is the result of our policy, which must be the starting point in the correct Marxist evaluation of a problem.

A number of other important questions were also taken up at the pre-Congress conferences and meetings. Some remarks were made concerning the pre-Congress meetings, party conferences and membership meetings in the factories; they were criticized for having at times practically turned into production meetings. It is, of course, a political error if the essential political questions are not discussed at such gatherings. But it is not accidental and not even so bad if working people, and creative people in general, do not meditate too much on the question of whether putting non-party people into leading posts is a Marxist or a liberal act if instead they simply state that "the situation in our country is generally normal, one can go ahead and work, and as we are building socialism, let us discuss the ways, and means of construction". This is not such a big problem. In this case the factory worker has the same viewpoint as Lenin had. As is well known Lenin stated that capitalism defeated feudalism by ensuring a higher productivity of labour and a greater abundance of goods for society. Socialism will also finally and completely defeat capitalism by creating a higher productivity of labour and a greater abundance of goods. This shows that the workers and Lenin are on the same platform. And we can learn from them!

How do we stand now with regard to labour productivity? We stated, during the meetings last spring and in connection with the congress directives, that we should use two kinds of yardsticks: our past standard, which we have left behind, and the world standard. We have started to do this, and the Central Committee also took steps in this connection. The question of productivity was examined and we found the following: at present the United States of America is way ahead in standards of labour productivity. Then come the advanced western capitalist countries, the Soviet Union, the German Democratic Republic and Czechoslovakia, all more or less on the same level. Then comes a considerably lower standard, and this is where we, the Hungarian People's Republic, stand. I trust everybody understands that the most essential problem of our entire work is the raising of labour productivity in industry, agriculture, and everywhere else where people carry on productive, creative work. Because our objective – to surpass capitalist society and defeat it in peaceful competition – can only be reached in one way: through a victory attained in the field of labour productivity – and through nothing else!

Interview Given to André Wurmser, Correspondent of "L'Humanité"

JANUARY 6, 1963

ANDRÉ WURMSER: No single government has gone through birthpangs such as yours. It was not recognized by many states in 1956 and was by no means popular. Six years later you are praised by the most varied organs of the press, often quite unexpectedly. How did you get so far so quickly?

JÁNOS KÁDÁR: Let me begin with the story of another interview. In November 1956, when anarchy was at its height, with shooting going on almost everywhere, I was notified that a journalist wished to interview me. An interview? That was all I needed! I asked for the name of the journalist and was told that André Stil wanted to see me. All right, let him come. Stil came and I told him that there would be no interview, but I would describe the situation to him and my stand on matters. If he wanted to make use of it, he could. My intention was to inform the French comrades of what was happening through him. He made an interview from our talk which I was only able to read two months later. It was very good, and quite useful at that time.

A. W.: I shall never forget the week when we did not get any direct news from Hungary at *l'Humanité*. Our only "source of information" was the enemy. That is why André Stil came to Budapest.

J. K.: Frankly speaking, there were not many people in Budapest at that time who knew what was going on in the country. You are asking me now why and how the situation changed so radically within such a short time. You also mention the question of popularity. This is extremely important for us, not in the everyday sense of the word, but from the point of view of gauging the approval and support of the people for government policy. The popularity or unpopularity of the government is a yardstick of the party's authority when the party is in power. There are a few non-party ministers in our government, but it is no secret to the Hungarian people and to foreign public opinion that the government is implementing the party's policies.

We can state that the popularity of the party and government is incomparably greater than at the end of 1956. Experience has proved that in order to raise its influence among the masses the party must take a stand based on principles on all questions. We must always take into consideration, of course, the response to our resolutions, but this cannot be the starting point for us. We were compelled to take a number of measures at the end of 1956 which were disapproved of by many people; had we yielded at that time to confused and erroneous ideas, these same people would have cursed us a year later.

The essential thing is that the working masses should realize that our policy corresponds to their best interests. They saw this and understood it. Expressing this in terms of ideology we can say that the working masses have identified themselves with the ideas of socialism; moreover they demand, on the basis of their own experience, that this policy be really Communist, devoid of distortions, abuses and inconsistencies.

Our people became familiar with the extreme forms of the two deviations: with dogmatism and sectarianism on the one hand, and revisionism on the other. They paid a high price for this double and bitter experience. Our people have not only learned the ideas of socialism, but also how it is implemented to the full in practice, and they are ready to work for its complete realization. But they do not want either revisionism, which leads in the long run to class betrayal, the betrayal of people's Hungary, or dogmatism which results in isolation from the people and in the long run also in the destruction of the fundamental achievements of socialism.

People call for consistency in our policy. They have not forgotten the deep crisis which appeared, beginning with the summer of 1953, throughout the party, the working class and the entire country. It is their conviction that there must be no basic change in the political line over short periods of time, because then, in the end, they can neither know what is expected of them, nor what they are working for.

Finally, the policy of the party and the government must be open and above-board. Our entire people must always be told clearly what the objective is, and what the road leading to it. They have to be told openly who we rely on, who we are fighting against and what methods we wish to apply. One cannot gloss over the difficulties to be surmounted, nor the mistakes which were made.

The masses not only expect frankness from us, they demand unity of word and deed; that they should look upon politics as something which consists of declarations and speeches, while the reality is something entirely different, must be avoided.

You must have noticed that there is really very little new in our ideological theses, our methods and style of work. Our party can attribute the effectiveness of its work to its return to the teachings and practice of Marxism–Leninism. It rid itself of the distortions of the personality cult, and also of the burdens of revisionist class treason. But neither the Central Committee of our party, nor the government, at the state level, has discovered anything new.

A. W.: Allow me to interrupt you, Comrade Kádár. You undoubtedly belong among those persons of the socialist world who today are least criticized by the Western press; it happens that democrats and liberals present you as a model to the French Communists whom they blame for always harping on the same string. Yet you attribute your wonderful successes from the very outset to strict adherence to the "by no means new" Marxist–Leninist line. This is piquant.

J. K.: Yes, I know... But let us only speak about Hungary. Many kinds of people now support us in Hungary, from different considerations. The majority are conscious supporters of socialism. But we are also backed by people with a relatively low social consciousness, who are primarily interested in their own and their family's living conditions. They are not much interested in ideology, the personality cult is profoundly unintelligible to them, and they have very little notion of revisionism either; all they say is that life has become easier and better, therefore they are in agreement with us. But we know that other people, the spiritual relatives of the men mentioned by you, also speak about us at times with a certain amount of recognition. Why is this so?

For two reasons. First because they tried in 1956 for something more to their liking, a sort of a coalition consisting of Mindszenty, Imre Nagy, Ferenc Nagy and their kind, but it did not work out. They resign themselves therefore to something which exists and which — as they say — is not the worst. The second reason is that they lull themselves with illusions. They believe that we are facing a development which they gladly label liberalization; they imagine and hope that we will swerve from the fundamentals of socialism.

A. W.: They still keep on confusing freedom with liberalism.

J. K.: Yes, that is what it is all about. They keep on hoping. Well, let them keep on hoping... The development which took place in Hungary during recent years repeatedly proved the correctness of the Leninist idea that nothing is as important for the masses as their own experience. Our people lived through all imaginable experiences: they became familiar with a more or less correct Communist policy during the first three years after the Liberation, then they lived through the years of the personality cult, followed by a period of revisionist treason and the counter-revolutionary insurrection; finally during the past six years they could learn from day to day how correct the principles of Marxism–Leninism are.

A. W.: To top it all, what has happened is exceptionally daring and new. Your government threw open the doors at all levels of state life to every Hungarian, making only one demand: that they should be qualified, honest and loyal to the system. The social origin of those applying for admission to universities is no longer considered. Since June 1, 25,000 Hungarians with passports to travel abroad were given seventy dollars each in return for the required sum in forints. Your theatres put on satirical programmes which spare neither the government nor the system, and which are playing to capacity audiences. And these are only some of the characteristic novelties. I have a number of Hungarian friends. Frankly, some consider these measures as the guarantees of socialism's stability in Hungary, while others wonder whether this confidence and liberality is not premature and risky.

J. K.: You are right to raise this question and I will give a straightforward answer. This problem is being raised here, too: in fact some people even say that this or that of our measures is not correct in principle. We do not resent this, since it is quite natural that at certain stages of development such questions should be raised by some people in such a form. I will therefore try to answer you.

The measures referred to are parts of a whole. What we are faced with is no less than the Leninist answer to *topical* problems, that is, answering problems which Marx, Engels and Lenin could not deal with, because they could not guess that they would arise in Hungary in 1962. We have to solve them with the aid of the compass they bequeathed to us.

Our resolution springs from two sources: our faith in the justness of socialism and our confidence in the masses.

A. W.: Only good manners stop me from applauding.

J. K.: Is this faith and confidence justified? Everyday reality answers this question. For six years the party has been repeating that Communists must join forces with non-party people, and the party carries out this principle in practice. Is this right? One cannot answer this question without knowing the reason for this cooperation. If party members and non-party people were to join forces in order to destroy the achievements of socialism, this cooperation would not be correct. If they unite in building a socialist society, then joining forces in this way is correct. Communists and non-party people know, of course, that the purpose of this alliance is to build socialism.

For six years the party has not boasted daily about its leading role and has not delivered long-winded speeches about the dictatorship of the proletariat. Moreover, we took a stand against the thesis of Stalin that Communists are people of a special mould. This thesis is incorrect. Communists are of the same mould as any other people, with the difference that they have a scientific outlook on the world, a clear-cut objective and a high level of social consciousness. Finally, for the past six years the party has been urging that non-party people should be given appreciation and congratulated when they do good work, and that paeans of praise should never be sung about Communists...

Well, what is the result? There is no question about the leading role of the party. Our People's Republic, the expression of the proletarian dictatorship, is vigorous; Communists enjoy a reputation which is higher than ever; we have laid the foundations of socialism. The cornerstone of our entire concept is the expropriation of the means of production and their social ownership. Well, the social ownership of the means of production has undergone a great deal of expansion during the last six years; more than 95 per cent of the population is working under socialist production relations, with means of production belonging to the community.

That is why we feel that it is right for Communists to continue to congratulate non-party people and for non-party people to maintain their high regard for Communists; we think this a more wholesome situation. For this reason we believe that the above measures were taken on the basis of principle and by no means impetuously.

A. W.: I knew that sooner or later such measures would be taken, but did not expect them so soon. Perhaps I was not optimistic enough?

J. K.: My answer is as follows: I was convinced that such measures would be taken sooner or later, but I did not expect that they would be taken so soon either. We Communists were convinced, even during the most critical moments of the counter-revolutionary insurrection, of the victory of Communism, but we could not say how and when we would succeed in setting right the questions of principle and policy in people's minds. But this was accomplished faster and better than anticipated. And this holds good for everything, the consolidation of the People's Republic, the restoration of law and order, the results of the 1958 elections and the socialist reorganization of agriculture.

What does it prove? That the socialist idea has struck deeper roots among the masses of people than we thought and that not only the Central Committee, the government and the Communists, but the entire people, have undergone a tremendous political advance in the hard school of historical trials and tribulations.

We had confidence in the people, but these six years have taught us that we can have still greater confidence in them...

A. W.: Can we draw other lessons from what you say, Comrade Kádár? If a determined and wise policy made it possible for socialism to accomplish such rapid results, it is certain that this holds good the other way round: the mistakes, exposed and corrected by the Twentieth Congress, acted as a brake on success and retarded the victory of socialism.

J. K.: I will only deal with the experiences here in Hungary which I know best. We are indeed working in the spirit of the Twentieth Congress, whose fundamental feature was the return to the Marxist–Leninist line, free of all deviations and all concessions to the class enemy. The Twentieth Congress, by freeing the international Communist movement from the curse of the personality cult, brought about a regeneration; we Hungarians are also enjoying the benefits of this, which is expressed in the onward march of the international Communist movement. Because the mistakes did indeed check, hold back and, in fact, fundamentally jeopardize the achievements and advance of socialism — especially in Hungary.

A. W.: They did jeopardize it... and yet when all is said and done, whereas in 1876, five years after the Commune, MacMahon refused Victor Hugo's request that the deportation of a young communard journalist be postponed, you declare, six years after the Budapest events, that 95 per cent of the political prisoners are free and the defectors have been invited to return. Does not this throw light on the October 1956 events?

J. K.: Our views have not changed... We have been proclaiming since November 4 [1956] that the party and the government are not guided by the spirit of revenge and we must determine through thorough analysis the forces which rallied against the People's Republic. They included, first of all, our sworn class enemies: the domestic bourgeoisie and international imperialism. Then came the rabble: the counter-revolution released 9,000 murderers, thieves and criminals of all types from prison. What stand must be taken against these people? The answer is clear: the class enemy, if it uses violence, must be answered with violence. As to the criminals, they should be sent back, as far as possible, to where they came from.

There were many other people, however, who came into conflict with the People's Republic; yet the prime responsibility for their attitude lies not in themselves, but in the wrong policies which for years undermined the rule of law and violated many things without which people cannot live and work. The revisionists also played a detrimental role and misled people by stating that they wanted to implement the spirit of the Twentieth Congress in Hungary, while in reality they leagued themselves with all kinds of enemies of people's democracy. The fact that so many totally different forces could be rallied against us is a proof of the excellent tactical sense of our enemies. Their real objective was obviously the abolition of socialism and the restoration of capitalism. To accomplish this goal they wanted to sever Hungary's ties with the Warsaw Treaty, thereby depriving her of protection and delivering her to the mercy of international imperialism. At the beginning they kept these objectives hidden, but later proclaimed them openly, during the days of the open counter-revolutionary insurrection, as was done, for instance, in the infamous radio statement of Cardinal Mindszenty on November 3.

But what slogans were used during the preceding period when the hostile forces were consolidating and rallying, that is between summer 1953 and October 1956? During the summer of 1953 they demanded the restoration of democracy in the party, and of socialist law and order in the country; in 1956 they called for the implementation of the spirit of the Twentieth Congress. They pushed Imre Nagy and his group to the forefront; they were followed by people who were not able to differentiate politically between the Right and the Left; further in the background were the bourgeoisie and imperialism. We have, by the way, many telling statements from the summer of 1956; in connection with Imre Nagy, the counter-revolutionary leaders of the Hungarian émigrés pointed out to the press that it did not disturb them in the least that the movement was headed by a Communist; the important thing was that they should achieve a breakthrough. Thus came October 23 when Imre Nagy and his group acted as doormen: they threw the gates wide open. Then everything changed with amazing speed. The forces standing in the background moved into the front line, while those who till then had stood in the forefront were pushed increasingly into the background. On November 3, the principal role was already being played by Mindszenty.

We had had a similar experience once before: our enemies' 1956 tactics repeated those of 1919 with amazing precision. In 1919, too, there was a counter-revolutionary grouping in Hungary, which was supported by international imperialism. In 1919, Horthy's counter-revolution had the direct backing of the French imperialist army, whereas in 1956 the Americans played that role. And what happened in Hungary in 1919? The enemies of socialism advocated that it was socialism they wanted, but it should be a democratic socialism! They overthrew the Republic of Councils and replaced it by a so-called "trade union government" headed by a certain Peidl. The Peidl group was in power for only six days. On the sixth day about fifteen counter-revolutionaries entered the government building and declared: now you are to get out. And the ministers took their hats and coats and left. This was the beginning of the Horthy Fascist terror which weighed the Hungarian people down for twenty-five years. I presume that Imre Nagy was destined to play a similar role. He, too, would have been told after six days: get up and get out. And he would have taken his hat and coat and left.

Coming back to your question, the essential problem was not to put the sworn enemies of the system in the same category as those who, either because of ideological confusion or for some other reason, came into conflict with the People's Republic. Our state meted out severe punishment to the major criminals who were arrested, was less severe with others, while other people, the great majority, were told to go home and think matters over. The majority of those penalized have been amnestied – and as you pointed out: 95 per cent of the political prisoners have been freed...

Then again, when inviting emigrants to return to Hungary, we do so in the conviction that the majority will be able to find their place in our society and get along properly in their homeland. As for those who do not want to return to Hungary for some family or other reasons, we call upon them to live decently in the country in which they will become naturalized citizens, and to support the cause of peace and progress. One group of émigrés – the smallest in number – simply sold out to reaction. But we want even these people to find their way back to decent life.

A. W.: Your humanism and patriotism prompt me to ask another question. You have stated that the time has come to replace the notorious catchphrase "He who is not with us is against us" with the phrase of trust: "He who is not against us is with us." We know how much trouble came from vigilance changing into systematic distrust, but undoubtedly you are taking up the cudgels against more than just suspicion when you speak so emphatically about "the party of the entire nation".

J. K.: Let us look at this question more closely. The Hungarian Socialist Workers' Party is the revolutionary vanguard of the working class. However, the party is developing and its role is changing. We can state now that our party is on the road to becoming the party of the entire people, while socialism is becoming the objective of the entire nation. With this we wish to demonstrate that socialism will bring into being the national prosperity forecast by the greatest Hungarian patriots. Socialism is no more the exclusive goal of the party or the working class, it does not serve only the cause of the working class, but is being achieved for the good of the entire people, and can only be achieved by the entire people.

There are no longer classes in our country whose interests conflict with socialism. The ideas of socialism and Communism are widespread. Moreover, there is a growing certainty that socialism ensures prosperity and coincides with the interests of all working people. We can therefore say that understanding is also rising constantly and people are becoming, ever more consciously, builders of a socialist society. These facts cannot be reconciled with a lack of confidence in the masses, or with a distrust of people belonging to various social categories, something which prevailed under the personality cult. Distrust engenders distrust, while confidence generates confidence. I can cite two examples.

Early in 1957, when we still could not entirely isolate the anarchistic elements and there were still a large number of weapons about, though we did not know where or in whose hands they were, we organized and armed the Workers' Militia. The Workers' Militia, by the way, does not consist of workers only, but also includes peasants, office employees and intellectuals. Thus many Hungarians have possessed weapons for the past six years. When we provided them with weapons we could not guarantee that they were in complete agreement with us, and on every question; we were merely convinced that they were supporters of people's democracy. This is why we told them: "Hold on to your weapons, and defend the regime, if necessary!" As the people we armed saw that we had confidence in them, they, on their part, answered with confidence, too. In not one single case, not once, was one of these weapons turned against the regime.

Let us now speak about the countryside. We have approximately 4,200 cooperative farms. Discussions were carried on with some peasants for eight to ten years, and many who did not join the cooperatives were excellent farmers. Such a peasant finally makes up his mind and joins. When it comes to the election of the president of the cooperative farm, members vote him into office. Our man just cannot make sense of it; how does it happen that he who until recently was farming on his own and disputing with cooperative members is now elected president? But the members keep on insisting: "Never mind, just accept it, since we know that you are the right man for the job and we have confidence in you." Hundreds of such cases took place and the "presidents" had the same idea in every case: if the entire community, including the party organization, trusts me, I cannot disappoint them. A few of these leaders — perhaps less than five in the entire country — were later replaced by the cooperative farmers but this was because of incompetence, because there is quite a difference between farming on nine holds and managing a farm of 2,500 holds. But let me repeat, never in a single case was the replacement because of political reasons or opposition to our regime. A policy of confidence always pays off, whether it is a case of providing weapons to the Workers' Militia or the appointment of somebody to the leadership of a cooperative farm.

A. W.: In other words, confidence brings in returns. But can one draw the conclusion from your remarks that the party's role will diminish?

J. K.: The party's role has not diminished during recent years; on the contrary, it has increased, and will continue to do so during the entire period of socialist construction. What will change is the character of the problems coming to the forefront: the principal task of the party organizations will be concentrated ever more on the problems of economic and cultural construction. Social control must be organized and the people mobilized to solve the tasks at hand; and this must be done by the party.

A. W.: Will the party membership, in your opinion, grow or decline in the coming period?

J. K.: It will increase.

A. W.: And is it increasing?

J. K.: In this respect Hungary's position differs somewhat from that of the other socialist countries. We reorganized the party between early November 1956 and May 1, 1957. But the issuing of new party cards was not done automatically, it was controlled. Following reorganization, party membership was approximately 40 per cent of that preceding the counter-revolution. This truly qualitative change had necessarily to be followed by a certain growth. We are faced, first of all, with the young generation, to whom we could not close the doors of the party. Moreover, our policies attracted people who did not join the party before; 38 per cent of our present membership did not belong to the party before 1956.

A. W.: While we are on this subject, what is the relationship today between former Social Democrats and Communists in the Hungarian Socialist Workers' Party?

J. K.: The Communist Party of Hungary, one of the first Marxist–Leninist parties, was formed on November 20, 1918. Prior to this, however, the Social Democratic Party was for a long time the vanguard of the working class; it was the first workers' party in Hungary, born during the last decades of the last century. The merger of the two parties fourteen years ago was a great victory for the working class.

After unification, a number of former Social Democrats suffered under a repression which incidentally did not spare Communists either. We condemn these measures and consider restitution for the damage caused by them our responsibility. At present there is unity in our party. I could cite a number of former Social Democrats who are members of the Central Committee, hold important state positions or are functionaries in social and trade union bodies, e.g. Comrades Kisházi[17], Nyers[18], Rónai[19], Szakasits and Szurdi[20]. One has to think hard today to recall who were Social Democrats before unification; such categories belong to the past. This is logical, too, since a long and desperate struggle has been waged over fourteen years, first against dogmatism, then against revisionism, later against counter-revolution, and finally for the actual building of socialism. There have been so many changes and so many ideological clashes that selection has taken place on its own. It is not necessary now to differentiate between party members on the grounds of whether they belonged to the Communist or the Social Democratic Party in the past; it is sufficient to know their conduct during this period, in these struggles. Unification, internal cohesion, has become an accomplished fact.

But now let us leave topical problems. Relations between socialists and Communists go back to an earlier period. During the Horthy regime, when Communist party organizations were driven underground, I first joined the Federation of Young Communist Workers. Then I was given an assigment to work in the Social Democratic Party and the trade unions. In that epoch we cooperated with the progressive elements of the Social Democratic Party on the basis of agreement. I was also a trade union shop steward. I got to know thousands of Social Democrats; some of them were conscious and staunch partisans of the working class, others professed petty-bourgeois views, while some were progressive liberals who became Social Democrats as they developed.

I had plenty of discussions in those days with Social Democratic comrades about the lessons of history. There was a country where the Communist Party was in power; in that country they had nationalized the means of production and laid the foundations of a socialist society. That country was the Soviet Union. Then there were other countries with socialist, Social Democratic or labour governments, like Great Britain, France, the Weimar Republic, the Scandinavian countries... I maintain that it is by no means a matter of indifference to us whether a country has a Social Democratic or a conservative government. If I had to choose between the rule of a socialist or conservative government in a capitalist country, I would always "vote" for the socialist government. Yet what does history teach us? These socialist governments secured at times considerable benefits for their people. In Britain, for instance, five million people received free dental care. It is by no means a matter of indifference to these five million people whether their teeth are good or bad. But history also shows that the structure of capitalist society did not change in these countries. I believe that we Communists must unite with the socialists, as we must unite with all progressive forces, to achieve some democratic institutions and push through some social measures.

A. W.: This is also the attitude of the French Communist Party.

J. K.: The Communist Party of Argentina cooperates with the Peronists, and they are right to do so. One can cooperate with all kinds of petty-bourgeois, radical and other movements, but when all is said and done, the socialists are the closest to us. But there is a question that faces the socialists – and they have to answer it themselves: for their struggle to go beyond free dental service, if they want to achieve a new social order, they have to accept the helping hand offered them by the Communists.

Our experience proves that there are many socialists who will understand this when history poses the question. Our parties, which were both illegal at the time, worked in the fullest unity after May 1944. After the Liberation the Communist Party, driven underground for twenty-five years, regained its legality, and the Social Democratic Party was also reorganized as a legal party. Then the struggle began for the seizure of power by the working class, a struggle which lasted for three years, from 1945 till

1948. During this period the two parties were in alliance, but also fought against each other.

The bourgeoisie brought pressure to bear upon the Social Democratic Party in order to draw it into their anti-Communist front, but the working class, under the slogan "Together with the Communists, for the seizure of power", also exerted pressure on them. We fought, shoulder to shoulder, for three years against the bourgeoisie on issues like the nationalization of the mines, and we also fought against each other for three years, in the factories and in the countryside, to secure a hold on the working people. During that period I was for two and a half years the Secretary of the Budapest party organization and presided at the weekly meetings of the district secretaries. I often told them: Comrades, go ahead and argue with the socialists whenever necessary, quarrel with them when you must, but never lose sight of our obligation to give first consideration to the interests of the working class. Do not overlook the fact that we have many allies in the socialist party who are in agreement with us on the nationalization of the means of production. One day we shall all be members of the same party; you must therefore quarrel with them in such a way that you will be able to patch it up.

When I look back on my fourteen years of work during the Horthy era, and on the three years following the Liberation, I can draw only one conclusion: whenever relations between socialists and Communists become strained, it becomes quite easy for the bourgeoisie to carry on; whenever we march shoulder to shoulder, it becomes extremely tough for the bourgeoisie. The unity of our forces is not a matter of simple arithmetic; when two progressive parties unite, one and one does not make two, one and one may equal five or even ten. To my knowledge the history of the entire working class movement teaches a similar lesson.

A. W.: It is a fact that we in France did not make any significant progress, except during two periods, when Communists and socialists joined forces: in 1936, during the Popular Front, and in 1945, at the time of the Liberation.

J. K.: The history of the French working class movement shows, as does that of the Weimar Republic, that whenever reaction or Fascism secures a foothold, to start with they speak about the annihilation of the Communists only. Once Fascism and reaction succeeds in striking hard at the Communists, they do not wait even a week to strike down the socialists as well.

A. W.: In 1958 [Roger] Frey, De Gaulle's minister, declared that the U.N.R. would launch an attack against those municipal councils which were controlled by the Communist Party — and only against them; in 1962, he was already attacking all the other parties.

J. K.: Your experiences bear out our own. We are familiar with the unceasing struggle of the French party for unity of action; we are convinced that this correct policy will bring results.

A. W.: I would now like to put my last question. Not so long ago, at the Eighth Congress of the Hungarian Socialist Workers' Party, the various ideological trends in cultural life came up for discussion. What is the present position of Hungarian intellectuals? This question is especially important because, as you know, international reaction took advantage of the stand taken by a number of Hungarian writers in 1956.

J. K.: The relations between the party—and, let us add, the government—and the intellectuals are good. It is indisputable that the intelligentsia does not always have correct ideas about socialism, but when they are asked whether they want capitalism or socialism, the great majority takes a stand for socialism. This means that they have a certain social consciousness; they are aware of the tremendous change socialism has already brought about in the life of the Hungarian people, in the development of the country, and of culture. They also take part in the building of the socialist society. But the intellectuals are human, too. They want to know what is expected of them, they want to be treated as adults, they expect us to tell them the truth, they want the elementary requirements of their intellectual life and creative work to be ensured, they want us to take their opinions into account, they do not want their dignity to be insulted...

A. W.: These are all justified demands.

J. K.: In this respect the situation is a good one, and the intellectuals are satisfied.

A. W.: Confidence has paid off here as well.

J. K.: That is perfectly true. As a result of all this, there is a very significant political *rapprochement*. Once the proper atmosphere for creative work is established, the intellectual accepts, indeed demands, the ideological guidance of the party. We do not wish to imply by this that there is complete unity on ideological matters. The change is considerable, but there are still confused views, including ideas about a "third road" and long-standing intellectual dreams of living in a country where there is neither capitalism nor socialism.

A. W.: Something like *Le Bourgeois Gentilhomme*, who neither wished to write in prose nor in verse.

J. K.: Exactly. Neither the dictatorship of the capitalists, nor the dictatorship of the proletariat. Well, of course, that will also come about in the future... but right now a choice has to be made between the two.

A. W.: I don't want to offend your national pride, Comrade Kádár, but these are not solely Hungarian phenomena.

J. K.: Yes, they are indeed prevalent in other countries. If we had wanted to engage in a discussion at the Congress on the views of the minority of intellectuals who do not agree with our principles, we should have taken up the cudgels against at least sixty erroneous views, some of which have only a handful of supporters in the country. For us the essential thing is that Marxist ideology should permeate the masses. Six hundred thousand people—a hundred thousand more than our party membership—are taking part in extra-curricular party education which embraces the study of Marxism–Leninism. Moreover, four hundred thousand young people attend classes on Marxism–Leninism. This adds up to a million people, and approximately three-fifths of them are neither party members, nor members of the Young Communist League. And this million includes several tens of thousands of intellectuals who registered for the classes of their own free will.

We are witnessing, in addition, a great ferment in our entire cultural life, which has its repercussions in literature and drama. A perusal of the recent lists of publications reveals the names of all our living authors. There is not a single writer in Hungary who keeps silent. You should have the programme of our theatres translated; classics are especially popular. Shakespeare is played perhaps more often in Hungary than in Britain.

A. W.: And Molière is played more than in France.

J. K.: But six to eight Hungarian plays are also being staged; they deal with topical problems and the playwrights are often non-party people. Last week I saw a play by the Communist Dobozy[21], and yesterday a very interesting one by Thurzó[22], who I understand is a Catholic writer. Three plays by László Németh[23], a well-known non-party writer, are featured in our theatres at present; one of them, *The Journey*, deals with topical problems. It took some time after the counter-revolution for our writers and artists to get their bearings. Some of them took a stand, in their works, for socialism and for people's power as early as the spring of 1957. I emphasize: in their works. We don't need any political declarations from them. We do not exert any pressure on a single writer or artist to produce a statement for the press. Only their works matter. The previously mentioned group was quite small in the spring of 1957. Then came a period of discussion, reflection and ferment, which we did not hurry. The intellectuals must solve their own problems, and this is a slow and often painful process. But we now have a second wave of development, which can be described as being of a mass character; alongside well-known artists and writers many younger men have emerged and matured during the last six years.

Our Congress deliberately did not take up these questions in detail, nor problems of method or of style. We are obviously adherents of socialist realism, but neither the party nor the government prescribes a definite style. We are of the opinion that one must have plenty of discussion with the artists and also a lot of patience. Ideological unity in the arts and literature calls for a great deal of time and much patience.

At the beginning of the struggle waged against the counter-revolution we concentrated our forces on winning over the workers and peasants. Once the masses of the nation are on our side, what can the intellectuals do? Where can they go? I am deeply convinced that they will follow the masses, because their ties with the people and their honesty prompt them to take this direction.

All told, one must be optimistic. The French comrades told us about their expectations in the second round of the elections, and we were overjoyed about the results. They told us how you were implementing the unity of the democratic forces, as we have just discussed. You were highly successful; the outcome was above expectation. This will surely have its repercussion in the international sphere. Consistent Communist policy, let me repeat, will bring its fruits sooner or later, in all questions and all spheres.

A. W.: I am convinced of this, dear Comrade Kádár, but ... I have reached a certain age, and I would like to be around when these fruits are picked.

J. K.: I understand you ... but I was 33 years old when the Liberation came. I never expected to live to see the day, but was of the opinion that then everything would go smoothly and easily. Well, nothing was simple, I even had to go through bitter disappointment. As far as you are concerned, your position will be difficult until the day of victory, but then your sailing will be much smoother than ours. The enemy never speaks about it, but we make the mistake of speaking too little about our starting point, the semifeudal, medieval state of affairs which prevailed here eighteen years ago; we had no industry worthy of note, and no civilization in the real sense of the word. This was not the fault of our people, but of our past. Indeed, we still have to make considerable progress in order to stand comparison with France.

A. W.: How can I thank you for all the time you have given me, Comrade Kádár?

J. K.: There is nothing to thank me for. Ours is a common cause.

A. W.: That is my only excuse ...

Speech at a Mass Meeting Held on the Occasion of UN Secretary-General U Thant's Visit at Csepel

JULY 2, 1963

Comrades,

The government of the Hungarian People's Republic invited the highly esteemed Secretary-General of the United Nations Organization, Mr. U Thant, to visit Hungary. The Secretary-General accepted our invitation.

The gates of our country are thrown open today to friends, to impartial men of good will, and even to our ill-disposed critics. Although we are by no means satisfied with our achievements, we are convinced that what can be seen in our country is bound to give strength and encouragement to our friends, while the well-meaning inquirers get somewhat closer to understanding our people, and even an ill-disposed critic cannot spread lies about conditions here with the same conviction as before his visit.

We consider the Secretary-General as a representative of the positive impartiality standpoint. We recognize him as a man who has friendly feelings towards all peoples, including our people, and the Hungarian People's Republic.

One must say that the Secretary-General occupies a highly complicated position where he is expected to do the most diverse things, and it is very difficult for him to offer solutions which are satisfactory to all parties. During his term of office Mr. U Thant has been serving the cause of progress and peace, and has taken a fair stand towards our country, too. We trust that Mr. U Thant will better understand our position on the basis of his experiences here and perhaps will also get somewhat closer to our people in sentiment.

I had the good fortune to have a very pleasant talk with the Secretary-General yesterday. I told him in detail about our history in order to make him better acquainted with the present situation in our country; I told him about important questions to acquaint him better with our present-day life. The eighteen years since the Liberation have been a period of tremendous creative work. Unfortunately, this eighteen years of advance has not been unbroken. There was a stage, which we characterize as that of the personality cult, when many harmful and negative features interfered with our socialist development. As a result of these political, economic and other mistakes, bitterness and dissatisfaction justly accumulated as far as part of our public opinion was concerned. This was utilized by the enemies of our system, and by international imperialism, and through misrepresentation they succeeded in turning justly embittered and dissatisfied people against us, and in unleashing a counter-revolutionary insurrection. But the Hungarian people overcame this, too. We found our way back to the straight and bright path of socialist development, and now our people are advancing along this path with self-confidence, chalking up new achievements, from year to year.

Our industry has developed at a rapid pace since the Liberation, and output is three-and-a-half times as high as in 1938. Many new factories were built, and we are exporting a number of products we could not even think of manufacturing in our country in the old days.

In Hungarian agriculture we carried out the highly complicated task of socialist reorganization and, braving the inclemencies of the weather, we have also raised agricultural production to a higher level. We can record similar outstanding achievements in public education, too, in culture and many other spheres.

In order to implement lofty, socialist ideas and to build a socialist country we have to consolidate working class power, the most important task at the present stage of historical development. Because as long as we have this, we can carry on our work, draft and implement our plans, and can do everything. But if something goes wrong with the power of the working class, we cannot carry into effect our socialist ideas.

I would like to make special reference to something of extreme importance to our constitutional and legal system: we restored the socialist rule of law in our country. We cannot allow this lawful order, the Constitution and laws of the Hungarian People's Republic to be violated by anyone, neither by the enemies of the system nor by those who bear ill will towards it, nor by those who act on behalf of our power. In this sense we have restored the socialist rule of law one hundred per cent on both counts.

Now the Secretary-General of the UN is in our midst. He must have heard much about those who were jailed, and those who were not, and the reasons why some people were not released. It is our sacred duty to protect our People's Republic; we are fighting for this with fire and sword and, if necessary, we also punish. But there has been no single individual during this entire period who was imprisoned for something he did not do. We were tough when it was necessary, but we reached a point when an amnesty could be granted. The amnesty indicates the very strength of our regime. No one is imprisoned in Hungary today because of political offences.

When meting out punishment we were also guided by humanitarian considerations. When we were compelled to take drastic measures we felt it much better to keep a tight rein on a few individuals than to have many ordinary people misled either by their own stupidity or by deception fall victim to something which they themselves did not start.

I also told the Secretary-General about the number of people freed through the amnesty. We could tell him, but I told him as well why we did not publicize it in the press. It was because we are under no obligation to give an account to anybody, to the government of any country or any international organization, because the Hungarian People's Republic is a sovereign country. That is all there is to it. We do not wish to mislead the Secretary-General, our esteemed guest.

The fact of the matter is that people's power is firm in our country and our people are working in unity for the achievement of socialist objectives. Are we really satisfied or dissatisfied? It depends on from what angle we are looking at things. If we consider the state of affairs in April 1945, when our country was liberated, I can say that we are happy with our achievements.

Or if we go back to the morning of November 4, 1956, then I can again state that we are happy with what we have achieved through hard struggle. But if we start out from what we want to achieve in industry, agriculture, public education, culture and living standards, then we must be very dissatisfied.

In so far as future perspectives are concerned, we were able to point out with a great deal of satisfaction and approval at the Eighth Congress of the Hungarian Socialist Workers' Party, the leading force in Hungarian society, that we have laid the foundations of socialism in our country; we also declared that our people's advance has reached a stage when the completion of a socialist society is the objective. This is our common responsibility, and this is what we are working for.

Our other aim, our international objective, is the safeguarding of peace. Hungary is not a big enough power on her own to be able to influence decisively the destiny of the world and its nations. But Hungary is advancing resolutely, in alliance with our closest and best helper and friend, the Soviet Union, and we are in friendship with the great community of socialist countries. Thus we have ourselves become a part of the mighty international force which is now playing a decisive role in influencing the destiny of mankind. This mighty force is in alliance with all progressive forces, with the peoples liberated from the colonial yoke, and with all those who are still fighting for liberation from colonial oppression; we are allies of all decent peoples the world over who agree with us on one question, the safeguarding of peace. We are adherents of the peaceful coexistence between countries with differing social systems. Yes, with all countries, and I must state – it is no secret – that we wish to maintain normal relations with the government of the United States, too. Frankly speaking, we do not ask anything from the United States. We are going to build our socialist society without their assistance, just as we have been doing so far, in the face of their opposition and interference. We support the UN resolution calling for an international conference on world trade, because we believe that this is beneficial to the cause of peace and to all the countries of the world. We are in favour of widening and increasing trade relations and the exchange of goods between countries.

The small Hungarian People's Republic, disparaged at first by the imperialists, is gaining in strength and is advancing. Even those who have so far failed to realize the benefits of mutual trade may perhaps understand by now that it would help us speed our development, while letting them make their profit as well. We view the work of the United Nations Organization with a certain amount of expectation and hope. Our expectation is that the United Nations Organization will indeed serve the interests of mankind, and not become an organization in the service of one or another group of powers. We hope that it will be so, and the United Nations Organization will be able to play a positive role for the benefit of mankind. The people and government of the Hungarian People's Republic wish to promote this end.

I am convinced the Secretary-General's visit to Hungary will contribute to the lessening of cold war problems in international affairs, and to the increase of all those things which bind people together in advancing the fundamental and common interest of peace.

Our policy and methods do not change. The Eighth Party Congress laid down the line for us. Experience has shown that we are moving ahead on the right path, and this is the path we are going to follow.

I would like to speak on one more question. We agreed previously with the Secretary-General on the date of his visit, because he is a very busy man and must travel a lot. In the meantime it so happened that we decided to go to Berlin to extend, in a fitting manner, our best wishes on his 70th birthday to Comrade Ulbricht who has a record of over fifty years of struggle in the German Communist movement. We simultaneously expressed our solidarity with the German Democratic Republic, which at last represents an anti-imperialist, anti-militarist workers' and peasants' state on German soil, and which is also building socialism. I had to come back quickly from Berlin to Budapest lest our honoured guest should get here ahead of me, because it is bad manners for the host to arrive after the guest.

You all know that Comrades Khrushchev, Gomulka, Novotny, Zhivkov, Fajon and other representatives of the international working class movement were also in Berlin. We had some talks there, of course. We talked about our common problems and came to the conclusion that the cause of socialism and peace is not going badly. The major necessity is to continue along the lines which have proved to be correct in the international field, to keep on carrying out a policy of peaceful coexistence and to maintain our unity; then our cause will triumph.

I thank you, comrades, for your attention. Although I do not like to make prophecies, yet I believe that, just as we have been advancing during the last few years in all spheres and in all respects, so we will continue to do in the coming years. In order to achieve this, our forces must be united. The government must do its job properly, and the same applies to you. We cannot get anywhere separately, we can only advance by our united efforts. I wish all the workers of the plant good health, good work and plenty of success.

Interview with AP Correspondent Preston Grover

JUNE 1965

PRESTON GROVER: At about the same time as I left Moscow the East European countries started to examine the West more seriously than previously. What is the meaning of this interest in the West on the part of the East European socialist countries and how are they studying the situation there? At the same time there are definite signs in the Western countries that they also want to have a "new look" at the East European countries.

JÁNOS KÁDÁR: Our countries have always taken what is happening in the West into account. This was true even in the period of isolation. In my opinion the reason for the change is that there have been certain changes both in the international situation and in the evaluation of issues in recent years.

The best way I can put it is that both sides have realized more forcefully over the past years that the outbreak of a world war has to be prevented and peaceful coexistence somehow achieved. I am thinking of the past four to five years. This is the situation which made the East European countries, including the government of the Hungarian People's Republic, study how to implement peaceful coexistence with greater attention and in greater depth. But I must also add that the development which can, to a certain extent, be regarded as breaking the ice of the cold war, does not go in a straight line. There are situations hindering the process, and there are events which can even set it back. At the moment there are several factors on the international scene which are unfavourable to this process. I mean first and foremost the situation which has arisen in the Vietnamese area and the aggression of the United States, which we condemn. In connection with this I should like to state that the Hungarian government continues to be of the opinion that peaceful coexistence and normal diplomatic relations are necessary and that it is possible to establish contacts in trade, culture and in other fields between the socialist and Western countries. In my view it is still true that the only alternative to a possible new world war is peaceful coexistence. The interests of the Hungarian people and the Hungarian People's Republic call for peace. But we are convinced that this is the interest of every nation in the world.

P. G.: I do not know if you have adequately studied the American opinion that aggression in Vietnam comes from the North to the South.

J. K.: I know this American view, at least the one that is officially proclaimed, and I find it unacceptable. In our judgement there are two clearly distinguishable things in Vietnam. One is the question of South Vietnam. What is happening in South Vietnam is that the United States is interfering in the internal affairs of the Vietnamese people. The other is the issue of North Vietnam, the military aggression against North Vietnam, an act running counter to all international norms.

P. G.: The Americans have the feeling that their position is not understood in this part of the world . . .

J. K.: I think those who believe that this is the only place where the American point of view is not accepted are wrong. The view of the United States Administration is accepted nowhere in the world by thinking and progressive people. The starting point of the present conflict is well known in all parts of the world; it is quite clear, simple and comprehensible. The issue of Vietnam had been discussed and negotiated in the proper way in Geneva. At that time all the interested parties came to an unanimous agreement. This agreement was torpedoed by the United States, its implementation was prevented and the United States began to spread her own theory. This is the core of the conflict. There are several examples illustrating that it is not only we who cannot understand the position of the United States Administration. I could list the official position taken by the French government and the debates in the British Parliament on this issue, and several similar opinions and points of view. We are also aware of the fact that even in the United States the approach to the question is not unanimous and many criticisms are voiced against the dangerous theory of the American government.

P. G.: The United States is fully aware of the fact that there are very many reasonable things in the criticism of her Vietnam policy. She also knows that there is a certain isolation in this field detectible all over the world and that the United States is practically alone. In spite of this she would not agree to anything that would mean abandoning her position.

J. K.: Regardless of how many times one thinks about this problem, one's conclusion is always that there is an agreement which complies with all the norms of international law and which refers to the so-called Indo-China issues.

All the government of the United States has to decide is to adhere to this agreement which is internationally valid. In my view, the realization which has made the intensification of relations between countries with different social systems possible continues to be valid. But peace is one and indivisible. It is quite impossible to imagine, for example, that while aggression is taking place in Vietnam or anywhere else in the world, and interference in the internal affairs of other states, peaceful coexistence can make progress in another part of the world. This is a naive and dangerous illusion. One cannot talk in the same breath and with the same emphasis about the fact that the government of the United States gave some sort of nameless guarantee to a South Vietnamese government, and the question of what the main direction in the world situation is: whether it's moving towards a world war, or in the direction of peaceful coexistence.

P. G.: The conclusion which can be drawn from what you have said is that if the United States carries on with her Vietnam policy, this will mean the prevention of the further improvement in East-West relations?

J. K.: I am not an oracle, so I cannot tell what is going to happen. I can only emphasize my opinion that this already curbs and hinders normal and manysided relations and cooperation between countries with different social systems.

P. G.: There is a situation in Vietnam which is extremely unpleasant; it is unquestionably more unpleasant for the United States than, for example, for Hungary, because it is the United States which is involved. But I would like to add that in spite of the present Vietnam situation, I really wish there were a "sideline" which would make the settlement of certain problems possible, for example, the diplomatic, trade and cultural relations between, let's say, the United States and Hungary. I am aware that the situation in Vietnam hinders and slows down the process of settlement. Still I would ask whether it is possible to make progress in these questions in spite of the present situation in Vietnam.

J. K.: At the moment there are two simultaneous conflicting tendencies and I can clearly describe them to you. In my opinion it has been the intention of both sides to improve the relations between the Hungarian People's Republic and the United States for some time. An important although not decisive indication of this was that the United States had her own pavilion at the Budapest International Fair in May. I should like to stress that this was in line with our intentions as well. Six to eight days before the opening of the Fair, the Vietnam problem gave rise to an event which made the government of the Hungarian People's Republic, in accordance with their standpoint, condemn the aggression of the United States in Vietnam. Then the Fair was opened by an official representative of our government and, as is customary in such a case, he welcomed the exhibitors at the Fair, and among them, of course, the countries which participated with their own pavilions. We do not act contrary to our principles. Both the official statement of our government condemning the United States, and the greetings extended to the exhibitors of the Fair are based on our firm convictions of principle. I think the above example shows clearly that at present there are two conflicting tendencies. This is disturbing; and let me add that it will not be possible for them to run parallel for long. This is my belief. One of the trends has to gain the upper hand. Since you deal with political questions by profession I do not want to give you a lecture on what the idea of peaceful coexistence means, nor on the meaning of cold war, aggression, and the danger of war.

P. G.: In your opinion which of the two tendencies is going to dominate, to gain the day in the long run, say in about two to three years, as it is impossible to forecast further ahead?

J. K.: Peaceful coexistence. This is my conviction. I would also add that the Administration of the United States will be obliged to revise their position on the issue of Vietnam. Though you did not say so, you referred earlier to the problem of prestige. The United States is a big country and of course prestige is important. But it is not the right way to approach things logically. There was a given situation in June 1954. Negotiations took place and an agreement was concluded between the warring parties. If the agreement was reached between the sides who had previously fought against each other, then an acceptable settlement was reached. Not only for the two sides, as there were fourteen states represented. There was no kind of prestige problem involved for the United States; she had no presence in Vietnam and had not fought on either side. Now you have hinted that the problem of prestige is involved. But who created this problem of prestige? The government of the United States gradually ran into a situation which I do not envy, as I do not know how they can get out of it. But the United States created the problem for herself, as there was no prestige involved in June 1954. It was really the French government which had to face the problem of prestige, but they took a rational position, weighed up the situation and found the point at which they were able to withdraw without losing face.

P. G.: I can understand this position, but this is not the American one ... What I am more directly interested in now is the following: how are relations between the socialist countries and the United States going to develop, considering the presently given situation in Vietnam?

J. K.: In our opinion, and according to our intentions and efforts, there should be normal and indeed good relations between the United States and the Hungarian People's Republic at some future date. Our peoples have no reason to be angry with each other, we can have no special demands on each other and geographically we live far from each other. But I am convinced that we also have common interests. It is in our common interest to live in peace. It is not our task to change the social system of the United States. In our opinion it is possible and in fact necessary to have relations in every field where it is to our mutual advantage. In economic or other areas. Of course we do not think that good relations with, for example, the Hungarian People's Republic is of vital importance to the United States. Nor do we think that the Hungarian People's Republic can be a major business partner for the United States. But there is another aspect to be considered. The Hungarian People's Republic has existed for 20 years. In the major part of this period we have not had good relations with the United States and there has not been any *de facto* communication and trade between the two countries. In spite of this, however, the Hungarian People's Republic has existed, has become stronger and has developed. But if relations are normal, it is to a certain extent to the advantage of and useful to both sides. I think that on the economic scene you also are governed by the rule that international turnover is necessary. We too need partners, we are looking for them and we find them. I have lived the greater part of my life in the capitalist system, I worked with capitalist companies, I also know trading companies and I know the rules of the game. Undertakings and companies with reasonable management know that they have to reckon with every customer, with the small ones as well as the big ones. I know that you have five and ten cent stores, but even there the customer is made welcome. That is the American side of the thing. The Hungarian side is very simple, too. The Hungarian People's Republic is obliged to have a considerable volume of foreign trade. This follows from the position of the country. A considerable part of this trade is with Western countries. For us it is all the same in theory and practice, whether our business partner is Italian, French, English, West German or American; the only important thing is mutual advantage. I want to mention something else as well: trade relations between the United States and the Hungarian People's Republic are on a very low level and within very narrow limits.

But I also know that besides trade proper, there have been more considerable indirect economic relations between the two countries over the past twenty years. The ways of commerce are very complex and I know about certain channels through which West European enterprises buy goods from Hungary and re-export them to the United States or the other way around. It is all a question of approach which is the more rational: to pay commission to the go-between or to eliminate him.

P. G.: Coming to the situation in Hungary; there is obviously a tendency to have less concentrated central planning and to make certain companies more independent, either on a regional or on some other basis. How much has this trend developed in

Hungary and can this be compared in scope with similar tendencies in Romania or Czechoslovakia?

J. K.: In 1957, when we reconstructed the economy, we paid special attention to changing certain economic restrictions which were not useful. At that time we introduced certain methods; among other things, we made it possible for several big, important companies to carry on independent foreign trading. We made some other changes of a similar nature compared to the previous practice. Later we also introduced certain measures which promote the independent economic activities of companies. I cannot make an exact comparison with the economic management of, say, Czechoslovakia, the German Democratic Republic or other countries. Work is now going on in our country which we intend to continue with further measures when it is finished. The starting point is that we count on bringing about more changes in the excessively centralized system in order to give more independence to the individual economic units and to allow the internal economic laws to play a more important role as against administrative control. This is the essence of the problem. Articles are often carried in your press in connection with this, alleging that we are moving closer towards capitalist methods. This is not true. The point is that in the past twenty years certain basic processes were completed. After the devastation of the war, the reconstruction of the economy was finished and the basis of a socialist economy was established. During a further period we had to overcome a certain historical backwardness, and to ensure quite a rapid development of industry. These processes have been completed for the most part or in the latter case have reached a certain stage of development. So naturally study in greater depth and working out methods of economic management which will ensure further progress have now come very much into the picture. A particular period which was in a certain sense inevitable, i.e., industrialization at any cost, has come to an end. Our country has been transformed from an agrarian into an industrial one. Now a more economic system of management is the order of the day. By the way, this will partly answer your first question about the reasons why we are taking more interest in relations with the West. Because in our opinion it would be wrong for the socialist countries to try to establish some sort of self-sufficiency on their own. Therefore in this new period of development, more efficient international division of labour is coming into the focus of attention both in respect of economic relations between the socialist countries and of world trade. In my opinion the heart of the matter is that it would not be expedient to allocate investments to develop the production of goods which are certainly and constantly available in international trade on the basis of the mutual advantages I have already mentioned.

P. G.: There were reports in the international press about an agreement between Poland and the Krupp Company. Is it possible that a similar agreement will be made between Krupp and Hungarian companies on the basis of which there would be some form of joint manufacture of goods mainly for export?

J. K.: In theory this is possible. I can mention that there are already similar cooperation ventures with certain companies on a small scale. Cooperation has been established with Austrian companies, for example, and the products manufactured jointly are sold on a third market. The volume is not really considerable, not earth shattering, but it is already going on in practice and in theory we consider it possible to develop cooperation of this type. If my memory serves me well you have hinted at the relations of socialist countries with one another. And you mentioned certain things such as "now that the monopolistic unity of the Communist countries does not exist any more..."

P. G.: I did not say that it does not exist, I only said that it had changed. Experience shows that this unity is still stable.

J. K.: The point is that relations between socialist countries have naturally developed parallel with the development of the socialist countries themselves. It is a fiction and a mistake for anybody to think that there has ever been the kind of contact in which a button is pushed in the Soviet Union, and all sorts of forces in different parts of the world "jump". The heart of the matter is that relations linking the socialist countries to each other, and within that relations between the Soviet Union and the Hungarian People's Republic, are based on independence and respect for sovereignty.

P. G.: There are three more questions I would like to have discussed in detail. I should like you to talk about the Mindszenty issue in more detail.

J. K.: I should like to say that if fewer questions had been asked about this matter at a certain period, and if the international press had not created such excitement about it, perhaps this issue would no longer exist. In my opinion, the Mindszenty issue is not the same as the problem of religion. Although Mindszenty is a cleric by profession, the Mindszenty issue has been a political problem from the outset. In our view it is of much less importance than it used to be and in itself it is not of great significance. At one time it was an important domestic issue. Now we can say it no longer exists as a domestic problem.

P. G.: Why not?

J. K.: Politically, Mindszenty is a has-been. The waves which he caused by different conflicts and clashes have receded; they have flown down the Danube and disappeared. It is a fact that at that time the basis of the conflict was that Mindszenty demanded his part in the executive power on the grounds of the old feudal legal system. He was opposed to the land reform, the nationalization of industry and the separation of church and state. In Hungary these problems have been settled from the point of view of both the public and the church. That is why I say that the problems themselves in this sense are outdated. In spite of this, however, the Mindszenty issue as a problem with international implications still exists, but not the way it did ten to fifteen years ago. In this matter prestige also has a role to play. There are issues which are not of very great importance, but still they are matters of prestige. This is a problem of prestige for the Vatican, for the Hungarian state and, though it is rarely mentioned, for the United States, too, which got involved in this matter in a very awkward manner. And perhaps even for Mindszenty himself there is prestige at stake. But I do not know for sure, as I have never talked to him. In our opinion, this problem can be solved satisfactorily. But patience is necessary. I should like to repeat that if there had not been a large-scale international campaign which aggravated the case, in my opinion we would have already solved the problem. The issue is being dealt with through the proper channels. It is more difficult to find a solution because all the sides involved behave as if the matter were not urgent for them. We behave the same way and as I know our underlying reasons very well, I can tell you that the matter is really not particularly urgent for us.

P. G.: My next question is one that is sometimes difficult to put. I should like to write something for the press of the United States about you as a private person.

J. K.: It is not usually customary for us to deal with personal matters in the way and style you often adopt in the United States...

P. G.: Perhaps something about your way of life, or what you like to read.

J. K.: I have plenty of work which follows from the post I hold, but not only from that. Even someone with the simplest job works a lot if he takes a responsible attitude to his work. I have little time, but I find time for reading because I am a student of the old school. I rarely watch TV or listen to the radio. I am in favour of reading. If I have time to spare and I want to have a rest, I read fiction. I read books from the most diverse countries. I know progressive American fiction and prose writers and I like them. The way I read? I read several books at the same time, two or three of them synchronously. Fiction relaxes me; I read it until I fall asleep.

I sometimes even read a book six times, for example Jack London's works. Probably because I like nature and know nature quite well and like to read about people who have had a life of many ups and downs. I like and know Upton Sinclair and Sinclair Lewis very well, too. As for other pursuits? I like to play chess. At the age of 16 I used to play competitive chess as a beginner, but I had to give it up because my circumstances did not favour competing. But I like playing chess even today for relaxation. I have few opportunities to play, but I always have a look at the description of a new game of chess in the newspapers.

P. G.: I feel there would be many more topics to discuss, but I am afraid I have already taken too much of your time.

J. K.: Let me finish this interview by saying that I hope that the journalists of the American press, who certainly work very hard in their profession, will serve the right cause, the issue of peaceful understanding. At the same time let me take this opportunity to wish all the best to the American working people.

P. G.: Is there, perhaps, a possibility you might visit the United States to discuss such questions?

J. K.: I link this to your question concerned with me personally. By nature I am not much of a traveller. Travelling is not my favourite pastime, but I understand those who are keen on it.

However, I am ready to travel anywhere and any time if I can render service to the cause I believe in. In this case I have in mind better relations between the United States and the Hungarian People's Republic, general understanding and peaceful coexistence. Of course several conditions are necessary for this.

Conversation with Henry Shapiro, the Moscow-Based Correspondent of UPI

JULY 2, 1966

HENRY SHAPIRO: What are Hungary's major achievements in the political, economic and intellectual fields since the events of 1956?

JÁNOS KÁDÁR: I consider the restoration of the constitutional and legal order of the Hungarian People's Republic at the end of 1956 as the first and most important result. This ensured the preconditions of life and of the work of building socialism under which the Hungarian people with resolute effort have consolidated the political and economic foundations of the socialist state and system over the past ten years; and they have scored a new victory of historical importance by solving the problem of the socialist reorganization of agriculture.

The political strength of our system made it possible to bring the struggles of the past to an end by giving a general amnesty, and to bring about a really broad, patriotic cooperation in creative work. And this has borne fruit.

Hungary's industrial output in 1965 was twice as high as in 1955. In spite of the inevitable difficulties arising from the reorganization of agriculture and under unfavourable weather conditions, agricultural output between 1961 and 1965 was 25 per cent higher than ten years earlier, between 1951 and 1955. The living conditions of the population improved considerably. There was a 60 per cent increase in the real wages of workers and employees, and a 46 per cent rise was recorded in the real income of the peasantry between 1955 and 1965.

Sound development took place in science and technology, public education and health care and in the creative fields of literature and the arts, and the results achieved have also won international recognition. During the ten years in question there was a three-fold increase in the number of young people attending secondary school, while the figure for college and university students doubled. In Hungary, a country with a population of ten million, 4,000 books were published in 45 million copies in 1965. Last year a Hungarian film, the short entitled *Overture*, was awarded a prize at the Cannes Film Festival; the same year saw our feature film *Twenty Hours* winning an award at the Moscow festival, and this year another feature film *Cold Days* won a prize at the Karlovy Vary Film Festival. The results of the lively, intellectual, creative work carried on in Hungary is receiving its due measure of attention on the international cultural horizon as well.

These are the facts and I think they speak for themselves. From 1960 on evaluation of the situation in Hungary has been helped by the increasing number of published writings by responsible representatives of the Western bourgeois press who try to present a true picture. We consider it even more important that, within the framework of a broad range of the mutual personal visits which the Hungarian government has intentionally encouraged, hundreds of thousands of foreign tourists have come to our country and have been able to obtain firsthand information about the real situation in Hungary today.

When taking stock of results achieved over the past ten years, we must not forget that ten years ago the plight of both the country and the people was very serious. When the party and government stated that they would lead the country back to the path of socialist development many people maintained that they had undertaken an impossible task. Since then even our opponents and our enemies have had to admit that we have accomplished this task. Today the Hungarian People's Republic is strong, she is making progress and she commands an appropriate international authority. The world at large is aware of the fact that on the international plane our people are taking their due share in the struggle for a better future for mankind, for progress and for peace.

H. S.: Is there any institutional or other type of guarantee that the cult of the personality will not revive?

J. K.: Yes, there is. I see this guarantee as embodied within the socialist system itself. In addition, on the basis of historical experience the laws have been appropriately supplemented so that they can ensure the lawful order of the state simultaneously with the protection of its citizens.

H. S.: What are the limits to the freedom of intellectual and artistic expression?

J. K.: There are only the limits which are prescribed by law. In other words, works of art which incite against the existing legal order are not permitted. Nor are works which arouse hatred against other peoples and other races, nor those which incite war. There are legal limitations of these and a similar kind but in other respects creative work is free.

H. S.: Is abstract art acceptable?

J. K.: In our country there is no state law or decree designed to regulate the style of works of art; therefore there is freedom of style — and this applies to abstract art as well. To complete the picture, however, I should like to point out that although abstract works are put on display at certain exhibitions, a large section of the purchasers are public institutions or social bodies and when they make their purchases, they do not give preference to abstract works. There is no ban on them, however. Individual citizens can buy whatever piece of work they like.

H. S.: Yes, it is a matter of taste. Abstract works will go out of fashion in the same way that any fashion comes and goes.

J. K.: They had already gone out of fashion but the fashion has revived. Periodically it keeps returning, like the waves.

H. S.: In 1962, the same question was put to Fidel Castro and his reply was this: it is not abstract art which is our enemy. Do you agree with this reply?

J. K.: Yes, I do. We are interested in the social aspects of the arts and cannot name any style as being in itself an enemy of society.

H. S.: Is the Hungarian party of the opinion that "those who are not against us are with us"?

J. K.: I can reaffirm that.

H. S.: You said it, Mr. Kádár, about ten years ago.

J. K.: My memory for dates is not quite accurate. At one of the meetings of the National Council of the Patriotic People's Front where political questions were being considered, this expression came into my mind. It met with approval and was accepted. However, personally I think it essential politically, too, and it also describes the way things are. In a socialist state every citizen who earns his living from work and practices his profession honestly is also contributing to the work of construction which is going on in the given country without his own, separate, political decision to that effect. In a political sense it would be harmful and unjust to describe a person who does not take an interest in certain questions of ideology and ideas, or who is indifferent to such issues, as an enemy. In general I consider it unreasonable to increase the number of our enemies by designating people as such, and therefore I am opposed to it. I have a good subjective reason for this, for I was also designated an enemy of socialism some time ago although I knew that I was not.

H. S.: May I make a subjective remark?

J. K.: Yes, go ahead.

H. S.: There are not too many people who were in a situation similar to yours Mr. Kádár, and who would draw the same conclusions as you do.

J. K.: There are some though.

H. S.: Are there political prisoners in Hungary?

J. K.: Yes, there are. When the time was ripe, there was a general amnesty in Hungary under which all political prisoners were released since they were amnestied. At the same time we made it clear that the amnesty applied to acts which had already been committed and not to the future. Since then there have been cases, though not many, in which some citizens have committed criminal acts of a political nature against the system. Legal action was taken against them and so some of them have been arrested, sentenced and are now in jail. Their number is very small; there are not more than a few hundred, and, as far as I know, there are about two dozen recidivists among them, people who had been amnestied before. Now, under the provisions of the amnesty, their previous sentence has been reimposed as well.

H. S.: Do you consider freedom of travel an inalienable right, or a prerogative, a privilege?

J. K.: We do not treat this issue in this sense. As in every organized state, every citizen in Hungary has the right to apply for a passport. According to our present practice, if there is no legal obstacle, he will be given his passport. Naturally, there are certain regulations which the state imposes. When general decisions are made on this question, economic considerations – questions relating to foreign currency and foreign exchange, etc. – may play a role too, in the same way as in any other state. But what might be of interest in this respect is this: some years ago, as is well known, a comparatively broad range of opportunities for personal visits involving Hungary and the Western capitalist countries was developed; this will be maintained in the future.

H. S.: In both directions?

J. K.: Yes.

H. S.: Does Hungary intend to introduce the system of workers' councils of the Yugoslav type?

J. K.: No, we do not. Certain similar problems were settled in Hungary in a different manner from that adopted by Yugoslavia. This also applies to questions which the Yugoslavs intended to solve by the establishment of workers' councils. We do not follow this practice; instead we have adopted practices which have been developed on the basis of our own experiences. We maintain that these and similar questions must be settled in every socialist country in accordance with the given conditions and characteristics.

H. S.: What is the importance of the reform of economic management in Hungary?

J. K.: I have already spoken about the results. We can be satisfied with the achievements if we look back on the path which has been covered. But we are encouraged to make new efforts, to increase work efficiency if we look ahead at our more distant objectives and into the future. The fact that we have entered a new stage of socialist development calls for a reform of our economic mechanism. What do we mean by this as far as economic activities are concerned?

In the past twenty years, when the ruins had to be removed, when centuries of backwardness had to be made good through the industrialization of the country, the top priority issue was to make a certain quantity of products available. Questions like economic efficiency, how much the goods cost, whether our articles met international standards and whether they were competitive or not were not in the focus of attention. When we completed laying the foundations of a socialist society the initial stage of development ended. Today our construction work at home also calls for the better utilization and more rapid development of the forces of production, and this is what is demanded by the international market as well. A strict and high degree of centralization in management was necessarily a characteristic of the stage of economic development which has ended.

The economic mechanism must be changed so that it will be capable of meeting new demands. That is why the Central Committee of our party called for the relevant reform to be worked out, has approved the resultant draft and has decided to introduce the reform. One of the essential elements of the reform is that the systematic development of the national economy in the future will not be ensured by central instructions which specify the last detail, but by economic methods, through increasing the material interest the companies and the working people have in production. Companies will be given a larger measure of independence; there will be more scope for taking the initiative and for the realization of the democratic rights of the working people.

As a result of the reform, socialist property relations will grow stronger in Hungary along with the systematic development of the national economy. The pace of technological progress will be accelerated, production and productivity will increase, the assortment of goods will become wider and their quality will improve.

The reform of the economic mechanism is a necessity objectively and has become possible subjectively because today there are adequate numbers of highly experienced economic leaders in Hungary, people who are loyal to socialism and who possess the appropriate professional knowledge. On my part I consider the reform of the economic mechanism timely, expedient and a factor of immense importance from the point of view of the economic and social development of the Hungarian People's Republic.

H. S.: How can you ensure that the directors and the company managers will really work honestly, well and effectively when they are given more independence?

J. K.: The independence of companies and within this the range of authority of the managers, will be considerably expanded in the near future. We believe that this will be advantageous for the country. We think that the guarantee that the managers will take advantage of their wider range of authority in a correct manner lies in the economic system, in the fact that the overwhelming majority of managers subjectively and sincerely want to build socialism. They possess the adequate management experience and professional knowledge for this. In addition, we want to make them interested to a greater extent than before, both personally and in material terms, in using their wider range of authority correctly for the benefit of the country.

H. S.: What are Hungary's present relations with the socialist countries and countries with different social systems?

J. K.: The Hungarian People's Republic is tied to all the socialist countries by an identity of fundamental interests and objectives. She maintains good relations with them and endeavours to develop these further on the basis of mutual advantages and the principle of comradely assistance. Our political, military, and economic cooperation is closer with the socialist countries belonging to the Warsaw Treaty Organization and affiliated to the Council for Mutual Economic Assistance, in line with the function of these organizations. Hungary's development is inseparable from cooperation with the other socialist countries and from the assistance we can derive from them; this applies, in particular, to the Soviet Union, to whom our people are greatful for ridding them of the Hitlerite invaders and the sufferings of the war.

Our ties with the Asian and African countries recently liberated from colonial rule are developing favourably. We maintain mutually advantageous economic relations with India, the United Arab Republic, Algeria and others among them. We support all their endeavours to strengthen their political and economic independence and we respect the fact that they are non-aligned. Imperialism is the common enemy of the socialist countries and the countries liberated from colonial rule and peace is in their common interest. That is why we struggle shoulder to shoulder with them on these issues.

Our relations with the Western capitalist countries, including those affiliated to NATO, have been settled and are now developing. Recently we have raised the level of our diplomatic representation with some of them and are developing economic contacts and cultural exchanges with them. Our foreign policy with regard to the capitalist countries is based on the principles of peaceful coexistence, respect for sovereignty and the development of mutually advantageous economic relations.

We think it regrettable that we have not so far been successful in settling our relations with the United States, so that they correspond to the interests of both the American and Hungarian peoples. We have not been able to solve this problem to date because the United States Administration discriminates against us and does not observe the generally accepted principles and norms governing relations between countries as far as we are concerned.

This is the way in which the Hungarian People's Republic develops her international contacts with the individual countries and with other organizations as well.

As is known, in line with our policy towards the churches, which ensures liberty of conscience, and through our efforts to solve outstanding issues, our government was the first of the socialist countries to conclude an agreement with the Vatican which is acceptable to both parties.

H. S.: Regarding relations between Hungary and the capitalist countries could you say something about how ties between the United States and Hungary could improve?

J. K.: In my opinion, if both parties approach the outstanding issues with the sincere intention of solving them, there will be no unsurmountable obstacles, and the relations between the two countries could be normalized.

There are certain problems, certain material demands on both sides, commercial restrictions and the like; these are what I mean when I said that the gaps between the two positions on various issues can be bridged.

By the way, negotiations on this problem between the two countries have been in progress for some time.

H. S.: Since when?

J. K.: For about two years now. They are in progress right at this moment.

H. S.: President Johnson's policy of building a bridge towards the East European countries is well known. Have you any comment on this, or anything to add to it, Mr. Kádár?

J. K.: We know these statements which have been made by President Johnson. However, his performance as president (of the United States) gives rise to doubts about the sincerity of these statements, because the actions which we see exert an influence in the opposite direction. The expression of the desire itself falls in with our sincere intentions; in fact we try to coexist peacefully with every country, irrespective of what social system they have.

H. S.: Does the case of Cardinal Mindszenty constitute an obstacle to the development of good relations with Hungary's Roman Catholic Church, the Vatican and the United States?

J. K.: The Mindszenty question has been at a standstill for years. I cannot say anything new on the heart of the matter. But so far as your question is concerned, I can say in reply that Mindszenty's position is well known. He now lives as the guest of the American people.

H. S.: Do you mean to say that he is a welcome or unwelcome guest...

J. K.: Life has gone past him and past the Mindszenty issue as well. Our relations, the relations of the state with the Roman Catholic Church of Hungary, are tolerable and acceptable. This applies to both parties.

In essence the situation is similar as regards our links with the Vatican. The so-called Mindszenty question has not been settled. We have, however, conducted negotiations with the Vatican and a certain agreement has been reached.

There is one more element involved in the problem: to a certain extent the Mindszenty issue acts as an obstacle to normalizing our relations with the United States; it has a disturbing effect on our relations.

H. S.: Can the unity of the socialist community be achieved despite the differences of opinion between the Soviet Union and China?

J. K.: What you are alluding to is the difference of opinion between the leaders of the Communist Party of China and practically all the other parties of the international Communist movement, and not between the Soviet Union and China.

Our starting point is our principles and our fundamental common interests. The Soviet Union and along with it the Hungarian People's Republic and the Communists of other socialist countries strive for unity with the Chinese Communists. This unity will sooner or later be realized. In our opinion it will come about even if differences of opinion prevail for some time; united action against the imperialists is possible and necessary especially now, to assist the Vietnamese people who are waging a heroic struggle for their freedom.

H. S.: It appears – and this came out at the Bucharest Conference, too, – that the efforts to achieve unity are very much on one side, and the Chinese reject every endeavour aimed at unity. At the same time they say that the Soviet leaders are renegades. How is unity possible under such conditions?

J. K.: As a supplement to what has been said I can mention certain historical experiences. The international workers' movement and the Communist movement itself have existed since Marx. During the past 120 years there have been differences of opinion and debate, but they have always been ironed out or settled. Everything in life changes, including the circumstances, and the evaluation of questions; thus the debate carried on right now and which is often a heated one is a problem associated with a certain period of time and so it will be settled.

H. S.: It is true that since Marx there have been debates in the international working class movement, but over the past 10 to 20 years the antagonisms and disputes in several socialist states have also come to assume the form of conflict between socialist states. Does not this bring about a change in the picture in a certain sense?

J. K.: In a certain sense it does. On the basis of the principles of Marxism and in line with interests held in common they can also be settled. The current debates cause problems for the adherents of socialism and afford pleasure to people who are hostile to socialism and so they attach different hopes to these debates. Now, as you mentioned, the socialist system exists, but there are also debates, and problems may also arise in the relations between socialist countries. Well, so far as I am concerned, if around 1930 when I became a Communist someone had asked me: "In the 1960s there will be socialist systems in many countries but there will also be debates; do you want that or not?" I would have been only too pleased to raise both my hands to express my approval.

H. S.: Mr. Kádár, you are an optimist.

J. K.: I am. This seems to be a matter of constitution and ideology. I have seen and lived through a lot of very bad times and then they were over; things have invariably taken a turn for the better. Therefore I cannot be anything but an optimist.

H. S.: What role is played by nationalism in promoting or slowing down socialist development, with special regard to the coordination of the policies pursued by the socialist countries?

J. K.: Communists are internationalists on principle, for this is at the heart of their ideals. Therefore they also follow this principle in the international relations of those countries in which they govern. They also try to implant this principle more clearly in the thinking of their own people. Building a socialist society runs parallel with major ideological and political work in every country; this necessarily includes the strengthening of internationalism in the thinking of the masses.

Since socialist cionstruction takes place within the national framework of each country, necessarly the successes achieved justifiably contribute at the same time to an increase of national self-esteem and patriotic pride. This, however, is not the same as nationalism. It may happen that reactionary, chauvinist elements, which are to be found in the socialist countries too, distort justified national pride into nationalism. This must be fought because if nationalism and chauvinism flare up in one country this can result in the same thing elsewhere, leading to upsets in international relations. And it can impede and, in the final resort, can undermine the successes and achievements of socialist construction in the country concerned.

Since so many of their other attempts have ended in failure, the imperialists are now trying to bring about confrontation between certain socialist countries by inspiring and encouraging nationalism, or at the very least to drive a wedge between them and the Soviet Union and the whole of the socialist world system. These manoeuvres are also doomed to failure because the identity of interests of our countries and the ideas held in common are stronger than any kind of attempt to influence public opinion to nationalism and they will gain the upper hand over such attempts.

It is possible to coordinate the policies pursued by the socialist countries on questions of common interest because this does not require any country to act against her own interests. The individual socialist countries are sovereign and independent states and as such they, too, have their own specific interests. However, these can be coordinated because the fundamental interests of the individual socialist countries coincide and are the same as the common interests of the socialist community of nations.

H. S.: So far as nationalism in the socialist countries is concerned, there are quite a few unconfirmed rumours in circulation. Romania in particular is mentioned. Why is it that the Romanian leaders especially, but the leaders of the other socialist countries as well, emphasize independence and sovereignty whenever they speak. Is there any real problem in connection with this?

J. K.: I do not think I am competent to comment on what the Romanian leaders say and how they say it during their individual political appearances.

H. S.: Does nationalism cause a great problem in the socialist countries?

J. K.: Nationalism has taken centuries to develop in the European countries and in the minds of their peoples. This way of thinking had a positive role to play at a certain stage of history, in the period when nations were emerging. In my opinion, however, it no longer has the same role in Europe. In the case of the socialist countries, nationalism can even play a negative role. The ambitions which emerged in times past under the banner of nationalism – taking the form of efforts to ensure the existence of the nation, and the essential conditions for its continued existence and development – assume a different guise in our times. As you know I am a Communist. It is my conviction that in our age the best possible guarantee of prosperity and of friendship between peoples and of peace is to overcome nationalism and to respect other peoples, in short, friendship and a socialist policy.

H. S.: Mr. Kádár, you've spoken about the historical development of nationalism. Is it not the remnants of nationalism which are involved today in the conflicts between China and the other socialist countries? Doesn't nationalism have a role to play in the conflict, as well as ideological factors?

J. K.: As I have said in connection with the issue in question, there are certain nationalist elements and remnants in the socialist countries, too, but they are playing a negative role.

H. S.: Are there socialist countries in which the interests of the international working class movement are given priority over their own national interests, or do national interests invariably gain the upper hand whenever they run into conflict with internationalism?

J. K.: Socialist policy always finds the coordination of national and common international interests that is possible and correct. In reality, if questions of really major importance are involved there is no need for either one to be subordinated to the other because on fundamental questions the national and international interests of our countries always coincide.

H. S.: In what manner should territorial issues involving socialist countries be settled? Is there any territorial problem for the Hungarian People's Republic?

J. K.: It is interesting that today, when the United States is not in an enviable position as far as foreign affairs are concerned, you have time for such problems. This reminds me that after the First World War Woodrow Wilson, the then President of the United States, was the principal figure (along with the other three "great" men, Clemenceau, Lloyd George and Orlando) who inspired and guaranteed the imperialist dictates of Versailles and Trianon which dismembered the territory of Hungary.

The overriding objective of the "territorial settlement" carried out by the imperialists has invariably been to plunder, to sow the seeds of discord among peoples, to divide them and to play them off one against the other. We Communists are struggling to bring this practice of the imperialists to an end once and for all. Today I know of only one highly industrialized country which, guided by peace-breaking and *revanchard* motives, openly disputes existing borders; this is the Bonn government of the Federal Republic of Germany. We come out in opposition to this endeavour because we want the security of our people and the peoples of Europe, and we want to safeguard peace.

As you know not long ago the representatives of Bulgaria, Czechoslovakia, the German Democratic Republic, Hungary, Poland, Romania and the Soviet Union declared in Bucharest that they have no territorial claims on any of the European countries.

H. S.: Perhaps the issue of territorial revisions was not raised officially, but there have been several declarations and indications on the part of China that that country has territorial claims against the Soviet Union. Chairman Mao Tse-tung is said to have told a group of Japanese Socialist Members of Parliament that China regards certain territories of the Soviet Far East and Central Asia as belonging to her. At the same time, certain obscure allusions were made in the Romanian press in connection with Bessarabia. Apart from China, can it be said that the member countries of the Warsaw Treaty who attended the Bucharest Conference do not have territorial claims on each other?

J. K.: I do not want to add anything to my reply. That declaration was made in respect of European security and it should be understood in terms of Europe. On the part of our countries it was a completely unambiguous official statement, based on appropriate consideration, and as such it must under all circumstances be taken seriously.

H. S.: Can the policy of peaceful coexistence be compatible with support for the national liberation movement?

J. K.: Only a few years ago John Foster Dulles, the former Secretary of State of the United States described the principle of peaceful coexistence as "Communist propaganda". To the great good fortune of mankind we've gone beyond that and today the majority of the peoples and governments – practically all of them – in principle understand that peaceful coexistence is the only alternative to a new world war.

However, the principle of peaceful coexistence is not designed to govern relations between the exploiters and the exploited ones, the colonizers and the oppressed, the aggressor and the victim of aggression, but to act as the foundation of the interstate relations between countries with different social systems. This is the way we have always interpreted it; in this manner and in this sense we are the unswerving supporters of the policy of peaceful coexistence to this day.

In other respects we are on the side of the exploited, those suffering under colonial oppression, the victims of aggression and peoples struggling for their national independence; we consider their struggle and support for that struggle legitimate. On the other hand there is good reason for asking whether the struggle against the national liberation movements (in the Congo and the Yemen) and the armed aggression against sovereign states (the Dominican Republic and Vietnam) are compatible with the policy of peaceful coexistence.

H. S.: In different countries there are conflicting views as to what is meant by a national liberation movement. Who is to define what is a genuine, true national liberation and which side should be supported in a given area?

J. K.: If someone is sincere in posing this question, then it is possible to give a completely clear and unambiguous answer. War designed to achieve national liberation is a struggle waged by a people for liberation from the colonial yoke, or, on another level, to ensure independent national existence or to defend the sovereignty of an existing state.

H. S.: Thus this is a question of interpretation. What I have in mind are the different groups, for example, in Iraq and Syria among the Arab countries. One group overthrows the other, but both of them say that they are struggling for national liberation.

J. K.: In cases where the point at issue is within the borders of a country, then other countries have nothing to do with it, they have no right to interfere.

H. S.: What is the position of the Hungarian People's Republic on the question of military blocs? In the present circumstances is it necessary to strengthen further the Warsaw Treaty?

J. K.: The Hungarian People's Republic is in favour of abolishing military blocs. Our country is a member of the Warsaw Treaty Organization. The background to the problem includes the fact that, on the initiative of the United States, the aggressive North Atlantic Treaty Organization was established first and afterwards the threatened European socialist countries formed the Warsaw Treaty for defensive reasons. As long as NATO exists, it is also necessary to maintain and further strengthen the Warsaw Treaty.

H. S.: Romania is said to have proposed the implementation of a number of reforms in the organization. As a result of the Bucharest Conference can it be said that all the participants are in complete agreement on the issue of maintaining the Warsaw Treaty with its present command, structure and system of operation?

J. K.: We can say so without reservation.

H. S.: Is it the unanimous opinion of the states affiliated to the Warsaw Treaty that the Warsaw Treaty must be strengthened?

J. K.: Yes.

H. S.: Excuse me, Mr. Kádár, for coming back to this question, but so much has been written about Romania's possible withdrawal from the organization, and no reliable information is available.

J. K.: Well, now I have given you reliable information. I was present, I know what happened.

H. S.: Can the national economies of the socialist countries be coordinated or integrated?

J. K.: The unification or integration of the national economies of the socialist countries is not a timely question and is not on the agenda; none of the socialist countries is contemplating or intends to contemplate such a plan.

H. S.: Is there any essential difference in the system of cooperation between the CMEA countries and that of the countries affiliated to the European Common Market?

J. K.: The two integrations of an economic nature, the Council for Mutual Economic Assistance and the Common Market are completely different in purpose and nature and in the methods they have adopted. As far as the CMEA countries are concerned, the integration of the national economies of these countries, to a lesser or greater degree, is not on the agenda.

H. S.: Yes, I understand it is not on the agenda, but is it not going to be on the agenda in the foreseeable future?

J. K.: It is not.

H. S.: There were rumours to the effect that a reduction in the numbers of the Soviet troops stationed in Hungary or withdrawal of these troops from Hungarian territory is envisaged. Are these troops stationed in Hungary on the basis of the Warsaw Treaty, or on the basis of a bilateral agreement? Do you consider the continued stationing of Soviet troops here as essential?

J. K.: The Soviet troops provisionally stationed in Hungary are here on the basis of the Warsaw Treaty and on the basis of a separate agreement signed by the Hungarian and Soviet governments to this effect. Looking at the question more closely, it must be understood that the member states of the Warsaw Treaty and the Hungarian People's Republic as a sovereign state must equally agree to it.

The continued stationing of Soviet troops here at this given moment is, in the opinion of the Hungarian government, correct and necessary, but the reasons for this are not those of domestic policy. The fundamental reason for the continued presence of Soviet troops here is to be sought in the international situation. Since in general quite a lot of people are interested in this issue in your part of the world, I want to mention that at the moment there are countless initiatives and proposals on the part of the Warsaw Treaty countries in this connection, ranging from the possibility of withdrawing troops stationed abroad to within their national borders, to what was collectively repeated recently in Bucharest by the Warsaw Treaty countries: that we are prepared to negotiate the disbanding of the two opposing groups, the military organizations of NATO and the Warsaw Treaty, and the liquidation of the two treaties and groupings as well. This is how the question of the Soviet troops provisionally stationed in Hungary stands at the moment, and this question can only be negotiated in substance in the context mentioned.

H. S.: This means that the rumours...

J. K.: Are without foundation.

H. S.: Can an effective plan for European security be elaborated without the participation of the United States?

J. K.: Definitely yes, both in principle and legally, since the United States has neither mandates nor trusteeship territories in Europe. In addition, it is the European peoples and countries who are primarily and directly interested in the issue of European security; they know better than anyone else what they need for this security.

In the sense that the question of European security has an influence on world affairs as a whole, naturally the United States is also affected by the issue and could have a say in the matter.

The most important problem today, however, is not whether an effective plan for European security could be worked out faster and better with or without the direct participation of the United States. The problem is that during the period which followed the Second World War, the United States did little to contribute to the security of this continent, but did many things which threatened and still threaten it.

The things which constitute a threat to the security of the peoples of Europe today are, first of all, the United States military bases which have been established and maintained for offensive purposes in several European countries: her troops who are stationed there, her aircraft and warships which are supplied with nuclear bombs and which "patrol" European air-space and European waters, and German militarism which has been revived in the Federal Republic of Germany with the support of the United States. It is no secret that, ignoring the opposition displayed by even her allies, the United States is aggravating the situation still further by wanting to make nuclear weapons available to the West German militarists. This policy of war and cold war should be abandoned by the administration of the United States and then it would immediately be easier to tackle the problems of European security.

H. S.: Mr. Kádár, you did reply. However, could I hear a little more about the problem of whether any of the responsible world powers can be omitted from European and other security plans, apart from moral questions and those of international law? In the space of one generation the United States was twice forced to take part in a world war involving the future of Europe. Can there be peace in Europe without fundamental agreement between the United States and the Soviet Union, naturally with the agreement of the European powers directly interested?

J. K.: I repeat what I have already said. In my opinion in any part of the world — even if continents are involved — regional problems can be settled on the basis of negotiations conducted and agreements concluded by the countries concerned, without the participation of any country situated outside the region in question. At the same time it is also true that owing to the importance of certain issues, or because of the size of the region in question, they may have an impact, or play a considerable role in the development of the world situation. In my view, in this sense some of the great powers have and must have a say in matters exercising an influence on the world situation as a whole. Thus, for example, in my judgement such important problems as ending the arms race, preventing the expansion of nuclear armaments, or the destruction of nuclear weapons, general disarmament and so on, cannot be tackled without the participation of the Soviet Union and the People's Republic of China on the one side and the United States, Britain and France on the other.

H. S.: For instance, wouldn't it be necessary for the whole anti-Nazi coalition to take part in conducting a German peace treaty?

J. K.: In the sense I mentioned the representatives of the United States are involved in certain questions of European security. For example, in connection with the issue you mentioned, the problem of a German peace treaty, the United States has not only rights but also obligations; that is why her voice must undoubtedly be heard on this issue.

H. S.: However, the Soviet standpoint on the question of German reunification is a matter for the two German states.

J. K.: German reunification is another matter. What I said was concerned with the question of a German peace treaty.

H. S.: The difference between the standpoint of the East and that of the West lies in the fact, although I am not qualified to state it, that the West asserts that the question of reunification is also part of the issue, while the East asserts that it is not.

J. K.: The problem of the reunification of the two Vietnams would also be healthier and simpler if finding a solution were left to the two Vietnams as was agreed by the 1954 Geneva Conference.

H. S.: The leaders of North Vietnam have made it clear that they will carry on fighting until the reunification of the country is achieved. I wonder if this creates a precedent for divided countries that military force must be used if there is to be reunification? I have in mind Korea but such a precedent might also have an impact in Germany.

J. K.: I have paid attention to quite a number of the statements made on the areas in question. Declarations have been made by responsible persons in the Democratic Republic of Vietnam and the People's Democratic Republic of Korea that they will do everything in their power to bring about the reunification of their peoples. I consider this a legitimate position which they have every right to take. However, I have never heard any statement that they are preparing to make an armed attack in the interest of reunification. The statements made by North Vietnam repeatedly emphasize, even under the present conditions, that they are struggling for the removal of the intervention forces, so that the people of South Vietnam can decide on their own future.

H. S.: I would like to refer to a report saying that about a week ago Ho Chi Minh explained why they are supporting the South Vietnamese, and that then he stated that there is only one people, only one country and reunification must be brought about.

J. K.: This is a just and correct endeavour, but so far as I know no statement to the effect that you referred to has been made by Ho Chi Minh either in the speech in question or in any of his speeches. Official statements reaffirm that the Geneva agreement must be observed.

I maintain that the Geneva agreement is correct; it settles the Vietnam issue and in general that of Indo-China accurately and explicitly. We fully agree that a return must be made to the agreement and it must be observed. The agreement contains explicit items and articles setting out the process for settling the issues involved. According to Article 1 foreign troops must be withdrawn from the whole of Indo-China and the countries in the region, including Vietnam and South Vietnam, must not be included in any military grouping.

H. S.: This means that both North Vietnamese and US troops should be withdrawn from South Vietnam?

J. K.: So far as I know there are no North Vietnamese troops of any kind in South Vietnam.

H. S.: It is said that there was a report from Hanoi saying that certain regular military units were deployed in South Vietnam.

J. K.: There was no such thing. The troops of the National Liberation Front of South Vietnam are fighting in South Vietnam.

H. S.: There are no North Vietnamese?

J. K.: There are none.

H. S.: When the socialist countries speak of sending volunteers, do they mean sending them to North Vietnam?

J. K.: Yes.

H. S.: It appears to me that there is no shortage of servicemen in North Vietnam. What would be the importance of sending volunteers, except for technical personnel?

J. K.: This statement indicates an intention to give assistance in every respect. It means precisely that if the government of the Democratic Republic of Vietnam thinks it necessary and requests it, the governments of the countries which made the statement are prepared to allow their citizens to go there as volunteers. At the same time, the government of North Vietnam has so far reacted to this a number of times by saying that it is grateful for the assistance offered but at the moment does not request the sending of volunteers. Thus the question is clear and so is the present situation in relation to it.

H. S.: I asked this because in the Western press there have been several reports that perhaps combat infantry troops will be sent to Vietnam.

J. K.: The matter is clear and it now depends on whether the government of the Democratic Republic of Vietnam thinks it necessary, and if so, what form the despatch of volunteers should take and how many should go.

H. S.: According to reports, Marshal Malinovsky declared in Hungary that the Chinese are hampering the shipment of arms destined for North Vietnam. The

Chinese flatly rejected this allegation. What do you think of it? Is it possible to increase the military and economic aid given to North Vietnam without the cooperation of the Chinese or at least without their hampering such shipments?

J. K.: It is possible and this is what is actually happening.

H. S.: Can there be a way out of the Vietnamese situation through negotiations?

J. K.: We have always maintained that disputed international issues must be settled through negotiation and this obviously applies to the situation in Vietnam as well. However, in Vietnam today the problem at issue is not simply a disputed question but that the United States is waging a colonial war in South Vietnam and is committing armed aggression against the Democratic Republic of Vietnam day after day, thus infringing international law.

Many people have realized that the United States will not be able to achieve anything in Vietnam with weapons, apart from political and military fiasco, and if she wants to negotiate, there is no alternative for her but to acknowledge the four points proposed by the Democratic Republic of Vietnam and the five-point proposal of the National Liberation Front of South Vietnam, and accept them as a basis for negotiations.

But the United States can also end the whole matter on her own without fighting and negotiations: she should withdraw her interventionist troops from South Vietnam, cease her aggression and in that same hour there will be peace in the whole of Indo-China.

H. S.: What are the possibilities of avoiding a third world war?

J. K.: Today mankind is protected against the outbreak of a new world war by the superiority of the peace-loving forces, or if I want to be more polite, I can put it like this: by a certain kind of balance of forces. This, however, is not sufficient on its own in the final resort to save mankind from the threat of a third world war.

A reassuring situation will only be created in the world if the parties interested in various issues set about seeking a solution to the problems with sincere readiness to reach an agreement. In addition, it is also necessary to observe international law, to refrain from aggression and to respect the sovereignty of countries. In order to avoid major problems and trouble — and this is an acute question now — it is necessary to end the aggression committed against the people of Vietnam without delay. It is also necessary to prevent the proliferation of nuclear weapons, to end the arms race and to solve the problem of disarmament.

None of these issues is easy and every effort must be made to prevent a new world war, not only by those sincerely anxious about the fate of peoples but also by every man with a sound mind, irrespective of the country in which he lives. For my part I believe that this will be the case, that is why I am confident that mankind will be able to save itself from a new, third, world war. For our part, the Hungarian people, our party and government will do their utmost to this end.

H. S.: I have no more questions, but perhaps you Mr. Kádár would like to say something more?

J. K.: I repeat that there is a question which is common to every country and every man: the prevention of the outbreak of a third world war. The way to solve this problem is through peaceful coexistence between countries with different social systems. In order to accomplish this genuinely and completely not the least important is that peoples living in countries with different social systems should get to know and understand one another better. A wide variety of factors can come into play to promote this. They range from appropriate work from the press to reciprocal visits by tourists. That is why we have accepted the initiative taken by the news agency you serve in seeking this interview. And if it can contribute just a little bit to the better understanding of the real situation and opinions on either side, then I am not sorry for a single minute that has been devoted to it.

So far as the people of the United States are concerned, with them we have no problems whatsoever. We wish that the American people may prosper through their work and may settle their social relations according to what they consider most appropriate for them. We think it possible, and it would also be a good thing for relations between the Hungarian People's Republic and the United States to be normalized. I sincerely wish it; and I thank you for your work.

It is said that the news agency you represent tends to be fair in its reports. If this is the case, only good will come of it.

Report by the Central Committee of the HSWP to the 9th Congress of the Party
(Excerpts)

NOVEMBER 28, 1966

Distinguished Delegates, Dear Comrades,

Over the past four years our party has been working on the basis and in the spirit of the resolutions passed by the 8th Congress and has been leading the Hungarian people's constructive work in the country in accordance with its historic mission. The policy pursued by the party, the assistance given by the masses, the work of organization and guidance given by the Communists and the purposeful efforts made by the workers, peasants and intellectuals have yielded outstanding results: the country has become richer in material terms, living standards have been improved for the working people, the socialist social order has been strengthened and the international authority commanded by our country, the Hungarian People's Republic, has increased.

Our party has made adequate preparations for the 9th Congress. The Central Committee made the directives and proposals for the modification of the party rules available to the party organizations in good time. The membership meetings and party conferences at which the Congress documents were discussed and the new leadership was elected were attended by over 90 per cent of the membership and some 160,000 contributions were made to the debates. The membership expressed their agreement with the party's policy and called for its continuation and more consistent implementation.

In response to our invitation the directives were discussed and opinions on them were given by the Presidium of the National Council of the Patriotic People's Front, the Central Council of Trade Unions, the Central Committee of the Young Communist League, the Executive Committee of the National Council of Hungarian Women and the Presidium of the Hungarian Academy of Sciences. The bodies listed have said in their written replies that they agree with the party's policy and the objectives outlined in the directives, and are prepared to cooperate in their implementation.

A large number of proposals were sent to the Central Committee by the membership and the social organizations. We have examined them and the appropriate proposals have been taken into account in the draft resolutions of the Congress and in the draft document containing the proposals for the modification of the party rules. The others must be utilized in our day-to-day activities.

A nationwide socialist emulation programme was launched in honour of the party's 9th Congress. Hundreds of thousands of working people with the members of the socialist work brigades in the forefront made pledges in every area of the national economy and of creative work, according to the needs of the country. By living up to their pledges they have achieved magnificent results. Let me greet from the forum of this Congress those who initiated the socialist emulation, its participants and all people who support our party's policy by deed and by performing creative work.

Dear Comrades! Conditions are favourable for the 9th Congress of the Hungarian Socialist Workers' Party to do successful work for the benefit of the people and the country. The Central Committee requests the Congress to evaluate the work which has been accomplished, and to analyze, summarize and utilize the practical experiences gained by the party on the basis of Marxist–Leninist theory. We propose that the Congress should approve and further develop all the elements in our party's activities which provide their constancy, continuity and strength, and should change everything that has to be changed to meet the new requirements of the time and changing conditions. Our membership, our working class and our working people expect the Congress to define the objectives of our work of socialist construction for the period lying ahead of us, the paths leading to the achievement of our objectives and the way to carry through our tasks.

Distinguished Comrades! Before discussing the report of the Central Committee in detail, let me extend my cordial greetings to our guests, the delegates of the fraternal parties. I also greet the veterans of the Hungarian revolutionary working class movement and the non-party representatives of the Patriotic People's Front who are with us today. In their person our Central Committee welcomes our international class brothers, the pioneers of Communist ideals here at home, and our non-party allies who work shoulder to shoulder with us in day-to-day activities.

I welcome the delegates to this Congress, those who have been invited and the comrades engaged in its organization. In their person the Central Committee greets the whole membership, Communists, people who work unselfishly and untiringly for the community, for our system and for the socialist future of our people, without sparing themselves, and who are always prepared to give the assistance which is the key to every success achieved by the party.

I
THE INTERNATIONAL SITUATION AND OUR FOREIGN POLICY

Distinguished Delegates, Dear Comrades,

The Central Committee has been paying great attention to the international issues which are of decisive importance from the point of view of the socialist construction work carried on by the Hungarian people. A contradictory development has taken place on the international scene over the past four years. This Congress is meeting under complicated international conditions. The complexity of the situation during the period under review is indicated by such critical events as the Caribbean crisis, the American aggression in the Dominican Republic, the continuous attack carried on by the imperialists on the people of the Congo, the reactionary terror in Indonesia, the right-wing coup in Ghana and other events, and presently and most crucially, the barbarous war waged by the United States against Vietnam, which is colonial in its objectives. The principal results of the policy pursued by our party and the government is that in cooperation with our powerful allies and in complicated international conditions we have been successful in safeguarding the peace of our people and ensuring the international conditions necessary for constructive work, thus upsetting all those plans of the imperialists which constitute a threat.

The fundamental contradictions in the world today are: firstly, between capitalism and socialism, between the international bourgeoisie and the international working class; secondly, between imperialism and the peoples struggling for the elimination of the colonial system; thirdly, between the monopoly capitalist, militarist circles engaged in armaments and drawing up war plans and those struggling for peace. It is the struggle waged by these forces which determines the development of the international situation.

Since the 8th Congress of our party the forces of peace and socialism have continued to grow. The socialist countries have a decisive role to play among them.

The characteristic features of the economic growth of the socialist countries are as follows: between 1950 and 1965 industrial production in the Soviet Union increased fourfold. During the same period industrial production in the socialist countries grew to 510 per cent. Meanwhile the corresponding figure for the rest of the world, that is all the non-socialist countries put together, is 225 per cent. In terms of the rate of development we can hold our own in the competition with even the most industrialized capitalist states, for while the annual growth of industrial production since 1950 was 7.2 per cent in the Common Market member states, the annual increase in industrial production in the countries gathered in the Council for Mutual Economic Assistance amounted to 10.9 per cent. Twenty-six per cent of the area of the world is occupied by the socialist countries whose production amounted to as much as 38 per cent of the world's total industrial output in 1965.

It is obvious that the economic and, naturally, the military strength of the 14 countries making up the socialist world system has become much more substantial not only in absolute terms but also in comparison with that of the capitalist countries. The above facts fully support the highly important statements made at the 1957 and 1960 Moscow meetings that the socialist world system is becoming a decisive factor in the development of mankind.

This is the most important and, for peace and socialism, most favourable factor in weighing up the international situation. However, we cannot keep silent about the fact that at the moment the increased and invincible strength of the socialist world system is divided and its full effectiveness is hampered by lack of unity. The present disruptive policy pursued by the Chinese leaders, whatever their intention may be, in practice serves the ends of the imperialists. The temporary disruption of the unity of the socialist countries offers a tactical opportunity to the imperialists, but it cannot alter the fact that historically our age is one of transition from capitalism to Communism.

Asia, Africa and Latin America constitute essential areas in the worldwide struggle taking place between the forces of progress and reaction. Following the establishment of the Soviet Union and then the socialist world system there was a force in the world which the peoples under colonial oppression could rely on; they were able to launch their victorious independence struggle against the imperialists who subjugate them. The imperialists fought desperately to defend their colonial empires, but the struggle waged by the peoples rising to annihilate the colonial system is irresistible. After the Second World War sixty new independent states were born in the place of the former colonial territories. Fifty years ago 66 per cent of the world's population occupying 77 per cent of the world's total area lived under the colonial oppression of the imperialists; today colonies in the classical sense of the term occupy as little as 4 per cent of the world's territory and their population accounts for only 1 per cent of the world's total.

In the countries where there is undisguised colonial rule and open oppression, such as the Portuguese colonies, Rhodesia, the Republic of South Africa and elsewhere, the struggle waged by the oppressed is growing more intensive. The newly independent countries are strengthening their independent national economies and the other guarantees of their independence. In this situation the imperialists adopt new, camouflaged "neo-colonialist" methods and use economic influence and blackmail in an attempt to continue exploitation of the countries who recently gained their political independence. In recent years the imperialists have organized counter-attacks in their former colonies, waging a "secret war" in the form of criminal attempts, conspiracies and coups. In some places, like in Ghana, they have succeeded.

The plundered economies and backwardness of the newly independent, former colonial countries and the fact that the working class in them is not developed have and do offer a certain opportunity to the imperialists to carry out their counter-attacks. Territorial and tribal division, division by language and religion, often created and induced artificially, plus internal conflicts between groups and individuals boil down to the weakening of the resistance of the newly independent countries. As is known, such conflicts created consciously and intentionally and left as a heritage by the colonizers were responsible for the armed conflict between Pakistan and India.

In the newly independent countries the issue of which path social development should follow comes very much into the picture; in other words, the problem of choosing the capitalist or non-capitalist path. There are places where the internal feudal, bourgeois and militarist elements and the imperialists have made an alliance in order to prevent social development. And where the progressive forces were not sufficiently organized or vigilant, they have been unable to prevent reaction from gaining the upper hand temporarily. A striking example to this effect is the crisis which occurred in Indonesia in September last year; the carnage involving masses of Communists and other progressive people. The division of the Indonesian people who were united earlier against the imperialists is an unprecedented national tragedy. We are filled with profound grief over the tragic fate of our Indonesian comrades, the best patriots of that country. It is our conviction that the revolutionary forces of the Indonesian people will be able to rally their ranks and will again be important factors in the anti-imperialist struggle which is being waged for national advancement and for the cause of the international working class.

In the last four years the activity and effectiveness of Hungarian foreign policy have increased. Our growing foreign political activity and even more the stability of our regime and the fact that we can come forward as a member of the great socialist community have further increased the international weight of the Hungarian People's Republic. This shows itself in the country's growing bilateral relations, in the international organizations—the UN and UNESCO—and in the work carried out in other fields. In the United Nations Organization, as is known, the so-called "Hungarian question" has dropped out of the reports and representatives of our country have had the honour of being elected to chair one of the main commissions last year, and to serve as one of the deputy presidents of the General Assembly this year.

Among our foreign relations, the cultivation and development of the closest cooperation with the Soviet Union is of particular importance, as well as our direct association with the socialist countries who belong to the Warsaw Treaty and the Council for Mutual Economic Assistance.

The foreign policy objectives of the Hungarian People's Republic are unchanged. The principles underlying this policy are as follows:

1. We defend our national independence and the sovereignty of the Hungarian People's Republic against every attempt on the part of the imperialists.

2. We struggle for the unity of the socialist countries and to increase their political, economic and military weight.

3. We are in solidarity with our brother workers who live in the capitalist countries in their struggle for democratic rights and liberties, for peace and for social progress.

4. We support the fight of the national liberation movements against old and new colonialism and against the oppression and aggression of imperialism.

5. We are determined to cooperate with the independent countries of Asia, Africa and Latin America.

6. We struggle for the realization of peaceful coexistence between countries with different social systems.

7. The unchanging focal point of our whole international activity is to prevent the outbreak of a world war in collaboration with all peaceloving mankind.

II

THE DEVELOPMENT OF HUNGARIAN SOCIETY;
CHANGES WHICH HAVE TAKEN PLACE IN CLASS RELATIONS.
THE PARTY'S ALLIANCE POLICY

Distinguished Delegates, Dear Comrades,

Now I move on to the discussion of Hungary's social development, the changes in class relations and the results achieved in domestic policy.

With regard to social development, which is a major issue, it was stated at the 8th Congress that the foundations of a socialist society had been laid in this country. This opened up a new stage of development, the period of the complete building of a socialist society. It was also concluded by the 8th Congress that the period of major class conflicts had ended in Hungary. The preconditions had been established for the realization and strengthening of the unity of all the creative powers of the people and the nation by strengthening the alliance of workers and peasants under the leadership of the working class on the basis of the programme for completing the building of a socialist society.

The profound changes which have taken place in the class structure of our society can be measured by figures. Compared to 1949, the following changes have taken place by the current year:

There has been an almost threefold increase in the number of people employed in socialist industry. The actual growth was from 521,000 to 1,480,000 during the period under review. At the same time the total number of workers and employees rose from 1,630,000 to 3,400,000, which is more than double. Similar increases were recorded in the agricultural cooperatives where the membership rose from 10,000 to 1,050,000, and in the industrial cooperatives where the corresponding growth was from 8,000 to 192,000. Meanwhile there was a sharp decrease in the number of small producers: the figure stood at 2,322,000 in 1949 and has dropped to 142,000 by now. In line with Hungary's large-scale industrialization, which has gone ahead rapidly, the proportion of people employed in agriculture has dropped from 52 per cent of the total manpower in 1949 to 31 per cent.

These figures indicate that, after the expropriation of the landowners and capitalists, exploitation came to an end in this country and there are only working classes in today's Hungarian society. At a subsequent stage socialist transformation was carried out in all fields of the national economy as a result of the establishment of agricultural cooperatives. The above figures also reveal that the industrialization of the country has brought about a tremendous increase in the numerical strength of the working class and a substantial change in its composition. There has also been a considerable growth in the total number of workers and employees, a process which has run parallel with a substantial decrease in the number of people employed in agriculture. The remarkable changes which have taken place in class relations are attributable to the development made by society and they are, at the same time, the new foundations of and conditions for completing the building of a socialist society.

The overwhelming majority of today's Hungarian working class were not workers before the Liberation in 1945 either because they were too young at the time or for some other reason. This accounted for a certain lack of political schooling in the previous years. Today there is less inter-class mobility and this has resulted in the consolidation of the country's working class in recent years. A large proportion of today's workers were brought up under the conditions of our people's democratic system; they have been reared and trained in working and struggling to build socialism. Their basic schooling is of a higher level than that of the proletariat under capitalism; hundreds of thousands of them acquire political and professional education after working hours. The working class is fitted to carry through their historic mission as the leading force of society both in its numbers and composition.

The fundamental political basis of our people's state is the workers' and peasants' alliance. Following the socialist reorganization of agriculture, the Hungarian peasantry set out on the road of socialism; the workers' and peasants' alliance grew stronger in qualitative terms, that is, as far as the objectives and content of this alliance are concerned; as a result, the political foundations of our state have continued to grow stronger in recent years: it is the constant duty of our party to strengthen continuously the alliance of workers and peasants. The conditions for this are now more favourable than ever before. However, we must take note that strengthening the workers' and peasants' alliance does not depend merely on the intention to do so and political statements to that effect; it calls, first of all, for an economic policy that will promote the proportionate development of the national economy and for the correct coordination of the interests of the two fundamental classes involved.

In this country the socialist reorganization of agriculture took place in accordance with the common interests of the two working classes, the workers and the peasantry, and as a result of the accomplishment of a double task: successful reorganization and a simultaneous increase in production. We did everything in our power to make it easier for our peasantry to take the decisive step; democratic measures were introduced for the establishment and management of agricultural cooperatives. Besides introducing the system of paying land rent, old age pensions, and social insurance, a quota system also became widespread in order to reward skill and hard work. As a result of all this the foundations of socialism have been consolidated in Hungary's rural areas. Our peasantry managed to find their place in the collective farms; they work honestly and are now better off than before. Since, work has acquired a new dignity in the Hungarian villages, and is valued above everything else; a united socialist cooperative-minded peasantry is on its way to becoming a reality.

As part of the reform of the economic mechanism, agricultural organization and the system of production contracts must be strengthened and developed. To this end it is proposed by the Central Committee that a national congress of agricultural cooperatives be convened for next year to consider the principal questions relating to the operation and production activities of the agricultural cooperatives. It is proposed that a National Council of Agricultural Cooperatives be elected by that congress, which should also advocate the establishment of regional agricultural cooperative associations. Following the formation of the proposed National Council of Agricultural Cooperatives the state bodies should work out the legal provisions and fundamental economic policy issues involving all cooperatives together with the Council.

In Hungarian society today, in addition to the workers and peasants, the two fundamental classes, there are other working groups and strata such as the intellectuals and the petty bourgeoisie who are taking part in building a socialist society as our allies. Our party pays proper attention to fostering alliance with them, and to their specific problems.

The number of intellectuals and the social importance they command go hand in hand with the growing role played by the sciences, technology and culture. Hungarian professional classes work shoulder to shoulder with the workers, the peasants and the people to achieve the common objective, socialism. The most progressive professional people in political terms work and struggle to achieve our goals as members of the party. The overwhelming majority of the professional classes agree with the policy pursued by the party and government and with the way socialism is practised at home. This is confirmed by the work they do. The result of their work constitutes part and parcel of the people's newly created works, higher standards of training, culture and education. Over the past four years the Hungarian professional classes have contributed to the reputation Hungary commands in the international arena by several outstanding scientific and technological achievements, as well as literary and artistic works. However, the party must take into account the fact that certain groups of the professional classes react sensitively to the difficulties which have arisen, and to the impact of bourgeois ideology and policies. That is why it is essential to be untiring in popularizing Marxist–Leninist theory in their ranks, in establishing and strengthening community-mindedness and the spirit of revolutionary firmness and constancy.

The petty bourgeoisie who are active as craftsmen and retail traders are also respected members of our society. Without abandoning the struggle against the spirit of parasitism and its occasional manifestation, everyone should understand that in the period of building socialism there is a need to have the socially useful work of a certain number of craftsmen and retail traders, and since their activities meet social demands they will also be necessary in future.

Experiences gained over the past few years have confirmed as well the correctness of the policy which has been adopted towards members of the former ruling classes. All the people who have abandoned their past prestige and are doing an honest job of work can adjust themselves to a society engaged in building socialism.

The party is paying special attention to the diversity of problems involving women and young people.

In Hungary, women have equal rights under the law, and the social role they play is constantly on the increase. Since 1949, the number of women working in the national economy has risen by more than 900,000. During the same period the proportion of women in the total work force has grown from 30 per cent to 39 per cent. This sharp increase is largely attributable to former housewives going out to work in larger numbers. It is a welcome development that the ratio and the absolute number of women are steadily on the increase in the ranks of trained and skilled working people, including skilled workers, primary and secondary school teachers, nursing staff and medical doctors. The party has to continue to work consistently to ensure that the equality of women assumes ever more real dimensions, and is actually and fully enforced in society. That is partly why it is necessary to take further measures designed to assist and defend women as mothers and the member of the family carrying the heavier household burden.

In recent years there have been quite a few debates on the way of thinking and the attitudes of Hungarian youth. Extremist views have also been voiced in the course of these debates. By generating debates on the generation gap some people have attempted to bring about a confrontation between the young people and the adults of this country; others have painted a dark picture of the moral and political attitudes of Hungary's young people. The Central Committee condemns these extremist views and false generalizations. What are today's young people like? Naturally, they are not alike, they are different, in the way that the adults of today are not alike but different.

The overwhelming majority of young Hungarians learn honestly or work honestly whichever the case may be; they carry out the duties expected of them by their country; their thinking is moulded by the socialist society. However, it must be taken into consideration that the state of our society is a provisional one and, for that matter, young people are subjected to different influences. The fact that the system in which they live is a socialist one is insufficient on its own automatically to make them socialists. The fundamental shortcomings of our society which still exist exert a particular effect on our young people, and in the absence of an adequate experience of life, they do not always draw correct conclusions from these drawbacks. It is a primary political task of our party to give socialist education to the youth. We have to work so that young Hungarians will see a meaningful life, the only life befitting a man or woman, in the building and service of their socialist homeland.

Our social system is based on solid foundations; order and security provided by the law prevail in Hungary. Our fundamental laws are good and socialist lawfulness is appropriately enforced. A law-abiding citizen is given complete protection; at the same time we keep constant watch over our socialist achievements and allow no one to endanger our social system in any way. This is the case today and will be so in future, too.

The socialist joining of forces on the part of our people has been well served in recent years by our party's domestic policy, which professes and implements the alliance of the working classes, the joining of forces and cooperation of Communists and non-party people, the strengthening and development of the socialist character and the democracy of our state and society.

The Patriotic People's Front has been taking an active part in the accomplishment of all the major tasks facing our society. It has been successful in implementing political cooperation between Communists and non-party people, and in rallying all patriots who are prepared to take action to serve the major national goals of the complete building of socialism. As international experience confirms, in principle the operation of more than one party is possible under socialism. In Hungary, the situation has arisen historically that one party, the revolutionary party of the working class, operates and leads society. This state of affairs involves the party in increased, not decreased, responsibility in respect of working in the closest possible cooperation with the masses, and winning the support of the representatives of the different classes and strata of society for the accomplishment of objectives of common interest; and this includes people who still have reservations on one or another political issue and who are still reluctant to accept our world outlook *in toto*.

Full equality is ensured by the legal system of the Hungarian People's Republic for every citizen. Our state represents and serves the interests of the whole people. International experience and our own history both give evidence that the functioning of the state as the embodiment of the power of the working class will be necessary during the whole period of long historic transition from capitalism to Communism. If there is no aggravation of the situation for one reason or another in this particular period the state's oppressive functions will gradually decrease and will increasingly give way to a simple management of affairs, to organizing creative, economic and cultural work and to attending to the everyday problems of people.

With this concept of the role of the state in mind, the party considers it necessary to strengthen and further develop the state and its different bodies in a democratic manner. The role of Parliament, the supreme legislative body of the country, must be further developed. Its law-making activities must be increased and its range of authority over fundamental social issues must be expanded along with its supervising role. In connection with the work performed by Parliament, a new electoral law is considered necessary; with the introduction of constituencies represented by individual MPs it will be possible to establish closer contacts between a Member of Parliament and his voters and this will have a favourable impact on the work of Parliament.

Our people's state as a whole – our government bodies, state economic and cultural management bodies, as well as the local bodies of people's power and administration i.e. the local councils – is operating successfully and, since it serves the people's fundamental interests, it is also a democratic one. However, although it is basically sound there are also unwanted bureaucratic features to be found in the work of state administration, and it is partly because of this that there is "string pulling", and the use of so-called "socialist connections" and other unhealthy influences; even bribery and corruption at times.

The further strengthening of democracy in our state affairs and of the efficiency of state and local administration, and the elimination of incorrect features and weaknesses in their activities call, above all, for the improvement and development of the system and methods of management in general, and the simplification of the system of administration in local government in particular. It is the conviction of the Central Committee that the fundamental principles underlying the reform of the economic mechanism can help effectively specify clearer, better defined and more independent spheres of authority involving a greater measure of responsibility at every level of state administration. The bureaucratic approach and other abuses can only be eliminated if the right to take economic decisions is delegated to the place where political responsibility rests. It will thus be unnecessary to have an army of signatures verifying agreement on each substantial decision.

The strengthening of democracy in our regime means that the working people, the population, are offered the opportunity to an ever increasing extent to have a say either directly or indirectly, through their representatives, in matters in which they are interested. In order to make this more effective than it is today, a broader range of authority must be delegated to companies and institutions as well as to county, district, town and village councils in economic, cultural and social matters and also in a number of questions of state administration. This is the path along which the work of our state administration must be developed.

The false belief that the complete realization of our social endeavours, the observance of our laws and seeing that they are not broken by others, the ending of abuses and injustices, are the exclusive tasks of the top management of the country is quite often found even among people most loyal to our regime. It goes without saying that both the Central Committee of the party and the government have their own specific tasks in this respect, but effective action can only be taken in matters of this kind if the leadership and the masses act jointly and simultaneously. Our socialist endeavours and the democracy of our system can be enforced to the fullest possible extent and the possibility of abuses occurring can be eliminated completely only when the central and local forces of socialism and democracy are unanimous and firm in taking uncompromising action. This is the key to finding a real solution to the problems, along with the development of our institutions and methods of management and a better-defined spheres of authority.

So far as social issues are concerned, I want to make mention of the demographic problem. As is known there has been a sharp decline in the birthrate in our country in recent years. This can be traced back to several reasons, and in this context quite a few exaggerations can be heard. Although the decline came to a stop about two years ago, and a slight improvement can be detected since then, we still hold that it is an important issue for our state and society, and must be treated as such. Many people tend to confine the question of boosting the birthrate to the material implications of the issue (shortage of crèches and kindergartens, the housing problem, low family allowances). Beyond any doubt there is more than that at issue, for the question has social, health and financial implications as well as those of outlook.

The Central Committee is of the opinion that since this is a problem with diverse implications which seriously influences a number of aspects of society and of people's lives, measures suitable for promoting an increase in the birthrate can only be taken after a thoroughgoing and very considered examination, and on the basis of detailed consultations with the interested parties. It seems essential that the issue of demographic development should be treated by the competent government bodies and that all the measures which are in line with the interests of women, mothers, the family and society as a whole, and which cover the social, ethical, public health, material and financial aspects of the problem should be worked out with the cooperation of the social organizations.

All the major resolutions passed by our party recently are designed to promote the complete building of a socialist society. This objective is also served by the new draft resolutions to be considered by this Congress. To achieve our major objective which is the completion of building a socialist society, the following tasks must be accomplished:

1. The power of the working class, of the people, must be strengthened and further developed.

2. Socialist property relations must be further consolidated and developed.

3. The forces of production must be increased and their more rational utilization must be organized.

4. The Marxist world outlook must become predominant, socialist social awareness and community spirit must be strengthened.

5. The gap between physical labour and intellectual work, and that between town and country must be further narrowed, while working for higher overall standards.

6. The productivity of labour must be increased chiefly by raising technological standards and by achieving a higher degree of organization of labour.

7. Economic production must be increased in industry, agriculture and in all the major fields of the national economy.

8. The level of professional knowledge, general knowledge and culture of the working people and of the whole nation must be further increased.

9. Our system of distribution must be improved, and consumption patterns and living standards must be raised.

III
THE TASKS OF COMPLETING THE BUILDING OF SOCIALISM. THE REFORM OF THE SYSTEM OF MANAGEMENT OF THE NATIONAL ECONOMY. QUESTIONS RELATING TO ECONOMIC CONSTRUCTION

Distinguished Delegates, Dear Comrades,

In the period of completing the building of a socialist society the most important area of our party's activity is the economy. It is the task of the leading party bodies to work out correct economic policies, and the party as a whole should mobilize and organize the working masses for the accomplishment of these economic tasks.

Our activities in the economic sphere have been guided by the economic policy goals set by the party's 8th Congress. Starting out from demands for the intensive development of the national economy, the Congress specified increased economic efficiency, the raising of productivity, the lowering of production costs and the improvement of quality as the guiding principles for economic activity.

Over the past five years industrial production has grown by 47 per cent, the output of the building industry and transport has gone up 35 per cent, while there has been a 10 per cent increase in agricultural production compared to the average for the previous five year period. A 25 per cent increase in the national income has made for a 31 per cent rise in the fixed assets of the national economy and a 22 per cent increase in the consumption funds. The living standards of the population have been raised, social insurance has become universal and there has also been an improvement in housing. The rise in the living standards is largely due to the increase in the number of people earning and to the substantial growth in social benefits. The savings of the population have increased fourfold over the past five years.

During the same period there has been a 37 per cent increase in the value of the fixed assets of the national economy. Production has been modernized, as has technology, and the productivity of labour has improved. There has been a 21 per cent rise in the use of electric power per worker in industry over the past five years. In the course of the fulfilment of the second Five Year Plan the increase in the productivity of labour was responsible for two-thirds of the growth of industrial production.

Taking into account unfavourable weather conditions and difficulties during the initial stages of large-scale farming, the 10 per cent increase in total agricultural output in five years is a remarkable achievement of socialist development. This is all the more so if we consider that in 1965 the total production of the agricultural co-operatives was 27 per cent higher than in 1961, the year which saw the end of the socialist reorganization of agriculture. Collective property, which is the indivisible basis of the agricultural cooperatives, more than doubled during the second Five Year Plan period. Calculated in units, the number of tractors almost doubled during the same period.

Increased industrialization in the provinces was designated a separate task by the 8th Congress. Accordingly, about three quarters of the sums allocated for industrial investment were used first of all in the major provincial cities such as Győr, Székesfehérvár, Miskolc, Szeged, Debrecen and Pécs during the second Five Year Plan. As a result of the development of the forces of production in this direction, the rate of growth of industrial employment in counties which formerly were industrially backward was almost twice as high as the national average and was four times higher than in Budapest. Development of industry in the provinces continues to be a priority issue since 41 per cent of Hungary's industrial workers are still employed by industries located in Budapest.

In view of the fact that more than a third of our country's national income is derived from foreign trade, the exploitation and development of the potentials of international economic relations constitute an important part of our economic activities. Accordingly, special attention has been paid in recent years to economizing on imports and increasing exports and, in general, to improving Hungary's foreign trade balance. We have lived up to our international trade and financial obligations. At the same time we have had to face the difficulty of the unsatisfactory development of our foreign trade balance.

During the period under review the Central Committee made a critical and comprehensive analysis of Hungary's economic development. This examination revealed the viable foundations of our national economy, and the substantial progress which has been made, but it also disclosed considerable shortcomings.

The major drawbacks of our economic activities can be summed up as follows: the effectiveness of the exploitation of the resources available in the country lags behind the potentialities. Compared to the previous years, the rate of economic growth has slowed down. The utilization of the production forces in the industrial and agricultural enterprises has not been satisfactory. The fact that storage, processing and transport have failed to keep pace with the increase in production has hampered progress in important branches of the economy. This, in turn, has led to substantial losses. All this has revealed shortcomings in planning.

The national income was lower than planned; consumption funds grew according to plans while the accumulated assets increased at a rate higher than planned. This meant that the total sum of consumption and accumulation exceeded the national income which resulted in an unfavourable change in the foreign trade balance.

The rate of growth of the national economy and on the basis of this, the pace at which the living standards increase, do not primarily depend on a quantitative increase in industrial output but rather on the extent to which we succeed in manufacturing products which are very much in demand both at home and abroad at a lower cost, by using less material and labour. It also depends on the way in which the efficiency of our work can be improved at the investment stage and in turnover, that is by taking advantage of all the means of the national economy at our disposal.

In the economic sphere the fundamental and direct task ahead of us is to realize the objectives of the third Five Year Plan. In the course of working out the plan, the current and long-term activities which have to be carried out in the service of building socialism were taken into account. The overriding objectives of the plan are: continuing to build a developed socialist society; augmentation of the country's resources; and increasing the national income in order to bring about further systematic growth in the population's consumption and further improvement in their living conditions, and in their cultural and social welfare. A 19 to 21 per cent increase in the national income, a 14 to 16 per cent growth in the real income of people living from wages and an 18 per cent rise in the real consumption of the peasantry are envisaged under the third Five Year Plan.

Increasing the efficiency of labour is an important feature of the third Five Year Plan. The relevant objective of the plan is that 80 per cent of the rise in production should be derived from increasing the productivity of labour. The success of economic activities should no longer be measured just by increasing production, but rather by their real contribution to the national income: by the increase in profits, improvement in the quality and technological standard of products, and their yield of foreign currency. It must be fully understood that it is not sufficient for the national economy if there is a general growth in industrial output, even if the figures are quite impressive. The proportion of industrial production that can be allocated for consumption and the amount of income productive work provides for distribution are the important factors from the point of view of the national economy.

In the field of exports a larger measure of adaptability and flexibility must be ensured in order to meet the diversity of export demands which change at a rapid rate and cannot be assessed in advance. It is also in the interests of the domestic market to achieve a greater flexibility in industrial production than is the case today.

So far as agriculture is concerned it is necessary for agricultural production to grow more rapidly than during the past five years with large-scale farming which has grown stronger, with better materials and technology and with the reasonable policy which has been pursued in connection with household plot farming.

Our party considered the improvement of economic management and defined what had to be done in important matters as early as at the 1957 Party Conference and then at the 8th Congress. Since then our system of economic management has been enriched by a number of new elements.

In May 1966, the Central Committee passed a resolution on a comprehensive reform of the economic mechanism. The objectives of the reform include better exploitation of our resources, acceleration of the rate of development and of the pace at which living conditions improve. The reform makes it possible for a substantial proportion of the decision-making jurisdiction to be delegated to the enterprises and local councils, instead of coming under the authority of the government and the individual ministries. By delegating a large number of economic questions to the decision-making jurisdiction of enterprises and local councils it is possible for the government bodies to concentrate their attention on supervisory activities, on a more scientific establishment of the main proportions of the national economy and on drawing up long-term plans.

Central planning will continue to play a primary role in future, too. The central plan must determine the ratio of consumption and accumulation, the main proportions of investments, the technological development of the branches of the national economy, the pressures on consumption structure, questions relating to the development of our participation in the international division of labour, changes in the siting of the forces of production, and the most important factors associated with social and cultural matters and living standards. On the other hand, the mechanisms of production and of the market are expected to ensure that the manufacturing and supply of the individual products are adjusted to demand more flexibly and that enterprises make every effort to exploit the economic resources at their disposal in the wisest possible manner.

In principle, the position occupied and role played by enterprises will undergo changes in the further developed, new system of planned socialist economy. So far the socialist enterprises have essentially done no more than execute the duties allocated to them by the national economic plan in quite a mechanical manner, and they organized the prerequisites for the execution of the tasks. In the new system of management they will have financial resources, investment funds and incentive funds at their disposal, to be used in harmony with the main objectives of the central state plan. They will also be engaged in their own market research, will conduct direct negotiations with their suppliers and will build their relations with the parties which placed orders with them. Direct relations between enterprises in the acquisition and sale of the means of production through the customary commercial channels must become the general practice to an increasing extent.

In the new system of economic mechanism in general no obligatory plan indices will be specified centrally by the state for the individual enterprises. Companies will have to draw up their plans on their own on the basis of information obtained from central bodies and on the grounds of their own knowledge of market conditions. In the capacity of proprietor the state will regulate the operation of enterprises but the method and form of regulation will undergo changes. In general the state will not adopt the method of issuing instructions directly to ensure that the objectives of the plan are accomplished; instead, economic methods, a suitable credit policy, regulation of the utilization of company net profits and some other methods will be used.

The goal of a socialist planned economy is to meet demand. Enterprise management can best serve the interests of society if their activities are focused on satisfying financially sound demands in the most economic manner and if they manufacture the goods needed by society. Enterprise profit is a means to an end. Following the introduction of the new economic mechanism the development of profit will be the most important though not the only index of the efficiency of production, and of the quality of the economic activities carried on by the enterprises.

The reform of the economic mechanism calls for producers' prices that are in harmony with the social labour necessary for producing the goods, which is what the actual value is. Producers' prices will have to undergo general changes and an overall settlement must be reached by January 1968. The method of pricing must also be changed.

The reform will also be extended to other essential issues of socialist construction, such as material incentives and the more consistent application of the socialist principle of distribution according to the work performed. We must endeavour in future to increase, first and foremost, working people's wages and to see that everyone pays the equivalent of the value he happens to be consuming. Wages should reflect working people's actual performance: this is what is meant by the more consistent application of the socialist principle of distribution according to the work performed. That is why we shall have to assume a more courageous attitude in going ahead with the differentiation of wages and incomes.

In the course of the reform of the economic mechanism it must be made possible for an enterprise working successfully to give surplus pay, up to a specified extent, to those workers and employees who are doing a good job, in addition to the normal profit sharing which they are entitled to. This is the manner in which incentives for doing good work can be strengthened. More consistent distribution according to the work performed, and adjustment to the actual individual and enterprise performance enhances the honour of work.

As a result of our planned socialist economy we will be able to ensure an appropriate level of social employment and its subsequent development, an increase in real incomes and an improvement in living conditions. But there are also other economic means which can be used to achieve these objectives so that a more obvious distinction can be made between poor and good performance on both the enterprise and the individual level, between the presence and absence of expertise, between zeal and the lack of zeal.

We have good reason to expect that the new economic mechanism will contribute to the authority commanded by the guiding bodies of the state. State discipline will assume a new content, the practice of shifting responsibility will be discontinued along with quarrels over petty problems of detail, but actual management will grow stronger in their stead. Today we have to do everything in our power in order that the partial application of the reform of the economic management be in harmony with the fundamental principles which have been approved and that the reform in its full effectiveness might be introduced as of January 1968.

Dear Comrades! During the period between the 8th and the 9th Congresses a substantial increase was recorded in working people's living standards which is indicated by a 9 per cent growth in real wages, an 18 per cent rise in real incomes and a 38 per cent increase in social benefits. The figures envisaged by the third Five Year Plan for raising the living standards include a 9 to 10 per cent rise in real wages and a 14 to 16 per cent increase in real incomes.

Further improvement in the living conditions of workers and working people is an issue to be considered by the party and government in a number of respects. Recently the Central Committee has made a thorough study of some of the problems belonging to this sphere in the conviction that in the coming years certain questions awaiting settlement can be solved by doing purposeful work to raise the necessary funds.

The working hours in Hungarian industry, totalling 48 hours per week, constitute an essential issue in the living conditions of workers and employees. The Central Committee proposes that Congress should pass the following resolution on working hours:

1. While maintaining the present performance and wages, the 48 hour week for all working in industry should be gradually reduced to 44 hours on the average in individual enterprises and factories by the end of 1970. It is proposed that the process should begin in 1968.

2. So far the working hours of 170,000 people engaged in extremely heavy physical labour and under conditions detrimental to health have been reduced to between 36

and 42 hours per week. This programme must be continued and by the end of 1970 a corresponding reduction in the working hours of another 60 to 70 thousand working people employed under similar conditions will have to be brought into effect gradually.

In order to ease the situation of working women, mothers and parents bringing up children, our party and government have constantly been pressing for the development of the system of family allowances and they will continue to urge improvement in the future, depending on the availability of the funds necessary for this programme. In addition to what has been done to date, further measures to be introduced straight away are also proposed by the Central Committee. They are as follows:

1. It is proposed to make it possible for a working woman who has a baby to stay at home for a period of two years on extended maternity leave in order to look after the child until it is two and a half years of age. While ensuring her rights arising from employment, she should be given a sum of 600 Forints as an extended child care allowance for two years.

2. The system of child care allowances must be extended to women working in agricultural cooperatives who carry out the duties which arise from membership.

3. The possibility must be studied that not only the mother living on her own but also the father bringing up a young child on his own should be entitled to a child care allowance.

In line with the policy pursued so far and in order that the living conditions of the working people in the countryside be brought close to those of the urban population, the following are proposed by the Central Committee:

1. The system of social provision and health care for members of cooperative farms should be raised to the level of that for people earning salaries and wages during the third Five Year Plan period, while retaining the present terms for cooperative farmers in respect of old age pensions and sick pay.

2. It is proposed that the amount of the family allowance which cooperative farmers are entitled to be raised to the level of people earning wages and salaries by the end of 1970.

Further improvement in the housing situation is an important social issue. It is common knowledge that a 15 year housing programme has been worked out, envisaging the building of one million new homes by 1975. Originally, the construction of 250,000 new homes had been envisaged under the second Five Year Plan. This figure was increased to 300,000 by the 8th Congress of the party. Actually 282,000 homes were built as part of the programme. The building of another 300,000 new homes is envisaged during the third Five Year Plan. Basically this meets the rate projected by the fifteen year housing programme.

Under present conditions economic construction work constitutes the central issue for the party and the revolutionaries. Whether or not we achieve our socialist objectives, as well as the further raising of the workers' and working people's living standards, are dependent on how successful this work will turn out to be. In this connection the tasks lying ahead of us are as follows:

1. We must make every effort to work for the successful fulfilment and overfulfilment of the third Five Year Plan.

2. The preparatory work for the reform of the economic mechanism must be finished by the deadline set, with the principles of the relevant party resolution being observed.

3. We must make sure that the reform of the economic mechanism is introduced and that its effectiveness is ensured.

4. By defining the tasks to be accomplished correctly and eliminating unnecessary duplication, it must be ensured that on the one hand the party and mass organizations, and on the other hand the economic bodies of the state and the local councils, are able to work and cooperate successfully and most efficiently in accomplishing the tasks facing the national economy.

5. The party must play the leading role even in the field of economic activities; it is the duty of the central and regional party bodies and the party branches in the locality to see that our economic policy is made good both on a nationwide and local scale and that national and local interests are appropriately coordinated.

IV

THE PARTY'S IDEOLOGICAL ACTIVITIES.
RESULTS AND TASKS
IN MOULDING SOCIALIST AWARENESS

Distinguished Delegates, Dear Comrades,

Our party which leads our society ideologically and politically is guided by Marxism–Leninism, the revolutionary theory of the working class, in carrying on its activities. Like every real science Marxism–Leninism is developing constantly, interacting with practice. It is our party's fundamental task to carry on comprehensive ideological activities:

a) Marxist theory must be applied and developed in a creative manner to give answers to the new questions posed by progress; b) Marxist–Leninist theory and the Communist world outlook must be propagated and spread and a struggle waged against hostile views; c) by purposeful activation of the masses, theory should be converted into a material power in society.

Under the conditions of acute class struggle in the period of laying the foundations of socialist society, the party found itself faced with a number of questions of theoretical importance and, as practice proved, managed to give correct Marxist–Leninist replies to them. This achievement came to light, among other things, in the most important issues such as the struggle for power and the socialist reorganization of agriculture. In its theoretical activities at the moment the party is giving top priority to the examination of the economic problems of socialism.

Both the party and party cadres are making progress in ideological work. The revival of this work is indicated by the party's resolutions touching on theoretical matters, the national conference on ideological work and the meetings of Marxist historians, economists and Marxist representatives of other disciplines. A lively debate has begun on the correct interpretation of our national past, on questions of socialist economy, socialist democracy, ethics, the ethics of labour, sociology, demography, the family and other problems.

The Central Committee partly initiated and partly encouraged these debates. It is true that different ideological views existing and exerting an influence in our transitional society were reflected in the debates; wrong standpoints also showed up, but all this is natural in the clarification of problems. It became apparent that, having freed themselves from a schematic simplification of everything, Marxist researchers are capable of penetrating to the core of a problem and guiding the debate into the right channels. At the present stage of our development the new questions arising during the completion of the building of a socialist society, the present development of the international situation and the international working class movement demand that our party should carry on intensive theoretical work, take a stand on and take part in the clarification of debated issues.

I wish to touch quite briefly upon some of the questions in the ideological field, first of all the implications of socialist awareness, and the relationship between material interests and money-grubbing. Quite recently several people have voiced the anxiety that partly because of rising living standards and partly because of different negative influences, the revolutionary spirit is running lower, a selfish money-grubbing attitude is increasingly gaining ground and our society is threatened with the danger of becoming "bourgeois-minded". Parallel with the call to strengthen socialist awareness and public-spirited thinking, the party often voices the need to give people material incentives, and indeed wants to increase these through the reform of the economic mechanism. In our opinion there are different issues involved. They include two phenomena; one of them is harmful and as such should be done away with, while the other is in complete harmony with socialist theory and practice.

The well-known earlier mistakes and counter-revolutionary demagogy brought about temporary disappointment in the ranks of the vacillating supporters of socialism, and caused them to move away from socialist ideals; in some cases they also led to the attitude of "let us live for the day". It is beyond any doubt that the substantial increase in living standards in 1957, the certain degree of boom in small-scale industry and retail trade, the purchasing of plots of land, the building of family houses, the buying of cars, the advent of mass foreign travel, and wide-ranging contacts with Western capitalist countries, have all helped to strengthen petty bourgeois ways of thinking and the attitude of selfish materialism.

Petty bourgeois thinking stems, among other things, from the existence of the petty bourgeoisie. But in the circumstances of today all the private initiatives which contribute to the achievement of socialist objectives must be allowed. But the distortions which hamper this process must be done away with. This is a Leninist policy. The result will be the strengthening of the socialist state and system and the further development of the socialist revolution.

Petty bourgeois ways of thinking, self-seeking and the spirit of selfish money-grubbing belong to another category. They are alien to socialism and, for that matter, uncompromising struggle based on firm principles must be waged against them. Giving working people material incentives to build socialism is another matter. It is in complete harmony with socialist ideals and practice and so we want to strengthen it. We declare and proclaim that the building of a socialist society calls for conscious action on the part of the masses, their readiness to make sacrifices, their unselfishness and the strengthening of community spirit. However, these two things do not run counter to each other. Quite the contrary: they supplement each other. While working to strengthen and deepen socialist ideals the party is simultaneously proclaiming that the building of a socialist society must go hand in hand with the regular raising of working people's living standards. At the moment our immediate task is the more effective enforcement of the principles of the socialist wage system, in other words, we want to give the working people more material incentive, that is to say, we want to ensure that those making a greater contribution to society through their work should have a larger share in the wealth produced.

Practice has proved that the party's position is correct on this issue too. In the years which saw a considerable increase in the living standards of the working masses — workers, peasants and the clerical and administrative workers — there were hundreds of thousands more Communists and non-party people who did not hesitate to take part in carrying out our major social tasks as conscious builders of socialism. These people who were the active members of the party, the mass organizations, the local councils and the Patriotic People's Front, were ready to contribute without any material recompense and they sacrificed not only their leisure time but quite often their health, too. It was in those years, for example, that the workers' militia was established and became a strong organization. Its members have been and are prepared to defend our regime at home, people's power, and our socialist achievements with arms in hand, without exacting any material recompense; they do this unselfishly and out of social awareness, while they carry out their duties at their place of work in an exemplary fashion. These years also saw the birth of the socialist brigade movement, this new magnificent movement of the conscious builders of socialism, of people in the forefront of socialist construction, which soon assumed mass dimensions.

Strong patriotism is a characteristic of our people, in the sense that they guard and foster our historic past and the valuable traditions of our national culture.

Our party considers working-class internationalism and friendship towards other peoples an essential part of socialist patriotism. The identity of the interests of our socialist homeland, of the international working class and of the socialist world system and loyalty to them are united in the idea of proletarian internationalism.

Among the ideological questions, I wish to touch upon are our attitudes towards the religious outlook, religious people and the churches. Basically the position our party took on this issue has been correct throughout.

Our party's world outlook is opposed to an idealist world outlook of any kind including that of religion. This involves a battle of ideas. In Hungary there is freedom of religion, and our party avoids everything that would hurt the feelings of religious people, but it refuses to relinquish the struggle for an enlightened approach and to spread a scientific world outlook. In our opinion the front line of the class struggle was never between believers and non-believers; nor is it there today. Whatever denomination they belong to, believers are free to practise their religion; they are not discriminated against, and they are citizens of this country who have equal rights.

There has been a further increase in the culture of our people in the last four years. Statistically speaking, 42 out of every 100 primary school leavers go on to secondary school, while another 41 go to apprentice schools. Today the number of people graduating from colleges and universities annually is 50 per cent higher than the whole college and university population in the 1937–38 academic year. In terms of the absolute number and the proportion of college and university students attending day-time courses per ten thousand inhabitants, we are ahead of such highly industrialized European capitalist countries as, for example, the United Kingdom, France, Italy and Sweden. These facts can be counted among the finest achievements of our socialist construction.

One of the decisions of major importance taken by the 8th Congress was the abolition of the classification of people according to their family background and the introduction of a new system of entry into higher educational institutions. The correctness of this decision has been verified by practice. The demands to be met in the admission system, that is knowledge, talent, aptitude and good conduct, stimulate young people to hold their own increasingly, and to study better, and they inspire them to develop their abilities and skills. At the entrance examinations in the current year (1966) talent, aptitude and good conduct were taken more intensively into account than earlier, in addition to the applicants' knowledge. There has been no decrease on a nationwide scale in the proportion of students coming from the families of manual workers: it stands at 44–45 per cent, although students from originally working class or peasant families which have a different status today are not included in the above figure. However, mention must be made of the fact that their proportion is still low at certain universities, particularly those operating in Budapest.

The sphere of cultural and artistic activities is one of the important and, at the same time, the most complicated domains of the ideological struggle. Its development and inherent contradictions reflect the contradictions of the whole of Hungarian society. That is why it is influenced, in the final analysis, by the remoulding and transformation of social reality and its immediate guidance is based, in the first place, on consistent struggle waged in the field of ideas.

Over the past five years the value of the turnover in books has grown from 554 million forints to 778 million Forints. During the same period the number of readers registered in libraries run by factories, enterprises and the local councils has increased to over two million and there has also been a substantial parallel rise from 30 million to 49.5 million in the number of volumes borrowed from them. It is also noteworthy that in recent years the number of people visiting museums, exhibitions and art galleries has grown by two million, that half of the music audience of 1,200,000 attended concerts of classical music last year and that 65 to 70 per cent of the cinemagoers saw films made in the socialist countries.

But it is perhaps even more important that in the recent past public opinion in this country has considered works of art, the phenomena and the events of cultural and artistic life as public issues and they have been discussed widely and, understandably, critically. The most significant new result of our cultural revolution is that the wider public is no longer only a mere passive recipient, but is increasingly an active participant in cultural activities. It must also be noted that the major progress which has taken place has also brought new problems to light. Rising living standards, the socialist transformation of agriculture and technological development have made it possible for new strata of society to join in cultural activities. However, there is still considerable fascination with petty bourgeois tastes, trash and sentimentalism.

Foreign classics are being widely distributed, and we are more aware than ever before of the rich heritage of our national culture and, within that, our socialist traditions. It is a welcome development that in our socialist society an appropriate way has evolved for keeping local traditions alive in an increasing number of places. The horizon of our cultural and artistic life has broadened. The Hungarian public has got to know not only European culture but has also become better acquainted with the culture of the peoples of Asia, Africa and Latin America; besides this more diverse information is available about 20th century literature and the arts from the realm of both socialist and valuable bourgeois works.

The fact that cultural life has been guided, above all, by the means of ideas, that it is decentralized and democratic in structure, that there is no forceful interference in questions of style, and that the freedom to experiment has been ensured has led to a considerable improvement in the creative atmosphere. It is largely attributable to this that works outstanding both artistically and in their message have recently been produced; most of them have contributed to strengthening the international authority of our socialist arts.

Our cultural policy must make it clear both in principle and in practical terms what we are in favour of: socialist culture must be made available to our people engaged in building socialism. We will continue to give every assistance to humanist works of art, socialist in spirit, which have an appeal to the broad masses. They must be spread and propagated in more definite terms than hitherto by the radio, television, and press, in the dissemination of knowledge and in the various forms of adult education. We also support those path-finding and experimenting efforts which are seeking something new within the sphere of socialist ideas. Our starting point in this case too is that what is important is the message and the ideas expressed, not adherence to the customary forms.

V

THE FURTHER DEVELOPMENT OF PARTY WORK

Distinguished Delegates, Dear Comrades,

Over the past four years the party has made sound progress; the membership have grown by an average of 3.5 per cent annually, with a total of 73,000 new members in four years. At the moment the membership stands at 584,849, including both full and candidate members. Basically, the composition of the membership is appropriate:

42.5 per cent of the members are blue collar workers and white collar members account for 37.3 per cent; 7.9 per cent of the members serve in the armed forces, 3 per cent belong to the category of miscellaneous professions and students, and old age pensioners account for 9.3 per cent. Women represent 22.9 per cent of the membership.

The strength of the party lies not only in the size of its membership but first and foremost in the awareness of the members, their knowledge, training and active work, and in the unity and concord of the party. That is why we will not aim at a massive increase in membership in the future. We will try to recruit new members first of all from the ranks of workers who have excelled in production and voluntary work and from among cooperative farmers, women and young people.

The Central Committee reports to Congress that in our party the Leninist norms are the determining factors of party life; the principle of collective leadership is in force. However, in our party work personal responsibility has to a certain extent weakened in recent years. Strict adherence to the principle of collective leadership is desirable when it comes to passing resolutions and taking decisions, but the principle of individual responsibility should be better enforced in implementing resolutions and in party work.

Our party operates on the basis of the principles of democratic centralism: the higher party bodies actually carry out the work of direction while the lower ones operate independently within an appropriate sphere of authority, and party life is carried on in a democratic atmosphere and within a democratic framework. Party democracy developed further and grew stronger in the course of the preparatory work for this Congress. The prior election of the nomination committee turned out to be a good method, and the party membership effectively cooperated in the selection of nominees. The extension of vote by secret ballot for the election of the officials of the party committees and the secretaries of the branch organizations further strengthened democracy in party life. These new features of party democracy must in future be further developed and strengthened.

A critical spirit is very much alive in our party. In this atmosphere of being able to voice criticism freely, it is ever more striking that there are conceited people who are satisfied with everything. There are still quite a few party officials who can explain everything, who thank people for criticizing them, but do not forget it.

Our party acquires respect by using power well; if instead of ruling, it plays the role of leader and serves the people. This attitude is binding on every official and member of the party. Whether the opinion of ordinary people about the party is good or bad is to no small extent dependent on the work and behaviour of Communists whom they know personally. The overwhelming majority of our party officials and the rank and file members live and work as befits Communists. We take the most resolute action in the sporadic cases in which someone has abused the power delegated to him, and shall continue to adopt this practice.

We have also seen that a petty bourgeois way of life and morals — manifested in money-grubbing, pressing for and accepting unauthorized advantages, pretentiousness, and an immoral life style — can have an influence on individual party members as well. It is the paramount interest of the party to guard our party and public life firmly and effectively against every symptom which injures the purity and honour of our party.

Some of our party members show a lack of understanding of the new way in which problems can be solved in accordance with the present stage of development and present conditions. Differences of opinion have been detected with regard to the abolition of classification according to family background, over the question of the equality of citizens, and the interpretation of our policy towards the churches, as well as in judging the economic situation and the development of living standards. Basically, the differences of opinion in judging the individual partially arises from the complexity of the age in which we happen to live and of our situation, and partly from the present state of our society and economy. These differences are often associated with the fact that quite a few party members mistakenly believe that the period of transition to socialism will be a brief one free from conflicts. That is why they are at a loss to find an explanation for several — often contradictory — phenomena in our life.

The Leninist view that ideological and political unity must be established again and again, day after day, through frank and open exchange of views on each new conclusion to be drawn and each new measure to be taken is truer today than ever. For this reason patient persuasion is the correct and effective method to adopt with people who fail to understand certain details of party policy.

There are people who tend to interpret the leading role of the party as if it were the duty of party organizations to take a decision even on matters of minute detail, confining the role of the state and social bodies to mere execution. This is an incorrect view. Such a concept of the leading role of the party would lead to the decline of the independence and responsibility of state and mass organizations.

Others tend to identify the leading role with the use of force and the instruments of power. This runs counter to the fundamental Leninist principles of the leadership of the party, especially in the present period of socialist construction. There are quite a few party members who identify the leading role of the party with the role to be played by, and the range of authority of, the individual party organizations. There are others who believe that it is a condition of the party's leading role that every leading position should be occupied by party members. The party's leading role is in force everywhere where the party's policy is being implemented. In some cases and in some places, however, the party's resolutions are not translated into practice with sufficient consistency, or they are sometimes even distorted. Where the party's policy is not implemented, the leading role of the party is obviously ruled out. In this sense, in some places — and in more than one or two cases — the party's leading role is not enforced. But it is wrong to generalize from certain exceptional cases. Local problems can and must be settled. But this should not be confused with the fundamental issue which is that the party is leading the country, and its policy is being implemented.

Our Central Committee decided on a reform of the system of economic management in May 1966, which, in itself, justifies the further development of the party's leading role. A review and the scientific analysis of complicated processes, the disclosure and elimination of contradictions and continued guidance in the development of socialism are only possible under the leadership of the party, which should be more effective than has been up till now. The major tasks ahead call for the development of the party's leading role and improvement in the methods and forms of party leadership as well as organizational activities in harmony with social development.

Increasing the party's leading role makes further development of the party's guidance of state and government work necessary. The present practice slows down decision-making as well as the administration of affairs, and quite often makes it impossible to identify responsibility. For this reason the parallelisms, the interpenetration to be found in the organizational setup, and the overlapping of areas of compentence must be done away with at both the upper and lower level of the party and state bodies. The individual responsibility borne by the leaders of state bodies for work in the area they have charge of must be increased.

The mass organizations and mass movements of the working people, which take an active part in shaping party policy, in realizing its objectives and strengthening the relations between the party and the masses, are important links in the enforcement of the party's leading role. At the same time they also act as organizational frameworks to rally the forces of the people, the nation within which the working masses carry on a diversity of activities in the building of socialism. Our party has established the principles governing party guidance of mass organizations and movements in compliance with the Leninist principles. Party guidance is effected by using the vehicles of politics and ideology, while organizational independence is respected. The fact that the resolutions of the party are binding not on the mass organizations but on the Communists active in them can result in more effective and more spontaneous work.

Our most important, working-class, mass organization is the trade unions, which embrace the overwhelming majority of wage and salary earners. It has become necessary to settle and expand their sphere of rights and, at the same time to give them increased responsibility. The unions have an increasing role in and bear growing responsibility for taking decisions involving the material, social and cultural circumstances of the working people, and in controlling the execution of these decisions. They cooperate in the work designed to eliminate differences of opinion and contradictions arising between the state administration bodies and the economic and union bodies in the course of work for the common objectives. The inclusion of working people in management and practically all other activities carried on by the enterprises must be ensured by relying on the assistance of the unions so that they feel themselves responsible for the successful work of that enterprise. In representing the workers, they have a role in evaluating factory managers and in confirming them in, or relieving them of, their positions.

While making preprarations for this Congress the Central Committee made an analysis of how the party's cadre policy is being implemented. This established that the principles adopted by the 8th Congress have proved to be correct. A generation of leaders have been brought up in our party who are capable of making an independent judgement on and implementing the party's policy even under complex conditions. During the period under review there was a considerable increase in theoretical knowledge and ability to lead among the party's cadres. However, the directives of the

8th Congress relating to the work with cadres have not been implemented consistently enough; quite a few errors and misunderstandings can be found to occur.

At the 8th Congress great emphasis was laid on the issue of suitability for specific tasks. By misinterpreting this, in certain places professional knowledge is given a one-sided priority when filling leading posts in the state and the economy, and is separated from the requirements of ideological steadfastness and the ability to lead. The party refuses to accept this attitude and practice. What society is in need of are not "experts" indifferent to politics, nor is it in need of "politically-minded" people who are incompetent professionally; suitable leaders are needed. Qualification for carrying out the tasks in all the leading posts of our society calls for a combination of devotion to socialism, appropriate professional knowledge and an ability to lead.

When selecting cadres, it remains a fundamental principle that people loyal to our people's democracy, with appropriate political and professional knowledge and possessing the ability to organize and give directions should be chosen for leading positions. When decisions are taken on matters of personnel, it is demanded by the party that the above requirements be observed, that every type of statistical approach be discarded and that a strictly situation-specific decision be made by every person, every organization and every forum authorized to deal with such matters.

VI
OUR PARTY FOR THE UNITY OF THE INTERNATIONAL WORKING CLASS MOVEMENT

Distinguished Delegates, Dear Comrades,

Now I am going to discuss questions relating to the international working class movement.

The Hungarian Socialist Workers' Party is an internationalist party whose past and present are closely knit with the international Communist movement and these ties will be indissoluble in the future too. Our party can serve the Hungarian working class, the people, the nation to which it owes its birth faithfully and successfully on the basis of the principles of Marxism–Leninism, and if it is imbued with the spirit of internationalism. That is why we always pay great attention to the international working class movement in which our party is an active participant and as such a responsible factor as well.

The world Communist movement is the most influential political force of our age. The number of Communist parties in the world today approaches ninety; they are active in almost every country of the world, and the influence of the ideas of Marxism–Leninism is to be felt everywhere.

It is extremely important that there are lively relations between the Communist and workers' parties, and that fraternal parties exchange their experiences and coordinate their actions on the international scene in the struggle against imperialism, the common enemy. It was this consideration which guided our party when in the period under review it had meetings and conducted talks with several parties belonging to the international Communist and working class movement. We had repeated meetings with the representatives of the Communist Party of the Soviet Union and of the Communist parties of almost every socialist country, with the representatives of the majority of the West European Communist parties and quite a number of Communist parties operating in other continents. Each of these discussions was fruitful and useful. We want to carry on similar talks in the future, too, and we are pressing for bilateral and multilateral meetings and discussions between the fraternal parties.

It is a factor disturbing the unity of the international working class movement that the Marxist–Leninist approach, and treatment of issues are, in places, marred by nationalist tendencies alien to our world outlook. If we examine the characteristic features of these false ideas, we will immediately find that a misunderstanding or misinterpretation of national interests is what lies behind them. In places it is a matter of consideration whether national interests should be subordinated or given priority over the common interests, although it is completely clear that they must and can be coordinated.

An anti-Soviet attitude has always been, and is still today, the common feature by which pseudo-left-wing and right-wing deviation can be identified in the international working class movement. International imperialism and the bourgeoisie have always regarded the Soviet Union as their main enemy, and this still applies today. Whatever their intention might be, those who deviate to the right or "left" willy-nilly promote the ends of the imperialists with their anti-Soviet attitude.

The Central Committee and the membership of the Hungarian Socialist Workers' Party are deeply concerned by all the issues on which debates are taking place today and in which there are differences of opinion in the international Communist and working class movement. We maintain that it is possible to remain neutral on a given issue in relations between states, but it is imperative to adopt a position on the most important questions of Marxism–Leninism and the international Communist movement. The representatives of our party have made our position on the disputed issues clear on every occasion, and this is what we are doing now at our present Congress. We condemn every action that is designed to disrupt the unity of the ranks of the revolutionary working class movement. At the moment the hegemonist endeavours of the Chinese leaders, their anti-Soviet attitude and disruptive activities cause the greatest damage. In an effort to crush the opposition to their incorrect views they have in recent months launched what they call the "proletarian cultural revolution", and have established organized "Red Guard" squads recruited from students to act as the commandos of this movement. All this cannot simply be regarded as an internal matter for the Chinese party or Central Committee.

Being true internationalists we most firmly denounce the anti-Soviet attitude, an anti-Communist idea, along with nationalism and all its anti-socialist manifestations. Nationalism and chauvinism are not unknown in Hungary. Our country and people were oppressed by foreigners for centuries, while the Hungarian ruling class was the oppressor of the national minorities living within the borders of the country. The imperialist dictate of Trianon after the First World War was a pretext for the ruling classes to whip up to the maximum nationalist and chauvinist passions, along with hatred for the neighbouring peoples.

Today there are socialist countries existing alongside one another on a significant tract of the earth. As a result of the establishment of the socialist social order it is possible once and for all to eliminate national hatred from the relations between peoples; it is a factor which has caused immeasurable damage to the oppressed and exploited working people of every country for many centuries. The Communist parties also have a duty to pull out nationalism by the roots. Only socialism is capable of finding a solution to the questions of the past, because it can create an order in which cooperation and fraternity, based on the equality of peoples and nations and on their common interests, can evolve.

When drawing up the independent policy of our party, we invariably set out from the historic, social and economic conditions of our country, but since we are an internationalist party, we always take into account the international experiences of the proletarian revolution and the building of socialism. Our party takes into consideration the common interests of the socialist world system and also reckons with the interests of the fraternal parties operating in the capitalist countries and struggling under difficult conditions. We are of the opinion that a revolutionary party is responsible for the work it performs not only to the working class and people it belongs to, but also to the international working class and to mankind.

Distinguished delegates, dear comrades: I have come to the end of the report. I ask the distinguished delegates to discuss and subsequently adopt the report of the Central Committee and the draft resolution which has been submitted. During the period under review the Central Committee endeavoured to implement the policy which was defined by our previous Congress. Our work has its successes and shortcomings, but the policy being pursued is a good one. The 9th Congress is requested to reaffirm the main direction of the policy which has so far been pursued by our party. This is the policy in which the working class and the people have confidence, and this will earn respect for the party and will bring about good results for the country and the people in the future as well.

Conversation with Lajos Mesterházi,
Editor in Chief of "Budapest" Magazine

FEBRUARY 1967

LAJOS MESTERHÁZI: Comrade Kádár, we know that you are not Budapest born. First of all we would like to ask you what your first visit to Budapest meant for you?

JÁNOS KÁDÁR: Until I was six I was brought up in a small village in Somogy County consisting of thatched-roof houses lit by paraffin lamps. It was a tiny mudbound nest, but it was my world; I knew every living soul, every tree, bush, hill and stream. In the autumn of 1918 I moved straight to the capital from there, at my mother's wish because she wanted me to go to school here and become a townsman.

When I stepped out of the Déli (Southern) Railway Station and caught a glimpse of Budapest which I later became so familiar with, it had an indescribable effect on me; but this is understandable enough. It was here that I first saw asphalt, hardsurfaced roads, electric lamps, multi-storied buildings, trams, the underground, motorcars, aeroplanes, cinemas and other formerly unknown wonders. And it was here that I first saw enormous crowds of people who were strangers. All this was at once wonderful, alien and awe-inspiring for me; I confess that Budapest remained alien to me, something I didn't like very much, for quite a number of years.

I lived in the Inner city, and then later in the 13th, the 7th and the 6th districts; gradually, I came to know Budapest quite well. Particularly so, since my mother was an unskilled worker bringing up her two children by herself, and I had to work a lot after school, at home and also running errands about the city. But I liked to walk all over the city in my free time, too. In the countryside, I took to the forest, to the fields, and plains, so in Budapest, too, I was always trying to move towards the outskirts where one could breathe more freely and where the horizon was not blocked by a multitude of houses. I discovered the shore of the Danube, the winter docks, Lágymányos, Kelenföld, Gellért Hill, Sas Hill, Városmajor, Szunyog Island, the City Park and the People's Park one after the other, and they all became favourite places. Of course, besides studying and working I liked to play with friends of my own age; we played ball games when, where and with whatever we could. Once I knew my letters fairly well, reading became my passion; I read every book I could lay my hands on. There was not enough room in the flat, we used paraffin lamps here in Budapest too for a long time; so I used to sit on the kerb stones late at night and read by the dim light of the street lamps.

L. M.: In one of your memoirs you related that you had read *Anti-Dühring* in this fashion when you were sixteen.

J. K.: Yes, that's right. This great work by Engels was the first Marxist book I got hold of. I won it at a junior chess competition held by one of the trade unions in Havas Street. It was a hard job for me to get through such a difficult book as my first Marxist reading. I got hold of it through playing chess and was urged on by my vanity to read it several times over eight months, until eventually I thought I understood it. In those days I did not yet know that a basic Marxist work should not be "read" but studied thoroughly.

L. M.: When would you say you became a "Budapest citizen" in your feelings and views?

J. K.: For about the first ten years of my stay in Budapest I led a kind of "double" life. During the school year I went to school and worked here, like any other "Budapest resident"; in the summer months I lived in the country on the farmsteads, for the first years in Somogy, later in Pest and Békés Counties. I also worked in the country and received flour and bacon as a payment. In this way, in addition to four years of elementary school I managed to complete four further years of study which was a great thing at that time for a poor child like me. When I became an apprentice, and then a skilled worker, my summer trips to the country were over, since there were no holidays of any kind for the industrial worker at that time. The drawback of the "double life" which I led in my childhood was that I suffered a lot for it; in Budapest I was called a "country boy" while in the village I was a "city boy", so that in fact my contemporaries looked upon me as fundamentally alien both here and there. I have considered myself a Budapest citizen since the end of the 20s, since I was sixteen. I am grateful that fate allowed me to get to know nature, the country and country people as a child, and also eventually to become a townsman, a worker here in Budapest. Apart from these basic experiences, I owe thanks for everything I consider valuable in my life to my being a worker and a Budapest citizen, to my life here.

L. M.: How did the meaning of the word "Budapest" change and acquire new shades in your feelings and views?

J. K.: It was almost fifty years ago that I first encountered Budapest, and since then not only I but the city has changed very much. The population of Budapest has grown considerably; industry, trade, and traffic have proliferated, and its culture has flourished. Man's creative talent has enhanced its natural beauty, it has become a genuine city, a great capital, a metropolis.

Over the past half century, together with my whole generation, I have witnessed and later actively taken part in historical events in Budapest. In the long fight during those years, we lived to see the Michaelmas Daisy Revolution, the Republic of Councils, the counter-revolution in the autumn of 1919, the Nazi invasion, the Arrow Cross terror, the rising sun of liberty and the long awaited liberators. After the Liberation the new founding of the country by the people was a common experience for us all.

Our fate was united with the city in a rich, mutual coexistence: we, the citizens of Budapest, shaped the city, and the city shaped us in return. At one time I came here as a stranger, and Budapest was also strange to me. Today I know the people here, I know the stones too, as well as the beautiful landscape surrounding us. I know and feel that here people whose names I do not know are no longer strangers to me; somehow they are all fellow townsmen and acquaintances, because we are all strongly linked by our city, by the common past, present and future of Budapest.

L. M.: Comrade Kádár, looking at the changing face of the city, how would you evaluate the work of our architects and our city planning?

J. K.: In general we can be satisfied. We all realize that our building industry creates good and beautiful buildings, although not always inexpensively. Our city planners have done a good job, and we can see year by year how the overall appearance of the city is improving.

L. M.: Can you see anything in Budapest today which we can hope will eventually become historic landmarks, and representative of the urban development of our age?

J. K.: Oh, yes, I certainly can. And not only the Elizabeth Bridge. We can think of some of our public buildings already completed, and of others under planning or construction. I do believe, however, that mention must be made not so much of certain buildings, but of the housing estates, the new quarters of the city. These estates, with their great variety of houses, parks and public buildings may become "historic landmarks" which will truly represent the life of today's man for the succeeding generations.

L. M.: Comrade Kádár, please speak about your work at the time when you were directly involved in matters concerning Budapest.

J. K.: I was actively involved in our movement and did community work in Budapest before the Liberation. At that time, however, we Communists, fighting in a situation of illegality, could be concerned with the problems and matters of the city only to a limited extent. Some Communist party members, including myself, carried out their activities within the Social Democratic Party between 1935 and 1942. Then, in cooperation with the progressive wing of the Social Democrats, we also dealt with the questions of city development.

I worked in the interests of the city directly and more effectively after the Liberation. As the deputy of Comrade László Sólyom, Chief Commissioner of Police, I was to help re-establish public order and to try to establish the power and order of the working class state. This was of great importance at the time. It was not easy to establish even basic public order. The difficulties caused by the war, the ruins, deserters, those in hiding and the members of the underworld at large had to be tackled in an exemplary way by our newly organized democratic police who were without pay or suitable equipment.

On my next assignment, as the Budapest Secretary of the Hungarian Communist Party, for three years I took part in the work and fight to establish working class power, to reconstruct the capital and to provide sufficient supplies for the population of the capital. As is well known, we managed to resolve the basic problems successfully with the exemplary sacrifice, work and struggle of the working class who suffered under post-war inflation; it took the cooperation of every honest worker in Budapest. Anybody remembering the first socialist emulation campaign which started in March 1945, the first free May Day, the construction of the Kossuth Bridge in freezing winter, the propaganda in the villages, knows that the work and the struggle were not only extremely difficult but beautiful, and inspiring as well.

I had the chance to became directly involved in the construction and development work in Budapest and also in the political life of the city as an elected and active member of the Municipal Council for several terms. I am proud that in certain periods and on certain occasions I could take my share in work which promoted the progress and development of Budapest.

I believe that everybody who attended the magnificent mass rally on May Day 1957 will always remember the enthusiastic atmosphere of that day. In a way I think that half a million people, citizens of Budapest, who met there again were those who decided early in 1945 to rebuild Budapest and to rebuild it for the working people, those who in the tragic autumn of 1956 decided that they would not allow the destruction of all that the working people had created with their own blood, sweat and toil here on the two banks of the Danube so that the future might be socialist and a beautiful one. Budapest gave clear evidence on this beautiful spring day of 1957 that it is not only the lawful capital of the Hungarian People's Republic, but in fact the heart, the driving force of the country, of the socialist revolution.

L. M.: Comrade Kádár, you have mentioned the relationship of Budapest to the rest of the country. How do you see the problem of local and national interests with regard to the special position of Budapest? One fifth of the country's population lives here, 40 per cent of Hungarian industrial products are manufactured here.

J. K.: The very facts mentioned in your question mean that everybody should pay due attention to resolving the problems of the capital, the largest administrative unit of the country, when settling national affairs. We know that during the past ten years a larger amount of money was spent, even relatively, on maintaining, building and developing Budapest than over the previous years. This was inevitable, necessary and right. On the one hand certain matters neglected earlier had to be reconsidered, so that a better solution could be found to meet the demands of the population of Budapest. On the other hand, not only the problems of Budapest citizens were considered when dealing with the affairs of the capital.

In some people's opinions, the finances available for local development should be allocated in a ratio of five-to-one between Budapest and the rest of the country. This is an exaggerated misconception of the question. It is true that a fifth of the country's population lives in Budapest; however, not a fifth but a quarter of the country's population work and do their shopping in Budapest. Scores of central institutes dealing with nationwide matters are located here. The medical centres of Budapest take constant care of more than a quarter of the whole population. Almost a third of the country's students study at Budapest colleges. Budapest transport, roads and bridges not only benefit the capital, but are at the disposal of the freight and passenger services of the whole country. Over the past ten years we spent more on protecting and conserving national monuments than in the previous hundred years. Care for the historical heritage of the Hungarian nation and the self-respect of the people both demand this. Important work in this field is being carried out in Budapest, Visegrád, Esztergom, Szombathely, Kőszeg, Siklós, Szigetvár, Gyula, Sárospatak, Diósgyőr, in fact almost all over the country. A bit more than a fifth of the whole amount available for this purpose is being spent here in Budapest. Buda Castle and the cultural institutions to be located there will belong not only to Budapest, but to the whole country, to the entire Hungarian nation.

The protection and coordination of the "local" interests of Budapest with those of the country is an ever-present task which can be resolved, because the major institutions of the capital are of national importance, so their development is in the interest of the whole nation. Suitable coordination and harmonization of national and local interests in this respect is clear to see. For at the same time as there is development in Budapest there is comparatively rapid industrialization in the provinces, comparatively rapid development in our provincial towns, urbanization in the countryside and a rapid improvement in cultural facilities in rural Hungary. At the same time as there is growth in Budapest, other towns like Miskolc, Debrecen, Szeged, Pécs, Győr are also becoming urban centres. This is in the interest of both the provinces and Budapest itself, which is overcrowded in many respects.

L. M.: Our magazine has published several documents about the internationalist role of Budapest. We would like to hear your opinion on this and some words about your personal reminiscences.

J. K.: The research and publication of documents related to the internationalist traditions of Budapest and the relations between the national minorities here are undoubtedly right. Thinking about the past, we can say first of all that Budapest — although the capital of some kind of "Hungarian empire" — created living and progressive relations between various peoples because of the circumstances at the time. In this relationship the progressive elements of the peoples living in the Danube Valley were brought together, and contacts and mutual assistance were established. The word "internationalism" does not exactly apply to this initial period, but what developed at that time could provide a basis for these relations when the working class and its revolutionary party were emerging to acquire an internationalist character in the present meaning of the word. As I have said the research and publication of documents concerning this period are very useful in giving the public appropriate information, therefore such endeavours are always welcome.

Of course my comments on this question only concern the period and history of World War II. It is common knowledge that the events which arose out of the various actions of Nazi imperialism and the role which the Hungarian ruling class played within this evoked a reaction from the working class and the revolutionary parties here and in the neighbouring countries in line with their strength. Hungarian, Czechoslovak, Romanian and Yugoslav Communist organizations established contacts to create a united front on the territories which at that time were under Hungarian rule, in accordance with the aspirations of the working class of Hungary and other nations. The aim was to fight against Hitlerism, to struggle for independence, democracy and social progress. These efforts were met with an appropriate response among a great many workers.

Various meetings took place here in Budapest as well, organized contacts were established and plans for various actions were worked out. We, Hungarian Communists, and progressive Hungarian forces in general, considered the Hitlerite Vienna Awards to be temporary. We were aware that the aim was to play off the peoples living in the Danube Valley, one against the other. A firm commitment was immediately made to bring together and unite illegal organizations and active revolutionaries in a common fight. This was carried out with the Communist organizations in Slovakia and Transylvania and with the Communists we could contact in Yugoslavia. The Hungarian Communist Party in Budapest put out leaflets for the inhabitants of the temporarily occupied regions. They were translated into the mother tongue of the people living in the areas in question and they were distributed in two languages.

L. M.: Finally, Comrade Kádár, how do you evaluate the relationship between patriotism and local patriotism?

J. K.: Patriotism and local patriotism, the devotion one feels towards the region one was brought up in, depend on and complement each other. The meaning of the words fatherland and homeland are closely related in our langage. In the broadening mind of a child knowledge of and devotion to his closest, everyday environment widen and gradually turn into knowledge of his fatherland and love for his country. It is hard to believe that someone can love his fatherland without loving his native village or town. Local patriotism is coupled with a certain pride. What is important is that we should always know what we are proud of.

The mere fact that someone was born and is living in a certain place cannot be a reason for pride. The citizens of Budapest can be proud of the historic monuments and buildings of their capital. The struggle and work of our ancestors, our difficult history and today's anxious care are embodied in them. We can be proud of the Elizabeth Bridge, since all of us have contributed to it in one way or another. We all worked to see the capital rise from the ruins, to create new and beautiful city areas to replace the Valéria slums, in Lágymányos and Kelenföld too, and before long in Zugló, Békásmegyer, Óbuda. We can be rightly proud of all we created with our hands and minds, each of us of his share in the work. This is right and just, this we deserve. This is the essence and real meaning of our local patriotism. However, the reverse of my former statement is also true: nobody can be a good local patriot if he neglects the general interests of the country. Let us love our home town, let us love Budapest for the sake of the whole country! And let us love our country as befits our responsibility to humanity, as befits our historical mission and socialism.

I think that most of the matters we have touched upon are questions constantly on the agenda regarding our city and our public life. These problems will be duly discussed and decided upon in parliament, at the sessions of the Municipal Council and the District Councils of Budapest where qualified and dedicated persons will find the right solution for the benefit of Budapest and the country – of our homeland.

34. *Going to vote in the company of his wife, 1973*
35. *At the polling station, 1973*

36. With his wife in Havanna, 1975
37. In Cuba, 1975
38. Signing the Final Document of the European Conference on Security and Cooperation in Helsinki, 1975
39. In Helsinki, with the members of the Hungarian delegation, 1975

38

39

40

41

40. Meeting President Kreisky at Schwechat Airport, 1976
41. In Bonn with Chancellor Schmidt, 1977
42. With his wife in Rome, 1977
43. Received by Pope Paul VI in the Vatican, 1977

44

45

44. At the 12th Congress of the Hungarian Socialist Workers' Party, 1980
45. At the Congress, 1980
46. During an intermission of the Congress, 1980
47. Delivering his closing speech at the 12th Congress, 1980

46

47

48

48—52. *Delivering his closing speech at the 12th Congress, 1980*

49

50

51

52

53

54

53. With President György Lázár at the 7th Congress of the Patriotic People's Front, 1981
54. At a Moscow art exhibition, 1981
55. Speech at the 26th Congress of the CPSU, 1981

56

57

56. At the 1982 May Day Parade
57. Visiting downtown Budapest, 1982
58. Visiting the Budapest Party Committee, 1982
59. A village visit, 1982

58

59

60

60. *At a session of Parliament, 1982*
61. *Visiting Pest County, 1982*
62. *With his wife at a reception held in honour of his 70th birthday, 1982*

61

62

63

63. 1982

Address to the Session of the Central Committee

NOVEMBER 24, 1967

Distinguished Members of the Central Committee, Dear Comrades,

We are now in the last phase of the preparations for the reform. The checks which have been made confirm that the measures appropriate to this phase fully correspond to the earlier Central Committee resolutions on the principles and the general objectives of the reform. I agree with them, I accept them and I propose that we should support them.

It has been said many times that—as far as the party's struggles are concerned—we are now dealing with one of the biggest undertakings of the past thirty years. Both our fight for power and the socialist reorganization of agriculture had their own social timeliness and necessity, and so has this reform. The difference between these three is that the timetable of our fight for power was not decided by our Central Committee, but they did set the date for the socialist reorganization of agriculture and they did decide when that work should begin. When I recollect those days now, I can only say that the time was chosen well from an historical point of view too, because—for well-known reasons—the reorganization had not been successfully carried through earlier. If we had missed the opportunity then it would have been much more difficult to put into effect later. The reason why I mention this is because I believe that this reform is timely and necessary now, and it seems to me that it cannot be put off. Some people say it should have been done earlier. I do not think we would have been able to carry it out earlier, but now we must set to. If we don't do it now, we should certainly have to do it in a few years' time, but by then conditions would be more difficult.

We have dedicated nearly three years of work to the preparations of the reform, because in fact certain questions and how they could be solved were discussed at the December 1964 Central Committee session; these eventually became the basis of our reform, even though the subject of our discussion then was not the reform itself. It has taken three years of intensive work and on this occasion I would like to say: all those comrades who directed this activity in the Central Committee apparatus, and in the government and its apparatus, and all those comrades—both managers and economists—who joined in this work and took an active part in it, have worked well and successfully. I say this with conviction. I should also like to add something which follows from what I have said: in my opinion the Central Committee of our party has handled and directed the elaboration of the reform with due responsibility and proper thoroughness, and I am convinced that this will be proved by the results.

I have already spoken about the timetable of the reform, as well as the fact that the reform of the economic management, which we plan to introduce on January 1, is an unavoidable necessity. As far as the essential features of the reform are concerned, I believe they cover the most important and most timely questions of our socialist national economy. First is the question of profitable production. We must stress this openly, because it is not in opposition to socialism, rather it is a need and requirement of socialism, to have profitable production. I can confidently extend this principle to other fields as well: it is necessary to have profitable sales both on the domestic and the foreign markets. Obviously in this context, too, I am referring to a profit which can be made on the basis of the principles of a socialist national economy. The elements of the reform concerning the decentralization of distribution and management are also essential. Summing up, I believe I can say that the reform is a Marxist reform, a socialist reform.

This is something which must be emphasized and we must not get lost in the details; we must make sure that even those sections of the general public who are unable to take a comprehensive view of the details should be given decisive answers to the major questions. This is a Marxist, socialist reform of our economic management, it has socialist goals, it is aimed at developing socialist production, at increasing consumption, at constantly improving the standard of living of the workers and finally at promoting the completion of the building of a socialist society. In fact this is now our party programme.

I believe it is right and necessary to introduce the reform in an ordered way. I also think that sufficient guarantees have been attached to the reform as far as our commitments and potentialities are concerned, up to the limit which will still allow for a real reform. It was clear from our debate that it is impossible to introduce and establish a price system reflecting real values immediately, because the implementation of such a system can only be the culmination of a process. In certain fields this is a programme for decades. Nevertheless it is extremely important that we have already taken this direction and that the work has begun. The principle of gradual change is necessary and correct in this case; some of our measures, for instance, are deliberately aimed at curbing imports from the capitalist countries — controls which may be reduced or completely abolished in the future. It is a good and important thing to introduce the reform in an ordered way.

Ever since these questions were debated by the Central Committee one aspect of the preparations which has constantly been raised — and rightly so — is that the government, as the supreme executive body, must have sufficient reserves when the reform is introduced. We need reserves in raw materials for production, and in consumer goods, as well as in both national and foreign currencies. We do have some reserves but for preparations to be ideal — if such a thing is possible — we would need to have more. It would be better to have more; still I want to stress that we have ensured all the reserves we possibly can, and we can say that in a whole variety of respects our reserves are bigger now than in any year before we started a new plan period. I should also like to add that if we were to introduce the reform three or more years from now, then we would have smaller reserves because the continuing unfavourable tendencies would certainly absorb even the reserves we now have. So, as far as reserves are concerned, I can only say that although they are not too sizeable we do have the guaranteed minimum which is needed for the introduction of the reform.

One of the positive features of the reform is that we have made serious efforts to provide information for, and to get the support of, all those leading officials who are working in the state economy, in the local councils, in party organizations, in the trade unions and in many other fields. I can confidently say that mutual confidence — a feature which has always been considered very important by the Central Committee — has been characteristic of this activity, too. I think it is an essential and very important feature of the introduction of the reform that the Central Committee and the goverment are working together with the two or three hundred thousand leading officials on a basis of mutual confidence. This is a very important fact. We have given information — and we shall continue to do so — about the essential points of the reform to millions of workers and farmers, and to thousands of the intelligentsia; we want to convince them of its necessity and ask for their support.

Because of the nature of economic management only two or three hundred thousand leading people can affect its course; the millions of workers cannot exert any direct influence. And it is not their fault. We can tell people, we must tell people, to pay attention to what is happening in the workshops in the spirit of the reform, to voice their comments on it, to stand up to any attempts to oppose it, and so on. But the workers who actually operate the machines, the farmers who cultivate the land, those many white collar workers who have ordinary jobs ... well — because of their position — they cannot exert an operative influence on the realization, implementation or management of the reform. These things will mostly depend on those two or three hundred thousand leading people. I am glad that our relationship with them is based on mutual confidence, because in this case it is indispensable. Because most people are not able to get to know, accept and follow each detailed element of the reform; they are familiar with some parts of the reform and they accept the rest of it on the basis of confidence. Based on the experiences of many years they will say: "The party and the government have never deceived us so we have confidence in them." This confidence is our biggest moral and political capital in introducing the reform, because millions do not have — and will not have in the future either — enough factual knowledge for it to be a substitute for this confidence.

One of the exceptionally important, decisive conditions for the successful introduction of the reform is our unity. I can say that we do have that unity in the Central Committee, in the government, in the leadership of the major social organizations. We have unity in general on the major issues of our policy, as well as on the principal questions of the reform. When we discussed the reform more than two years ago there was a great diversity of opinion, even on the principal questions, not only among economists but among those present here. We took the proper course in line with the principles and practice of the party; we conducted our discussion in a comradely, principled manner without any personal disputes; we discussed and clarified all the basic questions one after the other and achieved a unity of opinion in a normal, partylike way. This unity, which is demanded and expected of us on all major issues by the party's rank and file is our guarantee that we speak the same language and we will strive for and stand up in unity for the same cause.

We have been reassured by our comrades, the ministers who took the floor — in case we had been worried — that there are going to be mistakes. And indeed, in a certain sense there is a critical period of the reform: the first six months or even the first year. But I believe that even this initial period will be far from being as critical as some people are inclined to think. The basic tendencies in our economic life, from production all the way to consumption, are not going to go through a radical and abrupt change. If we act in the spirit of the unity which has developed during the period of preparation and which can be now regarded as total as far as the principles are concerned, if we speak the same language and if we work for the same goals then we shall be able to overcome the difficulties which may arise; then the real results of the reform can prove ever more effective and ever stronger year by year as we progress.

I am confident, that we will already achieve this result in the first year and will be able to reduce the still existing negative trends in our economic life to a considerable extent. I can say this because we are going to introduce the reform under good time and – considering the circumstances – after sound preparations and in good conditions.

The introduction of the reform will also be made easier by the decisive fact that, as with all major social changes in our social system, it will necessarily be pioneered and directed by the party. When I speak of the party I mean both our Central Committee and our party organizations, as well as the rank and file of our party. To this I must add as a second precondition: we must continue to take the same attitude to the leading role of the party, to the methods we have already worked out and introduced in practice with good results. In the upper, medium and lower levels alike there is a proper division of labour between the party leadership, the state administration and the officials of the social organizations (the trade unions, the Young Communist League and other mass organizations).

We will continue to interpret the leading role of the party in the following sense: the party does not want to assume all the responsibilities, or to take upon itself every sphere of authority; in other words, we want a proper division of labour. Indeed, the independent but at the same time coordinated activities of the party organizations, state officials, the local councils, and the trade unions, the mass organizations, as well as the management of industrial plants and cooperatives – this is the healthy, multi-stage system of our management, already in existence, which will have to function in implementing the reform as well.

Communist party history shows that when the necessary policies, economic and cultural, have been worked out successfully, then the question of cadres arises, because there is a need for people who are able to implement a specific policy in practice. This holds true for our reform, too. Cadres have been, and still are being trained, something which was indispensable during the preparations. But there is some contradiction here because the training of cadres in preparation for the reform was done using the same system and nomenclature which is in force now, before the introduction of the reform. We will solve the question of cadres because we have to, and I think the solutions will in general be the right ones. For we will continue to rely on those people who have been leading our economic activities and who have worked successfully. But later a certain selection will no doubt have to be made.

Let us not think that our work on cadres will be completed on January 1, just because all the appointments will have been made and approved. I propose that we should show a certain patience on the question of cadres. Those who supervise the activity of these cadres should follow their work with attention and help them; and within a year or eighteen months they will have to examine whether their appointments were good or not. Certain changes may have to be made, but we must not begin by doing that, although we must be aware that a certain selection will be necessary. In a year or two we'll see how widespread it will be.

There is a further question. So far we've had interests on two levels — the interests of the society as a whole and the interests of the individual. Now this will be modified by another element, and we will speak of three levels of interest: the interests of the nation, the whole country; the collective interests of a workers' community; and the interests of the individual. As Comrade Gáspár has pointed out, it will be a complicated and difficult task for the party, for the trade unions and for the leading officials in general to guarantee the most suitable answers to problems. As far as these three levels of interest are concerned, they do coincide with each other — and this is the decisive factor — but also they may be in conflict with each other. So how will these questions be solved? Who will solve them? I do not think it would be right to make arbitrary distinctions between party secretaries, trade union officials and general managers. The real differences which exist among them are due to their different tasks, to their particular scope of activity. I think it would be difficult to draw a line between whether they are responsible to the state or to the workers' community. They are responsible to both. There is no way to wriggle out of that responsibility.

So what is going to happen? There are mandatory resolutions: party resolutions, state decrees, trade union decisions. These are mandatory for party officials, managers and trade union officials respectively. I hope that the party, the government and the trade unions will issue consistent central directives keeping in mind the public interest. These are mandatory for everybody, and everybody should be required to act accordingly. But I think the Central Committee and the goverment will have to reckon with the fact that local interests will crop up and will try to get hold of a somewhat bigger share of the national wealth to improve matters for a particular factory. Every local management, every factory community — including the party secretary, or the general manager — is interested in improving its performance, which does not necessarily involve only profit but moral incentives as well. Indeed, they want to be proud that their factory is doing well, that it produces a profit and that it needs no state subsidy. We must reckon with this and fundamentally it is healthy. But it is also important that they should endeavour to do so by honest and straightforward means, by working better, by doing their best to exploit the given opportunities.

We will have to oppose all attempts to improve the achievements of a small community at the expense of the community at large, the country or the general interests of the people. The medium level has a very important role here. Let's take as an example, the party committee, the trade union committee, and the management of a particular factory. Their activities must be supervised by their respective superior authorities who are responsible for preventing the formation of an unhealthy, local united front which could be harmful to the national economy. I don't want to enter into details but in fact it might easily happen that, for instance in industry, it will be the district or town party committee, in agriculture it will be perhaps the local council, that will have to be on guard and see to it that the right principles and public interest predominate in the factories, the state farms or the cooperatives. As a matter of fact one cannot deny one's own interest; although there will be individual examples to the contrary, it wouldn't be realistic to expect local functionaries in general to challenge the local public opinion of a factory. This is something which the superior authorities will have to deal with, acting in unity. Should such problems arise, then they will have to be examined at the next session or meeting of the party, the government or the trade unions; unanimous and fitting conclusions and solutions must be found and—if necessary—instructions will have to be given to the local officials. This can be an effective attitude. But we must not allow situations to arise in which a state body tells people: "Do this"; when the party organization says: "Not that way", and the trade unions wait and see which standpoint proves the stronger.

There is a big question which concerns everyone: the question of consumer prices. Comrade Háy[24] mentioned during the break in our session that while the party leadership, the economic organizations and the trade unions are well prepared for the reform, this is not so in the case of the consumers. Our Central Committee has passed a resolution in which we have instructed all organizations which can influence public opinion to conduct an intensive publicity campaign on the essential points of the price reform. Let's publicize our price policy because it is a just, socialist price policy: it protects the interest of the workers, the interest of the national economy. Basic consumer goods will have centrally fixed prices—and, I can add, they are quite low prices; on other goods will be prices ceilings, while there will be some products where the prices are free. It is our price policy as a whole, and the principles it is based on, rather than the prices of individual articles, which the party and the social organizations will have to publicize and persuade the public to accept.

I want to mention again here that we will have to enforce all elements of the reform, and consequently statutory provisions must be prepared and issued in good time, stipulating severe punishment for fraud, profiteering and price speculation, no matter whether these are committed on behalf of a collective or simply by an individual. This is something that can be and must be done without fail. Fraud, profiteering and price speculation all have their well-known characteristic features so they should be described in legal terms and the consequent provisions should be made public as soon as possible, even before January 1. It is difficult to arm oneself in advance against minor manipulations but we'll fight against these, too, as they arise; but we must make sure that there is no fraud, profiteering or price speculation, and we will guarantee this by legal sanctions.

I would like to raise another question of a different nature. Our reform has certain international connotations as well. Much has already been said about the capitalist market. Our relations with the capitalists are quite simple: they don't buy anything from us they don't need, or which we offer at unacceptable prices, and we pursue the same practice with them. We have nothing to do with the capitalist system as such. The situation is quite different with the socialist world. Our existing economic relationship with the socialist countries is of a superior nature from an economic point of view as well, and is not only of a commercial character. A reform of economic management quite similar in nature to ours is being discussed in several socialist countries. I think many people in the socialist world system have in mind similar principles of economic administration and management both within the individual countries and also in terms of trade and cooperation between the socialist countries. I believe this is an international necessity demanded by development. I think this present resolution can be interpreted by our Central Committee as an obligation for our comrades who work in the CMEA and in general for our comrades who manage our economic affairs vis-à-vis the socialist countries, to represent the principles of our reform and to work in their own respective fields in this spirit in the interest of even more effective economic cooperation.

Now that the reform will come into force it is very important that continued suitable party and state leadership is guaranteed so that the aims of the reform can be achieved. We must keep control of affairs and we must have a good system of information so that we can follow the whole process. We must also play a leading role — as many speakers have said — in the sense that we will have to take some necessary measures and make corrections on certain questions which will inevitably arise during the implementation of the reform. I cannot say exactly in what way we will be able to find the answers but it has already been decided that after the first three months the results and experiences of both the introduction of the reform and the new economic management will be examined by the government. Later this will have to be done at regular intervals by the responsible bodies of the party and of the economic leadership.

We have some other difficult tasks in addition to the reform and the national economy.

Firstly, the international situation — whether we like it or not — always sets us some tasks. We must not fail to deal with them. In addition to that there are thousands of questions in the Hungarian People's Republic that need to be answered on a regular day-to-day basis in the fields of public education, culture, scientific life and so on. Now that the question of power is solved and socialist agriculture and economic management are on our agenda I would like to say — without any intention of making it urgent — that I think that before long we have to examine our scientific and cultural life (together or separately) just as we did our economic life. We did pass some resolutions concerning this, but most of them are no longer really up-to-date. I think we should conduct the same critical analysis of the situation and of the new developments in science and culture as we did for economic management. We will include all interested parties in this study as well as in working out what has to be done; we will consult them and we will put this subject on our agenda within two years or even within eighteen months.

As a matter of fact the economic activity we are discussing now is very much influenced by the various factors of our scientific and cultural life. It was stressed at our party congress that nothing can be achieved without conscientious, political commitment. We also emphasize that our major objective is a constant improvement in the standard of living of the working people. True though this is, it is not enough to profess this objective on its own. We must strengthen the view that it is of vital importance to safeguard our socialist achievements, to guarantee a future for our people, and to complete the building of a socialist society and in the meantime to improve the standard of living of the working people. If our socialist achievements, our regime, the security and future of our people are threatened, then everything else must be subordinated to their protection. We need a public attitude which gives priority to the interests of our socialist homeland and which is ready to sacrifice everything for it — even life, if necessary.

This is something we must keep in mind. This is where socialist consciousness plays an important role, and that is why we must deal regularly with questions of ideology, science and culture. This consciousness has been strengthened more — we are glad to say — by the 50th anniversary of the victory of the Soviet socialist revolution than by any number of resolutions. But we must not feel content: it will be a long time before we can believe that our task of influencing people's awareness is done.

Besides, our party is an internationalist party — something we are proud of — and this often entails duties in the noble sense of the word. We were the hosts to the conference on the Middle East and we will organize the next CMEA general assembly meeting; we will also host a large international consultative meeting which will have limited programmes but which will be attended by some sixty or seventy party delegations, with a lot of work to do. So we, the hosts, will also have many tasks. There are duties of this kind for the Central Committee and the government too. This is an honour that we can be proud of, but they still involve tasks which must be done. This is something we are used to because we have always had to cope with various tasks. I am confident that the party and all those bodies which have manifold tasks — the government, the trade unions, the mass organizations and so on — can tackle them, because today we are working under better conditions than in the past.

Let me remind you how we started: the fight for power was not merely a timely topic on our agenda, we had to wage a real battle to the finish; now we can enjoy the fruits of that struggle. Power is firmly in the hands of the people, the party is widely respected, people have confidence in the party and it is followed by the masses of the people. Consequently we are working under better conditions. The socialist reorganization of agriculture involved three years' hard work, but we completed it successfully and now we can enjoy its advantages with the existence of a certain number of state farms and three and a half thousand cooperative farmers — compared with the earlier 1,700,000 farmers working on their own. What a difference it makes to solving the large variety of agricultural problems such as what to sow on the land, and whether the product should be sold to the state and when.

The conditions of our activities have been greatly improved even in the past ten years by the significant achievements of the historic struggles of our party, our working class, our people. So if we rely on a firm, principled policy, on the confidence shown in the party and the government, on our good relationship with the masses of the people and on our socialist industry and agriculture, then we really don't have so very much and such difficult work to do. Keeping these important things in mind, I am confident that the reform, which we have now decided to introduce, will work well and will achieve what we expect from it.

A Radio and Television Interview

JANUARY 1, 1968

JÁNOS KÁDÁR: I'd like to welcome my radio and television audience. I feel honoured that so many people have addressed questions to me through the *Rádióújság* (Radio Weekly). I hope my answers will be of some use; so please go ahead and ask.

QUESTION: Many of the questions addressed to you concern the cause of peace. Many people would like to know how you, Comrade Kádár, evaluate the international situation — especially the Vietnam war — on the eve of the New Year.

J. K.: I think it is quite understandable that on the eve of the New Year most people are primarily concerned about peace. All honest working people all over the world are united by a common desire for peace. It's not surprising that this question is raised with anxiety. In this modern age our society has practically never experienced total peace, and the present generation has suffered the severe hardships of two world wars. The anxiety and concern can be justified by the fact that — following a slight temporary improvement — international relations have, to a certain extent, again become tense. This has found expression in several different events which are certainly familiar to all who read the papers, listen to the radio or watch television: coup d'états, so-called local wars and especially the Vietnam war. People can see and realize that imperialism still rages, that its leading power — the United States — is waging a barbarous, aggressive war against Vietnam, a war which everybody condemns. The United States wants to bring the people of Vietnam to their knees.

I am a Communist and — as most people know very well — the world Communist movement has always linked its struggle for the ideals and the social system of Communism with a fight for general and lasting peace. We are fighting for peace with optimism. We consider it one of our duties to join forces with all progressive-minded people throughout the world in order to prevent a new world war and to make it impossible for the imperialists to endanger and undermine peace, even if they fight local wars.

The Vietnam war is a constant topic of discussion nowadays. I am convinced that the government of the United States won't achieve the goals that made them start that war. The people of Vietnam, the people of Indochina, will not accept the reimposition of the yoke of colonialism. The United States is committing horrible cruelties in this war, she is waging a war which is inhuman in the extreme but she has not been able — and won't be able — to crush the people of Vietnam. The whole world is witness to the fact that even the biggest imperialist power is unable to defeat a relatively small nation if it fights bravely for its liberty, shattering all attempts to oppress it.

The people of Vietnam will win, the people of Vietnam will be free. It is my deep conviction that the strength of the countries of the world socialist system, the efforts of the progressive-minded people of the world and the vigilance of the peoples of the world can prevent a new world war.

QUESTION: Last year Hungary's role and prestige in international political life continued to grow, and most people expect — as they write in their letters — that 1968 will be another year when we will take further steps on this road.

J. K.: In the past few years or — to specify a period which is easier to grasp and to evaluate — in the last ten years the international reputation and prestige of the Hungarian People's Republic have strengthened considerably. When you examine what accounts for this fact you'll find that the prestige of the Hungarian People's Republic was boosted and strengthened as a result of new progressive and consistent policies — a policy at home which promotes social freedom and a policy abroad which serves the cause of socialism and peace. The Hungarian People's Republic is indeed among the leading progressive countries and nations of the world and although this country has a relatively small population and territory, she can exert some influence on international developments through her policy and by belonging to the socialist alliance, thus serving peace, peaceful coexistence and social progress.

I should also like to mention that in the complex world of today there are large power groups fighting in the international arena, and naturally there are also attempts to set the socialist countries against each other and to disrupt the unity of the progressive forces. There are certain voices which sing the song of sirens, so to speak; they ask quite frequently why doesn't Hungary have a more independent foreign policy. What they actually mean is why Hungary doesn't move away from the Soviet Union and in general from the community of socialist countries. The only answer I can give to that question is: we do not deviate because in the long run only a policy true to its principles can be successful; by adhering to our principles at home and in our foreign policy we can gain and maintain both the respect of our friends and to a certain extent even the esteem of our enemies.

QUESTION: The population of the country has been concerned for quite a long time — quite understandably, I think — with the problems of the introduction of the economic reform. There are a lot of questions expressing the same thought: what can we expect from the new economic management? Some people phrase it this way: is the standard of living going to go up?

J. K.: Today a large section of the general public shows great interest in the reform of the economic mechanism, and this is in harmony with the intentions of the Central Committee of our party and the government. We are implementing a necessary and timely change not only in economic management but in fact in our whole economy. It is quite natural that most people link this question to the standard of living, but I cannot restrict myself to this aspect only. I want to emphasize, if I may, something which I never fail to mention when I speak about questions like this. According to the laws and logic of life, I feel the following to be the correct order of importance: by means of the reform of the economic mechanism we will improve our economic efficiency, we will develop production and productivity and in this way we will be able to raise the standard of living. As we have said many times, we expect the reform to speed up the development of production, the improvement of the standard of living and the pace of building socialism in Hungary. We are convinced that this is indeed going to happen.

QUESTION: I think it is a welcome phenomenon that the people of this country want to take part in public affairs and want to be well-informed, even though some of the ideas are a little pedantic. Like the correspondent who asked who first came up with the idea of this new mechanism?

J. K.: I can answer that question, although it's not easy to do so. First of all the new mechanism is not just an idea, consequently it was no one particular person's idea. The establishment of the new mechanism was a process which began at a certain time — about three years ago — with the recognition of certain characteristics in the development of our economy. We realized that if we failed to change certain things then we would not be able to ensure the rate of development at the pace achieved so far. So thousands of people began to examine the methods of our economic administration and management in order to trace the factors which either hindered or facilitated development. These studies brought together a lot of experience which was then systematically compiled by the Central Committee of the party and by the government, and repeatedly discussed by economic experts, scientists, economists and the party bodies concerned. It was concluded that our system of economic management needed to be overhauled.

QUESTION: One of our listeners linked the new economic mechanism to the problem of housing, and he would like to know whether the reform of the economic management is expected to solve the housing problem in Hungary.

J. K.: The question of housing is one of the most important social issues today. We have already done much to solve this problem, but we have not found a satisfactory solution for society as a whole. Even the completed large-scale housing projects have failed to provide — as we stipulated in our earlier aims — a home of their own for every family. People often raise the question whether the housing problem can be solved by means of our economic reform, by means of the new economic mechanism. I think the answer is positive; we will use the word "reform" for another year maybe, but after that we won't speak about any sort of reform but about how to use it as a new method which can help us solve the problem of housing, too. I think the measures of the reform which enable production units and factories to use some of their revenues and profit directly to finance the housing of their employees are very encouraging signs. On the one hand this will increase the funds available; on the other it will be possible for large concerns to establish a certain number of houses from their own building capacity. But this won't be enough to solve the housing shortage. As I have said before, we expect the reform to promote more efficient, more profitable production and this will create the surplus capacity which can be utilized — among other things — to solve the housing problem within the foreseeable future.

As you know, a fifteen year plan to build one million flats is already being implemented. The rate we're proceeding at, we are at the present more or less where we projected to be, though not 100 per cent.

I would also like to mention — because if I get the chance I usually take the opportunity to speak — that the Central Committee is presently dealing with the question of housing, examining aspects of construction. I have personally raised the issue many times, stressing that we should also deal with demand and distribution rather than restricting ourselves to the question of construction. In order to distribute the flats we build according to real needs and on a fair basis, we first of all need a true picture of the situation. If everything goes on like it has in the past then even though we have built one million flats in fifteen years, the numbers on the housing lists will be the same or even more than now. If all you need to apply to get on the list is to go to a stationer's shop to buy a piece of paper and a pen for a few *fillérs*, if this is enough to put you on the housing list like anybody else, then we won't be able to achieve any progress. But if we speed up the construction of new blocks of flats and if we—at the same time—set things right as far as applying for a flat is concerned, in other words if applicants are allocated a flat under a fair system of distribution, based on their real needs and conditions, then we can solve this problem satisfactorily.

QUESTION: It is well-known that most of those who write letters to us so diligently are women and pensioners. So my question now refers to women and pensioners. What will their position be like under the new mechanism?

J. K.: I feel great respect for the working women of our socialist society because they are just as diligent in work as in writing letters. Women are our equal partners both in life and in work and they deserve the greatest appreciation. When I say that our new economic method will improve the conditions of the working people and make life easier for them, then the same applies to women, too. The general public is surely aware of the fact that our government and our social organizations pay constant and proper attention to the social problems and special questions of working women. In line with the resolutions of our party Congress, further measures have been taken to ease the conditions of working women and especially those who are mothers. Our attitude is not going to change in the future and we will always devote special care to these issues.

QUESTION: And what about pensioners?

J. K.: I could say almost the same about pensioners. Boasting is not usually a characteristic of our party or our government. I don't like to boast either, but now that you have mentioned this topic I think I should say that our pension system would bear comparison with that of any country. Everybody must be aware of the fact that we are very concerned about the problems of elderly people, taking into account both the social and the specifically financial aspects as well. I must refer again to the main resolution of our Congress, as a result of which several measures have been taken to improve the conditions of several hundred thousand pensioners.

But I should also like to say that honest intentions in themselves are not enough. I must start with the basic elements of the reform: the conditions of life for pensioners will also continuously improve in the future, because it is the reform itself which will enable us to create larger and more reliable financial resources for the care of pensioners. The essence of the problem is easy to understand if you make a simple calculation. In this country of ten million people, one million two hundred thousand people receive a pension of some kind. To illustrate this ratio along with the economic and financial questions involved, let me tell you that the number of workers and employees in industry, too, is about one million and two hundred thousand. So this is not a minor question. Good intentions—and good intentions we have—are not enough for further improvement. We need certain financial conditions, too. We hope that within a few years we will have bigger resources than we have today and then we will be able to examine the problem which has been voiced for some years now by a certain group of the pensioners, namely the issue of pensions determined by laws which are now outdated.

QUESTION: A lot of young people are curious about you; many would like to know how you lived when you were young and more specifically about how and when you joined the youth movement.

J. K.: I am in a position which doesn't leave much time for contemplating the past, and I usually don't spend much time on questions like that. But the time when I joined the labour movement, more specifically the Communist youth movement, was a memorable stage in my life, and I don't have to think too hard to remember it. In 1930 I was already a journeyman in industry. That was the time, as many people can still remember, of the Great Depression. Hungary, a semi-feudal agrarian country was hard hit by the crisis both in industry and in agriculture. The conditions of the working people were simply desperate and I was one of those who were in that situation. It was my desire to live a decent life through my own work that took me, as a young worker, into the labour movement. Through my trade I came into contact with the members of the ironworkers' opposition movement, as it was called. They represented the revolutionary wing of the trade union movement under Communist leadership. This is where I got to know how the labour movement worked in practice and what its political struggle was. I took part in the demonstrations against unemployment and later on I contacted some of my friends and acquaintances who were — as I learnt — members of the illegal Communist youth movement. They gave me information about the movement and then I asked them to admit me to the Young Communist League, which was working underground in those days. My admittance was a memorable event in my life. I can remember it quite vividly. It was in September 1931 on a Thursday evening at a so-called illegal street-meeting in Paulay Ede Street that I was introduced to the cell which discussed my application for membership and which then decided to accept me as a member of the Young Communist League.

QUESTION: How old were you then, Comrade Kádár?

J. K.: Nineteen.

QUESTION: Here is an interesting question from a young man who is twenty years old. He wants to know what you, Comrade Kádár, think of his generation. He'd like to know whether you thought when you were twenty that you'd be a leading personality one day, and also what is it like to be responsible for the fate of ten million people?

J. K.: Let me begin with the personal question, that's the one I can answer more easily and briefly. Did I think when I was twenty that I would be a leader? Naturally not, at least not in the sense that a young twenty-year-old man thinks of the question today. There was a cruel, stormy struggle in those days. There were sharp clashes arising from the class struggle and everybody had this battle on his mind. Our activities and my own place in the Communist youth movement of those days took a turn which led to me — with a membership of less than a year — being invited to join first the district committee then the Budapest city committee of the movement. I was twenty years old when I became the secretary of the central committee of the underground Communist youth association and I became a member of the party. So in a sense I can say that I was appointed to a leading post at the age of twenty.

This brings me to the second question which is linked to the previous one, namely: what is it like to care for the fate of ten million people. I must say honestly that it is a great responsibility although I almost never look at it in the way in which you asked the question. What I have in mind is that I am assigned to a specific post with certain tasks, which I have accepted to do. Instead of too much soul-searching and contemplation I consider it my major duty to do the job I was entrusted with well and conscientiously. In this post I have to take a stand on questions of great importance, and in this respect it is not an easy job. But the feeling itself is not so difficult to understand, a lot of people can feel the way I do if they want to. We are living in a more developed society and a wide range of people have a certain social awareness; there are tens, no, hundreds of thousands of people who concern themselves not only with their own problems and affairs but also with the fate of their ten million fellow countrymen. They can judge for themselves what this feeling is like. It's a feeling of great and heavy responsibility.

As far as our youth is concerned, I would gladly have a long talk about this if we had more time because it's one of my favourite topics. I have worked a lot with and among young people and I have always liked to do so. People often ask me what Hungarian youth is like today. It's a very difficult question to answer because there are hardly two people alike among adults or elderly people. Young people are also very different. But if you want to answer the question in general, it is useful to quote some statistics. Only a tiny fraction, a barely recognizable percentage, of our youth is without some decent work. So the great majority are studying, or working in industry, or in agriculture; you can find them in a great variety of fields of production. I believe our youth have found their place in the building of socialism or — as students — are conscientiously preparing to do so.

But there are problems too, and they have nothing to do with our social system. One of the laws of life is that the age groups farthest apart do not easily understand each other in certain matters. I always draw the attention of people —and not only young people—to the fact that being young, just like being old, is simply a certain stage in human life. It's neither a sin nor a merit to be young or old, so once we accept that we should not make either a sin or a merit out of it, then it will be much easier to approach this question and to do so more sensibly.

Youth is an extremely important stage in human life; this is the time when with relatively little experience you have to take a stand on great questions, stands that will influence your whole life. Already as a young man you must define your relationship to society and start looking for a partner—as they say— you must lay the foundations of your family. So young people must live accordingly: when a job is to be done, they must do it; when a serious matter is to be decided they must give it serious thought; and when they have a little spare time left, let them spend it enjoying themselves the way young people usually do.

Many people attach too much importance to superficial things, clothes and fashion, when judging young people. I believe our society should not make a radical, crucial issue of these; because fashions come and go. I have already seen trousers loose, and then tight. Occasionally we see some young people with unusually long hair; some consider them fashionable, others say it is not in fashion. I think, whatever the fashion is, the important thing is to keep within the bounds of cleanliness, health and good taste. We don't want our youth to look like bums. And our young people are not going to be like that. Those who let their hair grow long will probably have it cut.

QUESTION: You've gone through a lot of hardship. Where does your cheerful optimism come from?

J. K.: It may come from the very fact that I have indeed gone through many things, many severe hardships which have helped me gather strength. Optimism or pessimism may also come from one's character. I think people in general are optimistic, although some of them may deny it while others are shy about it or just like to play prophets of doom who say: It's not going to work; and if it really does fail they can say: You see I was right. But if it works out no one is going to blame them. This is the advantage of those who call themselves pessimists. I think human nature has been the same for a long time. As the old saying goes: As long as there is life, there is hope. I never deny that I am optimistic and I am not saying it because of this interview. I was optimistic in the most difficult situations too, and I attribute it to my belief in a materialist ideology, to the fact that I am a Communist. Communists are optimists.

QUESTION: Optimism is closely linked to a liking for cheerfulness and humour and since Budapest is famous for its humour, the following question is far from surprising: is there any humour in politics?

J. K.: I like healthy humour. If you are angry for some reason, go ahead and be angry; but if there is also a humorous or funny side to it, don't fail to recognize it. Politics are something different; it's a word of Greek origin indicating the state in its primary meaning, and later the affairs of the state or — in today's terminology — public affairs. And there's no humour in public affairs. Naturally there are humorous events in political life too, but that's another story. There's no place for joking when it comes to state affairs, public affairs.

QUESTION: Here's a personal question for you, Comrade Kádár: Quite a number of people would like to know if you have time to read, to go to the theatre, to have some rest.

J. K.: To tell you the truth, I haven't got too much leisure time. Naturally, like everybody else, I do have some time for leisure, not much, though. On workdays practically none, but I do try to keep some of my week-ends free if I can, and I usually spend them in a traditional way and I read regularly. Since my early childhood I have always enjoyed reading novels and they help me relax and get some rest. I don't want to lag behind the developments in the world and sometimes I go to see a good film and — though not too frequently — I go to the theatre, too. I am fond of chess, sports, nature. I like to attend — if I can afford the time — a chess tournament or any sports event, especially a good soccer game; I like to take a walk in the woods, or in a park; and I admit that I love hunting—or, rather, I should love it if I had the time. I believe that recreation means spending your leisure time with something different from what you're doing at your job. I like woods and parks because there's no telephone there, and I don't have to read briefings there. These few hours are a real rest for me.

QUESTION: Thank you for your patience, Comrade Kádár. Today, on the first day of the New Year, we whole-heartedly wish you and your wife good health and a Happy New Year. Finally let me ask you on the first day of 1968: what message would you like to give to the people of Hungary?

J. K.: First of all, I thank you for your New Year's wishes and I also wish you all the best. When I think of the year to come and the people of our country, I think of the amount of work we shall have to do, which will not be less than in 1967. We will have to work for progress; in the domestic field we will have to challenge old-fashioned views, and often even ourselves, too; in the international field we will have to face the forces which threaten socialism and peace. Our nation can look forward to the New Year with justified confidence and hope, and now may I refer to a previous question. If ten million people concern themselves with the happy future of ten million people, if they work, think and try to influence each other accordingly, then we will protect peace and continue to build socialism. There will be work and there will be achievements. And now let me take this opportunity to wish with all my heart a Happy New Year to my radio and television audience, and to the whole nation.

Speech Made at the Cultural Centre of the IKARUS Body and Vehicle Factory (Budapest)

FEBRUARY 1968

Honoured Assembly, Comrades,

I am happy that, in accordance with the programme of our visit to your factory, we now have an opportunity to speak at this mass meeting on matters of common interest, on questions which are engaging our Central Committee and government.

First of all, some brief words about the internal political situation, the state of our country. The internal relations of the Hungarian People's Republic are in good trim: our country, our society, is at work implementing a commonly determined, clear programme; there is broad agreement in our homeland.

This agreement is firmly established. However, we are not in the habit of entertaining illusions, nor of deluding others. When we say that in Hungary the political situation and the atmosphere are good, we are also very well aware that not everyone takes the same attitude to the main objective, the main efforts. In Hungary, besides people of political awareness and socialist convictions, there are also others, though not in large numbers, who do not agree with even the fundamental objective, the building of a socialist society. Then there are some people who are quite indifferent to what kind of social system there is. But I dare say that even people who have a hostile attitude towards socialism have become resigned to the fact that socialism is being built in Hungary, for there is nothing they can do about it.

Among people who do not harbour hostile sentiments, but do not regard the building of a socialist society as their life's aim, one hears opinions — you are aware of this too — such as: it is all right, as long as it does not get any worse than at present. If we take this into consideration too, and appraise the situation realistically, we can still say with full justification that the working class, the peasantry and the intelligentsia, in other words, the overwhelming majority of our people do not simply acknowledge the fundamental socialist aims of our party and our people, but support them with devotion, honour, enthusiasm and deeds.

This is the situation in the country. It is reflected, for example, in the report on the realization of the 1967 national economic plan, which was made public two days ago, and in which the work, effort and impetus of socialist construction is also expressed in figures.

You know the main data relating to the fulfilment of last year's plan. I might add that the Hungarian People's Republic can quote these figures with assurance and confidence before the whole world. After all, the Hungarian national economy underwent extensive development last year. As we know, industrial production went up by 9 per cent and productivity in industry by 7 per cent in one year. We reached our target for agricultural production and, considering the particularly difficult circumstances and the not very favourable weather, this is a great achievement. In the same year, 1967, we invested 15 per cent more than in the previous year. Consumption also went up by an adequate amount and the money income of the population in 1967 was 7 per cent higher than in the previous year. Retail trade increased by 10 per cent, real wages per head of population by 3–3.5 per cent and real income per head of population by 6 per cent. To sum up, the overall fulfilment of the plan, taking into account the difficulties which are frankly admitted in the report, is such that we can state in the final analysis: we fulfilled the plan better and to a greater extent than originally envisaged.

The fulfilment of the 1967 plan in the IKARUS Factory fits into the general development well. The IKARUS Factory overfulfilled its target by 0.6 per cent, and delivered 2.5 per cent more products for export than planned. If we take into consideration that last year life in the factory was burdened with great difficulties, which you overcame, then we can only speak of this result with appreciation. For certain changes have taken place in the orders, while at the same time there were also hitches in the deliveries needed for production here. Meanwhile reconstruction went on, or more precisely: large-scale development and investment work was carried out. Taking all this into consideration, for my part I value these achievements highly and welcome them.

In my opinion, great political and moral results have attended this process. When I was here on a visit six years ago, one of the many reasons — and not the least — which brought me was that here at the IKARUS Factory the socialist brigade movement got going with great vitality. The six years that have passed have shown that the promising beginning of that time was no flash in the pan, but was the lasting and firm determination of the workers. Because since then three workshops, and indeed one of the office sections too, have won the title "socialist". Taken as a whole we may say that the factory reflects very well and accurately the socialist work which is in general going on in the country. Life at this factory, here on the outskirts of the capital, is otherwise such that one might almost say that the entire population is represented in it: workers, working people commuting from the countryside, even whole families, and intellectuals live and work here; and the nature of their work and its results are similar to those of the whole country. Please allow me to congratulate you with all my heart on your results for the year 1967 on my own behalf and on behalf of the Central Committee.

The IKARUS Factory is an important plant not only for the Ministry for Metallurgical and Engineering Industry, but also for the Hungarian national economy as a whole. This follows from the size of the plant, from the character of the products and from the fact that quite a considerable part of these products, some 80 per cent, are manufactured for export. The importance of the plant also derives from the plan for large-scale development envisaged in the government resolution on the IKARUS Factory. At present the plant — taking the entire premises into account — employs about 7,000 people, but long-term ideas envisage the growth of the plant, a large-scale increase in production and the development of technology. As you surely know and have often discussed, more than two years ago the government took a decision that more than 800 million Forints must be invested in developing the factory. During the past two years investments worth some 300 million Forints have already been put through, and it is envisaged that the rest will also be completed in the course of the current Five Year Plan. If we carry out this development, then I believe it will be proper to say that IKARUS is Europe's largest, or at least one of its largest, bus factories. This already indicates the enormous national economic importance of this plant and the work going on here.

Comrades in the party organization and at workshop conferences are now dealing more and more with the plan for 1968. The fact that the total value of production will have to be increased by more than 42 per cent within one year, that productivity will have to be raised by 20 per cent and meanwhile the capital construction will also have to be continued — that is, that you will have to produce and build simultaneously — means, frankly speaking, that you will have no easy task.

There are many young people in the plant, but there are also some older workers to be found who must in particular have experienced that, generally speaking, the tasks do not become easier but always tend to grow more complex and difficult. Somehow this is one of the facts of life. Naturally this should not be interpreted mechanically, i.e. the varying problems are not identical in character. When we spoke with the comrades, managers and workers here six years ago, the central issue then was: what will happen to the factory? Is there any need for it at all?

What will it manufacture? Who will it produce for? How will it produce? And from what? In other words, it was a question of the life and future of the factory. Well, just compare the problems of six years ago with those of today when the future of the factory is assured for decades to come and its development is provided for. These are not mere words, for it is already going on.

I should like to recommend to the workers of the IKARUS Factory what I once recommended to the scientists of the Academy of Sciences. I asked them to look to the future and let their thoughts soar to the skies, but at the same time to keep an eye on what was at their feet as well, because if they did not, they would stumble and would not reach either the heights or the distances. I should like to ask the large and powerful working collective of the IKARUS Factory—always keeping in mind the great and long-term goals of development—to devote suitable attention to the tasks of today. If I might be allowed to use a commonplace expression, let them put their shoulder to the 1968 plan and, if possible, let them fulfil it even better than the way they carried through the 1967 plan. However difficult the tasks for 1968 may seem, every condition needed for their solution is there. As far as I am concerned I am confident that you will also fulfil the 1968 plan with honour. On my part I wish you good health and much success in the implementation of the 1968 plan.

Naturally certain conditions are necessary for this work. When I said that you have the required conditions at your disposal, I was thinking first of all of conditions within the plant. But naturally other conditions are also needed for work, conditions which are not dependent on the factory community, the managers and the workers at the plant. These conditions for your work also exist and will be at hand. Again I am thinking of our greater community, first of all the Hungarian People's Republic, and its general situation and state. Because this is the primary background for your work also. The position of the Hungarian People's Republic is encouraging, and in my opinion, the future too looks heartening. We have firm working-class power, we have a goal which the Hungarian working people have adopted: the further and complete building of a socialist society; and in pursuing these socialist aims our society is united. As the result of our struggle and work up to now we command better conditions for our future work than in years past.

As far as the most important basis of our society and our political and cultural life is concerned, the economic foundation, the work and struggle up to now have yielded the following result: with the socialist transformation of agriculture, a socialist national economy with a unified structure has come into being. On this socialist foundation, the socialist national economy is growing and will become stronger from year to year. Therefore when we review the present tasks and sigh: "Good heavens, will there never be fewer of these tasks?" we must recall that everything which is already behind us, and the battles we have fought, have borne fruit and are helping us in our further struggles. I do not wish to go back too far. Let us recall what a great job it was at the end of 1956 and the beginning of 1957 to defend and consolidate working-class power; and then the next task, the socialist transformation of agriculture, was also not easy from a political point of view, when our two basic labouring classes argued a little on whether cooperative farms should be created now or later. This obviously came up and had its effect here too at the IKARUS Factory. Because people also talked about it among themselves.

It is not a simple process for the individual to arrive at approval for a socialist society. Among journalists and people working in similar political spheres comparisons are sometimes made which show that in the bourgeois countries addresses at meetings, speeches in parliament and even newspaper articles are "shorter" than in our country. I thought about this and arrived at the conclusion that to a certain extent this is inevitable. For bourgeois society to survive and indeed even to grow somewhat stronger the system of concepts already in people's heads is completely sufficient. Such is idealist ideology. Such is the primitive concept of life, the survival of the fittest attitude of that society: "Root hog, or die; I have no concern for either God or man, so long as I have mine!" Such concepts exist in capitalist society. People instinctively gather this point of view bit by bit, starting at an early age, and of course through the way in which the capitalist system is taught in the schools, churches and various other places. Our task, however, is not so simple, unfortunately. We have to do double or triple work. First we have to uproot from the thinking of a great many people the weeds which are bad and cannot be used when living and working in a socialist society; and then we have to implant and strengthen new ideas. We beg for forbearance; but this is why our speeches and articles are "longer". Because the ideologists and political spokesmen of capitalism operate quite easily. One does not like to offend the sentiments of religious-minded people, because we have no need of this, but if we were able to preach and say: "This dictatorship of the proletariat and this whole socialism has been ordained by God, one has to do what fate has decreed, forever, amen", then our speeches would also be shorter.

Every politically conscious person in the party, and in our society in general, has done great work in past years. Great results were born of this and today these are helping us too. Because when one does not have to argue with people any more about what kind of system we should have, and whether there should be socialism in agriculture, or individual private farming, then the fundamental questions of society are already in order and we can better concentrate our attention on matters which everyday life brings with it and which we also have to solve.

Undoubtedly there are people in the great capitalist countries who scorn Hungary: what is that poor little country capering about, what has she been able, and what does she want, to achieve? But we who are living our own lives remember what a great many things our people accomplished in two decades. That they created life out of the ruins of the war, smashed capitalism, built a new, socialist social order, defended it in a separate, by no means easy, battle, then laid the foundations of socialism and are now working on completing its building. We may rightfully say, therefore, that our people are both strong and rich, not only in spiritual matters, but they also have material resources the like of which the Hungarian people never possessed in their history.

Not long ago I met a Western diplomat. He said to me: Do you claim that if there had been no socialist system here, then there would have been no development? I replied: I do not claim that if there had not been some change in the system they would not have managed somehow to scrape away the war ruins, production would not have got started, and the country would not have developed to some extent. But, I said, what our people have achieved is, first of all, that they have become free, then that everyone has bread, if he wants to work for it; that what lawfully belongs to him cannot be taken away from him; that he has human dignity; that as far as material development is concerned, in twenty years we made up the handicap of at least eighty years which the capitalist system caused in Hungary—this could not have been accomplished in Hungary by any kind of old regime. For this a new system, a socialist system, was needed.

Such, therefore, are our general conditions—good and encouraging. Naturally we need to continue both the work of building, and the ideological and political work. Because it is very rare that a person who thinks in a Marxist manner ceases to be a Marxist, but before someone becomes a person thinking in a Marxist way, a man with socialist concepts and morals, great work is required. And it requires even greater work to turn all the sons and daughters of a whole people into such persons. In order to achieve this we must continue our efforts. We cannot say that we have already convinced our people of everything. Life raises its own problems every day, and for this reason the work of political enlightenment and convincing must be continued unceasingly and constantly. Here at the IKARUS almost everyone is studying, which is very right and good, because development always brings with it new things, which must be recognized and mastered.

You are familiar with the party's general policy and you are well aware that the Party spares no effort whatever in working to strengthen our regime and power, and to make our socialist aims understood. In our party, in the mass organizations and even in state and economic leadership, it is a general rule that people must be persuaded. Power must be ensured and defended with arms—this belongs to the nature of power. At certain times it is not the propaganda brigades, but the armed forces which have the say. But for the solution of the everyday problems of construction and development, bayonets are not the suitable weapons. Here the only help is that the aims must be good and the masses must agree with them and support them of their own accord. It is possible to fight for power with force of arms, power can be defended with force of arms, but it is not possible to build a new society with force of arms. This is our general standpoint, this is our endeavour and whoever examines our domestic policy carefully knows very well that this marks the course of our action.

On the question of defending power and socialism, our standpoint is unequivocal: we will not allow force to be used against our regime, against socialism. When someone has acted with force, we have responded with force. When they understood this to be our rule and abandoned force, then we too stopped using force immediately. To ask questions, to argue, to bring up ideas, to carry on a genuine exchange of views—not only do we not oppose this, but indeed we want and actually need it. In keeping with the needs of our society we want people who reason and express their ideas, because from this meeting of ideas must emerge what is indispensable for action: decision.

Well-considered, proper decisions are forged in debate. But we also have a fundamental rule with respect to debate. We debate various matters at suitable forums, but when we have concluded the debate we say: comrades, we have reached agreement, so we must no longer debate, but work, let us put into effect what we agreed upon. If we do not debate at the outset and do not clarify just what we want, but simply declare that this and that is the assignment, come on, get to work—then people will debate during work and at the expense of work. But if we have debated and have reached a decision on the basis of this about what we are going to do, then let us not start to debate again instead of working; this is not our method. Everything has its time and place. Whether we go this way or that, it is customary to ask before we start out, but once we have started off in the direction decided, then let us go that way.

We will continue the policy which people in our country already know well and approve of. Communists have a difficult and heavy responsibility: they have to lead. In addition, they have to work and stand their ground in an exemplary manner. The building of a socialist society is a joint task. It is not dependent on party membership, because the complete socialist society will not be a society of party members, but a socialist society of working people; therefore, everyone will have to share in its construction. Our political endeavour at home, as the Congress also proclaimed, is to regard everyone, every force, and every person who plays his or her part with honest intentions in the building of socialism as our friend and ally, and we wish to work in sound understanding with them. This is the essence of our policy.

The Patriotic People's Front is to hold its congress in the near future. In our country the people's front movement is the social framework for the political rallying and cohesion of Communists and non-party people. We are convinced that if this People's Front Congress is fruitful, then it will further strengthen our patriotic popular unity — I would not even know how to describe it otherwise — which is being realized through socialist aims.

A question of primary importance for Communists is how we judge people. Some comrades have said that in this matter our new leadership is very liberal. We are not liberal, we are Communists, therefore we maintain that it is impossible to judge a man only on the basis of papers, whoever he may be, because paper is one thing and a human being is another. For the very reason that I am a Communist I believe that people can be changed, i.e. that ideology influences people, and if ten years ago someone was not a supporter of the socialist idea, he could have changed in ten years. A man must not be pictured as a little statue carved out of stone, but really as a living man, whose thinking changes and develops.

You are aware that when the struggle for power was going on we had some problems with certain writers, artists, church and non-church people. But just look at and reflect on how and in what manner we settled these matters. I dare to claim that this was done scrupulously and in a Communist manner. Here is the latest Christmas issue of *Népszabadság*. If you will recall, in addition to Comrade Zoltán Komócsin[25], Gyula Illyés[26] and Péter Veres wrote articles in this issue and György Lukács[27] gave a statement. As I read the issue it occurred to me that eleven years ago it would have been difficult to imagine that they would appear together in one issue of the party's official paper.

In this I see something that warms me to the bottom of my heart. It means that our party really has learned its politics. It has learned what we most profoundly needed in 1956, how to distinguish, to differentiate between people. Because the matter is not simply that someone is now on this side, and the other person is on the opposite side, and then either we wipe out those on the other side to the last man, or they exterminate us. Here the front was more complex and difficult. Fortunately our party was able to differentiate, to split people who were temporarily gathered on the other side, and was able to lead those whose real place was on this side to the right road. This is what genuine Communist work is all about. Because if I say of a person that he is conservative, reactionary and antisocial, and with this I have concluded my social work, this can be finished in a moment. But sometimes it may happen that we have to take pains for years on end to guide someone on the road to us. And anyone who does this kind of work may be pleased with the strength of our ideas and the correctness of our party's policy. Because he will be able to perceive that people do indeed develop and, except for a few incorrigibles, they ultimately find their place. This is the work we must continue to do in future too both on a national and a local scale. This is real Communist work. In this sphere too, the party organizations here locally, the youth league, the trade union and the rest of the social organizations are working in the right way and getting suitable results. From the standpoint of fulfilling the 1968 plan and realizing the more long-term plans, this is just as necessary and important as, for example, the development of technological processes in the various workshops.

Our goals are such that every person with honest sentiments and straightforward ideas can concur with them. We hold it our responsibility to rally these forces, organize them, guide them in the proper direction and work in sound harmony with them. And when somebody works honestly and decently we appreciate it. Because if we again began to deal with who did what nine, fourteen or twenty-seven years ago, we would return to our own past. Over a certain period of time we have established a clear situation and we have concluded this battle, so now let everyone adapt to matters in a new manner. As he adapts, so will our attitude to him; we will deal with him on the basis of his merits or his sins. We must hold ourselves to this.

Speaking of the situation within the country, I should like to touch upon the reform of economic management and some of its social bearings. According to the Central Committee the reform was necessary and it was time that we decided to carry it out. Naturally the reform of economic management brings many new problems with it for both managers and workers. The first thing I should like to emphasize is: the Central Committee did not work out and approve the reform merely to devise something to make people's lives more difficult. The reform of economic management had to be worked out and decided upon because our social development and the development of our national economy had reached a point where we had to make up our minds: either we want to continue ensuring a suitable impetus and pace for socialist construction and economic development, or we get bogged down and must reconcile ourselves to bumping along by one or two per cent annually. Because the essence of the reform is that we shall try to work with greater energy and get further ahead. This applies in every respect: the development of the means of production, of the national economy and of living standards. Because these go hand in hand: if one rises or increases only slightly, then the others can only rise or grow to a slight extent also. If we are able to advance at a proper rate in the development of the means of production and the relations of production, then and only then will we be able to make progress in consumption also and in the living standards.

One of the aims of the economic reform is to introduce methods in the sphere of production prices which until now had been determined by government decisions and decrees. Earlier production prices were determined on the basis of criteria which were then perhaps acceptable and necessary. But the prices were not on a par with actual values, and they did not express them precisely. Consequently there were factories and there were products which were nominally lucrative, but in reality, with prices calculated according to their real value, they were unprofitable. And conversely: there were some factories and certain products that were listed as unprofitable according to the old price; on the other hand, at prices corresponding to their real value it will turn out that they were lucrative. A certain length of time will be needed and years will pass before production prices come close to the true and actual values, but this will have to happen. If we hand out equally and to everyone the task of producing more quickly, at lower cost and in greater quantity, but without their being in the same circumstances, then not everyone will be able to fulfil his task.

To mention only a single question — and this also affects people in the IKARUS Factory — there is, for example, the question of three shifts. Anyone who knows women working in the textile mills is well aware that for twenty years this has been an everyday issue there. Women in the textile mills say: why must it be a law that we women in the textile factories have to work three shifts? We understand that the means of production must be better exploited, but why is it a law that my husband and my grown-up son in the metal factory opposite work only two shifts? Are the means of production there not just as expensive as they are in our mill? Should they not be striving to make better use of the newly purchased means of production there?

The reason I mention this is to make it clearer that this economic reform does not by any means only consist of how much soap and bacon cost, but it touches on the substance of the economy as a whole. It is very important that we learn to work with the means of production intelligently and effectively. This is generally done, of course, but in many spheres and in many places it has not yet been achieved and this situation is intolerable. One comrade related that in the old days among the horses hitched to a coach was a trace horse, which had to do no more than to look good, because the other four pulled the coach. A country, a people cannot live in such a manner that four pull, and one just handsomely waves its mane and in the meantime eats a double portion of oats. This is not just, things will not work out this way.

The issue of consumption is a part of this question. We claim that man in a socialist society should receive a bonus as producer, and not as consumer. Because the very same person who goes into the factory to work is both producer and consumer. We ought to see to it that this man should receive more for his work than up to now, he should earn better, but naturally in proportion to the work done. In this respect, if possible, he should be given an even greater incentive as producer, and not as consumer. Because it is a strange thing when we give him an incentive as a consumer; a quite extreme example of this was that six years ago a man went into the tavern and asked for two decilitres of wine and received a state bonus of 80 *fillérs* for consuming it. For the winedrinker paid less for the wine than what it cost the state. And as far as production is concerned, people do not all work the same way. If someone's earnings are largely the same whether he works more or less, then he would have to be

Saint Paul at least to work himself to exhaustion in spite of it all. Because if it is all the same how a person works and there is no tangible result of his good work in the form of earnings, then after a time he loses his ambition.

What we would like to achieve in production is that if someone does not work he should not earn, but if he works a great deal he should also earn a great deal; and in consumption what we want to attain is that if someone consumes something he should also be the one to pay for it. This essential aspiration is also embodied in the reform. Of course, this cannot be done in one day, nor even in five years, at least fifteen years will be needed for this, but the prices which have become quite independent of the real values must be adjusted gradually at all events, because this too belongs to equitable distribution.

The question is connected with the socialist morality scale of values too.

Our society needs a set of standards which will hold someone who likes to run beside the coach as a side horse suitably close to the coach, on the basis of "you must pull too, brother". And whoever does not pull after all should be ordered out of the queue when distribution takes place, because he was not here when we queued up for work.

With the help of the economic reform we wish to get much closer to our fundamental aims. Naturally this will not happen from one day to the next, and in a certain sense a little patience is also needed. Waiting for a miracle will not get us anywhere, but time will have to be allowed for everything, so that matters develop suitably and our plans are realized.

A few years ago I visited a cooperative farm beside the Ipoly river, the Rákóczi Ferenc Cooperative Farm, where we talked about all kinds of questions freely and quite informally. One of the brigade leaders asked: "When will we become equal citizens?" "What do you mean?" I asked. He replied that they wanted the same kind of old-age pensions as the industrial workers. He put forward the old arguments which others usually mention at such times, that a worker goes into the factory, does his work, and when his time is up he goes home and has no more worries about anything else; but we, the peasants, he said, work from dawn to dusk. I told him that years ago we were out here to campaign in favour of cooperative farming. Then you people told us that you agreed with socialism, that you would definitely organize a cooperative farm, but not right away, let's wait a bit. We acknowledged that then; what could we do, we had to wait. Now I say this, I replied, you people will have the same kind of retirement pension system as the workers in industry, only wait a bit: a little time will be needed, because the conditions for everything have to be created.

Nowadays many workers raise the point that our government, our Central Committee, somehow seems to be quite pro-peasant and to favour the peasantry in this and that. I should like to reply to this: in this respect our Central Committee is not on the side of a single social stratum; we concern ourselves with the problems of society, of working people equally. Otherwise we are indeed endeavouring to stimulate agriculture by various means so that we should make some progress there too, which is in the interest of our working class and the entire people. If things were really so fine in the countryside, the way some city people presume they are, then the people in the villages would not be migrating to the cities, but the other way around.

Careful regulations are needed so that certain classes and sections of workers may live in certain ways and not otherwise. There must be proper proportions in this respect. The most important thing we would very much like to achieve is that every working person earn in accordance with the work he does, that is, in keeping with the principles of a socialist wage system. Another thing: in the sphere of consumption we also require regulations that will provide guarantees that Communism will not be realized too early, and only for a few. We want to realize Communism for all of society. In the meantime we have to establish an intermediate order that will be in conformity with the character and stage of development of our socialist society. Until then, let there be free benefits only where the interests of society require it, and at the same time conditions make it possible. Such are infant welfare, public health, and so on.

It was with such thoughts that we embarked on this great undertaking. We are certain that we will attain the aims of the economic reform in the same way as those of the earlier great battles, the struggle for power and the goals of the socialist transformation of agriculture. We still have a great deal of work to do for this, but this too will come to pass.

The transition, the conditions under which we start the reform of economic management, were favourable. Since we were unable to set for ourselves the goal of creating an entirely new situation in production from January 1 immediately and at once, we were intent on entering the first reform year without any hitches either in the sphere of production or consumption. And this was how it is. By now the first experiences are to hand, and I am able to inform you that both in respect of production and consumption completely normal conditions prevail within the country. What is more, the 1968 plans are better founded now on a national average than earlier ones. The quantity of orders placed is no worse than in other years. The enterprises have also prepared themselves with materials, and production results correspond to the normal and customary increases. The same is true of consumption. The defeatists and the hostile tried to frighten us by claiming that because of the reform there would be unemployment. What the "unemployment" is like in this factory, you know well. Campaign plans have to be drawn up in a manner of speaking, to decide where to get manpower. But even if this is not general, throughout the country the tendency is to a shortage rather than a surplus of labour. Therefore the foundation of the reform was sound and the transition proved to be healthy.

As far as public morale is concerned, the situation is one of calmness and confidence. One sign of this is the fact that in the first two weeks of January savings accounts grew by 361 million forints, which is three times as big an increase as a year earlier. There was a certain amount of growth then too, but now it has trebled. I can add that at present there are somewhat more reserves of the most important goods in the country than at the start of other years. The conditions, therefore, which are necessary for work are assured.

Speaking of the international situation, again I do not wish to go into detail. In general, people interpret and handle these questions properly. Our domestic and international aims are in harmony. Just as we are working for socialism and democracy and prosperity for the people here at home, similarly we are fighting for the same thing in our international endeavours. We regard the promotion of progress and the prevention of world war as our most important international aims. We desire peace; this is what we have worked for up to now, and this is what we will work for in the future.

The international position of the Hungarian People's Republic is firm, her prestige has increased, she enjoys international respect and her words have weight. This is due in part to our correct standpoint on foreign policy, and also to the results achieved by the Hungarian people, and the fact that we are a socialist country, part of a tremendous force.

As far as the imperialists are concerned, everyone knows that in some respects they also have grown wiser. They do not do the same things in the same way as they did fifty years ago. In those days they still declared outright that they wanted war. Now the imperialists say that they want peace, but in the meantime their minds are concerned with war. Or take another example. I have read Horthy's memoirs. The title of one chapter was "Counter-revolution". See how much the world has turned, I said: in 1919 they called the counter-revolution openly by its name. But in 1956 they described it as a revolution. Because the imperialists can no longer openly reveal that they are fomenting a counter-revolution, they are compelled to call it a revolution. However, today all thinking people throughout the world know that the meaning of words is given by deeds and facts. For this reason they also know what the truth is in this question.

At the present time the grave provocation which the largest imperialist power, the United States, is committing and continuing in Vietnam, is the focus of international attention. This imperialist aggression seriously endangers the peace of mankind. Not long ago a war was unleashed in the Middle East. Most recently fresh tension arose over an American spy ship which the coastal defence forces of the Democratic People's Republic of Korea captured. The imperialists, while always referring sanctimoniously to international law and representing themselves as the angels of peace, sent a spy vessel into Korean waters. The Koreans captured her and took her into their harbour. At first the United States was outraged. Now the captain of the captured ship and the government of the United States also have confessed that she was a spy ship equipped with instruments which had the task of carrying on espionage against the socialist countries. The ship lurked in Korean coastal waters in order to provoke a war. Now a discussion and a tussle are going on to decide what the future of the vessel will be. You still no doubt remember the U-2 spy plane, which was shot down over the Soviet Union. And what did the United States do then? First it denied the existence of the spy plane, claiming that such a thing had never existed, either now or in the past. For they did not yet know in the United States that the pilot was alive and had been captured. When the world learned this too, the Americans then declared that for "purposes of self-defense" they had the right to spy over the territory of every country. Yet they obviously have no right to do this, and international conflicts stem from just such unlawful acts. The position of the socialist countries, that they will allow no one to encroach upon their sovereignty and territorial integrity, is justified. The imperialists are endangering the peace and calm of mankind with their provocations, and are bringing great suffering to various people with their local wars. The whole world is indignant about what the American aggressors have been doing to the Vietnamese people for years. Large-scale massacres and killing and every possible kind of imaginable villainy are being committed there.

As far as the Hungarian People's Republic is concerned, our desire is to serve the interests of peace and progress in every way possible through our international policy. Therefore we are working and acting in very strong solidarity with the Soviet Union, the Warsaw Treaty countries, and the socialist nations, in the sphere of foreign policy too. We are in solidarity with the Vietnamese people, the anti-imperialist Arab peoples of the Middle East, as well as the recently provoked people and government of Korea. We oppose and condemn imperialist aggression.

Our aim and endeavour is that the peoples should live in peace. We are striving for friendship among the peoples. And with the capitalist countries we desire peaceful coexistence. The victory of Communism does not call for the instrument of war, because Communism will win in accordance with the laws of social development, as the result of the class struggle of the exploited. Our foreign policy is also suited to this. We support every international action which promotes the easing of tension, peaceful coexistence, and in general rapprochement, friendship and cooperation among nations.

For this reason we also support the proposal which the Soviet government has now submitted in Geneva that suitable treaties and regulations be worked out to prevent the proliferation of nuclear weapons. Actually only the Soviet Union and the United States possess significant stockpiles of such weapons, and Great Britain to a lesser degree. However, if twenty or more countries have nuclear weapons, then naturally the danger will grow that a conflict might break out in which atomic weapons will also be used. In that case the horrible destruction of mankind and civilization would follow. Naturally we oppose this and we are fighting against such a danger.

Our foreign policy, like our policy in general, is a principled one; it is a Communist policy based on Marxist analysis, which expresses the well-considered interests of our people. The great historic experience of our party and our people finds expression in this policy. A fundamental element of this policy is that one is free to think of the destiny of both our own and other peoples only with great responsibility. This firm and steadfast principled policy is a long-term one, because only in this manner can people establish their own future securely.

Hungary is a faithful friend and ally of the Soviet Union. For us this is a question of principle, and not a matter for a season. When we tell someone that we are their ally we mean this literally. Because if I am a friend today and not tomorrow, if today I am an ally and tomorrow act the contrary, then nobody will want the alliance and friendship of such a country, because it cannot be counted on or relied on in critical times. That the Hungarian People's Republic is the friend, good ally and comrade-in-arms of the Soviet Union, the Warsaw Treaty countries and the rest of the socialist countries is very good for us and fits in with our outlook and the interests of our people. This friendship and alliance ensures the future of our people.

It was often mentioned in the past that the Hungarian people, who have lived in this part of Europe for more than a thousand years, have no relatives whatever near by. Here is this small poor people, all alone, orphaned, wedged in amongst Slavs, Germans, Latins, Turks and other peoples. As far as blood relations are concerned, this is actually true, as the Hungarians have blood ties only with the Finns, the Estonians and a few other small peoples. But these are not the only kind of relationships in the world.

When we use the expression: the fraternal Soviet people, the fraternal Vietnamese people, and so on, naturally the intelligent, thinking person knows that this is not a blood relationship but a relationship based on common ideas, on solidarity and a community of interests. This is a true fraternal relationship. We know that in the family, in human personal relationships it is not always the ties between blood brothers or sisters which are the best. True, unbreakable fraternal relationships can, however, come into being pursuing the very same noble aims and in fighting together shoulder to shoulder. Such a fraternal relationship binds the Hungarian people to the Soviet people, to the Vietnamese people and other peoples.

Now for the first time in history we can say at last that the Hungarian people are allied with forces who have the common characteristic of being in the vanguard of social progress. Now our allies are countries which are leaders of social progress. The peoples with whom we live and cooperate in fraternity know where the Hungarian People's Republic stands. Since we pursue an open, principled policy not only those who are pleased by our affiliations can reckon with this, but also those who are not pleased by them.

On the other hand, I can say that people who dislike our affiliations also raise their hats higher than in, let us say, 1957, because they acknowledge that, although they have done everything they could, still they have been unable to cause the downfall of the Hungarian People's Republic. And if the Hungarian People's Republic exists, she will have to be reckoned with. I am thinking of the United States. It too has normalized its relationship with us, as this is the trend of things today. The United States is a great and developed country; it has more than 200 million inhabitants; it is the greatest imperialist power. Not long ago I said to a United States diplomat, in the course of a conversation: If it were up to me the regime in the United States would fall within two hours, and if it depended on you, our system would fall within five minutes. But it does not depend on me or you. Whatever we do, the United States exists and is what it is, and whatever you do, we too exist and will continue to exist. Do whatever they can, the imperialists of the United States are unable to turn back the wheel of history, and they never will be able to, because now they will always have to reckon with the invincible might of the Soviet Union and the world socialist system. It is in the light of this knowledge that we pursue our foreign policy, that we work to rally the socialist countries, the other progressive, anti-imperialist countries and all progressive forces.

We are working to unite, to join forces and rally the strength of the Communist and workers' parties also. We are striving so that the whole world Communist movement might be united. At the present time, unfortunately, this is more a goal than reality. There are differences of opinion among the socialist countries too. This is the kind of situation we have to live and work in. If we were united, it would be better, but there are problems.

We hold that the differences in views appearing on various ideological questions should not be allowed to prevent us from acting in unity against the imperialists. This is our opinion. Unfortunately we do not agree with the Peking opinion on this either. The socialist revolution has produced such results that already fourteen socialist countries are in existence. This is good, this is a tremendous force upon which we are able to rely. Let us not forget either that there was a time in history when there was a dictatorship of the proletariat only in the Soviet Union and in Hungary, but the Hungarian working class still fought!

The political line of the Hungarian Socialist Workers' Party and the Hungarian People's Republic in foreign affairs is widely known internationally. Everyone is familiar with our position; they know that we always speak unequivocally. Stemming also from this, a special sort of confidence finds expression in the fact that when the fraternal parties decided that representatives of the Communist and workers' parties ought to meet again, they proposed Budapest as the site for their exchange of views in this connection. This also means they have faith in our internationalist policy. We are honestly working for the success of the consultations, so that we may democratically compare our views and take some definite steps towards initiating a large and extensive international conference. We support the view that the main forces of progress, the Communist and workers' parties, should constitute a united anti-imperialist front, rallying the other forces of progress as well, because a leading nucleus is needed; and today there can be no substitute for the role of the Communist and workers' parties in taking the initiative on a worldwide scale. Various progressive endeavours exist, there are progressive countries, but nothing can replace the initiative and the vanguard role of the Communist and workers' parties, and the socialist countries. So this is the way in which we look forward to the consultations and are working honestly for their success. Naturally this will be a joint meeting and joint consultation of the participating parties. Our party will also be only one amongst the rest, and will put forward its views and represent its position. But the office of host devolves on us and we want to discharge it with honour.

Every party is independent and every socialist country is sovereign, but in our opinion it does not follow from this fact that they should go in as many directions as there are parties, or that there should be as many discrepancies as there are countries. Independence and sovereignty mean that in the framework of a constructive exchange of ideas we should draw together our experiences, compare our views and formulate a common endeavour and political line which will meet with all our interests. We are convinced that this is not only possible, but also necessary; the interests can and must be harmonized. In our view independence means that every party must decide with even more responsibility on the major issues which have an influence on the fate of their own country and the life of their own people. Because independence also means great responsibility. Therefore it is not a centre that is needed, not a leading party, but unity, the joining of forces on the basis of Marxism–Leninism, the common Communist ideology and viewpoint, internationalism. We have worked in the interest of this up to now, and shall continue to do so in the future.

In touching on these questions my intention was mainly to remind you of certain of our essential aspirations, and to ask that in the future you take these into consideration in both your political and production work. Once more I would like to salute the workers of the IKARUS Factory. Although we have been to many parts of the factory, unfortunately I have been unable to meet with everyone. I would ask you to be so kind as to convey my greetings and best wishes to all those whom we did not meet today. And please be so kind as to pass on what you have heard in some way; perhaps it would be even better if you added your own conviction and belief that whatever the mechanism is like, and however the economic management is reformed: it is necessary to work. And if we work properly then the reform will create better conditions for making our work really more productive and more effective, so that better results might be achieved, and we might distribute more and distribute it more equitably than up to now.

If everyone at his own place, the workers of the Central Committee, the Budapest Party Committee, the Ministry for Metallurgical and Engineering Industry and the IKARUS Factory, carries out his part of the tasks which await us, then we shall prosper. If someone among them does not stand his ground at his own post, does not carry through his own work, whatever it may be, then we will not be able to achieve good results. I believe that among them all, and between the Central Committee and the workers of the IKARUS Factory in particular, the necessary unity exists; we are all working for the same purpose. Retain this spirit, this manner of thinking, and there will be new results and we will make progress.

In the international sphere, of course, we still have many battles to fight. The present international power relations are such that the imperialists are committing provocations and will continue to commit provocations, and we have to struggle against them. But so far it has been possible to prevent the outbreak of a world war and we will continue to prevent it if we fight properly. And just as we have until now, we will continue to strive that our people may live and build in peace, because this is what we need. We want no gifts nor anything else from other peoples, only this, that we have the conditions in which we can work, and then we shall create what our people require. In cooperation, we will work and fight shoulder to shoulder with those of our allies, the Soviet Union and other socialist countries, with whom we have fought together up to now, and with whose help we have come thus far. Everyone can work in tranquillity and honesty, and the results will follow.

A few more words to the Communists. For some years I have often repeated over and over again that one should respect non-party workers, and I have never mentioned that one should honour the Communists. In this I am guided by the opinion that it is much better if non-party people say of the Communists that they march in the vanguard, are ready to make sacrifices, are worthy of respect and should be followed, than if we said this about ourselves. We have had to earn respect for the party, for party membership, for the name Communist in a difficult situation. I dare to assert that great results have been achieved. Our society is united, and this is due to the fact that the party, the leading force of society, enjoys great prestige and great respect among the people. The masses of the people in truth have confidence in the party, and they follow it. I believe that Communists, each and every one, feel this.

We should not preach that "we are of a special mould", because by this alone we are unable to convince other people. We are of the very same mould as are the working class, the people, but we have become Communists, we have Communist convictions and principles. This, the name Communist and party membership, goes with certain obligations; moreover, with the obligation that we have to live and work in a way worthy of this. Now in factory and village, everywhere, the name Communist enjoys respect, and we should very carefully safeguard this respect. Belonging to the party does not entail additional pay or anything like that. But it does go hand in hand with something extra on the moral side, which none of us would exchange for however many thousands of forints or any kind of bonus. This also adds something to a man's conscience, to a man's aspect; apart from this it adds something to society which is indispensable to it: the fact that such a force exists and there exist such men as can be followed.

I would ask you, all the workers of the IKARUS Factory, to strengthen our common cause with your work and attitude, your deeds and words. Work in such a way that through your results the factory and the country may thrive, and that the honour of the party may grow – that party which will help your work, your struggles and your successes in the future as well.

Thank you for your attention and your cordial welcome, and once again allow me to wish you the very best and much success.

Closing Speech at the 10th Congress of the Hungarian Socialist Workers' Party

NOVEMBER 1970

Honoured Congress, Comrades,

The four-day debate, and the 56 contributions made in the course of it, demonstrated complete unity on the main issues. There was not one contribution which differed on any essential question from party policy. Therefore, my first words to the comrades who spoke in the discussion, to the congress delegates, is to thank them on behalf of the Central Committee and the Central Control Committee, for their completely unanimous support.

In addition to the delegates to our party's 10th Congress, all the delegations from our fraternal parties addressed the Congress. We are grateful that they accepted our invitation and sent representatives and we are grateful that the Communist Party of the Soviet Union and in general all the fraternal parties who took part at our Congress honoured our party – perhaps even more than was merited – by the composition of their delegations and with their speeches.

I cannot mention each speech of the fraternal party delegations. On behalf of our Central Committee, we express our sincere thanks for their putting such emphasis, both in a general and in an international sense, on the 10th Congress of our party.

The internationalist standpoint taken by the fraternal parties, as far as the efforts of our party are concerned, is support of vital importance to our struggle which we can in no circumstances do without.

The contributions of the congress delegates and the debate were of a high standard and worthy of the mission of the Congress. One of the contributors to the debate remarked after his speech that it was difficult for him to make a start, for this was the first time he had faced such a forum. I told him that the second time would not be easy either. This is because a person who appreciates and knows in the good sense of the word the kind of forum he is addressing, who knows that every word he utters here will have an impact, cannot help feeling a sense of responsibility. In my opinion, the reason that the comrades generally wrote out their contributions is mainly because of this sense of responsibility, a fact which can only be welcomed. But another circumstance played a role in this too. In our opinion, the political preparation for the Congress was more thorough and better than that for previous Congresses. This time it was even more apparent that, although the delegates gave expression to their own thoughts, they were not representing solely their own position. The Congress delegates know and feel that each one of them — even statistically — represents one thousand Communists and speaks on their behalf.

In one of the intervals I had the opportunity to talk to outstanding representatives of our scientists and artists. Two of them — one a party member and the other non-party — cutting into each other's words explained that they wanted to ask for the floor, but did not do so because what they wanted to say had already been said, word for word; I only mentioned this as an illustration, as an example of the high level of the general debate at the Congress, and of the fact that every speaker felt responsibility and spoke in a prepared and suitable manner about the questions on the agenda.

The contributions expressed the growing political maturity which, as the result of everyday work, is one of the characteristics of our party members and activists, politically active workers, and, one can even say, of our whole people. The people's horizons have expanded, the understanding and unity of our party and the general public have grown.

In connection with some of the speeches it was said that the delegates knew how to speak. I think they not only know how to speak, but — whether we like it or not — to teach us economics. I recognized one or two of the speakers from old, and I know they have not only learned how to speak, but to count, to reckon with reality and life. This was adequately reflected in the debate.

The discussion touched on all the important questions of the two reports concerning the struggle and activity of the party. Therefore I feel, and the comrades will understand this, that it is not possible to refer to all aspects of the discussion. Permit me, then, not to answer and not to refer separately to the various remarks since they were all so unanimous and clear-cut.

The response to the Congress, in our judgement, is good and realistic. The response was just like the Congress itself. This is naturally also due to the fact that through the press, radio, television and with the help of those who work there, the congress hall was extended beyond its confines. With a very slight time-lag, the exchange of opinions during these days took place not only in this hall, but in the entire country. And there were discussions, as we know from the response, along the same lines and on the same questions throughout the entire country; the broad masses of the people were making their views known, just as we did here at the Congress. This is a very good thing.

Congress also heard the addresses of the fraternal parties which showed the internationalist position from which the various parties evaluate our party. Our Congress has met with a broad response in the fraternal socialist countries and in all countries where our fraternal parties could ensure publicity for it.

Our political opponents and our enemies also followed the 10th Congress of the Hungarian Socialist Workers' Party with attention. Our deliberations surprised them. Their guesses were all over the place. Finally, they reached almost the same conclusion as our camp, our own party membership and people, the fraternal parties and the fraternal peoples building socialism. Adversaries and foes alike consider the 10th Congress of the Hungarian Socialist Workers' Party as the consistent continuation of the path our party has followed so far. It may be useful for them to know this from the point of view of their practical work.

Agreement with the report of the Central Committee and the Central Control Committee is very widespread. It is quite obvious from the speeches at the Congress that the 56 comrades who took the floor not only expressed their own opinion, but the views of the Congress as well.

But the agreement is still broader; it has met with the accord of our entire party membership, public opinion, our allies, the working class and of our people. With the concurrence of all those who in a good and noble sense, consider the cause of the party and socialism their own. And as I have already stated, the basic position and the main line of our Congress meet with the approval of the great majority of the Communist and workers' parties and of the fraternal peoples building socialism. This agreement and solidarity – both domestic and international – is a great source of strength for the future work and struggle of our party.

After this, permit me to reiterate – this time factually – what emerged in the course of the preparatory work for the Congress as the opinion and demand of our party membership and working people, what we only proposed on Monday in the report of the Central Committee and what has been confirmed now: the party will continue its political line even more consistently and will implement it more firmly. This concurrence is a new source of great strength to our party: it shows encouragement, approval and is at the same time a compelling demand from those whom we wish to serve according to our best conscience, and on whose behalf our party often speaks, takes a stand and issues statements. We have to regard this as the demand of our working class, working people and of all the positive forces of our society, as the obligatory task of our party. This united stand at the same time provides us with new opportunities to accomplish even more consistently and more thoroughly what our party has to accomplish.

I should like to touch briefly upon a few specific questions which have arisen in the debate. Several people spoke about coal mining. It is just four years since the unquestionably correct programme to transform the energy structure of the national economy was one of the important themes of the 9th Congress; this set as its aim the reduction of coal consumption and an increase in the use of oil and gas.

We set about realizing this unquestionably economically correct objective and we achieved good results. At the same time, the process was not smooth, because energy requirements increased with unbelievable speed—perhaps to an even greater extent than calculated—while the expansion of energy sources did not keep pace with the emerging needs.

It must be stated that not only in our calculations, but also in our propaganda, a small error occurred. The 9th Congress stressed the need to reduce gradually the production of low-calorie coal which was being mined at great cost, but to continue mining coal of high-calorific value. We also took care of our miners who could no longer be employed in the mines, taking into consideration their great merits in rebuilding the country and in the socialist revolution. We made sure that they found jobs in other areas of work. All of this, however, gave the appearance of the general scaling down of coal mining. This was a mistaken interpretation. Internal, local changes will also have to be made in the future in order to increase the mining of good coal at lower cost, at the expense of lower-calorie coal at higher cost. But even though coal will constitute a smaller proportion of all our sources of energy, Hungarian coal mining, in the face of the increasing energy requirements of the national economy, will remain at about the present level.

Several speakers brought up the question of the Hungarian textile industry, linking it with the position and earnings of women. As far as the textile industry is concerned, anyone familiar with the new, fourth Five Year Plan for the development of the national economy is aware that the Hungarian textile industry has a great future. We are planning large-scale reconstruction of the industry and this will be put through. This reconstruction will extend not only to the modernization of the means of production, but also to an improvement in the situation of the textile workers. The Hungarian textile industry will be a strong, healthy and rapidly growing branch of our national economy, and it is necessary that the situation of the people working in this industry should correspond to this.

The present state of the cooperative farm peasantry and this year's difficulties also came up in the debate. I am thinking now not only of the cooperative farms damaged by the floods. It is well known that owing to the adverse weather conditions there were serious losses in crops. Cooperative farms where the main source of income is crop growing suffered a perceptible loss in income.

Agriculture needs more than good planning, the conscientious work of man and the necessary material resources; for the time being, and I believe for a long time to come, it will depend to a large extent on natural conditions, among other things on the weather. This holds good for crop growing in particular but indirectly for animal husbandry as well. Our peasant brothers are accustomed to the fact that in agriculture there are good and bad years. Who would have thought in the eighth month of this year that by the tenth month we would be crying out for rain. That is how capricious the weather has been. And it will always be like that. For the time being we are unable to do anything about this with human resources. By the way, the national average yield in wheat is about 12 quintals per *hold*. Not long ago this was celebrated as a national record. But in the meantime our agriculture has developed, we had a good year, then an even better one and last year was really magnificent from this point of view. Now that we have fallen back a degree we are disappointed by an average which five or six years ago was celebrated as a national record.

Let me note here that those cooperative farm members, who, in their exasperation at the transitory difficulties, would try to solve the problem by changing the management are mistaken. If their managers are working well and decently, they should keep them and continue to work with them.

And as far as the difficulties and the way to overcome them are concerned: first of all our agriculture based on socialist foundations is full of vigour and has changed into a branch of the national economy which is also able to endure difficulties. More than once during a drought or flood we found that were it not for the collective force in agriculture, and I may add the power of the workers' state, the results would have been disastrous. As things are, however, we can overcome the unforeseen obstacles.

In their awareness and self-confidence, the peasantry are also different from what they were even ten years ago. The Congress also heard that in the eastern counties which were most severely affected by the floods, as soon as the waters receded and the people were able to pull themselves together, they carried out the necessary agricultural work in full measure, according to plan and indeed even overfulfilled plans. This is the principal and best remedy for every kind of trouble.

The peasantry have greatly developed in awareness — and I may say in their collective and socialist awareness. This is proved, for example, by the fact that about two thousand agricultural cooperatives gave direct assistance to the cooperatives affected by the floods, according to their means, to a total value of 140 million Forints. I believe that people who know the minds of human beings, especially of the peasants — and there are also writers here who say they do — are able to appreciate fully what this means in terms of awareness. This all proves that the working class are correct when they decide and resolve to reckon on the peasant class as a fraternal class, to form an alliance with them, and advance together with them on the road to the building of socialism.

There are perhaps people who had doubts about the decision of the 9th Congress to increase the income of the peasantry through the common efforts of the working class and the peasantry and the united strength of our people to the level of that of the working class, nationally and on the average. That, comrades, was a historic step. Not a single working man must begrudge this; on the contrary, we should be proud of it. We will enjoy the fruits of this in the future in the solution of all our serious problems.

With regard to this year's difficulties: the working class has never let the peasantry down. Today they are also supported by their state, party and government. We have frequently criticized the building industry, and I think we will continue to criticize it for a long time. Still, if one looked at the flood-stricken area, even if only on television, after the water had receded, and now one looks at the beautiful, modern lines of houses, worthy of man, which have been built since, one sees proof that what our party, government and working class said and promised to those in distress has been fulfilled — and in a very short time at that. The Central Committee and the government took the necessary steps and has appealed to the cooperative peasants to mobilize their own forces; but what they can not do themselves they will be assisted with. We shall not allow any cooperative to fail merely because they have difficulties at the moment.

Many speakers dealt with the social position of women. They spoke about really current and burning issues, for example, that it is still difficult for women to attain leading positions, that the principle of "equal wages for equal work" has not yet been successfully implemented everywhere; and there are difficulties with regard to nursery and kindergarten places. This is all true and it is good that it was mentioned here at the Congress.

The Central Committee, as was stated in the report, laid down the principles and the Council of Ministers approved comprehensive resolutions on all these questions. Long years of consistent work are needed for their complete fulfilment, because these are not things which can be solved in a week by one resolution. What is involved is a great question of social justice, which has not been solved over thousands of years. It is no wonder that socialism also needs a little time. But the situation will improve as the signs already indicate.

Let me mention, for example, the place and role of women in public life. Only a short time has elapsed since the party resolution, and not enough has happened for a considerable change already to be noted. But certainly there was one event, within the party at that, and this generaly serves as an example. During the preparations for the Congress, in consequence of the political and moral weight of the Central Committee resolution, the number of women elected to the newly formed party committees increased by 33 per cent, by one-third compared to the former situation. More than 19,000 — about 21 per cent — of the 90,000 members of the party branch leaderships are women. If we really follow this example and implement the Central Committee and government resolutions concerning women in other fields and in all other respects, then the social problems of women will be more tangibly solved year by year.

However, there are questions which cannot be solved by Central Committee or government resolutions and not even by a congress resolution. It cannot be prescribed by resolution, for example, whom people should respect and how they should show this. But when everywhere, and also here in the debate at the Congress, the speakers point out that 41 per cent of all the active workers taking part in production are women — and in addition everybody knows how this 41 per cent of the active earners are also involved in the household and in raising a family — then all of us who consider ourselves Communists, or enlightened people, have to say that, although no resolution can be passed concerning this, working women have to be respected!

This has another aspect which, though perhaps not so obviously important, concerns behaviour — one might say etiquette. How many times do we see that backward people — I will not say men, because why should we accuse ourselves unnecessarily — interpret equality as the man forgetting to greet the woman first in a proper manner, although hundred-year-old manuals of etiquette prescribe: that if a man meets a woman he should greet her first; or if there is no empty seat on the tram, he should offer her a seat. All this may seem to be trivial, but it is extremely important: equality does not lie in, and our struggle should not be confined to, the fact that women are free to work just like men so we do not greet them, just like we sometimes do not greet each other. After all, the laws of nature cannot be changed by anybody, and when it comes to carrying weighty things in the physical sense of the word, women will always be weaker; they have to be helped and must always be respected when they take on great burdens.

Such a fundamental position will help us to advance a bit faster in some specific questions, such as the implementation of the principle of equal pay for equal work, and in others.

I am very happy that important male executives of large industrial enterprises spoke seriously about this question at the Congress, since not only the central bodies have the ways and means in their hands to do something, but local ones as well. If not a 23-member government or a 100-member Central Committee, but ten thousand, a hundred thousand, responsible executives seriously tackle these questions, then they will on the spot find unutilized possibilities, reserves and resources to improve the situation. This, comrades, is already a party resolution, unlike the question of etiquette, which I on my part nevertheless recommend for serious consideration.

While on this question, I should like to say a few words with respect to mothers. The 9th Congress passed a decision in principle regarding the introduction of a childcare allowance for mothers. This was carrried out. We still need many other things: crèches, nurseries, and the like, to realize the intention of complementing properly the original, and it seems successful, idea of child-care allowances.

I would like to express here my deep conviction that material resources are needed to increase families and to bring up children. We materialists realize that it is extremely difficult to exist and bring up children on sighs alone. But I dare to say, comrades, that we must also change a quite widespread – though not dominant – outlook. If someone is weighing up, according to his or her own conscience, the choice of buying a TV set or a car, rather than having children, that is his or her business. There are no compulsory laws on this matter, but if this degenerates to the point of speaking disparagingly about expectant mothers because they have not looked after their own well-being, then we Communists must oppose this. Those who live according to the normal laws of society, the noble traits of human nature, cannot be scoffed at; this cannot be condoned. Of course, there is such a thing as vanity too; there are women who think that giving birth to a child will spoil their figures. This may be so, but they will be more beautiful in a human and general sense.

Those who like to calculate should do so, if it is necessary and if they have the time for it. But the decision whether to have a child or not cannot be simply a matter of calculation. One must always reckon with the cost of a pair of socks, a baby carriage and diapers, but the existence of the future generation cannot be a matter of simple calculation. We realize how difficult it is to ensure a young couple even one room to start their independent life. Then, once they have got it, they continue to live there for a long time saying that if they get another room then they will have a baby, too. Those present here who were born before the Liberation must realize that if people had calculated that way at that time, very few of us would be here now.

Many demands were brought up in the discussion — such as raising the pay of textile workers, teachers and others, and similar problems. Demands can be handled in many ways. Let me mention, for instance, the question of provisions. The comrades certainly remember times when food supplies were very poor throughout the whole year, but were improved on important occasions — such as on Liberation Day, for the party congress, Christmas, and so forth.

We — as you may have noticed — have turned aside from this path. We do not pretend that supplies are first-rate throughout the year, but we have at least seen to it that they are not better on national holidays, and during the time of the Congress, than at other times. But I dare to assert that today the average level is as good as it used to be on holidays in the past. Let me add: we must not forget that at the time of this incorrect practice we were in another stage of development.

I could enumerate what we need at length: where we require most investments, increases in pay, and the faster the better. But I believe it to be a good practice that the party congress is not a day for re-stocking the shops, for distributing investments, and for raising salaries.

The party congress should deal with the problem of satisfying material demands when this has a general political, social reason and significance. When it is a question of a normal and systematic improvement of living standards — for example, increasing the pay of certain strata — it is not for the party congress to make decisions.

Four years have passed since the 9th Congress. I do not want to list all the measures we have taken since then to improve living standards. We did not have to wait until the 10th Congress: many questions were in the meantime solved by the Central Committee, the government and our enterprises. This was the proper, the sound, the normal road for developing living standards.

It also follows that if there is no decision at the Congress now we shall not have to wait with these questions until the 11th Congress, because the Central Committee and the government have never hesitated for a minute, they have always granted according to the possibilities and needs.

Comrades! We have mentioned this year's plan in the report; we outlined the anticipated results of the fulfilment of the third Five Year Plan. But anyone who has anything to do with even the smallest household budget knows very well that each fiscal year must be brought to a close. I ask you to recall what the country's leadership had to do at the time of the spring floods, how fast it had to act in order to ensure production, supplies, the conditions of normal life; and we can say that it did ensure them successfully and thoroughly. Even where the floodwaters were gushing, the people had warm meals in the evening.

I would therefore ask the honoured Congress to accept the standpoint put forward in the report of the Central Committee; and allow the competent authorities the opportunity and time to work out this year's balance accurately. The reason, comrades, is that what is anticipated does not figure in the same way on both sides of the balance sheet. If we, for example, had envisaged an increase of 40 per cent in the national income in the fourth Five Year Plan in place of the 30–32 per cent which could realistically be planned, this would have been wishful thinking. But as soon as Parliament passes the bill, the envisaged plan becomes law, and since in our country there is law and order, every law has to be carried out. Should we nevertheless begin to distribute what we do not yet possess, this would undermine the living standard of the working people – the textile workers, the metal workers, the teachers, and the rest. A responsible leadership cannot take this course.

Many speakers dealt with questions that may be listed under the main title of public morals. In the report, too, the relationship between political consciousness and material incentives received proper emphasis. Both are necessary. The building of socialism requires the strengthening of socialist awareness, the spirit of selflessness and readiness to make sacrifices; moreover, the spirit of enthusiasm, and also that incentives should exert an influence in the same direction. And inasmuch as this is a question of public morals, it is our opinion that it is difficult for socialism to be built by even one man as a secondary job, but a whole people certainly cannot regard as a secondary job the completion of building socialism; it is their main job. Fortunately this is the way we do it and this is how we are building it.

At the party conference in Csepel, one contributor to the debate, speaking of work morals, said work was once a compulsion, that is under the capitalist system, then it became an honour and now some people see it as a favour. In our society it is work which is the basis of all rights. Socialism is a society of labour in which people who are able to work must do so in order to enjoy rights. This is not only the opinion of every conscious supporter of socialism, but also of every decent person. In our country work must also be a matter of honour. And if there should be some who do not accept this, then, just as in the past work was a compulsion for some social classes, now it will be a compulsion for certain people. We shall prove to them that they cannot live without work, and live well at that, at the expense of the working people.

Comrades, the report was unable to detail every field of party activity. From the point of view of party work, activity carried on in the different mass organizations, in the state and social organizations, everything, without distinction, is of equal importance. This is also valid for non-Communists. We respect and credit the work of everyone who carries on useful social activity, no matter in what field.

I should like to address the Communist leaders, the heads of the party branches, as well as the leaders of the district party committees. This year I paid a visit to the Eighth district (of Budapest). In the meeting room of the Executive Committee, where we were talking, there was a portrait of Lenin. Time passed and afterwards I told the comrades that something was missing from that wall: a clock. At the Central Committee we have both a portrait of Lenin and a clock on the wall. This expresses a lot. If we look at them, Lenin and the clock together tell us what to do and in what direction, in what spirit and when. The clock also tells us that time passes, we should make haste as much as we can.

Here at the Congress, it was a pleasure to hear that almost all comrades emphasized – and if it was not expressly said it was implied in their contributions – that they themselves and the collective they were representing were ready to work for the realization of the resolutions of the 10th Congress. Every day hundreds of telegrams and letters of greeting arrived at the Congress from workers, peasants, intellectuals, from all strata of society. These letters informed us of the readiness to work for the realization of the resolutions of the 10th Congress. This also is a manifestation of trust and of the workers' honest outlook: we have not only to agree, but we must also do what has to be done.

Our party already put down its programme in writing at the time when the two workers' parties united. This programme – of which much has already been realized – states that the aim of our party is the building of a socialist society. We have a Marxist–Leninist policy which we must continue to follow. We have a sound policy of alliances, which we must continue to adhere to so that Communists and non-party people might be able to rally even closer. The party works in close contact with the masses; it must work in even closer cohesion with them in the future. We are working with the people, for the people, that is why we must work to implement the resolutions of the 10th Congress. Our party has always struggled in internationalist unity with the Communist and workers' parties – in the future we must cooperate with the fraternal peoples building socialism in even greater unity.

Comrades! The discussion at the Congress has proved that we are of the same opinion on all the main questions and this is most important for our future work. I ask you, comrades, to accept my reply and to authorize the newly elected Central Committee to make use of the advice of the comrades who have taken the floor as well as of the strength, the unity of outlook, the working and fighting ability, the truly Marxist–Leninist way of thinking and the Communist consciousness and internationalism which have characterized the 10th Congress of our party. I am convinced that the Central Committee will utilize all this for the good of our common cause.

I thank you for your attention.

Speech at the April 1972 Session of the National Assembly

Honoured National Assembly, Members of Parliament, Comrades,

We are all aware that we are participants in an event of extraordinary importance: our supreme legislative body, the National Assembly, is today debating the amendment of the basic law of our state: the Constitution. The Bill concerning the amendments has been prepared and submitted by the committee appointed by the National Assembly, and has been outlined and explained in all its aspects by the chairman of the committee, Comrade Gyula Kállai[28], in his report. I want to speak, with reference to his report and on the basis of the stand taken by our party, of the Constitution and of a few questions which are closely connected.

The Constitution is the law of laws, the foundation of the state, the basis of the legal superstructure of society. The amendment bill before the National Assembly well expresses the historical continuity of the Hungarian state and society which is over a thousand years old, and the revolutionary changes and the unshakeable and indissoluble unity of socialism and Hungary's statehood which exists today. The Bill which has been submitted, if it is made law by the National Assembly, will be the Constitution of the independent, sovereign and socialist Hungarian state, the Hungarian People's Republic, and will be the summary and inviolable law of all the historic achievements of the Hungarian people who have entered on the road to socialism and have become a nation.

Now as our National Assembly debates the Constitution, we remember the struggles of many generations and the great historic personalities: King Stephen[29] and Mátyás Hunyadi, Rákóczi, Kossuth and Széchenyi[30], Dózsa, Petőfi, Táncsics[31], and others. We remember with respect the guardians and reformers of our nation, of our national language and culture: the outstanding leaders, martyrs and simple militants of the people's revolutions and of the revolutionary workers' movement. Speaking of the past, we think first of all of the Hungarian working people, who through the centuries, with their toil, sweat, and blood, maintained, kept alive, and carried forward our country, our state, on the path of progress. For overcoming the immeasurable difficulties of our history, and thus enabling us to get this far, eternal glory and the gratitude of the living are ever due to the generations which preceded us, the known and unknown sons and daughters of the people who lived with honour. Their integrity, their example, inspire and bind us.

Speaking of the historic past, we must also remember that the rulers of the old Hungary often liked to refer to "the thousand-year-old constitution of the nation". But the truth is that neither the nation nor the country had a written, clear and unequivocal constitution for a thousand years. Single laws existed which significantly and for a long time influenced the life and development of the country, but a true constitution had never been evolved. The majority of the Hungarians living and constituting a state in the region of the Danube and the Tisza, the people who maintained the country, were excluded from legal rights for a thousand years; the laws were always made by the oppressors and exploiters for the protection of their own power.

The eleventh-century statute books of the founder of the state, King Stephen, which were progressive in their own day, and which served to protect the young feudal state then being organized together with its institutions, protected the interests of the feudal ruling class which was emerging at that time. The Golden Bull, enacted in the thirteenth century, summarized and ensured the rights and privileges of the nobility and of the freeholders. The infamous Tripartitum framed by Werbőczi[32] in the sixteenth century, the summary of Hungarian feudal law, already served with brutal frankness to bind the peasant serfs to the soil and to exploit and oppress the people for centuries.

The last big settlement of the public law of the old bygone world was in the last century, after the defeat of the 1848–49 War of Independence; it was the "Compromise" which was instituted in 1867 but never codified. This settlement, which was the concordat of the Hungarian ruling classes with the Habsburg dynasty, with the

Austrian ruling classes, meant the ambiguous conclusion of the Hungarian bourgeois revolution; it meant the abandonment of national independence, for the sake of protecting their class rule, and maintaining the oppression of the workers and peasants. Then the rulers of the country, betraying the ideas and goals of the fight for freedom, thereby ensured, within the framework of the state of the Austro–Hungarian Monarchy, the rule of the landowning and capitalist classes over the workers of Hungarian and other nationalities for a further half century. It was to their shame that the Hungarian ruling and exploiting classes were unable to give the country a genuine basic law, a constitution, so that the labouring classes, the people, lived for over a thousand years deprived of their rights; and it was to their shame also that they often betrayed the whole Hungarian nation, the country, for a mess of pottage.

Honoured National Assembly! Our history took shape in such a way that, following the Hungarian Republic of Councils of 1919, it was only in 1949 that the great idea of millions — which Petőfi formulated — the unity of homeland and legal rights, could be realized by the working Hungarian people. The adoption of Law XX:1949, the Constitution, was an achievement of historic importance. It sanctioned the power of the working class, of the people, and enacted as the programme of the nation the construction of a society free from the exploitation of man by man, and the building of socialism.

In order to have a constitution, and a constitution of this type, the Hungarian people had to free themselves from the vicious and reactionary Horthy regime which ruled for over a quarter century, from the capitalists and the landowners, and form the foreign oppressors who occupied the country in the Second World War, the Hitlerite Fascist army of occupation.

Our country was liberated from foreign oppressors by the glorious Red Army of the Soviet Union, and the people liberated themselves from their own oppressors. The Constitution accords the liberation its historic importance and expresses the never ceasing gratitude of our people towards their liberator, the Soviet Union.

The liberated people took their fate in their own hands, and under the leadership of the Communists, and of the working class, achieved power and created their state, the Hungarian People's Republic. The 1949 Constitution summarized the achievements realized till then through our struggle and work, determined the structure of the new state, its basic institutions, the rights and duties of the citizens, and declared that the Hungarian People's Republic was the state of the working people. The historic experience of nearly a quarter century has proved that the 1949 Constitution met its purpose.

More than twenty years have passed since the adoption of our constitution; they have told the story of the creative work and self-sacrificing struggle of the working people and of the rise of the nation, although some stages of the road were extremely difficult; nor was the period since 1949 free of conflicts. The adherents of socialism stood their ground in growing numbers; the work and struggle of our party, our working class and of our people have brought powerful progress and great, truly historic achievements. The power of the working class, of the people, of the Hungarian People's Republic is today more stable than ever before. We have laid the foundations of a socialist society, socialist production relations have won out throughout the entire economy and our people are working today for the building of a completely socialist society.

As a result of our planned socialist economy, of the work of economic construction, our stock of means of production has doubled in industry in the last ten years alone; the socialist industry of our country today produces nine times as much as capitalist industry produced in 1938. Socialist agriculture produces today, with 40 per cent less labour force, 43 per cent more than capitalist agriculture produced in 1938. The bread supply of the country has been solved and, as far as the most decisive crops are concerned, the results of agriculture can justly stand comparison with the yields of capitalist agriculture.

The cultural revolution has turned our people into an enlightened, educated people. It has opened up the possibilities of learning and of education, to the working masses who until then had been artificially shut out of culture; it has opened up to them the ennobling values of literature, theatre, music and the screen, has stimulated the progress of the sciences and the arts, has opened the road for the radiant talent of our creative artists and scientists. Socialist public thinking and the link between the individual and the community have been strengthened. Socialist trends play a leading role in our cultural and artistic life and assist successfully in the realization of our great social goal of a human life rich in content.

With the advance of socialism, the standard of living and the way of life of the Hungarian people, their security and well-being, have improved almost immeasurably compared to the conditions before Liberation. Penury on a massive scale, starvation, the Hungary of "three million beggars" are just a bad memory. It is characteristic of conditions today that throughout the country there is a washing machine in 50 households out of every 100, a refrigerator in 39 and a television set in 58. In 1949 the number of kindergartens and of places in them was insignificant; ten years ago 337 children out of 1,000 could be placed in kindergartens; today even more: 600, or 60 per cent of the age group concerned, are assured of a place in a kindergarten. We know that this is not enough either, but it is a very nice achievement.

The results of the socialist work of construction do not simply express the superiority of industry, of the cooperative farms and state farms and of large-scale production, but also the diligence, talent and devotion of the Hungarian working class, of the cooperative peasantry, the scientists, creative artists and professional people who are consciously building socialism with their deep sense of responsibility towards our cause and our entire people. We may speak proudly of the achievements, and from time to time we must do so, because they testify to and extol the creative ability of a liberated people building their own future and the steadfastness of the working millions; and they are at the same time a guarantee that, however great the tasks that still face us, we will solve them too.

A path similar to the progress of the Hungarian people building socialism would not have been possible in the old Hungary. The results we have achieved in twenty-seven years stand comparison to the rate of growth of any capitalist country. And if we consider that this does not involve the message of the figures alone, but above all what is behind the figures, how we lived earlier – however many years we look back – and how we live today, we again declare with full conviction that, as for every people, socialism is for the Hungarian people too the only certain road to social progress, to the prosperity of the nation.

Hungarian people, who have entered on the road to socialism and are advancing along this road, have already attained and bettered the conditions existing in the most advanced capitalist countries in respect of the rights of workers, health care, social security, culture and many other respects. We will also catch up with them and overtake them in those fields of technological norms in which we still lag behind. But technical progress must take place here and is taking place in another way, in a socialist way. We shall not build a dehumanized, barren mechanical age, which blots out the individual and leads to moral bankruptcy. We shall not compete with them in the supply of narcotics to our youth and in the tolerance of a gangsterism armed with modern technology. In these and similar respects we do not wish to, and will by no means, "catch up with them". We wish to, and will, develop science and technology for the benefit of the human person, with the maintenance of what is humane in life and safeguarding the real achievements of culture and civilization. Thus we advance on our road.

It is in this sense that we plan the modernization of the economy of our country, and to raise it to a higher level. It is a significant fact in the competition between the social systems that the semi-feudal Hungary, with a backward industry which the people inherited, has — as a result of socialist development over hardly more than a quarter century — entered the ranks of the economically medium-developed countries. An important statement for the future made at the 10th Congress of the Party was that, within the foreseeable future, our country will enter the ranks of the advanced industrial countries. It is our deep conviction that the conditions for this exist, that this aim is realistic and that we will achieve it through the power of our socialist system.

Honoured National Assembly! The socialist development of our country is the result of twenty years of hard work and steadfast struggle; this struggle took place in politics, in the economy, in culture, in all spheres of social life, in the whole country, in every community, often even within the family. In our circumstances this was inevitable and necessary, because here the transition from capitalism to socialism took place in the midst of sharp clashes between the classes. In the course of this the privileged landlord and capitalist classes ceased to exist, regroupings affecting masses of people took place within society, and the working class and the peasantry, which have fashioned and are the foundation of the new order, also developed considerably and became transformed in the process.

In the struggle for the new Hungary, the working class — capable of taking a grand, long-range view of things — was justified in acquiring the rank of the leading class in society. In the struggles fought against the class enemy they won the support first of all of their principal and natural ally, the peasantry, and, in addition, of the best members of the professional classes and of all strata engaged in work. The struggle for power tested individuals too and shaped them politically. There are people who stood up for the true cause at the beginning of the revolutionary transformation and who have stuck by it from beginning to end. There are others who turned against it in the course of the struggle and failed. And there are a great many who in this same struggle, recognizing the truth, became comrades instead of opponents, and with whom we now work and fight together for our common aims.

By conquering the remnants of the prejudices fomented by the capitalist ruling classes, and armed with the experience of the great clashes between the classes, the Hungarian worker, the peasant and the intellectual, finding each other in a recognized community of interest, are active together today in the building of socialism; Communists and non-party people, believers and non-believers work in common for the good of the country. Only in the conditions of working-class power, in the people's republic, on the basis of the programme of socialism, and through the assertion of the Leninist policy of alliances, has it been possible for the citizens of our homeland to find each other in this way. One of the greatest achievements of our revolution is the socialist national unity comprising all fundamental classes and strata of our society; everything must be done to strengthen this unity still further in the future.

Socialist national unity is a reality. Today the socially active millions gathered in the vanguard of the working class, the party, in the mass organizations and mass movements, and in the Patriotic People's Front, the great majority of the adult population of the country, profess with one will and prove in joint action that the Hungarian People's Republic is our true homeland; socialism is the programme and future of the Hungarian people.

Looking over the road covered since the enactment of the Constitution in 1949, we find that we have achieved the objectives which we set ourselves so far: we have laid the foundations of socialism and have achieved important results on the road to building of socialism. Our programme is clear. Our most important goals are declared by the Constitution itself. Our immediate tasks have been formulated by the 10th Congress of the party, by the election programme of the Patriotic People's Front and by the fourth Five Year Plan enacted by the National Assembly.

The wheel of history has made a great turn: Hungary has ceased for ever to be a country of parasitic lords, of exploiters; the capitalists, the imperialists have lost the country and never again will a single inch of Hungarian soil belong to them. Our class enemies will never forget this, but our people are aware of it too. It is a moral imperative for every son of the socialist homeland to defend the power and achievements of the people in all circumstances and every way. The homeland must be served with the mind and the heart, with word and deed alike; we must continue to develop, to strengthen and to make flourish the Hungarian People's Republic, which is dearer to us than anything else, because it ensures the peace, the socialist present and future of our people.

When we sum all this up, we are fully justified in saying; our party, our working class, our people have not struggled in vain; the sacrifices have not been in vain, the work and the struggle have been worthwhile. Everybody who in the past quarter century took part in the struggles and in the building of socialism may be proud of it. He has devoted his youth, his faith, his strength to a good cause. He deserves the respect of everybody, because he has fulfilled his duty to the Hungarian people and to the homeland faithfully.

Honoured National Assembly, Comrades! In the course of preparing to amend the Constitution a great many questions have necessarily arisen, and the proposals submitted by the committee themselves also recommend a number of essential amendments. By the nature of the thing, each of these is very important and a matter of principle; they demand careful consideration and decision by the National Assembly. Of the questions which have arisen in the course of the preparatory work, and which are among the proposals submitted, I wish to deal with only a few. I shall take them one by one.

The opinion of the Central Committee of our party is that, in spite of the very considerable progress which has taken place since 1949, it is not necessary to draft a new constitution; but it is necessary to modify the text of the existing Constitution, the basic tenets of which are fully correct, in accordance with the changes which have taken place in the meantime.

The amendments submitted are appropriate; they refer to the changes which have taken place in the life of the state, in the activities of the National Assembly, of the government, of the councils, of the institutions of the state in general; they define more exactly the rights and duties of citizens at the present stage of building socialism. The modifications are suitable in their entirety so that the National Assembly can approve the new, uniform text of the Constitution.

The 10th Congress of our party also examined whether the name of our state should be changed, and decided that the time had not yet come for our country to be declared a socialist republic in name as well. Setting out from the principle that the Constitution must essentially and in principle set down the achievements which have already been attained, and is not the declaration of a programme, it is right if this principle is also manifested in the official name of our state. The name "Hungarian People's Republic" expresses well the greatest achievement of the struggle of our working class, of our people. The name of the Hungarian People's Republic means, and proclaims unmistakably everywhere and to everybody, the power of our working people, their state, their homeland and the new socialist world which is being built.

Seeing, however, that in its main characteristics, in respect of property and class relations, our social system is already socialist, it is right that the new text should state in some less declarative way that the Hungarian People's Republic is a *socialist* state.

In our age the working class is the most revolutionary class of society. It can realize its own liberation and historic objectives only by liberating at the same time every other oppressed class and stratum, and by opening up the road to general progress for the whole of society. This is what has happened in Hungary too. In our country today there are already only allied, fraternal labouring classes. The Constitution deals with the relationship of the labouring classes to each other in a way which corresponds to the actual situation, and to the theoretical and political importance of the question, and correctly lays down that the leading class of society is the working class.

The working class of our country have accepted responsibility for the fate of the nation. It is the first time in the course of our history that power is possessed by a class which does not use that power to ensure a privileged position for themselves but demand and accept a responsibility commensurate with their rights.

In the past quarter century our working class have solved tasks of historic importance: they have gained power; they have expropriated the expropriators; they have organized and are developing socialist industry; they have taken the land from the landlords and given it to the peasants, and then assisted them in the socialist transformation of agriculture; they have broken the cultural monopoly of the old exploiting classes; their theory, ideology and morals affect the entire society; they lead and show an example in the building of socialism.

In everyday speech we often quite correctly use the expression "the power of the working class, of the people". This expresses too that the power of the working class serves the interests of the entire people, and they exercise power as the leading class of society in alliance with the peasantry united in cooperatives, with the intellectuals and the other working strata of society. Our party approves of this being also clearly formulated in the new text of our Constitution.

The amended text of the draft constitution declares: the Marxist–Leninist party of the working class is the leading force of society. The working class's political organization of the highest order is the party, which leads as a vanguard, and through which this class solves its governmental duties and realizes its historic goals. Our party has always considered it its duty to express simultaneously the historic goals of the working class and to represent the day-to-day interests of the workers. The proposal of the preparatory committee that the new text of our fundamental law should record the leading role of the party is a great honour for our entire party, and for every Communist.

Our Party has always stressed that it does not consider its leading role in society, and its governmental tasks, as some sort of "reign", but as a service, an honest and faithful service, to the people. We interpret the relevant formulations of the Constitution primarily as an increased responsibility for the Hungarian Socialist Workers' Party, for every member of the Party, to the whole of society. Hungarian Communists will endeavour to deserve this confidence in future too, to serve the people faithfully and to lead the way as true patriots in making the Hungarian People's Republic prosper.

An important characteristic of our Constitution is the equality of citizens. Our state, the Hungarian People's Republic, ensures equal rights and prescribes identical obligations to all its citizens from political rights to social security.

One of the greatest achievements of our political struggle and work of construction over more than a quarter century is that our Constitution on the one hand widens the range of rights, and on the other extends numerous existing rights to the broadest sections of society.

The amended text of our Constitution includes respect for human rights; the exercise of rights in harmony with the interests of society; the indivisibility of rights from duties; the ensuring of participation in public affairs. It extends to the whole of society and makes the right of assembly a civil right serving the interests of socialist society; the right to recreation, to the protection of life, limb and health, to social insurance and to education are also extended to the whole of society.

In harmony with our socialist endeavours, the Constitution emphasizes more than before the importance of certain civil rights: the right to work, the protection of the institution of marriage and of the family, the protection and socialist education of youth and the obligations connected with them are given greater emphasis.

Concluding my remarks on the individual propositions, I would like to stress: the Central Committee of our party maintains that if the proposals of the preparatory committee are adopted, the new text of the Constitution will express in every respect the achievements attained so far by the work and struggle of our people, will express their goals and will strengthen still further the foundations of our people's democratic state.

Honoured National Assembly, Comrades! Our Constitution will be sanctioned today through the resolution of the National Assembly. In the new recommended text, the Constitution summarizes more exactly than before, and ensures through the full force of the law and the state, the historic achievements of the Hungarian people who have taken the road to the building of socialism; it confirms the lofty principles which regulate the life of the Hungarian People's Republic, of our society, and it serves our further socialist progress.

From the moment of enactment, it will be the sacred duty of every organized force of our society, of every Hungarian citizen, to observe and make others observe the letter and principles of the amended Constitution to the full. The enforcement and effectiveness of the principles of the Constitution is for us a lawful duty not only in the legal sense of the word. It is that too, but beyond that it demands of all of us that we defend and enhance the achievements of our people, which are laid down in the Constitution, by deeds, by the work done at home and by our international activity alike; and that we serve even more effectively the earliest possible attainment of our long-term socialist goal.

The discussion of our Constitution today does not demand and its scope does not permit that we should here and now enumerate our tasks in domestic and foreign policy and on every internal question of our building of socialism; therefore I also wish only to touch on them in my speech.

Our socialist progress and the future of the nation are influenced by the combined effect of many factors. Our domestic policy efforts are centred today on the further development of state life, of socialist democracy. The amendment of the Constitution itself is an important act in this process. The full effectiveness of the principles of the Constitution depends not least on the extent to which we succeed in drawing the masses, even more than up to now, into the management of public affairs. We know full well that this does not happen either on its own or from one day to the next. It depends on us and therefore we must work in such a way that socialist democracy, thinking and acting together, should be an even stronger driving force in our progress than has been the case till now.

Our socialist progress is unimaginable without advanced science and technology, without industry, agriculture and services of a high standard, without the constant improvement of material circumstances. But socialist progress is much more than this. Our ceaseless intellectual efforts and making culture a common treasure are indispensable parts of the building of socialism. We must never forget ceaselessly to spread socialist ways of thinking and socialist morals, the many-sided unfolding and enrichment of human life, and that children should be brought up in well-balanced, happy, large families, in a socialist spirit, well prepared for the role that they are to fill in society.

We are building the kind of new world which realizes the dreams of the best sons of our nation, a new world in which the homeland is indeed a loving parent to all its citizens, in short, a society which is socialist, and which is at the same time Hungarian and an equal member of the fraternal community of progressive peoples.

We are at a stage in the building of socialism when our further progress depends in a decisive way on the successful solution of the economic tasks. We have all the necessary conditions for the continuation of the work of construction at our disposal: in our country the power of the people is stable, our economy is developing in a healthy way and we can and do make use of the benefits offered by socialist economic planning. In recent years our system of economic management has been developed further and we have a realistic national economic plan.

Our economy has great vitality and it is our task to develop it in a planned and many-sided way. We must increase the productivity and rentability of labour in industry and in agriculture alike; we must develop the technical basis of production and raise its technological level. We must raise the standard of leadership; in formulating our requirements we must set out from the realities and not from our desires; we must improve our investment policy and balance the budget, and through all this we will further enhance the strength of our economy, the good reputation of our work and respect for our workers.

The aim of our work is that the standard of living of the people should rise, and that their living conditions should improve in accordance with the policy of our party and in keeping with the results of our work.

The systematic raising of the standard of living of our people may be justly included among our great historic achievements. At the same time we know also that there are still strata of the population and families who live in difficult material circumstances and whose lot it is our duty to improve step by step. This is why the 10th Congress of of our party resolved – what, incidentally, our Five Year Plan also includes – that certain social benefits should increase to a greater extent than wages, so that the differences of income between families should be reduced in this way. Said in another way: we want a greater differentiation in wages depending on the work done and a further levelling up of family incomes.

In our circumstances this means that everybody should receive of the wealth produced in proportion to his work. Those who work more should receive more, and those who are missing from work should not queue up on pay-day either. This is our justice, the justice of the working people.

The key to our economic and cultural progress, to the further improvement of our living conditions, is in our own hands. The 10th Congress of our party gave a clear and realistic programme which our prople endorsed last spring through their vote at the elections, and which they have actively supported since. The resolutions are being carried out in the political, economic and cultural fields, in all important areas of social life. Seeing that the party will soon arrive at the half-way mark between two congresses, the Central Committee will in the near future survey where we stand in the execution of the congress resolutions; and where we are lagging behind or new tasks have emerged, the necessary measures will be taken.

For the raising of work standards, we still have reserves at our disposal in all spheres of life. We know that the implementation of our plans does not always go without hitches; it is well known that there are negative symptoms, too. In our society, which is a society of socialism in construction, conservative views still exercise an influence, and from time to time in certain places they are even being reproduced. It is not rare to find leisureliness, irresponsibility, incompetence, and indulgence towards negligence and the negligent. The organized forces of society, the great majority who feel and shoulder responsibility, must come out everywhere, and resolutely, against these adverse symptoms.

The main driving force of progress is the working man himself, and our main trust is in the steadfastness, the conscious discipline and the sense of responsibility of our working class, of our working people.

We witness day after day the mass manifestations of human steadfastness, of duties fulfilled with self-respect, but at the same time without ostentation. The increasing host of the activists working selflessly for the sake of society, the rebirth and progress of the socialist brigade movement, the gradual spreading of the socialist way of thinking are obvious evidence of the maturity of our society, of the enhanced responsibility felt for the affairs of the community, for the fate of the homeland.

It is certain that our battle-hardened working class, our people, who have lived, worked and fought sometimes in very difficult circumstances and were nevertheless able to change the face of the country radically in twenty-five years, will solve those new tasks too, tasks which derive from today's higher level of development, from the further building of socialism.

Honoured National Assembly! We must fight for progress not only within our boundaries but in the arena of international politics as well. We will ensure the international conditions for the realization of our plans in future too. For this purpose we will on the one hand strengthen our socialist homeland, because domestic progress is the primary source of all foreign political activity and international influence, and on the other we will broaden and deepen the fraternal relations linking us with the world socialist system, and first of all with our devoted friend and reliable ally, the Soviet Union.

We declare our goals openly: in the Hungarian people, the peoples of the world may see an active militant and reliable ally in the struggle against imperialism, for the liquidation of all forms of capitalist, colonial exploitation and for the prevention of war. At the same time we have been urging and continue to urge peaceful coexistence between countries with differing social systems. The Hungarian People's Republic wants regular, normal and mutually beneficial relations with the capitalist countries too.

Thus the letter of the Constitution becomes a living reality when according to the Bill it declares: the Hungarian People's Republic, as part of the world socialist system, develops and strengthens friendship with the socialist countries, and in the interest of peace and human progress wishes to cooperate with all peoples and countries of the world. Our actual deeds and the stands taken serve as security for our principles; we want to promote the solution of the burning problems of the international situation, as far as we can, in the interest of the peoples, socialism and peace.

In Europe we work together with the other member countries of the Warsaw Treaty to bring about a security system built on the acceptance of mutual obligations.

Events will be influenced in this direction by the adoption of agreements between the Soviet Union and the Federal Republic of Germany, between the Polish People's Republic and the Federal Republic of Germany, as well as by the coming into force of the quadripartite agreement on West Berlin and the agreement between the German Democratic Republic and the Federal Republic of Germany. The Hungarian People's Republic is interested in the ratification of these agreements, because they strengthen the relations between European states, and the perspectives for cooperation, peace and security. The ratification of the agreements is in the interest of all European states without exception, not least the Federal Republic of Germany.

We consider a conference of governments an important stage on the road to a European security system, and the conditions are ripening for the convening of this conference. The proponents of the conference enjoy the many-sided support of the social forces of our continent. The opponents of security, and thus of the conference, are being gradually isolated and are exposing themselves.

On the European front-line of the international class struggle, our party and our government—representing the national interests of our people—are fighting on the side of those who want to turn the continent, at present divided by military blocs and fraught with relics of the cold war, into a continent of security and cooperation, in accordance with the interests of every European country. The general situation offers opportunities to the countries of our continent to close a tragic chapter of the European past, a period in the history of the continent which has led to bloody wars and caused the peoples so much suffering.

We are guided by our principled, internationalist policy in our stand against the aggression of imperialism in Indochina and in the Middle East.

We help the just struggle of the heroic people of Vietnam in every way we can, because only respect for the freedom and independence of their country, the granting of the right of self-determination to the peoples of Laos and Cambodia and the discontinuation of American intervention can bring an actual solution to the problems of the area and serve at the same time the general interests of peace and security. The proposals of the Democratic Republic of Vietnam and of the Provisional Revolutionary Government of South Vietnam are directed to this aim; they are just, they provide a realistic foundation for the termination of the war and deservedly enjoy the far-reaching support of the progressive countries, including our own.

The offensive of the Vietnamese patriots unfolding at this very time is bringing further success to the liberating forces of the people and is causing heavy losses to the American aggressors and their Saigon satellites. The victories won so far by the Indochinese people's war are also proof that no extension of its military adventure can help American imperialism to extricate itself from the dead-end in Vietnam.

The Vietnamese people, the peoples of Indochina, have attacked nobody: they do not threaten the security of anybody, but fight on the soil of their homeland for their freedom and independence against invaders and mercenaries. The Hungarian People's Republic categorically condemns the aggressive actions of the American imperialists and the outrageous resumption of terror bombing; and we resolutely demand that the United States should stop prevaricating, should stop sabotaging the lasting, just and peaceful solution of the Indochinese question through negotiations, a resolution which respects the inalienable rights of the peoples of the area. Our Vietnamese brothers may count in future too on the selfless support of all progressive mankind, of the socialist countries, including our people. We believe and proclaim that the heroism and immeasurable sacrifices of the Vietnamese people, of the peoples of Indochina, are not in vain; whatever the aggressor does, the day of victory for their just cause is approaching.

In the Middle East we are in solidarity with the Arab states fighting consistently against the Israeli aggressors and their imperialist supporters. It is our decided view that only a political settlement — ensuring the independence and sovereignty of the Arab countries and the national existence and development of every state in the area — can meet the interests of peace and security. We are convinced that in the last resort the forces of imperialism and aggression will fail in the Middle East too.

We are proud that in the arena of international politics Hungarian people and the Hungarian People's Republic are resolutely fighting in the ranks of the progressive forces of the world, for the true cause of safeguarding the future of mankind, for socialism and peace. We will continue our international activities in future too in the spirit of our Constitution, meeting our international obligations to the full in the knowledge that, in spite of all the efforts of international reaction, the world advances in the direction of social progress, that the cause of the peoples fighting for their freedom will be victorious, and that the most ardent desire of mankind, a lasting and stable peace, will be achieved.

Honoured National Assembly, Members of Parliament, Comrades! Our people are confronted with the great and inspiring aim of building socialism; our present is encouraging and our future full of hopes. Our goals serve the progress of the working class, of the people, of the entire nation; every citizen of our country, who lives and works honestly, may look towards the future with confidence.

It is worth living, planning, working, struggling in the Hungarian People's Republic, in that state and for that system which has managed to harmonize the interests of the individual and of society, which serves the happiness of the entire people, and it is worth accepting responsibility in the day-to-day matters of life, for the lot of the narrower community, family and colleagues, and for the wider community, for the fate of the homeland and of mankind.

In the words of the poet, it is not sufficient to wish for our great social aims, for socialism, for Communism, for the happiness of our people, for the progress of our nation; we must also act to realize them. In our society, which is building socialism, everybody is weighed according to how much he gives to the community. The homeland demands devoted work and steadfastness in the struggle from everybody and promises general progress. If our entire people work in full awareness of this, all that we endeavour, which is comprehensively expressed in the draft constitution in front of us, will be fulfilled. We are convinced that this Constitution is a bridge which leads from the thousand-year-old past, fraught with tribulations, through the present, to a more beautiful and happier future.

Honoured National Assembly, Comrades! The Bill before us is good, and recognition is due to all those who — as befits the task — have worked with care on the amendments to the Constitution; thanks and recognition are due to the committee appointed by the National Assembly, who have completed this great work.

It is well known and I repeat it now: our party, the Hungarian Socialist Workers' Party, has always stood guard over the observance of the Constitution, has acted in the unconditional observance of its letter and spirit; we will do so in future too. The aim of the amendments to the Constitution, the main questions of principle, are known and supported by the broader public too.

In the spirit of these thoughts, I accept the Bill on the amendments to the Constitution, and in the name of the Central Committee of the Hungarian Socialist Workers' Party recommend its adoption to the honoured National Assembly.

Closing Remarks at the November 1972 Session of the Central Committee

Twenty-seven comrades have spoken in the debate on the agenda and five other comrades have submitted their comments in writing. Over and above this, a number of proposals and comments have been made regarding the draft resolution.

All those present can confirm that the comrades speaking in the general debate have, without exception, agreed with the Political Committee's report, analysis of the situation, and proposals regarding both the implementation of the Congress resolutions and the national plan and budget for 1973. These comments have touched upon practically every area of our work. If I were to categorize them according to some sort of time factor, I could say that one group urged quick, immediate, action; others spoke of things to do in the present period between congresses; a significant part of the comments however touched on general lines to be followed over a longer period, the remaining years of the fourth Five Year Plan, and in some cases to an even longer period of time.

The oral and written comments have, without exception, touched on very important questions. Even if not all can be accepted, all deserve attention, because they have dealt with topics which are timely and very important from the point of view of the work being done in the party, the state and society.

We have all followed the debate with attention. The remarks, comments, observations and proposals have been made in a room where the representatives and officials of the main leading bodies of the party, the state, economic, cultural and social life are present. I think that they will all take these remarks seriously and will endeavour to make use of them in their work. We do, however, assure you that the remarks and proposals will be systematically worked on and studied as well.

The very wide-ranging debate makes it impossible for me to deal with every important question raised by the speakers. Therefore, I should like to deal with a few general topics which are part of the agenda discussed and which most of the speakers have touched upon.

I shall put the general spirit within the party and in our society first, because this belongs among questions that entail no short-range tasks, but, on the contrary, a constant task of the first priority for us.

For the sake of easier review, I should like to make a few comparisons between – how shall I put it – still photos, in order to make explicit the changes and the development in public spirit. The history of our party and of the country can be broken down into certain periods. I want to recall the prevailing public spirit of three different periods within the party and the country.

I will start with the beginning of 1953. In that period, the cult of personality was in full bloom. In theoretical and political work, in the daily life of the party, in the public life of the country, and in other areas of social life the following phenomena were dominant: subjectivism, dogmatism in politics, sectarianism, and, in the life of the party and the state, centralization to the limits of absurdity.

These were accompanied by certain other phenomena. At the top – one could say – there were arbitrary decisions, while at the local level – and this has to be said as well – there were petty monarchistic ways. This was complemented by a type of behaviour which was dubbed exemplary and was to be copied, which one could call pseudo-revolutionary. For the sake of a clearer picture, I must mention that at the time it was considered treason to the course of revolution if a party worker or state official remarked, say, at five or six in the afternoon: "I have to leave the office, because I want to meet with my wife; I have to pick up my child," or if he made similar excuses. Meanwhile, on the surface and formally, within the party and the whole political public life of the country, there seemed to be unity and agreement. There were no debates, questions were not really posed, arguments or persuasion were virtually absent. This is how things stood at that time.

For the next snapshot I would take the time of the 1957 party conference. What was the public spirit like then within the party and country?

Perhaps it is no exaggeration if I say that our party had reached back to Leninist sources and had carried out a Leninist turn in its practical work. Everything that was bad was rejected; subjectivism, dogmatism and revisionism in theory, sectarianism and liberalism in politics and in other areas as well.

As far as the demands on the behaviour of Communists and party life were concerned, democratic centralism had again come into force and was operating. The party demanded proper Communist, and at the same time human, behaviour. Simultaneously the real and true Communist policy of alliance, the alliance of the working class with other working classes and strata, the honest manner and treatment of our allies, had become a reality. We had undertaken to spread the policies of the party through persuasion, thus recruiting true adherents to socialism. We did ask Communists to put the cause of the community and work first, but this was complemented by saying that human happiness was not forbidden. According to our ideas this is something which is natural and self-explanatory; it goes with Communist party membership just as much as it goes with public activities and the honest building of socialism.

Of course one must see the full picture in order to understand the links and the differences between the beginning of 1953 and the summer of 1957. The practices which still lived unbroken in the beginning of 1953 had been liquidated by the ruthless criticism of history. As a result of the counter-revolution and the offensives of the class enemy, our own forces were not capable of resistance and fell apart under the blows of the enemy. However sad it is to tell of it, in the autumn of 1956 the party had disintegrated into atoms, the regime was in danger and anarchy reigned in the country. That this could come to pass, and that it could come to pass on such a massive social scale, demanded drastic, radical rectification from the party. This is what we have carried out in the theoretical and practical work of the party, in fostering our relations with the masses, and in the full practice of socialist construction in Hungary. Readjustments always have one special trait. I am at a loss to find another analogy: if a resistant sheet of steel becomes warped and if it has to be bent back to its original form it is always bent to the other extreme and only then will it spring back to its original shape. This is the normal nature of readjustments and I think everybody can confirm this.

What is the situation like today, in the autumn of 1972, in this respect? We have safeguarded all the basic achievements of this Leninist turn as far as the prevalent public spirit within the party and society is concerned. In party life, in the mass relations of the party, the basic Leninist norms predominate and in the public life of the country socialist norms are prevalent. It is not possible any other way. For we have to see that the prevalence of socialist norms in society does not hinge on whether someone takes half an hour off at his workplace or not, whether he is moonlighting or not. Our party — we avow this with full conviction and the present meeting and the preparation for our present session of the Central Committee are evidence of this — works on the basis of Marxist–Leninist theory, carries out a Communist policy and applies Marxism–Leninism in practice in a fruitful manner. This is why we can already assure the lasting, unbroken construction of socialism in the country and this is the reason for our great victories in this present period of development.

Somebody has remarked here, and I will repeat it, that beyond the defence and the consolidation of power we have been able to carry out the socialist reorganization of agriculture in a manner which is not only praised by our friends, but in such a way that our enemies have been compelled to lay down their arms in this particular battle. The imperialist propaganda machine cannot attack in any way the socialist reorganization of agriculture.

Enemy propaganda at one time had difficulty in accepting that the nationalization of major industries is irreversible and that great landed estates cannot be reinstituted. Finally, they have had to come to the point of recognizing in their propaganda that the basic achievements cannot be touched, and neither in fact can these achievements be successfully attacked.

The real socialist norms of society are first of all embodied in basic things. In today's picture, however, one can find undesirable things as well. These can be found in inner party life and in the mass relations of the party, just as much as in the prevalent public spirit of society. I am speaking first of all of ourselves, of the party. With the progress of consolidation — and I have the consolidation of the party, its reorganization, and the restoration of its leading role in mind — along with the growth of respect, and the increase of achievements, the old mistakes have to a certain extent reappeared and resurfaced: self-satisfaction, formalism and bureaucracy in work, presumption and conceit, "illusions" that work is somehow equal to official display; in some individuals an acquisitive spirit has come to the forefront; they want to multiply the jubilees, the celebrations on all possible (and impossible) occasions and preferably with public money. These trends are not as widespread as at the time of the cult of personality, because if the basic Leninist norms are alive and well — and they are in fact alive and well and are growing stronger in the party — such mistakes cannot become prevalent; but on the surface they again adhere to our public affairs, and to the public spirit. We must rid ourselves of them.

There are harmful manifestations in basic attitudes as well, and it is possible that the key to the matter lies precisely in this question. Speaking of Communists, party members and party functionaries I would say that the root of things is in the relationship between being faithful to ideals and being materialistic. Projecting this on a social scale, I could say that the ratio of moral to material incentives in society is not entirely appropriate.

If somebody says that he wants to be a Communist and a member of the HSWP then we must look on him as a person who, having taken the solemn oath on the basic principles of Communism, will live, work, and if need be die for this ideal. This is a basic demand on Communists. To be added to this are certain standards of human behaviour. Devotion to and work for the cause of socialism and Communism should go with standards of behavior which before long will be acceptable to the entire people and to which adherence may be demanded of everyone. And this is where we still have shortcomings.

I have taken part at very many meetings for socialist brigade leaders and at gatherings of Communist activists. These are generally very good in spirit and give one food for thought. But it jars on one's ear to hear somebody say that we are earning quite a lot but we want to earn even more money, therefore we will step on it, you can count on us. To such a statement I will say that from Communists, from people who really sympathize with Communism, I will always accept only one order of priorities. The public good must come first! Now, should somebody add to this that he supports the common cause, the cause of socialism, also because it meets his material expectations, I don't find anything insulting in this. But if the order of priorities is turned around — and the "I" comes first and "we" comes later — then neither the individual nor a smaller group or collective will develop in a straightforward manner, even though he considers himself true to the party and a member of the vanguard of those building socialism.

Objectively we consider the engineer, the intellectual or anybody else — and I am not speaking of the Communists now — who is building socialism without any conscious intention, that is to say is working decently, to be a builder of socialism. From him we cannot demand the above standards, but we can ask that these people separate what they say at home during the Saturday evening bridge-game from what they say publicly, at a meeting, where it has the impact of a public utterance. Let us not allow anybody to preach the spirit of gross materalism. Let us not tolerate having gross materialism grow to be more important than socialist ideology and elementary decency. Today every grown-up and thinking Hungarian citizen understands, with more or less of an inner conviction, that the way to happiness is through the building of a socialist society. And he also knows that this will not be a wedding procession but an amalgam of sweat and toil, of struggle and happiness.

I would characterize the present situation thus: the foundations are sound but there is quite a bit of sediment which has been once again regenerated and settled upon them. The involuntary — but otherwise proper — turn-around and change which we had to carry out at the beginning of 1957 in a number of things have opened the way to certain undesirable petty bourgeois and right-wing phenomena. We know quite well that the road was also opened to egoism and material calculation. Still, this step was revolutionary and imperative. Only after and at the cost of such a turn of events could the basically normal situation be reestablished, in which the party leads the people in the construction of socialism. To this end peace had to be made with our allies.

There was a time when in our actions we gave greater appreciation and rank to our allies than to our own party members. This was necessary, because we wanted the whole people to side with socialism. Here was a leading force, here stood the Communists without allies; such difficult moments do exist. We simply had to win allies, sometimes even wavering allies, over to our side. I shall mention an example: you comrades will recall that I have honoured and continue to honour Péter Veres, and his memory as a man. I knew him quite well. We had always been debating allies. We did not always agree on ideological matters. But we always agreed when it came to devotion to the people, in our passion for public affairs and in matters of basic integrity. There have always been, and continue to be, many people like him. They constitute the great army of allies led by the party. And this is a very strong camp. In Hungary the adherents of socialism have a strong camp even among the non-Communists. This is why I feel that the unrest and the concern which has appeared in our public opinion, expresses, in the final analysis, that the great majority of decent people are concerned for the major guidelines of the party.

The errors, the wrongs which have been reproduced in our ranks — including, for example, Communist conceit — will have to be pruned. The various right-wing and petty bourgeois phenomena — which are the results of the otherwise necessary opening of the gates — will have to be overcome in our public life. Mainly through good political work, through propaganda in the true and noble sense of the word, with the intelligent use of the mass communication media.

It is true that in Hungary every person has a personal vested material interest in proper and good progress towards building socialism. Nevertheless, the ideals must be cared for and cultivated. This is how we can have non-Communists accept that we can be very good friends and very good allies even if, ideologically, we wish to guard Marxism in its pure form.

It has always been our task and will continue to be so in the future to try and influence people in all ways possible in order to hamper petty bourgeois distortions.

It is a shame if, because of the weaknesses in our work, we are occasionally unable to counteract these harmful processes properly.

We will maintain and defend against one and all the appropriate public spirit in the party and the socialist standards of public life, primarily through good mass political work and, in the case of party members, through warnings and disciplinary action. The Leninist norms within the party can only be maintained in their purity, and socialist norms within society on a mass scale can only be assured, if the phenomena alien to our principles, to socialism, disappear from our party. If we work hard for the guidelines and the policies of our party, if we continue to represent them without compromise everywhere and on every occasion — starting with party life, through public life and including our circle of friends — there will be no problem in adhering to standards. But if this is not the case, no sermon of any kind will be of any use.

Taking the second group of questions, I would like to mention a few economic topics.

We have worked out our system of economic management together, we have voted for it together and, I dare say, not only we here in this room are its originators but many tens, and hundreds of thousands of people in this country. We did it together, and it is good that we did it. This management mechanism, however, has to be continuously, constantly, corrected, developed and refined in such a way that we maintain and strengthen its essentials as we polish it further.

This is not the first time that we have spoken about propaganda for the reform. We have established that at the outset this propaganda was not of the very best. We have since partially corrected this error and today we properly emphasize the socialist traits of the mechanism. Today, when we debate about one or other of the elements of the mechanism, we can give the proper answer. But let us beware of national conceit. We have consolidated power, the socialist reorganization of agriculture has been successful and the reform — the third major undertaking of the party since 1956 — again seems to be a successful matter. We should not, however, forget that in these very same years the Soviet Union, the German Democratic Republic and other socialist countries have also developed rapidly although their system of economic management is different from ours.

The new economic mechanism in Hungary is a better, more efficient implement than the old one. It is a major factor in assuring that we stand better today as far as the economy and the growth of living standards are concerned. But we would not have perished without it, either. There are socialist countries which can live under other systems of management. So we should not preach to others. And the press should also be cautious in what it writes. Our system of economic management should be propagandized honestly. As far as the capitalists are concerned, we must always point to the socialist traits of our system of economic management; they must accept Hungary as a socialist country the way she is, whether they like it or not.

The planned development of the people's economy is an important task. We want to go forward here, too. We must prepare better plans, national, branch, company and local council plans, which take interrelationships, links and chains of relationships into better account. We must devote greater attention to the practical implementation of the plan.

We can safely say that today, four years after the modification of economic management, plan fulfilment in our people's economy is stronger than it was earlier both with respect to production processes and of goods produced. It is, however, also true that there is room for improvement. The Planning Office has a great role to play in this, and a perhaps even greater role will fall to a Planning Committee which is to be established later. For, figuratively speaking, if a Planning Office sits in a calm crater on the Moon and prepares marvellous plans but is not in live contact with those who carry out these plans, then that office cannot prepare good plans. If, on the other hand, the day-to-day operative leaders are too far removed from the problems of national planning, then they cannot do their work well either. This is why contacts between planning and practical economic activities must be brought closer.

The proposed draft resolution makes reference to economic regulators. We must make adjustments in them here and there, as we go along. A wider-ranging, more thought-out adjustment must come later so that we may begin the new Five Year Plan with the economic regulators brought into harmony with the new situation. The reason we must put things into periods in this way is that if we were to change important economic regulators every two years, the factories would not be able to work properly and we would disturb the continuous flow of production. Let us strive for stability as far as economic regulators are concerned, too. Simplifying things in the extreme, there are two, indivisible means available to us: the socialist economic plan and the economic regulators.

A further question is production and distribution. These two are equally important, inseparable from each other, they are twins, so to speak. But production is primary. We must not forget this even for a moment, not only in our work, but in propaganda, in agitation, in cultivating our relations with the masses. If there is no production, there will be no distribution either.

In production, and in economic work in general, our guiding principle is a more efficient economy. An important part of this is better factory and work organization. There is a resolution which deals with the subject, but we have virtually not even started to implement it. This means that the final stage of our management system is missing. It is as if three-quarters of the components of a machine unit were modern, but there was a wooden club at the end of the production line. Direct factory management and the organization of work are indispensable parts of the system of management. Yet in this respect we live in the "Middle Ages". Let us show that we can honestly solve factory organization, because otherwise we will only limp along.

Why cannot we fight against superfluous administrative manpower? We have radically decreased the number of administrative workers in the central bodies two or three times in the past ten years; but we have injected them, and also some more, into medium-level administration and into the factories and plants. I accept that the relative decrease in the number of manual workers is in line with the laws of the development of society. I agree that this goes hand in hand with technological progress. I accept that the proportion of intellectual work increases. But I definitely cannot accept the rate of growth of administrative labour. We are far ahead of the field in the production and ballooning of administrative manpower. Unquestionably this matter must be dealt with seriously.

Ceasing to turn out inefficient products has also come to the forefront. We must inevitably deal with this, but we must also tie it to the increase in the production of efficient products, for we have not done this sufficiently either. The two really constitute one process.

A few practical questions of economic work have also come up in our session. I would like to contribute to that discussion. How should the party lead, what should the party do, in the daily practice of the economy? The party—from the Central Committee down to the individual local party organizations—will always deal with economic questions because these are the questions of building socialism. And the party will always deal with these questions in the manner which is necessary: it may take a decision on principle, it may organize a special shift on Sunday and it may help to harvest the corn. This is one half of the question. The other half of the question concerns the form appropriate for party organizations to deal with the economy.

They may manage to procure something there is a shortage of, they may fight for something, they may help to obtain labour, or credits, but there must be an appropriate system in order for the party organizations to deal successfully with questions of the economy. I believe nobody can say that the smartest party organization is the one where it is the Communists who produce whatever is necessary. As in the case of every other task, great attention must be devoted to a healthy division of labour. We must know what the party will undertake to do, what it does, and what the economic organizations and the mass organizations will undertake and will do in the field of the economy. There are certain things which, by the nature of things, will fall to the party organization, while others will fall upon the state, the economic organizations or the trade unions. Here, as in the case of every normal form of the human division of labour, the machinery as a whole will operate best if everyone knows what his own task is, and is aware of his responsibility.

A number of speakers have spoken of the significance of community work. Naturally we cannot dismiss this. One of the strengths of socialism is that people are willing to work unselfishly for the whole of society, for the common good, for certain communal goals, even in their free time and without any remuneration. We see many fine examples of this, especially when it comes to building kindergartens or other children's establishment and the like. Still, often this volunteer labour winds up in a dead-end. There is mobilization, people offer their services, they want to work and still the matter is not in order. Either a tool is missing, or the work is of such a nature that it cannot be done through volunteer labour complementing some kind of state activity. For volunteer work is generally only a complementary part of some economic activity—except when we are talking about something like the planting of flower beds.

Community work should not be abandoned, but should not be led into a blind alley either, because by doing this we could harm the principle involved. Therefore, volunteer work should be called upon regularly and in an organized manner, but only in well-founded cases, when all the conditions are met. If the necessary conditions are missing, let us rather not do it, for we then harm normal economic activities just as much as the fine principle of volunteer labour.

In summing up the results of the discussion I am very pleased to state that full agreement has been expressed at this session of the Central Committee.

This fact in itself expresses very well the unified interpretation of the guidelines of the 10th Congress, and the prevailing and living spirit of the party; and it reflects the ideological and political unity and concord of the Central Committee. If today, at the start of our great political work, the spirit of unity radiates out, it will be an important factor for the appropriate execution of the present resolution by the party.

We are starting a very significant political campaign, and great work, following the meeting of the Central Committee. Everyone will have assignments enough related to the resolution. The contents of the political campaign will be given by the full, published text of the resolution. The working out of the local tasks will follow the publication of the resolution. Local tasks will have to become part of the action programmes, the working programmes of every party organization, of every local branch.

This is the task facing state, economic and cultural leaders as well. We will request something similar — naturally according to a healthy and normal division of labour — from the social organizations and movements, the trade unions, the youth federation, the Women's Council, the People's Front.

We are convinced that this session of the Central Committee has fulfilled its role in deciding those questions which require a decision at the halfway mark between Congresses. Let us consider this resolution to be a working, fighting programme which will give an impetus to our work and will help in the realization of the Congress resolutions. I believe everyone will agree that the times ahead are not times for meditation, for philosophizing, for desires, and for unresolved debates, but for vigorous work. We will have to do everything in order that this clear stand by our party succeed and be realized without reservations. Right now the main task is its fullest possible implementation and the continuous supervision of this implementation.

The Central Committee, the medium-level party organizations and the full membership of our party must stand up and act as one man. Right now it is this demand, this unified stand and action which is the most important thing. If we do not fail, then we will have done a lot in the interest of the better execution of the resolutions of the 10th Congress and in the course of our work we will have eased a number of our other daily concerns.

At the close of the Central Committee session may I join those comrades who have expressed their deep conviction that we will implement the resolutions of the 10th Congress with good results.

Quo Vadis, Europa?

JUNE 1973

The word Europe has been used as the name for our continent for some three millennia now and is a geographic, political, and cultural concept. It is also the home of over thirty peoples and nations, and stands for their historical past, present and future. The fate and future of Europe is also the fate and future of the generations alive today, of hundreds of millions of people of various nationalities.

Along with the accelerated sequence of historical events and the accelerated development of social progress and science and technology, there has come the recognition that the fate of social classes and of peoples is not exclusively determined within the boundaries of a nation, but is increasingly and to a growing extent determined by the international situation and its general development. This is why far-sighted members of the bourgeoisie, people like Voltaire, Rousseau, Byron or, more recently, Mann and Russell were just as concerned with the fate of humanity, and that of our continent, Europe, as were the giants of the working class movement, Marx and Lenin, or such great Hungarians as Kossuth, Petőfi and Ady.

Today everyone is concerned with the question of Europe. On the basis of personal experience I naturally enough know the thoughts and thinking of the generation of which I am a part, those people who grew up in the inter-war period and who are still active today. It was in the early thirties that as a member of the young iron-workers' movement I came into contact with socialist ideas and that I realized the need for political action. This, of course, had broad ramifications, including how I regarded our continent then and how I see it today.

The Hungary of that inter-war period was sorely burdened with semi-feudal remnants and economic underdevelopment. There was a brutally repressive political regime headed by the Fascist Miklós Horthy. There was a major economic crisis. On top were the big capitalists, the large estate owners and the privileged classes, living a life of ease, while at the bottom of the social scale were the millions of people, workers, peasants and intellectuals, whose lot in life consisted of exploitation, unemployment, hunger, misery, injustice, and police terror. These were the things that we, young Communists, Social Democrats and other progressives, seeking and working for a better world, fought against. Dealing with the vital questions facing the working class and our people, we necessarily had to take Europe into consideration, as well as the world as a whole. We all know just how bad things were at that time in Europe.

The change, the fact that there is a new situation and a favourable trend is signalled by an event which may not seem all that significant, but which really is one of great importance. At the end of last year—let us note the date—in November 1972, the representatives of the nations of Europe and of the United States and Canada met to discuss the specific agenda for the convening of a meeting on European security, and I think that our hopes that the meeting itself will take place this year, in 1973, and begin its highly significant work are not unfounded.

The fact that such developments have come about reflects the recognition that the cold war is a cul-de-sac and carries within itself the constant danger of actual conflict and war. The conviction is growing and is gradually becoming generally accepted that in the present phase of historical development, at the present level of military technology, in the age of nuclear weapons, the only alternative to the incalculable, or rather quite easily calculable, risk of war is the peaceful coexistence of nations with different social systems, and the settling of still open questions to the satisfaction of all European states.

Needless to say, a European conference on security, not to mention a strong security system, requires the solving of numerous questions. Partly due to historical reasons and partly due to the differences in our social systems, there are several very complex questions still outstanding, involving inter-state relations. These are not beyond solution in a mutually acceptable way, but a prerequisite for this is that everyone responsible for the fate of Europe and her peoples should take sober account of the realities and draw the lessons of the history of her recent past. In this case it is especially valid to point out that history is the teacher of life.

What have been the factors involved in hindering the establishment of collective security in Europe so far? Why has it not been possible to create a lasting peace and what makes this a possibility today?

There are still some old-timers around today in Europe who recall the years preceding World War I and call them the "peaceful years" when in fact they were not all that peaceful and idyllic. The relationships between the European countries were governed by an armaments race, various conflicts, and manoeuvres for spheres of influence and markets, which were often accompanied by violence. There was no way this could have resulted in a peaceful Europe; the World War was the only natural outcome. World War I ended with the defeat of German imperialism and its allies, who were responsible for the outbreak of the conflict. The United States, Britain, France and their allies emerged victorious, but capitalism as a global system suffered a blow from which it would never recover. The war had also led to the liquidation of Tsarist Russia, the chain of imperialism was broken, and the world's first workers'– peasants' state, the Soviet Union, was born.

The chief characteristics of the inter-war period were the conflicts among the imperialist powers, and the conflict between the imperialist powers on the one hand and the Soviet Union on the other. Following World War I, the competing capitalist states were still in control of Europe and large parts of the world, determining the main trends of development, but nevertheless they did have to take into account that newcomer to the world political stage, that consistently anti-imperialist and peace loving major power, the Soviet Union.

During the inter-war years, the growing strength of the young Soviet state, and the enormous political and economic successes achieved by the planned socialist economy filled Hungarian Communists and progressives, as well as the anti-fascists of every European country, with enthusiasm and hope. The foreign policy of the Soviet Union was designed to assist the progressive forces, to block the Fascist danger, and to aid all endeavours to prevent the danger of war. The Soviet Union fought for security, disarmament, and peace in the League of Nations, too.

Events accelerated from the middle of the thirties on; the leading Fascist states, Germany and Japan, concluded a so-called "anti-Comintern" pact, and voiced their imperialistic designs with increasing frankness. In fact, they soon began to realize their goals. The Soviet Union gave assistance to the Spanish Republic which was fighting the onslaught of Fascism. It offered to enter into an alliance with Western governments and urged joint political and military steps to protect Czechoslovakia and Poland. However, the Western powers were blinded by their anti-Communist and anti-Soviet views and instead of acting in concert to stop aggression they sought to appease it at Munich, which willy-nilly meant opting for the further strengthening of Fascism and the horrors of World War II.

The Munich Pact failed to satisfy the predatory Fascists, but, on the contrary, emboldened them. The threatened peoples and the politically conscious saw a lot more clearly than many of the politicians just how much this pact was worth, and they prepared for the hard times and for the struggle to come. As Fascism grew in strength and openly revealed its aims both here in Hungary and in other nations of Europe, domestically and world wide there was a growing circle of people ready to take action in order to shake off the yoke of Fascism and to stop the world catastrophe. In France, in Spain, and in other countries of the world, the best of mankind took a stand against Hitler and his ilk.

As far as the policies of the various governments were concerned, the situation only changed in the course of the war. The Western powers only abandoned their anti-Soviet stand when Hitler attacked them and threatened their power and existence. The entry of the Soviet Union into the war allowed the establishment of the coalition of anti-Fascist powers and lent it the character of a liberator. The Soviet Union, the United Sates of America, France and Britain defeated Hitler and his regime.

The end of this terrible war and the defeat of the Fascist powers introduced a new historical phase and new opportunities for the peoples of Europe and the world. After Hitlerite Germany surrendered unconditionally at Karlshorst, the Allied powers took only three months to prepare for the Potsdam Conference at which they had set forth the framework for the future development of Europe. They were able to reach an agreement despite the fact that there were major differences in opinion between the socialist Soviet Union and the capitalist Western powers about the post-war shape of the world. These differences notwithstanding, they signed the Potsdam Agreement, because they could not leave the results of a war which brought victory to the forces of social progress out of account, and because their starting point was their basic common interests.

Regrettably, events soon took another turn. The ideal of European security – almost immediately after the Potsdam Agreement – seemed dead. The numbing winds of the cold war blew over Europe. The forces of reaction sought to use the outcome of the war for their own ends and feverishly sought for any means to achieve their aims. The Truman Doctrine, the Marshall Plan, NATO, the boycott of the newly established socialist countries, subversions and other hostile acts were the results of these endeavours.

The reactionary circles of the capitalist world – forgetting the lessons of the Second World War – once again started their propaganda campaigns against the Soviet

Union and against Communism and tried to scare the peoples of Western Europe, who longed for progress, stability and peace, with stories alleging Soviet plans for world domination. The false philosophy and shady political practices of McCarthy, Dulles, Adenauer and Co. increasingly gained ground. Europe, which had barely tasted the fruits of peace and had only a glimpse of the opportunities offered by cooperation, was severed in two by mutual mistrust, isolationism, the cold war, and the so-called "iron curtain". The Damocles' sword of war, and this time a nuclear war, was again hanging over Europe.

Fortunately for Europe and her peoples, the world was different after World War II and at the time of the cold war than at the time of Hitler's ascent to power and the outbreak of the war. The Soviet Union was growing in strength at an unprecedented rate; the new socialist countries of Europe were becoming consolidated and were developing; the socialist countries established their own mutual assistance agreements; the class struggle was sharpening in the capitalist world; and the colonial empires of the capitalist powers were beginning to disintegrate. There was such political, economic and military force defending socialism, democracy and peace that every effort of the cold war warriors was frustrated and the imperialists were dissuaded from the use of armed force in the European arena.

With the passage of time, with the bankruptcy of the infamous plans for "liberation", the 1953 East Berlin and the 1956 Poznan events, and the failure of the 1956 Hungarian counter-revolution, the Western strategists had to face the fact that there was no way that the aims of the cold war could be realized. By the beginning of the 1960s it had become clear once and for all that the post-war European political situation was here to stay. At that time, the socialist countries issued a series of new and realistic proposals for cooperation which helped others to realize that there is only one sensible course to follow, that of peaceful cooperation among all countries of Europe, to establish an atmosphere of mutual trust, and on that basis to guarantee peace and stability for all Europeans.

As far as the governments of Western Europe's capitalist countries were concerned, there were an increasing number of sober-thinking politicians and other public figures who took a realistic view of the situation, who had learned the lessons of history, while those who "had forgotten nothing and learnt nothing" were gradually being relegated to the background.

It had become clear that the anti-Communism which had become government policy was unrealistic because it failed to cure the ills of capitalist society, it could not hold up the socialist countries' development, and was no longer an effective tool for misleading the masses. The peoples of Europe had paid a high price for this during the war and had learned that anti-Communism and opposition to the Soviet Union could only bring misery and suffering, regardless of how the demagogues sought to mask their real intent. They have also learned that the warnings of well-meaning people and even the courageous stand of some individuals are far from being enough in the face of the adherents of violence who threaten the peoples of Europe. Millions of people had to pay with their lives for the lesson that violence must be met by the combined strength of the peoples.

History has also taught us that anti-Communism is a weapon directed not only at the Soviet Union, the socialist countries and the Communist parties, but also against the freedom of all peoples, every progressive movement, and all people who believe in peace. At the same time, the wartime alliance and cooperation of the Soviet Union, the United States, Britain and France, as well as the broad anti-Fascist movement in Europe, prove that peaceful cooperation is possible among nations with different social systems and between people with different world outlooks and party affiliations in the interest of a mutually recognized major goal. This is the most important historical experience, the strongest memory, and the greatest tradition that the peoples of Europe and our generation leave for future generations.

Recently we have seen realistic prospects opening up for the creation of a collective security system and for strengthening peace in Europe. Europe today — since World War II — is composed of nations with different social systems, different political interests, of different sizes and geographical locations. For historical reasons, these nations have to coexist and nobody can alter that fact.

In today's circumstances the responsible statesmen of the European nations and other social bodies must take these historical experiences into account. But what we must be concerned with now is not trying to find out who was right and who was wrong, pondering the glorious and the shameful aspects of the past. We must not be concerned with trying to find out who is responsible, and to what extent, for the yet unsolved questions. The countries and peoples of Europe must take as their starting point the realistic interpretation of the real questions and, keeping their mutual interests in mind, create the solid foundations of a secure future by making the best of the present favourable historical opportunities. No other way is acceptable to the peoples of Europe. If we can do this in the European context, we shall have served the interests of all mankind.

To get matters moving, the Warsaw Treaty countries proposed that we should work out together and create a European collective security system, or to put it another way, the basis for a lasting peace. The Warsaw Treaty nations seek no special advantages for themselves. What we want is to see Europe rid of violence and the threat of violence and to have the parties to the agreement establish a system which would guarantee the protection of every nation against aggression and which would serve the interests and prosperity of all peoples.

Our objectives have been clearly expressed in the repeated statements issued by the political council of the Warsaw Treaty and in the specific proposals in the "Budapest Appeal". The Warsaw Treaty member states want a Europe where the differences in social system do not pose insurmountable obstacles to nations living together in peaceful coexistence, and to the all-round development of relations on the basis of mutually advantageous cooperation. We are seeking a Europe in which countries do not have to live in the poisonous atmosphere of the arms race but rather under conditions of agreement and cooperation which will enhance the maintenance of international peace and security and the development of friendship and cooperration among the nations.

With this proposal, the countries of the Warsaw Treaty have placed on the agenda a question ripe for an urgently requiring solution. This is best indicated by the fact that the idea of a security conference was received with approval by the progressive social organizations and broadest public opinion of Europe and by the responsible bodies of almost every NATO country and European nation. There is a growing recognition of the fact that a well-designed and firmly established European security system, and the development of economic, scientific, technological and cultural ties and expanding tourism is in everyone's interest. It is therefore understandable that besides the socialist block, there are in Western Europe increasing numbers of governments, parliaments, parties, and socially and politically active individuals voicing responsibility for the peaceful future of the present and future generations. These forces are moving in the same direction as the socialist countries and they are taking an increasingly decisive stand in the interest of Europe becoming a continent of fruitful cooperation between equal nations.

On the road leading to security, we must first arrive at the next station, the meeting on European security. The reason why we attach so much hope to this conference is because we are convinced that if that meeting adopts the basic principles of peace and security and the noble ideals and objectives they embody and makes them the basis for the relationships among the nations of Europe, then it will surely make a major decision of historic significance.

Our expectations are realistic. This is also indicated by the fact that there are ever growing forces in Europe which take a stand in favour of a security system and for convening the meeting leading to it. These forces have succeeded in getting the European governments – due, among other factors to the influence of the clear and unambiguous policy of the socialist nations – to take a more realistic view of the main questions facing Europe. They have also been successful in following up the favourable changes which have taken place in attitudes with the beginnings of the practical implementation of the mutually acceptable principles. By way of example to illustrate the significant forms this can take, let us mention the agreements which have been signed and ratified between the Soviet Union and the Federal Republic of Germany, and between the latter and Poland, or the four power agreement on West Berlin, the treaty signed between the German Democratic Republic and the Federal Republic of Germany, and the fact that the NATO governments have granted recognition to the German Democratic Republic. Negotiations have begun in Vienna on the possible reduction of the opposing armed forces and arms in Europe.

One can say without exaggeration that today the question of collective security and the security conference is on the daily agenda of European statesmen, politicians, diplomats, and the leaders of various social organizations, both in their domestic work and at various international forums throughout Europe. Public opinion in the countries of our continent is keenly interested in and actively supports their activities. The justified hope of the peoples of our continent is rising that Europe, which for centuries has been the starting point and the theatre of so many wars and so much destruction and misery, is turning in the direction of peace, security and cooperation and that she will attain this much sought-for goal.

Our expectations are realistic primarily because the peoples of Europe do not want war. Significant numbers of people with different world outlooks and party affiliations have been struggling for the past 25 years against war mongering politicians and for the creation of a lasting peace. The social movements supporting peace in Europe and a policy of security are concrete proof of this.

It is a historical fact that the world, and in it, the peoples of Europe, have come to a crossroads. Basically, there are only two genuine alternatives. One is an increased arms race and a new thermonuclear world war, and the other is a ban on the use of force in international relations, negotiations on all outstanding questions, and the peaceful coexistence of nations with different social systems. It is obvious that people are interested in the development of mutually advantageous economic contacts between countries with different social systems, in cultural exchanges and in the all round development of peace and friendship among the peoples. This is the people's way.

These historical realities necessarily lead to the situation whereby the idea of peaceful coexistence and the policy of peace and security become historical reality. We are optimistic about the future of Europe. But our trust is not blind. We know that there are still forces active in Europe that are interested in maintaining tensions. Their presence surprises no one, since it would be deluding ourselves to think that the forces of reaction would voluntarily surrender their positions. At the same time, we are certain that, given today's balance of power, the subversive activities of the enemies of détente can be defeated if we work together, consistently, to strengthen peace.

As one of the directly interested parties and as a member of the Warsaw Treaty, the Hungarian People's Republic has been an active participant, convinced adherent and fighter for the progress of peace and security in Europe. In the light of the basic interests of the Hungarian people, in harmony with the interests of all other European peoples, and keeping in mind the security of our continent, the Hungarian government is doing everything it can in the interest of détente and cooperation in Europe.

The Hungarian people are building socialism and they have great and splendid plans for the prosperity of the Hungarian People's Republic. In order to realize these plans, we need peace and stability. We are prepared to defend our national independence and our freedom in the face of all imperialist threats, but we do not want war. In close unity with the rest of the socialist block we are endeavouring to achieve friendship and mutually advantageous cooperation with all peoples and nations who are interested in conducting business with us on the basis of the principle of peaceful coexistence.

Our fate cannot be divorced from the fate of the peoples of Europe and of the world. This knowledge guides us in our independent foreign policy steps to achieve bilateral contacts and when the representatives of our government actively participate in the various multi-faceted conferences and meetings on European security, and when the emissaries of our society speak at the various international forums expressing Europe's public opinion.

We are still at the early stages of the process aimed at creating a European security system, but the political atmosphere has already changed as the peoples of Europe regard the future with renewed hope. Europe has already taken a significant step along the way leading to peace and security. Preparations for the European conference are under way, and the peoples rightly expect that all obstacles in the way of convening that meeting—due to be held this summer—will be overcome. All the forces threatening the peace of the continent are being defeated, and the forces which fill all of us with hope have grown tremendously. I can say with conviction that all the prerequisites are present for Europe to head in the direction of peace, security, and cooperation.

Address at the November 1974 Session of the Central Committee

The Central Committee resolved to convene the 11th Congress of the party at its March 1974 session. Since then the usual, continuous work in the party has been complemented and expanded by preparations for the Congress. This preparation is an extra task; the everyday activities of the party, however, must not suffer because of it, for this day-to-day work is also a significant, perhaps the most important, part of the preparations for the 11th Congress.

Nowadays, the best possible fulfilment of the national economic plan is on the agenda. It is absolutely clear that the economic plan is at the same time a programme for our entire work of socialist construction, since the national economic plan provides the material basis, the framework and the possibility of economic and cultural construction. I would like to emphasize that our work done to fulfil the economic plan has brought good, satisfactory results. The data relating to economic construction is, I believe, known to all, as the statistical reports for the first half of the year have been published; in fact, the data for the third quarter are also known. In industrial and agricultural production, in production as a whole, we have achieved results over and beyond the plan. The same goes for other areas basic to the life of society such as public education and the health service. This enormous, continuous work must not be interrupted in any circumstance. The central issue of preparation for the 11th Congress is to fulfil this year's plans for socialist construction with the best possible results.

In connection with current work, I will mention that preparatory work on the 1975 national economic plan is comparatively advanced—at least on the part of the central bodies. Parallel with the drawing up of this plan, work on the new Five Year Plan has also begun. The circle has, therefore, become wider, since this work was, naturally, begun by government agencies—the National Planning Office and the Ministry of Finance—but by now wide-ranging planning has begun for the year 1975 at the local councils and at the production units, the factories, as well. This work deserves attention, on the one hand because it will determine the further conditions of our socialist construction, and on the other, because the preparations for the 1975 economic plan and laying the foundations for the new Five Year Plan are being carried out under particularly difficult conditions. It is necessary to speak of these particularly difficult conditions, as they demand great effort and serious work from the whole party, from the government and from the economic organizations.

As I have mentioned, we are executing our 1974 plan in a satisfactory manner; one might even say with good results. However, as we do not work in isolation, and as the international background to our economic efforts has changed, we have not been able to reach our aim of balancing the economy in our current national economic plan, including, of course, the international balance: in this respect we have fallen far behind the goals set in the plan. It is widely known that about 50 per cent of our national income is generated by international trade, by our export and import activities. In the past two or three years, and especially in 1974, international conditions have deteriorated badly as far as we are concerned. About one-third of our international trade in goods is with the Western capitalist countries. In this trade recent changes on the world market have been greatly to the detriment of the Hungarian national economy: the critical situation in relation to raw materials, energy resources and energy carriers, the big increase in the price of energy carriers and raw materials, as well as the inflation which is reaching more and more dangerous proportions in the Western world, have all affected us adversely.

This process on the capitalist market naturally affects also the other half of the international background of Hungary's national economy, the socialist world market, which is likewise not completely independent of the world capitalist market. We must, necessarily, count on price changes on the socialist world market as they will to a certain extent be aligned – as they must be aligned – with general international price levels. This matter is already under consideration.

It is well known that the Hungarian national economy is very poor in raw materials and energy resources. Even to maintain continuous production, we depend on imports of large amounts of raw materials and energy. We cover our needs mostly from the socialist world, but we need continuous imports of raw materials, semi-finished goods, machines and equipment, and energy carriers from the Western market to cover the demands of both our industrial and agricultural production. Those who deal with economic affairs know what the prices are today. Oil, for example, at the moment, costs six times as much as it did only a short time ago. Or the world price of sugar – which is not a very special commodity – has jumped to incredible heights; it has increased tenfold in the past year and a half to two years.

At one time we exported sugar and we now need to import it. According to calculations next year we will have to import even more than this year and this certainly is a great burden on the Hungarian national economy. The drawing up of the national economic plan for 1975 is therefore no easy task for the Central Committee and the government, nor for the production units and local councils, either. In the course of our work, our party, our government and the Hungarian People's Republic must meet their international commitments which range over a great area and demand a great amount of activity. Our central bodies, therefore, have to grapple with the burdens of international activity. Of course I am not saying this by way of complaint, since this is an indispensable organic part of the activity of our party, our state and our people, and of the building of socialism: in order for us to be able to build we must fight for a more peaceful, more settled world.

All this constitutes a part of the whole situation, of the conditions under which our party is preparing fo the 11th Congress. May I therefore emphasize: Communists prepare for the 11th Congress in the appropriate manner only if they do their utmost and if they utilize every opportunity in the interests of meeting our political, economic and cultural plans this year so that we can present a satisfactory balance to the Congress. Daily work and the preparation for the Congress naturally puts heavy demands on the party, the state, the economic bodies, workers in cultural and scientific life, mass organizations, members of the party, and activists.

Those sympathetic to the cause of socialism are working vigorously, and are making great efforts. This is all expressed splendidly in the socialist emulation which our workers have initiated across the country in honour of the 30th anniversary of our Liberation and the 11th Congress. It is fitting to speak here of this year's autumn agricultural campaign, of the work done under extraordinarily difficult conditions. Luckily, thank God, though it is really thanks to the efforts of the workers, we are approaching the end of this campaign. We can all recall that earlier a campaign of this sort looked quite different, as did the mobilization for it. There were times when the people in the villages struggled, while others watched them struggle. And then we rallied the people in the cities, who went to help out, while some people in the villages watched them. This time, however, the workers in agriculture have made an enormous effort — one worthy of honour and recognition — and the urban workers have gone to help them out in a natural manner — in the true sense of the word. This campaign, just like a military campaign, demanded large-scale mobilization and complex organization. But it has succeeded splendidly; the goals set have been reached and the results achieved. It seems that in harvesting crops, for example, we have got caught up. It is particularly important — and here mobilization cannot give any direct help — that the autumn sowing be completed properly now. Six weeks ago, Hungarian agriculture and the country were facing awesome difficulties. But as a result of special efforts we have succeeded in overcoming them.

It is part and parcel of the description of the situation that the festivities in connection with the 30th anniversary of the Liberation of the country have begun in the midst of such efforts. We have aptly commemorated November 7, a great day for the working class, for all peoples building socialism, including the Hungarian people. The commemoration has been characterized by a good atmosphere and mood, and fine ceremonies with an appropriate political content.

These are the conditions under which we are preparing for our Congress. In keeping with the 1974 March decision, the executive bodies of the Central Committee, the CC apparatus and other invited comrades have immediately begun the work of preparing all Congress material and all organizational matters. The executive bodies of the Central Committee have had to deal with three Congress documents. I shall mention the draft programme declaration first because the Central Committee has appointed a committee to draw up this document. Naturally, the draft documents concerning the guidelines and the changes in party rules are also the results of wide-ranging and collective work. Committees are at present working on these documents.

The committee appointed to prepare the programme declaration has held six meetings; the committee dealing with the guidelines has also met a number of times;

and the comrades dealing with party rules have also held innumerable meetings. The final preparation and coordination of the three Congress documents has been carried out by the Political Committee which has put the final touches. This was necessary because these documents are closely interrelated with each other and it would not have been proper if their preparation had been done independently. The Committees appointed have, therefore, done their work. This is why the Political Committee has been able to finalize the documents in such a way that they can be presented to the Central Committee. As part of the work of preparing for the Congress the executive bodies of the Central Committee have accordingly informed party organizations of what has to be done. Congress preparations are progressing in an appropriate manner, and at an appropriate rate in the party organizations, as well as at the party headquarters.

As far as party meetings are concerned, the methods approved by the Central Committee and used during the period before our last Congress are being used: that is, there will be two meetings dealing with the Congress. At the first one the party organizations will discuss and weigh their own activities while at the second they will deal with the Congress documents. The first party meetings are already taking place and according to plan they will be completed by the middle of December. Again according to plan, the second set of party meetings, where the membership of the party will take a stand on the central questions and documents of the Congress, will be completed in the first half of January 1975.

To sum up: on behalf of the Political Committee I can report to the esteemed Central Committee that preparations for the 11th Congress are going on properly, according to the decisions of the Central Committee. Today's session of the Central Committee and the stand which it takes will be another big step forward in the process of the congressional preparations.

I would now like to expound on the draft resolution concerning the organizational preparation of the Congress, for which we are seeking approval from the Central Committee. The system of representation at the Congress is determined, in accordance with the party rules, by the Central Committee. Our proposal this time is the same as that which was in force at the time of the 10th Congress, i.e. the party organizations should elect one congress representative for every 1,000 members. According to the tested practice of our party this is a normal ratio of representation. The new proposal we have submitted is that 19 large-scale industrial concerns, where the number of party members is above 1,000, be given the right to direct congressional representation. This is a deviation from earlier practice, but it is really very simple: the industrial concerns will elect their own congressional representatives, so that along with the territorial representatives at the Congress, certain large-scale concerns will be directly represented. We request that this proposal be supported by the Central Committee. At the same time we do not wish to contravene the generally valid territorial principle; therefore, it is proposed that while these large-scale industrial concerns elect their congressional representative directly, their election should be confirmed by the territorial party conference. Although this may seem to be a formality, it is not, because it is an expression of a certain right. I should mention that the earlier party resolution continues to stand: accordingly, members of the Central Committee and the Central Control Committee, that is, members of bodies elected directly by the previous Congress, will take part in the Congress with full rights and not just as consultative delegates. They will take part in the work of the Congress with full rights, including voting rights.

The proposed agenda may seem to be somewhat complicated. The reason for this is that the Central Committee will have to submit a number of documents to the Congress and the topics touched upon in these documents are closely interrelated. It would not be practical, therefore, to discuss these documents individually, as separate points on the agenda. We therefore propose that as a part of the first point on the agenda we list the three documents which the Central Committee will table at the Congress for debate alongside the report of the work done, with the request that the Congress adopt all of them. However, since these documents are very important in their own right we propose that at the end of the debate the Congress vote on each document separately. It is definitely desirable that the programme declaration at least be adopted on its own as a Congress resolution. These documents will then be tabled at one and the same time; they should be debated together but, at the end, the Congress should vote on them separately.

According to the previously adopted practice we should like congressional delegates — in the interests of suitable preparation — to receive the basic documents of the Congress soon after their election. We propose that we should keep to the tested practice that the Central Committee and the Central Control Committee prepare a written preliminary report. In this we can list a great number of facts and figures which would then not burden the oral report of the Central Committee. A statistical publication which will help the delegates to get ready for the Congress is also under preparation.

We have also worked out a proposal on the procedure regarding the two main Congress documents. As far as the guidelines are concerned, we believe that this document should be published by the Central Committee now. And when the party meetings have discussed them, the Central Committee should look at the subject once again. The Central Committee can then finalize the guidelines in the light of the discussions among the party members, taking these experiences into consideration and utilizing them. It can then declare this document the one that will be introduced at the Congress as a draft resolution.

Regarding the programme declaration the idea is that should the Central Committee adopt the text already introduced as a basic draft text, we shall soon be able to put it into such a form that we will be able to consult on it with various bodies and with between something like 2,000–3,000 party leaders. The Central Committee should deal with this programme and finalize it in February although, naturally, this will not be a definitive finalization because that is work which must be done by the Congress.

To be specific, our proposal is that this programme declaration be referred for discussion to the Budapest and the 19 county party committees, to the city committees with county rights and the district party committees of Budapest, to the party committee of the five large-scale industrial concerns which have the most local party organizations, to the Rector's Council of the Political Academy, as well as to the leading bodies of the Institute of Social Sciences and the Institute of Party History. These bodies should also give their opinions. They will be able to study the guidelines along with the programme declaration, they can form an opinion on the two documents at the same time, as they are interrelated. In other words, they should discuss the programme declaration and offer their opinion to the Central Committee.

We propose that we should seek the opinion of a few other bodies, including the National Council of the Patriotic People's Front and the Presidium of the Academy of Sciences on the guidelines and programme declaration. In reality this is a way of appreciating our allies, it is in line with the work style of our party and it is also proper politically that we seek the opinion of these two bodies. Beyond this, however, it is certain that we will receive tangible help from them.

Concerning the exact timing of the Congress, the Political Committee proposes that the opening day be March 17, 1975. By this time all preparations will have been made. According to our thinking the conference of the Budapest and county party committees should be held at the end of February and the beginning of March. The site of the Congress will once again be the headquarters of the Construction Workers' Trade Union. The order of procedure will be roughly the same as at the last Congress and the one before that.

We propose that for the 11th Congress—as for the 10th—we invite the representatives of the fraternal parties of the socialist countries as well as the representatives of the European Communist and workers' parties.

A major task of the Central Committee is to judge the political situation as we approach the Congress. If this judgement is a united and clear one it is easier and simpler to take a stand regarding the documents.

Now I would like to speak on a few important features of the congress documents. The first thing to which I would wish to call your attention, comrades, is that there are relatively few critical statements in the documents, although, as it will be clear from the list of things to be done, there are a great many tasks to be solved. You will recall that the 10th Congress clearly stated: in our socialist society, under the conditions of socialism there are contradictions, although not antagonistic ones. This was a necessary and justified statement but, as often happens in the case of such statements of principle, it has become fashionable. There are opinions which suggest that if we really got down to it, then half the guidelines and the programme declaration would be devoted to these contradictions and we still would not be able to list all the contradictions which persist under the conditions of socialism and which need to be resolved.

There is much to be criticized in economic, in cultural construction work, in fact, even in political work. And yet, we are putting forward the documents we are. The departure point in our thinking is: can the Central Committee and the party state that we have implemented the resolutions of the 10th Congress? Can we say that we have successfully fulfilled them? I believe we can. We could go on for hours listing the party resolutions, the government, the economic, the cultural, the domestic political and the foreign political decisions which, without exception, were ways of implementing the resolutions of the 10th Congress. And the results are not meagre ones. In all major areas of the life of our society we have implemented the resolutions of the 10th Congress with great results. In this sense, the Hungarian People's Republic today is not identical to the one four years ago. It is different, it has changed, because in the past four years we have successfully worked for the achievement of our major aims.

We must also give an answer to the question of whether the political guidelines of the 10th Congress have proved in practice to be correct. It is the opinion of the Political Committee, and I am convinced the Central Committee shares this opinion, that the answer to this question is: yes. But if this is true, then we simply cannot give an ambiguous answer to the basic question. We must give an unequivocal answer!

At the same time nobody should draw the conclusion from the text of the documents that the Hungarian Socialist Workers' Party, which has so far judged its own situation realistically, now wishes to convince itself that it has solved all problems and so it can rest on its laurels.

The Central Committee, in reporting to the Congress, is justified in stating that it has worked on the implementation of the resolutions of the 10th Congress, it has succeeded in rallying the whole party, the working masses, other workers, the adherents of socialism — and great results have been achieved. The Central Committee can also say that the political guidelines of the 10th Congress have been proved in practice. In party life Leninist norms prevail, the relations of the party with the masses are alive and strong and have become even stronger in the past four years: the party is enjoying the support of the masses. It can state that we have significantly progressed in economic and in cultural construction, in the field of raising living standards, and in the foreign affairs field as well. Our struggles have brought results. Our international activity has played a role — naturally, to the extent appropriate — in that the situation in Europe today, and in the world as well, is different from that of four years ago. All our work and struggle was not in vain because we have come one step closer to our goal: a more peaceful and settled world, something that is of prime interest to our people and an indispensable condition of socialist construction. It follows from the above — and this is the first and basic conclusion — that we propose to the Central Committee that it should ask the 11th Congress of the Party to strengthen and continue this political line.

Naturally, we do have problems and when judging the situation the Central Committee must size these up as well.

I am convinced that the party has developed, has grown, has become stronger: on the whole it works better today than four years ago. There is development in the work of the party organizations and of the local party organizations as well.

Our society has developed in the past four years in a positive direction: its basic socialist character has strengthened. In the political sense one can say that the socialist unity of our society has become stronger and has become firmer.

I am not speaking on behalf of and at the request of the Central Control Committee. But when we examine the sense of responsibility of people holding public office, as reflected by the experiences of the Central Control Committee for example, we can notice certain symptoms which are incompatible with Communist morals. There are certain such phenomena and problems within the party and — necessarily to a greater extent — in society as well. Undeniably, there are certain things which we will have to improve and with which the party must deal very seriously. The Congress will have to do work which will strengthen the positive features, will strengthen the party, and which will eliminate the negative features or will relegate them to the background.

The tasks of the 11th Congress — and naturally the Central Committee must help to carry them through with its own resources — is to strengthen the Marxist–Leninist character, the ideological, political and organizational unity of the party; to set the next goals in building socialism; and to strengthen the socialist traits of society. It must also point to the socialist perspectives of our society, of our people. In everyday practice people can see positive and negative phenomena at the same time. The question arises: fine, but which way is our society going? The 11th Congress must provide an answer to this question. Naturally it will have to provide the answer to existing concerns on every topic on the agenda. The role of the programme declaration of the party, however, is explicitly to set out the direction in which we are proposing to go. This is very important now also because it helps to clarify where people stand.

As I have already mentioned, the links between the three congressional documents, the programme declaration, the guidelines and the party rules, are close. There are very many questions which we are discussing in both the political documents, in the guidelines as well as the programme declaration. This is a necessity, because here we are dealing with tasks on which we must work continuously, but whose final solution is a long-term goal. The Congress therefore cannot remain silent on these subjects, either in the guidelines which will set the tasks for the next five years, or in the programme declaration which sets the perspectives. Certain important basic questions must be discussed in both documents. The preparatory committees, as well as the Political Committee, have attempted to work in such a manner that if these topics are discussed in both documents then in the guidelines they should be formulated as continuous tasks, and emphasized as elements which constitute daily tasks, while in the programme declaration we should deal with them as long-term tasks.

There are only a few new elements in the party rules, and for the most part there are modifications which will improve and correct them; these seem to be appropriate on the basis of practical experience, so I do not want to deal with them at length. A new element is that our party life will switch from the present four year- to a five-year cycle. This change will concern the Congress and the work of other elected party organizations as well. Linked with this is another change in party rules: up until now elected bodies could co-opt up to fifteen per cent of their membership. We propose to raise this percentage to 20 in view of the fact that from now on we will work on a five-year cycle. It is justified that over five years we should be able to co-opt new forces to up to 20 per cent of the total membership.

The five-year cycle does not cause problems regarding the Congress, since in a certain sense of the word it deals with long-term questions. The arguments in favour of the five-year cycle are well known. The congress cycle should be five years in order to be in harmony with the economic planning cycle. In the work of elected bodies the five-year period is slightly long. Legally, however, there are no obstacles and we can accept the five years also because at the "critical level", in the local party organizations, there are so-called reporting meetings every year, where, when need arises, the composition of the leadership can be corrected — on the basis of the appropriate ruling. This is really necessary, since local party organizations are directly touched by the transfer of personnel and other things. There — for various reasons — fluctuation is greater.

The right of the party member to leave the ranks of the party is unchanged; what is new is that this resignation from the party may be initiated by the party organization. In practice, therefore, it becomes possible for a party organization to tell a party member who, perhaps has become opposed to party policy: "Comrade, if you do not agree with the policy of the party, please resign." The only change in party membership dues is that a new category is established for those earning above ten thousand forints a month.

I will now speak on a few topics which are dealt with both in the guidelines and in the programme declaration. I will not deal with questions of foreign affairs in detail. I propose, and perhaps I need not present a separate set of arguments, that the Central Committee approve the direction of our foreign policy absolutely.

On the questions of principle I would first like to mention that we are proposing a change in one of the basic tenets accepted by the previous Congress. At a number of Congresses — and at the most recent one as well — we have stated that our aim is the completion of the building of a socialist society. This time this expression does not appear in the document. In its place, however, there is another expression — formulated with greater emphasis in the programme declaration — "the building of a developed socialist society". The reason for the change is that the leading slogan, or rather, the leading principle, the completion of building a socialist society, is a somewhat mechanical concept. We have often discussed this: in our language it has a certain nuance which could lead to the conclusion that if one can complete building socialism, then, obviously, at one point or another we can state that the building of a socialist society has been completed. It would seem, however, that the development of society does not take place so mechanically; there is no clear borderline, there is no fixed date in the calendar when and where we can say that a socialist society has been fully built. Even less so, because in the course of the development of a socialist society, for example in the area of distribution, certain elements which reflect certain principles of a Communist society evolve relatively early: there are certain things which are distributed not according to performance but according to need. It is probable that such elements will multiply. Society will not change on a "stop-go" basis, but rather quantitative changes will merge into qualitative changes in the course of organic development. This is the reason why we propose changing the earlier statement of principle.

We believe that the single most important political question for us is appropriately reflected in the document: this is the leading role of the working class, the worker-peasant alliance, the policy of alliance and the People's Front policy. We touch upon these in both the guidelines and the programme declaration. The wording must be such as to demonstrate that the leading role of the working class, the worker-peasant alliance, the policy of alliance and the People's Front movement as the form of a political alliance have great perspectives; and that this is related to the state and situation of our society. In other words: as long as there is a class society, this policy will stay in effect, or, to put it in yet another way, it is valid for the whole period of the building of socialism. We propose that this must be expressed appropriately in the documents.

As far as socialist democracy is concerned, we have expressed our main aspirations at the last Congress by stating that we must further develop state life and socialist democracy. This time this question is accorded the status of a basic societal demand. The key to our entire socialist progress is the further development of socialist democracy. As a part of that topic we mention and discuss workplace democracy, which has been on the agenda for some years now. We have been dealing with the questions of workplace democracy for a number of years in party organizations concerned with theoretical questions, in the trade unions, and in other organizations in order that, if it is possible, we may go forward to some extent.

In our documents we have specified some very important requirements, including new principles, in the interest of strengthening workshop democracy. The Political Committee has adopted a special programme: on the basis of a joint letter and guidelines from the Central Committee, the National Council of Trade Unions and the Council of Ministers, certain changes in the development of workshop democracy must be experimented with and tested in certain large industrial concerns. We must wait and see what experiences will arise from this practice because the results of the theoretical studies do not go far enough for the Central Committee to come to a decision of greater consequence. This is such an important question that we should not experiment with it all over the country at once because this could lead to confusion and then not only would we not develop workshop democracy further but instead, we could damage the principle, the idea itself. This is the reason why the draft documents state only that the party organization should have the right and the duty to make comments on enterprise plans. Such a right and duty has not existed before. And then there is the question that workers' delegates should be elected into such important leading bodies such as the Board of Directors and the Control Committee. Regarding another area of workshop democracy we are only indicating what we would like. Instead of the term "production meeting" we are using the term "workers' meeting". The two, of course, are not the same. This is to indicate that in large industrial concerns a certain body of workers' representatives will have to be established. We are not yet proposing the general introduction of this body because practical experience is needed. We believe that in the coming months such institutions will be established in an appropriate number of enterprises while their general introduction will demand at least one or two years' experience.

Both documents, the guidelines and the programme declaration, discuss a few basic questions concerning the ownership of the means of production, the very important topic of state and cooperative ownership. In the guidelines we have primarily emphasized the tasks and aims which concern the present congress cycle: the strengthening of the results achieved so far and the further strengthening of state and cooperative ownership.

What is new in our proposal are the new forms of association, with new forms of common ownership which will mean higher level cooperative associations. This is a practical matter and should our Congress adopt this without changes, measures will then have to be introduced. An even greater innovation would be the combination of state enterprises and cooperatives: this would be a new form of state and cooperative ownership. Among the socialist countries the Soviet Union and Bulgaria have taken certain practical steps in this direction and the results are worthy of attention and very promising.

In both the guidelines and the programme declaration the question of personal ownership is discussed and this—as I need hardly prove—is very important from a number of viewpoints. The two documents therefore shed very sharp light on both aspects of personal ownership. One aspect is the growth of personal ownership which we consider to be a necessary and useful concomitant of socialist construction. As follows from the above the guidelines state that our system will defend personal ownership. But the other aspect, the limits of personal ownership, must also be decisively shown. This finds expression in this statement that personal ownership must be limited should its measure go above and beyond personal and family needs.

A further proposal is that the sale and purchase of real estate must be brought under state control; must be, in practice, given into the hands of the state. Real estate, thus, would only change hands through state channels because otherwise it is impossible to forestall speculation and a harmful accumulation of wealth, of income without work— something which our party opposes.

Economic and cultural construction work are given appropriate emphasis in the documents. I must mention that the major indices of the new Five Year Plan have not yet been fully drawn up; this is a vast and difficult job. It is, however, the opinion of the Political Committee that it is absolutely necessary that the major features of the Five Year Plan, the ideas of the party, be included in the guidelines, so that we can mobilize the masses in their support.

In our opinion the situation in our society, in the Hungarian economy—despite all difficulties—is such, that we can definitely ensure progress in the economy, in the raising of the living standards and in the fulfilment of other demands of socialist development even though only by really serious and hard work. To achieve this, we must naturally plan very precisely; and as the situation so demands, we must mobilize our resources more resolutely and more efficiently. We primarily have in mind the better utilization of production equipment.

Once we have elaborated our plans we must then paint a proper picture to the public in our country in order that everyone might understand that we undoubtedly must take steps to mobilize our forces and our reserves better.

Naturally, a further condition of our progress and development is the better utilization of possibilities inherent in cooperation between the CMEA countries. The new Five Year Plan—which will be enacted—will only be completed and finalized by the end of 1975. The draft will be on the agenda of the Political Committee, and obviously the Central Committee, too, by the middle of the year. Despite this we propose and request that the Central Committee ask Congress to approve a certain number of the important indices which can be projected with the necessary conscientiousness, realism and, obviously, socialist thinking. Ours is a socialist country; it is therefore necessary for our Congress to give us a working programme. Questions regarding living standards also appear in the guidelines. To ensure a certain growth in real wages and real income in the future remains a very important task. According to the surveys the rate of growth will probably be lower then in the past few years but there will still be growth. This can be assured. The level of supply must also be maintained under all conditions. These are the kind of aims expressed by the figures.

A certain development of the pension system and social insurance appears in the document, not in an itemized, direct, way but in a form of a reference. We believe that in this field — independently of our other problems — we must make progress. Serious considerations are involved here, including the problems of pensioners of longstanding, which above all mean very great difficulties for the older workers. An adjustment in the pension age for the peasants is also mentioned here. Our idea is to bring this down to the pension age for workers and employees over a period of five years. And a number of other social security matters are also involved including the settling of a number of benefits. These are social questions of great importance. It is therefore proper for the Congress to state that we wish to make progress here and for it to go into specific details.

The housing problem is also included in the guidelines. In the short run we will set a certain housing construction programme, while in the long run we will set our sights on constructing one-and-a-half to two million homes. The actual housing plan will only become final at the time the sixth Five Year Plan is approved but objectives of this order can be included in the document because the actual situation demands that housing construction go ahead at approximately this rate.

In ideological work our efforts are clear. We can state: we have reached the stage where Marxism plays a leading, hegemonistic role in Hungarian intellectual life as a whole and we are aiming to strengthen this further in the social sciences. I believe it is a justified demand that in social sciences Marxism–Leninism should enjoy a monopolistic position; I believe this does not limit the freedom of research and the freedom of creation. Those working in the sciences should do research, should debate in professional circles and I do believe that polemics are also justified in scientific journals. However, what we propagate, what we publish in tens of thousands or even millions of copies, and what we teach at the universities must be Marxist–Leninist. Work on an enormous scale must be done in the defense of the purity of Marxist theory. Repelling imperialist attempts at destabilization is a separate task, and we also have important tasks and aims in shaping people's views, and overcoming egoism. In the fight against egoism we must continue to use persuasion and exhortation; but above all we must fill in and eliminate the gaps in our legal code in which the egoism of no small section of society's members finds its roots. Our general goal in ideological work is to continue to work, and where necessary, fight for the general acceptance of real socialist social standards. The slogan "Live, work, study in a socialist manner" vividly expresses this aim. This needs to be made as widespread a social standard, in as short a time, as possible. And now a few more words regarding questions of principle in the programme declaration. Our departure point is that the aims set in the programme declaration of the 1948 Congress of Unification have been reached and, in fact, in a number of respects surpassed, by our party, our working class, our people. Since in such a document historical continuity must be demonstrated the question naturally arises: what proportions should a programme declaration devote to the historic past, the present and the future? We believe that we have been able to establish the right proportions. I would like to emphasize: the decisive thing, naturally, is whether this programme declaration shows the perspectives of the future. If it is able to do so, then it has in a certain respect fulfilled its function. And perhaps it is worthwhile mentioning that the reason why we call this document a programme declaration and not a programme is because it only indicates the most important aims and endeavours. The function of this document is to set out our endeavours in the future. The analysis of our historical past and the present is useful and necessary inasmuch as we build our references to the future on it.

The programme declaration contains stands on principle concerning important questions — in certain cases these are not even new — but what it contains has a certain significance; it is a document of a different character than an intermediate party resolution. The programme declaration speaks of the party in the sense that it is the party of the working class. However, not only the working class needs the party, but rather the whole people, the whole of society building socialism. It fills an indispensable function and it becomes the party of the entire working people.

This programme declaration also takes a stand regarding the state. This, although it is not a new topic, cannot be omitted. At one point it states that our state is a state of the dictatorship of the proletariat, because, if we look back to 1948, and furthermore if we speak of the present and look ahead to the next twenty years, then to say that our state is that of the dictatorship of the proletariat is a scientifically well-founded statement. The programme declaration appropriately speaks of how the working class has achieved power, how it exercises power and whom it includes in the exercise of power.

One also needs to declare that the nation and socialist construction require the state. A number of views have come to surface even within the working class and here and there in the Communist world movement as well. Recently, even the Voice of America and Radio Free Europe complain and ask why socialist countries do not follow Marx, when will the state wither away? We must say, and we must give our reasons, that the internal situation and socialist construction both demand and require the existence and operation of the state. The programme declaration sets the perspectives as well; that in the final analysis it will become a state of all the people and elements of Communist self-government in society will appear and grow stronger. We therefore consider it proper to say in a Marxist manner that our state is the dictatorship of the proletariat and that eventually there will be Communist self-government in society.

In connection with ownership, the programme declaration goes a little further in discussing socialist ownership than do the guidelines. Land is a separate question — it deals with this appropriately. It states — in harmony with the guidelines — that we will strengthen ownership relations in their present form. At the same time it also states that land is national wealth. This is not a legal definition but is linked with and calls attention to the fact that land is not something which can be bought and sold or traded at will, its ownership changed from state to cooperative ownership, from cooperative to private ownership at will. In the final analysis this is not the perspective, but rather that state ownership as well as cooperative ownership exist and gain in strength. Land in the use of cooperatives should definitely become indivisible wealth and their sale and purchase be forbidden.

The forms of state and cooperative ownership — naturally not only in the context of land ownership but in general — must develop and must come closer to each other and in the final analysis—this is also stated by the document—must take the form of all-national Communist ownership. I believe there is no need to explain: it is immensely important politically that the party in the form of a programme declaration delineate clearly and in so many words the developments in ownership relations in the long run.

The programme declaration includes specific, programmatic plans. It states that in fifteen to twenty years production and productivity should grow by a certain amount, vocational training should be broadened, education and vocational training should be developed. Our aims regarding living standards and housing construction are also included and there are general references to certain major investments: power plants, energy resources and others. It was not easy to include these because, for example, people responsible for economic affairs will not willingly put down on paper specific commitments when neither the Five Year Plan nor the fifteen-year long-range plan is finalized, when neither is in a ready state. Following debates and considerations in the good sense of the word, however, the view that without these the document would not be a programme statement prevailed. Because if I omit programmes for the growth of production, living standards, housing, other investments and education, what will remain is a scientific Marxist document which will be read perhaps by people intensely interested in Marxism but not by others. In our country, however, where the full responsibility of leading the whole of society rests upon the party, and where socialism is being built, the programme declaration of the Communist party must be such as to give a programme to non-Marxists, to all the working people as well. This is why specific plans have been included and why this was necessary.

I will repeat that in our opinion the Central Committee can face the Congress assured, because the party—in its own sphere of activities—is really working to meet the tasks set by the 10th Congress and does so with the appropriate results. It is also part of the situation that, naturally, the enemy is also preparing for the 11th Congress. The enemy's press and radio, the capitalist news media—perhaps they also have a programme of preparation—deal a lot and in detail with our problems. They attempt to project the image that nowadays the Hungarian Socialist Workers' Party, the Hungarian People's Republic, is in great trouble, is faced with great difficulties. They also round out the picture by saying that there are debates, differences of view, that the policy of the party will change in this or that direction, that the reform will die and will be followed by a hard line, etc. They complement this picture with various combinations of personnel.

One cannot speak of opposition, of inimical tendencies in our party. It is well known, however, that there really are some debates within our circles as well on how to approach and solve one question or another. We are convinced that this is necessary, natural and normal. On the basis of this and the objective situation, there are those not only in the West but here at home, too, who look at the Congress in such a manner. There are people of petty bourgeois thinking and views who are perhaps not even on bad terms with socialism. But as petty bourgeoisie they begin to feel insecure when they should not. Our party is not without such people: there are some in our party, too, who have recently become a little more insecure than they were before. They are spreading various views of varying credibility. But this is usually what takes place. A few months before each Congress those who feel they have to sing their song will begin: will policy change or not change? what kind of changes in personnel will there be? will this person stay? will that one not? This is so today as well, although I have a feeling that perhaps this time around there is a little bit more guessing than there was before the 10th Congress. The most varied combinations of personnel are in circulation. But then you, comrades, know these rumours, which have become political to a certain extent. It is a fact that even in the case of responsible people there is a certain reservation, a "who knows" attitude. This is also a part of the actual situation.

Taking even these circumstances into consideration I am convinced that we can work calmly. The conditions for the preparation to the Congress are not bad. It depends on the Central Committee, on the party to make the Congress campaign successful, that the Congress might be a good one that makes appropriate decisions. It is my profound conviction — and I may state this on behalf of the Political Committee as well — that the 11th Congress of the party will give appropriate answers to all the matters that some have put question marks to, or to questions which really need an answer, a decision or an orientation. I believe they will be answers which will reassure the true adherents of socialism in our country and beyond our borders. They will cool our enemies and our ill-willed critics. We must do everything to ensure that the 11th Congress of our party strengthens the Marxist–Leninist principles and guides the activities of our party, and strengthens the progressive, practical use of these principles and our tested policies. Holding to our main line, let it develop this policy as every Congress in the past has done, and as is necessary and inevitable. And the party will carry on with its activity as it has so far.

I believe the Central Committee will agree that our party continues its way down the road which it has trod for a long while now, and from which it will not be diverted. We will defend, strengthen and develop our achievements in every field of economy, culture, domestic politics, in the policy of alliance and, naturally, in our international relations as well. We will defend and we will add to our achievements for the benefit of the country, of the people, of socialism and the international cause of socialism and progress.

Address at the Closing Session of the Conference on Security and Cooperation in Europe

AUGUST 1975

From the outset public opinion in Hungary has been following the activities of the Conference on Security and Cooperation in Europe with close attention and active support. We consider it to be of historic significance that the common effort has not been in vain and, in agreement with all those concerned, the final stage of the Security Conference has now convened at the highest level. This Conference is an expression of the expectations of the peoples, their best hopes for a better future, and, without doubt, it opens a new, important page in the history of Europe.

We are attending this historic conference as representatives of the Hungarian people, who established their state 1,100 years ago between the Danube and the Tisza, in the centre of Europe, and whose past and future alike are linked to the fate of the other peoples living in Europe. We are convinced that the most ardent desire of all European peoples is peace. If possible, this is even more true of the Hungarian people, whose home was for centuries at the crossroads of campaigning armies and who had to suffer enormous sacrifices to survive and protect their state against the threat of destruction. In this century, following the useless sacrifices of the First World War, the territory of vanquished Hungary was reduced to one-third of what it had been; in World War II her rulers were responsible for bleeding her dry on the side of evil forces, causing the loss of 8 per cent of the adult population and reducing the country to ruins.

Thirty years ago the fate of the Hungarian people took a new turn for the better in the wake of the historic victory of the anti-Fascist coalition, after the Soviet army and those fighting by its side drove the Hitlerite fascist occupation forces from our country's territory. Ever since the Hungarian people have been living in peace, having won back their national independence and state sovereignty. They are progressing along the path of their own choice, firmly and with determination, building today a developed socialist society. We have learned the lesson of our history. It will be evident to all that for the socialist Hungarian People's Republic the peace, security, friendship and cooperation of the European peoples are not just empty words but a long-term policy founded on firm principles and solid historical experiences and expressing the vital interests of the Hungarian people.

The past sufferings of the European peoples, the terrible ravages of the two world wars, both of which broke out on our continent, are common knowledge. Considering all this, and particularly the fact that in case of conflict the modern weapons that have been accumulated threaten the peoples of Europe and the world with unprecedented horror and destruction, the responsible elements in every country must contribute effectively to making the recently manifest détente permanent and to guaranteeing and consolidating peace.

We feel that upon the success of the Conference on Security and Cooperation in Europe and upon the work to be carried on in the spirit of the current Conference will depend the future of our peoples, of the continent of Europe, and it may not be an exaggeration to say, in no small degree the future of mankind also. It is the hope of the peoples we represent that the Conference will complete its work successfully and that the future will be peace. The Hungarian delegation has been sent here to contribute to the success of the Conference and we will strive to carry out this mandate.

The Hungarian People's Republic is a staunch supporter of peaceful coexistence between countries with different social systems. Together with the Soviet Union and other socialist countries, she was an initiator of and a signatory to the 1969 Budapest appeal which proposed the convening of the Conference on Security and Cooperation in Europe. Together with our allies we have ever since done our utmost to bring about that Conference. Our representatives have participated throughout in the preparatory work and in the drafting of the document submitted for signature to the present Conference.

The Hungarian People's Republic is convinced that every effort must be made to find peaceful solutions to all problems that involve the threat of armed conflict so as to eliminate the possibility of a new world war.

Our Government is of the opinion that further efforts have to be made to promote general disarmament. We support all serious endeavours towards disarmament, including the Soviet proposal to convene a world disarmament conference.

We welcome, and from the point of view of international détente regard as decisive, the improvement in relations between the Soviet Union and the United States of America and their agreement and continued negotiations on the limitation of offensive strategic weapons.

All rational human beings realize that at the present stage of human development there is no realistic and acceptable alternative to avoiding world war other than peaceful coexistence, the solution of controversial issues by negotiation, halting the armaments race, arms limitation and then disarmament, normal relations among states, cooperation on questions of common interest, rapprochement and the friendship of peoples.

With full knowledge of this and in this spirit, the Hungarian People's Republic develops her international contacts and works in the United Nations and in nearly 600 other international organizations.

The document before this Conference reviews many important and complex issues of European security. The Hungarian delegation holds it to be of outstanding importance to lay down the principles governing relations and cooperation among states. There are 35 sovereign states attending the Conference, among them large and small states, industrially advanced and less advanced states, socialist and non-socialist states, aligned and non-aligned states and neutral states. Respect for and the practical implementation of the principles governing relations among states – sovereign equality, refraining from the threat or use of force, the inviolability of frontiers, and the other basic principles – correspond to the interests of the 35 different participating states and guarantee peace. By observing these we can banish war and armed conflict from our continent. The Hungarian People's Republic is willing to comply consistently with these principles.

In the view of the Hungarian Government, the endorsement by the Conference of the principles governing relations among states and the practical application of those principles will strengthen political confidence, which in turn will facilitate the reduction of armed forces and armaments in Europe rationally and on the basis of equal security.

We also welcome the recommendations concerning scientific, economic and trade cooperation. Hungary already maintains extensive economic relations with many European countries and participates in the international economic division of labour. For reasons of principle and because of her position, the Hungarian People's Republic is in favour of the continued expansion of international economic cooperation. We consider that mutually advantageous economic cooperation is a solid basis for political contacts among states in general and those with different social systems in particular. Hungary is ready for mutually advantageous economic cooperation free from discrimination and based on long-term agreements with all interested countries.

In the preparatory stage of the Conference there was a wide discussion, involving the expenditure of much time and energy, on working out proposals concerning cultural cooperation, the broader dissemination of information, the extension of human contacts, and the solution of certain humanitarian problems. The Hungarian People's Republic is ready to accept the recommendations on those issues also and to expand the contacts which exist in this field.

It is the conviction of the Hungarian Government that peaceful coexistence and the rapprochement and friendship of peoples facilitate fruitful cooperation among states in the fields of science, public education, culture and information. A shining example, which is of great significance for all of us, of interstate scientific cooperation for the good of mankind has been the magnificent achievement of the joint Soyuz–Apollo space programme..

In Hungary people value all the real treasures of human culture. Access by everybody to universal culture is being assured, among other things, by the publication in large editions and the staging of works by great authors and poets like Dante, Shakespeare, Molière, Goethe, Tolstoy and others. What is valuable in the current cultural activity of the West is also being made accessible to all in Hungary.

We are in favour of human contacts, of improving international tourism and travel, of making it still easier to see as much of the world as possible. In effect those who come to us in good faith will find the gates of the Hungarian People's Republic wide open. Two-way tourism to and from socialist and non-socialist countries is considerable. Every year, Hungary, with a population of ten million, receives more than eight million foreign tourists, and over three million people of Hungarian nationality travel abroad.

The Hungarian People's Republic has already proved herself to be a supporter of cultural cooperation, of expanding the circulation of information, and personal travel, and of all sensible steps which can promote better mutual understanding between peoples and countries. Additional positive steps in this direction can be taken only if we respect the sovereign rights and laws of the partner countries reciprocally, in conformity with what our Conference and the jointly drafted document before us expect from every participating state.

Ideological differences are particularly evident when it comes to cultural cooperation and the exchange of information. We too, who are deliberating here, represent parties with different ideologies and countries with different political systems. But clearly we have not assembled here to approve one another's ideologies or state and political systems. The peoples we represent expect us to reach an agreement despite the ideological and political differences which do in fact exist; they expect us to work together and agree on the common tasks which we have to fulfil in order that peace and security may prevail in Europe, and that states and countries may usefully cooperate in matters of common interest for the benefit of their peoples.

We have come a long and difficult way to reach the present, third, stage of the Conference on Security and Cooperation in Europe. There has been much discussion and argument, even struggles. Détente and peace have not only supporters but opponents as well. We have had to overcome many a stumbling block so far and, obviously, the same is true for the future.

This Conference closes a stage of the past and can go down in history as a milestone of a new, better and more peaceful world. If the governments represented here carry on with a sense of responsibility and if the peoples perseveringly struggle in the future for the good cause, then we shall be capable of solving the tasks of tomorrow also.

Press Conference in Vienna

DECEMBER 1976

At our meeting today I would first like to greet the esteemed representatives of the Austrian, international and Hungarian press. I am glad that in the course of my visit to Austria I can meet members of the press, radio and television. As you know I am paying an official visit to Austria at the invitation of Dr. Bruno Kreisky, the Federal Chancellor of the Republic of Austria. The fact that the relations between the Hungarian People's Republic and the Republic of Austria are developing and that we have all the opportunities for the further diverse development of these relations has provided good grounds for my trip. I can say with satisfaction that during our talks with the highly esteemed leaders of the Austrian state, which were congenial in atmosphere, there was a mutual effort to deepen and expand good neighbourly relations further and to utilize existing opportunities in this field better.

Our visit to Austria is in complete harmony with the principled socialist policy of the Hungarian People's Republic. Our aim is to facilitate the course of social progress and peace and to contribute to the peaceful coexistence between countries with differing social systems and the widening and consolidation of détente.

Correspondent of Népszabadság: How do you evaluate your talks in Vienna, the prospects for Hungarian–Austrian relations and the effect of the talks on asserting the spirit of Helsinki?

János Kádár: The two sessions of talks conducted with Chancellor Kreisky and the meeting with the Federal President confirmed me in my conviction that this trip is useful; it enhances the development of many-sided Austro–Hungarian bilateral relations and contributes to the realization of the recommendations approved in Helsinki.

During the talks, which had a very friendly atmosphere, we touched upon the specific question of the further development of our relations, and it was my impression that both sides are striving to develop these relations. On the Hungarian side we consider our present relations good: our political relations have been normalized, our economic and cultural relations are developing. They can genuinely be characterized as being more and more in harmony with the principle of peaceful coexistence between countries with different social systems and with good neighbourly relations.

Correspondent of the Corriere della Sera put a question concerning the alleged anti-Soviet character of so-called Eurocommunism.

J. K.: I do not share the view expressed in the correspondent's question.

Correspondent of Le Monde: In your judgement is there any improvement in the relations between the socialist, the social-democratic parties and the Communist parties following the Geneva Congress of the Socialist International; and what are the obstacles to the future improvement of these relations?

J. K.: The relationship between the Communist and the socialist and social-democratic parties is not simple. We are and without doubt we must be cooperating partners with the European countries in which there are socialist or social-democratic governments.

The more so because we represent countries, we are talking about state interests and questions related to the interests of peoples, and in such cases one must rise above narrowly interpreted party views. Therefore we must cooperate by necessity primarily in the interest of facilitating European security and peaceful coexistence. In this respect the cooperation between Communist and socialist and social-democratic parties has been developing well.

Perhaps it won't seem immodest if I say that in a certain respect this was well exemplified by the day we spent in Vienna yesterday. Chancellor Kreisky – I can probably say – is my contemporary whom I know to be a man of strong convictions. Everybody knows that he is a social democrat. I am a Communist. And we met, we conducted talks with a good atmosphere, but it was the purpose of neither of us to exchange ideologies or philosophies.

This is not our task, either. We dealt with the question of good relations and cooperation between the two countries and the two peoples, and with the promotion of the general course of European peace and security.

Relations are maintained between Communist and socialist, or social-democratic, parties in cases when one or the other side or neither is a member of the government of the given country. The Hungarian Socialist Workers' Party, for example, has established relations in recent years with a number of socialist and social-democratic parties which are not in government, for example, with the Italian Socialist Party, the Finnish Social Democratic Party, the Belgian and French Socialist Parties. Just as I was leaving for Vienna a delegation from the Hungarian Socialist Workers' Party left for Denmark, to return the visit to Hungary by a delegation from the Danish Social Democratic Party.

What is the sense and the use of these relations? It was declared at the Berlin Conference of European Communist and Workers' Parties that the promotion of European peace and security and of social progress is considered the central task. In the course of our talks with the socialist and social-democratic parties mentioned earlier, they also declared that in the interests of their peoples they would like to advance profitably the cause of European peace and security and of mutually advantageous relations. In addition to this, in my view the Communist and socialist and social-democratic parties have other, in a certain sense, common problems. It would be, for example, desirable to develop the relations and cooperation between the trade unions of European countries in order to promote peace and security and facilitate the cause of good relations between peoples and of progress.

Correspondent of FRANKFURTER RUNDSCHAU: How do you evaluate the situation after the signing of the Helsinki Final Act? How do you view the relationship between Hungary and the Federal Republic of Germany and is there any specific plan as to when you will visit Bonn?

J. K.: As far as the implementation of the Helsinki recommendations is concerned, I consider the situation to be good. Many do not share this view. I myself, however, am thinking of the historical antecedents and the special difficulties which arose before the Helsinki Conference. I am thinking of how much effort has been made by all participating countries to bring the conference about. We consider the Helsinki Conference to be of historic significance; a success for the efforts of all participants and a triumph for common sense. At the same time we view Helsinki as a beginning and not an end; this demands renewed efforts from everyone who desires détente. But it is also common knowledge that not everyone is in favour of détente.

I am convinced that the conference is in itself of enormous significance; the very fact that countries with such different social systems and governments with such diverse ideological and political aims as the thirty-five participants at the Helsinki meeting sat down at the same table and were able to come to a common denominator regarding important fundamental issues, such as the enhancement of European peace and security, is very significant.

Of course the realization of the recommendations and their practical implementation demand time, patience and consistent effort. There are already certain results. The relationships between several European countries have improved in the period since the Helsinki Conference and the practical implementation of the Helsinki recommendations has started.

It is my conviction that the further improvement of the cause of European peace and security demands that those who took part at the Helsinki meeting should act as advocates for an appropriate, constructive approach at the planned Belgrade meeting, too. One can hear various ideas, expectations and views in connection with the meeting to take place in the Yugoslav capital. We are against anyone making the Belgrade meeting into some "complaints' day"; we believe that the participants of the Helsinki Conference must prepare for the Belgrade meeting with a positive programme. The starting point must be one which would allow a review in Belgrade of the questions of the improvement of state relations and of the development of economic relations: a study of such important questions, serving the interests of peoples as the European energy situation, the better solution of the tasks related to transport, and environmental protection. It is such and other similar current topics related to a general rapprochement between peoples which feature in the Helsinki recommendations that must be adequately prepared and discussed in Belgrade.

I believe that a significant part of the responsible elements in the European states agree with this idea. I am glad to say that yesterday when we touched upon this question with Chancellor Kreisky we expressed similar views.

As for the bilateral relations between the Hungarian People's Republic and the Federal Republic of Germany, these go back a while in the economic sphere and have evolved on quite a broad front. I believe that we can make our state relations more settled in the present period. This is in harmony with the interests of the Hungarian people and the population of the Federal Republic of Germany and with the recommendations adopted in Helsinki and it is my impression that such efforts are mutual.

Of course the development of relations goes hand in hand with mutual visits by the persons responsible for these relations, economic leaders, diplomats and government officials, for them to meet, to talk, to negotiate. The plan for my visit which is in the phase of preparation fits into this process—that is, the development of the relations between the Hungarian People's Republic and the Federal Republic of Germany.

In connection with my present visit to Vienna, the press has honoured me by dealing with me as a person, and they have stressed that I seldom travel and was in a capitalist country for the first time yesterday. With regard to the official nature of my visit, to a certain extent this is true. But non-officially I have been to several capitalist countries; moreover I spent the larger part of my life in a capitalist country. I have had the opportunity of going to New York which, as you know, is unfortunately not the great city of a socialist country. There are of course several reasons why I am in Austria in an official capacity for the first time. People are different. I know enthusiastic travellers. I am not one of them. But I always go when and where a visit is politically useful from the point of view of developing the relations of the two countries and where it is necessary. That is why I came to Vienna now and that is why I am going to the Federal Republic of Germany.

Correspondent of ARBEITER-ZEITUNG: Hungary is surrounded by friendly countries, among whom Austria can be included. Why therefore are Soviet troops stationed on the territory of Hungary?

J. K.: As far as our neighbours are concerned, I think you have correctly characterized our relations. I know it can be said of all our neighbours that they have friendly aspirations towards us and are striving to maintain good relations.

As for the military aspect of the question, I should like to mention that I started my military "career" at the outbreak of the Second World War: I was a deserter in Horthyite fascist Hungary and I went underground. I have not advanced all that much in my military career and I have not become a great "strategist".

Of course I have become familiar with and have learned certain elementary things, for example that just as there is no longer a notion of "infantry" in the old sense, so it would be just as naive at the present level of military technology to imagine that the security of a country depends only on the aspirations of her direct neighbours. The reason, therefore, for the presence of the Soviet troops who are temporarily stationed in Hungary is not that we fear some sort of an attack from Austria, which has pledged her neutrality voluntarily. There is no domestic political reason, either. It is related to the general world political situation; and a reassessment of this question, a change in the situation, is related to the cause of peace and security.

As is known, a whole series of fundamental and important issues featured on the agenda of the recent Bucharest meeting of the Political Consultative Committee of the Warsaw Treaty member states. We repeated publicly that we were ready for the simultaneous dissolution of the Warsaw Treaty organization and NATO. We proposed that if the time was not yet ripe for this, at least we should not strive to expand the two military groupings. There was also a proposal for the thirty-five states approving the recommendations hammered out in Helsinki to declare that they will not be the first to use nuclear weapons. In addition we have made a number of other practical proposals. We have said earlier and say today that we are for the simultaneous withdrawal of all foreign troops stationed abroad. Therefore if we are able to make progress on this fundamental issue, the general situation would be further improved and then obviously there would be no need for the presence of Soviet troops in Hungary.

Correspondent of DIE PRESSE: You have implied that your talks in Vienna facilitated the practical implementation of the Helsinki recommendations. What were the specific results at the talks and is there any prospect of lifting the need for visas between Hungary and Austria?

J. K.: We had been conducting talks for many years, well before the Helsinki Conference, and have put the results into effect. This time we have indeed touched upon a number of important questions of Hungarian–Austrian relations. We referred to the Helsinki Conference specifically because the measures which we have taken and intend to take in the future to improve Austro–Hungarian relations are in full harmony with the Helsinki recommendations and with their spirit.

The question of visas directly affects large-scale foreign travel by our citizens and in particular travel between Hungary and Austria. We had tried to promote the increase of tourism and mutual visits to different countries on a large scale already a good few years before the Helsinki Conference. I will also tell you that we were led primarily by political considerations. First of all we wanted to help people to get to know the neighbouring countries better. When we decided to lift earlier restrictions on foreign travel, we were also thinking of the fact that Hungary had a very bad press in Western Europe at the end of the fifties and at the beginning of the sixties. Well, we changed the earlier practice and a fairly busy tourist traffic started with the Western European countries. This produced political gains for us. Hungarian citizens who earlier had had no opportunity to travel to any of the Western European countries can now go there. And the several hundred thousand Hungarian citizens who annually spend their holidays in Western European countries return with a good feeling. They realize that the streets are not paved with gold in the developed West European capitalist countries, either. They see phenomena which they have already forgotten about at home in Hungary. They see, for example, unemployment and the resulting fear and insecurity. Then they see a number of new products which perhaps they could not have seen earlier; but now they know that all this is available at home in Hungary too and perhaps at a cheaper price than in the shops of West European countries.

Our impressions of West European tourists in Hungary are very good. I don't know exactly what the dialectical relationship is between the press and tourism, but there are two things we have experienced. The first is that a tourist arriving in Hungary from Western Europe is usually pleasantly surprised, because no matter how critically he looks at things, his experiences are necessarily better than what he had been led to believe by what he read in the Western European capitalist press. The other thing is, and this is probably connected with the first: the assessment of Hungary in the Western European press has improved since tourism has increased. For not even those with the worst intentions can describe what is diametrically opposed to what millions of Western European citizens can see with their own eyes.

Within the tourism with Western European countries Hungarian–Austrian tourism is one of the most significant. Hundreds of thousands of citizens from the two countries travel to each other's country and feel mutually at home and comfortable. We have been working hard to achieve this among other things, and in the future will do our best to see that tourism does not shrink but increases further.

But beyond the political implications tourism has an economic aspect, too. We continue an open-door policy in tourism. But we are unable as yet to utilize tourism economically, we are just learning to do that. If we had as much experience in the tourist field as Austria and if we were able to generate as great a proportion of our national income from tourism as Austria can, then we, too, would have considerably wider tourism. It is easy to understand that Hungary, where tourism on a large scale goes back only a few years, is not prepared economically. Since we would like to ensure an appropriate level of services, we have been rapidly developing hotels and other tourism and catering facilities, almost at a forced rate.

In principle we are in favour of lifting visa obligations between Hungary and Austria. But we are still at a disadvantage with regards to certain economic conditions. We have to examine these conditions together with our Austrian partners. But the situation is ripening and the time is near when the need for visas between the two countries can be abolished.

Correspondent of PRAVDA: What are the prospects for the so-called small European countries in the political, economic and cultural field following the Helsinki Conference?

J. K.: Both Austria and Hungary were victims of the Second World War. Both countries lost many lives and suffered great economic damage, regrettably not in the service of a good cause. If there is a nation which desires peace, then it is the Hungarian nation. I believe the same can be said of the Austrian people. This is manifested in the policy of the Austrian state which has declared eternal neutrality.

The Hungarian state was established more than a thousand years ago. It seems that our legendary leader, Árpád[33], whom we call the Founder, in many respects chose a good place for the Hungarian people. The climate is good, the country is beautiful, for us the most beautiful in the world. But I think, in one respect Árpád had not enough foresight. This place does have a drawback: it is situated at the crossroads of marching armies. Possibly the Austrians think similarly about their own country. It is beautiful, for them probably the most beautiful in the world, but Austria, too, is quite a "busy" place. I believe it requires little proof that the Hungarian people, and, I think, the Austrian people, too, want peace most of all. In our opinion it is a further, and this time a political reason, that the Hungarian people do have a splendid programme, the programme of building a developed socialist society, and realize that peace is required above all. Therefore Hungary is without any doubt interested in the practical implementation of the Helsinki recommendations and I think that goes for Austria, too.

I want to mention another factor. It is a characteristic of Hungary not only that she is a small country, but also that she is poor in raw materials and energy. Therefore she is interested in developing international economic relations to a significant degree. In certain respects we envy countries where only six per cent of the national income depends on international trade. Forty-five per cent of the national income of the Hungarian People's Republic is realized in the sphere of international trade. One of the items of the recommendations approved in Helsinki which is of vital importance to us prescribed the wide expansion of mutually advantageous economic relations which satisfy mutual interests.

This is another reason why we attach great expectations to the recommendations of the Helsinki Conference: we have an interest in their implementation, we are making efforts to realize them and we wholeheartedly support all international efforts which serve this aim.

Press Conference in Rome

JUNE 1977

I am glad to have this opportunity during my visit to Italy to meet representatives of the press, radio and television. I greet you, the honoured representatives of the Italian and international press, and I am glad to have this opportunity to thank the Italian Press for the equitable job they have done in connection with my present visit. True, one of the papers wrote of me that I was a slave of compromise, but I would like to say that I did not find this derogatory. For a long time I have supported any compromise which promotes the cause for which I have worked and struggled.

As you know, I have come to visit Italy at the invitation of the Prime Minister of the Italian Republic. Recent healthy developments in the relations between the Hungarian People's Republic and the Italian Republic have created a favourable ground for this visit and there is every opportunity for the further diversified development of this relationship in the future.

Now that the official programme is over, I can say with satisfaction that at our talks with the esteemed leaders of the Italian Republic, which were conducted in a cordial atmosphere, there were mutual efforts to deepen and expand cooperation between the two countries and to make better use of the existing opportunities.

It is my conviction that the development of Hungarian–Italian relations serves the interests of both peoples well, enhances the cause of peace and contributes to peaceful coexistence between countries with different social systems and to the consolidation of détente.

As is known, this morning I called on Pope Paul VI in the Vatican and had a useful exchange of views with him on current international questions, on the relationship between the Hungarian state and the Church, and on relations between the Hungarian People's Republic and the Vatican.

Correspondent of NÉPSZABADSÁG: At the end of your official visit, how do you assess the results of the talks and what possibilities do you see for the further diverse development of Hungarian–Italian relations?

JÁNOS KÁDÁR: I consider my visit to be a success. During the short time available, I met several leaders of political life in the Italian Republic and it was my impression that both sides want to develop Hungarian–Italian relations in a diversity of fields. This applies to interstate and political relations, to economic cooperation, to the sphere of culture, to the widest possible contacts between citizens of each country, to tourism, and to other similar areas. We both found that we have very good opportunities to develop our relations further in many ways. I am convinced that making good use of these favourable opportunities suits the interests of both peoples and of both countries.

I attach great significance to the fact that although we are two countries belonging to different systems of alliance there is nevertheless the opportunity for very good cooperation. It is common knowledge that Italy belongs to NATO and the Common Market, while the Hungarian People's Republic belongs to the Warsaw Treaty Organization and the Council for Mutual Economic Assistance. Nonetheless our cooperation is a good practical example of cooperation and peaceful coexistence between countries with different social systems.

Correspondent of CORRIERE EUROPEO: Can any specific results in economic cooperation be expected as a follow-up to the visit?

J. K.: Talks of the kind we had yesterday and the day before with the leaders of the Republic of Italy usually cannot be aimed at discussing specifically and in detail individual problems of economic cooperation. We did treat the main areas and subjects, each side asking the other to pay special attention to them. The rest is up to the experts concerned. The Italian leaders promised to encourage the representatives of Italian economic life to seek cooperation. I myself met some of the leaders of economic life. I found a readiness to develop economic relations which serve our mutual interests. There was a positive reception for our proposal that we should not limit Hungarian–Italian relations simply to the exchange of goods, that is, to selling and buying, but that we should take every step, beginning with scientific research, to seek out the opportunities for more advanced economic cooperation. Examples are (for instance) production cooperation or even Hungarian–Italian cooperation on third markets. I am sure that our present talks – and not least the constructive contribution by the press – will give a new impetus and a new stimulus to Hungarian–Italian economic relations. And since the interests are mutual, I am certain that the subjects discussed here will soon enter the phase of actual realization.

Correspondent of OSSERVATORE ROMANO: How do you assess the relationship between the Hungarian state and the Church, and can further developments in these relations be expected following this visit?

J. K.: I think you know my ideology, so you will accept my opinion as objective: the Roman Catholic Church is a significant moral factor. The Vatican is one of the smallest states of the world in respect of area and population – one which has no armed forces but does have political weight. I considered it was only proper for me to visit Pope Paul VI when I came to Rome. I may say that I gained some very good impressions during the few hours I spent in the Vatican. I thought it was permissible and proper for me to thank the Pope for the efforts he and the Vatican are making for the cause of peace, for peaceful coexistence, for détente and particularly for the Helsinki agreement. I made the request that we should prepare for Belgrade in the same spirit. I had in mind the well-known fact that more people listen to the Pope and to the Vatican than there are Vatican citizens.

In Pope Paul VI's assessment, our meeting today was a significant event in our relations: it completed the process of settling relations between the Catholic Church and the Hungarian state, and this is to be welcomed. Personally I am convinced that the socialist Hungarian state, the Hungarian People's Republic, will last for a great many generations and that the churches will also exist for generations.

We consider it our duty – it is also in our interest – that the relationship between the state and the church be settled. No instrument has yet been invented which can register who is a true believer and who is not. The exact number of believers in Hungary cannot be determined. But there certainly are religious people there. A sharp confrontation between state and the Church would cause them insoluble problems of conscience. I can say that there is no such dilemma in Hungary.

True, we have worked for many years with the representatives of the Vatican to settle the relations between the state and the Roman Catholic Church in Hungary. But believers in our country are not faced with a moral dilemma. We do not interfere with the free exercise of religion and the life of the churches. Everyone does as he deems fit: if he wants to, he goes to Mass or to a religious service on Sunday; this does not bring him into conflict with the state.

The Hungarian spokesmen of the Roman Catholic Church have officially declared that they will observe the constitutional law of the Hungarian People's Republic and that they will do what they can to support the constructive plans of the Hungarian people. We ask nothing more from the people of the Church.

I thanked the representatives of the Pope and, of course, the Pope himself for their efforts to settle our relations. We spoke with mutual satisfaction of our present relationship. Of course, difficult problems sometimes come up during negotiations, talks last for a long time and agreement is reached slowly. But I was glad to be able to say that both sides have been scrupulous in carrying out whatever we had reached agreement on. We were both able to register it with satisfaction that our intentions coincided: the Vatican and the government of the Hungarian People's Republic will both strive to continue this favourable process in the future, too. Let us listen to each other, let us take into consideration and respect the other side's interests.

A lasting settlement has been reached in the relationship between Church and state in Hungary.

You will probably understand that, from the point of view of the state, serious questions are often at stake. I myself understand that sometimes things do not look simple from the Church's side either. But we must look further ahead, and we must take general interests into consideration. I have left the Vatican convinced that this is the road we are travelling.

Correspondent of CORRIERE DELLA SERA: What is the situation of the other churches in Hungary?

J. K.: What I have said about the settled state of the relations between state and Church applies to all the Churches operating in Hungary.

During the thirty years which have elapsed since the Liberation, our relation with each other has been settled. The basic principle is the same: the Churches respect the fundamental law of the state, and the state respects the autonomy of the Churches and guarantees freedom of religion.

In Hungary we settled our relations with the Protestant Churches earlier. I am not competent to pass value judgement on Church personalities. Cardinal Mindszenty played a considerable part in making the relationship between the Hungarian state and the Roman Catholic Church in Hungary complicated and difficult. Probably this was why our relationship with the Catholic Church was the last to be settled. But about two years ago our relationship was normalized, and this is very important and beneficial for us.

There are no special disputes today with any of the Churches. Of course, problems may always arise and some certainly do arise. Such things occur between partners even in the best of families. Tolerance is the most effective recipe in this respect, too. To settle matters one must understand the other partner. I am very confident that as we have no problems at present, we shall have no serious conflicts with any of the Churches in Hungary in the future, either.

Correspondent of LA NAZIONE of Florence and IL RESTO DEL CARLINO of Bologna: Do the socialist countries coordinate their policies on Church affairs?

J. K.: I would not say that they are coordinated, but they do exchange experiences from time to time, since an important social matter is concerned. The socialist countries generally display an interest in the experiences of Hungary, and we are glad to make these available to them. But each country handles the affairs pertaining to the Churches—just as it does other problems—by itself as it sees fit.

The representative of ITALIAN TELEVISION: The great work done in Hungary in twenty years is well known; it is known that human rights are taken very seriously in Hungary and also that Hungary is an independent country. After these preliminaries I ask whether the stationing of Soviet troops in Hungary could still be regarded as temporary?

J. K.: I have already had the privilege of encountering this question. I repeat what I have already stated on several occasions, that the stay of Soviet troops in Hungary is temporary. Right now I am unable to tell you exactly for how long. That depends on international détente, on trends in the international situation, and is related to the existence of NATO. It is not my habit to make prophecies, and I do not wish to do so now, but no one should count on people's power becoming imperilled following the withdrawal of the Soviet troops temporarily stationed in Hungary. The socialist system is firmly founded and enjoys the support of the entire people.

As for the observance of human rights: we do not believe that what we have achieved so far is ideal; our aim and task is to develop socialist democracy further. Slogans about human rights are very much in fashion nowadays. I myself could make a long list of the fundamental human rights, for example the right to life and to work, the right of women and of young people to equal wages, the right to free medical care for all citizens, the right to recreational holidays, and several other rights which exist in our country not only on paper but are guaranteed in practice. Other countries perhaps can refer to other human rights.

There is freedom of opinion in our country; we are not afraid of people's views and opinions, in fact we seek them on every possible occasion. Human rights do not pose an internal problem. But when they are raised as a pretext to interfere in our internal affairs, we are compelled to repudiate such attempts. We hold that whoever is for the fullest possible observation of human rights should support détente, disarmament and security. Then we shall be able to solve the problems facing us better, more smoothly more easily and faster. The road of progress leads to the universal recognition of the need to observe human rights. This depends on the spread of détente and on states feeling that they are no longer threatened.

The correspondent of NEWSWEEK: Can the journalists who reported on the events of 1956 in Hungary go back to Hungary at any time, even as ordinary tourists?

J. K.: The lessons of history must be kept in mind and taken into consideration. That is what we are doing. As I have just been to the Vatican, appropriately the biblical story of Lot's wife comes to my mind for it expresses profound human wisdom. Namely, that he who wants to live and to go forward, should look forward and not back. For Lot's wife looked back and became a pillar of salt.

The foreign journalists who reported on Hungary in 1956 can generally and in principle return to the country. In the dramatic days of 1956 a number of Hungarian journalists wrote many things, not all of which they would have liked to identify themselves with, say, a year later. I myself think that it is not worth looking into who wrote what ten or twenty years ago, whether we speak about people of the Hungarian or of the foreign press. What is important is what they write today, whether they contribute to the cause of progress. We have a human memory, but not a blacklist of foreign journalists.

The correspondent of IL MESSAGERO: Do you maintain the remark you made at the Vienna press conference that you did not agree that the concept of "Eurocommunism" was an anticommunist one?

J. K.: As far as my opinion on "Eurocommunism" is concerned: I went to school a long time ago, but in those days we learned in geography that, from the west, Europe stretched from the shores of the Atlantic Ocean to the Ural Mountains. Therefore the Communist Party of the Soviet Union is just as much a component and a part of the European Communist movement as let us say the Polish United Workers' Party, the German Socialist Unity Party, the German Communist Party, the French Communist Party, and so on, that is all the European Communist and workers' parties. I commend this fact to your attention.

The term "Eurocommunism" is often used nowadays in respect of certain Western European parties. In our view identical situations create similarities among certain parties. Those parties are fighting for a socialist future under the conditions of capitalism, under the dictatorship of monopoly capital. It is only natural under the circumstances. It is just as natural that they seek their own roads to social liberation in accordance with the historical past and social conditions of their society. This is not only their privilege, but also their duty; we do not argue about it and we cannot even have anything to say about it. For, so to speak, it is a matter in their own competence what kind of a road they are looking for to win liberty for the working people.

The position taken by some parties regarding the dictatorship of the proletariat and pluralist socialism did, of course, produce reverberations within the world Communist movement. Marxist–Leninist theory clearly charts the road of social progress. It states unequivocally that in accordance with the laws of social development all peoples shall inevitably embark on the road of socialism.

This can, however, take place in a great many different ways. Even up till now, the socialist revolutions have each triumphed in different ways in accordance with the historical development and specific characteristics of the countries concerned. As a result of the victory of the Great October Socialist Revolution, a dictatorship of the proletariat was established in Tsarist Russia. Then people's democratic regimes also filling the role of the dictatorship of the proletariat were established.

I do not want to make *ex cathedra* statements. On my own part I wish the Communist and workers' parties struggling and working in the capitalist countries a great deal of success in carrying the struggle against the dictatorship of monopoly capital on to victory, in rallying the working people and the democratic forces, and — I say this, as my personal opinion, if you like — whether with a proletarian dictatorship or without, by way of a pluralist or of some other kind of socialism — they should open up the socialist road to their peoples.

It is my conviction that mutual and full solidarity must and will prevail among all the Communist and workers' parties of Europe working either in socialist or Western European capitalist countries, and that no one will be able to disrupt this solidarity.

The representative of HUNGARIAN TELEVISION: What obstacles must be removed in the economic relations between member states of CMEA and the Common Market for the development of mutually advantageous cooperation?

J. K.: A few years ago the Hungarian side noted with regret that the dynamic development of Hungarian–Italian relations was halted – primarily because of certain restrictions applied by the Common Market. In this respect the Council of Mutual Economic Assistance is an organization of a different character from the Common Market; it does not limit or regulate the economic transactions of member states with various countries.

We agree that the building of contacts between the CMEA and the Common Market must be continued. It would be desirable to work out and conclude agreements between the two economic groupings which do not slow down but ease and promote the economic cooperation of member countries and the expansion of trade. This coincides with the universal interests of the peoples. Peaceful coexistence makes it imperative that fruitful economic relations develop between the different countries. As I have said, we were in agreement with our Italian partners in this respect.

Hungary is one of the small countries. Our economic conditions make us largely dependent on the development of international economic relations, which we are going to pursue with particular care in our Italian relations.

The correspondent of PAESE SERA: What can Italy and Hungary do together to contribute to the success of the Belgrade Conference?

J. K.: On the basis of our current talks it is my impression that the approach to issues from the Hungarian and Italian sides are similar. Responsible Italian spokesmen have stated that the continuation of détente is in the interests of the Italian people and of the Republic of Italy. We have also established that we are in favour of handling the Helsinki recommendations as an integrated whole. The Belgrade meeting must be a constructive conference which promotes the further practical realization of the Helsinki recommendations.

Answers to the Questions of the "Frankfurter Rundschau"

JULY 1977

QUESTION: Speaking of yourself, you once said that you were not an enthusiastic traveller in political matters. As you go to Bonn on one of your rare visits to the West, what significance do you attribute to this visit in respect of European politics, and what does it promise you specifically in the field of Hungarian–West German relations?

JÁNOS KÁDÁR: I have indeed said that I am not an enthusiastic traveller; but I have also said that I will go everywhere where I can serve a good purpose. I regard the visit to the Federal Republic of Germany which is going to take place in the next few days as a necessary step promising development in the relations between the two countries and peoples.

The fact that the relations between the Hungarian People's Republic and the Federal Republic of Germany are settled is a favourable basis for this visit, and we believe that there is an opportunity to develop our bilateral relations further in the field of state, political and economic life, in science, culture, tourism and other areas.

The cooperation between the Hungarian People's Republic and the Federal Republic of Germany can serve as a good, practical, example of cooperation and peaceful coexistence between countries with different social systems belonging to different alliance systems and to different economic groupings; thereby the two countries can contribute to the improvement of the international atmosphere and to the strengthening of détente.

QUESTION: Hungarian policy several times pointed to the dialogue between the two world powers, the Soviet Union and the United States of America, as a most important precondition and one of the first order for the policy of détente. How do you see the prospects of this policy in the light of the activities to date of the new American president, Mr. Carter?

J. K.: During the past half a century we have been the suffering protagonists of the various hot and cold wars, while in recent years we have been witnessing détente. It is certain that the peoples who have lived through the wars are in favour of a halt in the arms race and the consolidation of détente.

It is widely known that after President Carter and the new American administration entered office there was a halt in the very important Soviet–American talks. The peace policy of the Soviet Union and her efforts for a reasonable agreement have not changed. Reality and the fundamental interests of the peoples cannot be disregarded by any responsible politician, including the President of the United States of America. We hope that sobriety will prevail and that the difficulties which have emerged in the relationship between the Soviet Union and the United States will prove to be temporary.

QUESTION: What are the tasks of the medium-sized and smaller states alongside the dialogue of the world powers; what is Hungary's role in East–West relations, on which one Western theory holds that her very careful faithfulness to her alliance in foreign policy ensures her greater room to manoeuvre in domestic policy?

J. K.: It is a reality of our age that the Soviet Union, the United States and a few other large states carry the greatest responsibility for the way the international situation evolves. This however does not mean at all that the medium-sized and small states could not and do not play an important role in deepening and consolidating the process of détente. I would go even further: it is simply unimaginable without them. Let us only think of the Helsinki Conference, the results of which are the fruit of the joint efforts of 35 large, medium-sized and small states.

As for us, Hungarians, we do not judge the foreign policies of the various states by the country's size. Our starting point is the extent and manner in which they contribute to international détente and the consolidation of peace and security. Accordingly the Hungarian People's Republic is aware of her own responsibility, too, and has put forward a number of proposals to the governments of the European capitalist states aimed at deepening détente and confidence and, implementing the Helsinki recommendations.

As is known, in all states foreign policy is eventually determined by domestic policy. Accordingly, we do not have two policies either; our domestic and foreign policies are unified; our domestic policy, our work of socialist construction, unequivocally demands the consolidation of international peace and security and the development of cooperation with all states and peoples. Therefore if anyone wants to get to know Hungary without prejudice, he can easily see that our foreign policy, our national activities, stem from the essence of our socialist system and are in complete harmony with the aims of our work of construction and with our national interests. The basic essence of our commitment to our alliance is to create favourable international conditions for our work of construction, for the welfare of the Hungarian people, for the full predominance of our national interests in close cooperation with the other socialist countries, and simultaneously to serve the universal interests of the peoples.

QUESTION: In relation to human rights, so much referred to on the eve of the preparatory conference in Belgrade, you have reasoned that the Helsinki Final Act with its three baskets must be handled as a unified whole. Does this mean that a greater rapprochement in respect of questions related to Basket Three can only be imagined if there are simultaneous advances in the field of political security and economic cooperation?

J. K.: Experiences so far give unequivocal evidence that to handle the Final Act as a unified whole is the only way to fair and well-intentioned implementation, and not the opposite, the arbitrary selection and over-emphasis of certain questions. We believe that the various parts of the Final Act are organically interlinked and simultaneous and equal attention must be paid to the implementation of each and every provision.

Our experiences of recent years have proved that the normalization of diplomatic and political relations between states, and the development of economic relations, are followed by the widening and extension of cultural and humanitarian contacts without anyone setting it as a precondition. There are numerous such examples in our relations with the Federal Republic of Germany.

It is well known that the Helsinki Conference itself, which is of historic significance, was created by the alleviation of the cold war atmosphere, the appearance of confidence, and the efforts of 35 states to draw close together and to reach agreement. However, by now facts show unequivocally that the implementation of the provisions of the Final Act is to a decisive degree influenced by the further strengthening of political confidence and the shaping of political relations between states. At the same time, the non-selective, correct implementation of the provisions of the Final Act enhances the strengthening of confidence, too.

QUESTION: In contrast to a few other states, Hungary has remained singularly free of the phenomenon of explicitly political dissent. How can this surprising phenomenon be explained in view of the complicated situation in which you embarked on leadership?

J. K.: We have never said that everybody agrees with everything in Hungary. We consider it natural that there are some who do not or only partly agree with us on certain issues. Everyone may hold a different view on one condition: respect for our laws. In the various forums of our public life, we listen to people's opinions and we take them into consideration to a great extent in our political decisions.

It is indeed true that it was a long road to the present balanced, calm, domestic political situation. We embarked on the work of overcoming the difficulties of the past and its complicated conditions after a great shock and a historical trial. But we have learned from our own losses and we have not forgotten what we have learned.

Our starting point was, and we stick to this even today, that the most important precondition of successful work is the establishment and development of mutual trust between the party and the people. In resolving various questions, in determining the rate of socialist construction, we take into consideration the fact that we can only set aims which are understood and consciously supported by the great majority of the public. In the last twenty years we have tried to avoid the shocks which can be avoided and we unceasingly work to make the practice of socialism good for the whole people and within that for each individual, for each of the country's citizens. It was in this way and for this reason that our people have been forged together into a socialist national unity, with all progressive, patriotic, creative forces ready to work for the community irrespective of ideology.

In comparison with what was the case more than twenty years ago the situation has indeed changed fundamentally. Levelheadedness, patience and a great deal of work were necessary. During this time the party and the leadership of the country were doing their own work, but recognition and tribute for the development must be accorded to the Hungarian working class, to the Hungarian peasantry who embarked on a socialist path, to Hungarian intellectuals who displayed a high degree of responsibility, and to our people. Today, the Hungarian people, together with the people of countries building Communism and socialism, are consistently advancing on the road they have chosen, the road of building a developed socialist society.

QUESTION: With the appearance of Eurocommunism it seems that the question of the legitimacy of a separate national road in the building of socialism and of the primacy of internationally binding conformity has entered a new phase. How do you view Eurocommunism after your recent trip to Italy and how do you see its significance in the development of Communism?

J. K.: My visit to Italy has not changed the opinion which I put forward in respect of the nowadays fashionable expression "Eurocommunism".

In respect of the phenomenon called "Eurocommunism", it is evident that there are hostile factors opposing the working class movement which would like to use this notion to drive a wedge between certain West European Communist parties and the Communist parties of the Soviet Union and the socialist countries. Everything must be and will be done to frustrate this attempt.

As for the essence of the thing, the desire for change is strengthening in the peoples of Western Europe and the Communist parties are searching for the best way to progress and social development leading to socialism. This is not only a right but also a duty of Communist parties. It is the duty of each party to take into consideration the traditions of the historical path of their people, the characteristics of the given country and society and at the same time the experiences of the international working class movement. This is not Eurocommunism, this has always been so; this is how it is, and it is how it will be in the life of all Communist parties whatever part of the globe, in whichever country they work. A new element in the situation is, and it is making many people nervous, that there is an upswing in the revolutionary movement in Western Europe and a strengthening of the Left. Hungarian Communists heartily welcome this and are in solidarity with the struggles which are being waged by the Western European Communist parties who represent the interests of the working masses for progress and social transformation. And if you have raised this question in respect of my visit to Italy, let me tell you that at the meeting with Comrades Luigi Longo and Enrico Berlinguer, the leaders of the Italian Communist Party, we were able to establish with mutual satisfaction that the relations between the Hungarian Socialist Workers' Party and the Communist Party of Italy are free of disturbance and the two fraternal parties are linked together by the ideals of internationalism and mutual solidarity.

QUESTION: Hungarian newspapers have acknowledged that Communism and political pluralism are reconcilable, although not for Hungary. Would this, in your opinion, apply not only to the phase of the acquisition of power, but also to the phase of the change of power, so that in the system of political pluralism the Communist parties in government would be obliged to return executive power after losing elections? How could this be reconciled with the claim to represent a historical progress?

J. K.: First of all I will deal with the introductory sentence of the question. There was a multi-party system in Hungary after 1945. Those who know the history of our country are probably aware of this and of how historically the one-party system emerged in Hungary. Our experience has convinced us that neither the one-party, nor the two-party, nor the multi-party system are criteria for either socialism or bourgeois democracy. There was a multi-party system in Hungary before the Liberation. Yet, who could say that that made the Horthyite Fascist system democratic?

In some of the newly established socialist countries there are one party systems, and multi-party systems in others. This proves that it is not a question of principle but a practical, political question, depending on historical development.

Within the pluralist political systems of Western European countries it is not we who are competent in the methods of the transfer of power, but the Communist and other left-wing parties in a given country.

Practice is always the test of theory. Another question arises therefore which is more timely and exciting than the case which you have suggested. Do the forces holding executive power today consider it their duty to transfer this power to the left-wing progressive democratic parties, if the majority of the people supported them with their votes in a coming election?

QUESTION: The normalization of European conditions through the Conference on Security and Cooperation in Europe and through the *Ost-politik* of Bonn has made lasting changes in the political climate on our continent. In the context of this development, do you see a possibility that the question of the withdrawal of Soviet troops stationed in Hungary will come on the agenda?

J. K.: I agree that positive development has taken place on our continent. The political climate has significantly improved, particularly in comparison with the years of the cold war. At the same time I believe that we still have to do a lot to create mutual confidence and genuinely stable relations ensuring political and military security alike.

The temporary stationing of Soviet troops in Hungary is dependent on this international situation. The troops of the Soviet armed forces stationed in Hungary fulfil jointly coordinated and determined tasks in cooperation with the Hungarian armed forces within the framework of the Warsaw Treaty, for the defense of the peace and security of the peoples of the socialist countries.

The usage of the word "temporary" expresses our conviction that the process of détente and the development of the international situation will reach a stage when, among measures guaranteeing political and military détente, the withdrawal of military units stationed abroad can take place, as can the simultaneous disbanding of the two military alliances, NATO and the Warsaw Treaty.

QUESTION: During their history, the Hungarian people have lost the opportunity of national self-fulfilment as a unified state. Hungarian minorities living in every neighbouring country are a result of this. Do you believe that peoples can give up their demand for a nationally unified state and are the Hungarians reconciled to this? What is the position of the Hungarian minorities and what can Hungary do to improve their situation?

J. K.: History has resulted in a large number of ethnic fragments living beyond the borders of given countries, not only in Europe, but in many other parts of the world. Great attention from the governments of the countries involved is needed to solve the resulting problems and it also places a great responsibility on their shoulders.

In the 20th century the nationality question cannot be resolved by the methods of the 19th century. In Europe today the feasible way is the development of the cooperation of peoples. The fate of the minority cannot be separated from that of the majority. The nationality question will be finally settled by socialism, by ensuring free development for the whole society, that is including the national minorities. In present-day Europe it is not the citation of "the glorious past of bygone days" which constitutes a solution for the problems of nations and national minorities but the application of the lessons of history. The anti-national revanchist policy of the former ruling classes, professing hate against other nations, caused immeasurable harm, first of all to the Hungarian people themselves, and almost resulted in the destruction of the whole nation. Our government is not following this path. Our ambition is to provide a new national prosperity for our people and of course to the national minorities living in our country; while advancing on the road to socialism our aim is that the national minorities living in Hungary and in the neighbouring countries should be more and more a bridge between our countries and peoples.

It is common knowledge that many Hungarians live not only in neighbouring countries, but also in a number of countries in Europe and overseas. It is part of the official policy of the Hungarian People's Republic that the assimilation of Hungarians living beyond our borders into the life of the given country is considered natural; at the same time love for the homeland and the old country is nurtured within the limits of what is permissible and possible. This purpose is served by the promotion of travel and visits, the development of cultural relations and the nurturing of ethnic traditions on the basis of agreements concluded with many different states. The signatories of the Helsinki Document were right to agree that one of the preconditions for tranquillity and security is the inviolability of present borders. We, on our part, also expressed our conviction at this historically significant conference that this principle corresponds to the interests of the participating 35 states and adherence to it will ensure peace.

QUESTION: On one occasion looking back at the events of 1956, which you had called a national tragedy, you spoke of the "spiritual torment" of politicians which was not understood by the majority of people. Two rather personal questions in this connection: which political decision caused the greatest "spiritual torment" during your long political career and what do you consider the greatest achievement of your policy?

J. K.: The Communist Party struggles and works for the masses. In our country it also carries the responsibility of government. For this reason, Communist leaders, myself among them, are aware that all important decisions have an effect on how the life of the masses develops. So the great decisions always mean a question of conscience, or to use your expression, "spiritual torment", for a leader. But I would rather call it the weight of responsibility for a decision. I myself as a convinced Communist, have been doing political work, that is work demanding a great degree of responsibility, for more than 45 years. The most difficult case is when our decisions are not understood or are not immediately understood by those in whose interest they are being made. During this long period, unfortunately, I have had more than one such case.

I cannot reflect on the greatest achievement of my policy, because nobody is able to judge his own work objectively. I am not pursuing an individual policy, I am working as a member of a collective leading body.

I consider that the greatest achievement of the Hungarian Socialist Workers' Party and of our country's government is that we have solved all basic questions together with the people, so I can say that our most significant achievement is the activity, the readiness and consensus, with which our people solve the everyday domestic and international tasks in the work of building socialism.

Address at the April 1978 Session of the Central Committee

At this session today the Central Committee wishes to fulfil the obligation undertaken at our Congress. Allow me to remind you, comrades, of the Central Committee declaration at the Congress, in which we undertook to survey, at more or less the half-way stage, how the resolutions adopted by the Congress were being implemented. Three years have elapsed since that Congress, and the next is two years away. It is my belief, therefore, that we are within the appointed time-limit, since intensive preparations for this session have been going on for some eight months.

The Central Committee executive has chosen to prepare this session in a way which will enable the Central Committee to examine important questions on the basis of social reality and facts, instead of wishes and subjective ideas. This is why the party's medium-level bodies—the Budapest Party Committee and the county party committees—were asked to assess how the implementation of the adopted Congress resolutions was going by analyzing both the main general issues and their own specific areas, without previous conclusions and instructions from the centre. This assessment has been carried out in a very thorough and responsible manner.

The preparations were even more comprehensive because the annual report-back meetings of the party branch organizations served this same purpose; they not only considered their own work but also assessed the overall tasks more comprehensively. Apart from this, the Political Committee asked the Central Control Committee, the Central Council of Hungarian Trade Unions and the Council of Ministers to draw up their own balance-sheet and to submit their conclusions to the Central Committee. Thus the Political Committee prepared its report to the Central Committee taking the opinions asked for and collected into consideration, but without itself taking any preliminary stand.

This item on the agenda is headed: "Report on the work completed since Congress and the tasks ahead". On behalf of the Political Committee I report to the esteemed Central Committee that the resolutions adopted by the party's 11th Congress are being successfully implemented in all the main fields of life. Let me say that implementation is in certain cases uneven, partly because of objective difficulties unforeseen at the time of the Congress or which have emerged since then and partly because of subjective reasons. I wish to reiterate, nevertheless, that the most important conclusion, from the general observations of the survey, is that the resolutions of the 11th Congress are being successfully implemented in all the main fields of life. Therefore, the Political Committee recommends the Central Committee to make this known both to the party membership and public opinion throughout the country.

When speaking about the main fields, the Political Committee has in mind not only questions specified and discussed in the draft resolution, but also spheres not mentioned. Some important spheres of social life, party and state work and the activity of the masses have not been included in the written material or, for certain reasons which

I shall explain later, are not discussed in detail. All things considered, however, I would stress that progress has been made in all spheres as a result of our work.

Working class power, our people's democratic system, has strengthened, and people's socialist collaboration and cohesion have developed. Significant positive changes have taken place in the domestic affairs of the country as a result of the ideological and political impact of the party's 11th Congress. The work aimed at implementing the programme announced at the Congress has further consolidated our state, the Hungarian People's Republic and the basis of our economy. All the main spheres of culture — including scientific work, public and general education, the arts and literature — show signs of progress.

We can claim with complete responsibility that advances have been made in all spheres. I would just add that the draft resolution does not contain statistical data concerning our economic development, since they are well known, and in the cultural sphere progress often cannot be measured in terms of statistical data, because of the specific nature of this sphere. Successful work has been carried out in developing our national defences, in the ramifications and rather complex spheres of the activity of the Ministry of Home Affairs, and in the workers' militia. The socialist brigade movement has also yielded excellent results. An example which illustrates these results is the socialist work emulation carried out to commemorate the 60th anniversary of the Great October Socialist Revolution. Fine work has been done in the party's youth organization, the mass organizations and mass movements too. Or, in a nutshell, significant, worthy results have been achieved in all the main spheres.

To keep the record straight I should like to mention another matter. The Central Committee executive, and first and foremost the Political Committee, considered at the initial state of the preparations for today's session how the assessment should be carried out. Our sister parties in the other socialist countries have all adopted differing practices. Some have convened a party conference, others have made their assessment at a session of the Central Committee. Seeing that a large-scale party conference allows for a type of debate which may differ from what is required, the Political Committee considered it appropriate to carry out this work at a Central Committee session. Naturally, this explains our decision only as far as procedure is concerned.

Another even more important consideration was the probable result of this stock taking, namely, that no radical or essential alteration was required in the main lines determined by the Congress as regards domestic and foreign policy, economic and social policy, cultural policy and other issues. Since we regard a party conference to be a higher party authority than a session of the Central Committee, and since this matter does not justify a decision by a higher party authority, the Political Committee decided at an early stage not to recommend the convening of a party conference, but considered it would be sufficient and in a way more effective to make this assessment at a session of the Central Committee.

The Political Committee has drawn up a draft resolution and has distributed it among its esteemed members. At this session today our main task is to discuss this written draft resolution. Once accepted, the resolution may also serve as a public stand. The draft resolution contains matters we consider expedient to publish as the Central Committee's standpoint. Therefore we recommend that only a short communiqué be published now about the Central Committee session, while detailed information should be provided in the form of the full text of the resolution adopted by the Central Committee.

In connection with the written draft resolution I wish to add that, as no doubt the comrades also realized when they read it, this document does not cover everything. As I have said earlier, the proposal does not deal with party work and many important questions of public life. The principle governing this draft resolution is that no second, complementary congressional stand is needed. The aim of the Central Committee resolution is to evaluate the work done to date and to call attention to tasks which require the most effective endeavours in order to implement the resolutions of the 11th Congress before the next Congress. This explains the choice of subjects.

Comrades will have observed an important feature of the draft resolution: although the real situation indicates that the general balance is positive, this document is mostly devoted to the discussion of problems. Furthermore, it offers a brief but serious self-criticism on the part of the Central Committee, which, in drawing up the balance of its own activity, states that its work is reflected in achievements and shortcomings alike. I believe this self-critical tone is expedient and correct.

Still on the subject of the draft resolution allow me to mention yet another of its constituents: it contains extremely important questions concerning the whole of society, which have not yet been the subject of decisions by the Central Committee. For instance, the long-term development of the price system, a subject I shall come back to later on. The Political Committee, therefore, submits the inclusion of this in the resolution for consideration, since without discussing this subject, our session today cannot consider the work performed since the party's 11th Congress and the tasks ahead in a responsible fashion. If the Central Committee should find it to be a matter of such importance that it wishes to examine it in future, the open policy of the party makes it imperative that, rather than concealing it, we should refer to it as one of the significant problems of our country's economic and social life in the party's public declaration.

The overall tone of the draft resolution is, of course, optimistic. This is necessary and well-founded. The draft resolution can justifiably state that we have created or can create in the time left the conditions required for the successful implementation of the resolutions adopted by the 11th Congress. So much about the document.

Together with the draft resolution, the members of the Central Committee have received a supplementary summary which faithfully reflects the observations made by the Budapest Party Committee and the county party committees. They speak with appreciation about the party's general activity, about the work of the Central Committee and the central bodies, but they also point to the great number of shortcomings in our work — in a comradely manner, of course. We thought it right and proper to give the Central Committee, with the best intentions, a true picture of the opinion of the party's main leading bodies concerning the implementation of the resolutions adopted by the last party Congress.

Although this assessment is first and foremost intended to provide the Central Committee with information, every department of the Central Committee must study and take note of the most important questions raised, so as to keep in evidence all that has to be done about them, and to solve them satisfactorily through the work of the central or local bodies. This is what we think about the series of questions collected in the supplement.

Finally allow me to say a few words about the aim of this introductory address. The written draft resolution proposes that the Central Committee should not deal with all the questions of the Congress one by one in its resolution, since at the moment this would not help our work sufficiently. During my consultations with the Political Committee on the topics I should deal with in my address, we agreed that I would not introduce the draft resolution item by item, because everyone has a written copy of it. So, please, regard this document as the basis of our discussion. Allow me to touch upon just some of the themes contained in it, rather as a means of argumentation, justification and perhaps amplification. Therefore I beg your pardon in advance for not mentioning all the topics.

First I propose to say a few words about the conclusions of the draft resolution because these are, in fact, the most essential conclusions of the document. I repeat these in order to call attention to them.

— The first main conclusion to be corroborated was that the party resolutions and programme adopted by the 11th Congress have stood the test of time.

— Secondly, Hungarian public opinion, our party membership, the working class, together with our people, and international public opinion — here I am referring primarily to our fraternal parties — welcomed the resolutions adopted by the Congress when they were made public. The declared programme of our party was received with similar enthusiasm. I mention this because it is no trifling matter. The written statement bears ample witness to how Hungarian public opinion received the documents of the 11th Congress. Therefore it seems expedient that the Central Committee should now return to it, openly appreciating the attitude to the Congress of our mass organizations, mass movements and the most varied factors of our society.

As far as the international reception is concerned, comrades will no doubt recall that the socialist countries were represented by top level delegations which addressed the 11th Congress. The fact that the 11th Congress was hailed, particularly by the Communist Party of the Soviet Union, as a truly Marxist–Leninist party congress and that this view was given serious and repeated expression after the event is no small recognition for us. The resolution and the programme were also referred to in terms of praise. To my way of thinking it is good for us to know that the Hungarian Socialist Workers' Party is not the sole repository of Marxist–Leninist truth. But it is our conviction and intention to try and follow a truly Marxist–Leninist line, and the opinion of our brother parties is undoubtedly a test of this. The opinion of our fraternal parties confirms our confidence in ourselves and in our views.

— Our third conclusion is that following the Congress, the Central Committee and its executive, the government and the social bodies took up the important matters raised by the Congress which required further, specific decisions. Experience has corroborated that these decisions were correct and helped the practical implementation of the Congress resolutions.

Considering the guidelines of the Congress as well as the resolutions of the Central Committee which gave them substance, the fourth main conclusion is that we are pleased and satisfied to acknowledge that the party membership and our whole nation not only welcomed the stands taken by the Congress and the resolutions and decisions complementing them, but actively supported their implementation. Consequently, our country has gone from strength to strength, our party and nation have gained greater international prestige.

International respect for the Hungarian Socialist Workers' Party has increased among those whose opinion is vital to us. The last three years have witnessed talks between our party and 65 fraternal parties. I don't think it is necessary to give details of these now. The party's sound, principled and at the same time practical, realistic and flexible policy has met with increasing recognition since the 11th Congress. Similar features characterize the international relations of our mass organizations and mass movements; international recognition of them has also grown by virtue of the work they have carried out in the spirit of the 11th Congress.

The World Federation of Trade Unions is at present in session in Prague. A serious proposal nominating a Hungarian candidate for one of the top posts of the world federation has been put forward. Need I say more as to the kind of recognition this implies?

Comrades will, no doubt, have been informed about certain changes in the leadership of the World Federation of Democratic Youth. There the representative of the Chilean Young Communist League was elected president and a candidate from the Hungarian Young Communist League was nominated secretary-general. A whole series of other examples come to mind. In conclusion I can state that the work of Hungarian delegates is valued highly in all spheres of the peace movement, which is at present of vital importance all over the world and which is obviously intensifying the activities carried on in the most varied fields. The same applies to the international activities of Hungarian church representatives, too: prominent Hungarian churchmen take a very positive stand within the great social and international movements, which is very heartening. In a certain way this is also linked with the party's policy and day-to-day practice.

It seems to be superfluous to enlarge upon the improving international reputation which the Hungarian People's Republic has been enjoying as a nation in the years since the Congress. This is also due to the resolutions of the Congress, to our principled, steadfast but nevertheless realistic and flexible policy. I don't want to give any further illustrations.

Yet another extremely important conclusion is that the resolutions and programme adopted by the 11th Congress, as well as the complementary decisions taken and measures introduced by the party, state and social bodies, continue to be completely valid without needing to be changed. The task now is their further, successful, implementation. This needs to be called to the notice of the party membership emphatically and adequately. Some may feel disappointed that now, at this time of assessment, there are no sensational statements. On the other hand, I think it is precisely this lack of sensationalism that is natural and welcome news to our people, our socialist allies and partners. The party shows no signs at all of changing direction as far as national and international activities or methods of work are concerned.

We must refer to the Congress resolutions because they are, by the nature of the subject, of extraordinary weight, and valid not just for today. The Congress resolutions embrace a whole series of tasks which can only be fulfilled with purposeful work over a long period of time. This is all particularly true of the party's programme.

Perhaps it will not be superfluous to recall some of the fundamental stipulations made at the Congress: the fact, for instance, that we are a Marxist–Leninist party, the vanguard of the Hungarian working class, in a period of development when – naturally over a period of historical time – it is becoming the vanguard of the working people. Our state is ruled by working class power, it is a state of the dictatorship of the proletariat, a people's democratic regime, which has gradually developed into a state of the whole population. These significant statements continue to hold good.

The party Congress resolutions, and even more so the programme, contain extremely important and topical statements concerning state ownership and production relations, together with prospects for their further development. These statements are still true, just as they were laid down in the programme at the party Congress.

Before the session I had the opportunity to meet and consult with comrades who had already read the draft resolution. One asked why the draft resolution does not deal with important observations of the Congress such as the development of property and production relations. Indeed it does not deal with these questions, so allow me to explain briefly why not. The programme has been worded clearly and categorically, and covers future prospects in terms of decades. Fundamental changes cannot be expected to show in spheres such as the development of property and production relations in two to two and a half years. Therefore to follow this up is not yet justified. Certain measures necessary for long-term development and rooted in the Congress resolutions have, of course, been introduced and put into effect. Here I am referring, for instance, to the prevention of further fragmentation of landed property belonging to the state and the cooperative farms.

Naturally, all the main aspects of building a developed socialist society featured in the resolutions of the Congress, which are still valid without alteration. The Congress expressed its opinion concerning the guidelines of the fifth Five Year Plan, too. This statement gave a basic definition of the tasks involved in building a developed socialist society during these five years. I must remind you that the guidelines had to be revised to some extent; the fifth Five Year Plan was prepared according to schedule, has been enacted and is being successfully implemented. The implementation of the fifth Five Year Plan with good results continues to be our unaltered task.

Finally, the resolutions of the 11th Congress have stood the test of time; they have proved to be fitting Marxist–Leninist decisions when it came to implementing them too, which makes any alteration unnecessary. And since this is so, it logically follows that questions concerning their implementation are bound to arise regularly. And the questions of implementation are closely connected with the work of the masses, the activity of the cadres and solving the cadre problem.

The above are the main conclusions of the draft resolution. Our activity still relies heavily on making sure that the Congress resolutions are well implemented through the work of the masses, party members and cadres.

struggle, I am merely suggesting that we maintain this two-way sensibility. One must always be sensitive to more than one thing. Let us be sensitive to dogmatic, sectarian views, as well as to revisionist, opportunist, rightist or any other harmful views and attitudes. The Central Committee, its members and in general every public figure must keep this in view.

While on this subject allow me to indulge in a little historical retrospect and illustration: in December 1956 – at the time of the decisive session of the Central Committee – the Central Committee had 23 members. These comrades had had varying experiences. Many were meeting at this session for the first time after a very long time. They were all Communists, but, naturally were all adjusting their views to their own experiences. The 23 of them agreed on two things at the time, I believe: they were the partisans of socialist, Communist principles and were ready to fight for a people's democracy, to maintain and strengthen working class power. This leadership has since then become unified. It was basically this leadership and – let us not beat about the bush – the party's 1957 conference that laid the foundations for our present platform. Those present at that party conference surely remember that sharp clash with the main trend of dogmatism; the reorganized party was free of revisionist elements. The party leadership became more united at the party Conference and subsequently party members naturally followed suit.

I would mention the debates of December 1958 concerning the socialist reorganization of agriculture. We were unified, we all wanted socialism, and yet three, clearly distinct views still confronted one another, although none of the approaches could be said to have been against the socialist reorganization. You may recall the tendency whose representatives asserted that the middle peasants had to be divested of everything they had, and treated hard-heartedly, since that was the only way to create order, so to speak; that was the only way to establish socialism in the countryside. Another trend claimed that the appropriate conditions for the reorganization were lacking, and if fine, large-scale socialist agriculture could not be created, it was better not to begin at all so as not to compromise the principle itself. The Central Committee adopted a resolution at that session and we have recently discussed the achievements of that decision over the last twenty years. Looking back on that session of the Central Committee, I must say it was a momentous session. I mention this because there was a heated debate at that session, a clash of views, and finally a correct decision was made. So we should not be afraid of occasional polemics either. We encourage the nation, the people to discuss, debate; let us take heed of this encouragement too. We should not be afraid sometimes of debating here at our sessions: here we have the right to debate. And if anyone knows a better solution than the one suggested, he should come forward with it, just as he is bound to voice his disagreements.

Of course, we carried on the debate, even after the party's 1957 Conference and the 1958 session of the Central Committee, about the reform of economic management and other issues. That is quite natural. So what should we take heed of today as we debate? Here I am not only talking about those present: we have a considerable number, many thousands of party, state, economic and mass organization activists. Really a lot depends on their behaviour, on how they influence the masses. What I have said concerning our debate also applies to them. We must take care that during the debates no one should designate himself the independent representative of the working class, no one should designate himself the representative of the interests of the peasantry, of the intellectuals. We know anyhow where everybody belongs. No one should persuade himself into believing this theory of separate representation. It is impossible to live and work with such a division of spheres. Everybody should understand that neither the Central Committee nor the Political Committee as corporate bodies, nor their members, can side with the workers or the intellectuals alone. We must side with the workers, peasants, and intellectuals together, that is with all of the people at the same time. Nobody should designate himself, or, in a bad sense, someone else, the representative of one group or another. Those who respect state property should also respect cooperative property, and those who respect cooperative property should respect state property; those who support one sector should support the other sector too. The resolutions to be implemented are very clear and save us a lot of other inconvenience. I must say that we have settled all these polemics in a positive fashion with appropriate party resolutions, while certain issues were concluded by the extremely important resolutions adopted by the 11th Congress. We are all obliged to take these resolutions literally and to work in their spirit.

I know a great number of people and I respect everyone subjectively. I do not respect those who have no views or who are cynical. Among us there are no such people. In politics, in struggles I respect those who have their own views and are convinced of their correctness, their own truth. Everybody should expound their views, we should exchange opinions, debate and, if necessary, clash in order to reach the appropriate decision. I am absolutely convinced that those who participated in the above-mentioned debates, going back as far as December 1956, were subjectively honest and well-meaning people, though many of them are no longer on the Central Committee. We say "subjectively honest", so no one can entertain doubts as to their human integrity.

The party has worked for a long, long time in this way, in this spirit, showing a high degree of sensitivity on important questions. And we have been working hard in this fashion since the 11th Congress too, and not without results. We have managed to solve our basic tasks. The principled directives of the 11th Congress are precise, clear, Marxist directives and served the interests of the country and the people well. We must work on firmly and indeed with increased effort and expertise to implement these resolutions even more successfully.

Although the resolutions are binding on everybody, no one should be more Catholic than the Pope. I am not saying this because I happened to be in Rome some time ago. Even before that I stated that no one needed to be more imbued with the spirit of class struggle than the Central Committee: we have a fine, class-struggle minded party and Central Committee.

I would end the list of conclusions with something that is my personal conviction and has been expressed by the Political Committee too: namely that if we maintain and strengthen our guiding principles, continue our policies and fulfil the tasks ahead together with the people, for the people and with good results, then the party can prepare for the 12th Congress adequately and can report with a clear conscience to the Central Committee on the work accomplished between the two Congresses.

Since members of the other corporate body elected at the Congress, the Central Control Committee, are also present, I would like to take the opportunity to thank them on behalf of the Central Committee for their work which helps and supports the activity of the Central Committee in the spirit of the guiding principles of the 11th Congress.

I would like to conclude by asking the esteemed Central Committee to discuss, support, accept and adopt the draft resolution submitted in writing.

Press Conference at the Crillon Hotel

NOVEMBER 1978

It is a pleasure for me to meet the distinguished representatives of the French and international press, radio and television, and I thank you for your interest.

As you know I came to the French capital at the invitation of M. Giscard d'Estaing with the intention of exchanging views on the development of relations between the Hungarian People's Republic and the French Republic and on current international issues.

I am glad to say that in the past few years our relations have to our mutual satisfaction become richer and more extensive. We hope that this will continue in the future.

We should like France to take a greater part in our foreign trade relations.

Our talks with the distinguished President of the French Republic took place in a congenial atmosphere, including exchanges on the most burning international issues. This is natural, as both countries have committed themselves to the policies of peaceful coexistence and détente. This led us to take an active part both in the preparatory and effective work of the Helsinki Conference on Security and Cooperation in Europe, together with the leaders of 33 other countries. We signed the Helsinki Final Act and we are making every effort to realize it to the full.

All this is naturally only just a brief reference to the topics I discussed during my two days with the President of the French Republic and with the outstanding figures of the French government and political life. At the conclusion of our talks we signed a declaration with President Giscard d'Estaing. Our mutual intention to develop further Hungarian–French relations is included in the declaration. I hope that as a result of our talks our relations will expand, serving the interest of our peoples well, and will further the cause of peaceful coexistence and détente.

Correspondent of Népszabadság: Comrade Kádár, how would you evaluate your present visit and how does it fit into the history of Hungarian–French relations?

János Kádár: The expression "summit meeting" has long been accepted in the international use of words and it seems that we have to accept it. When we received the invitation we appreciated that if this meeting took place it would be the first summit meeting in the history of Hungarian–French relations. The invitation itself indicates a political resolve as far as the Hungarian People's Republic is concerned, a mutual endeavour to deepen the cooperation between the Hungarian People's Republic and the French Republic in the political, economic, cultural and every other important field. As a result of our talks I am confident that our discussions will give an impetus to our relations. We think—and we met a similar resolve on the French side—that the expression of mutual intentions and the marking out of the specific things to be done in many individual areas can give—and I hope it really will give—impetus to Hungarian–French relations. Naturally this will require that both parties make intensive and consistent efforts in the working days which follow our present meeting. In other respects I feel that our meeting and talks, as well as serving the interests of our peoples, are a good example of how European countries belonging to different alliances can work together actively for the improvement of bilateral relations and at the same time help solve the focal questions of international politics—détente, and arms reduction—for the benefit of the European peoples, and better relations between the nations of the world.

Reporter of FRENCH TELEVISION: How would you evaluate your meeting with Georges Marchais and what is your opinion of "Eurocommunism"?

J. K.: On Thursday I met Comrade Marchais, General Secretary of the French Communist Party and M. Mitterrand, First Secretary of the French Socialist Party. The two meetings had a common feature. We in Hungary examine our relations with France—beyond their political topicality—from the aspect of their historical development. We do not consider this an exclusively party matter at home. We hope that the development of relations between the two countries, and the two peoples is not simply a party issue here in France either. As the statements on our meetings show, these two opposition parties also back the many-sided development of Hungarian–French relations.

As far as the explicitly inter-party questions of these two meetings are concerned: we have lasting, normal, and good relations with the French Communist Party; we are linked by the principles of mutual solidarity. We have had normal relations with the French Socialist Party and personally with the First Secretary M. Mitterrand for a number of years. This is in keeping with the system of relations maintained by the Hungarian Socialist Workers' Party. Our party—being a Communist party—strives for cooperation with socialist and social-democrat parties too on questions of common interest and particularly on issues concerning Europe. Among these parties is the French Socialist Party. The Thursday meeting thus fits into a whole series of talks which we also intend to continue in the future. I think that the question of relations between the Hungarian Socialist Workers' Party and the two French parties are simple and clear.

The concept of "Eurocommunism" is a rather dubious and much debated one which is not interpreted uniformly by Western European Communist parties either. There are suppositions that the flourishing of some kind of Eurocommunism would make the life of Communist parties in the socialist countries more difficult. I think there is more fantasy in this than reality.

There is another supposition and anxiety which is not often mentioned, although we know it exists: what happens if so-called Eurocommunism takes root and the Communist parties of Western Europe gain further strength, knock at the door, and make their claim to power? Nevertheless we do not deal with this question, let those deal with it where it is topical.

Communist parties work in full independence nowadays. Every other supposition is without basis. Each party is marking out its own strategic aims and deciding on its own tactics. According to our principles, every party has to consider the historical development of its own country, and the conditions of its own society, as well as the historical experiences of the international working class movement. But they make their own decisions.

The Hungarian Socialist Workers' Party – in accordance with its principles – follows the practice of maintaining normal and systematic relations with Western European Communist parties and that will be our aim in the future as well. We are linked by mutual solidarity and we want their struggle for social progress to be successful. But that is the internal affair of every country, of every people. We are against the export of revolution as well as the export of counterrevolution. We believe that the Communist parties of Eastern Europe and the Communist parties of the advanced capitalist countries in Western Europe do have common tasks. All this was put into words at the last Berlin meeting.

Our common task is cooperation on the most important and basic questions of mankind: on the continuation of détente, on maintaining peace, in the field of social progress, in promoting friendship between peoples and in many other areas.

That is the basis of our policies towards, and our practice in our relations with, Western European Communist parties, including the French Communist Party. As far as differences of opinion on questions of ideology and similar issues are concerned these too have their own system of clarification.

We are of the opinion that Eurocommunism as such is a fiction. As we learnt at school a long time ago we believe that Europe spreads from the Atlantic Ocean to the Urals and we ourselves are Europeans, too.

Correspondent of HUNGARIAN RADIO and TELEVISION: How would you evaluate the perspectives for international détente in the light of the sudden standstill in the process of international détente?

J. K.: This group of questions is linked with the Helsinki agreements. We consider those talks to have been an event of historical importance, which came about as a result of great efforts, and had the goal of promoting European security, and the strengthening of peace and the process of détente. The realization of the Helsinki agreements has its tangible examples. Those who follow political events can observe, for example, that in the international activities of the Hungarian People's Republic the realization of the Helsinki agreements has promoted and made it easy to establish bilateral relations between the Hungarian People's Republic and West European countries.

I met M. Giscard d'Estaing, President of the French Republic, for the first time in Helsinki, at the Finlandia Palace where we signed the same document as representatives of Hungary and France respectively. And now we meet for the second time here in Paris; during the talks we invited the President of the French Republic to Hungary. That, too, is a specific manifestation of the Helsinki spirit.

I am not particularly surprised that the course of détente has slowed down recently and some difficulties have arisen. Every great cause has its supporters and enemies. The Helsinki agreement owes its existence to the joint efforts of all the forces represented there. Its enemies were not there, although they existed, and then they went into counter-attack. Those who have been dealing with international issues for a long time, like me, know well that this is the dialectics of struggle.

It is my deep conviction that the trend towards détente will overcome all obstacles, and will finally triumph. This has been realized not only by Communists, by the responsible leaders of the socialist countries, but by a wide range of bourgeois politicians who think rationally and realistically. All the more so as mankind has no other alternative. The main task is to prevent a new world war. If we aren't able to agree on that, I can not imagine what prospects are left for the representatives of mankind to think of. I'm sure that nobody would choose collective suicide.

Correspondent of TASS NEWS AGENCY: Just recently Hungary took steps in the interests of disarmament.

J. K.: The Hungarian People's Republic, with the Soviet Union and the other countries of the Warsaw Treaty, have taken part in every effective disarmament talk which might promote the matter. We support a slowdown in the arms race and in keeping with the concept of equal security we want a balance of power — if possible — at a lower level of armament.

We attach great importance to the Soviet-American talks aimed at the limitation of strategic arms, and we wish them success. We ourselves are taking part in the work of the Geneva disarmament committee and are present at the Vienna talks on the reduction of armed forces in Central Europe. As is known, we put forward a number of proposals aimed at the prohibition of certain types of arms at the Geneva conference and these met with a favourable response. During our present talks in Paris we also devoted time to questions of the talks in Vienna on the reduction of armed forces. Both parties agreed on the importance of these talks and that the progress of these negotiations must be promoted.

The President of the Republic mentioned that just recently there was a French initiative to call together an all-European disarmament conference. We told him that we are now studying this French initiative. But we stressed, however, that we consider it extremely important to push the disarmament talks already in progress out of the present deadlock. The Hungarian People's Republic supports every realistic effort in the field of arms reduction.

Correspondent of TÉMOIGNAGE CHRÉTIEN: What are the relations between church and state in Hungary like?

J. K.: Perhaps it is not so well known that historically the Catholic Church was strong and influential in Hungary: about 65 per cent of the population belonged to it. But there were also quite strong Protestant churches — Calvinist and Lutheran — as well. Historically that was the position, but now nobody knows for certain what sort of influence the churches have because — parallel with democratic progress — all state, school, or any other kind of questionnaire on which you had to declare your faith was abolished. All citizens are equal in this respect; there is no discrimination.

After World War II we also came to that great historical task which the French Revolution solved in 1789: that is, the separation of church and state. This process was not without obstacles but finally it was completed. According to earlier laws in Hungary the church enjoyed exceptional status by virtue of state decree. We Communists said that we did not want to be worse than the bourgeois revolutionaries in their own time and we also decided to settle this question. Following this we had substantial talks with all the churches which lasted over a number of years. Our work brought results: the relationship between state and church has finally been settled. In connection with the Catholic Church, we carried on talks with the Vatican for 14 years and last year, during my visit to Pope Paul VI, the Vatican — so to speak — also gave its blessings to the settled relations between the Hungarian state and the Church.

We have settled our relations with the free churches, as they are known, as well, which was demonstrated by the visit of a world-famous Baptist preacher to Hungary last year.

What is the basis of the settled relations between state and church? On the one hand the state respects the autonomy of the church, it does not interfere with questions of faith. On the other hand there is an agreement that the church with its own means is ready to help in the programme of building socialism. As you probably know, we have a one-party system, but this isn't a simple way of governing either. Our work is backed by the people's front movement, which has its local as well as national leading bodies. The representatives of the churches, among them the Catholic Archbishop of Esztergom, have their role in the national leadership of this movement. The settled relations are indicated by the fact that during the last congress of the Patriotic People's Front — when they discussed the essentials of the people's front programme, the building of a socialist society in Hungary — the head of the Hungarian Catholic Church also made a contribution.

We consider the settled relations between state and church a great achievement. There were struggles during the shift from the capitalist to the socialist road in Hungary too, and at the end of the 1940s the new workers' state had to face a church clinging to old, feudal institutions — like, for example, the system of large landed estates. What went on in the mind of a believer at that time? When he thought of his happiness in this world he wanted to back the cause of the socialist revolution, but when he thought of his happiness in heaven — at least that's how I imagine it — he wanted to march with his church. But he couldn't tear himself in two. Well, by now we have already solved the great problem of conscience for the Hungarian citizen who is a believer, and that's very important. Today the believer can live in peace without fear because both state and church have proposed that he should back the work of building socialism. If his conscience requires it, he can live according to his faith. The correspondent of *Le Monde* put an additional question in connection with the Vienna talks and the French standpoint.

Of the disarmament talks at present in progress we mentioned the Vienna and Geneva talks. Although France is not taking part in the work of the Vienna talks, we have expressed the view that attention should be devoted to all serious talks and that we want them to achieve success. However, when I met the President—as I had the opportunity—I welcomed the certain measure of change recently evident in the official French standpoint, the approach to and interest in certain disarmament talks in connection with which France had earlier been reserved.

Report by the Central Committee at the 12th Congress of the HSWP
(Excerpts)

MARCH 1980

We have arrived at a political event of exceptional importance in the life of our country: the 12th Congress of the Hungarian Socialist Workers' Party has opened and has started its work. It is my task to present the Central Committee's report in the preparation of which account has been taken of the preliminary written report already distributed to the Congress delegates, as well as of the draft resolution.

I

THE INTERNATIONAL SITUATION AND
OUR COUNTRY'S FOREIGN POLICY

During the period under review, our party and government have pursued their international activities in accordance with the stands taken at the 11th Congress. In representing the interests of our country and people and in following the principles of proletarian internationalism and peaceful coexistence, we have endeavoured to contribute to the spread of détente, to the consolidation of peace and the growth of the forces of national independence, socialism and social progress.

The representatives of the Hungarian People's Republic carry out widespread activity both in international organizations and in the field of bilateral relations. We attach great importance to our work in the United Nations and its specialized agencies. This country is a member of the Food and Agriculture Organization (FAO), the International Labour Organization (ILO), the United Nations Educational, Scientific and Cultural Organization (Unesco) and the World Health Organization (WHO). Our representatives take part in the work of more than 900 international organizations. We maintain diplomatic relations with 125 countries.

We attach special significance to our relations with the socialist countries. The countries of the socialist community have achieved substantial results in the building of a new society; their internationalist unity and joint stand are a decisive factor in the worldwide struggle for peace and social progress. Our relations with the other socialist countries have shown a healthy development during the period under review, and we shall continue to do all we can to make sure that the unity of the socialist countries and the political, economic, cultural and ideological cooperation between them are further strengthened.

It is with great satisfaction that the Central Committee can report to Congress that our internationalist unity with the Soviet Union, our liberator, the first socialist state in the world, and the main bulwark in the cause of human progress, has continued to grow firmer over the past five years. There has been a vigorous development of our many and varied relations and a strengthening of the indissoluble bonds of friendship between the two peoples.

One historic event in the period under review was the victory of the Vietnamese people, who had been fighting for their freedom, and the birth of a united Socialist Republic of Vietnam. The successful struggle of the Indochinese peoples has brought about a new situation in Southeast Asia. The road to independent development and national advancement has also been cleared for the peoples of Cambodia and Laos.

The national liberation and democratic revolutionary movements have gained momentum. In Africa, the peoples of Angola and Mozambique, former colonies of Portugal, have won their independence. Ethiopia is marching successfully along the road of its own choice and, recently, after long years of struggle, the patriots of Zimbabwe have scored a significant victory. In Latin America, there has been an upswing in the struggle by democratic and revolutionary forces against Fascist dictatorship and semi-colonial oppression, while the cause of the people has emerged victorious in Nicaragua. With the fall of the Iranian monarchy, imperialism has lost an important ally in the Middle East. The people of the People's Democratic Republic of Yemen have defended their independence. The revolutionary forces of the Afghan people are waging a resolute struggle to defend the independence of their country against the counter-revolutionaries, who are being aided and abetted by imperialists.

There can be no disputing the right of peoples to struggle to attain and consolidate their national independence and to make social progress. We reaffirm the solidarity of Hungarian Communists with the peoples of Asia, Africa and Latin America in their rightful struggle against neo-colonialists and every kind of aggressor.

The Hungarian People's Republic considers the movement of non-aligned countries a significant factor in international life. The Havana summit conference strengthened the anti-imperialist features of the movement, and the resolutions taken there constitute a major contribution to the defense of peace and to the cause of national independence and social progress. We are backing the struggle of the developing countries to consolidate their national independence and achieve social progress, and also their endeavour to change the international economic order so as to provide more equitable conditions for the development of all countries than it does at present.

As for the factors that influence the international situation, one must also mention that in recent years the general crisis of capitalism has further deepened, the internal contradictions in the capitalist countries have sharpened, and their struggles among themselves for energy, raw material resources and markets have intensified. The result of the financial crisis which permanently afflicts the world capitalist system, of the economic setbacks which occur in even the most developed capitalist countries, of inflation, and of the permanently high rate of unemployment, is to make the burden imposed on the working people still heavier and to heighten political tensions. World economic relations are further destabilized by attempts to gain unilateral advantages through protectionism, a growing tendency in the capitalist countries. It is a tendency that also has an adverse effect on the relations of the capitalist countries with the socialist and developing states.

The international situation has recently become more tense; voices familiar to us from the cold war period are again making themselves heard. At present – on the pretext of the events in Afghanistan – reactionary circles are waging an all-out anti-Soviet, anti-Communist propaganda campaign directed against the socialist social system. They are taking a stand against détente, and their stand against the Moscow Olympic Games serves the same purpose. As for Afghanistan, it is common knowledge that the legitimate government of that country, in the face of external threats and on the basis of a valid treaty between the two countries, asked for military assistance, which was granted by the Soviet Union in keeping with international law. The Soviet Union has already made it clear that if and when the reasons for the request and the granting of assistance cease, she is ready to withdraw her troops from Afghanistan.

The foreign policy moves of the Chinese leaders have also heightened international tension. Guided by their nationalistic, hegemonistic aspirations and disregarding the true interests of the Chinese people, they openly collaborate with the most extremist and aggressive circles of international imperialism. Our people resolutely condemned the Chinese aggression against socialist Vietnam, which caused great damage not only to the Vietnamese and Chinese peoples, but also to the socialist cause as a whole.

Every country has its own specific interests. There are, however, interests which are fundamentally important to every country, regardless of whether it is attached to either of the alliance systems or to the movement of non-aligned countries, or whether it is neutral. The vast amounts spent on armaments impose increasingly grave burdens on the peoples, and by reducing these sums, considerable resources could be released for the benefit of the peoples and for solving the common vital problems of mankind. Besides the preservation of peace, these are tasks that require joint efforts: the solution of the raw material and energy problems of the world; the development of transport and communications; protection of the environment; combating grave endemic diseases, famine and poverty; and the eradication of illiteracy in various regions of the world.

The international activity of the Hungarian Socialist Workers' Party and the foreign policy of the Hungarian People's Republic continue to be determined by internationalism, solidarity, the lofty idea of friendship among peoples and the principles of peaceful coexistence. Our people give full support to our international

II
THE DEVELOPMENT OF SOCIAL RELATIONS, OUR POLICY OF ALLIANCE

endeavours and our foreign policy. We continue to strive to add weight to our words in international life by doing good work at home; by doing so we serve the interests of both our people and homeland, and the cause of overall progress and peace.

The domestic political situation in the Hungarian People's Republic is well balanced, and the power of the working class, of the working people, is firm. The leading role played by the party dominates life in our society, and mutual confidence marks the relations between the party and the masses. The party's policy is actively supported by our people; socialist national cohesion is strengthening. The political unity of our society is our great historic achievement. This is the first and foremost requirement for successful domestic construction, just as it is for the favourable international opinion of our country.

The party, the Central Committee and the government, on a basis of confidence, reveal the genuine situation to the public, speak openly about the problems and difficulties, and take into consideration well-founded and justified criticism. We do not hesitate to do this in spite of the existence of a tiny minority who for one reason or another do not agree with our socialist system and our policy; in fact there are some who uncritically take over the propaganda slogans of imperialism, who underestimate the achievements of our people and who try to sow doubts.

During the past five years there has been no change in the class structure of society in our country. The present pattern shows a ratio of 59 per cent workers, 13 per cent cooperative peasants, 25 per cent intellectuals and employees and 3 per cent peasants and small craftsmen working on their own. Irreconcilable class antagonisms have ceased with the elimination of the exploiting capitalist and landed classes. In this country there are only working classes and strata in alliance with one another; the continuous harmonization of their interests is a constant political task never to be neglected.

Our invariable aim is to continue bringing the classes and strata of our society closer together and to further their specific interests on the basis that the interests of society take priority and that differences between town and village, mental work and physical work need to be reduced still further.

In the period under review, the party has been dealing appropriately with the position of women. According to this year's census, women make up 51.5 per cent of Hungary's population; 79 per cent of women capable of working are employed, and 45 per cent of all active earners are women. In work, in the family and in public life, women meet their obligations with increasing skill, estimable discipline and diligence. Their social equality is gaining ground. Nevertheless, we cannot be satisfied; we must continue to watch the position of women closely; improved economic and cultural conditions and mental attitudes must be created to ensure equal opportunities for women, to help them do their jobs as both workers and mothers. These aims must be promoted by raising their qualifications, by social measures, by the extension of services and by overcoming conservative views which underestimate the social role of women. It is important that the proportion of women in leading positions and in elected posts should increase, in accordance with the part they are playing in society.

In our party's view, the overwhelming majority of young Hungarians support socialism and see it as ensuring their future. Their position and attitude also reflect the general condition of society.

Caring for the younger generation and educating young people concern the whole of society. In doing this, schools, work places and social bodies are essential elements as are the young people themselves, and the Young Communist League. However, the gravest responsibility invariably rests with the family — the smallest unit in our society, but an essential one from the point of view of the future. Our party and our socialist state give support and protection to the institution of the family. Efforts should be made to ensure that the family plays an increasing role in personality development and in the general acceptance of the socialist way of life.

Our party is well aware of the problems facing young people. It works, and encourages the state and social bodies, to grant young people more equal opportunities to study, to choose their careers, to obtain jobs in line with their qualifications, and to improve the conditions under which they can establish families, obtain housing and set up a home.

The well-balanced situation of our society is reflected in the well-ordered relationship between the state and the churches, a relationship to which both state and church must pay close attention. In the spirit of the Constitution, the state guarantees freedom of conscience and the conditions under which the churches can operate autonomously. Religious believers play their part in the building of socialism and in public life as citizens with equal rights. The churches respect the laws of our state and support the country's construction work. Just recently the church leaders affirmed that the relationship between state and church had continued to develop over the past years, and at present it is not simply a well-ordered relationship, but a joint work for the benefit of the people. The current settled relationship between state and church has arisen out of the fair implementation of agreements drawn up jointly and that is the way it can continue to develop in the future. For our part, we wish to proceed along this same path, on a principled basis.

An important element in the cohesion of our society, an element that is based upon socialist foundations, is that the national minorities who live in this country take part in the construction work and in political life as citizens with equal rights. They are free to use their mother tongue and are given appropriate assistance in fostering and developing their national cultures. Here the national minorities have found a place to live and they feel at home in their own country, in socialist Hungary. Our party considers the consistent implementation of the Leninist policy on nationalities as an important matter of principle. It does its utmost to ensure that the national minorities remain active participants in our social and political life and preserve and enrich their national traditions and cultures. Our aim is that the German, Slovak, South Slav and Romanian minorities in this country, and the Hungarian communities in the neighbouring socialist countries, should contribute to strengthening friendship and internationalist cooperation between our peoples.

Our history has been such that today about a third of all Hungarians live beyond the borders of this country; there are Hungarians to be found in almost every corner of the world. When we consider them, it is good to know that most, as far as they can, preserve and foster their mother tongue, their national culture and traditions, and respect socialist Hungary. We expect that, while fostering their national culture, they be honest citizens of their countries, and promote social progress and friendship among peoples.

Further cutbacks in the still widespread bureaucracy should be considered one of the main tasks in developing state administration. The public can see the improvements in state administration, but they justly censure the often protracted and sometimes soulless procedures. In order to improve this, it is necessary to reduce the number of regulations passed by law, to streamline and simplify state administration in every field and to increase the role of public supervision.

An essential feature of our social system is socialist democracy, which stimulates the political activity and development of a people liberated from capitalist oppression, and the evolution of their creative forces. Our party has devoted great attention to this development in recent years. We are pleased to note that the population takes an increasing part in public life by expressing their views and making suggestions and critical comments. The public bodies of trade union stewards set up in accordance with the resolutions of the 11th Party Congress have done a good job. Democracy within the cooperatives has strengthened and is gradually acquiring forms adjusted to the increased size of farms. Community forums are also enriching public life.

But we cannot be satisfied with the achievements of socialist democracy attained so far. We must see to it that the forums of socialist democracy function in accordance with their purpose and effectively. Workers' participation in solving problems, including the submission of suggestions and the exercising of control, and wherever possible and necessary, decision-making, should be increased in all jobs and in all units of public administration.

Socialist democracy should not weaken individual responsibility. It is improper that worthwhile decisions are often postponed with the excuse that it is a collective responsibility, or that the responsibility for wrong decisions cannot be traced. Socialist democracy should not become a refuge for shirkers or the undisciplined. It implies order and discipline, harmony of responsibilities and rights, carefully considered opinions expressed on public affairs, active participation in work and a personal sense of responsibility for the common good.

We must examine how to place the activity of appointed managers under more substantive public supervision while increasing their individual responsibility. To this effect, it is necessary to define more precisely the responsibility managers have to report to the democratic forums, and to find ways of taking better account of the workers' opinions when appointing managers.

The deepening of socialist democracy, that immense source of strength to our social system, and the discontinuation of its merely formal manifestations, call for a strengthening of party guidance and party democracy, an increase in the role of public and representative bodies and increased public control.

III
THE TASKS OF ECONOMIC CONSTRUCTION

We are in a position to report to Congress that in the period under review the common efforts of the party and the people have brought about great achievements in economic construction. The productive forces have developed, and the material and technical basis of our society has been strengthened. National wealth has grown and living conditions have improved. Provided the plan targets for the current year are fulfilled, within five years the national income will have risen by 21–28 per cent, industrial output by 24–25 per cent and housing construction by 13–14 per cent, while the volume of agricultural production will have increased by 15–16 per cent as compared with the previous five-year period.

The productivity of labour is growing at a faster rate than the efficiency of production. Initial results have been achieved in making hitherto uneconomical production profitable, or in terminating it. In the last five-year period, about 80 investments, each exceeding 500 million Forints, were made and these allowed production to expand and facilitated the transformation of the production structure.

Yet we must report that despite all the efforts made and essentially because of the more adverse than expected conditions, the results of our economic development will lag behind the targets envisaged in the fifth Five Year Plan. The growth rate of the national income, and consequently of living standards, is slower than planned. The present-day situation is more complex, and work on the economy requires greater efforts and organization than previously. The drastic and lasting changes which have taken place in the international economic arena since 1973–74, an adverse change in the terms of trade on the world markets and the discriminatory measures taken by some capitalist countries have unfavourably affected Hungary's national economy. It is a proof of the strength and viability of our socialist economy that we were in a position to withstand the gravest external economic effects of the last three decades.

We must also note that the adverse changes in the external economic conditions have shown up the weak spots in our economy and the shortcomings in our work more clearly. Although we realized that the adverse changes in the market had to be combated by a change in the product structure and selective industrial development, economic management in practice was unable to adjust well enough, fast enough and with sufficient flexibility to the changed conditions. The switchover to intensive methods of economic management, the improvement in the efficiency of production and the streamlining of production and the product structure lag behind the rates required by the circumstances and that made possible by the present-day technical and technological level of the national economy.

The Central Committee proposes to Congress that the chief economic objective in the period of the sixth Five Year Plan should be an improvement in the balance of the national economy and a consolidation of the standards of living already achieved at a slower development rate, and this by improving the qualitative factors of economic progress and increasing the international competitiveness of production. Now, for the time being, we can realistically set ourselves this objective. A very important task to be faced in the coming years is to improve our foreign trade balance and our balance of payments, to establish an equilibrium between commodity stocks and purchasing power, manpower and jobs, allocations for investments and construction capacity, by consistently fulfilling the guidelines of our economic policy. It is to these objectives that the growth rates of industrial output and the internal utilization and distribution of the national income should be subordinated. A more rapid increase in industrial production can be allowed only if significant results are achieved in updating the product structure and in improving the efficiency of production and realization, thus creating more favourable terms of trade in our export–import work.

In recent years, the industrial production base has undergone substantial modernization, and the technological level as well as the professional expertise of the workers have improved. Industry and the construction industry produce 61 per cent of the national income. The picture is not a homogeneous one at present, but it is encouraging to perceive and to know that there are already an increasing number of industrial concerns which operate and produce in line with the requirements of the age and which bear international comparison. We have to develop industrial production in a more differentiated manner than so far, keeping our own production capabilities in mind. First of all, there has to be an increase in the ratio of products which require less material and energy, so as to enable us to economize on imports and achieve a greater net income for the national economy. Every industrial concern should shape its product pattern in the knowledge that only efficient work and up-to-date, high-quality and competitive products are really valued on both the domestic and the world market. This is the only type of production that has a future.

Agriculture is highly important to the development of our entire society. Food production is increasing in importance the world over. Without boasting we can proudly say we have a historic achievement in that Hungarian agriculture is now based upon socialist foundations and is progressing dynamically. At present the country has 131 state farms with 143,000 workers and 1,350 cooperative farms with 618,000 workers. Agriculture today produces 61 per cent more, on a 7 per cent smaller land area and with 48 per cent less manpower than it did in the years before socialist transformation. When speaking about progress, it is sufficient to mention that in the fifth Five Year Plan period, the aggregate figure for maize and cereal production amounted to approximately 1,200 kilograms per capita, while per capita meat production was 190 kilograms dead weight. This is a very good result even by world standards.

Increasing reliance upon the power inherent in science is of particular importance at the present stage of our development. Speedier and larger-scale application of research achievements can only be achieved through good cooperation between the research institutes and the units of economy and production. Mutual interest in the application of research achievements has to be increased. More attention has to be devoted to taking over foreign know-how which can be put to good use in this country, and also to adapting it and developing it further at home. These activities should be accorded a suitable place and adequate recognition by research workers and experts involved in technological development. Scientific and technological results need to be put to practical use more rapidly than they are now.

We must economize better on manpower, our most important resource, and on the knowledge and diligence of our people in production and in every other field of life. There has recently been a rational regrouping of manpower in a number of enterprises. Manpower requirements have decreased, and there are fewer unmotivated changes in place of work. The anomaly of a considerable surplus of jobs over manpower has to be ended. We cannot go on having superfluous manpower in some places and a shortage in other important areas of the national economy.

Full employment is a major achievement of our system. It will remain so in the future, too. However, the present requirements of the economy are for more effective employment of manpower, better work organization and the strengthening of work discipline. Alongside the transformation of production and product patterns and the reduction of uneconomical production, we must see to it that there should be a planned regrouping of manpower, and that entails the retraining and further training of workers. These tasks have to be accomplished consistently and with great circumspection. Here the party and social organs should give far-reaching assistance.

Our economic development and the natural endowments of our country both require that we should take an increasing part in the international division of labour. Our economic and foreign trade relations are already widespread and extend to approximately 150 countries. Our exports now account for 50 per cent of our national income.

Multilateral cooperation with the socialist countries is of outstanding importance to our economic development. The share of the socialist countries in Hungary's foreign trade turnover has amounted to more than 50 per cent in recent years. Almost one-third of our foreign trade is with the Soviet Union and almost a quarter of it with the other socialist countries.

We will continue working for the further development of our country's economic relations with the capitalist countries on a basis of mutual advantage and equality. In addition to traditional foreign trade, we wish to advance in cooperation, which should include production and marketing, too. This accords with the interests of our people and our policy aimed at the practical realization of peaceful coexistence.

The developing countries are playing a steadily increasing role in the world economy and we are advancing our cooperation with them in keeping with our domestic endeavours and in harmony with the specific features of each country. We want to expand our turnover and our economic cooperation with these lands significantly. We are assisting the former colonies in developing their forces of production and in establishing their economic independence through economic cooperation which is mutually advantageous.

Our economic development requires us to adjust our economic management system better to changing conditions. Our system of economic management, the fundamental principles of which were worked out almost fifteen years ago, takes into consideration both the general objective laws of building socialism and the specific features of our country. A socialist planned economy based upon social ownership and bound up with the autonomy of enterprises and cooperatives, which asserts group interests and the material interests of individuals equally, greatly promotes the implementation of our economic policy. However, the functioning of our system of economic management leaves something to be desired from certain points of view. Management, national economic planning and the system of organization do not adjust flexibly enough to changing conditions, and sometimes there is a delay in making the necessary decisions.

The functioning of the governing bodies must be made more effective and their responsibility in solving the basic problems of economic policy, in working out and coordinating plans and in bringing about the conditions for implementation must be clearly defined. Central economic management should be made more flexible and efficient; it should direct the main economic processes consistently, with the appropriate coordination of economic decisions and with the necessary efficiency. The work of decision-makers must be improved, the number of transpositions in management should be reduced and the spheres of activity and responsibility of each and every body should be better defined.

Our management system guarantees the autonomy of enterprises and cooperatives; the link between material interest and better performance is a feature of its operation. Successful accomplishment of our economic assignments this year and in the years to come will depend decisively on the autonomous work of enterprises and cooperatives, their spirit of initiative, their economic success and their better organization.

The price system plays an important role in the regulation of economic processes. Prices must adequately reflect socially necessary and justified input. This is an indispensable requirement for clear-sightedness in the economic sphere, for making good economic decisions and for the satisfactory regulation of production and consumption. The economy of production can be judged on the basis of realistic producer prices which express world market value judgements. Only profitability based on such prices can give the economic units the correct stimulus to increase efficiency, to advance technology and to improve quality. We took this into consideration when we introduced a comprehensive reorganization of producer prices at the beginning of this year.

As far as consumer prices are concerned, our rule is that the prices of fundamental goods and services are fixed centrally, in harmony with decisions determining trends in living standards. However, the price system can fulfil its role in the economy only if there is an organic link between producer and consumer prices. The two cannot be kept separate from each other for any great length of time. This is an important requirement if consumption and the consumption pattern are to develop in harmony with our economic potentialities.

IV

LIVING STANDARDS

It is a fundamental tenet of our policy that in the course of building socialism, the living standards of the working people must rise regularly. It is also a rule that the resources have first to be produced and can only afterwards be distributed and consumed. An important condition, if we are to maintain an adequate level of supply, is that there must be a balance between the commodity basis and purchasing power. Our party and government have implemented their living standards policy and have fulfilled the obligations undertaken in this respect.

Looking back over the past twenty years of building socialism, it is obvious that the population has become considerably richer both in material and intellectual resources. Since 1960, consumption and per capita real income have more than doubled. About 1,500,000 dwellings have been built. Almost half the country's population have moved into new homes. Household appliances, washing machines, vacuum cleaners, refrigerators, radio and television sets, tape-recorders and other durable consumer goods are now used on a wide scale. Almost one family in four has a car. Our people's nutritional level and standards of dress are good by international comparison. Our system of public health and welfare accords with our level of economic development. In real terms we now devote four times the sum to social benefits that we did twenty years ago.

Our work over the last five years has brought about a considerable improvement in living standards, even in the midst of the economic difficulties. The targets set in the fifth Five Year Plan will not be fully reached, yet per capita real income will have risen by 9 per cent, and consumption by 14 per cent. The commodity supply is basically balanced. From this year on, the retirement age for cooperative farm members is the same as that for workers and employees. The lowest pensions have been raised. The 44-hour working week has become general. If we include this year's targets, then 440,000–450,000 new dwellings will have been built in the present Five Year Plan period, together with 107,000 nursery-school and 17,000–18,000 day-nursery places. The health network, public transport and other services are improving.

We have still not been able to fulfil all the justified demands, although the living standards of our people have increased over the past five years. We are aware of the burning problems of those awaiting accommodation, of young people starting out in life and laying the foundations of their family life, of the troubles of retired people living on a small pension, or of those in a difficult situation for other reasons. The solution of these problems must remain on the agenda. Evaluating our situation, however, we can state that our people live a secure life, enjoy acceptable living standards and have a lot to cherish, preserve and protect. We have a basis for building our future.

Assessing our economic situation, the foreseeable possibilities for our development, only the maintenance of the results we have achieved, the stabilization of living standards and the establishment of the preconditions of their further increase can be set as realistic objectives for the forthcoming sixth Five Year Plan period. According to the available information, the per capita real income can increase by 6 per cent and public consumption by 8 per cent.

The principal aim of our policy on living standards has remained unchanged: to maintain the security of life through ensuring full employment and social allowances, to differentiate wages according to the work performed, to make further, gradual reductions in the unjustified differences in family incomes, and to ensure a proportionate growing share of the social assets for all classes and strata of society.

Work, effective production and economic activity are the only ways to consolidate living standards and to ensure the moderate increase that can be planned for on the basis of our present knowledge. In assessing our tasks, we must take into account the fact that over the past five years the number of active earners has decreased by 3,000, while the number of pensioners, mothers staying at home on child care allowance, children of school-age and other dependants has increased by 204,000. In our country there are at present 5,083,000 active earners, whereas we have 5,627,000 old-age pensioners, women on child care leave and other dependants.

A more consistent implementation of the socialist principle of wages according to work performed has become especially timely. We should resolutely combat the appealing notion and easy-going practice of egalitarianism. Social justice requires the creation of greater differences than the existing ones in the remuneration for work on the basis of the quality and quantity of the work performed. Wages cannot mean payment merely for being present at one's workplace. We have to ensure that at all levels in the division of labour — in leading positions and in lower posts — the incomes deriving from work clearly reflect the differences in work performed.

We must self-critically admit that, despite the positive efforts and endeavours that have been made, we have not been able to achieve appropriate results in removing anti-social phenomena like sharp practice or parasitism, which justifiably cause indignation among honest people. The consistent implementation of our socialist principles requires that we restrict and restrain the opportunities to acquire income without work or a disproportionately large amount of money compared to the work performed. We must take energetic measures to preclude income which originates from speculation or abuse, and which is not the reward for honest work.

Our society makes considerable efforts to ensure appropriate care for old people who, in past decades, contributed to the building of socialism with their honest work. Basic security is provided for them by the pension system and health and social care, but this does not and cannot replace the attention and care provided by their families and their children. Elderly people should be cared for both by society and by their families. Low pensions should be raised in the course of the sixth Five Year Plan. Social institutions which make life easier for senior citizens should be further developed.

In improving living conditions, a great role is played by local initiative. In future, we should rely on the activity of the public to a greater extent, using local resources in improving supplies of goods and services. Party and social organs and the local councils should stimulate and support these efforts. We have to devote major attention to ensuring that we lead an intelligent and cultured way of life, and protect, care for and decorate our homes, buildings and environment. Our party does its utmost to ensure that our people continue to live in security in the future, and can live and work in a balanced, peaceful, constructive atmosphere.

V
THE DEVELOPMENT OF SOCIALIST CONSCIOUSNESS

After the 11th Congress, under conditions when the international ideological struggle became sharper, and the domestic conditions for building society more complex, our party continued successfully to guide and organize ideological and cultural work.

A survey of the situation as far as ideology and public thinking are concerned demands that we examine the development of the ideological and moral state of our society, and its consciousness, that we see today's features in their full reality, and critically evaluate the present ideological work of our party.

The overthrow of the capitalist system, the elimination of the remnants of feudalism, the creation of the power of the working class and the laying of the foundations for a socialist society have resulted in fundamental changes in our people's way of thinking. The conclusion of this historic process was the successful socialist transformation of agriculture, which resulted in further profound and favourable changes in the thinking, not only of the peasantry, but the people as a whole. With this, the economic basis for the many centuries-old conservative views, way of life and customs ceased to exist. The rapid rise in the political, professional and general educational level of the peasantry is unparalleled in our history. With regard to consciousness, too, the worker–peasant alliance has been able to rely on an increasingly united socialist basis.

The economic policy which we have been pursuing for more than twenty years has also had a major effect on the evolution of social consciousness. In addition to moral incentives, this economic policy has made material interests an important social driving force. Personal interest in the building of socialism has become more perceptible, and it has also become obvious that the individual can only prosper in conjunction with the community. The new system of economic management introduced in 1968 opened up new vistas for initiative and for independent and responsible thinking and action. All this allowed new progress to be made in socialist democracy and public life.

The present state of society's consciousness is basically determined by the positive changes in the thinking of our people. This is true even if we bear in mind that this process was not and is not devoid of contradictions. Our practical experience has proved the long-standing Marxist truth that the consciousness of society, the thinking of people, advances more slowly than the changes in the conditions of life. However, we cannot use this as an excuse for inconsistencies in social practice, for shortcomings in our educational work, or for the fact that we have not yet been able to give satisfactory answers to numerous questions in our ideological work. The intensification of the international ideological class struggle puts increasing demands upon ideological work.

Attention has to be centred on the ideological and moral issues most important from the point of view of the development of society: to increasing the prestige of work, to respecting and serving the public interest, to strengthening the community spirit, to consolidating socialist patriotism and proletarian internationalism and to defeating conservative views which are ideologically harmful and hostile to the socialist system and socialist principles.

We have to strive to ensure that the moral face of our society now becomes that of a society of work. Everything that we possess has been achieved and defended through the hard struggles of our working class, of the Hungarian people, and has been created with their own hands. Society expects each of us to protect and enhance the socialist property of the community and of the people, and to work devotedly to the best of our ability and strength. Workers who fulfil the obligations they undertake and who live and work sincerely should be respected and honoured, and prosper in their place of work.

There is one sure way to achieve personal prosperity and realize individual wishes and plans, and that is to recognize the public interest, to accept it, and to promote its implementation. This is the basic moral norm of a socialist society. All honest and justified human demands and aspirations are accumulated and expressed by public interest, which is formulated and represented by the party in its policy. If public interest is manifest, the country will advance on the road of development, and the citizen will not be disappointed, either in his work or in his future.

VI
THE PARTY'S WORK AND INTERNATIONAL ACTIVITY

The party's leading role prevails. Relying upon the scientific theory of Marxism–Leninism, using the real situation of society as a point of departure and keeping in mind the opinions and proposals of the people, the party determines the main direction and chief tasks of building socialism. In the future, as in the past, our party will assert its leading role through the influence of its ideology, through argument and discussion, through political guidance and organizing work, and by the mobilization of the masses. The party considers its own activity as a service to the people. It guides but it does not command, it leads but it does not rule, and it condemns even the slightest manifestation of misuse of power.

Five years ago, at the time of the 11th Congress, our party had 754,000 members, and on December 31, 1979, it had 812,000 members. The vast majority of the new party members, prior to their admission, had performed selfless voluntary work in the mass organizations, in the socialist brigades, in the Workers' Militia and elsewhere. The social composition of the party membership also expresses the fact that our party is the vanguard of the working class, the party of the working people, the party of the masses. If we consider present occupation, over half of our party members are workers and peasants, and if we consider original occupation, nearly three-quarters of them come from these classes. The proportion of women among the party members has increased continuously in proportion to the role women have been playing in society, and has now reached 28 per cent. The proportion of young people under 30 admitted to the party in the past five years makes up 60 per cent of total admissions.

A noteworthy fact is that nearly three-quarters of the membership have joined the party since 1956. This all strongly underlines the importance of the task of helping to mould the level of preparedness, general and political culture, and the experiences of the revolutionary movement of Communists of different age groups into a well-knit unity. We must do everything in our power to help the younger generation become acquainted with the historical road covered by our party and with the most important lessons of the battles it has fought.

The correct Communist conduct is unflinching firmness on matters of principle, and flexibility in practice. We must take care that elements of our policy which have stood the test of time, continue to be observed in full, and that no one distort them, either in the direction of dogmatism or revisionism. Nor can we permit our former correct decisions and positions to become dogma. We must be open to new issues, and we must continue to take the initiative on everything in which the interests of the people, the country and general progress require change. This is our concept of the continuity of the main trend of our policy: we must maintain and advance what promotes the progress of the country and effectively serves the people.

The further advance of party democracy is an essential condition for well-founded resolutions which take reality into account, and increases the responsibility and activeness of party members in their implementation. In the future, there must be more of the spirit and style of work which enables discussion of all issues, large and small, at the party forums – all issues affecting the life of the party, of the country and of the people. Every member of the party should consider it his or her responsibility to express his or her views and positions at the party's forums. And in all cases party members should receive replies to their questions and information on the outcome of their proposals.

The operation of party democracy is an essential condition for a critical and self-critical examination of our work. This will protect the party and its officials and members from errors, mistakes and self-satisfaction. In our party, criticism and self-criticism are not satisfactory in all respects, despite the progress that has been made. The need for this is admitted in words, but in reality, many do practice it.

It is the party's duty to the people to solve cadre issues in time, and when solving them, to take into consideration the interests of the community. It is correct and just that those who are unable to work according to the higher requirements, and who thus harm the working community, should not be allowed to continue in leading posts. Striving for stability is only correct up to the point when it means employing people who can be relied upon – people who are politically stable but not rigid; who are competent in their jobs; whose horizons are wide; who take initiative but are not prone to follow fads; who are disciplined and who demand discipline from others; and who at the same time respect and consider the views of others and are able to face up to their own weaknesses; who live and work in an exemplary manner and who are respected for this by their colleagues and the community. Leaders like these are needed in all posts. It is high time to have no hesitation in promoting young people who were born and brought up in this political system of ours, who learned their jobs from us and have become adults capable of leadership.

When speaking about the party, it should not be forgotten that it is our duty to develop our work style, to reinforce the working class movement character of party work and to reduce its formal and bureaucratic features. The tasks we are facing require lively political work among the masses and not a stack of reports and resolutions. The party branches, and the party committees at all levels, which have efficiently accomplished their work in the past period, can do a great deal to implement the party's policy and to strengthen their contacts with the masses. The wish often stressed at report-back membership meetings that more, and more effective, support be given by the higher bodies to the party branches, including community party branch organizations must be considered a justified one.

In the period we are reporting on, our party, which is part of the international Communist movement, pursued lively international activity in keeping with the resolution of the 11th Congress and with our internationalist principles.

The present situation of our Communist movement is characterized by the fact that the parties are independent and each party elaborates and implements its own policy. This increases the responsibility of each party to apply Marxism–Leninism in a creative way, to strengthen solidarity, to study one another's experiences, and to advance cooperation in the struggle for our common goals. Our party consistently holds the opinion that differing views emerging from within our movement must be clarified in principled and tolerant exchanges of opinion, which must always consider that the goal of these discussions is to promote cooperation among the parties and to strengthen the movement, while contributing to the enrichment of the scientific theory of Marxism–Leninism. Our party's general concept of international activity will continue to be the further consolidation of the unity of our movement through a common stand and joint actions, and through strengthening bilateral and multilateral relations, always in keeping with the principles of Marxism–Leninism.

Our party, guided by the principles of Marxism–Leninism and of proletarian internationalism, strives to strengthen its cooperation with the fraternal parties. In the five years since the 11th Congress we have conducted useful bilateral discussions with the delegates of 78 fraternal parties working in different parts of the world.

Over the past few years, our contacts with most of the Western European socialist and social democratic parties have further expanded. This helped to improve our relations with the countries concerned and made for the development of relations between European countries with differing social systems. This proves that ideological antagonisms and differences of political views do not preclude opportunities for cooperation on such vital issues of common interest as peace, security and the promotion of disarmament.

The international Communist and workers' movement is a huge and constantly growing force in our times; it promotes the progress of human society as a whole. Communists have no other aim but to serve the cause of socialism, progress and peace in the interests of their peoples and the whole of mankind. Our party continues to strive, in harmony with its patriotic and internationalist policies, to serve by its entire activity the progress of our country and the attainment of the common goals of the international Communist and workers' movement.

The Central Committee asks the Congress to approve the work accomplished over the past five years, to discuss and accept the report and the submitted draft resolution.

Closing Address at the 12th Congress of the HSWP

MARCH 1980

As the chairman has announced, 156 comrades asked to take the platform and 57 comrades were actually given the floor in the debate on the two items on the agenda. Representatives from every area of party life and the life of our society have expressed their opinions. The first speaker spoke on behalf of the Communists in the capital, but every county in the country, and almost our entire society — by occupation, too — has been represented in the debate: we have heard the voices of workers, miners, agricultural workers, intellectuals and artists at the Congress. Some people in uniform spoke as well; we heard the Minister of Defense, a lance-corporal in the army; the first secretary of the party committee in the Border Guards who spoke on behalf of the services under the Ministry of Home Affairs, and many others.

One speaker mentioned that we were listening here to the words of three generations. I believe this should be amended slightly, because if we take every participant into consideration, we shall find that perhaps five generations of party militants are represented at this Congress of ours. I also include in this the charming children who greeted us in the name of the Pioneers and Little Drummers.

I should like to mention the most important items raised in the contributions we have heard. I attentively followed each of the 57 speakers. All of them have approved the Report of the Central Committee, the Report of the Central Control Committee and the submitted draft resolution as a basis which needs some supplementation.

Our Congress Secretariat have informed me that the 99 comrades who submitted their contributions in written form also approve of the Report of the Central Committee. The principled, political and organizational unity which is tangibly present at our Congress is our main strength! But we can also state that not only our Congress, but our entire party is united.

During the Congress we kept a dutiful eye on outside response to our debate, and the plenum of the Congress was also informed of this. We ascertained that public opinion was attentively following the work of the Congress. Thanks to the work of the press, radio and television, the entire nation was able to follow the deliberations of the Congress. As the response shows: the nation approves of the line of the Congress and supports its work. Convincing proof of this are the numerous telegrams which were made known here. From various fields of social life, the Congress has received more than 700 domestic telegrams from manual workers, socialist brigades, intellectuals, scientists, research workers, young people, students and Pioneers. In addition to greetings and good wishes for successful work, almost every telegram announced the fulfilment of Congress pledges and what is more, informed us of further pledges. It seems that the young people were the quickest, or the most ingenious, because they have already named a socialist brigade after the 12th Congress. This means that our people and public opinion support the work of the Congress and the policy of the party not merely politically and verbally, but in deeds as well.

I have just spoken about the unity of the party, because this is the source of the unity in our country. But knowing the response of public opinion, I believe we can repeat what the Central Committee declared in its report: the party has living contacts with the masses; the party and the masses are welded closely together, and on the fundamental aims of socialism the Hungarian working people, irrespective of their party affiliation, ideology, profession, occupation or status, are united and active.

Our distinguished foreign guests have also voiced their impressions of our Congress and their opinions of our debate. They spoke warmly and appreciatively, stating that our people have attained great achievements through their work. The 12th Congress of our party met with a favourable response in the Soviet Union and the other socialist countries. The international Communist movement, the Communist and workers' parties of the world, look with solidarity upon our Congress and wherever they have had an opportunity to express it they have voiced their positive opinion of it. We invited representatives of our fraternal parties from the socialist countries and from the other European Communist and workers' parties to our Congress, but, as was stated during the debate here and as was reported by the press, the Communist and workers' parties of the other continents, North and South America, Asia, Africa and Australia, also expressed their solidarity with our Congress and with our party. This is excellent, and we are grateful for it. It is also a sure confirmation that the 12th Congress of our party has been carrying out its activities appropriately.

The capitalist press took a stand which roughly tallies with reality, naturally expressing it in their own terminology. They say of us that in foreign policy we joined forces with the Soviet Union. They also say the Congress is being very realistic and courageous over economic issues. That we take note of as well. The summary of their commentaries is that the Hungarian People's Republic continues on the path it has pursued so far. And how right they are!

Our Congress has taken a stand for continuing our principled policy. We are continuing our tried methods of realizing the leading role of the party, of which the main feature is persuasion.

In essence, our foreign policy is to continue our international activities in the interest of social progress, socialism, the freedom of peoples, and for peace. Communism and socialism are now being built on three continents. As a result of the course of history, the majority of peoples who are at present building socialism have inherited a grave legacy from their previous ruling classes. Largely for this reason, and because these peoples pursue a new, untrodden path, difficulties also arise during the building of socialism.

Forces hostile to our ideology and to socialism seek to claim that even socialism has turned out to be different from what is seemed it would be at the start; it has not had such great successes; on the contrary, it has difficulties. To that I can only say: let them delight in their daily propaganda to their hearts' content. It is our profound belief that humanity has no other path, future or hope than in peace and a socialist society.

Peace is needed! When we reached this topic in the report, we began by saying how the international situation has now sharpened. This is true, and this worries the sincere supporters of peace, not just here, but in every country in the world. But then, I am deeply convinced that there will be no new world war, that this can be prevented by humanity. Humanity's strength derives from the will which links the better half of the peoples of the world: let us have no war! Naturally, there are also other impressive means in reserve to prevent the launching of a new world war.

We state – thinking particularly about the seven long years of laborious negotiations by which the representatives of the Soviet Union and the United States worked out the SALT 2 agreement – that a balance of forces has been reached. This is the basis for negotiations and why it is sensible to halt the mad arms race. In fact, not only the peoples building socialism have an interest in doing this; the people of the United States and the people of every country in the whole world have an interest in it. There must be peace, there must be a balance of power, but at a lower level of armaments. Each state and every nation should feel itself secure. This is what we struggle for on an international scale.

In the report of the Central Committee we also expressed our support for the solution of disputes by negotiation. We also said (and not for the first time but it may not be superfluous to say it again) that the working class is no unyielding adherent of armed rebellion. Transformation of the social order by peaceful means is the most advantageous for the working class, but whether this can be done or not does not depend on the working class. I mention this, because while we deliberate here, the bourgeoisie have been illustrating how they interpret the class struggle and the means to which they stoop. Think of the Archbishop of San Salvador, who could hardly be called a Communist revolutionary, I suppose, but who, because he spoke out against the fascist terror of the junta, was murdered by gunmen in a chapel, which even in the Middle Ages was considered a sanctuary. Our standpoint is unchanged: we do not wish to export revolution, but we will not stand the export of counter-revolution.

We are frequently referred to in the West as "satellites". We are nobody's satellite, and nobody asks us to be a satellite! The Hungarian People's Republic is a sovereign, independent, socialist country! It is in this knowledge that our party and our people live and work, and we shall continue to work like that. We ourselves work out our policy – whether it is a matter of domestic policy, foreign policy, economic policy, living standards, social policy, culture or methods of management. Naturally, we favour discussions, consultations and exchanges of experience between the fraternal parties and fraternal peoples. When we go to conferences, we do not have the preconceived intention, regardless of what is said there, of maintaining our position unchanged. We take part so that we may listen to everybody. We confer on the basis of collective wisdom, so that we may become wiser, see more, know more, and if necessary adjust our own standpoint.

Pressmen dislike and readers are bored by the rather frequent official communiqués on international affairs that run: "This person met that person and an exchange of views took place." I prefer the term "exchange of views" to the other term "exchange views", because at times I cannot help talking to people whom I would loathe to exchange views with... But we do have an exchange of views, and it is useful and necessary to do so. When people read brief official communiqués, they claim that these fail to tell them what the meeting was about. Quite true. Yet if all the news of international events were to be printed in detail, it would fill up every page in the newspapers. You may rest assured that, wherever we are represented, whether at closed or at open sessions, whether here at home or abroad, whether at the seat of the United Nations or at the Helsinki Conference, whether in Moscow, Warsaw, Prague, Berlin, Bucharest, Belgrade, Sofia, Vienna, Rome, Bonn or Paris, we advocate the same policy, we uphold the same position. By saying this, we should like people whose thinking is close to ours and those whose thinking is far from ours to know and understand that when Hungarians say yes, they mean yes, and when they say no, they mean no. What we have pledged to do we adhere to in honesty, and when we cannot pledge to do something we say so. In politics responsible leaders keep their fingers crossed that they will have a predictable partner. As for us, we are firmly resolved to be a predictable partner. We want to be, and we are, loyal to our allies. We want to be, and we are, faithful to our friends. If we sit down to talk and come to an agreement with the other party, we are fair, abiding and honest partners, and we want to stay that way.

We have never concealed our stand from anyone, anywhere. Moreover, we have correctly presented ourselves in the Western world too, by saying: "You know that we maintain close cooperation, true friendship and brotherhood with the Soviet Union. We want to comply honestly with our obligations undertaken within the framework of the Warsaw Treaty to which we are and shall remain a party until similar alliance systems are simultaneously disbanded." Those who have established contacts with us know this of us and we can only assure them that we will remain so in the future. We are a willing partner to any reasonable suggestion or proposal that is in keeping with the interests of our people, or with mutual interests, or with the general interests of the peoples, and our desire is to serve any good cause in the future as well. I think the Congress will add international credit to the pronouncements of our party, and that is a fine thing.

We Communists are optimistic people who are deeply convinced that the idea of peace and socialism will emerge victorious. As Engels, our great classic, put it, mankind will arrive from the realm of necessity to the realm of liberty, and that's where the true history of mankind will begin.

Very many speakers have referred to questions of party work. That is understandable, since that is the central concern of the Congress. Comrades who hold different posts have clearly explained the essence of party work in its various aspects and pointed out what action they think necessary to improve it further. We have also heard statements to the effect that the trade unions unfortunately waste a considerable part of their energies on "internal self-administration", to the detriment of real work.

This statement can be applied not only to the trade unions but also to our party organizations and mass organizations. But this time we should not bother to inquire which ones, and to what extent. Everyone can improve his own method or style of work so as to avoid, as in the case of a bad furnace, 80 per cent of the energy being used for self-heating and only 20 per cent for real operation, and everyone can make sure that as little energy as possible is used for self-administration.

This is something I would particularly like to call to the attention of young people, of leaders of the Young Communist League. They should be even more resolute and eliminate bureaucratic traits from their work. Young people who have spoken here have given good advice on how to do this. I would only add that they should not learn from older people things that are wrong. They see what is wrong anyway, they see red tape here and there, they see big piles of paper all around us. That is something they should not learn from us. They should learn what is good, so they can cut red tape to the minimum in political work, especially in work with young people.

The question of cadre work has been a matter of great political importance throughout the discussion. Many speakers pointed out the need to make better use of the inherent capacities of man as a matter of decisive significance at the present stage. This applies in general, but it is of still greater importance in cadre work. By the way, I am not a big eater myself, but I like a good meal. When people ask me what I would like to eat, I call the dish by its name. If it is called potato soup, call it that. I am only telling you this to draw a parallel. Our cadre work should be such as to ensure that an official or a leader is indeed what he is meant to be in the full sense of the word. If he is a party secretary he should be that, and not a bureaucrat; if he is a director, he should direct; if he is a scientific worker, he should produce something of scientific value, and so on. Everyone should fulfil the function expected of him. I think that is valid for the work of our party organizations and office holders and, by extension, for our social life as a whole.

I agree with the speaker who said we need to invest, for we cannot do without technological development, or without the development of science, public education and health services; but our funds fall short of our needs, so now the key to improving faster is to use human resources, both in respect of cadres and in general.

During the discussion we have heard many concordant remarks on the Patriotic People's Front, chiefly that there are satisfactory conditions for work in it and for the implementation of our party's policy of alliance. As was also stated in the report to Congress, in this country there are only labouring classes, whose fundamental interests coincide. The class base of our political power is constituted by the worker–peasant alliance in which intellectual workers also join. So the conditions are good.

The fact that Hungary has undergone far-reaching historic change, that the working class has won power and retains it, and that its revolutionary vanguard is the ruling party of the country may cause many Communists to become complacent. Let us take, for example, the fact that we have a strong army and police force. There is generally little talk about their work. We are glad to know that almost every fourth family in Hungary has a car. But we hardly consider the burden shouldered by the people who keep the traffic running smoothly. At an earlier congress we decided to open the gate to tourism, to let Hungarians see for themselves the so-called "Paradise of the West" and to be happy once they got back home; but also to let people from the West gain an insight into the life of the Hungarian people and enable them to know how to treat the lies published about Hungary in their papers. However, those who do not know their work have no idea what tourism means to the Border Guards and the Customs Authorities.

So we have power, we have strength, and we can maintain law and order. But I still say we should not rely on this to maintain order in our society; instead we should rely on political work and persuasion. Believe me, an experience we once gained in underground work is still valid; only the people we have convinced are really, wholeheartedly and fully with us. What a convinced person is able to do for a good cause cannot be done by command, by briefing and least of all by threats. For the implementation of our policy we must continue to rely on persuading people.

Among the officers of the Patriotic People's Front, there are 500 church people of different denominations. When the Central Committee's report was being prepared some comrades suggested that I should, once again, include a sentence reaffirming that in Hungary non-party people may hold any public office, with the exception of party offices, of course. I thought, why should this be restated, since it is an absolutely normal practice with us, as everyone can see? Still, I am glad of that suggestion, for it is proof that the relationship between the state and the churches is sound in this country and that any public function is open to non-party people as well.

Our policy towards the national minorities was another topic discussed in plain and specific terms, illustrating with practical examples the relevant statements in the report of the Central Committee. It so happened that we also heard contributions from two women comrades who spoke about their villages, which are inhabited by national minorities. I back the proposal that the resolution should include due appreciation for the work of the federations of national minorities, because they deserve it. May I add – and this was clearly shown in these contributions – that people belonging to different nationalities live, work and prosper as fully-fledged citizens of Hungary in accordance with the principles of our Leninist policy towards the national minorities, with our laws and with our Constitution. We wish the same for the Hungarians living beyond our borders.

As for what is outstanding about this Congress, I have not yet been able to make a full appraisal, but a few things have given me food for thought. It struck me, for example, that the speakers, except for those who work in these fields, did not dwell on the details of our domestic and foreign policies. I find this to be a positive phenomenon, for I am deeply convinced that the domestic and foreign policies of our party are part and parcel of the life of the masses, are well understood by the people, who know them from experience, endorse and support them and agree with them, while adding that "the resolutions and policy of the party must be better implemented".

It is only natural that economic questions received great attention during the discussion. That is in accordance with the position of the Central Committee. It is the key issue now. While work should be improved in all fields, attention needs to be focused on the economy.

Questions of training, further training and culture were also discussed. The role of general culture and the human factor were similarly given great emphasis. I am glad that a comrade from Pest County and other workers who understand the interrelationships have dealt with cultural questions correctly and in detail. This is important, because we need people who are educated and able to think and act accordingly.

Hardly anything was said this time about the social position of women. I consider this, too, as a positive symptom. Were it an acute issue, it would be impossible to force it out of the congress hall of the HSWP. As almost no complaint was voiced in this respect here, I draw the conclusion that our party, the state and our system have done a great deal in improving the position of women. Much can be mentioned here; progress has also been made in implementing the principle of "equal pay for equal work".

It is said that the relatively smaller number of skilled female workers poses a great problem. That is true, but we realize what cares and tasks women have to shoulder. Therefore, we cannot demand that they become skilled workers in the same proportion and numbers as men, but we shall try to help them more than at present.

The substantial increase in the number of nursery-school places alleviates the burdens shouldered by mothers in childcare, like many other things accomplished by society in order to improve the situation of women. We are pleased to sum up what has so far been accomplished; however, our Congress should resolve that this endeavour will continue, so as further to improve the position of women, and in particular of mothers.

Each one of the 57 speakers spoke from an honourable standpoint and with convincing force. I am rather sorry for my colleagues, the county party first secretaries, because they also had to deal with obligatory subjects. Each and every speaker enriched the Congress, but, if I may, I should like to point out some of them. I believe it was a pleasant experience for every one of us to listen to the speeches of the woman comrade from the Ajka glass factory, the university student from Pécs, the scientific research worker from Budapest and other women comrades. In the espousal of the cause, in the steadfastness of principles, in candidness and political courage, and I must apologize to my male colleagues, the women comrades appear to have carried the day. That is the truth. The entire country saw and heard it.

The woman student from Pécs springs to mind. If I am not mistaken, I believe she is the one who has been a party member for scarcely more than a year. I mention this as proof of the proposal concerning the party rules: it is certainly also worthwhile to engage those who have been party members for scarely more than a year in our work.

Just a few words about the older generation. The position of pensioners represents an important social issue. It was mentioned in the report of the Central Committee, it will also be mentioned in the resolutions of the Congress. Unflinching efforts should be exerted to improve the situation of the elderly, the pensioners, in particular of those long retired on low pensions.

I cannot resist saying that I infinitely rejoiced to hear Comrade Andrásfi's[34] speech. I noticed that everybody was spellbound by it. Without his words, our Congress would have been poorer. He spoke out on behalf of a generation and represented the voice of the old veteran Communists. It appealed to me immeasurably, and I consider his as exemplary behaviour typical of a Communist. Just recall what he said. He related that he had been a county lord-lieutenant and an ambassador, and had gained many distinctions, and now he is proud, rather than ashamed, of being the party secretary in a district area organization. This proves that snobbery is alien to the true Communist; he just serves his cause with all his might.

There is no denying that I had qualms of conscience at not having spoken of the district area party organizations. So far we have not been able to improve the situation of these party organizations. Yet he (Andrásfi) pointed out, convincingly and beautifully, the importance and attraction of this kind of work, instead of us, instead of the

Central Committee. I strongly recommend that you take note of what he said. The comrades working in other party organizations should go and visit the district area party organizations every now and then. They should exchange opinions with those working in those places; attention which will be received gratefully. I, too, now take the opportunity to thank the older generation of Communists for their attitude, for their inspired service to the cause.

Youth was a subject touched upon in almost every speech. I believe this can primarily be attributed to the fact that the party members and our entire society are aware of the extraordinary importance of the role of youth. Secondly, we appear to have qualms of conscience about not having done everything necessary as far as the education of youth is concerned.

I agree with the speakers who said that our young people can, fundamentally, be positively appraised. They study, work, fulfil their army service duty and live up to the expectations. I speak with strong conviction when I agree with the speakers that our party – the socialist revolution – has a rising generation. And the new generation is a good one! This magnificent feeling must inspire us to care for young people with an even greater sense of purpose.

Speaking of youth, it is also necessary to stress the important role of the family. We should ask parents at least to do one thing: not to spoil their children by lavishing on them whatever they lay their eyes on, and more, without demanding from them the fulfilment of even elementary, minor responsibilities.

In November, I read a small item in *Népszabadság* about a road accident. It began, "An 18-year-old inhabitant of Debrecen, an apprentice, swung his car onto the wrong side of the road ... etc." Once, when we were young, we demanded in our leaflets that apprentices should be taught their trade, be given equal pay for equal work, and so on, but we really wrote this only to irritate the bourgeoisie, because we ourselves did not believe that all this was possible. And now I read in *Népszabadság* about an 18-year-old apprentice in his car ... Providing the news item is grammatically correct, he owns the car ... And he is not the only young man in the country to own a car.

We heard a rector of one higher-education establishment tell us that we should give young people practically nothing free of charge. We should make them acquainted in good time with the necessity of giving something in return, at the very least decent behaviour and diligence in learning, to obtain what is due to them from society and the family. As far as the party is concerned, it should provide young people with revolutionary ideals and a guiding goal for life. This goal is socialism. In addition, it is necessary to give them specific assignments. I have mentioned many times that exemplary conduct is the best method of education. I should like to expand on this; giving assignments is an equally good method. Assigning tasks implies trust.

Our young people grumble about many things, sometimes even when they are not right. This is natural and is a concomitant of their age. But their most serious and most common complaint is that when they undertake work during the summer holidays – and there is more to it than just apple or grape picking – they are not entrusted with serious work. This needs to be changed. Our young people must be provided with a guiding ideal, with a goal in life. However, we cannot offer a more noble goal than socialism. Nor do we know anything better than irreproachable work accomplished together with the community. Young people must be given tasks in accordance with their age, because then they will be satisfied.

I recently visited Bábolna, and I was struck by two things. One: we reached the village at 11 o'clock in the morning. I took a look at the street and at the shops, and there was not a single soul to be seen anywhere. Three and a half thousand people live at Bábolna, and 5,000 people work there, but in this village one could not see a single person, young or old, strolling or meandering along the street at 11 a.m. Yet the people are healtly, because those who work well earn well, and those who earn well live well. Perhaps one can learn a lesson from that.

The other thing was that our host greeted us with his general staff. Well, comrades, I should tell you that the general manager was the "veteran"; the oldest member of the general staff of directors and people in such positions was 43 years of age, and the youngest was 37. It is an example to be followed: we should rely on youth, on our young people! They should be assigned tasks. They are particularly fired with ambition to show that they can work better. Let us make it possible for them to show what they are capable of.

In the report we heard, the expected profits at Bábolna were mentioned. It was said that the central deduction has got bigger now, otherwise the profit would be larger. In this respect, may I point out that the deliberations on the guidelines have a general implication which has been reinforced by this Congress. People ask us to stop bothering them with the enumeration of difficulties, with the problems of raw materials, with the price explosion and with the adverse world market prices. May I add that the managers should also stop reckoning how much bigger the profit would be this year if the deduction was retained at the level of the previous year. We should calculate with the international economic environment as it exists. That is the situation, that is how we should live, work and make ends meet. And in particular I ask the managers of the plants to count on this: the deduction will not decrease next year either. If they fulfil this year's plan targets, the deduction will remain as it is, if not, it will be even greater.

We have already said a lot about the circumstances in which we live. A frequent comment is: "They tell us we'll have to produce more efficiently, we'll have to be thrifty, we have a negative economic balance, and only a moderate increase in living standards can be expected." But instead of that, people are right in asking to be informed correctly about the tasks to be accomplished! That is what people demand from their leaders, and it is the obligation of the leaders to give a definite answer.

Sometimes I wonder why a resolution is being implemented with such difficulty. The only comfort I can think of is the story from the Bible, in which thousands of years ago, Moses took up the Ten Commandments. Maybe that was the first "party resolution", but its implementation is still going on. Necessity urges us to work at a somewhat quicker pace.

At our Congress, people from the most varied fields of occupation have expressed their views on what should be done to organize work better and to establish more satisfactory working conditions. Many people stressed this, we heard the stand of the government as well, and now, at the Congress, people whom we did not know before, and who work very well directly in production, have expressed their views too. Our objective is to improve efficiency and quality, and to increase thriftiness. Instead of calculating fictitious sums, we have to assess real costs, and the real international price, that is, what can be obtained for how much, and what can be sold for how much. We must meet this demand. I fully agree with the demand raised at the Congress that our party should fully support the collectives and managers who are ready to take this initiative. The connection between producer prices and consumer prices should be examined, but we do not intend to make any change to the price system itself. Concerning consumer prices: the prices of certain essential consumer goods will continue to be fixed centrally, but even in these cases there must be an organic relationship between the consumer and the producer prices. Otherwise we would not be able to guarantee a supply of commodities in accordance with purchasing power, although this again is one of our great achievements, which must be maintained.

Economic incentives should be maintained. But the delegate who said that incentives in agriculture should not be changed in the course of the year, or each year, but that the prevailing biological cycle should be taken into account, was right. Stability should be aimed at, coupled with flexibility.

The slowing down of the growth rate to a certain degree is a necessary reality, and not a source of joy for us. However, it does allow and encourage us to improve the quality of work. Neither the system of incentives nor the slower growth rate will automatically accomplish anyone's work; we have to make full use of our reserves.

Very often a lot of negative things are said about the construction industry, so that one wonders just how these gigantic building projects can go on in this country. During the past five years, 80 new investment projects were completed, each with a value of more than 500 million Forints; new housing estates, some of them of the size of a town, have emerged. So, the construction industry does function to a certain extent. At the same time, construction requirements and construction capacity have indeed failed to match: requirements surpassed capacity by 30, 40 or an even greater per cent.

You can tell me what you like about commerce: I still recall the truth of an old observation of mine, dating back to my childhood: if there is not enough meat, the customer says hello first, if there is a lot of meat, it is the butcher who first gives the greeting. The reduced growth rate will have a similar, that is stimulating, effect. Now fewer enterprises will launch new investment projects, storming the construction firms with orders. Then maybe fewer orders will be given to sub-contractors, too. Customers will not be crowding out the shops and traders' establishments. In the catering trade we can already see empty places in certain category restaurants. All this will stimulate real economic work.

Prices should also be regulated, and there may be, and must be, cases when certain producer prices and certain consumer prices not only increase, but decrease. Because prices may even go down if we work well and honestly. Of course, this cannot be a general tendency, because raw materials and energy are getting more expensive. The slowing down of the growth rate, and the removal of certain strains, will have a positive effect on the enterprises, on branches of the economy and on people.

Regarding living standards, I reiterate what was said in the report of the Central Committee: we have to devote our main efforts to consolidating the results achieved so far. There will be moderate growth, but conditions for further progress in the years ahead must be ensured. Most likely there will not be a "nation-wide" consensus on the introduction and application of wages according to the work performed. This, I think, also belongs, comrades, to the group of issues where a few good words are needed, where good propaganda and political work should be done.

The paying out of salaries or wages not based on real performance should be discontinued. If we carry this out appropriately, we will implement the general rule of socialist construction work. An advance in the work of building socialism will bring about a regular increase in the living standards of the workers. But everyone has to learn to honour his workplace, his work and his salary.

Those who work properly may feel themselves safe and secure, because they will get on. But people of working age and in good health who do not want to work honestly will and should have cause for concern. Our endeavours to this end also include, as was mentioned in the report, acting much more firmly and severely against those who cause damage to public property, and against parasitism. We stressed in the report that wages cannot be paid for merely being present on the job. People paid attention to this and sympathized with it. This should become the rule.

In connection with the Congress, the capitalist press mentioned (and volumes had been written about it earlier) that the Hungarian People's Republic has this-and-that sort of economic policy, such-and-such a system of economic management, and that it bravely applies capitalist methods. This is how they "praise" us. On the other hand, they criticized us for calculating profits, then they found fault with the Győr Wagon Factory because it dismissed workers it did not need. To this I can reply on the basis of my outlook: these are not capitalist methods, these are socialist methods. First of all, the essential question is whether workers have to economize for the benefit of a capitalist, or for the benefit of the people. If a worker is obliged to economize for a capitalist, then this is the capitalist method. If he does so for the benefit of the people, then this is the socialist one. If we calculate whether production is effective, that, in my view, is the socialist method. The issue of whether the work should be of good quality is, in my view, a requirement of socialism, because it is not a matter of indifference whether good or better things are produced for the capitalists or for a socialist society.

In the socialist system, public property should be handled rationally and thriftily, which is a revolutionary, socialist obligation, a norm of the socialist state. It has no connection with the balance of payments, which we cannot now be proud of. All we can say, and it is not a trifling thing to say, is that last year, for the first time after many years, we managed to improve it a little, and this should be appreciated. I think these socialist norms will continue to prevail when the international balance of payments has further improved.

It is a fact to be welcomed, and not only by the experts, that the role of public education and culture and also human factors were mentioned. The attainment of our economic objectives requires experts with higher and higher qualifications and continuous further training. Having this in mind, I greet the employees and representatives of public education, science and culture. During a break yesterday we had a short meeting with them. Our Congress is attended by the best representatives of the Hungarian intelligentsia, some of them as invited guests. We have here our non-party allies and friends. We belong together! We are of the same people, our homeland is the same, we live together, get on together, and have the same problems.

Our tasks are enormous, but anyone who has followed the work of the Congress with due attention and is familiar with the resolution or will study it, will see that the tasks are not just great and difficult, they are clear-cut too. And that is already a good start to our work.

Both on behalf of the Central Committee and the Central Control Committee, on my behalf and on behalf of Comrade János Brutyó I express my sincere thanks for your support, for the fact that the speakers endorsed our reports, and expressed in a number of ways their readiness to support actively the policy and objectives outlined here by the Central Committee, as well as by the Central Control Committee. In my view, all the speakers made excellent and high-standard contributions to both the reports and the draft resolutions during the discussion. This also reflects our united way of thinking, the strength of our party, its creative power, and its opportunities, and indicates the readiness for action of those who have joined or are about to join our ranks. There is unity within the party, the people are in full agreement with us and are ready to support the line of this Congress.

I ask everyone present to manifest the same unity in the work of implementation. Show an example, because your words will have special weight for the people, since it was you who adopted these decisions.

Confidence and readiness for action prevail both in the party and in the people. This is a logical link: our people are confident because they are ready to act, and we may feel confident because the deeds will back our optimism.

We Communists are optimists by nature, since our ideology is optimistic. We have chosen this ideology. The much respected and oldest delegate here, Comrade István Hunya, precedes all of us; he has been a member of the party for 63 years, while the youngest of the delegates has been one for hardly more than a year.

Fortunately, few people present can remember the 1929 Depression. Those were very hard, difficult times. Various ideologies emerged even among the working class and the peasantry. Philosophies and religious sects born of misery were popular. People living in hardship tried to find hope in whatever way they could. I do not want to blame anyone for that, since a person who believes in something is better than a cynically-minded person. There are certain sects which from time to time forecast the expected end of the world, and prepare for it. We Communists prepare ourselves not for the end of the world, but for life.

Communists always have confidence. This distinguishes them from the followers of other ideologies. Naturally, no one is born with a membership card in his hand. Non-party people will only later become Communists, party members. And there is another difference too. A Communist says: I would like to be happy, I would like my family to be happy, but not through trampling down or exploiting other people, not as a result of servile flattery to the exploiter; I would like to be happy as a result of my own work, on the basis of my own rights, within my own system, together with my comrades! The Communist wants to get everything from life that he is entitled to, but he wants to achieve it through work, and together with his class-brothers.

A Communist cannot live in happiness while others live in misery and under oppression.

That is a Communist characteristic; we must preserve it!

The Communist believes in the ideal; he never gives up hope and he is always ready for action. So let us have hope and take action. And if you decide to accept the reports and the resolutions, then let us show the same unity in putting them into effect!

Notes to the Speeches and Interviews

[1] Kardelj, Eduard 1910—1979
Yugoslav politician, member of the illegal Communist party from 1929. He was arrested in 1930 and received a two-year sentence. He spent three years (1934—1937) as an emigrant in the Soviet Union. After his return to Yugoslavia he became member of the Central Committee of the Communist Party (1938). During the war he was the organizer of the Slovenian resistance movement. His positions after 1945: Vice-President (1945—1948); Minister of Foreign Affairs (1948—1953); Deputy Premier of the Yugoslavian Federal Executive Committee (1953—1963); Speaker of the Yugoslavian Federal Assembly (1963—1967); Member of the Collective State-Presidency (1974—1979).

[2] Gáspár, Sándor 1917—
Hungarian politician, member of the illegal Communist party from 1936. Formerly an engine fitter, he became the member of the Executive Committee of the Ironworkers' Union in 1945. His positions from 1945: Deputy General Secretary of the Central Council of Trade Unions (1952—1956); General Secretary of the Central Council of Trade Unions (1956—1959); First Secretary of the Budapest Committee of the Hungarian Socialist Workers' Party (1959—1961 and 1963—1965); Secretary-General of the Central Council of Trade Unions (1965—). He became a member of the Central Committee of the Communist party in 1957, and of the Political Committee in 1959.

[3] Losonczy, Géza 1917—1957
Hungarian politician and journalist, member of the illegal Communist party from 1939. He was active in the resistance movement from 1940 to 1945. In 1946 he became a member of the Central Committee of the Communist Party. From 1947 to 1949 he was Undersecretary of the Cabinet, from 1949 to 1951 he was Undersecretary for Public Education. He was arrested on false charges in 1951. After his release in 1954 he worked as a journalist and became Chief Editor of the journal *Magyar Nemzet* (Hungarian Nation) in 1956. In October 1956 he was State Minister in the Imre Nagy government, and member of the Political Committee of the Communist party. In early November he was co-opted into the Executive Committee of the newly formed Hungarian Socialist Workers' Party. After November 4 he took refuge in the Yugoslav Embassy in Budapest from where he was taken prisoner. He died in prison.

[4] Z. Nagy, Ferenc
Hungarian peasant politician, member of the Smallholders' Party. He was Member of Parliament.

[5] Beresztóczy, Miklós 1905—1973
Honorary provost, politician. He was Head of the Department of Roman Catholic Affairs in the Ministry for Religion and Education (1938—1945), and Chairman of the National Peace Council

of Priests (1950—1956). He was Member of Parliament (1953—1973) and Deputy Speaker of Parliament (1961—1973).

⁶ Péter, János 1910—
Hungarian politician, priest in the Reformed Church from 1935, member of the Communist party from 1961. From 1949 to 1957 he was Bishop of the Transtibiscan Synod of the Reformed Church. His positions thereafter: President of the Institute of Cultural Relations (1957—1958); First Deputy Minister of Foreign Affairs (1958—1961); member of the Presidential Council (1957—1961); Minister of Foreign Affairs (1961—1973); Deputy Speaker of Parliament (1973—). He became member of the Central Committee of the Communist party in 1966.

⁷ Ilku, Pál 1912—1973
Teacher, Communist politician. Member of the Czechoslovakian Communist party from 1937. He collaborated with the Hungarian illegal Communist movement from 1939. After 1945 he worked in the Hungarian Communist party apparatus and from 1948, in the Army. He was Deputy Minister of Defense (1957—1958), Deputy Minister of Culture (1958—1961) and Minister of Culture (1961—1973). He was member of the Central Committee from 1958, and member of the Political Committee from 1962 till 1970.

⁸ Csikesz, (Mrs.), József 1918—
Communist politician, member of the illegal Communist party from 1942. In 1945 she became the Secretary of the IX. District Committee of the Hungarian Women's Democratic Association. In 1946—1947 she worked as a fitter, and in 1947 she became a Communist party employee in the apparatus. She was member of the Communist party committee of Budapest (1950—1952), and later became the Secretary of this committee (1954—1964). From 1965 till 1975 she was Deputy Chairperson of the Municipal Council of Budapest. She is member of the Central Control Committee of the Communist party.

⁹ Szigeti, Attila ?—1957
Publicist, active member of the National Peasant Party after 1945. In 1956 he became the Chairman of the Revolutionary Committee in the city of Győr. Following November 4, for a short time he collaborated with the new Kádár government. Thereafter he was arrested and committed suicide in prison.

¹⁰ Darvas, József 1912—1973
Writer and politician. He was a leading figure in the National Peasant Party founded in 1939. After the dissolution of his party, he joined the Communist party of which he was acknowledged as a member from 1932. He was Minister of Construction and Public Labour (1947—1949), Minister of Construction (1949—1950), Minister of Education (1950—1953), Minister of Public Education (1953—1956).

¹¹ One of the most important newspapers in the so-called Christian-National regime (1919—1944).

¹² Weekly journal edited by István Milotay. In 1919 it became a daily newspaper.

¹³ Parragi, György 1902—1963
Prominent Hungarian journalist. In the war years he contributed to the daily *Magyar Nemzet* (Hungarian Nation) revealing a strong anti-German stand. He was interned by the Germans in 1944. Following his return, he became a Smallholders' MP and, in 1947, he joined the newly formed Independent Hungarian Democratic Party. From 1957 till 1962 he was chief editor of the sole paper to appear on Monday, the *Hétfői Hírek*. He was Member of the Presidential Council from 1953.

[14] Mesterházi, Lajos 1916—1979
Writer, publicist. A bank clerk until 1945, he became an editor at the Hungarian Radio Company (1945—1949). He was chief editor of the journal *Művelt nép* (Cultured Nation) (1950—1955). He was then editor of the literary journal *Élet és Irodalom* (Life and Literature) (1957—1959). From 1966 he was chief editor of the journal *Budapest*.

[15] Formed in January 1957 by the Communist party, the circle was a forum of intellectuals active in post-1956 consolidation. The circle was dissolved in January 1958.

[16] The official newspaper of the Communist party started in November 1956. It appears daily.

[17] Kisházi, Ödön 1900—1975
Social Democratic worker, member of the National Federation of Iron Workers throughout the 1920's and 1930's. He became Deputy Chairman of the Trade Unions Council in 1945. He became Communist party member following the merger of his party with the Communists in 1948. He was arrested on false charges in 1952, and was rehabilitated in 1955. He was Minister of Labour (1957—1963) and Deputy Chairman of the Presidential Council (1963—1975). He was member of the Central Committee from 1962.

[18] Nyers, Rezső 1923—
Communist politician, member of the Social Democratic Party since 1940. He worked as a printer. In 1945, he became Secretary of the Social Democratic Party Committee of Kispest, and in 1947—1948 he was Secretary of the Social Democratic Party Committee of Budapest and its environs. After the fusion of the Social Democratic Party and the Communist party, he became member of the Central Leadership of the merged party, and from 1962 till 1974 he was also member of the Political Committee and Secretary of the Central Committee. He was Deputy Chairman of the National Council of Cooperatives (1954—1956); Minister of Food (August—November 1956); Minister of Public Supplies (1956—1957); Chairman of the National Council of Cooperatives (1957—1960), Minister of Finance (1960—1962). He is Member of Parliament since 1958.

[19] Rónai, Sándor 1892—1965
Social Democratic, and later Communist politician. As a bricklayer, he became member of the Social Democratic Party in 1910. In 1919 he was member of the Workers' Council of the city of Miskolc during the Republic of Councils. From 1922 he acted as Secretary of the Miskolc SDP Committee. In 1945 he became Minister of Public Supplies in the Provisional Government (July—November 1945); he was then Minister of Trade and Cooperatives (1945—1949). With the fusion of the SDP with the Communist party in 1948, he was co-opted to the Central Leadership of the merged party of which he remained a member until his death. He was Minister of Foreign Trade (1949—1950); Chairman of the Presidential Council (1950—1952); Speaker of Parliament (1952—1962); and Minister of Trade (Nov. 4, 1956—Feb. 28, 1957).

[20] Szurdi, István 1911—
Textile worker, Social Democrat and later Communist politician. Member of the SDP from 1936, and of the Communist party since 1948. He was member of the Central Leadership (1948—1950, and again from 1957. He was Minister of Domestic Trade (1966—1976) and Member of Parliament (1956—1975).

[21] Dobozy, Imre 1917—1982
Hungarian writer and journalist. Active in the anti-German resistance from 1944, he joined the Communist party in 1945. He worked as a journalist and became chief editor of the literary journal *Élet és Irodalom* (Life and Literature) (1961—1963). Since 1959 he was Chairman of the Hungarian Writers' Association. He was member of the Central Committee since 1975.

[22] Thurzó, Gábor 1912—1979
Hungarian writer and journalist.

[23] Németh, László 1901—1975
Prominent Hungarian writer and essayist belonging to the populist movement. He worked as a dentist and as a school doctor in the late twenties. From the early thirties he devoted his time to literary activities and contributed to many influential publications. His concept of social and national reform had a great effect on Hungarian intellectuals. In the late 1940's and early 1950's he withdrew from public life and began to publish his works again in the late 1950's.

[24] Háy, László 1891—1975
Economist and politician, member of the Hungarian Social Democratic Party from 1909. In 1919 he joined the Hungarian Communist party. He went into emigration in 1920 and returned to Hungary in 1945. His positions from 1945: Secretary of State for Foreign Trade (1945—1946); President of the Hungarian National Bank (1946—1948); Minister of Foreign Trade (1954—1956); Dean of the Karl Marx University of Economics (1957—1963). In 1959 he became a member of the Central Committee of the HSWP.

[25] Komócsin, Zoltán 1923—1974
Communist politician, member of the illegal Communist party since 1938. He was Secretary of the Communist party committee of the city of Szeged (1945—1948), Head of the Propaganda Department of the Central Leadership (1954), Party Secretary of Hajdú-Bihar County (1956—1957), First Secretary of the Communist Youth Organization (1957—1961), chief editor of *Népszabadság*, the party's official newspaper (1961—1965), Secretary of the Central Committee (1965—1974). He was member of the Central Committee and of the Political Committee from 1957. He was Member of Parliament from 1949.

[26] Illyés, Gyula 1902—1983
Prominent Hungarian writer and publicist, a leading figure among the populist intelligentsia of Hungary, from the 1930's. In the early thirties he collaborated with the left-wing workers' movement and visited the Soviet Union in 1934. He was collaborator and editor of highly influential journals, his writings were formative in the development of the so-called modern populist thought in the country. He was active in the National Peasant Party (1945—1949), and became Member of Parliament. He was Vice President of the PEN International from 1970.

[27] Lukács, György 1885—1971
Hungarian literary critic, philosopher, Communist politician. As a literary critic Lukács was an exponent of evolving modern Hungarian literature at the turn of the century. As a philosopher, he was an internationally renowned figure of contemporary German idealism. He joined the Hungarian Communist party at the end of 1918 and became People's Commissar of Culture in the Communist government of Béla Kun. Following the fall of the Republic of Councils, he fled to Vienna (1920—1929) and carried on his political activities in the Communist party. In 1924, he published *History and Class Consciousness* which is held to be the most significant Marxist work of the age. From 1929 he lived in the USSR and returned to Hungary in 1945 when he became professor at the University of Budapest and a leading exponent of Communist cultural policies. His major synthetic works were written in the 1950's. His *Aesthetics* was published in Hungary after 1965, while his *Ontology* appeared only posthumously. In 1956 he was Minister of Public Education in the Imre Nagy government and participated in the formation of the HSWP. On the 4th of November he went to the Yugoslav Embassy from where he was taken to Romania and held there until 1957. He lived in forced retirement after his return, but in 1967 he rejoined the party and was officially acknowledged as the most authoritative Hungarian Marxist philosopher.

[28] Kállai, Gyula 1910—
Journalist and politician, member of the illegal Communist party from 1931. He represented the

Communist party in the resistance movement during the war. He was Minister of Foreign Affairs from 1949 to 1951, in which year he was arrested on false charges. Released in 1954, he became Deputy Minister of Public Education. He was active in the reorganization of the Communist party after 1956, and became member of the Central Committee and the Political Committee. His positions following 1956: Minister of Cultural Affairs (1956—1958); Deputy President of the Council of Ministers (1959—1965); President of the Council of Ministers (1965—1967); President of Parliament (1967—1970).

[29] King Stephen c. 970—1038
Prince of Hungary from 997, the first king of Hungary from 1001. His historic achievement was the organization of the Hungarian royal state and the conversion of his people to Christianity. With his victory over the pagan chiefs he secured the power of the Monarchy, and, by adopting a peaceful policy towards foreign powers, he secured a better status for his people in Europe.

[30] Széchenyi, István, Count 1791—1860
Aristocrat, intellectual and political leader in the Hungarian reform movement preceeding the 1848 revolution. In his books he urged Hungarians to take the path of Western modernization. To this end he took the initiative in founding the Hungarian Academy of Sciences in 1825, in regulating the river Tisza, and in building the first bridge across the Danube. In the forties he increasingly disapproved of Kossuth's radicalism and suffered a gradual loss of popularity. In the 1848 government he accepted the transportation portfolio, but in a short while he withdrew from politics. He committed suicide in exile.

[31] Táncsics, Mihály 1799—1884
Writer and politician of peasant origin active in the reform movement before 1848. As a follower of Owen and Fourier, he preached the abolition of class distinctions. He was Member of Parliament from the spring of 1848, and editor of the *Munkások Ujsága* (Workmen's Journal). After the defeat of the Revolution, he received a death sentence, but managed to escape from the authorities. Captured in 1860, he was sentenced for 15 years. Released from prison with an amnesty, he again became an active politician as the head of the Hungarian Section of the General Workers' Union.

[32] Werbőczi, István 1458—1541
Chief Justice and Palatine of Hungary. He compiled the so-called "Tripartitum opus juris" codifying the Hungarian legal system. Although his work had never been enacted, it still served as a source of common law until the 19th century.

[33] Prince Árpád ?—907
The prince of Hungarians during the time of the conquest of Danubian Hungary.

[34] Andrásfi, Gyula
Communist worker, active in the resistance in 1944. He was Ambassador to Mongolia from 1961 to 1968.

Index

Adenauer, Konrad 360
Ady, Endre 89, 164, 357
Afghanistan 431f
Africa 43, 104, 249, 263, 265, 282, 431
Agriculture 78ff, 82, 114, 147, 178f, 205f, 267, 330f
Albania 211, 212
Algeria 249
Alliance policy 110, 219ff, 227ff, 265ff, 316f, 352, 433ff
Allied powers 43, 44, 66, 68, 154, 164, 359
Andrásfi, Gyula 452, 462
Angola 407, 431
Angyalföld (district of Budapest) 84f, 181
Anti-Dühring (Herr Eugen Dühring's Revolution in Science) 18f, 24, 289
Anti-Fascist Resistance 41ff, 47ff, 158, 159, 161, 163, 165, 184, 293, 357, 361
Apró, Antal 65, 162, 185
Aragon, Louis 27
Argentine 230
Árpád, Prince 388, 462
Arrow Cross Party 30, 44, 49, 50, 53, 55, 61, 95, 148, 154, 155, 157, 193, 290
Asia 249, 263, 265, 282, 431
Austria 9, 14, 17, 35, 59, 127, 138, 165, 180, 336f, 382ff, 408, 488
Austro-Hungarian Monarchy 9, 14, 127, 337
Axis powers 35, 66, 154

Bábolna 454
Bajcsy-Zsilinszky, Endre 42, 50, 52f, 58, 157
Bakó, Ágnes 196
Barbusse, Henri 27
Becher, Johannes R. 27
Belgium 91, 161, 165, 384
Belgrade Meeting 384f, 390, 394, 396
Bem, József 60, 90, 162
Beresztóczy, Miklós 181f, 458

Berinkey government 154
Berlin 138, 237, 346, 360, 362
Berlinguer, Enrico 398
Bessarabia 253
Bethlen, István 22, 24, 35, 42, 43, 53, 154, 155, 157, 158
Biatorbágy 27
Blum, Léon 27
Borsod (County) 194
Brecht, Bertold 27, 34
Brezhnev, Leonid 140
Brioni 100
Brutyó, János 457
Budapest 14, 17ff, 57, 194, 289ff
Bulgaria 17, 29, 44, 69, 100, 138, 253, 374
Byron, George Gordon 357

Cadres' policy 78f, 194, 200f, 217ff, 281, 285f, 298f, 420f, 450
Cambodia 28, 346, 431
Canada 130, 165, 357
Caribbean Crisis (1962) 262
Carter, Jimmy 395
Castro, Fidel 137, 246
Central powers 154
Central Statistical Office 80
Charles IV 35
Chile 28, 305
China, People's Republic of 68, 88, 100, 201, 211, 250ff, 263f, 287, 324, 410, 411, 432
Chotek, Sophia 9
Churches 14, 57f, 111, 123f, 174, 181f, 250, 280f, 389ff, 412f, 428f, 434
Churchill, Winston S. 68, 81
Clemenceau, Georges 253
CMEA (Council for Mutual Economic Assistance) 249, 255, 263f, 301ff, 374, 389, 394, 407
Coalition period 59ff, 172

Cold War 68, 69, 127, 238, 346, 360
Collectivization of agriculture 78, 114ff, 178, 207f
COMINFORM (Information Bureau of Communist Workers' Parties) 69, 86
COMINTERN (Communist International) 29, 36, 37, 46ff, 69, 153, 159
Committee of National Defense 78
Common Market, European 255, 263, 389, 394
Communist Party, Hungarian
(Hungarian Party of Communists: November 1918—June 1919, August 1919—1925 1927—1944; Socialist-Communist Workers' Hungarian Party: June—August 1919; Socialist Workers' Party of Hungary: 1925—1927; Peace Party: 1944; Hungarian Communist Party: 1944—1948; Hungarian Working People's Party: 1948—1956; Hungarian Socialist Workers' Party: 1956—) 15, 24ff, 27f, 29, 37, 45, 47, 48, 49, 52, 54ff, 62, 66, 67, 72, 74, 83ff, 94, 99, 102f, 105ff, 125, 140, 144, 145ff, 151f, 153, 154, 155ff, 174ff, 181, 185, 191ff, 200, 206, 210, 211, 212f, 216ff, 225ff, 231, 236, 260ff, 282ff, 293, 295ff, 304ff, 310ff, 324ff, 326ff, 339ff, 342, 348ff, 357, 364, 384, 398, 400, 401ff, 426, 427, 430ff, 446ff, 458, 459
Communist Party (USSR) 26, 82, 85ff, 106, 140, 199, 211ff, 226, 287ff, 393, 397, 404
Communist youth movement 24, 26, 33f, 67, 154, 158, 164, 165, 186, 200, 206, 230, 232, 261, 298, 307ff, 405, 434, 449f
Congo 254, 262
Consolidation of power after 1956 100ff, 169ff, 174ff, 183, 222ff, 225, 350, 422f
Constitution, Hungarian 145, 235, 335ff, 412, 434, 451
Corriere della Sera 383
Csepel (district of Budapest) 174, 176, 210, 241f
Csermanek, Borbála 9, 10, 13, 14, 23
Csermanek, Jenő 50
Csikesz, Mrs. József 182, 459
Csillag prison 39
Cuba 138
Cult of personality 86, 211f, 349
Culture 79, 245f, 281f, 338, 417ff
Czechoslovakia 9, 17, 35, 66, 69, 100, 127, 138, 160, 221, 242, 253, 293, 359

Dálnoki Miklós, Béla 52, 160
Dante, Alighieri 381
Darvas, József 184, 459
de Gaulle, Charles 231

Debrecen 293
Democracy 67, 69,113, 143, 208f, 223ff, 269f, 373, 398
Denmark 384
Dictatorship of the proletariat 122, 172f, 177, 199ff
Dinnyés, Lajos 66, 163
Diósgyőr 292
Dobozy, Imre 233, 460
Dögei, Imre 114, 166
Dogmatism 192ff, 196ff, 213f, 349
Dominica 254, 262
Dostoyevsky, Fyodor 73
Dózsa, György 20, 58, 154, 336
Dual Cross Blood Federation 35, 49, 156
Dudás, József 95, 164
Dulles, John Foster 254, 360
Dunaújváros 107

Eaton, Cyrus 137
Economic development 78ff, 128, 265f, 272ff, 311ff, 328ff, 337f, 413ff, 436ff, 455
Eckhardt, Tibor 158
Education 18, 80
Egypt 98, 249
Ehrenburg, Ilya 84
Elections 34, 53f, 62, 66
Élet és Irodalom 460
Elizabeth, Empress 9
Emigrés 101, 124, 187, 399f
Engels, Friedrich 19ff, 135, 224, 289, 449
Entente 14, 15, 20
Eötvös College 55, 160, 187
Erdei, Ferenc 60, 162
Esztergom 52, 57, 292
Etelköz Federation 34, 155
Ethiopia 407, 431
Eurocommunism 383, 393, 397, 426, 427
Europe 29, 256ff, 346, 357ff, 379ff, 383ff, 393, 407

Fajon, Etienne 237
Farkas, Mihály 54ff, 61, 64, 66, 71f, 78, 82, 85, 86, 87, 90, 125, 160
Fascism 36, 41, 42, 47, 68, 158, 187, 231, 359
Fauré, Paul 27
Fenákel, János 26
Finland 384, 408
First Hungarian Army 44, 52
Fiume (Rijeka) 9, 10, 153
Five Year Plans 78, 272ff, 312, 329, 333ff, 340, 344, 348, 354, 364f, 369, 375, 376, 377, 406, 413, 436ff
Foreign policy 111, 179, 238ff, 248ff, 262ff, 303, 408f, 430ff

Foreign trade 242f, 300f, 365, 388, 408ff
Foreign travel 124, 247, 381, 387, 408, 450
France 44, 55, 98, 153, 155, 159, 164, 227, 230f, 233, 234, 240, 257, 281, 357ff, 384, 408, 413, 425ff
Francis Ferdinand, Archduke 9
Francis Joseph I 9, 21
Frey, Roger 231
Fürst, Sándor 27, 43, 155

Garbai, Sándor 15, 153
Gáspár, Sándor 170, 172, 185, 299, 458
German Democratic Republic 138, 221, 237, 242, 253, 346, 353, 361ff
Germany 17, 30, 35ff, 43, 44, 45, 49, 53, 55, 57, 66, 69, 156, 158, 159, 160, 230f, 257, 357ff
Germany, Federal Republic of 68, 253, 256f, 346, 361ff, 384ff, 394ff, 407, 408
Gerő, Ernő 54ff, 71f, 78, 82, 85, 87f, 90, 94, 126, 160
Gestapo (Geheime Staats Polizei) 43, 157, 161
Ghana 262, 264
Gide, André 27
Giscard d'Estaing, Valéry 425ff
Goethe, Johann Wolfgang 381
Goldman, György 45
Gomulka, Wladyslaw 90, 237
Gorky 210, 215
Gorky, Maxim 210
Great Britain 35, 38, 81, 98, 156, 164, 230, 233, 257, 281, 322
Great Depression (1929–1933) 23, 41, 307, 457
Great October Socialist Revolution 210, 302, 393, 402, 411, 420
Grover, Preston 238
Győr 184, 293, 414
Gyula 292

Habsburgs 15, 20, 156, 164, 336
Háy, László 300, 461
Haynau, Julius Jakob 20, 154
Hegedüs, András 86, 90, 164
Hegel, Georg Wilhelm Friedrich 19
Helsinki Conference 138, 379ff, 383, 384, 390, 394, 395, 396, 398f, 407, 425
Hétfői Hírek 459
Hitler, Adolf 22, 35ff, 43f, 66, 68, 155, 163, 359
Ho Chi Minh 258
Horthy, Miklós 21f, 35ff, 42, 43f, 49f, 61, 66, 88, 95, 98, 154, 155, 156, 164, 169, 227, 321, 357

Horthy regime 16, 33, 53, 65, 77, 104, 137f, 139, 146, 147, 155, 156, 169, 187, 196, 197, 227, 230, 231, 337
Hoxha, Enver 211
Hugo, Victor 226
Human rights 247, 342, 392, 396
Hungarian Front 49, 50
Hungarian Historical Commemorative Committee 42, 184
Hungarian National Defense Society 35, 156
Hungarian National Independence Front 52, 184
Hunya, István 457
Hunyadi, Mátyás 336

Ilku, Pál 182, 459
Illyés, Gyula 316, 461
India 249, 264
Indonesia 262, 264
Intellectuals 231ff, 267, 412
International Communist movement 211ff, 229ff, 251ff, 286ff, 383ff, 393, 397, 408ff, 426f, 445
Internationalism 139, 184, 203, 293, 324
Iran 431
Iraq 254
Israel 98
Italy 9, 35, 43, 153, 154, 158, 164, 281, 388ff, 397f, 408

Japan 35, 359
Jews 35, 44f, 51, 101, 155, 156, 158
Johnson, Lyndon B. 250
Jordan 179
Joseph, Archduke 20
József, Attila 10, 11, 14, 31, 40f, 153
June Resolution of 1953 82, 350, 422

Kállai, Gyula 335, 461
Kállay, Miklós 43, 47, 158
Kapoly 10ff, 56
Kardelj, Eduard 170, 458
Károlyi, Mihály 14, 15, 58, 153, 154, 164
Károlyi government 21
Kéthly, Anna 59f, 161
Khrushchev, Nikita 85f, 100, 107, 136f, 139f, 210, 211, 237
Kilián, György 96, 165
Király, Béla 96, 165
Kisházi, Ödön 229, 460
Kiss, János 50, 159
Köböl, József 65, 162
Kollwitz, Käthe 27
Komárom 49
Komócsin, Zoltán 316, 461

Kopácsi, Sándor 96, 165
Korea 68, 100, 184, 257, 321, 322
Korean War 77
Korvin, Ottó 43, 157
Kossuth, Lajos 89, 164, 184, 336, 357
Kosygin, Aleksei 140
Kőszeg 292
Kovács, Béla 59, 62, 161
Kovács, Imre 60, 162
Kreisky, Bruno 382ff
Kulak 77, 79, 123, 163
Kun, Béla 15, 29, 37, 40, 153, 154, 155

Lakatos government 157
Land reform 14, 16, 57f, 207
Landler, Jenő 29, 155
Laos 346, 431
Latin America 263, 265, 282, 431
League for the Revision of the Trianon Peace Treaty 35, 156
League of Nations 35, 357
Le Monde 383
Lenin, Vladimir I. 41, 59, 68, 81, 112f, 115, 118, 123, 125, 143, 170, 199, 218, 219, 221, 224, 334, 357
Levente Organization 57
Lewis, Sinclair 244
L'Humanité 222
Li Si Man 68
Liberation Committee of the Hungarian National Uprising 50
Liberation of Hungary 16, 29, 32, 33, 45, 48, 51ff, 60, 62, 71, 73, 78, 82, 95, 96, 104, 127, 134, 145, 146, 147, 148, 169, 173, 189f, 197, 205, 219, 224, 230, 231, 233, 234, 235, 236, 266, 276f, 279f, 290, 291, 300f, 317ff, 333, 338, 366, 391, 398
Living standards 82, 127, 134, 173, 189f, 276f, 279f, 300f, 317ff, 338, 440f, 455f
Lloyd George, David 253
London, Jack 244
Longo, Luigi 398
Losonczy, Géza 176, 458
Lőwy, Sándor 43, 158
Lukács, György 316, 461

McCarthy, Joseph 360
MacMahon, Edme Patrice Maurice, comte de 226
Madrid 41
Magyar Nemzet 97, 165, 458, 459
Maléter, Pál 96, 165
Malinovsky, Rodion 258
Management of economy 111f, 127ff, 242f, 249, 272ff, 295ff, 304ff, 317ff, 353f, 436ff, 455f

Mann, Thomas 27, 357
Mao Tse-tung 253, 410
Marchais, Georges 426
Marshall Plan 359
Marosán, György 59f, 66, 87f, 98, 161f
Marx, Karl 25, 59, 80, 121, 122, 139, 144, 224, 251, 351, 357, 376, 417
Marxism–Leninism 18ff, 99, 120, 143, 170ff, 174ff, 192, 203, 211, 216, 220, 223ff, 232, 251, 261, 267, 278ff, 284, 286ff, 289, 296, 315, 324, 335, 342, 350ff, 371, 375f, 377, 378, 393, 404, 410, 411, 417f, 422, 442, 443, 445
Matuska, Szilveszter 27
Maximilian, Emperor of Mexico 9
Mesterházi, Lajos 195, 289, 460
Mező, Imre 97, 99, 165
Michaelmas Daisy Revolution 290
Mikszáth, Kálmán 6, 153
Mindszenty, József 57f, 73, 98, 124, 137, 161, 224, 226f, 243f, 250, 391
Minorities 21, 35, 399f, 434f
Miskolc 293
Mitterand, François 426
Molière 233, 381
Molnár, Erik 72, 163
Moscow 29, 40, 46, 48, 53, 56, 82, 95, 146, 155, 156, 157, 162, 164, 210, 238
Mozambique 431
Munkások Újsága 462
Münnich, Ferenc 99f, 165
Mussolini, Benito 43f
Művelt Nép 460

Nagy, Elek 175
Nagy, Ferenc 58f, 62, 98, 161, 224
Nagy, Imre 51, 59f, 62, 72, 82ff, 88, 89, 91ff, 96, 97, 98, 100ff, 104f, 157, 159, 160, 161, 164, 176, 180, 183, 196, 199, 224, 228
National socialists (nazis) 30, 35, 36, 45, 53, 55, 150, 155
National unity 113, 201, 221
Nationalism 112, 139, 202f, 252, 287f
NATO (North Atlantic Treaty Organization) 64, 249, 254ff, 359ff, 386, 389, 392, 399, 410
Németh, László 233, 461
Némethy, Jenő 61
Nemzeti Függetlenség 165
Nemzeti Újság 187, 459
Népszabadság 197, 316, 453, 460, 461
Népszava 42, 157, 159
New York 137f, 141, 385
Nicaragua 431
Nógrád (County) 173, 194

Novotný, Antonin 237
Nyergesújfalu 49
Nyers, Rezső 229, 460

October events of 1956 87ff, 169ff, 179, 182ff, 196, 226ff, 236, 321, 360, 392
Ógyalla 9
Old people 306f, 452
Orbán, László 61
Orlando, Vittorio Emanuele 253

Pakistan 264
Pálffy, György 71, 73f, 163
Paris Commune 17, 28, 143
Parragi, György 187, 459
Patriotic People's Front 60, 97, 113, 143, 144, 147, 150, 156, 165, 181, 184, 185, 204ff, 247, 261, 269, 280, 316, 340, 356, 369, 372, 413, 429, 449, 451
Paul VI, Pope 389ff, 429
Peace 86, 141, 240ff, 303, 357ff, 379ff, 383ff, 427f, 447f
Peace Party (see Communist Party, Hungarian)
Peasant Party 42, 48, 49, 53, 59f, 65, 66, 91, 98, 103, 156, 157, 162
Peasantry 11ff, 78, 110 118, 205f, 267, 319, 330
Pécs 293
Peidl, Gyula 153, 154, 227
Pesti Hírlap 164
Péter, Gábor 71, 84, 86, 126, 163
Péter, János 182, 184, 459
Petőfi Circle 89, 164
Petőfi, Sándor 42, 157, 166, 336f, 357
Peyer, Károly 24, 59, 155
Pol Pot 28
Poland 9, 17, 29, 35, 69, 87, 90, 100, 138f, 164, 165, 242, 253, 346, 359, 362
Portugal 263, 431
Poverty of Philosophy, The 25
Poznan 87, 360
Prague 37, 41
Provisional National Assembly 52, 53
Provisional National Government 52, 57, 158, 160, 161
Pusztaszemes 13

Radio Free Europe 103, 175
Rádióújság 303
Rajk, László 49, 52, 54, 55, 70ff, 85f, 88, 104, 153, 159, 166, 195
Rákóczi, Ferenc I 164
Rákóczi, Ferenc II 89, 164, 336
Rákosi Mátyás 39f, 48, 52, 54ff, 61ff, 65, 66, 70ff, 75, 77f, 80ff, 86ff, 96, 97, 98, 105f, 108, 118, 124, 126f, 140, 150, 156f, 192ff

Rankovich, Alexander 75
Red Army 29, 44, 48, 51, 52, 60, 68, 100, 165, 337
Reed, John 118
Renn, Ludwig 27
Republic of Councils (1919) 15ff, 54, 57, 59, 82, 83, 126, 148, 153ff, 160, 227, 290, 337, 460
Révai, József 54, 56, 67, 71f, 82, 85, 90, 106, 160, 192ff, 197, 202
Revisionism 197, 214, 226
Revolutionary Workers' and Peasants' Government 100, 105, 107, 169, 180, 185
Rezi, Károly 43, 158
Rhodesia 263
Rolland, Romain 27
Romania 9, 17, 20, 35, 44, 66, 69, 100, 104, 159, 160, 242, 252ff, 293
Rome 388
Rónai, Sándor 229, 460
Rónai, Zoltán 17, 154
Roosevelt, Franklin D. 68
Rousseau, Jean-Jacques 357
Rothermere, H. S. Harmsworth, Lord 156
Rózsa, Ferenc, 43, 158
Rudolf, Archduke 9
Russell, Bertrand 357
Russia 17

Ságvári, Endre 45, 48, 158f
Sallai, Imre 27, 43, 155
Sarajevo 9
Sári, Ignác 61
Sárospatak 292
Scandinavia 230
Schmidt, Helmut 407
Schönherz, Zoltán 43, 158
Second Hungarian Army 43
Seghers, Anna 27
Shakespeare, William 73, 233, 381
Shapiro, Henry 245
Shehu, Mehmet 137, 211
Show trials 63, 70ff, 84ff, 88, 126
Sicily 43
Siklós 292
Sinclair, Upton 244
Sixth German Army 43
Skorzeny, Otto 44
Smallholders' Party 43, 49, 53, 54, 58ff, 66, 95, 98, 103, 104, 158, 161, 162, 163, 164, 459
Social Democratic Party 15, 17, 24, 28, 29, 36f, 42f, 47, 49, 50, 53, 54, 58, 59f, 66, 70, 73, 85, 98, 103, 145, 146f, 153ff, 161, 174, 229ff, 257, 291, 357, 383ff, 417, 460, 461
Socialist International 29, 36, 383

Society of Awakening Hungarians 35, 156
Sólyom, László 71, 163, 291
Somogy (County) 10, 17, 159
Sophia, Archduchess 9
South Africa 263
Soviet Russia 16, 17, 143
Soviet Union 9, 26, 32, 36, 39, 40, 43, 44, 50, 52, 54, 55, 68, 69, 81, 98, 100, 104f, 138ff, 154, 157ff, 163ff, 179, 197, 203, 210ff, 221, 230, 236, 243, 249, 250ff, 256, 257, 262ff, 287, 304, 321, 322ff, 337, 345, 346, 353, 357ff, 374, 380, 395, 397, 407, 408, 409, 428, 431, 432, 438, 447, 448, 449, 458
Spain 28, 41, 55, 74, 126, 359, 417
Spanish Civil War 41, 55, 91, 126, 159, 160, 165
"Splendid winds" 78, 164
SS (Schutzstaffel) 44
Stalin, Joseph 68, 81f, 84, 106, 118, 211, 214, 220, 225
State Security Authority (ÁVH) 51, 71f, 74, 77, 88f, 92f, 95, 159, 163, 193, 198f
Stephen I 150, 336, 462
Stil, André 222
Suez Canal crisis 98
Sulyok, Dezső 60f, 162
Sverdlov, Yakov 26
Sweden 280
Switzerland 59, 62, 72, 161
Syria 254
Szabad Nép 64, 67, 158, 162, 165
Szabó, István (of Nagyatád) 158
Szakasits, Árpád 42, 47, 59, 60, 66, 98, 157, 229
Szalai, András 72, 74, 163
Szálasi, Ferenc 44, 66, 155, 158
Szántó, Judit 40f
Széchenyi, István 336, 462
Szeged 20, 39, 56, 82, 156, 293
Szekfű, Gyula 42, 157
Szép Szó 153
Szigeti, Attila 184, 459
Szigetvár 292
Szolnok 100ff
Szőnyi, Tibor 72, 74, 163
Szurdi, István 299, 460

Talpra magyar 104, 157, 166
Táncsics Circle 196, 197, 460
Táncsics, Mihály 336, 462
Teleki, Pál Count 35f, 53, 156
Thant, U 234ff
Thurzó, Gábor 233, 461
Tildy, Zoltán 58ff, 158, 161
Tisza, Kálmán 153
Tito (Josip Broz) 48, 61, 100, 137

Toller, Ernst 27
Tolstoy, Lev 381
Trade Unions 23, 28, 59, 90, 157, 169ff, 189, 261, 285, 298
Transdanubia 9, 20, 178, 184
Transylvania 22, 35, 162, 164, 293
Treaty of Trianon 21, 35, 66, 148, 154, 161, 253, 288
Trotskyism 154
Truman, Harry 68, 359
Turul Federation 35, 156
Turkey 164
Two-front struggle 112, 422f

Új Nemzedék 187, 459
Ulbricht, Walter 237
UN (United Nations) 38, 95, 98, 100f, 123, 136ff, 234ff, 264, 346f, 380, 430, 449
UNESCO (United Nations Educational, Scientific and Cultural Organization) 264
United Party 158
United States of America 38, 59, 68, 72, 98, 137f, 150, 155, 158, 161f, 165, 179, 180, 221, 227, 236, 238ff, 249, 250ff, 262, 264, 303, 321ff, 347, 357, 359, 361, 380, 395ff, 408, 448

Valóság 157
Varga Béla 59, 62, 161
Vas, Zoltán 52, 159
Vatican 243, 250, 389ff, 429
Veres, Péter 38, 60, 144, 156, 316, 352
Verne, Jules 19
Versailles, Treaty of 253
Vetsera, Maria 9
Vienna 29, 37, 98, 154, 155, 160, 161, 163, 362, 382f
Vienna Award, first 35
Vienna Award, second 35
Vietnam 104, 238ff, 254, 257ff, 262, 303, 321, 346, 407, 431, 432
Visegrád 292
Voltaire 357
Vörösmarty, Mihály 89, 164

War of Independence (1848) 20, 41, 42, 51, 52, 154, 157, 162, 164, 166, 336
Warsaw ghetto 44
Warsaw Treaty Organization 98, 179, 226, 249, 254f, 264, 322, 346, 361ff, 386, 389, 399, 407, 428, 449
Weimar Republic 230, 231
Werbőczi, István 336, 462
White terror 21, 148

Wilson, Woodrow 15, 253
Women's rights 268, 306, 331ff, 433f, 451f
Workers' Councils 170f, 202, 247f
Workers' Militia 198, 228, 229
Working Class 30, 186, 228, 266, 339, 423
World War I 9, 13, 14, 17, 66, 148, 153, 155, 156, 253, 357, 379ff
World War II 22, 32, 35ff, 68, 72, 81ff, 136, 153, 154, 156, 158, 160f, 165, 184, 256, 263, 293, 337, 357ff, 379, 386, 387, 429
Writers' Union 89, 120, 156
Wurmser, André 222

Yemen 254, 431
Youth question 112, 186f, 200, 217ff, 268, 307ff, 434, 453
Yugoslavia 9, 17, 36, 48, 66, 69f, 75, 85f, 88, 90, 100ff, 153, 156, 170, 247f, 293, 458

Z. Nagy, Ferenc 178f, 185, 458
Zelewsky, Erich von dem Bach 44
Zhivkov, Todor 237
Zimbabwe 431
Zola, Émile 19
Zrínyi, Ilona 164